ABORIGINAL MUSIC IN
CONTEMPORARY
CANADA

# Aboriginal Music in Contemporary Canada

ECHOES AND EXCHANGES

Edited by Anna Hoefnagels and
Beverley Diamond

MCGILL-QUEEN'S UNIVERSITY PRESS

MONTREAL & KINGSTON | LONDON | ITHACA

Legal deposit first quarter 2012
Bibliothèque nationale du Québec

Printed in Canada on acid-free paper.

This book has been published with the help of a grant from the Canadian Federation for the Humanities and Social Sciences, thorugh the Aid to Scholarly Publications Program, using funds provided by the Social Sciences and Humanities Research Council of Canada. Funding has also been received from the Memorial University of Newfoundland's Publication Subvention Program.

McGill-Queen's University Press acknowledges the support of the Canada Council for the Arts for our publishing program. We also acknowledge the financial support of the Government of Canada through the Canada Book Fund for our publishing activities.

LIBRARY AND ARCHIVES CANADA CATALOGUING IN PUBLICATION

Aboriginal music in contemporary Canada : echoes and exchanges / edited by Anna Hoefnagels and Beverley Diamond.

(McGill-Queen's native and northern series ; 66)
Includes bibliographical references, discography and index.
ISBN 978-0-7735-3951-8

1. Indians of North America – Canada – Music – History and criticism.   2. Indians of North America – Canada – Music – Social aspects.   3. Indians of North America – Canada – Interviews.   I. Hoefnagels, Anna   II. Diamond, Beverley, 1948–
III. Series: McGill-Queen's native and northern series ; 66

ML3563.6.A154 2012   781.6297071   C2011-906130-9

Set in 10.5/13.5 Calluna with Calluna Sans
Book design and typesetting by Garet Markvoort, zijn digital

CONTENTS

LIST OF TABLES AND FIGURES

TABLES

FIGURES

ACKNOWLEDGMENTS

From our hearts, we thank all Aboriginal people who have generously and patiently answered the many questions of researchers who seek to understand their powerful song and dance traditions and their vibrant contemporary creative work. We thank all Indigenous teachers, who, inevitably, help each of us on our own journeys toward understanding the injustices of colonialism and the strength of knowledge systems that underpin different worldviews. Those of us from settler communities have had, and still have, much to learn about the wisdom and resilience that enabled First Nations, Inuit, and Métis people to survive the devastating impact of discriminatory attitudes, acts, and institutions in order to reach a place of strength and leadership at the beginning of the twenty-first century. This resilience, in no small part, emerged through song and dance culture – both the traditional practices that underpin ceremony, heal, or offer thanks for the gifts of the earth and the new artistic creations that have played a huge role in articulating histories hidden or denied, inspiring audiences through powerful art and ideas.

The realization of an anthology such as this requires a great deal of work, patience, and commitment to the final outcome on the part of many people. Foremost, we want to thank all of the contributors who believed in the importance of this project and responded positively and patiently throughout the review and editing processes. Of course, many scholars in ethnomusicology, Indigenous studies, and other disciplines have informed concepts and theories that shaped the chapters that follow, and we are grateful to them as well. We especially acknowledge Sam Cronk for his ideas and enthusiasm during the initial stages of this project.

We also offer our thanks for the encouragement and shrewd advice of Jonathan Crago, Robert Lewis, Ryan Van Huijstee, and the staff at McGill-Queen's University Press for their exceptional support during the entire process from preliminary ideas, through preparation, to printing. We appreciate the anonymous reviewers for McGill-Queen's University Press who offered valuable and insightful feedback to the authors and helped to find a stronger structure for grouping chapters. We are very grateful to Julie Leblanc and Anna Guigné for their assistance with the translation of French texts, to Rosalind McCanny for the preparation of the manuscript, and to Kristin Harris Walsh for creating the index. In addition, the supportive and ever efficient staff of the Music Program at Carleton University and of the Research Centre for Music, Media and Place at Memorial University were always there for us, even when not directly involved with this project.

Above all, we owe our families and close colleagues thanks for accepting our distractions when academic projects have consumed our attention. There are those who help us to hone ideas or write more convincingly, but we cherish most those closest to us who sustain our spirits through their ongoing love and support.

This anthology was generously subsidized by the Aid to Scholarly Publications Program of the Canadian Federation for the Humanities and Social Sciences and by the Memorial University Publication Subvention Program. Through Beverley Diamond's position as a Trudeau Fellow, we also benefited from support for translation from the Trudeau Foundation. We thank them all.

ABORIGINAL MUSIC IN
CONTEMPORARY
CANADA

Introduction

BEVERLEY DIAMOND AND
ANNA HOEFNAGELS

Interaction between the scholarly community and culture bearers, creative artists, and elders of First Nations, Inuit, and Métis people of Canada has been extensive in the late twentieth and early twenty-first centuries. This period marks an important time in Aboriginal culture in Canada characterized by renewal and revitalization of Indigenous heritage and cultural expressions. At the same time, Aboriginal communities are struggling over land rights and seeking improved systems of health and education that other citizens of Canada enjoy. Indeed, since the mid-twentieth century Indigenous rights in Canada have become a priority for communities and individuals, shaping discourses and exchanges by and among First Peoples in Canada. In the context of this period of both struggle and celebration, there has been a shift in the ways researchers engage with culture bearers, elders, and creative artists as researchers seek more collaborative models of exchange and ways to speak with, not for, our Aboriginal colleagues. We struggled to find the right metaphors to frame the diverse studies in this anthology, studies that reflect a part of this extensive interaction. The subtitle *Echoes and Exchanges* contains two that are pertinent. "Echoes" reference historical traces, ways that traditional song and dance resound or influence contemporary artistic production. At the same time, the metaphor of "echoing" points to concepts that underpin traditional knowledge in many Aboriginal traditions: the circularity of life, the interconnectedness of all things, and the recursiveness of history. Points of return are marked and observed, each one simultaneously referencing past experiences and future possibilities. The metaphor of "exchanges" points to the dialogic nature of many of the sections in the anthology and to the varied meeting points that facilitate exchange. The word is akin to others in postcolonial scholarship: for example, the phrase "intellectual trade routes," coined by the distinguished Native American literary critic Robert Warrior (2005); and the term "contact zones," defined by Mary Louise Pratt as the "social spaces where cultures meet, clash, and grapple with each other, often in contexts of highly asymmetrical relations of power, such as colonialism, slavery, or their aftermaths as they are lived out in many parts of the world today" (1991, 34). The metaphor of exchange also points to the processes of collaboration that ethnographers have attempted to critique or to redefine in recent decades (see Lassiter 2005 for one attempt to survey collaborative strategies in historical and contemporary ethnography).

This anthology of research essays, interviews, and personal reflections of Aboriginal musicians presents a multifaceted representation of First Nations, Inuit, and Métis music in Canada at the beginning of the twenty-first century. The chapters illustrate ongoing negotiations of identity organized around three broad themes: (1) Innovating Tradition, (2) Teaching and Transmission, and (3) Cultural Interactions and Negotiations. The subjects addressed by the authors include the influence of new technologies, modes of transmission, intercultural processes, and intellectual property implications. The authors discuss musical styles associated with nation-specific and intertribal repertoires, popular music genres such as country and hip hop, and a wide array of hybrid expressive cultural practices involving not only music but also theatre or dance. They demonstrate that music continues to be a powerful tool for articulating the social challenges faced by communities and an effective mode of affirming Indigenous strength and pride.

The anthology is innovative in its focus on the processes of knowledge production. It does this primarily by juxtaposing perspectives that emanate from scholarly study (by both Aboriginal and non-Aboriginal authors) with those that are rooted in artistic practices (in interviews with and personal reflections by Aboriginal musicians). Of the twenty-seven authors or interviewees, fifteen are Aboriginal people. They offer a range of perspectives reflecting the specific histories of their ancestral people and their interaction with others. The interviews are mediated in various ways. Some are informal, recorded conversations more or less structured by both parties in the moment and subsequently in the (minimal) editing process. Some are shaped by the medium of radio. Some are edited compilations from several interviews and hence more "constructed" after the fact. As a result, we hope to demonstrate that conversations and interviews are never self-evident but shaped by different media and kinds of encounter. In many cases, interviews and scholarly articles are inter-linked, permitting a rare view of how conversations are reframed within academic study. The compilation of interrelated types of text – academic studies or personal accounts, insider or outsider perspectives, individual or dialogically produced narratives – is, then, intentionally diverse in order to ask how questions are framed, how research is conducted, and how interpretations are constructed about Aboriginal expressive culture in Canada at the beginning of the twenty-first century. Each style of discourse has its own strength, its own story.

Themes and Theories

An overriding theme is Indigenous modernity. Within this broad subject, the three sections focus on different phases of musical practice, phases that we might label production, transmission, and interaction. They are preceded by Beverley Diamond's bibliographic review of trends in scholarship over the past two decades.

As indicated above, the first group of chapters addresses the significant issue of innovating tradition, considering new creative opportunities and challenges that result when new technologies, new audiences, or new contexts emerge. Some chapters deal with continuity and change, indicating ways that musicians and culture bearers choose to modify traditional cultural expressions so that they become particularly meaningful and relevant to Aboriginal people today, as well as to new audiences. The interlinked chapters by Amber Ridington and by Garry Oker with Ridington are a significant example. Ridington, who has had privileged access to collections made in the 1960s by her father, anthropologist Robin Ridington, has been working with the Dane-ẕaa community to create Internet access to traditional song knowledge, and Oker has produced new arrangements on CD, among other projects. An important issue that emerges as a result of the commodification of traditional song in both cases is the complex challenge of respecting traditional protocols relating to intellectual property. The innovating that Janice Tulk addresses relates to revitalization initiatives in Mi'kma'ki (Mi'kmaq territory in Atlantic Canada). She demonstrates how intertribal traditions have been combined with local ones and made locally significant. Her work calls into question the firm cultural boundaries that are sometimes ascribed to specific First Nations by demonstrating their permeability and the sharing in which different First Nations engage. Tulk's is the first of three chapters in the section that address the powwow, the most widespread intertribal tradition in North America. Anishnabe producer Gabriel Desrosiers and ethnomusicologist Christopher Scales engage in an extended discussion of recording studio practices and issues relating to competition. Both have been involved with the powwow circuit as singers and CD producers; their conversation nicely defies a clear boundary between them since, although their histories differ, their powwow experiences are complexly intertwined. Finally, Anna Hoefnagels presents a range of viewpoints about the gendering of powwow singing, not only offering respect to the traditional teachings that justify women's exclusion but also acknowledging new perspectives of women who want the right to sit at the big drum.

The second group of chapters focuses on ways of teaching and learning culture when the oral transmission of the past is recontextualized, complemented, or in some cases, replaced by new approaches. The first three chapters are written from the perspective of teachers (two Aboriginal and one non-Aboriginal). Haudenosaunee cultural leader Sadie Buck reflects on several decades during which she taught the traditional songs and dances of her nation, sometimes in new contexts such as university classrooms or arts centres. Mary Piercey writes an autoethnographic account of her experience as a non-Inuit music teacher in Arviat, where she was charged with teaching traditional music and dance to the Inuit children of the community. Her narrative raises candid questions about who is the teacher and who the learner. Métis musician and ethnomusicologist Annette Chrétien explores metaphors that she encounters in Ottawa Valley communities, using Métis ways of knowing such as trails, or ways of interacting such as *miziksharing*, to guide her representation of Métis identity. Like that of Ridington, Chrétien's project is Internet-based. The final two chapters in the second group are reflections by First Nations people on their own learning processes in urban communities. Both Beverly Souliere and Jimmy Dick actively sought ways to deepen their knowledge of traditional Aboriginal culture and to form new "communities of practice" (Wenger 1998) in Ottawa and Toronto respectively. Both have become important teachers.

The final section explores contemporary cultural interaction and the inherent negotiation processes that are part of any intercultural interaction. The authors speak about a wide range of genres, including classical music, music in theatre productions, popular music, and work that is not easily classified within existing genres at all. Although some of these chapters, such as the personal reflection of Lil'wat composer Russell Wallace, express hope about the opportunity afforded by intercultural work, others are warier about the play of power in such contexts. Dylan Robinson, for instance, develops a model for exploring the power relations between traditional Inuit performers and classical Baroque ensembles that have sought to integrate two disparate styles. The next three chapters all deal with artistic expressions that are associated with emotionally difficult social challenges of colonialism or with its violent consequences, including murder and suicide. Klisala Harrison describes the vibrant Aboriginal theatre scene in Vancouver, exploring the cross-cultural negotiation as well as the performer-audience relationships in recent plays. Interview excerpts with leading writer-performers Marie Clements, Sophie Merasty, and Columpa Bobb are among the research encounters that inform Harrison's chapter. Mi'kmaq elder Walter Denny Jr converses with ethnomusicologist Gordon E. Smith, revealing his own commitment both to Mi'kmaq traditions and to the Catholic Church as he struggles to enable his community to heal and deal with trauma. Byron Dueck has managed to find a way to discuss a controversial song by Chris Beach, who struggles to offer solace to the families of suicide victims. These chapters address tough social issues and circumstances, demonstrating how performance plays a strong role in struggles to heal and to claim full citizenship in Canadian society. Although lighter in terms of subject matter, the remaining chapters address no less significant issues. Marcia Ostashewski's biographical portrayal of Arnie Strynadka challenges usual definitions of "Métis" by giving voice to Strynadka's personal and professional negotiations as a person of Cree and Ukrainian descent. Charity Marsh explores the work of two Saskatchewan hip hop artists, contrasting their ways of articulating identity issues. Véronique Audet similarly examines popular music, this time in the context of Quebec Innu songwriters who were among the earliest creative artists to adopt popular styles in the Indigenous pop music renaissance of the late twentieth century. Two interviews originally presented for a radio audience, one with pioneering musician Florent Vollant and the other with playwright-musician Gilles Sioui, explain their perspectives on some of the same issues. Together, the chapters of the third section implicitly raise important questions not only about cross-cultural interaction but also about performance context since the venues for the musical performances considered range from widely intimate spaces to highly public ones, including festivals and theatre productions.

Suggestions for Classroom Use of the Anthology

We hope that the focus on different types of text, different authorial perspectives, and different styles of cross-cultural interaction will facilitate classroom discussion. We find that questions such as the following elicit careful observations from our own students. What exactly do scholars decide to quote when they incorporate conversations into their writing? How does this citation work in the development of a scholar's ideas? What are the differences between intimate one-on-one interviews, such as those with Gabriel Desrosiers, Jimmy Dick, and Beverly Souliere, and those that are more public, such as the radio interviews with Florent Vollant and Gilles Sioui?

Similarly, each of the three sections provides a thematic focus that could easily be expanded through community- or library-based projects. Aboriginal students might be able to ask family or community elders about the ways that Inuktitut or a specific First Nations language conceptualizes "innovation." Are there words for this? Students could attend one of the many powwows in every region of Canada, comparing their experiences and reflecting on the issues discussed by Tulk, Desrosiers and Scales, or Hoefnagels. Students could consider the transmission processes described in the second section by comparing them to their own experiences of learning in school/university or elsewhere. They could listen for traces of cross-cultural interaction evident in the style of a contemporary Aboriginal songwriter or study the liner notes in order to analyze the teamwork in the production of an album. Additionally, however, teachers and students might regroup the chapters in other ways for their own purposes. Those interested in the powwow, for instance, could juxtapose readings of Dick, Desrosiers and Scales, Hoefnagels, and Tulk. Métis readers might choose to focus on Dueck, Chrétien, and Ostashewski.

Many of the chapters are about process not in the production of texts but in human lives: changes in the lives and musical practices of individuals or communities (Denny and Smith, Dick, Ridington), new roles for women (Hoefnagels; Souliere and Hoefnagels), ways that performers and audiences or performers and their collaborators influence one another (Harrison; Robinson; Clements, Merasty, Bobb, and Harrison; Dueck; Wallace; Vollant and Sioui), ways that the Internet influences the representation of Aboriginal song knowledge (Chrétien, Ridington), differences between insider and outsider expectations (Piercey), ways that technology or industry infrastructure mediates cultural production (Ridington; Oker and Ridington; Audet; Desrosiers and Scales), ways that social marginalization or, conversely, celebrity impacts the message (Marsh, Ostashewski, Audet), or ways that history is being reconceptualized in specific regions or time periods (Tulk, Diamond). Our assigning of the various chapters to this list of processes tells, in itself, an incomplete story since many of them speak to more than one process.

The anthology, then, may present echoes and exchanges, but it hopes also to have a ripple effect and to stimulate further interaction and sharing. We are grateful for the opportunities that scholars have been given to listen to and read the words of Indigenous musicians, elders, and culture bearers. We hope this volume conveys the respect we have for these opportunities and the dialogue that results.

1

Recent Studies of First Nations, Inuit, and Métis Music in Canada

BEVERLEY DIAMOND

At a recent meeting of academics and Indigenous musicians, dancers, and cultural specialists, a First Nations friend leaned over and commented on what is an old but still emotionally raw issue for Aboriginal people: "My god, we're studied so much!" Indeed, although the growing number of scholars of Aboriginal descent is a welcome, predictable, and socially significant trend in recent scholarship, the fascination that non-Native scholars have with the song and dance traditions of First Nations, Inuit, and Métis music seems as strong as ever. The roles we (both Indigenous and non-Indigenous scholars) describe for ourselves have changed. Early collectors often claimed to be "mining" communities for cultural gems. Postmodernists queried the differences between scholarly activity and the work of missionaries, at times, or tourists, at others. In recent decades, academics have hopefully been cognizant of reciprocity; many advocate collaboration with their Indigenous partners, jointly defining research objectives and methods.[1] But we should be prepared to query the terms of our (often self-described) collaboration. One of my "collaborators" recently asserted that she never collaborates; she says that she helps me out of friendship and because it is the way of her people to assist when asked. She stresses that it is my responsibility to use the knowledge she shares with me ethically. Collaboration, then, is not a verbal veneer that absolves anyone of individual responsibility.

Several surveys of published studies of First Nations, Inuit, and Métis music in regions that today comprise Canada provide good bibliographic accounts of historical literature relevant to this anthology. Since overviews by Wendy Wickwire (1985), Lynn Whidden (1998), James Robbins (1993), and myself and Robbins (1992) are now out of date, this chapter presents a bibliographic update with particular emphasis on Canadian-based work that has emerged in the past twenty years.[2] I offer observations about themes and styles of representation that have emerged in work by and about Canadian Aboriginal people, not with a view to demarcating any sort of national distinction but to see how specific relationships between people and places have influenced our narratives. Indeed, this is arguably the justification for compiling a volume of studies bounded by the contemporary nation-state. For although the traditional lands of some First Nations, Métis, and Inuit people cross the border between Canada and the United States,[3] nation-states are the sites and at times the determinants for different political contexts and social developments that have had an impact on the lives of Indigenous people.

This chapter's contribution to the volume's bibliography includes articles and books[4] by Aboriginal cultural specialists, ethnomusicologists, anthropologists, and other scholars since 1988.[5] Although dates are largely chosen for convenience, one could argue that this particular year was, in retrospect, something of a watershed for publications in Aboriginal music studies in Canada. It marked the appearance of Robin Ridington's *Trail to Heaven*, for instance, a book that influenced many of us to rethink styles of representation and to reflect on learning processes.[6] In the same year, beyond our borders, James Clifford's significant studies of museum practices and the legal ramifications of Indigenous rights in the *Predicament of Culture* stimulated further debate. A significant anthology on Native American music, edited by Whidden, was also published in 1988 by the *Canadian Journal of Native Studies*, with articles by Nicole Beaudry, Anton Kolstee, Wickwire, and others, and an anthology on "Fêtes et musiques"[7] was produced by *Recherches amérindiennes au Québec*. Publications by the SPINC[8] research group began to appear in the late 1980s. A very significant conference on ethnomusicology in Canada was also convened in 1988, the first national event that brought together the majority of academics working in the field of ethnomusicology as well as scholars studying music within cognate disciplines. In the middle of this productive "era" from 1988 to approximately 2010, volume 3 of the *Garland Encyclopedia of World Music* (Koskoff 2001) was published; it contains the most extensive reference coverage on Aboriginal music in Canada to date. Bookending this approximately twenty-year period is Tara Browner's *Music of the First Nations* (2009), the first North American anthology to contain a significant number of Canadian contributions, the appearance of massive and media-rich websites by Elaine Keillor (see http://native-dance.ca and http://native-drums.ca), and my textbook for the Global Music series of Oxford University Press, *Native American Music in Eastern North America* (2008). All signal a broadening transnational interest in the music of Aboriginal Canada.

Themes: Intercultural Interactions

It is not surprising that much of the scholarship of this period is marked by new considerations. The impact of au courant intellectual paradigms – postmodernism, postcolonialism, feminism, and ethnopoetics, in particular – is evident. The shifts in representation are also a reflection of the growing assumption of agency in Indigenous communities over research and representation. Scholars of Native American descent in Canada are producing groundbreaking studies of traditional knowledge and its potential impact on governance (e.g., Alfred 1999), education (Battiste 2000, Battiste and Semeganis 2002), selfhood (Anderson 2000), or the interpretation of texts (King 2003), to name only a very few areas. The centrality of song and dance traditions to decolonization initiatives (Young and Nadeau 2005) and to building/sustaining healthy communities (Amadahy 2003, Harrison 2008) is one of the most significant emphases of recent scholarship.

These topics imply that an ethical relationship among participants in the projects of Indigenous modernity is essential. Many individuals and community leaders have spoken about intercultural ethics in terms of access: topics (in)appropriate for the public domain, the negotiation of editorial input, and observations about errors in the public record. Other social issues concern the need to build common research agendas that enable the most effective social outcomes for Aboriginal people and the most powerful contributions of both Indigenous and non-Indigenous citizens in achieving an equitable and civil society in which Aboriginal participation is equal to that of "newcomers."[9] Although fieldwork has always been negotiative and has always relied on trust to be successful, the need to discuss research agendas with communities, to consider community priorities and issues, and to find ways to reciprocate have been emphasized with more urgency during the past twenty years. Fieldwork methodology is the focus of articles by Beaudry (1997), who describes challenges she faced in her own research in northern communities, and by Gordon E. Smith (2006) and Mary Piercey (forthcoming), who focus more on collaborative teaching. Intercultural ethics are, however, implicit in the writing of many other scholars. Discussions among members of the SPINC research group, in which I participated in the late 1980s, often turned into debates about the very right to know. Why were Euro-Americans taught to assume they had it? What were the responsibilities of knowledge? Why should we be interested in someone else's (traditional) knowledge? Questions of access and ownership that have become front and centre in ethnomusicology in the early twenty-first century were posed largely as fieldwork issues in the circles of scholars with whom I was working two decades ago. These questions are still fieldwork issues, of course, but also now extensively discussed as teaching issues, publication issues, and ethical issues.

Perhaps because of these various factors that influenced new directions in Canadian Aboriginal scholarship, it is not surprising that the very nature of cross-cultural encounter and particularly the impact of colonialism were themes scrutinized extensively in the past two decades.[10] Music taught and used in Christian churches received considerable attention. Christian repertoires in Indigenous languages were studied by Keillor (1987), Whidden (1985), and myself (1992, 1988) in the 1980s.[11] Keillor and I were both interested in the mediation of print, and we looked closely not only at the hymn books in use but also at the handwritten manuscripts or overhead projections used in some churches. Using information from my own work as well as that of Michael Sam Cronk and Franziska von Rosen, I wrote about the indigenization of hymnody in traditional Innu, Mi'kmaq, and Haudenosaunee contexts, documenting in music such things as dual religious affiliation and recontextualization, what others such as John Webster Grant (1984) and William Powers (1987) had written about in other spheres. Tom Gordon's (2007) more recent textual analyses of Moravian sources used, copied, and in some cases created on the Labrador coast give renewed attention to printed media. Local aesthetics and distinctive performance practices are revealed by his work on the hand-copied music used by Inuit in this region. Paul-André Dubois (2003, 2002, 2001, 1997a, 1997b) has conducted extensive studies of the history of missions in New France between the sixteenth and nineteenth centuries, including consideration of manuscript collections, language, social relations, and interactive beliefs. Complementing his work is that of Jean-Guy Goulet (2000). However, Christianity has always been a complex topic in Aboriginal communities, inspiring different responses from different people at different times: syncretism, indigenization, or resistance, among others. Elizabeth Chute (1992) as well as Mi'kmaq elder Mildred Milliea (1989) have written about the New Brunswick community's embrace of the Christian hymns associated with St Anne's Day, which continues to be an occasion for significant gatherings all over Mi'kma'ki and in other Aboriginal Catholic communities. It was not until more recent work, particularly that of Ann Morrison Spinney (1991, 1996, 1997, 1999, 2006, 2009), however, that the historical power negotiations between Indigenous medicine people, Christian clergy, and political leaders (in her case, among the Passamaquoddy of Maine) were represented with a focus on agency on both sides. Although much of her work is centred south of the Canada-US border, the people with whom she works travel into maritime Canada, and her work will inform Canadian scholarship (particularly in Atlantic Canadian Aboriginal communities) for its interpretive depth as well as its historical data.

Printed hymn books were but one material entry point to the subject of colonial relations. Museum collections were among the others. The SPINC research project, which studied Native American instrument collections in the Northeast, was already underway when James Clifford's mischievous claim that "cultures are ethnographic collections" (1988, 230) was published. Indeed, Clifford's "On Collecting Art and Culture," in *The Predicament of Culture* (1988), together with the important work of the late historian and museologist Deborah Doxtator, who curated the exhibition *Fluffs and Feathers* (Doxtator 1992) for the Woodland Cultural Centre and Royal Ontario Museum, helped to shape our study of sound-producing instruments in twenty-five museum collections in the Northeast. The resultant book, *Visions of Sound* (Diamond, Cronk, and von Rosen 1994), was shaped by the exchanges we had with elders and musicians about photos of these instruments and about museums themselves. We learned the ways that materials embodied meaning and the ways that design and image were "read" either in relation to shared systems of symbols or in relation to individual experience. Ultimately, however, the project and process were about the colonial enterprise. Sound-producing instruments (Leroux 1992, Matthews and Roulette 1996, Williams 1996) or other artefacts relevant to song traditions, such as Mide song scrolls (Fulford 1990, 1989), have drawn the attention of scholars interested in the rich symbolism of image and design and in the fascinating histories of provenance. Recent work on specific collectors, such as Marius Barbeau (Smith 2008, Jessup 2008, Nyce 2008, Keillor 2004, Nurse 1997) and James Teit (Wickwire 2001, 1988, Thompson 2007), adds new contextual layers.

Studies of "entertainments" involving Native Americans (e.g., wild west shows and exhibitions), about which Philip Deloria (2004) has written so cogently with particular attention to the Lakota, have emerged with reference to Indigenous people living north of the 49th parallel, although with less detail about musical performance than I might hope for. Trudy

Nicks (1999) and Kaley Mason (2004) have explored the significant and understudied world of Aboriginal involvement in tourism as both crafts people and performers, and Lynda Jessup (2002) has studied the world of exhibitions. Jim Zwick's *Inuit Entertainers in the United States* (2006) is curiously lacking in information about musical performance, and Quebec folklorist Olivier Maligne's (2006) broad-ranging study of the Indianist movement identifies important processes but few that are place-specific. One music-focused study, however, is Keillor's (2002) article on "Amerindians" in rodeos.

Cross-cultural encounter has also been addressed through studies of the representation – indeed, the stereotyping – of Indigenous people in classical music, film, and popular music, with particular attention to hybrid and borrowed styles. The most comprehensive to date, by Michael Pisani (2005), has laid the groundwork. Both Keillor (1995b), who examines the use of Indian music by Canadian composers, and Olivia Bloechl (2008, 2005), who reinterprets Native American song in the colonial encounters particularly of the sixteenth and seventeenth centuries, similarly study cross-cultural "translation" in musical style and technique. More recent work by Pamela Karantonis and Dylan Robinson (Karantonis and Robinson 2011) differs in its framing of hybrid (Native classical) practices by focusing not only on style but also on social action and impact. Music's role among the complex responses to colonialism and its potential as a tool for decolonization are highlighted. A number of explorations of sheet music iconography, lyrics, and musical gestures (e.g., Cronk 1990, Green 1989,[12] Nicks 1999) have analyzed the power-laden nature of aesthetic representations. Studies of Aboriginal film representations through sound (e.g., Gorbman 2000, Deloria 2004) are far fewer than those that look at cinematic image and narrative, but Canadian scholars have been among those who have written about such topics (Diamond 2005b, Tulk 2010). Many Canadian ethnomusicologists, however, have explored production (especially popular music production) rather than representation by others, as I discuss below.

Finally, *métissage* is a type of "cultural contact" that has emerged strongly as a theme in the past two decades (see the chapters by Chrétien and Ostashewski in this volume). Contemporary studies consider both contact between and among Indigenous people and contact between individuals or families of mixed Aboriginal and non-Aboriginal people. Recognized as an Aboriginal people in the repatriated Canadian Constitution of 1982, the Métis have grown in numbers and political significance in the intervening years. Regional diversity – both linguistic and cultural – has been a major theme in this growth. The prairie Métis have been recognized for their Michif language and shared history stemming from the Red River settlement. Lynn Whidden (2003a, 2003b, 2000, 1993) has written about their song traditions. In Saskatoon the Gabriel Dumont Institute has played a major role in producing anthologies of prairie Métis music (see Dorion-Paquin 2002 for one of its most popular publications). Many studies of Métis culture emphasize, however, that self-identifying either as a member of a First Nation or as a Métis is a complicated process, one that is historically and politically contingent. The distinctive features of Métis instrumental music (heterometric fiddle tunes in particular) have been described in numerous publications. Some scholars, such as Anne Lederman[13] (1988), Byron Dueck (2005), and Sarah Quick (2008a, 2008b), have tackled the difficult job of analyzing this distinctive musical style. Dueck has been particularly instrumental in changing the interpretive model by stressing how contextual elements shape aesthetic decisions, identifying variable degrees of "public intimacy" and different publics. Craig Mishler's (1993) important study of northern Athapascan fiddle traditions complements the Métis studies that have been conducted in southern Canada.

Métis scholars from regions other than the Prairies (Chrétien 1996, 2002, 2005) as well as from other disciplines (e.g., the Cree/Métis writer-educator and oral historian Kim Anderson [2000] and the Mi'kmaq/Métis sociologist Bonita Lawrence [2004]), however, have questioned the boundary making, observing the dispersion of the Métis and emphasizing that Métis cultures cannot be reduced to the prairie Métis paradigm. The music of Métis from regions other than the Prairies and also from families with other ethnically mixed ancestry has begun only quite recently to attract scholarly attention.[14] The definition of "mixed" Aboriginal cultures, however, remains contested.

In some regions of Canada, the nature and temporal extent of intercultural contact (among Aboriginals as well as between Aboriginals and non-Aboriginals) challenges the discrete nations model altogether. Particularly in Atlantic Canada – where inaccurate myths, such as those about the extinguishment of the Beothuk[15] and about the "mercenary" Mi'kmaq, have implied a history of unmitigated conflict among First Nations – music scholars have presented counterevidence. The important play between nation-specific and intertribal identities is particularly evident in work by Janice Tulk (2008) on the music of Newfoundland's First Peoples. Also presenting evidence of cultural exchange is John Hewson's and my (2007) analysis of a "Beothuk song," a shard of evidence of the continuity of Beothuk music, albeit in a family of mixed descent. Nicholas Smith's study of Wabanaki Confederacy exchanges in such practices as "trading dances" (1996) and chief-making ceremonies (2004) further nuances the intertribal history of Atlantic Canada, which, like other parts of the Atlantic seaboard, experienced the earliest phases of colonization.

Academics have become increasingly attuned to intercultural differences in expression as they relate to issues of representation. Robin Ridington was part of the ethnopoetic movement that also included Dennis Tedlock, Barre Toelken, and Harold Broomfield, among others. His work with the Dane-ẕaa (known in earlier Anglo terminology as the Beaver Indians), especially in the Doig River community, enabled many to see how the positivist paradigms of a certain era of scholarship had limitations not only for explanations of the "dreamers" with whom Ridington had the privilege of working but also as a representation of how he himself learned about the culture. In *Trail to Heaven* (1988) and other more recent publications (1996), he examines his pathway from the "science" of anthropology to the narratives of the Dane-ẕaa, permitting his readers to see his vulnerability while showing us how song, narrative, and life events are interwoven. He is also one of the few scholars of his generation to write about changing soundscapes in Aboriginal communities (Ridington 1988b).

Especially influential as a comparative theorist of narrative styles is anthropologist Julie Cruikshank. Her groundbreaking work with elders of the Tagish community in the Yukon, published in *Life Lived Like a Story* (1990), acknowledges the agency of powerful women and also demonstrates that life and expressive culture are inseparable. She reveals how Angela Sidney, Kitty Smith, and Annie Ned moved fluidly between "narrative" and reportage in a way that defies the genres of folklore and the boundaries between song, speech, politics, and dream worlds. In one chapter of the *Social Life of Stories* (1998b), Cruikshank focuses explicitly on how a narrative can be adapted for new social purposes in her account of Pete Sidney's salmon "song." Her work goes well beyond conventional oral history by challenging the way stories of lives unfold and the way experience and personal narratives intersect. Her more recent work, *Do Glaciers Listen?* (2005), on the intersection of narrative (including song) and the science of glaciers, continues in the same vein, albeit with a more urgent agenda relating to environmental survival.

Themes: Contemporary Culture and Technological Change

Among the studies of contemporary musical practices is an array of pow-wow studies, each of which nuances the North American picture in important ways. Based in Winnipeg during his doctoral fieldwork, Christopher Scales (2002, 2004, forthcoming) studied the studio mediation of a powwow aesthetic, particularly its emphasis on "liveness." Scales (2007) critiques but ultimately finds "pan-Indianism" a useful concept for the work he does. Others, such as Anna Hoefnagels (2001a, 2001b, 2002, 2004, 2007a), Sylvie Berbaum (2000), and Tulk (2006, 2007a, 2007b, 2008), who have explored the powwow beyond its Plains heartland, nuance the picture with regional studies that emphasize localization (see also Ellis et al. 2005). Like that of other contemporary scholars such as Browner (2002), their work challenges the overarching dichotomy of "northern" and "southern" singing styles by demonstrating regional practices that use elements of both. Patricia Albers and Beatrice Medicine (2005) offer a personal account of changing magnitudes and structures of powwow performance on the northern Plains, suggesting that different issues emerge at events of different scale and substance. Media emanating from powwows in the form of CDs or DVDs,[16] as well as the mediation of powwow culture in the press, have been studied by Scales (forthcoming, 2007, 2004, 2002), Mark Ruml (2000), Kathleen Buddle (2004), and Whidden (1992). Dance is described in many of the aforementioned studies as well as by Nina De Shane (1991). The separation of music and dance in scholarly studies is frequently challenged in powwow literature. Playwright Drew Hayden Taylor (2004) has written a humorous first-person powwow account, a significant First Nations perspective on the powwow experience. Canadian powwow scholarship is, of course, closely interconnected with studies in the United States (see Browner 2002, Hatton 1986, Heth 1992, and Vennum 1989a). Both Thomas Vennum Jr (1989b) and Browner (2000) have written about song forms, the latter specifically about powwow songs and the former about songs of the Ojibwe dream dance that were among the antecedents of the powwow. Their work is not specific to Canadian communities, of course, but directly relevant to these cross-border musical traditions.

Other cross-cultural performance spaces, such as festivals, have been explored comparatively by Véronique Audet (2005a) and by myself, Cronk, and von Rosen (Cavanagh [Diamond], Cronk, and von Rosen [1988] and Cronk, Diamond, and von Rosen [1988] are slightly varied presentations of the same study, one in English and one in French). Traditional protocols in West Coast festival contexts are discussed by Klisala Harrison (2000).

Indigenous popular music, worldwide, has become a subject of extensive interest to scholars in several disciplines in recent decades. The Canadian contribution to this burgeoning literature has been substantive and, in many cases, pioneering. A boost to these studies was the appearance of a major discographic reference work compiled by Brian Wright-McLeod (2005).

Contemporary popular music as a medium for articulating a range of identity issues has been the theme chosen by many scholars (including Audet 2005b, Baxter-Moore 2000–01, Cain 2006, Chrétien 1996, 2005, Diamond 1999–2000, 2001, 2002, 2008a, Dueck 2005, 2006, 2007, Janke 1992, Keillor 1995a, 1988, V. Morrison 1996, Neuenfeldt 1996, 2002b, Patterson 1996a, Scales 1996, 1999, 2002, 2004, Tulk 2003, Valentine 2003, von Rosen 1998, Whidden 2007, and Wright-McLeod 1996). Among the identity studies, however, the foci have varied a great deal. Whereas some (e.g., Chrétien, Dueck, and Tulk) explore specific Aboriginal or regional groupness (e.g., Ontario Métis or Newfoundland Mi'kmaq), others (e.g., Baxter-Moore, Neuenfeldt, V. Morrison, Patterson, and Wright-McLeod) address Native American identity more broadly, often with an emphasis on sociopolitical issues articulated in song. Laurent Jerôme (2005) explores Atikamekw youth culture but with an emphasis on the Atikamekw's use of the traditional drum, the *teueikan*. Karl Neuenfeldt (1996, 2002a), whose work is usefully informed by his knowledge of both Canadian and Australian Indigenous scenes, has written about the ways that song texts articulate social issues. Wright-McLeod (1996) has published an important article on popular music and political activism, and interviews by E.K. Caldwell (1999) further explore this theme. The success of the Innu duo Kashtin has been studied most intensively by Line Grenier and Val Morrison (1995a, 1995b), who have explored how the mediation of Kashtin's music articulates with the rise of Quebec nationalism. Both Scales and I have examined debates about the definition of "Aboriginal music" that accompanied the inauguration of the Aboriginal Music Award within the Junos. Several studies of both contemporary pop and the recontextualization of traditional social music emphasize community (re)vitalization (Krouse 2001, Tulk 2007a, 2007b, Valentine 2003).

Recent attention to hip hop (Lashua 2005, 2006a, 2006b, Lashua and Fox 2006, 2007, Krims 2000, Ullestad 1999, Marsh forthcoming) has broadened the range of practices studied. Furthermore, these studies shed light on the urban experience of Aboriginal youth and, at the same time, challenge the assumed "natural" connection between hip hop cultures and urban locales; Aboriginal rap is being created in remote communities as well as cities. A handful of scholars have addressed other challenges and opportunities in urban contexts. Susan Krouse (2001) has studied processes of adapting traditional repertoires. Harrison (2008) has explored revitalization initiatives in the impoverished Downtown Eastside of Vancouver. Aboriginal urban spaces remain, however, an understudied subject.

A fruitful subset of Aboriginal music research has focused on technological change. Among the pioneering initiatives, Scales's work on recording and mixing technologies as they are adapted to powwow and other contemporary music is particularly noteworthy. His dual skills as producer and scholar provide him with insight into studio processes. His study of the recording processes of powwow music and the differences between powwow and popular music production illustrates how local aesthetics and traditional values continue to inform production. My work (2002, 2005a) has explored both the social relations of the studio (with particular reference to the gendering of these relations) and Aboriginal aesthetic views as they relate to recording and mixing techniques in four small case studies of CDs. Aboriginal music on radio and television has been studied both regionally (in the Yukon) by Janke (1992) and thematically by Michael Patterson (1996a). The proliferation of Native American music awards as well as their structures, systems of categorization, and impact have been related topics, studied in comparison with the parallel awards systems in Australia and Scandinavia (Diamond 2008b).

Themes: Stories of Individuals

Oral histories and autobiographical narratives[17] have been significant in their own right as means of giving song carriers and other culture bearers a voice about their own role in maintaining and revitalizing culture. The *Sound of the Drum* (1990), compiled by Michael Sam Cronk for the Woodland Cultural Centre, is an important anthology of interviews with First Nations musicians whose diverse practices range from Haudenosaunee song to brass bands. Franziska von Rosen's (1994) work with Mi'kmaw fiddler Mike Francis and with Maliseet singer and elder Maggie Paul (in Browner 2009) is a significant example.[18] Paul's story is narrated somewhat differently in a text edited by Peter Kulchyski and colleagues (1999). An emphasis on individual musicians has characterized work by many graduates of the ethnomusicology program at Brown University, where both von Rosen and Kevin Alstrup studied, the latter focusing on Rita Joe (Alstrup 2003, Smith and Alstrup 1995) and on Thomas George Poulette (Alstrup 2004, 2003). Of course, we meet individual musicians and elders in the work of many others.

The representation of pop musicians is arguably cast in a different mould, one influenced by the emphases of the marketplace and the industry. Some studies have focused on important individuals, including older popular musicians, such as fiddlers (e.g., Smith 1994, on Mi'kmaw fiddler Lee Cremo; von Rosen 1994, on Michael Francis), and newer bands (e.g., Tulk 2003, on Medicine Dream). Still others have concentrated on subsets of individuals (e.g., Diamond 2002, on women) or on specific genres (e.g., Cain 2006, on blues performers). Star performers such as Buffy Sainte-Marie (see Caldwell 1999 for one instance) have been the subjects of extensive interviews, film presentations, and journalistic initiatives. Sainte-Marie's current entry in Wikipedia lists seventeen references, among them a DVD entitled *Buffy Sainte-Marie: A Multimedia Life* (Prowse 2006), produced by CineFocus Canada. As mentioned earlier, the style in which popular music journalism tells life stories differs from that of the oral history studies of tradition bearers. Part of the production of "stardom," the accounts often feature achievements and awards as well as responses to specific songs, concerts, or recordings (including, for instance, important interview material on such things as the ban on Buffy Sainte-Marie's antiwar song "Universal Soldier"). The worlds of scholars and journalists, however, are hardly discrete, and close attention to the role that academics play in the global industry is an important topic that exceeds the bounds of this survey.

The distinctive styles of self-narration and the ways that life and expressive culture (including song) are integrated in such narratives are of special significance. Not only does self-narration enable us to celebrate remarkable tradition bearers and contemporary innovators, but it also reflects important concepts of selfhood that are rooted in systems of traditional knowledge.

Other Approaches

The directions in scholarship outlined thus far perhaps imply, incorrectly, that Canadian ethnomusicologists have moved away from the study of historic genres of "traditional" Inuit, Métis, and First Nations music in the past twenty years. Although fewer repertoire-oriented studies have been created in recent decades, there have been several significant ones, in addition to the aforementioned powwow studies. The potlatch within several specific First Nations contexts continues to be a subject of both historical (Anderson and Halpern 2000, Kan 1989) and contemporary (Beck 1993, Easterson 1992, Kan 1990, Padfield 1991, Teskey and Brock 1995) consideration. Knowledge of Dene drum traditions has been expanded (Abel 1993, Asch 1988, Beaudry 1992a, 1992b, 1997, 1999), as has the literature on the Ojibwe traditional dream dance (Kaczmarek 1998, 1999; Valentine 1995, which presents a range of communicative practices) and on the Inuit drum dance tradition (Conlon 2009, 1992, Vascotto 2001, Trott 2000, Piercey 2005). Based largely on archival material, John Enrico and Wendy Bross Stuart's (1996) detailed linguistic and musicological treatment of Haida songs is one of the few recent publications to attempt a survey of all song genres of a specific First Nation. Like Enrico and Stuart, Robert Witmer (1991) has demonstrated the importance of archival materials in the analysis of historical change in song repertoires. Richard Burleson (2004) has analyzed rhythmic dimensions. Arden Ogg (1988) has made an innovative study of Cree song texts in relation to melody. Language in the context of song and vocal style has been the focus of several other studies as well (Diamond 1998, Surmont 2004, Tremblay-Matte and Rivard 2001). The northern Dene have also collaborated with a number of ethnomusicologists in recent years in the study of traditional repertoires. Lucy Lafferty and Keillor (2009) have written about the Dogrib love and land songs, complementing Ogg's work on Cree love songs; Beaudry's (1992a) more anthropologically informed approach has focused on the prophecy tradition of Dene dream songs. A cultural analysis of the Mi'kmaq snake dance by Trudy Sable (1996, 1998) in the context of her master's thesis research on traditional scientific knowledge demonstrates how the disciplinary categories of the Western academy have often distorted the frames of Native American knowledge systems. Cronk's (1988) account of Haudenosaunee "socials" provides deeply informed description while also querying the relationship of scholar and community. Paula Thistle Conlon's (1992) Iglulik Inuit study uses the semiotic analytical method developed by Jean-Jacques Nattiez, and Nattiez's (1999) recent publication on Inuit throat songs, comprising his Seeger lecture to the Society for Ethnomusicology, continues his work of the 1970s. To some extent, however, the splurge of attention given to Inuit music in the 1970s slowed in subsequent decades.

Other important themes that have been addressed in recent decades include kinship and transmission processes (Asch 1988, Vascotto 2001), specific collectors (Wickwire 1988, on James Teit; Thompson 2007, with a useful listing of Teit's audio recordings; Smith 2008, on Marius Barbeau), teaching practices (Smith 2006, Whidden 2007), and intellectual property (Harrison 2002, Diamond 2008c). These studies indicate rich and significant topics that will undoubtedly benefit from further research in the future.

New technologies as well as new ways of integrating verbal and non-verbal information have had a significant impact not only on production, as described earlier, but on representation as well. Scholars have questioned the relationship of image and text, either explicitly or implicitly, by using multimedia presentation. Prior to the period under consideration in this chapter, explorations of musical transcriptions (e.g., Beaudry 1978; Charron 1978, who developed an innovative way of writing the sounds of Inuit throat games, or *katajjait*) raised issues that would emerge in Victoria Lindsay Levine's (2002) continent-wide compilation and interpretation of music notation of Native American song. Among these issues were the challenges of conveying such things as timbre or breathing patterns in visual representation. The SPINC project used photographic images as a way of mediating interviews during the research process (Diamond, Cronk, and von Rosen 1994) and attempted to integrate photographs and verbal text (sometimes drawn from interviews) in a collage-like presentation that had elements of hypertext in print. Particularly on the West Coast, a tradition of photo essays of the potlatch, one of the best of which is Ulli Steltzer's *A Haida Potlatch* (1984), offered an integrated presentation of image and text. An emphasis on integrating image, colour, and text is often evident in works authored by scholars of Native American descent (Heth 1992; Longboat 2010, which concerns residential school stories but with many references to expressive culture). Notable museum exhibitions (e.g., Jonaitis 1991, Martin and Boyer 2001) with richly illustrated catalogues have maintained their longstanding tradition of integrating image, text, and artefact (in the case of exhibitions) in representations of performance events.[19] More recently, imaginative websites have asserted, either implicitly or explicitly, the interdependence of image, sound, and verbal text. Significant among these are www.native-drums.ca and www.native-dance.ca, two massive sites conceptualized and overseen by Elaine Keillor in collaboration with a large number of Aboriginal organizations and individuals. Overview essays, interviews with significant Aboriginal elders and musicians, photographs, and videos present an array of voices and styles of representation on these sites. More limited in its coverage but deeper in its presentation of language and traditional knowledge perspectives within a single First Nation is the *Dane Wajich* website (Doig River 2007), created by the Doig River community with Amber Ridington and Kate Hennesey.[20] Like Keillor's websites, this site is a model of consultative practice and decision making since its design and content were carefully negotiated in the community.

Although one might applaud these new forms of mediated representation, perhaps describing them as something of a "postmodern" turn, the postmodern identity constructs that have, broadly speaking, been studied the most extensively – race, class, and gender – have been addressed less than one might expect in the Canadian-authored literature on First Nations, Inuit, and Métis musical identities, although all these issues interweave in the oral histories and personal narratives documented in important anthologies such as *Strong Women Stories* (Anderson and Lawrence 2003), *Sifters* (Purdue 2001), and *In the Words of Elders* (Kulchyski et al. 1999). In Canadian-based communities, gender has been studied more than class or race constructs by ethnomusicologists (Diamond 2002, Diamond Cavanagh 1989, Hoefnagels 2007b, Keillor 1996, Piercey 2005, Vennum 1989a, Vosen 2001), with numerous gender-related comments arising in other studies as well (e.g., Tulk 2008). The impact of colonial institutions on gender constructs, for instance, is only beginning to come to light. Expressive culture has been central for both men and women in their struggles to negotiate and survive social upheaval, but these struggles have rarely been equivalent. Building on pioneering work by anthropologists such as Eleanor Leacock (1980), scholars have presented growing evidence (e.g., McBride 1995, 1999, 2001, Diamond 2008b) that women in the Northeast and along the Atlantic seaboard played a crucial role as cross-cultural mediators. One might argue, then, that the complexity of traditional concepts of sex and gender, the Aboriginal emphasis on the complementarity of the strengths of men and women, and the radically different impacts of colonialism demand a new approach that has not yet been adequately articulated within Canadian ethnomusicology. The same might be said for the analysis of how social constructs of race and class have shaped musical practices.

At the beginning of the twenty-first century, new themes that concern Indigenous people globally are emerging as central concerns in ethnomusicology. Numerous gatherings are bringing Indigenous creative artists, dancers, and musicians together with (Indigenous and non-Indigenous) scholars to discuss a wide range of issues that are of transnational significance: the impact of digital technologies,[21] globalization's impact on traditional protocols and intellectual property issues,[22] community renewal, expressive culture's role in human rights struggles, arts practices as they relate to health, and many others. Engaged scholarship has become a shared obligation and an exciting pathway.

1 Luke Eric Lassiter's important overview the *Chicago Guide to Collaborative Ethnography* (2005) is shaped fundamentally by the collaborations he is involved in during his ongoing Kiowa research.

2 This chapter focuses on scholarly articles and monographs that present new research. In addition, during the past two decades, there have been many publications that synthesize existing information or offer bibliographic/discographic guidance. They include textbooks such as Elaine Keillor's *Music in Canada* (2006) and newer reference works such as volume 3 of the *Garland Encyclopedia of World Music* (Koskoff 2001), the *Continuum Encyclopedia of Popular Music of the World* (Shepherd et al. 2005), the second edition of the *Encyclopedia of Music in Canada* (Kallmann et al. 1992), Richard Keeling's *North American Indian Music* (1997), and Brian Wright-McLeod's *Encyclopedia of Native Music* (2005), all of which have extensive coverage of communities, individuals, or practices in Canada. Several reference sources compiled by Native Americans have included significant material on music-related topics and individuals; see, for instance, Rayna Green's *The British Museum Encyclopedia of Native North America* (1999) or Duane Champagne's *Native America: Portrait of the Peoples* (1994).

3 This volume's bibliography includes work on the northern powwow and other topics relevant to First Nations who live both north and south of the Canada-US border.

4 A number of very short articles in bulletins or newsletters relevant to this chapter are not included in the volume's bibliography.

5 During the same period, access to historical studies has often been enhanced by print or electronic publication. Among the older documents now accessible digitally are the Human Relations Area Files; see http://www.yale.edu/hraf (accessed 22 July 2011). These reprints of older material are not included in the current survey.

6 Much of Ridington's career-long scholarship about the Dane-ẕaa has been compiled in two significant anthologies (Ridington 1990, Ridington and Ridington 2006).

7 *Recherches amérindiennes au Québec* also produced an anthology on "Chants et tambours" in 1985.

8 The anagram stands for Sound Producing Instruments in Native Communities. With support from the Social Sciences and Humanities Research Council of Canada, I formed this research group at Queen's University in 1985. The group included Michael Sam Cronk, Franziska von Rosen, and myself.

9 Here, I use the term that Bruce Trigger coined for non-Indigenous populations in his groundbreaking book *Natives and Newcomers* (1985).

10 Curiously, several studies of residential schools have only passing reference to music.

11 In the United States Judith Gray and Charlotte Heth have also worked on hymnody.

12 Rayna Green (1989, 1999) has published extensively on non-Native visual, theatrical, and musical representations of "Indians," with particular emphasis on the representation of women in what she has called the "Pocohantas perplex."

13 Lederman has also contributed to the definition of "Métis" by writing numerous encyclopedia articles and through her one-woman show describing her fieldwork in Métis communities in Manitoba. As a skilled performer of Métis fiddle music, she also maintains the tradition.

14 As this volume goes to press, Marcia Ostashewski is undertaking a postdoctoral project on Ukrainian Aboriginal families and cultural connections.

15 Historians trace the end of the Beothuk to the death of Shawnadithit (perhaps the last pure-blood Beothuk) in 1828, ignoring that families of mixed descent thrive to the present day. Many histories attribute the demise of the Beothuk to the Mi'kmaq, overdrawing hostilities between the nations and ignoring many instances of collaboration and intermarriage.

16 Arbor Records' eleven-part DVD series *Powwow Trail* (2004) is a noteworthy example. More recently, First Nations Films' documentary *Beat of the Drum* (n.d.) has received an American Indian Film Festival award.

17 Publication of the oral histories of Aboriginal people other than song carriers has burgeoned, including the landmark bilingual (Innu-aimun and French) autobiographies of Innu elders published in the 1970s and 1980s by Lemeac (e.g., Antane Kapesh 1976) and shorter biographies of Native women in the arts (Brant and Laronde 1996). See also Anderson (2000), Anderson and Lawrence (2003), Caldwell (1999), Perdue (2001), and Kulchyski et al. (1999).

18 Margaret Paul has also presented a part of her life story in Kulchyski et al. (1999).

19 It should be noted that some studies of the potlatch focus on dimensions other than the music and dance performance. See, for example, Cole and Chaikin (1990) on the legal history relating to the bans initiated in the 1880s or Kan (1989) on the mortuary customs and beliefs.

20 This site won the Jean Rouch Prize, awarded by the American Anthropological Association.

21 A symposium on "Indigenous People and Digital Technologies" in 2010, organized by Royal Holloway University in Egham, United Kingdom, was one such event.

22 A colloquium on this topic in Toronto in 2008, sponsored by the International Council for Traditional Music, attracted widespread attention from Indigenous musicians and (Indigenous and non-Indigenous) scholars in eight countries. Paper abstracts are online at http://www.mun.ca/indigenousIP (accessed 22 July 2011).

PART ONE
Innovating Tradition

ANNA HOEFNAGELS AND
BEVERLEY DIAMOND

The concept of tradition has variable meanings, associations, and uses in different contexts, but although scholars have unpacked its complexity, frequent ambiguity, and randomness, it remains a designation that is widely used in most communities, especially Aboriginal communities. The term functions as a dance category, for instance, in reference to Men's and Women's Traditional dances at powwows; "traditional teachings" explain appropriate behaviours and guide younger generations as they learn about their culture and its practices; traditional music can be contrasted with contemporary music or with music that draws from mainstream music; traditional ways of life might be invoked when describing a person's or a community's way of surviving and living on a daily basis; and "traditional" is also frequently used to describe someone who adheres to "Native" spirituality in contrast to those who identify as "Christian." But although "tradition" may be spoken about as part of a binary construction (contrasted with "modernity" and "contemporary" expression or with Western life-ways, Christian beliefs, and commercial performance contexts), as the chapters in this section demonstrate, the labels "traditional" and "tradition" do not always imply such binaries in Aboriginal contexts. First Nations, Inuit, or Métis musicians, elders, and community members might see new forms or styles as adding new layers of meaning, referencing both the contemporary and older memories simultaneously. New musical arts, dance, and creative work may reflect "traditional" themes or social values. The ongoing development of "traditional" music often reflects local, and sometimes very personal, understandings of what is meant by "tradition." Furthermore, through these chapters, it becomes evident that innovation, whether deliberate or "accidental," has permeated the histories and creative processes of traditional musicians and repertoires for generations. The authors and musicians illustrate that innovation and renewal are ongoing processes in many Indigenous musical repertoires and practices. It is thus important to consider how the words "tradition" and "traditional" are used and why – and by whom. Equally, they explore how tradition changes as it is reshaped by innovative artists, new contexts, and media developments.

The first chapter in this section, "Continuity and Innovation in the Dane-zaa Dreamers' Song and Dance Tradition: A Forty-Year Perspective," by Amber Ridington, illustrates the variability in a traditional music genre by comparing the same song as performed by different singers in the same community over the course of forty years. She highlights the Dane-zaa's concerns with the impact of technological change (particularly websites) on their repertoires, forcing consideration of content, intellectual property, and song ownership. She explores emerging community protocols for protecting the sacred nature of the song tradition and for ascribing both group and individual performers' intellectual property rights to dreamers' songs. The issue of song ownership is usually very important in repertoires that are considered traditional, as the transmission of a song from person to person, spirit to person, and person to group (in person and through recordings and/or websites) is often governed by common notions of appropriate song uses and sharing. However, as Ridington illustrates in this chapter, experimentation with songs considered "traditional" is not always welcome by community members and often requires careful negotiation in order not to offend them.

Ridington's analysis of the issues of song ownership and the innovation/ change of traditional song performances is complemented by an interview she recorded with singer-producer Garry Oker. In this interview, Ridington and Oker discuss the creative process Oker used in the development of his CD *Dane-zaa Dreamer's Melodies*, highlighting the challenges of song ownership, audience/community satisfaction/evaluation, and related issues. Coupled with the more extended chapter, this interview illustrates both active and "passive" negotiations with traditional repertoires, negotiations that result in changes in the performance practices and musical features of selected songs of the Dane-zaa.

The powwow is a relatively new and ever-evolving tradition, particularly in north-eastern North America. Janice Tulk's chapter, "Intertribal Traditions:

The Powwow as Mi'kmaw Cultural Expression," highlights some of the strategies that Mi'kmaw powwow participants use to make a borrowed, "intertribal" celebration something that is localized and Mi'kmaq-specific. Although the powwow celebration and its music, dance, and cultural teachings originated in First Nations distant from Mi'kma'ki, the traditional territory of the Mi'kmaq, in the past two decades the powwow has emerged as a valued cultural expression. Like powwows held in other parts of North America, Mi'kmaw powwows are subject to processes that strive to make the events more locally meaningful. Drawing on fieldwork at various powwows in Mi'kma'ki and on interviews with powwow participants, Tulk identifies three means of localization. First, she highlights the incorporation of pre-existing Mi'kmaw or local songs (such as "I'ko") and dance genres (such as Ko'jua) into the structure of the powwow; next, she illustrates how borrowed powwow traditions are inscribed with local, or nation-specific, meaning through the embellishment of regalia, the use of a local singing style or language, and discourse that emphasizes tradition, or "the Mi'kmaw way"; last, she suggests that the recognition of local histories (including colonial histories referenced in Christian themes/prayers at powwows) in oration and in performance is one way that Mi'kmaw culture is used to create a localized powwow that is meaningful to Mi'kmaq in eastern Canada.

The interview of powwow musician Gabriel Desrosiers by ethno-musicologist Christopher Scales offers insight into three important topics related to northern-style powwow song and dance: (1) the relationship between "traditional" and contemporary, or "competition," powwows; (2) influences of recording technology on musical practice and on the development of musical style; and (3) issues of song ownership and song transmission, particularly vis-à-vis commercial and personal recordings of powwow songs. The conversational style of the chapter, which presents the personal reflections of two powwow participants and studio producers, affords exciting insights into various issues and ideas about powwow music drawn from their extensive experience and knowledge of this tradition.

The final chapter in this section also addresses powwows and tradition. "Aboriginal Women and the Powwow Drum: Restrictions, Teachings, and Challenges," by Anna Hoefnagels, queries the common practices and traditional teachings associated with making powwow music. At most powwows men strike the powwow drum and lead the singing of the song, and if women are present as musicians, they are usually restricted to the role of back-up singer, entering in particular places in the songs an octave higher than the men. Drawing on interviews with First Nations female and male powwow musicians, Hoefnagels explores various issues and considerations regarding the common practices and traditional teachings that define women's public music making at powwows, and she describes how women are, in fact, performing this repertoire contrary to common teachings or as reinterpretations of those teachings. Some all-female powwow groups are being well received in some regions and communities, and Hoefnagels examines the performance choices and music making of an all-female drum group in terms of where and why they choose to perform. As she demonstrates, it is clear that although Aboriginal women respect traditional teachings, many are seeking empowerment and a "reawakening" of their voices through their participation in the performance of powwow music.

Together, the chapters in this section of the anthology illustrate the vitality of Aboriginal traditions and traditional music. The sense of renewal and the engagement with innovative ways of thinking about and making "traditional music" demonstrate the dynamism of tradition. New technologies, revised interpretations of teachings, and the importance of local and personal histories in the construction of cultural understandings and ways of life are all part of this dynamism.

2

Continuity and Innovation in the Dane-ẕaa Dreamers' Song and Dance Tradition: A Forty-Year Perspective

AMBER RIDINGTON

Informed by performance theory,[1] this chapter takes a contextual approach to trace some of the ways that the Dane-ẕaa dreamers' dance[2] and song tradition has responded to and been affected by historical, cultural, social, and technological changes over the past forty years. I identify both continuities and innovations in the song and dance tradition over this period of time and relate these findings to responses of resistance and renewal to new social circumstances. The first sections of this chapter introduce Dane-ẕaa culture and history and place the Dane-ẕaa dreamers' dance within a broader Indigenous prophet dance movement associated with cultural changes brought on by European cultural encounters and colonization. Moving from a broad, ritualized context with a focus on dance movement, I outline structural elements of the dreamers' songs themselves and then trace continuities and innovations in the maintenance of these musical elements between the 1960s and the present. Taking this analysis a step further, I compare four performances of the same dreamers' song recorded between 1966 and 2008 by different performers in different contexts and discuss the implications of continuities and innovations, as seen in this particular song example, for the tradition's conservation and renewal. Finally, I discuss implications of recording and new media technologies in facilitating preservation, revitalization, and innovation of the dreamers' song tradition; I also address emerging intellectual property concerns and protocols that have arisen in response to this new electronically mediated era affecting the global transmission of Dane-ẕaa dreamers' songs. To provide the basic cultural and historical context for the materials discussed here, I draw on the writings and ethnographic fieldwork of Robin Ridington, Antonia Mills,[3] and Jillian Ridington relating to the Dane-ẕaa, along with relevant work by other ethnographers working in neighbouring Athapaskan communities.[4] I also utilize my own knowledge, experience, and work with the Dane-ẕaa.[5]

A Brief Introduction to the Dane-ẕaa

The Dane-ẕaa, also known as Beaver Indians, are an Athapaskan group indigenous to the Peace River area of north-eastern British Columbia and north-western Alberta. Today, there are approximately 1,000 Dane-ẕaa living in and around the Doig River, Blueberry River, Halfway River, and Prophet River reserve communities (figure 2.1). Until very recently, the Dane-ẕaa lived semi-nomadically, travelling seasonally to hunt, gather, and socialize with their kinship groups. After their first known direct contact with Europeans in 1794, when Rocky Mountain Fort was established in their territories (on the Peace River close to the current city of Fort St John), the Dane-ẕaa began participating in the fur trade and in cultural exchange with European traders and Cree middlemen and porters (Brody 1981; Burley, Hamilton, and Fladmark 1996, 30; Roe 2003).

After the 1860s the Dane-ẕaa continued cultural exchanges with Catholic missionaries, gold prospectors, government agents, and farmers, and they signed Treaty No. 8 in 1900. Despite these cultural interactions, as well as a drastic population loss due to smallpox and the Spanish flu, Dane-ẕaa traditional life-ways were not radically affected until their ancestral land was opened up for non-Native settlement and industry through the construction of the Alaska Highway in 1942 (Roe 2003). Since the Second World War, the Dane-ẕaa's life-ways and culture have undergone more rapid change. They have been forced to settle on reserves and to send their children to outside schools, have incorporated new patterns of hunting and community sustainability, have been heavily influenced by Evangelical Christian missionary efforts, and are now influenced by popular culture and media (Ridington 1988a, Doig River 2007, Ridington and Ridington 2006).

These changes have had serious consequences for the maintenance of the Dane-ẕaa's social networks and for the continuing relevance and use of the Dane-ẕaa language, as well as their song and dance tradition. Although the Dane-ẕaa still maintain a sense of identity and actively protect customs and practices deeply rooted in their culture, they struggle with the threat of cultural erosion and practical issues related to alcohol-

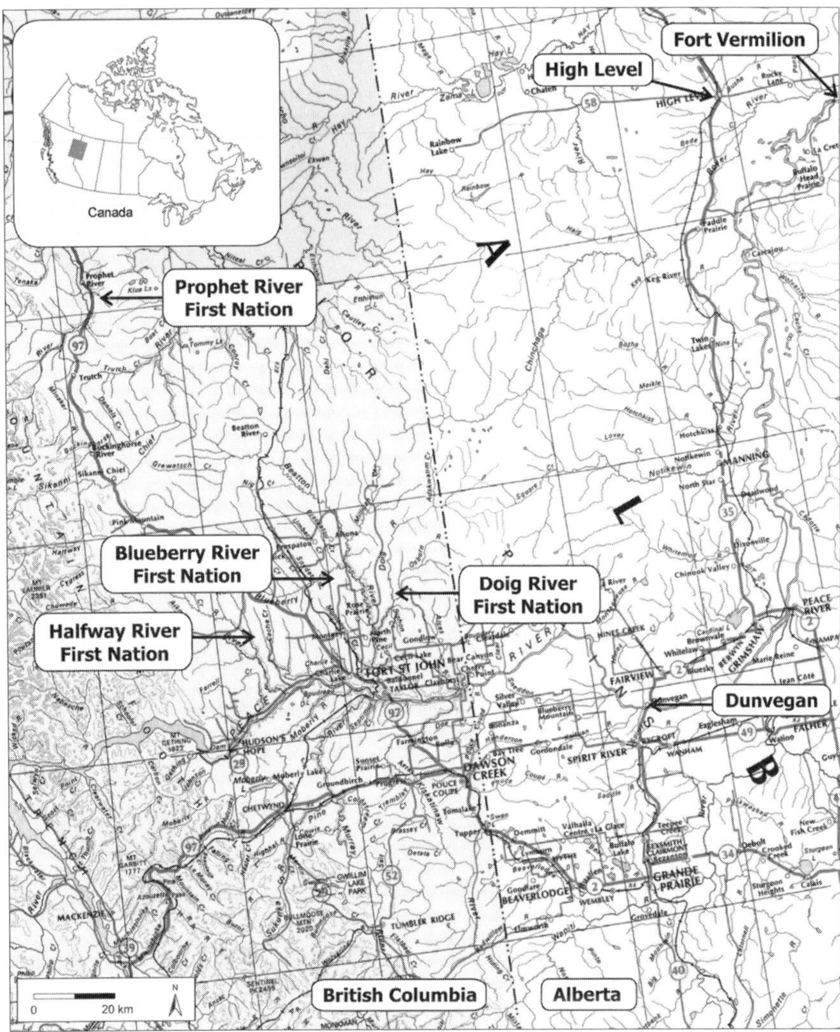

2.1 The four Dane-ẕaa reserves in north-eastern British Columbia and some areas of Dane-ẕaa traditional use and interaction in north-western Alberta. The Alaska Highway is Route 97. The Peace River runs west to east below the town of Fort St John and turns northward at Dunvegan, Alberta. Base map used with permission of the Ministry of Lands and Parks, Province of British Columbia, "NE BC" (1:2,000,000), 1991.

ism, youth support, employment, education, racism, and community cohesion. Robin Ridington and Jillian Ridington observe that over the past fifty years they "have been privileged to witness the Dane-ẕaa move from a purely hunting and trapping economy to one that is now integrated, in a dense and complex way, into the fabric of contemporary political and economic issues" (Ridington and Ridington 2006, 96). Indeed, many Dane-z̲aa leaders have become adept at negotiating their way through the labyrinth of colonial law to defend their peoples' Aboriginal and treaty rights. In 1998, after a twenty-year fight for justice, the Doig River and Blueberry River Bands received a settlement of $147 million after suing the federal government for breach of trust and lost oil and gas revenues from the 1945 "surrender" of their Indian Reserve (#172) at Gat Tah Kwą̂ (Montney)[6] by the Department of Indian Affairs so that the land could be made available for settlement by returning veterans of the Second World War. Doig River and Blueberry River people, classified as the Fort St John Band at that time, had chosen the reserve land in 1914 pursuant to land allotments set out under Treaty No. 8. They had chosen this land because of its significance as a summer gathering place for their people and be-cause of the dance grounds there called Suunéch'ii Kéch'iige yiné? (the Place Where Happiness Dwells) (Ridington and Ridington 2006, 104–5; Doig River 2007). Virtually overnight, the Doig River and Blueberry River Bands rose from a position of economic poverty to a position of monet-ary wealth.

The Doig River First Nation has utilized some of its newfound wealth to take a lead in using new media technologies to preserve, revitalize, share, and teach about Dane-z̲aa culture. This new electronically medi-ated era of cultural revitalization began with a number of digital heritage-preservation projects in the late 1990s. These heritage-preservation pro-jects led to the creation of a digital archive of Dane-z̲aa audio, video, text-ual, and photographic materials recorded by Robin Ridington, Antonia Mills, Jillian Ridington, and their colleagues since 1964, called the Rid-ington/Dane-z̲aa Digital Archive. Once digitally preserved, the archive materials were virtually repatriated to all the Dane-z̲aa communities on a 500-gigabyte harddrive curated by the Doig River First Nation in its community centre and accompanied by a password-protected Internet-based catalogue interface (Ridington, Ridington, and Doig River 2003, Ridington and Ridington 2003, Ridington and Hennessy 2008, Hennessy 2010). With new access to these digital cultural-heritage materials, the Doig River First Nation continued to work in collaboration with trusted ethnographers to produce audio CDs, videos, and websites for educa-tional use by its own community and the general public.[7]

The Dane-z̲aa dreamers' dance tradition has been greatly affected by all of the historical, social, and technological changes detailed above. The dances have ceased to be practised regularly in many communities. Cur-rently, the Doig River community, which contains a core group of singers and drummers, is the only remaining Dane-ẕaa group to regularly hold community-wide dance gatherings and to take an active role in revitalizing the song and dance tradition. Dynamic and conservative elements of the tradition are detailed in later sections of this chapter as examples of resistance and renewal in the face of changing social contexts.

Cultural Context of Dane-ẕaa Song and Dance

Like the worldview of most Indigenous northern hunting cultures worldwide, the Dane-ẕaa worldview has a cyclical perspective that reflects the natural cycles of the world and the natural cycles of life, death, and rebirth. The Dane-ẕaa worldview is also based upon a belief that there is an interdependence between people, animals, and forces of nature and that people gain power by learning how to communicate with human and animal spirits and forces of nature (Ridington 2006a, 171; Ridington 1968, 91). Dane-ẕaa songs reflect this practical and sacred practice and are used as a medium for prayer and communication with spirits and forces.

The Dane-ẕaa have two types of songs. Personal medicine songs, received during vision quests, are called *mayiné?* (my song) and are almost never sung in public or shared with others. They are used only when a person is in dire need of help. I will not be discussing mayiné? here.[8] Songs shared with the community and sung both by individuals on their own and during dreamers' dance gatherings are referred to as *nááchẹyiné?* (dreamers' songs), *Nahhatááʔyiné?* (God songs), or prayer songs. These songs are given to a dreamer in Heaven[9] by the Creator/God to help the dreamer guide Dane-ẕaa people through life and death and for use during their prayer and dance ceremonies (Mills 1982; Ridington 2006a, 172). In recent years some of these songs have also been shared with the public through public performances and on the Internet. A Dane-ẕaa *nááchẹ*, referred to as a dreamer or prophet in English, is a person who has gained dream-travelling and prophetic abilities only after a significant experience, such as dying and coming back to life. In the Dane-ẕaa dreamers' dance, which is described in greater detail later, the natural cycles of the world are symbolically enacted as people dance in a circle following the direction of the sun and retrace their steps through life so that they can eventually follow a dreamer's song along the trail to Heaven (Mills 1982; Ridington 2006a, 172).

The Dane-ẕaa dreamers' dance tradition can be seen as part of a broader Indigenous North American song and dance tradition. Similar ceremonial practices centred around the circle dance and world renewal have been referred to in various western North American Indian cultures as the prophet dance (Spier 1935, Goulet 1996, 1998, Ridington 1978, 1988a, 1990, Mills 1982, 2004, Cebula 2003, among others), the ghost dance (Vander 1997, Coleman 2000, Shea Murphy 2007, among others), the drum dance (Abel 1993, Asch 1988, Beaudry 1988a, 1992a), and the tea dance (Asch 1988, Moore and Wheelock 1990).[10] All of these terms have come to refer to messianic shamanic movements originating shortly before or after the contact period in western North America. Many dreamers/prophets associated with these traditions predicted the changes, disruptions, and diseases associated with white contact and directed their people to counter these changes by dancing to restore balance in their world (Mills 2004, 288). Although the Dane-zaa dreamers' dance and the other dance movements mentioned above can be seen as rites of resistance to devastating colonial policies, they can also be seen as examples of innovation and cultural syncretism that meld Indigenous and Christian cosmological philosophies. In many instances, the dance movements join Aboriginal shamanic principles about renewing the cycles of the world with Christian messages about the importance of clean living and forgiveness for one's resurrection/redemption on Judgment Day (Vander 1997, 76; Goulet 1996; Ridington 1978, 1988a; Mills 1982, 10; Cebula 2003, 47; Cruikshank 1998a, 119; Shea Murphy 2007, 47).

One of the first dreamers in the Dane-zaa dreamers' dance religion, born in the mid- or late 1700s, was named Makénúúnatane. Like Jesus, he is remembered in particular for his messages of mercy and compassion. Makénúúnatane is credited with predicting the coming of the "whiteman," a new pathway to Heaven, as well as the end of the world (Mills 1982, 10; Doig River 2007).[11] With the influx of Europeans in the late 1700s, the Dane-zaa's knowledge-based technology of the communal hunt was undermined by the introduction of the gun and by changing subsistence patterns. Dreamer Makénúúnatane's teachings and prophecies helped the Dane-zaa people to make sense of the new tools and worldviews introduced through non-Native contact and later colonial policies (Ridington 1978, 46–8).

Robin Ridington points out that the main difference between the Dane-zaa dreamers' dance tradition and the more widespread prophet dance tradition – as well as, I suggest, the adjacent north-western Athapaskan traditions documented by Jean-Guy Goulet (1996, 1998) and by Patrick Moore and Angela Wheelock (1990), among others – is that each song in the Dane-zaa tradition is rooted in the particulars of Dane-zaa experience, genealogy, and narrative tradition. All of the Dane-zaa dreamers can be placed in known family genealogies recorded both in oral tradition and in baptismal and fur trade company records, and all of the dreamers' songs in the repertoire of contemporary Dane-ẕaa singers derive from these twenty dreamers. Additionally, many of the dreamers' names convey titles that refer to a dreamer's particular influence or teaching (Ridington, Hastings, and Attachie 2005, 117). The Doig River First Nation recently compiled and displayed information about all of its dreamers on its *Dane Wajich* website and included audio examples of many of these dreamers' songs performed by singers and drummers from the community (Doig River 2007).[12] This electronically mediated transmission of dreamers' songs and their contextualizing narratives represent an innovation for the maintenance and revitalization of the Dane-ẕaa dreamers' song tradition. Indeed, as tradition bearers continue to pass away, CDs, harddrives, and websites are coming to be valued as new song keepers connecting the people with many of their teachers.

Dane-ẕaa Nááchẹyiné? Structure and Customary Use

Although there has been a great deal of literature about prophet dance movements and their development, as referenced in the preceding section, little work has been done to examine the songs that were and are central to these practices. An exception to this in the literature about the Dane-ẕaa is Brian Lillos's 1977 structural study of forty-five dreamers' songs recorded by Robin Ridington and Antonia Mills between 1966 and 1967. Lillos's study provides musical transcriptions and structural analysis to accompany the recordings of these nááchẹyiné?. However, Lillos acknowledges that an analysis of the cultural context and social message revealed by the song recordings he analyzed is beyond the scope of his work (Lillos 1977, 63).

In this section I make an effort to describe the basic structural pattern of nááchẹyiné? and the associated Dane-ẕaa hand drum playing styles in relatively simple language. Here, and throughout this chapter, I also make an effort to contextualize the songs in both Dane-ẕaa culture and practice from a number of perspectives (e.g., historical, social setting, individual) in order to identify actions, social messages, and symbols revealed by Dane-ẕaa nááchẹyiné? performances.

Vocables and Structure

Songs typically have anywhere from one to three distinct melodic lines that each start on a high pitch and end on a much lower one. These melodic lines with descending contours are made up of a series of vocables, primarily vowels and the letter *h*, which are common sounds used in the

Dane-z̲aa language. Song keeper Tommy Attachie explains the vocables and melodies used in Dane-z̲aa dreamers' songs in the following way:

> No words in it.
> Just sing like that ...
> This is no words in there, but the way Creator give to prophet.
> That is the way it is.
> No words. (Attachie 2007)

Attachie also tells me that traditional song keepers place a high value on recreating the song melodies as faithfully as they can. Dreamer and song keeper Ak'ize (Emma Skookum) also emphasizes the importance of maintaining the structure of each dreamer's song:

> Me, I don't change the song.
> I don't move it.
> Me, that's who I am. (Skookum 1966, trans. Madeline Oker 2003)

Although I have noted that the melody is recreated quite closely with each performance, the actual vocables used by each lead singer do have variation. Each singer seems to come up with a distinctive way of singing the song, tailored to his or her own voice and vocable preference, while at the same time maintaining the original melody.[13]

In practice, dreamers' songs can be sung once through, or they can be sung many times in a row, creating a continuous structural sequence. In the case of a two-line song, for example, this can be represented as AB AB AB and so on. The number of times a song is sung depends on the social context of the performance and the singer's preference. At dreamers' dances, for example, the songs are often sung many times in a row, especially if the audience is enjoying the dance and the singers' voices are strong. During more private performances or in instances when the singer sings for himself or herself, the songs tend to be repeated fewer times (Attachie 2007, Oker 2007). A variation to this melodic structure is the occasional addition of a few Dane-z̲aa words inserted into the last, low register, vocables of the song. Most often, words such as *Yaage Satiin* (Sky Sitter/Sky Keeper) or *Nahhatáá?* (Our Father)[14] are added to a song to emphasize the singers' worship and prayer through their performance (S. Acko 2007).

Although there are no words at the core of dreamers' songs, they are not without significance or meaning.[15] As mentioned earlier, dreamers' songs can be seen as a language – a medium for communicating with animal and human spirits, forces of nature, and the Creator. As well as being a mode of communication, each song has a meaning that is highly contextualized. Narratives, often told before or after a song performance, are used to contextualize the songs and to maintain their genealogical and historic associations. Knowledge about nááchęyiné? is accrued through time as people are exposed to the songs in different performance settings and by different performers with their own body of knowledge about the songs. Information typically associated with each song by song keepers and some community members includes its dreamer, its message from Heaven, and its significance in Dane-ẕaa history. Song connotations may also include the circumstances of an individual's personal use of the song during prayer.

Song Performers

Traditionally, both women and men, including adolescents, adults, and elders, knew and sang dreamers' songs and used them as part of their prayer practice. Today, women always sing *a capella*, whereas men often accompany themselves with a hand drum (S. Acko 2007, Davis 2007, Makadahay 2007). Many of the current elders remember that their fathers often started and ended the day in prayer by singing dreamers' songs.[16] As Sam Acko recalls, "That is everyday praying for Dane-ẕaa people" (S. Acko 2007). At dreamers' dances, including those held as part of memorial services, songs are typically sung by a group of male singers who accompany themselves on hand drums. Drumming begins before the singing, usually for just enough time to establish a clear and synchronized beat, and ends with the conclusion of the vocals. One of the song keepers leads the session, choosing the songs to sing and taking the vocal lead. The performers drum in unison and sing together in a monophonic style, without harmony. Lillos (1977, 77) points out that vocal tension is apparent in Dane-ẕaa dreamers' songs but not to the extent that it is seen in most other North American Indigenous music.

Hand Drum Accompaniment

The Dane-ẕaa have two types of drums: single-headed snare drums and double-headed barrel drums. They range between one foot and one and one-quarter feet in diameter, are typically made of cow moose rawhide stretched tightly across birch frames, and are secured with babiche (twisted sinew) (J. Askoty 2007, 01:25). Both types of drum are held by one hand and are beaten with a stick about eight inches in length.

The double-headed barrel drums are used only by dreamers or occasionally by others who have inherited drums after dreamers have passed away. They are about four to six inches deep and are held by a leather thong attached to the top side of the drum frame. Robin Ridington and Antonia Mills recorded dreamer Charlie Yahey performing with a double-headed drum made by dreamer Gaayęą and took a number of photographs of Charlie Yahey with this drum, which are now part of the Ridington/Dane-ẕaa Digital Archive (Ridington, Ridington, and Doig River 2003). Double-headed drums, like the one documented by Ridington and Mills, were often painted by dreamers with maps of the trail to Heaven that they received in their dreams.

The single-headed adjustable snare drum is the type used by most song keepers and singers. It has two thick strands of babiche strung across the bottom of the drum frame at a ninety-degree angle, which are wrapped/webbed at their intersection to make a handle. A thin babiche string, referred to as a snare, is attached to the inside of the drum frame so that it rests horizontally against the bottom side of the drum head but can also be pulled tight by the drummer's thumb. This allows the drummer to put varying tension on the snare as he plays and to create a range of buzzing sounds. Robin Ridington writes that the buzzing sound of snares on the drum head are meant to evoke the dream world and the dreamer's path to Heaven (Oker, Ridington, and Shaak 2000, liner notes). Beverley Diamond and colleagues describe how other northern First Nations, particularly the Innu, describe the sounds of snares as "spirit voices" (Diamond, Cronk, and von Rosen 1994, 87, 140). These examples, both from the Dane-ẕaa and other First Nations groups, indicate that the audience for songs often includes spirits as well as the people who are physically present during the performance. This is an important point that is often neglected, in part due to an etic/outsider perspective that does not take into account the basic worldview that most First Nations people have. Figures 2.2 and 2.3 show some typical single-headed adjustable snare hand drums, which have changed little in design over the years.

Drumming Styles

Before singing begins, drums are tuned over a fire, or sometimes over an electric stove, to adjust their pitch to the singer's voice. Although drumming is an optional accompaniment for dreamers' songs, the drumbeat is generally fixed for each particular song (Attachie 2007). The most common drumbeat, a steady, unaccented pattern (DUM, DUM, DUM, DUM, DUM ...), evokes the sense of walking over a long distance. The less commonly used drumming pattern, also unaccented, consists of a short percussive beat followed by a longer beat (daDUM, daDUM, daDUM, daDUM, daDUM ...). This short-long drumming pattern is called "jig time," or *Dishinni*, the Dane-ẕaa word for Cree people, as it is the same drumming pattern practised by Cree people who moved to, and often settled in, Dane-ẕaa territory during the fur trade. Dane-ẕaa use of this beat exemplifies how Dane-ẕaa people have incorporated new cultural patterns into their own traditions and have made them their own. Having presented some of the structural elements of Dane-ẕaa dreamers' songs, I now move on to outline stable and divergent aspects of the song and dance tradition over the past forty years.

The Dane-ẕaa Dreamers' Dance of the 1960s

In the 1960s there were still two Dane-ẕaa dreamers living: Charlie Yahey at Blueberry River and Ak'ize (Emma Skookum) at Halfway River (Doig River 2007). At that time, the Dane-ẕaa people were also more actively engaged in traditional forms of subsistence, such as hunting, snaring, and trapping. The adults of this era had not gone to school and had been raised in their small kinship groups travelling seasonally throughout their hunting and trapping grounds and meeting up with other Dane-ẕaa people at dreamers' dances in the summer months. One of the main features of the dreamers' dance of the 1960s was its sacred[17] nature. People believed in the teachings of the dreamers and followed customs to maintain the power relations between themselves and the other living and nonliving creatures of the world that they relied on for sustenance. Robin Ridington describes a typical Dane-ẕaa dreamers' dance from the early 1960s as lasting three or four nights. During the day, he notes, the dreamer may dream for the people or talk to them about his dreaming. Ridington writes,

> The Beavers dance, usually in a large tepee, clockwise, or as they say, "following the sun" around a fire. The fire is the center of the circle and its column of smoke joins heaven and earth, the axis of subjective experience. Extending horizontally out from the fire is a circle of people. The singers and drummers are mainly young adults, the hunters. They sit in the direction of the sunrise [east],

2.2 Dreamers' dance inside a tipi, Doig River, 1966. Drummer on far left is Tommy Attachie, and at centre is Tar Davis. Photograph by Robin Ridington (Ridington/ Dane-ẕaa Digital Archive, catalogue no. OS DDD 12), used with permission of Robin Ridington and Doig River First Nation.

> just as they sleep in their own camps toward the sunrise. Older men sit toward the north, and the very old, as well as the Dreamer, if he is present, sit toward the sunset [west]. Women and their children sit along the southern circumference of the circle, and the door is generally the dividing line between men and women. (Ridington 1990, 62)

Figure 2.2 shows gender division at a dreamers' dance in the 1960s. At very large Dane-ẕaa gatherings, the dances were held outside, and people would dance around an open fire with the same physical arrangement based on age and gender as described above.

Rita Makadahay, a current Doig River elder, recalls the sacred nature of dreamers' songs and the dreamers' dance during her youth and notes some of the changes in the current practice:

> I am probably about thirteen, fourteen.
> Then [dreamer] Charlie Yahey used to come to Doig, or Petersen's Crossing.
> They usually have a powwow for about seven days.
> I used to really like that.
> Like not only for dancing, but my mum said also,

"Think about God when you dance
    because you're dancing unto the Lord.
    This is not for fun!" ...
  It's very different now because most people just dance for fun or
    something ...
  Now there's no prophet so it's kind of hard.
  I guess the older people they still do dance the way they believe.
  But the younger people should be taught how to respect,
    not only elders, but the song ...
  It doesn't matter how you dance.
  It's how you think when you go into the dance.
  Like mostly people now they pick out songs so if they could dance
    good to this tune,
    but it's not like that, back then when I was young,
    it don't matter what kind of song,
        "Get up and dance."
  My mum used to tell us that.

The Dane-<u>z</u>aa Dreamers' Dance Today

In the quotation above, Rita Makadahay mentions one of the key differences between the dreamers' dance of her youth in the 1960s and that of today: the partial loss of reverence for the sacred and ceremonial nature of the dance. After the death of the last dreamer, Charlie Yahey, in 1976 and the death of Jack Acko, a respected elder and song keeper in 1979, the Dane-<u>z</u>aa people stopped holding tea dances[18] for a short period of time. As elder and song keeper Sam Acko recalls, "it seems like it slowed down for a while. We went pretty close to losing it" (S. Acko 2007). Sam Acko has explained that it took another death, this time of a young Dane-<u>z</u>aa man named Mackenzie Ben in 1981, for his community to restore the tea dance tradition. Mackenzie's death helped the community to remember that it had an obligation to help Mackenzie begin his journey to Heaven on a trail of song and that the dreamers' dance is an essential part of the Dane-<u>z</u>aa's traditional memorial practice. Revitalizing the song and dance tradition after a brief hiatus became an important affirmation of Dane-<u>z</u>aa cosmology despite significant pressure to adopt non-Native lifestyles and Christian funeral ceremonies during this era (S. Acko 2007). Revitalization was also facilitated by the community's access to recordings of the dreamers' songs that Robin Ridington and Antonia Mills had documented in the 1960s. As Sam Acko explains,

From there it picked up again.
And then we listened to a lot of these songs,
like reminder,
like what Robin Ridington did, those tapes ...
So that is why it picked up.
And today it is pretty good ...
But there is still a lot of songs from way back,
Makénúúnatane songs, people never hear it yet.
One day I would like to sing it.
Maybe next tea dance.
I would like to sing them all so people will learn from those
    songs. (S. Acko 2007)

Although all the Dane-zaa communities have access to the sample of
dreamers' songs recorded in the 1960s, the Doig River community is currently the only Dane-zaa group that publicly and actively maintains the
song and dance tradition. Doig River community members Tommy Attachie and Sam Acko are respected song keepers who lead a small group
of Doig River drummers, occasionally joined by singers and drummers
from other Dane-zaa communities.[19] Although they most often practise
and perform at their own reserve, the Doig River Drummers are often
called to the other three Dane-zaa communities to sing for memorial tea
dances after a community member has died.

Today, in contrast to the 1960s, instead of dancing, singing, and drumming for three or four nights, tea dances take place in one evening and are
usually over by midnight, in part due to the reduced number of singers in
the group, whose voices need a break after five or six hours of singing.
Additionally, the singers and drummers sit on a stage, speaker systems
are used to amplify the performance, and people appear to sit wherever
they like, forming groups related to friendships and kinship ties regardless of age and gender. In the past, when the Dane-zaa relied on hunting
and gathering for their principal sustenance, customs and taboos regulated the physical interaction of men and women to a far greater degree. I
suggest that since the economy has changed, the older customs that separated genders at tea dances are no longer as relevant and subsequently
are not maintained or are only selectively maintained. Although division
of the sexes is not maintained, the drummers are still positioned in the
east, the direction of the sunrise, and the people still dance around the
fire moving in a sunwise/clockwise direction, a symbol of the recurring
natural cycle of the sun and the seasons, as was the custom at large summer gatherings in the past.[20]

2.3 The Doig River Drummers performing on stage at Doig Day, 24 May 2007. From left are Brian Acko, Robert Dominic, Chief Kelvin Davis (in background), Freddy Askoty, Sam Acko, Tommy Attachie (lead singer), Leo Acko, and Johnny Askoty. Photograph by Amber Ridington (archived with Amber Ridington and the Whatcom Museum, catalogue no. ARDZDP-5-24-07-E-73), used with permission of Doig River First Nation.

Currently, in addition to holding tea dances as part of memorial services, the Doig River First Nation also regularly holds tea dances as part of its annual spring and summer gatherings. During the spring Doig Day festivities, in which the community invites hundreds of public school children from neighbouring areas to its reserve to learn about Dane-ẕaa culture, Dane-ẕaa children dance, accompanied by the Doig River drummers and singers, as part of a cultural performance (see figure 2.3). The traditional summer tea dance marking the summer solstice has become a relatively small part of the contemporary summer gathering festivities at Doig River, which revolve around the Doig River Rodeo. The rodeo, now part of the semi-professional circuit, takes place over two days and is preceded by a tea dance on Friday evening billed as a "cultural day." Almost all of the community members attend the two-day rodeo, but a relatively small number of community members, mostly elders and parents with young children, participate in the tea dance. Although the shift in focus from the dreamers' dance to the rodeo may seem to signal a change in Dane-ẕaa traditional culture, I recognize continuity in the traditional practice of Dane-ẕaa people gathering together from many different communities in the height of summer to socialize, renew their kinship links, and affirm their sense of identity as Dane-ẕaa people. The dreamers' dance still holds a firm spot in the annual Doig River summer gathering and is maintained by the Doig River drummers and singers, with the support of the chief and the council, even if it is poorly attended compared to the rodeo.

My recent work with Dane-ẕaa youth has shown that many have limited knowledge of, and intimacy with, the history and significance of each dreamer's song. Despite their lack of knowledge about the songs at this stage in their lives, youth do have experience and knowledge of dancing. They view dancing to be an essential part of their funerary practice as well as an important cultural display used to assert and affirm their Aboriginal identity. Indeed, for all Dane-ẕaa, the dreamers' dance and song tradition has become an important symbolic marker signifying their people's distinct culture. Dreamers' songs are not just performed at community events, such as memorial tea dances, Doig Day, and the Doig River Rodeo, but are also routinely incorporated into opening ceremonies and opening prayers at public meetings and gatherings with other First Nations as well as with provincial and federal government representatives.

Comparative Analysis: Recorded Performances of Dreamer Gaayęą's "Nedaheyiné?" (Prairie Chicken Song), 1966–2008

In this section I present and compare four recorded performances of dreamer Gaayęą's "Nedaheyiné?," referred to in English as his "Prairie Chicken Song," over a forty-two-year period by different performers and in different contexts. Because this song is referred to as both "Nedaheyiné?" and the more generic term "Jiihyiné?" (Grouse Song) by Dane-ẕaa song keepers, I use the English term here to avoid confusion.[21] The performance contexts include prayer, a memorial tea dance, a summer gathering, and a studio production. In my analysis of these recorded performances, I offer comments about continuities and innovations within the tradition and about the situated nature of song meaning and interpretation. To frame my analysis, I first share the historical context of the creation of Gaayęą's "Prairie Chicken Song," told to me by song keeper Tommy Attachie. This is a good example of how dreamers' songs and their narratives have functioned together to maintain Dane-ẕaa cultural history about people, places, events, and connections to the land.

As Attachie relates, Dreamer Gaayęą brought the "Prairie Chicken Song" back from Heaven in a dream he had in 1922 while camping at Sweeney Creek, Alberta, not too far east of the Doig River reserve. In the morning when he sang the song for the first time, a covey of prairie chickens appeared and began to dance. The male singers camped with Gaayęą at Sweeney Creek helped him to remember the song by following his lead and singing the melody over and over as they drummed. You can watch Tommy tell this story in far greater detail at Sweeney Creek in 2005 on the *Dane Wajich* website (Doig River 2007).[22]

1966 "Prairie Chicken Song" Performance

The first "Prairie Chicken Song" example I discuss here is a field recording by Robin Ridington performed by dreamer Charlie Yahey at his home at Blueberry River early in the morning on 2 January 1966. Other people present included a number of family members, both adults and children, four elders visiting from Prophet River, as well as ethnographers Robin Ridington and Antonia Mills. In his field notes, Robin writes that the weather was fiercely cold at the time and that drumming and singing were used to pray for and bring about a change in the weather (Ridington 1966). He further describes, "About 3 in the morning Charlie began singing and talking by himself. No one got up but everyone must have listened with interest. Paul [Notsetta] and Sally [St Pierre] said that maybe he had had a dream when we told them about it. He began talking, a very long serious uninterrupted speech in the morning. It was a very solemn atmosphere. Then the singing began, first Charlie and then Sam [St Pierre] and Jumbie, and I brought the tape recorder over and taped some of it and some oratory" (Ridington 1966). As part of this singing session, Charlie Yahey sang the "Prairie Chicken Song" three times in a row with the following structural pattern of melodic lines with descending contours: ABC BC ABC. He accompanied himself with his double-headed barrel drum given to him by dreamer Gaayęą using the steady, unaccented rhythmic pattern. Doig River drummer and singer Leo Acko translates Charlie Yahey's narrative surrounding the song as follows:

> Why are these spirit chickens gone?
> Even the last one prays.
>
> [Charlie Yahey drums and sings Gaayęą's "Prairie Chicken
> Song" three times in a row. For these three repetitions, the

structural pattern of melodic lines with descending contours is
ABC BC ABC.]

Even those animals, some time they say that.
And some people aren't afraid to pray.
Even with these prayer songs, I don't hear anybody pray with
    these songs in the evening.
You're all like white people now. Thinking like white people.
They all adapted to *Monias* (white man's) way.
But they won't be living forever.
It's long ways to Heaven.
(Ridington/Dane-ẕaa Digital Archive, catalogue no. CMC4-1,
    9:09–11:20, trans. Leo Acko 2007)

In his introduction to the song, Yahey does not directly name or reference Gaayęą as the dreamer of this song but refers to the "spirit chickens."
He knows that the majority of the audience already knows the historic
context of the "Prairie Chicken Song" and the narrative of how it came
to Gaayęą in a dream at Sweeney Creek. After singing the song, Yahey
warns about losing one's way to Heaven by abandoning dreamers' songs
and prayer traditions. Robin Ridington has written that dreamer Charlie
Yahey, in a prophetic way, understood the role of the tape recorder and
the role of the anthropologist as a messenger to help distribute his songs
and teachings. For example, in 1966 Charlie Yahey said, "I will not live
long. I am sending messages to other people with this tape recorder. God
made all those things for people (Ridington 1978, 88; Ridington and Ridington 2003, 62). This 1966 field recording is now part of the Ridington/
Dane-ẕaa Digital Archive, which is accessible to the Dane-ẕaa communities. The recording quality is crisp, and Charlie Yahey's strong, unaccompanied voice is clearly audible, making it an excellent audio example for
people to learn from.

1994 "Prairie Chicken Song" Performance

The second example of dreamer Gaayęą's "Prairie Chicken Song" was
performed almost thirty years later in 1994 by a group of drummers and
singers led by song keeper Albert Askoty at a memorial tea dance for his
wife, Alice Askoty. Albert Askoty, now deceased, was a respected song
keeper whom Charlie Yahey mentored. The memorial tea dance took
place close to the couple's former home at Petersen's Crossing, not far

from Doig River. This event was recorded by Garry Oker, who is Alice Askoty's grandson and Albert Askoty's step-grandson. Like Charlie Yahey often did, Albert introduced the song with a short narrative in his language to situate the performance and to guide the audience's interpretation of the song. Garry Oker has translated Albert's introduction to the song's performance as follows:

> In a dream, one will, one dreamer, will know us. One will quickly be aware, that's what they said, sing two songs, sing two songs, sing them all, sing two dreamers' songs. There are many dreamers, one will know us, they said. He is a dreamer, that is the way. (Albert Askoty, trans. G. Oker, in Oker 2008a, liner notes).

Following his verbal introduction, Albert begins drumming on his single-headed snare drum in the steady, unaccented rhythmic pattern. Then he and the group of drummers who had joined his lead sing the "Prairie Chicken Song" four times in a row with the following structural pattern of melodic lines with descending contours: ABC BC ABC BC. Alice's son, Freddy Askoty, told me that throughout this tea dance many of the audience members, both family and community members, danced in a circle to help Alice begin her journey to Heaven (F. Askoty 2007). Albert's introductory oratory is not specifically directed to Gaayęą's "Prairie Chicken Song" but rather is made relevant to the context of the memorial dreamers' dance. By directing his audience to "sing two songs, sing them all," Albert refers to the role of the singers and dancers present to help the deceased – in this case, Alice Askoty – to meet a dreamer who will "know us" and guide her as she begins to retrace her steps in life along her journey to Heaven. This autoethnographic recording by Garry Oker was included on the first of a series of audio CDs of dreamers' songs produced for the Dane-ẕaa communities by Garry Oker and various collaborators (Oker, Ridington, and Shaak 2000, track 21).[23] As well as being distributed within the Dane-ẕaa communities, the 1994 recording has been shared with the public on the *Dane Wajich* website (Doig River 2007).[24]

2004 "Prairie Chicken Song" Performance

The third example of dreamer Gaayęą's "Prairie Chicken Song" was performed by the Doig River Drummers, lead by Tommy Attachie, as part of the 23 July 2004 Doig River Cultural Day festivities, which preceded the Doig River Rodeo. The other drummers/singers are Brian Acko, Garry

Oker, Leo Acko, and Clarence Apsassin. After the death of song keeper Albert Askoty in 1994, Tommy Attachie took on a leading role as singer and song keeper. Tommy began drumming with his elders and singing dreamers' songs in his youth. He has never stopped practising and studying the dreamers' songs and is now recognized as a leader in revitalizing the dreamers' dance and song tradition as he teaches others about both the songs and their contextualizing narratives.

I recorded the entire 2004 summer tea dance, which took place between 7:00 and 11:30 PM and had about forty people in attendance. Dreamer Gaayęą's "Prairie Chicken Song" was sung twice that evening. The example discussed here was sung close to the end of the tea dance when the singers were becoming tired and their voices were getting a bit hoarse. Tommy was the only singer in that group who could take the lead, so by the end of the evening his voice was less strong. The melody was sung five times in a row with the following structural pattern of melodic lines with descending contours: ABC BC ABC BC ABC.

The singers accompanied themselves on single-headed snare drums and used the steady, unaccented rhythmic pattern. Much of the audience danced to this song, following the lead of elder Annie Oker around the fire. Typical of the other songs performed that evening, Tommy began the song by mentioning its dreamer, Gaayęą, and ended it by referencing two of the names used to refer to it, "Jiihyiné?" and "Prairie Chicken." Tommy's contextual comments were made so that his fellow drummers and singers would know what song he wanted to sing and so that they could continue to learn about the tradition. He mentioned the name of the song in both the Dane-ẕaa and the English languages. This could have been for the benefit of some of the younger drummers who are less fluent in the Dane-ẕaa language, or it could simply have reflected the increasing use of English words and phrases among Dane-ẕaa people. The comments were not made loud enough for the audience to hear and were not directed into the speaker system microphone. However, the comments were picked up by the lavalier microphone that lead singer Tommy Attachie was wearing and that I used to record the tea dance. This partial separation from the live audience distinguishes this performance from the more intimate performance context of dreamer Charlie Yahey's home in 1966, when everyone present could hear him speak about the songs. However, the 2004 field recording, including its contextualizing narrative, is now available to a worldwide audience through its inclusion in the *Dane Wajich* website (Doig River 2007).[25]

The 2008 example of dreamer Gaayęą's "Prairie Chicken Song" is a studio recording that samples from the 1994 field recording discussed previously and adds new content. The recording was directed and co-produced by Doig River First Nation member Garry Oker, a musician, visual artist, and one of the current members of the Doig River Drummers. Garry first started sampling from and re-mixing dreamers' songs in the recording studio to make a soundtrack for a video he directed, *They Dream about Everything* (Oker and elders of the Dane-ẕaa First Nation 2005, Oker 2005c, Oker 2007). Later, in 2007, Garry attended the Aboriginal Music Lab at Vancouver Community College, where he found inspiration and support for his sampling of, and experimentation with, traditional dreamers' songs from workshop leaders and other Aboriginal artists (Oker 2007, 2008b). In 2008 Garry partnered with producer Harris Van Berkel, who had mentored Garry at the Aboriginal Music Lab, to record and produce Garry's own CD of "recomposed" dreamers' songs for release and sale to the general public. The album, entitled *Dane-zaa Dreamer's Melodies* (Oker 2008a), is currently available for purchase online at the Apple iTunes store.

The first track on this recording, entitled "Sing Two Songs," uses the 1994 recording of dreamer Gaayęą's "Prairie Chicken Song" performed by Garry's step-grandfather, Albert Askoty (discussed previously), as an inspirational base. As with the rest of the songs on the album, it is credited as "Composed by traditional Dane-ẕaa Dreamers, Recomposed by Garry Oker" (Oker 2008a, liner notes). Although the specific dreamer and the performance sampled are not referenced in the liner notes, I was able to recognize the core section of "Sing Two Songs" as dreamer Gaayęą's "Prairie Chicken Song." I had become familiar with this song through listening to the recording of Albert Askoty singing it in 1994, which was included on the CD compilation of dreamers' songs mentioned earlier (Oker, Ridington, and Shaak 2000, track 21), as well as through listening to my own recording of the song by Tommy Attachie and the Doig River Drummers in the summer of 2004. In addition to recognizing the melody, I understood that the name, "Sing Two Songs," references Albert's introductory narrative to his 1994 performance, a translation of which is also included in the liner notes of the CD compilation. The connotations that I have for this particular song are a good example of the polyvocality of sampled songs. Listeners bring with them their own body of knowledge that helps them to find meaning and cultural associations in the samples. In Dane-ẕaa tradition, song keepers accrue knowledge about the songs through narratives passed along by their teachers and in turn carry forward the tradition by transmitting this knowledge through narratives during their own performances.

For an outside audience, Garry contextualizes the song as follows: "The message of the dreamers to the tribal members is to continue practicing songs, so that they will be able to recognize their spiritual path through these prayer songs" (Oker 2008a, liner notes). This general contextualization is in contrast to the way that song keeper Tommy Attachie uses narrative to place the song specifically in both genealogical and historical context and the way that dreamer Charlie Yahey and song keeper Albert Askoty addressed their community audience and directed its members to participate in traditional practices of prayer, dance, and spiritual connection through their framing narratives of dreamer Gaayęą's "Prairie Chicken Song."

"Sing Two Songs" is not initially recognizable as a Dane-ẕaa dreamer's song. It begins with piano, joined by electric guitar, flute, and synthesizer, all played by professional session musicians in a four-four metre. After twenty-six seconds Albert Askoty's introduction in the Dane-ẕaa language to his 1994 performance of the "Prairie Chicken Song" is added to the instrumental mix. His voice is electronically distorted so that it is slower and echoes and has the effect of sounding distant and otherworldly. This verbal sample is followed by the addition of a single Dane-ẕaa drumbeat played on the single-headed snare drum in the steady, unaccented rhythmic pattern. Shortly thereafter, Garry sings dreamer Gaayęą's "Prairie Chicken Song" three times in a row, with the Dane-ẕaa drumbeat dropped from the mix for the third repetition of the song. The structural pattern of melodic lines with descending contours is ABC BC ABC. "Sing Two Songs" ends like it began with an arrangement of new musical content, played on instruments from outside the Dane-ẕaa musical tradition and following the newly applied four-four metre.

Co-producer Harris Van Berkel explained the process of production and recomposition for this song, as well as the other songs on the CD, to me in an interview about the production. He recalls that Garry selected the traditional Dane-ẕaa dreamers' songs he wanted to use in the production from recorded sources and provided Harris with these recordings, as well as direction about the sound and feel that he was after. Harris then transcribed each traditional dreamer's song in musical notation and composed parts for additional musical instruments that would fit with the melody and rhythmic pattern of the original dreamer's song and Garry's vision for the recomposition (Van Berkel 2008). For "Sing Two Songs," Garry explained that instead of including the inspirational song as a layer in the mix, he laid down his own vocal performance by listening to the source recording through headphones and following Albert's lead while he sang and drummed along with it in the studio (Oker 2008b).

Although the beginning and ending of "Sing Two Songs" are not recognizable as parts of a Dane-ẕaa genre of music, the actual vocal performance at the centre of the song is very traditional, and the song melody is easily recognizable to those familiar with the dreamers' song repertoire as Gaayę̀ą's "Prairie Chicken Song." As with the previous examples from 1966, 1994, and 2004, the melody is sung through in its entirety, with no significant variation, and the steady unaccented hand drum rhythm used is consistent. The core structural sequence of melodic lines with descending contours – which for this song consists of three melodic lines, represented as ABC, with the first line, A, dropped with every second verse – is consistent in all four performances. Similarly consistent in all four performances is the variation in vocables used for the melodic lines by each performer, an attribute that is part of the Dane-ẕaa performance tradition. However, the 2008 recomposition as a whole is quite different from the other examples discussed here. It is a pastiche of musical styles that samples from and recreates a traditional Dane-ẕaa dreamer's melody but ultimately represents a new hybrid genre of music that iTunes has categorized as "new age."

To summarize, the first three examples of dreamer Gaayę̀ą's "Prairie Chicken Song," from 1966, 1994, and 2004, are similar in form and performance context. All are live performances by traditionally trained Dane-ẕaa musicians staged for a Dane-ẕaa community audience and within the context of a sacred tradition: as prayer, as a memorial, and as a summer world-renewal ceremony. The biggest differences between these examples and Garry Oker's 2008 recomposition include: (1) taking the performance out of a live and natural community context, (2) electronically sampling and manipulating the performance in the studio, (3) adding new musical content and performers from outside the Dane-ẕaa tradition, (4) copyrighting and commoditizing the material for global distribution beyond the Dane-ẕaa communities, and (5) altering the primary use from sacred to secular, noting that those familiar with the Dane-ẕaa dreamers' song tradition may still find sacred meaning in the dreamer's song at the core of the recomposition. Oker acknowledges that his recompositions are different from the traditional dreamers' songs but also asserts that they can still be used for personal prayer, even if they no longer fit within the dreamers' dance tradition as it is currently practised. He states,

> This is not dancing stuff.
> This is just more for getting into a groove.
> You can stand in one place and just do it.
> Just like a traditional song, they used to have songs like that
> where you just stand in one place and dance ...
> This is one of them. (Oker 2007)[26]

In comparing these four performances of dreamer Gaayęą's "Prairie Chicken Song" over a forty-two-year period, I have tried to identify patterns in the song structure and the context of the performances so that the meanings and connotations of the song for a variety of different participants – drummers, singers, lead singers, and various audience segments, both local and distant – can be better understood. As will be discussed further, some view the 2008 recomposition as a distinct break from the dreamers' song tradition, whereas others see it as a continuation of the tradition that ultimately renews it and makes it relevant for the current sociocultural environment.

Conclusion: The Emergent Nature of Dane-ẕaa Song Creation and Recreation

Singing, drumming, and dancing are still important ceremonial practices for Dane-ẕaa people, particularly as part of their funerary custom, personal prayer, and public cultural display. However, this is a critical time for Dane-ẕaa dreamers' songs because traditional song keepers are few and younger generations are less engaged than in the past with traditional culture. Recordings and new media tools, including digitization, databases, and websites, have emerged as new types of song keepers that connect the community to samples of the song repertoires and teachings of past dreamers and song keepers. At the same time as these electronic song keepers are maintaining the tradition, the new technology has also facilitated and inspired artistic innovation.

A current topic of debate is whether it is appropriate to change the songs and alter the tradition as Garry Oker has begun to do with his dreamers' song recompositions. Many in the community (B. Acko 2007, L. Acko 2007, S. Acko 2007, Attachie 2007, Davis 2007, Makadahay 2007) suggest that these innovations are inappropriate, as they change the form, accompaniment, and performance context of the song tradition from sacred, affirming the Dane-zaa's worldview and oral history, to a secular commodity. For example, Brian Acko, one of the younger members of the Doig River drumming and singing group (in his early forties), is an advocate for the maintenance of dreamers' song forms. He says,

> I don't agree with that.
> I was kind of choked for that, because these are prayer songs.
> Why you want to mix something with the songs that the
>   dreamer, that God gave them?
> Why you want to go play around with them? …
> They are just like gospel music, same thing.
> It is no different than that.
> That's what my grandpa used to say, my uncle Jack,
>   "These are Heaven songs …
>   You never forget it!" (B. Acko 2007)

A similar critical view of the sampled and remixed dreamers' songs was expressed during a community-wide survey earlier in 2007 to review and approve content for Doig River's (2007) *Dane Wajich* virtual exhibit, which I co-curated with Kate Hennessy. The initial storyboard for the "songs" section of the virtual exhibit had included one of Garry's recompositions along with numerous traditional dreamers' song recordings. However, the majority view expressed during our community consultation was that the remixed/recomposed dreamers' songs did not belong in the Doig River First Nation's public display of its sacred dreamers' song tradition, and it was removed from the exhibition's storyboard. Another discussion centred around whether it was culturally appropriate to circulate recordings of dreamers' songs outside of the community context at all, let alone to a global audience on the Internet. Following a debate, it was agreed that although nááchẹyiné? are considered to be powerful, and need to be honored and respected, they are given to dreamers to be used by everybody and that the power of the songs would not be compromised by their being shared publicly. It was also agreed that the benefit of asserting Dane-zaa identity and tradition by sharing dreamers' songs outweighed concerns of piracy or appropriation.[27] This community-wide content review for *Dane Wajich* also hastened intense discussions about how the community can control the use and distribution of archival recordings of dreamers' songs and other forms of digital cultural heritage, now more easily duplicable as part of the Ridington/Dane-zaa Digital Archive, and about who should have the right to control specific archival materials.

Although intellectual property rights have been antithetical concepts for this nonhierarchical hunting and gathering group, whose members have traditionally valued individual knowledge over material possessions, the creation of song recordings and the more recent use of new digital media (e.g., CDs, Internet) for the duplication and transmission of these heritage materials to an outside audience have prompted an interest in them as both individual and cultural property. The Doig River community, and other Dane-ẕaa communities with a shared interest in these cultural materials, have begun to develop and articulate their own cultural protocols for controlling the distribution and attribution of this valued heritage. The following provisional guidelines became implicit following the discussions during the production of *Dane Wajich*. The dreamers' songs themselves are considered to be collective heritage shared by the group. However, distribution of recorded performances of dreamers' songs outside of the community should be approved by the performer. If the performer is deceased, then the approval of the performer's family would be required. Kate Hennessy and I have written elsewhere about these developing cultural stewardship and cultural property issues surrounding Dane-ẕaa digital cultural heritage (Ridington and Hennessy 2008; et al. 2011, 235–7). Additionally, Kate places Dane-ẕaa people's engagement with their digital cultural heritage within the global context of Indigenous repatriation in her recent dissertation (Hennessy 2010).

Garry Oker has responded to these intellectual property attribution concerns by adopting the newly articulated kinship-based clearance guidelines. Currently, he samples only from the recordings of his step-grandfather, Albert Askoty, or from recordings of his own performance with the Doig River Drummers, as these are relatively clear for him to use under the provisional rights clearance protocol and aren't likely to be challenged. He has also started to avoid the clearance issue by recording his own performances of dreamers' songs instead of sampling from archival recordings. In response to community concerns about altering the accompaniment and form of dreamers' songs, detailed above, Oker has suggested that in order to revitalize the dreamers' song tradition, now actively practised by only a handful of singers, the songs need to be framed in a modern sound because, as he says, "if we don't explore and develop new traditions with the songs, people are going to forget about it, especially the younger generation" (Oker 2007). Although he continues to sample from and experiment with traditional Dane-ẕaa dreamers' songs,

Oker has made an effort to ameliorate some of the community concerns about altering the dreamers' melodies. For example, in "Sing Two Songs," discussed previously, he has been careful to faithfully recreate Gaayea's "Prairie Chicken Song" and use it as a base melody to mix with musical arrangements and instruments from outside of the Dane-ẕaa musical tradition, a process that he calls recomposition. He explains, "It is only adding and filling the spaces in between the beats. That is what I'm doing. I am not actually altering the sound, I'm just filling in the blanks to make it more contemporary" (Oker 2007).

The Dane-ẕaa dreamers' song and dance tradition has been dynamic since its inception as an Indigenous movement that has helped Dane-ẕaa people to adjust to cultural changes brought on by European encounter, the fur trade, and the impacts of colonization. With the rapid cultural, social, and technological changes since the Second World War, the Dane-ẕaa dreamers' song and dance tradition has continued to adapt. Although technology has been important in the preservation and revitalization of the dreamers' song tradition, the current era of easy digital reproduction and distribution of recordings, touched upon briefly in this chapter, has also inspired artistic innovation as well as resistance to these innovations. As Dane-ẕaa songs move onto a global stage through the Internet and public release on CDs, the Dane-ẕaa, like many other Indigenous groups, are being forced to find a balance between sharing and protecting their sacred musical heritage.

NOTES

1 Mary Magoulick summarizes performance theory as it is often applied in folk-loristics, and as I utilize it here, in her online article "Fieldwork/Ethnography and Performance Theory," http://hercules.gcsu.edu/~mmagouli/performance.htm (accessed 9 June 2011).
2 Throughout this chapter the terms "dreamers' dance" and "tea dance" are used interchangeably. "Dreamers' dance" is an etic (outsider) term used by scholars to categorize the tradition in relation both to the dreamers' songs, which are central to the dance, and to the religious and spiritual elements of the practice.

  Please note that Robin Ridington and Antonia Mills used the term "prophet dance" in most of their earlier writing about the Dane-ẕaa. However, "dreamer" has become the preferred Dane-ẕaa translation of their source word, *nááchẹ*, so in recent years the terms "dreamer" and "dreamers' dance" have replaced the terms "prophet" and "prophet dance" in their writings.

  "Tea dance" and "powwow" are emic (insider) terms used frequently by the current group of Dane-ẕaa people to describe their song and dance tradition.

The Dane-zaa's use of these terms should not be confused with the particulars of other Native North American tea dance and powwow traditions. Dane-zaa people use the term "tea dance" simply because "they make tea" when their communities gather together socially to dance (S. Acko 2007, Davis 2007). Similarly, the Dane-zaa have adopted the term "powwow" to refer to their dreamers' dances as a way of identifying them as a type of Indigenous dance gathering.

As is described further in note 10, throughout this chapter I have chosen not to capitalize the first letters of dance genres such as dreamers' dance, prophet dance, and tea dance.

3 Antonia Mills conducted her initial fieldwork with the Dane-zaa while she was married to Robin Ridington and initially published under the name Antonia Ridington. Since 1978 she has published under the name Antonia Mills.

4 Robin and Antonia began documenting the Dane-zaa in 1964 as Harvard University graduate students in anthropology and spent a great deal of time living in Dane-zaa communities until 1970. Since 1974 Robin and Antonia have continued their work with the Dane-zaa separately. As of 1978 Robin has been joined in his work with the Dane-zaa by his current partner and colleague, sociologist Jillian Ridington.

5 As the daughter of Antonia Mills and Robin Ridington, I spent extended periods of time with the Dane-zaa as I was growing up, primarily during the summer months. Since 2002 I have worked collaboratively with the Doig River First Nation, one of the four Dane-zaa bands, on a number of digital heritage projects. The first of these involved coordinating the digital preservation of the Ridington collection of Dane-zaa audio and video recordings and photographs compiled since 1964. My most recent collaboration is a participatory Internet-based multimedia exhibit entitled *Dane Wajich – Dane-zaa Stories and Songs: Dreamers and the Land* (Doig River 2007).

6 Linguistic anthropologist Dr Patrick Moore has provided orthographic transcriptions of the Dane-zaa words that appear in this chapter. Much of this linguistic work was done as part of the *Dane Wajich* project (Doig River 2007). Pat has kindly helped me with the new terms I use here. You can learn more about the Dane-zaa language and orthography at http://www.virtualmuseum.ca/Exhibitions/Danewajich/english/resources/language.php (accessed 19 April 2011).

7 These digital heritage projects include four audio CDs of traditional Dane-zaa dreamers' songs (Oker, Ridington, and Shaak 2000, Oker 2005a, 2005b, 2005c), videos (Oker et. al 2001, Oker and elders of the Dane-zaa First Nation 2005), a CD of Garry Oker's remixed dreamers' songs prepared as a soundtrack for the video *They Dream about Everything* (Oker 2005d), and two participatory and collaborative multimedia web exhibitions (Doig River 2004, 2007).

8 See note 6.

9 The word "Heaven" is capitalized throughout this chapter. I use it as a proper noun to represent the way the Dane-zaa think of Heaven as a tangible place. The Dane-zaa's use of the term appears to reference a hybrid concept that draws from both their precontact belief system and Christianity.

10 The use of capitalization to refer to these Aboriginal dance genres varies in academic use. Throughout this chapter I have chosen not to capitalize the first letters of these dance genres according to standard grammatical practice.

11 http://www.virtualmuseum.ca/Exhibitions/Danewajich/english/dreamers/dreamer.php?action=dreamer/makenuunatane (accessed 19 April 2011).

12 http://www.virtualmuseum.ca/Exhibitions/Danewajich/english/dreamers/dreamers.php (accessed 19 April 2011).

13 Elsewhere, I have described as "oral curation" this dynamic yet conservative process that underlies the transmission of oral forms of narrative and song (Ridington and Ridington 2011).

14 *Yaage Saatin* (Sky Sitter/Sky Keeper) and *Nahhatááʔ* (Our Father) are the two terms currently used to refer both to the Creator and to God in the Dane-ẕaa language. *Nahhatááʔ* (Our Father) is a translation for "God" introduced by Catholic missionaries. It is unclear whether the term *Yaage Saatin* is exclusively an Indigenous Dane-ẕaa term for the Creator, whether it is another term used to reference the Christian concept of God, or whether it represents a hybrid concept that draws from both the precontact Dane-ẕaa belief system and Christianity (personal communication with Robin Ridington and Patrick Moore, June 2008).

15 Charlotte Frisbie's (1980) work on Navajo vocables and the many ways they have meaning has helped me to think about and to inquire about the meanings of Dane-ẕaa dreamers' song vocables.

16 These elders include Tommy Attachie, Sam Acko, Madeleine Davis, Johnny Askoty, and May Apsassin.

17 I have applied the terms "sacred" and "secular" in an etic manner to describe my own categorization of songs according to their use.

18 See note 2.

19 Dreamer Charlie Yahey's son, John Yahey, from the Blueberry River community, has been an important song keeper for much of his adult life. His sons, who are now elders themselves, are also song keepers. Charlie Yahey's grandsons, along with a few other elders at Blueberry River, continue to sing dreamers' songs but seldom do so in public or for the rest of their community. Because of their predominantly private practice at this time, these singers can be seen as passive tradition bearers who do not publicly transmit their knowledge to the wider Dane-ẕaa community.

20 As was the practice in the 1960s, when dancing indoors in the wintertime, the community dances around a table placed in the centre of the room as a symbolic representation of the fire and its trail of smoke, which connects the dancers to the spirit world and Heaven.

21 My thanks to anthropological linguist Dr Patrick Moore for his orthographic transcription of the phrase "Prairie Chicken Song" and for the following explanation of variants in an e-mail on 7 February 2011: "*Jiihyinéʔ* translates literally as 'grouse song.' *Jiih* means 'grouse' and can be applied to any type of grouse, including ruffed grouse, spruce grouse and prairie chicken. *Yinéʔ* means 'song' when it is used in a possessed form. 'Song' on its own is *shin. Nedahe* means specifically 'prairie chicken' so *nedaheyinéʔ* would be 'prairie chicken song.'"

22 http://www.virtualmuseum.ca/Exhibitions/Danewajich/english/stories/
    video.php?action=fla/sweeney_chicken_dance (accessed 19 April 2011).

23 See note 7.

24 http://www.virtualmuseum.ca/Exhibitions/Danewajich/english/stories/songs/
    askoty_chickensong.php (accessed 19 April 2011).

25 http://www.virtualmuseum.ca/Exhibitions/Danewajich/english/stories/songs/
    drummers_chickensong.php (accessed 19 April 2011).

26 Jean-Guy Goulet notes that according to explorers such as Samuel Herne and
    Alexander Mackenzie, earlier Beaver dance styles from the beginning of the
    twentieth century tended to be more interpretive and individual, with partici-
    pants standing in place. The dominant symbols in the prophet dance – *the circle*,
    seen in the orientation of all participants around the fire, and *the path*, repre-
    sented by the dancers' clockwise movement around the fire – Goulet suggests,
    are relatively new among the Dene Tha and other related groups (Goulet 1998,
    226–7).

27 These discussions took place in concert with a parallel debate about whether it
    is culturally appropriate to display a digital picture of a sacred dreamer's draw-
    ing on the Internet, where it can be seen anytime by anyone. Traditionally, in
    order to safeguard the power of a dreamer's drawing, it is shared only with the
    community on special occasions and is cared for according to particular taboos
    and customs. Because some community members felt that uncontrolled access
    to the digital copies of these powerful drawings could be damaging, all images of
    dreamers' drawings were excluded from the online exhibition.

3

From Tea Dance to iTunes: Recomposing Dane-ẕaa Dreamers' Songs

INTERVIEW: GARRY OKER WITH AMBER RIDINGTON

The following edited interview was recorded on 14 January 2008 over dinner at a restaurant in Vancouver (Oker 2008b). At the time, Garry Oker was in the final stages of producing his CD *Dane-zaa Dreamer's Melodies* and was kind enough to talk to me about his music, his musical inspiration, and his process of production. On this CD, Garry mixes traditional Dane-ẕaa dreamers' songs with "modern sounds." During our conversation, as Garry explained his musical approach, the following themes surfaced: (1) innovation within tradition, (2) artistic expression, and (3) issues of intellectual property rights that emerge with commercial distribution of sampled traditional songs.

Garry's CD *Dane-zaa Dreamer's Melodies* can be purchased online at the Apple iTunes store. Since this interview, Garry has continued to create new music inspired by Dane-ẕaa dreamers' songs. Visit www.garryoker.com to learn about Garry's most recent productions.

My thanks to linguistic anthropologist Dr Patrick Moore for transcribing the Dane-ẕaa words in the interview using Dane-ẕaa orthography. My chapter in this volume may serve as helpful background information on Dane-ẕaa culture and music.

GO: My name is Garry Oker. I'm a descendant of a *nááchę* [dreamer]. I am also a Dane-ẕaa music keeper. I've been playing music for a long time, and I'm finally finding my own voice. Years and years ago my Grandma and Grandpa told me their last words before they left. They said,

Meháánetah.
Look for it.

Jii shin, jii shin edekede dǫtsi.
This song, don't let it go, don't let it go.

Mataawedesʔǫ lę.
It's very important, you got to use it.

Meháánetah.
Look for it.

That's what they told me. And these songs that they talked about were
the dreamers' [songs] that go back in time for many Dane-ẕaa people.
Over the years, I've always heard other sounds, and because I play in the
modern world, I really believe that we need to listen and hear the songs
as we hear the world today.

And so I started off with Makénúúnatane [a Dane-ẕaa dreamer] and
one of his songs. He was around in the 1700s, and he was teaching the
prophets. He helped people make sense of the world by opening the
doorway to the spiritual world and ... he started the idea that people
shouldn't be killing each other. And then Mak'íhts'ewéswą̈ą̈ [a Dane-
ẕaa dreamer] in the 1800s showed the way about [finding] the trail to
Heaven by dancing together. And I think that was the time when Christianity was coming in, around the 1800s, up there ... It seems to me that
the teachings and values come with the times of the world. So Gaayę̈ą̈
[a Dane-ẕaa dreamer], in the late 1870s, created celebration songs for the
world to renew itself in the seasons. And he used to come to Montney
all the time, the old travel area, the [traditional gathering] ground. He
wrote a song called ... What did he used to call it?

AR: "Suunéch'ii Kéch'iige"?

GO: "Suunéch'ii Kéch'ii yinéʔ." And then in the 1900s my grandpa
Oker [a Dane-ẕaa dreamer] created human prayer songs by teaching
the younger generation to continue dreaming their songs. There are
virtually [Dane-ẕaa dreamers'] songs for everything. Each time we play
them, it reveals a spiritual meaning. And that's why I believe it was time
for me to create my own versions of these songs, because today in the
world, we need to heal. And I [am] personally going through a healing
process.

So in Dane-ẕaa music the songs are narrative melodies. There's no words to describe exactly how you should think. It's just how you feel. And these songs can help you be able to get to that state, wherever you are. Similar to *naadaagaayiné?*, daylight songs. This is a place where the spirits meet the physical world, a place where relationships provide the thought of possibilities, the thought of moving closer to Creator and God, and the thought of your own action, of where you want to go. That is the power of these songs, and that's what I mean by [saying] they are healing songs.

3.1 Master designer and producer Garry Oker. Photo taken early 2011 by Andrew Tylosky of Motion Media.

So those [dreamers' songs] were my inspiration for recreating, or I would say, recomposing, these traditional songs … So what I wanted to do was harness the healing power of these old songs, and then preserve it in a whole new way so that in the modern world people can understand these healing songs. These songs are not meant to be kept to ourselves. They need to evolve with the world as we hear it … These Dane-ẕaa narrative melodies are now recomposed by me so that the world can hear it. And I believe that these [new] songs are very uplifting and soulful celebrations of Dane-ẕaa dreamer songs. And I know it's a beginning of something new, and it's totally refreshing, but it's got a familiar traditional sense to it. I'm respecting the traditions by maintaining the song structure but also shaping the future. The songs speak the language of our emotions without the words. This is what makes them uniquely Dane-ẕaa songs, that they convey these emotions without words. And the reason why I've added a lot of feelings when we recorded them.

[For my CD] we basically had them, the traditional songs from my grandpa, as a base. And we listened to it, and then we just used that as a foundational structure for the arrangement of these melodies. I just asked the guys [producer and session musicians] to allow themselves to feel that song, and that melody, and find a melody or that spirit of that song. And that's how we got to what we got.

AR: So by your recording of your grandpa's song, was that Albert Askoty? You brought in a recording of him singing?

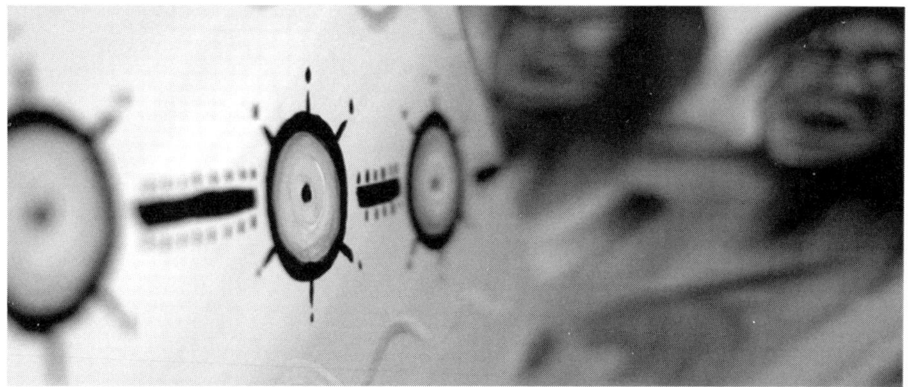

3.2 Untitled acrylic painting by Garry Oker, 2008. The painting incorporates elements of a dreamer's explanations of his musical journey to spiritual dimensions. The symbols are the translation of a dreamer's musical notes.

GO: Yeah, I searched my archives of music that I recorded over the years, and this particular one that moved me was when Grandma died. And those were the songs that I brought out, because it was so emotionally impactful. So those were the ones that I used as a foundation to create these modern melodies. I'm going from Indigenous-based [traditions] and adding modern sound ... I told the musicians, "Look, here are the songs. I don't want to change them. I want to remain true to it. So let's listen to it, and then let's create a music with it."

I was fortunate enough to find some really good people that are open enough to allow the spirit of the songs to come in. It's hard to identify what category of music it is. I did a study on it in Toronto at a big national gathering of First Nations people. A lot of people said it's soulful, spiritual. It's jazzy world beat. It's got a lot of things in it. And when I think back about it, I say, "Yeah, it is. It's got everything in it," meaning spirit. We hear the world through spiritual vibration. Now we have Dane-ẕaa melodies mixed with how we hear the world.

AR: Sounds good. So did you actually bring something like that [pointing to a series of drawings and notes on a long scroll of paper that Garry has been referring to as he speaks] into the studio and explain that to the musicians?

GO: Oh yeah, I came in with the drum and told them there is no musical notes. All we have is voices and drumbeats. Then I created a drawing of

Dane-ẕaa musical notes [figure 3.2]. We talked about it and I gave them a sampling of the recordings I had done in the past.[1] And they were totally open to it. They just got it. They just nailed it! A lot of these songs, the new ones that we recorded, a lot of them were just one or two takes. And it was amazing! It was so easy, how it came together. And even for them to find the melody and the timing of it. Yeah, everybody got into it. Even the singers, the girls that I got in. I would just sing them a melody and say, "Here's how it goes." And they would just pick it up and do it.

AR: So this was your first contact with Sal Ferreras,[2] is that right?

GO: Yeah.

AR: So what was his role with all of this?

GO: Well, Sal organized the Aboriginal Music Lab at Vancouver Community College. And I attended that. And that's where I met these guys [producers and session musicians]. And when I did my session with them, they totally loved it. They thought it was totally unique. Immediately after it was over, they said, "If you want to record, we want to be part of it." Because it was just magical. So then about two months later, I phoned Sal, I said, "Okay, I want to do it." So then he hooked me up with Harris Van Berkel, the guitarist [and producer] … So basically Harris actually pulled it all together.

AR: So he selected, or brought in, other musicians that he thought would be good for it?

GO: Yeah, he found the singers, the backup singers, the flute player, the jazzy stuff. I mean, it's funny how it came together. I mean, it's kind of jazzy, world beat music, right. It just came together like that.

AR: But wouldn't you say that that comes from all the musicians who are working with you? They're bringing their musical influences?

GO: Oh yeah, what they hear, and feel … It's a perfect match. I mean, it really captures the way I want to hear it … I did one Grandpa song, [dreamer] Oker song, and yeah, it is really coming together to what the message is. And the more I hear it, the more it starts to become clear. And that's what makes it unique, because it tells itself. Like the song, it forms itself.

AR: So when you go into the recording studio, does someone work on it a bit more afterwards? Or are you there for everything that's being mixed and recorded?

GO: Well the engineers and the producers, they just work with the sound. They make sure all the sound is even. You know, the technical stuff.

AR: That doesn't bother you that … Like I think of just a plain tea dance, usually there's no one messing with the sound levels. It's just what you hear is what you get from the ensemble. So does changing the way that the song is recorded and then changing the way people hear it …?

GO: I don't think it does. I think it just fine-tunes what you hear. Because we already nailed the sound. We know what we want. Some places, it's just that the bass may be too high, or you got to bring it down so that it's even. Sometimes the piano is too loud, so you got to bring it down. But the essence of the whole song is not changed. It's just fine-tuning. And sometimes it's mixed up too much. It's like too many sounds on one spot. And it just gets muddled up, and you got to balance it out so that the mixed sound, all those instruments become a whole, or become a melody in a pleasing way. That's the modern sound …

AR: Who do you see being the main audience for this, and are you going to make it available to the public? And who's going to market it?

GO: I'd like to market in Europe, Germany, because they like Indians over there.

AR: Right, yeah, they do.

GO: I'm looking at SOAR Records; they're interested in looking at it. They do marketing for Native people across North America. I'm [also] working on a big gig in Korea, for big tours and projects that I'm getting involved with. They're building a tourism resort in Korea. So, they love my music, and that's the kind of stuff they want to promote.

AR: … You'd actually go there and perform with this whole band that you've assembled [for the *Dane-zaa Dreamer's Melodies* CD]?

GO: I may bring in the traditional drummers, and the tourism activities … Part of this multipurpose thing that I'm doing with this [CD] is also part of the animation project that I'm working on. That's where the funding came from, to develop it … Plus for promotion for our [Doig River First Nation] companies. Yeah, so there's a lot of multipurpose use [for my music].

AR: Earlier today at your meeting with the animators you were talking about wanting to market these things [animated videos, videogames] and have them turning into a profit.

GO: Yeah.

AR: Do you see that with these songs?

GO: I hope so. Then we can have our own pot of money to create more projects. You know, we got to be sustainable about it. But it's hard to make money nowadays because of the changes in the industry right now. Everybody wants to download music. I hope that we can sell a whole bunch. I mean, I'm hoping that we can sell like thousands [of CDs] in Korea.

AR: So when this is produced, is it copyright Garry Oker? It's not copyright Doig River First Nation?

GO: Well it is Doig-funded, but it's my recomposition; it's my versions. So, as an artist, I own the rights to it … But any kind of money that's generated, I'm going to make sure that it goes back to the band somehow, so that there'll be a continuous fund for cultural programs. Then I could be able to create more music. There's a lot of songs to record, or to rerecord, like to recompose them.

AR: Something I was going to ask, sometimes for a traditional song, people will say "traditional" if there is no clear author. It just says "traditional" and then it says whoever is performing it. How do you anticipate this'll be?

GO: Oh, I'll just put the name of the dreamer that it came from.

AR: As the author?

GO: Yeah; original song composed by Makénúúnatane or Mak'íhts'ewéswąą, Gaayęą, Oker, or whoever, right?

AR: I've been reading a lot on digital media and complications that come up with intellectual property rights ... There's been so many issues with First Nations, like whether copyright even applies very well to First Nation philosophies?

GO: Well no, I think the copyright issue and all ... that's because of the money attached to it. If you look at and study why people do that, it's because the artist, or the composers, need to be compensated for that.

AR: I understand that, but then when it comes down to Makénúúnatane [a long-deceased Dane-ẕaa dreamer], or like someone who's deceased ... do you say, well, God created this song? 'Cause the song keepers say that the dreamer brought the song down from Heaven. So then it's like do you put God as the composer? Or like, how do you?

GO: Well, I don't know. I question the idea of that. But I mean, there's a lot of great artists in the world that create music. Where does that come from? Does it come from the spirit? Does it come from God? ... I'll pick up a guitar, and I can have a melody all of a sudden come there. It's right there. Where did that come from? I don't know. It's a creative, creation process, right.

The only thing that I could do about that is give recognition to those dreamers that brought it up and ... to make sure that whenever we make money, that there will be money going back to teach younger genera-tions. Or some kind of foundation that teaches Indigenous people how to modernize their music without being constructed on tradition. Because culture and tradition, sometimes people are so stuck in their framework ... We shouldn't be controlled by that.

AR: I wanted to ask about identity. Like how this helps build your identity as a Native person, or as a musician, or as an artist, or as all of those things?

GO: Yeah, I feel way better as an artist, as a musician, I'm finding my own voice. This is my own style. This is my own style. I can go out and I don't have to be in the shadow of the dreamers, and Tommy [Attachie], and all those guys [Dane-ẕaa song keepers]. If we're an artist, we should be able to create and develop if we're inspired by that idea – but not say, "Oh, we got to sing it exactly like that" … You know, that's what I'm struggling with right now, but I think I've overcome it. I said, "Okay, I'm just going to do my version of it. I don't care." I've gotten to the point where, okay, I'm going to maintain as much traditional idea or structure to that music, but I want to have my own identity in my own music. So I follow that [traditional base] but then I added all this other stuff to it. I mean, we got to evolve as how we hear the world. Back in the day, they only had drums and voices, so that's what they used. But today, we got access to all kinds of [instruments,] guitar, fiddles.

NOTES

1 Garry's prior music sampling and recomposition work with traditional Dane-zaa dreamers' songs began in 2005 while producing the soundtrack for a video he directed, *They Dream about Everything* (Oker and elders of the Dane-zaa First Nation 2005), and continued in 2007 while attending the Aboriginal Music Lab at Vancouver Community College.
2 Salvador Ferreras is a percussionist, a producer, an ethnomusicologist, and the current dean of music at Vancouver Community College, where he administers the Aboriginal Music Lab.

4

Localizing Intertribal Traditions: The Powwow as Mi'kmaw Cultural Expression

JANICE ESTHER TULK

Powwows have been celebrated in Mi'kma'ki, the traditional territory of the Mi'kmaq, since their introduction in Elsipogtog, New Brunswick, in the mid-1980s by members of the Birch Creek Singers, by local traditionalists, and by visiting traditionalists from western Canada and the United States.[1] Sometimes referred to as *mawio'mi*, or gatherings, powwows have gained prominence as Mi'kmaw[2] cultural events over the past two decades, and a Mi'kmaw powwow trail has developed, with powwows scheduled in different Mi'kmaw communities almost every weekend during the summer. For those who travel the trail, this style of song and dance has become an important mode of cultural expression through which they can acknowledge, create, negotiate, embody, enact, and maintain a sense of Mi'kmaw identity and community. How intertribal powwow traditions become meaningful expressions of a particular First Nation or regional identity is largely attributable to processes of localization.

Some early studies of the powwow employed reductionalist notions of "pan-Indianism," suggesting that the distinct characteristics of the communities involved were supposedly erased or minimized (see Howard 1955). More recent scholarship, however, has shifted the terms of inquiry to focus on local practices and the increasing variation displayed during such intertribal events (Fowler 2005, Goertzen 2005). In particular, the oversimplified binary between northern- and southern-style singing is being challenged, with regional or localized singing styles demonstrating the existence of a continuum of performance practices (see Goertzen 2005, Hoefnagels 2004, Keillor 2006). However, singing styles are not the only elements of the powwow that may have localized forms. The order of events at a powwow may differ from one context to another: namings of particular elements, such as the closing song during which flags are danced out of the arbour, may have local variants; and the timing of the Grand Entry and how often it occurs each day may vary from one region to another. Social events and even specials[3] that occur within the context of a powwow weekend also serve to inscribe local meanings, perhaps through the performance of other music forms that are locally or regionally significant, through lyric substitution in which local people and places are referenced, or through cultural presentations that honour important local historical figures.[4]

There are, then, multiple and varied processes for making intertribal traditions locally meaningful. In this chapter, based on Mi'kmaw powwows I attended between 2004 and 2007 in Miawpukek (Newfoundland), Eskasoni (Nova Scotia), and Elsipogtog (New Brunswick), I elucidate some of the processes of localization that are employed to shift powwows from borrowed intertribal practice to local and nation-specific expressions of identity. Three primary means of localization emerge in this study: (1) the incorporation of pre-existing Mi'kmaw or local song and dance genres into the structure of the powwow, which sometimes includes transposing them to a different instrumentation or singing style and sometimes not; (2) the inscription of borrowed powwow traditions with local or nation-specific meaning through the embellishment of regalia, the use of a local singing style or language, and discourse that emphasizes tradition or "the Mi'kmaw way"; and (3) explicitly referencing or implicitly performing local histories. Through discussion of a specific example of each of these localization strategies, I demonstrate how the powwow emerges as constitutive of Mi'kmaw identity.

The Powwow in Mi'kma'ki

Traditional gatherings throughout Mi'kma'ki, like those of many First Nations, combined elements of expressive culture, such as music, dance, and storytelling, with social functions that included feasting, matchmaking, and decision making by community leaders. Perhaps the best known of such Mi'kmaw gatherings is that held annually at Chapel Island (Bras d'Or Lakes, Cape Breton Island). Each year during the celebration of St Anne's Day in late July, the Sante' Mawio'mi (Grand Council) meets.[5] The site of a mission, Chapel Island is a space in which Catholic religion and Mi'kmaw culture and government coexisted for centuries.

Indeed, Mi'kmaq have danced at celebrations in this space for so long that a circle has been worn into the ground (Sable and Sable 2007).

This history of celebration at a single site over centuries, however, does not mean that Mi'kmaw culture was unaffected by forces of colonization and assimilation. As Sam Cronk and colleagues note, "Unlike the Iroquois and Ojibwe nations from Ontario, the Wabenaki nation (including the Micmacs, Maliseets, Penobscots, and Passamaquoddy) has lost many of its traditional cultural teachings, particularly with regard to ceremonies, rituals, songs, and dances" (Cronk, Diamond, and von Rosen 1988, 77). Although it is true that many traditional teachings were lost, some did live on in the memories of Mi'kmaw elders. In the 1960s and 1970s the movement to recover these traditions and to learn Native traditions and spirituality from other (distant) First Nations gained strength in Mi'kma'ki. Those involved in revival efforts were termed "traditionalists" because of their orientation toward "traditional ways" rather than those introduced and enforced by colonizers,[6] and they followed several complementary paths to achieve their goal. Some individuals, like the late Sarah Denny, were dedicated to the preservation of nation-specific traditions and focused their efforts on Mi'kmaw chants and dances. Others broadened their focus to revive Wabenaki-specific traditions and travelled throughout Maine and the northeast region. However, some traditionalists travelled more widely, receiving teachings and ceremonies from spiritual leaders and elders in Alberta, North Dakota, and South Dakota (Cronk, Diamond, and von Rosen 1988, 78).

The influence of these distant neighbours to the west was noted by James Howard in a description of the 1962 celebration at Chapel Island:

Edward Kabatty, Don Wells, and Kabatty's children donned their Indian costumes and proceeded to stage a small Indian dance in the grassy area before the church. Since Kabatty is Ojibwa, and since Wells' Indian lore also stems largely from the further west, this particular pow-wow was not particularly Micmac in flavor, though the Kabatty children are, of course, half Micmac. (Howard 1965, 9)

Such cultural exchange was observed not only in terms of music but also in terms of dress, which featured bustles and war bonnets (Howard 1965, 10).

Although Howard refers to this gathering as a "pow-wow," it should be noted that a central element of the powwow is missing in his description – a powwow drum and drum group. In Howard's description, an individual sings, accompanied by a hand drum. Indeed, the term "powwow" has been used imprecisely by insiders and outsiders alike to describe modern events that "combine music and dance, games, feasts, and fireworks" and/or include a powwow drum (Cronk, Diamond, and von Rosen 1988, 72–4). Nevertheless, by the 1980s the powwow as it is now understood had been brought to the Mi'kmaw people. Oral history collected in Elsipogtog indicates that the first Mi'kmaw powwow was held in that community in 1986 thanks to the efforts of the Birch Creek Singers (see Tulk 2008).

Although the Birch Creek Singers were an important Mi'kmaw powwow drum group (see Tulk 2007a), at early powwows Sarah Denny's dance troupe, the Eskasoni Mi'kmaq Dancers, also often performed traditional repertoire alongside them and other intertribal groups. A mixture of intertribal, regional, and nation-specific musical styles and repertoires was embraced; however, the powwow did not necessarily exclude Christian incorporations.[7] Thus, just as Chapel Island had provided a space in which Mi'kmaw traditions could coexist and fuse with those of other First Nations and elements of Catholic-traditional belief, the powwow provided a structure in which the same exchange and recombination could occur. After more than two decades of practising the powwow in Mi'kma'ki, practitioners of this celebration continue to incorporate intertribal and nation-specific traditions, some of which are reconfigured through processes of localization.

Transposing "I'ko" to Powwow Aesthetics

One way that the powwow is localized in the Mi'kmaw context is by incorporating pre-existing Mi'kmaw song and dance genres into its structure. I have discussed the way that Ko'jua, a Mi'kmaw song and dance genre, is incorporated into the powwow event as an element that is distinctively Mi'kmaw (see Tulk 2007a). This dance, announced by the emcee[8] as "*our* dance," is an important expression of Mi'kmaw identity and a source of cultural pride. When performed at a powwow, it is presented as a special and is sung by an individual who also provides the accompaniment of a rattle or hand drum. That is, Ko'jua is performed without alteration; it is not transposed to a powwow aesthetic in form, instrumentation, or singing style but is incorporated "as is" into the proceedings.

The singing style retained in such a performance displays characteristics that have often fallen under the classification of eastern woodlands.[9]

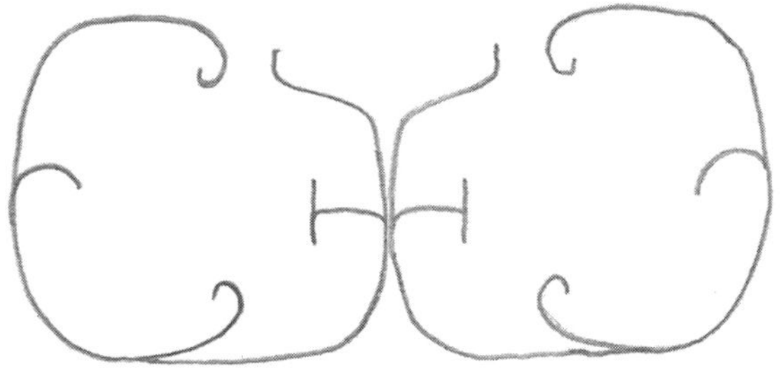

4.1 The double-curve motif.

In comparison to northern-style powwow singing, this vocal style features a "much more relaxed" technique (Goertzen 2005, 291). Indeed, these songs are sung at a more moderate tessitura, have a more limited range, employ less vocal pulsation, and make use of significantly less vocal tension in the production of sound. As Chris Goertzen notes, such songs are often accompanied by an instrument of "less imposing" timbre than the powwow drum, such as a rattle or hand drum. Differences are also observed in terms of a song's melodic contour, which is often more arch-shaped, and its rhythm, which features less "tension between drumbeat and vocal line" (Goertzen 2005, 291).[10]

Songs deemed to be "traditional"[11] Mi'kmaw songs, such as the "Gathering Song," "Friendship Song," and those of the Ko'jua genre, are primarily in forms other than the incomplete repetition form (A A[1] BC BC) associated with powwow singing. For example, Mi'kmaw songs often employ antiphonal structures throughout (rather than limiting this style to the one initial lead and response that is heard in powwow songs). The melodic contours employed vary from song to song; whereas the "Gathering Song" and "Friendship Song" display overall descending melodic contours, other songs, such as some versions of Ko'jua songs, feature several arch-like phrases that return regularly to the starting pitch. In Mi'kmaw material culture, this shape is called a rainbow or stepped motif (Whitehead 1982, 139–42). Still other songs, such as the "Partridge Song," are almost triadic in structure, regularly returning to an upper pitch and creating an upside-down arch not unlike the figure featured in the double-curve motif.[12]

When such traditional songs are transposed to a powwow idiom, like the northern style, modifications are often necessary. The form may be altered to be more in line with the incomplete repetition form, the tempo may increase dramatically, and honour beats may be added. Further, the rhythm and movement of the melodic line may be altered to better match the driving rhythm employed in some northern-style songs. Finally, the

Comparison of "I'ko" sung at a cultural workshop in Se't A'newey School and at the Eskasoni annual powwow

	I'ko	*I'ko*
Sung by	Two female students	Stoney Bear (male drum group)
Event	Workshop, Miawpukek, 19 May 2006	Eskasoni powwow, 23 June 2007
Dance category	n/a	Men's Traditional (straight)
Form of one push-up (verse)	A B	A B A^1 B^1 C A B A^1 B^1 C
Number of repetitions	3	15
Range	A3 to G4	B-flat 3 to A-flat 4
Instrumentation	Hand drum	Powwow drum
Tempo	50 bpm	160 bpm
Tail or coda?	Yes (B^1)	No
Honour beats?	No	Every second B^1 C

tessitura of the song may move to an extreme part of the range, and the production style may become more strident, in keeping with the aesthetic of the northern style.

One example of a traditional song being transposed to powwow aesthetics is "I'ko," often referred to as a song of peace between the Mohawk and the Mi'kmaq.[13] When "I'ko" is sung in its "traditional" style, as in a cultural workshop at Se't A'newey School on 19 May 2006, the form of one "verse" can be represented by AB, with the overall form of the song being AB A^{1}B AB B^1; it is accompanied by a steady beat, and honour beats are not employed.[14] At this particular workshop, dancing did not occur during the presentation of "I'ko." In the context of a powwow, however, this traditional song may be performed by a powwow drum group to accompany a Men's Traditional dance and, therefore, is subject to transposition suiting both powwow musical aesthetics and the specific dance category. When Stoney Bear performed "I'ko" at the Eskasoni powwow in 2007, the form was changed to more closely resemble the incomplete repetition form commonly associated with powwow repertoires, the tempo was substantially increased, honour beats were added, and the young men sang in the extreme of their range with a strident timbre.

Although significant changes may be made in transposing a Mi'kmaw song to a powwow idiom, when comparing a Mi'kmaw song to other northern-style songs that are not adaptations of traditional songs, one finds that there are still idiosyncrasies that may be indicative of a Mi'kmaw song style. For example, the antiphonal structure that is common in many traditional Mi'kmaw songs (such as the "Gathering Song") is maintained here. The A section is always sung as a solo, with all other sections sung by the group. The aural effect is that one hears two leads within each push-up, or round, of the song (which would not normally occur in the incomplete repetition form). Further, the addition of honour beats becomes essential for determining the form of this song, appearing in the second half of each push-up. Without them, this song would not be heard as having the incomplete repetition form (and the number of repetitions would double). Thus, although local repertoires may be transposed to suit powwow aesthetics, they may display at once elements of the local and borrowed styles and of formal structures.

Embellishing Plains-Style Regalia with Mi'kmaw Imagery

A second means of localizing the powwow inscribes borrowed powwow traditions with local or nation-specific meaning through the embellishment of regalia, the use of a local singing style or language, and discourse that emphasizes tradition. Regional singing styles may employ timbres, vocal ranges, and production techniques to achieve aesthetics different from those heard in northern- or southern-style singing. Traditional language specific to a nation provides another means of expressing local identity, particularly in contemporary, or "word," songs (see Goertzen 2005). Further, discursive practices, largely employed by the emcee of an event, may inscribe songs and dances with local meaning or emphasize the traditional nature of the proceedings and repertoire. An example of this is the exclamation "Swing and sway the Mi'kmaw way!" in reference to round dances within the context of a Mi'kmaw powwow. This expression makes a claim for the round dance, and, by extension, the powwow during which it is danced, as traditional to the Mi'kmaq (see Tulk 2007a). Through all of these processes, borrowed or intertribal powwow traditions are made meaningful to the Mi'kmaq who participate in the powwow and become expressive of Mi'kmaw identity. In this chapter, however, I would like to focus on the way that such processes of localization play out in Mi'kmaw regalia.

The style of regalia worn by powwow dancers is directly related to the style of dancing one chooses to practice; however, the dress associated

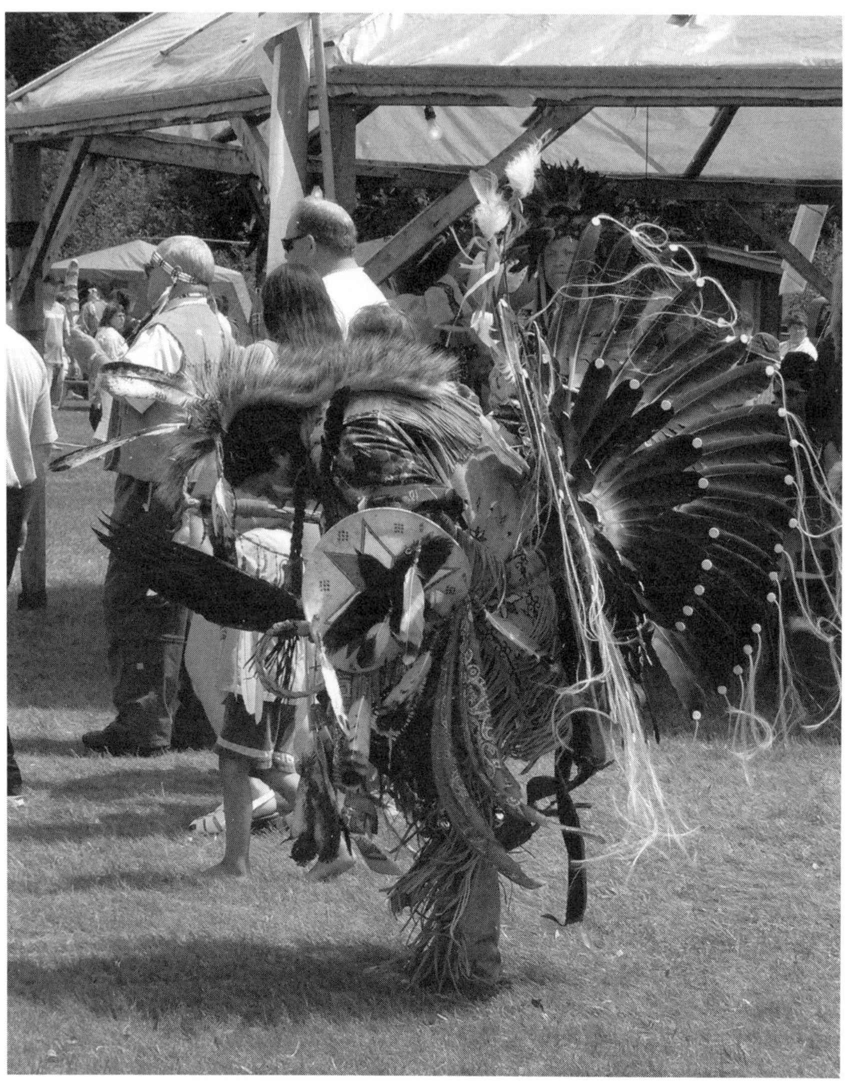

4.2 Paul Pike in his Newfoundland regalia at the 2005 Miawpukek powwow.
Photograph by author.

with a borrowed dance style may be localized through motifs that have
been used in Mi'kmaw expressive culture for centuries. Tara Browner
notes that "Each type of contest dancing has a pre-existing template for
regalia, largely determined by custom … The average dancer wears a mixture of homemade, inherited, gifted, and purchased regalia" (Browner
2002, 49). Although many styles of regalia are based on Plains dress, elements such as the materials used, the particular designs employed, or

the other ways that regalia are embellished may, and often do, point to a specific nation.[15] Regalia styles are primarily passed on via nonwritten forms of transmission, with dancers participating in events and seeing styles of regalia that they can replicate. They may also learn about styles specific to their nation by talking to elders. However, archival pictures from the past or books featuring various styles of regalia may also be consulted.[16] To demonstrate how borrowed regalia styles are both localized and personalized, I focus here on the regalia of one Mi'kmaw Northern Traditional dancer.

The conventions associated with Northern Traditional dancing have been described by Browner: "Typical contemporary Northern Traditional dance regalia includes a roach [pin] topped (ideally) with two eagle feathers, a bone-pipe breastplate, an eagle feather bustle, and a feather fan (made from bird-of-prey feathers) held in the left hand. All of these items were elements of the old Omaha dancer's regalia, but all were also used by most warrior societies" (Browner 2002, 25). She further points out that such regalia normally features "two cloth trailers hanging from the bustle" and that "modern dancers almost always wear full shirts and leggings, reminiscent of the dance clothing worn only in the winter months of the late 1800s" (Browner 2002, 51). It is this style of regalia that serves as a template for the dress of Northern Traditional dancer Paul Pike.

Over the past seven years, I have developed a close relationship with Paul Pike, who has provided guidance and served as a source of information and encouragement countless times. I was honoured to help him to prepare and dress in his regalia at the 2004 and 2005 Miawpukek powwows and also performed "spot checks" throughout the day. Pike, a non-Status[17] Mi'kmaw from Corner Brook, Newfoundland, who now resides in Alaska, was given permission to dance in the Northern Traditional style by the LaFever family (Northern Cheyenne). Due to the fact that he is non-Status, Paul has two sets of regalia, one for each of his homes. This is necessary because he cannot travel with eagle feathers as a non-Status person. The base of his regalia (i.e., leggings, vest, ribbon shirt, cuffs, moccasins, breastplate, shield, and other related items) is common to both sets; however, he has two of each element of his regalia that includes feathers (e.g., his bustle and roach pin).

In 2004 Paul spoke with me about the many personal elements of his Newfoundland regalia:

Paul: Does everything look okay?
Janice: Yeah, it looks great.

Paul: I gotta take a minute to catch my breath.

Janice: Paul, how long did it take you to make that?

Paul: [chuckles] Years.

Janice: It's a work in progress, I know, but …

Paul: A lifetime, yeah. Well, the beadwork, wampum, making the bonework, and the cuffs, and the staff. Just that took three years. And then, doing the vest – Dee [his wife] did most of this vest. And where else … Just preparing everything. It took a lot of time to put it all together. It's a major operation.

Janice: And are all the feathers found, or were they given, or …?

Paul: No. Yeah. This came from an eagle, a whole eagle. This claw and all these tail feathers were given to me from someone else. The outer part of my bustle came from a very old bustle from Lake Deer, Montana, from Northern Cheyenne Reservation. And it was pretty bad and I fixed it up quite a bit, and changed a lot, made it me. And I added inner feathers. That's from the same eagle as these came from [motions to eagle staff]. Then there's hawk feathers. These are red tail hawk feathers [on shield]. And they came from the original outfit that this came with. And I've got some small golden eagle feathers here, but I have some bigger golden eagle feathers in Anchorage, in Wasilla. Like these two little ones here. Those there and these little ones down at the bottom here, those are golden eagle. But I have large, very large ones up in Alaska. Hard to find around here. I think I heard there are some out around the Tablelands.

Janice: Really?

Paul: There are some golden eagles out there. They're usually high country type of animal, bird. [pause] This is two braids of sweetgrass that I've been dancing with since I barely ever danced. When I came out [as a dancer], the guy who gave me my bustle, my other bustle from Montana, he had died. K.C. [LaFever].[18] It was supposed to go to him. And out of respect for him, I've got two braids here – one for my family and one for him. So he's always with me when I dance. I wouldn't have gotten the bustle without him. (Personal communication, 2 July 2004)

Paul's description demonstrates the way that a dancer's regalia may be assembled from a variety of sources, especially through the process of gifting. Further, it demonstrates how a dancer's regalia can come from quite distant places and different nations and then be remade to reflect the individual and the nation of his own heritage. An event the following

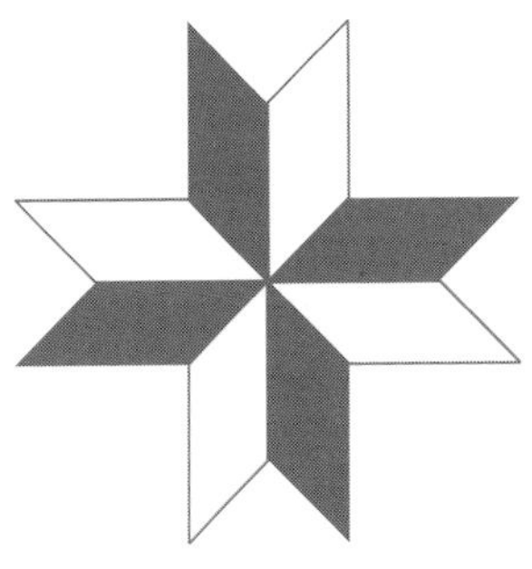

4.3 Mi'kmaw eight-point star.

year demonstrated the fluid and changing nature of regalia, which may be repaired, tweaked, revised, or added to over a lifetime. In 2005 Paul added eagle feather shoulder caps to his regalia when a dancer gifted them to him.

Items held while dancing, such as a double braid of sweetgrass, may have very personal meaning for a dancer – in this case, as a memorial to a friend. However, it is often the imagery used to embellish such regalia that is indicative of a particular locale, nation, or family. Paul's regalia makes use of three primary images that are of significance to him. The first is the crow, for his mother was of the crow clan. A crow is featured on the shield on his left arm, and smaller versions of this image are beaded onto the front of his vest. Both items also feature the Mi'kmaw eight-point star.

On Paul's shield, the crow is flying over an eight-point star (or is superimposed on it), and small red and white eight-point stars outlined in black are beaded onto his vest. An eight-point star is also found on his breech-clout, as well as on a clip that secures a red scarf around his neck. Finally, elements of Paul's regalia, such as his vest and cuffs, have edges embellished with black beadwork in the double-curve motif (see figure 4.1) and flowers. Although the image of the crow is a very personal expression of Pike's family, it also demonstrates kinship ties. Images such as the eight-point star and double-curve motif have broader meaning for the Mi'kmaw nation and have been in continual use for several centuries, if not longer.

Ruth Whitehead has studied the eight-point star as a decorative symbol and has determined that it was historically found only in one type of Mi'kmaw expressive form – quillwork on a birch bark base – and not in beadwork or earlier styles of quillwork.[19] She terms this symbol the *Kagwet*, or "Eight-legged Starfish," a term conveyed to the Nova Scotia Museum's curator in 1933 by a Mi'kmaw artisan (Whitehead 1982, 133). From her research, we are able to ascertain that the symbol has been in use as a quillwork motif since at least the early nineteenth century (Whitehead 1982, 176). The Louisbourg Institute notes that the eight-point star was located "as a petroglyph tracing at a rock site in Bedford, dating back more than 500 years," and served as a symbol of the sun, a figure of power in Mi'kmaw cosmology (Louisbourg Institute n.d.). The Nova Scotia Museum concurs with these findings and states that the eight-point star appears "in Mi'kmaq hieroglyphic writing as a symbol of the sun" (Nova Scotia Museum 1997). This symbol was later used to represent "Heaven" in a system of writing developed by Father Chrestien LeClercq and the abbé Pierre Maillard (Whitehead 1982, 180).

In describing this symbol in modern artwork, Mi'kmaw artist Barry Stevens claims that it represents the sun but also contains the four winds and the four seasons (see Houston North Gallery n.d.). Another artist calls it a symbol for unity, which shows the four directions. Each direction is said to parallel the four directions within a person; by doubling them (two points facing each direction), the star represents the fact that "there is more than meets the eye" (Invitation Project n.d.). This explanation goes on to point out, "Elders explain the eight-point star as representing the original seven Mi'gmaq [*sic*] districts plus the 1752 agreement with the Crown that made all inseparable from one another" (Invitation Project n.d.).[20]

This interpretation of the symbol as a joining of the Mi'kmaq and British in peace is given credence in an explanation provided by the Lennox Island First Nation Cultural Centre in Prince Edward Island: "The eighteenth century treaties on agreements between the Mi'kmaw nation and the British are still regarded by the Mi'kmaq as stages and renewals of a larger agreement *entitling Britain to join the Wabanaki Confederacy.* The Mi'kmaq symbolized this important relationship by adding an eighth point – Great Britain – to the seven point star representing the seven districts of the Mi'kmaw nation" (Moores 2003, emphasis added). Indeed, this was Paul Pike's explanation of its meaning when we attended a traditional powwow together in Chickaloon, Alaska, on 11 June 2002. This understanding of the symbol appears widespread at present. The Confederacy of Mainland Mi'kmaq has adopted this symbol as a logo for the Tripartite Forum, a group dedicated to securing equality and strengthening ties between the Mi'kmaq, Nova Scotia, and Canada. The confederacy explains its use of this symbol as follows: "The historic Mi'kmaq symbol had seven points to represent the traditional seven districts of the Mi'kmaq Nation. An eighth point representing the British Crown was added when the Mi'kmaq began signing treaties with the British Crown. All discussions of the Tripartite Forum will be guided by the spirit and intent of the treaties and the treaty relationship" (Confederacy of Mainland Mi'kmaq 2002). Thus, although the exact origins and period of emergence of the eight-point star in expressive culture are not certain, the star has nevertheless become a symbol of the Mi'kmaw people, which is currently understood in a variety of ways. It is not surprising, then, that this icon is the most common one seen on regalia at a Mi'kmaw powwow.

Regardless of which meaning is ascribed to this imagery, it remains identifiable as Mi'kmaw.

Both regalia styles and singing styles observed at a Mi'kmaw powwow, then, may be based on the conventions and templates dictated by more generally recognized styles of dance, music, and dress. However, these conventions do not preclude creativity, personal expression, or nation-specific aesthetics. With the categories of Women's and Men's Traditional dance allowing for particularly broad interpretation of their label "traditional," dancers are free to select a historic moment that they understand to represent their own experience, community, or nation. Likewise, although drum groups may be guided by general characteristics of northern-style singing, they may also inject nation-specific musical aesthetics, as well as language or antiphonal structures, into their own singing and compositions, thereby establishing a local or regional style.

Performing Local Histories

A third way that borrowed powwow traditions may be localized is through explicit reference to or implicit performance of local histories. As I have described elsewhere, local histories and important community figures may be explicitly referenced within the context of a powwow (see Tulk 2006). For example, at the Elsipogtog powwow in 2006, emcee Mike Doucette spoke of Tom Paul[21] and his role in bringing the powwow to Mi'kma'ki as a means of introducing a "Friendship Song" in his honour. Such speeches recount community and regional histories and (re)contextualize powwow practices and customs.

Unspoken local histories may also be performed within the context of a Mi'kmaw powwow. During this powwow in Elsipogtog, as with powwows in other parts of Mi'kma'ki, an opening prayer or invocation followed the "Veterans' Song." On the second day of the powwow, it was given by community elder Joe John:[22]

> Ni'n teluisi Musikisk. Welta'si mawitayk nike' kiskuk.
> [My name is Sky. I am happy we are gathered here today.]
>
> Elita'suatmek kiskuk alasutma'tinen. Mi'kmawita'sultinej.
> [We rely today on prayer. Let us think on our being Mi'kmaw.]
>
> Msit wulayiktn, aqq wulo'taqitinen. Knekk mimajuinu'k wejita'jik.
> [Let everything go well today, and let us be happy. People come
>   from far away.]

Nike' Kji-Niskam tamanej:
[Now, let us ask of God:]

Kji-Niskam, elita'sualnek, elita'suatmek ta'n telukutiek.
[Great God we rely on you, we rely on you for what we do.]

Apiksiktuinen, apiksiktuinen. Kepmite'lmu'kik aqq kepmite'tmek
    ta'n telukutiek.
[Forgive us, forgive us. We honour them, and we honour
    what we do.]

Alasutma'tiek nike' ukjit mimajuinu'k ta'n kesnukutijik, aqq
    wulo'taqitinew. Ta'n kesnukutijik, Wji-ula'siktn wktininewaq.
[We pray now for people who are sick, and for them to be well. For
    those who are sick, let there be goodness in their bodies.]

Alasutmelsewk mijua'ji'jk, wulo'taqitinew kiskuk, aqq wulayiktn
    kiskuk ta'n telo'lti'kw.
[Let us pray for the children, to feel good today, and for things to go
    well for the way we are.]

Alasutmelsewkik nike' amalkewinu'k, wulte'lsultinew kiskuk, aqq
    drummersik wji-wulayiktn kiskuk. Wulta'sulti'kw, wuta'sultinej.
[I pray for the dancers, to think well of themselves today, and the
    drummers, for things to go well today. Have good thoughts! Let
    us have good thoughts.]

Ke' Niskam tamanej wulo'taqatinew kiskuk.
[Let us ask God for things to go well today.]

Ta'n te'ioq, No'kmaq, wela'lioq.
[For all my relatives, thank you.]

The incorporations from Christianity are striking here, particularly in the way that this invocation asks for forgiveness and then prays for the healing of those who are sick, for the children, and for the drummers. In some ways, this structure recalls the part of the Liturgy of the Word in the Catholic Mass that is referred to as general intercessions. During this part of the Mass, petitions are made for the Lord's intervention, and the congregation replies with "Lord, hear our prayer." The lector who reads them, phrases them in this way: "For those who are sick, let us pray to the

Lord." This structure is very similar to that employed by Joe John in his prayer, even though there is no group response to his petitions.[23]

Christian incorporations are common at Mi'kmaw powwows, especially in Miawpukek, where the invocation may consist solely of a recitation of the Lord's Prayer. The name God may be used in place of Creator, and reference to those gathered as God's "children" may be heard in the English portions of some prayers. Such incorporations are not surprising, given that the Mi'kmaq adopted and adapted Christianity (specifically Catholicism) to their belief system very early on, starting with the baptism of Chief Membertou in 1610.[24] Many Mi'kmaq from all areas of Mi'kma'ki still celebrate St Anne's Day, and Christian hymn singing remains an important musical expression in many communities. The Mi'kmaw-Christian invocations heard within the context of a Mi'kmaw powwow, then, may be read as a performance of a local history of colonial encounter and response.

Conclusion

The manner in which the powwow becomes expressive of a particular First Nation – a group of people who share culture traits, are linked by local or regional histories, and have occupied (year round or seasonally) particular places and landscapes – is intricately linked to the modes of localization that are mobilized by participants. That is, the powwow becomes expressive of a nation-specific identity when nation-specific or local repertoires and styles are employed, processes of local meaning making are engaged, and local histories are performed.

Through localized expressions of the powwow, as with localized forms of other musical genres (e.g., popular music, hymns, fiddle music, and so on), individuals and communities connect to the past and tradition, and embrace exchange and new forms of cultural expression, while actively reconfiguring these traditions for the future. The powwow, then, is neither intertribal nor local but a process of negotiating two simultaneous modes of cultural expression. The power of the localized powwow lies in its ability to both enact and maintain a sense of nation-specific identity while fostering participation in a broader Indigenous community.

1   I am grateful to the Social Sciences and Humanities Research Council of Canada, the J.R. Smallwood Foundation for Newfoundland and Labrador Studies, and the Institute of Social and Economic Research for their financial support of this research. I would also like to thank my consultants for sharing their experiences with me and providing valuable feedback on early drafts of the material in this chapter. A greatly expanded exploration of the localization processes observed in the Mi'kmaw powwow can be found in Tulk (2008).

2   Regarding orthography, see 299n1.

3   The category of specials at a powwow may include nation-specific dances, display dances (such as the Hoop Dance), storytelling, craft demonstrations, or other activities that do not fall into the dance categories commonly observed at powwows, such as Fancy Dance, Grass Dance, or Women's Traditional.

4   For discussion of these localizations in a Mi'kmaw context, see Tulk (2006). See also Samuels (2004a) on the localization of transnationally known songs.

5   St Anne is the patron saint of the Mi'kmaq.

6   Angela Robinson (2004) indicates that three fluid categories of religious practitioners emerged in Mi'kma'ki: Catholics, traditionalists, and Catholic-traditionalists. These categories are perhaps best conceived of as a continuum, as individuals' personal belief systems may or may not combine two or more belief systems simultaneously to varying degrees.

7   For discussion of the relationship between Christian churches and the advancement of the powwow as a cultural expression in Ontario, see Hoefnagels (2007a).

8   I have attended six Mi'kmaw powwows, and there has always been a Mi'kmaw emcee present. At two of these powwows, a co-emcee of Anishnabe heritage was also present. Also, head dancers for powwows are almost exclusively chosen from Mi'kmaw communities.

9   First Nations musical styles and instruments were first mapped in terms of geographic distribution by George Herzog in 1928 and Helen Roberts in 1936. At mid-century, Nettl (1954) divided North America into six style areas, a classification system that was employed for the greater part of the second half of the century (e.g., McGee 1985). More recently, however, these style areas have been subject to revision. For example, Elaine Keillor (2006) has employed a classification system based on eight regions, setting the Mi'kmaq apart from "Eastern Woodlands" by grouping them with the Beothuk and Maliseet under "Maritime." Such notions of regional style have homogenizing effects and do not acknowledge the flexibility and variation inherent in singing styles and song forms.

10 Goertzen (2005, 291) notes that there may even be a metric feel to these songs.

11 The term "traditional" is used in a variety of ways in this context. It may refer to songs that were historically part of Mi'kmaw culture (such as Ko'jua songs) or to songs made in a traditional style (such as George Paul's "Gathering Song"). Further, the word "traditional" may be used as part of discursive practices to suggest an interpretive lens that connects songs to a "perceived past" (Bealle 1993, 64). As the particular histories of certain songs are erased and conflated, these songs

play a role in the recasting of history (Sarkissian 2000, 101–2). Consequently, there may be a discourse of "ancient" songs that are actually quite new.

12 The double-curve motif is a symmetrical image that employs a curve and its mirror image, which connect, intersect, or overlap in the middle. It is pervasive in Mi'kmaw iconography and has been interpreted in various ways (e.g., Speck 1914; Whitehead 1982, 133–5, 162–7).

13 Rita Joe recounts the story of learning "I'ko" from Sarah Denny and the response she got after singing it on one occasion: "Everything went well but the next day an educated individual put me on while I was hitchhiking in my community. 'I saw you on television last night. It was good, but the song you sang was Mohawk,' he said. That part was reasoned out that when the other tribes had dealings with us, the exchange was gift-giving. If you do not have anything you give a story or song which is true" (Joe 1997, 262). Kevin Alstrup notes that although the original text of "I'ko" is neither Mi'kmaw nor Mohawk, the song "has symbolic value to the Eskasoni Mi'kmaq as an invocation of Mi'kmaq traditional music culture, and perhaps as an allusion to historical ties between the Mi'kmaq and Mohawk nations" (Alstrup 2004, 5).

14 Here, each section consists of two short phrases. The slight melodic variation heard in A^1 occurs to accommodate a different Mi'kmaw lyric sung the second time through. B^1 indicates that the song closes with the second half of B (a coda). Other formal variations of this orally transmitted song exist.

15 For example, although painted regalia is not an element of the specific regalia described in this section, this style is worn by some members of the Mi'kmaw drum group Kitpu. Paint is believed to be a precontact form of embellishment that few people in the present practice.

16 The danger of consulting such sources may be demonstrated by the experience of Men's Northern Traditional dancer Paul Pike. Pike added an item to his regalia that he had seen it in a book and whose aesthetic value he appreciated, not knowing what it was or represented. At a powwow in Chickaloon, Alaska, another dancer told him he was carrying a "belly ripper," a weapon of war. Paul immediately decided to drop this item from his regalia because of its violent implications (personal communication, 25 May 2002).

17 At the time this research was conducted (between 2004 and 2008), thousands of Mi'kmaq on the west coast of Newfoundland did not have status under the Indian Act. In 2011 the Qalipu Mi'kmaq First Nation Band was established, and registration is ongoing.

18 Paul wrote the song "True Friends," which is on his band's first album, *Identity* (Medicine Dream 1998), about his friend K.C. LaFever, who, having lost his battle with drugs and alcohol, committed suicide. The proceeds from the sale of this album were donated to a memorial fund in K.C.'s name and his band, Medicine Dream, continues to contribute to recovery and sobriety programs. This song also appears on *Mawio'Mi* (Medicine Dream 2000).

19 A piece of quillwork featuring the Mi'kmaw eight-point star has been employed as a symbol for the contemporary Native group Medicine Dream and appears on its recordings, as well as on posters advertising its upcoming concerts. Medicine Dream has also had jewellery made featuring the same design (see Tulk 2003).

Paul Pike has explained, "I wanted people to know just by looking at the CD that ... the songs were composed by a Mi'kmaq person" (personal communication, 13 May 2008).

20 The 1752 treaty was a renewal of the friendship between the British and the Mi'kmaw people that was initiated in 1725, an agreement that marked the end of the fourth Anglo-Wabanaki war (Prins 1996, 138). While instituting peace between the groups, this agreement also made explicit guarantees of hunting and fishing rights, as well as provisions, if the Mi'kmaq upheld their responsibilities to encourage similar treaties among other Native nations, to defend the Crown, and to save any shipwrecked persons (Davis 1997, 67–9; see also Prins 1996, 145–7; Paul 2000, 119–23). The entire treaty is reproduced in Davis (1997) and Paul (2000). It must be duly noted that this agreement was not as amicable as it may appear; it was dissolved and reinstated multiple times over the course of history. Through contact first with European sailors who came to fish in Atlantic waters and then with the French in the sixteenth century, Mi'kmaw life changed rapidly in terms of rights, land ownership, and religion. The Mi'kmaq were allies of France at a time when France and England were both making claims to the land area that the Mi'kmaq occupied. When the English sold a band of Wabanaki as slaves to the Portuguese in 1676, the Mi'kmaq retaliated, and the first of many Anglo-Wabanaki wars ensued (Prins 1996, 123).

In 1713 France surrendered control of the area inhabited by the Mi'kmaq to Great Britain. Treaties with the English were signed and broken many times as the Mi'kmaq retained their allegiance to France. The 1752 peace treaty was short-lived, but in 1760, when the British had defeated the French, the Mi'kmaq reaffirmed their alliance with the British (Prins 1996, 151). Colonial oppressive rule continued to affect their culture and life-way. Nevertheless, it is this alliance that is referenced by the Mi'kmaw eight-point star as being a symbol of peace and unity. The historical sources consulted do not discuss the genesis of the symbol.

21 Thomas Michael Paul from Eskasoni, Nova Scotia, served in the American forces in Vietnam and was a "veteran of Indian protests at Wounded Knee, S.D., and Restigouche, Que." A supporter of the Mohawks at Oka in 1990, he died in 1992 at the age of forty-nine while awaiting trial (Nova Scotia Museum 1997, MP1113).

22 This prayer was transcribed and translated by Helen Sylliboy of Eskasoni, Nova Scotia.

23 Although it may be possible to further deconstruct these invocations – for example, another dimension that could be explored is that of sentence or phrase structures – my concern has been to demonstrate how these invocations are a performance of a particular localized history of contact and how the Mi'kmaw language is a marker to greater or lesser degrees of nation-specific identity within the context of a Mi'kmaw powwow.

24 Prior to contact, the Mi'kmaq practised their own religion, a spirituality Daniel Paul describes as being based on three fundamental principles: "the supremacy of the Great Spirit, respect for Mother Earth, and people power" (Paul 2000, 12). Within a tradition that followed the laws of the Creator, encouraged stewardship of the land, and advocated democracy among its people, the Mi'kmaq

flourished. The Mi'kmaq believed that after death they would be reunited with the Creator and their ancestors in the "Land of Souls" (Paul 2000, 19, 29). The Mi'kmaq perceived some similarities between their religion and Christianity: for example, a single God who was responsible for creation parallelled their belief in the Great Spirit, and saints who provided spiritual guidance were similar to the ancestors who provided guidance to the Mi'kmaq. For these reasons, the religions were not completely at odds with one another. Coupled with a loss of confidence in their own shamans because they were unable to protect the Mi'kmaq from recently introduced diseases such as smallpox to which the Catholic priests seemed immune, the Catholic religion was accepted by the Mi'kmaw people (Prins 1996, 44–7, 71). Conversion to Christianity was further encouraged by the creation of a writing system that could be used to teach the Mi'kmaq the underlying principles and beliefs of the Catholic Church. This system was developed by Father Chrestien LeClercq using ideograms to represent ideas (see Schmidt and Marshall 1995). Anne-Christine Hornborg notes that the introduction of St Anne further "increased the likelihood of their conversion" (Hornborg 2002, 238), for the Mi'kmaq regard St Anne, the grandmother of Jesus, as an elder, a person who is wise, has experienced life, and shares her wisdom and experience with others.

5

Contemporary Northern Plains Powwow Music: The Twin Influences of Recording and Competition

INTERVIEW: GABRIEL DESROSIERS AND
CHRISTOPHER SCALES

This chapter represents a part of an ongoing scholarly and pedagogical collaboration between Gabriel Desrosiers and myself. Mr Desrosiers is a well known and highly respected Ojibwa singer, dancer, and composer of both traditional Ojibwa song styles as well as modern powwow songs. Born 25 January 1962, he has been singing since the age of six, coming to prominence performing with and composing songs for the popular powwow group the Whitefish Bay Singers from the Whitefish Bay reserve in north-western Ontario. Gabe left that group in 1991 to lead his own group, Northern Wind, comprised of singers from the Ojibwa nation, many of whom grew up in the Lake of the Woods area in north-western Ontario. Gabe is also an internationally known dancer who has performed across North America, eastern and western Europe, and in the Middle East as a grass dancer and eagle dancer.

I first met Gabe in 2000 when I was carrying out ethnographic research and working as a recording engineer for Arbor Records, an independent music label in Winnipeg, Manitoba, that specializes in the Aboriginal music of North America. Our first collaborative project involved the creation of Northern Wind's 2000 CD *Ikwe Nagamonan: Women's Songs*, a project for which I served as recording engineer and producer. Since that time I have invited Gabe to several of the schools where I have taught to give various lectures, performances, and demonstrations. Each time we get together, we continue our ongoing conversation about the current state of powwow singing and dancing and the ever-changing nature of northern powwow culture.

This chapter presents a somewhat unvarnished transcribed and edited exchange between two individuals with quite different attachments and positions within the powwow world. The general theme of the conversation, contemporary developments in northern Plains powwow culture, was formulated through a series of e-mail exchanges between Gabe and myself prior to our face-to-face meeting. My interest in this topic stems from my own long-term academic engagement with powwow music and the Aboriginal recording industry in Canada, whereas Gabe has been deeply involved in powwows as a singer and dancer since he was a child. This conversation is, in part, an attempt to work across and between the discourses found on the powwow trail and in the academy, as both of us operate, in varying degrees and with varying degrees of investment, within both of these social and cultural spaces.

This transcription has undergone some moderate editorial work in its preparation for publication. All of the "ummms" and "ahhhs" and "yeahs" have been removed. Some informal speech patterns have been altered to suit the more formal style of an academic publication (e.g., "Like" used at the beginning of a sentence has been replaced with "For example," or "For instance," or "What I mean by that is"). Incomplete sentences, sentence fragments, and repetitive phrases have been deleted or altered to form complete and grammatically correct sentences. Part of the editorial process has also involved picking out and stitching together different moments of our longer conversation in order to group parts of the conversation that share similar topical foci. Overall, however, we have tried to retain the general arc and flow of the six-hour conversation, which was recorded over a two-day period in a room at the Mystic Lake Casino Hotel in Prior Lake, Minnesota, in the early autumn of 2007.

 CS: I know we've gone back and forth on e-mail about the goals for this project, but I think it's worth revisiting. What are your goals for this chapter? What do you want this to be about? What do you want to make sure is mentioned in this work?

GD: I think the main goal we should be working towards is educating people about Native American music. That's the main focus for me. Because I have found that, especially within non-Native communities, there are a lot of misunderstandings surrounding Native American music. They might think that it's all just noise, or chanting, or they think that it's all a "war cry" or "savage" sounding. My main focus, what is most important for me, are the *true meanings* behind Indian music. And this means not only my Ojibwa music that I was raised with and that I learn from, but also the life-ways that I was taught by my father, my relatives, and my grandfather. I want to be accurate about what Native American music is all about for me. And there are all different kinds of Native American music. You have ceremony songs. You have old traditional songs that are passed on that have had significant meaning for people in their lives. Maybe it was a song of hope. Or maybe it was a song about the death of a special individual that would otherwise be forgotten. Those songs keep on surviving and get passed on. And that's important. That's an important thing to know about a song. Because these days there are a lot of singers out there who could just make up a song right here, right now, on the spot. These new songs can sometimes overshadow the older songs, because at today's powwows it's all about being "contemporary." What I mean by this is that singers are worried about who's going to sound the best in a competition. And that's the main focus for a lot of singers now. A lot of the drum groups now are younger groups, filled with young people. And I think a lot of them don't know their roots as Indian people. For instance, a lot of them have lost their language; they don't speak their own tribal language. And as a result of this, a lot of the modern powwow composers go to older guys, like myself, or people older than myself, in order to get words for their songs and to get the meanings behind those lyrics. And for me, speaking as a composer, I think that's a problem. I wonder if that song is really from their heart.

cs: Wow. There's a lot of stuff in what you've just said that I think we need to talk about further. Just to pick up on one thread, why do you think it is that powwow song composition is changing so much now? What do you think accounts for the differences between newly composed songs and older songs? One of the factors that I think has played a large part in this is the increasing prominence and availability of powwow recordings. I know I've met a lot of singers who have told me that, especially when they are first learning how to sing, they learn a lot of songs from commercial cds and tapes, and not necessarily from other singers. And so there's a different kind of relationship to the music. Instead of learning the older songs from other singers, they're learning newly composed songs from cds. And so that's what they're basing their musical knowledge on. Do you think that's why they don't know the older songs, or some of the meanings behind the older songs?

GD: I think it is a lack of teaching. I mean, it's what you're saying. They don't have the guidance of the elders because somewhere along the lines I think some singers have lost those lines of contact. And, again, I think that a big part of that story is the loss of language. But related to this is also the issue of younger singers wanting to be more "modern." They want to be "modern-day singers." In my opinion, I think that a sense of spirituality has gone from the singing, the way it was meant to be. Back in the days when I began singing, you were supposed to listen to what the elders were teaching and saying. They used to begin the singing process by smoking the pipe and offering tobacco to the spirits and to the four directions. Now you don't see that as much at powwows.

And so I think you're right that a lot of singers learn by just buying a CD and listening to it, putting on headphones and learning songs. I teach song and dance at the high school where I work, and I've noticed that my students do that.[1] They'll come up to me with their iPod or CD player or whatever and say, "Hey I like this song, let's learn this one." So one day I asked one of the boys in my class, "Well, can you tell me what those words mean in that song that you want to learn? Can you translate the lyrics for me word by word so that you know what you're singing?" And he couldn't. So I think a lot of the young people now are doing the same thing. They learn songs by listening to a CD, but they don't know the meaning behind those songs.

So for me, with all songs, I think all lead singers – well all singers – should try to know what that song is all about: where it comes from, what region it comes from, what tribe it comes from. I think it's important for the people who originally composed those songs. So I think that singers should always be trying and learn these things. Our educators are our elders and they're passing on and we're losing the opportunity to learn from them. But at the real contemporary, competition powwows, a young singer is going to go over to a drum, and his first thought is, "does this sound good?" And the second biggest concern for that young singer is winning that big money. I think, sounding good, winning money, and trying to make a name for himself or for his drum are the three main concerns of a young singer today.

CS: How do you think those kinds of concerns are affecting powwows more generally? Do you think they are overshadowing some of the other kinds of responsibilities that drums have at a powwow, like singing an appropriate song for a dancer? Maybe instead of singing an appropriate song, they'll sing one that they know really well, where they know they're going to sound really good for a competition. I was down in Fort Berthold at a powwow a few years ago making a recording of Mandaree singers, and during the Saturday evening dance session they called on this young group of singers to sing for the adult Grass Dance competition. The emcee called for a Crow Hop, but this group sang a Chicken Dance song instead.[2] After the song was finished the emcee addressed the group and publicly scolded them for singing a Chicken Dance song and [said] that they should have been performing what the emcee had asked of them. And then they went to the host drum, and the host drum performed a Crow Hop for the dancers. And I don't know whether that drum just didn't know a Crow Hop song or whether they just decided to do a Chicken Dance instead.

GD: I've seen similar occasions where groups will just sing anything. For example, at one powwow I went to a drum group started singing a Jingle Dress song for Women's Fancy Dance. And maybe that was because the group was up and coming and they didn't understand what the appropriate songs for each category are or when to sing them. So maybe that's why that happened. And powwow people will know right away. But I also know from experience that if you're called upon to sing all of a sudden, sometimes you just can't really think of a song right away. And so you'll just sing whatever you can think of. But if you're a singer you should know what to sing. A lot of drum groups have one guy in that group who knows all the songs, who's like a songbook. We have one. B.J. Copenace. We go to him. Even though I compose all the songs and music, I can't always remember a song when we need it [laughs]. I don't know why but I just cannot do that. I don't have that ability. But for him, we ask for a song that we need and [snaps fingers] he just comes right out with it. And I think each group has a guy like that, a guy who knows all the songs and who can come up with them just like that. So in the case of the Mandaree powwow that you were talking about, that group just might not have had anybody like that. Or maybe they didn't have a complete repertoire of songs, maybe because they were a new group.

Sometimes you sing whatever you think will suffice for the situation. But sometimes if you do that, you can offend people. And so you need to learn more. At contest powwows this always comes up. If a certain drum group is not singing up to par, I will hear people say, "They need to go back to traditional powwows and practise more." So there is a feeling that a traditional powwow is where you first begin to learn about singing, and you sing there before you jump into the contest world.[3]

CS: What do you think about that idea?

GD: [Pause – sighs.] For me, when I was growing up and first learning about singing and about powwows, I would learn by watching elderly singers. I would watch the protocol they had at the drum, and I would listen to them talking with a pipe and walking around the arbour.[4] That's what they used to do a long time ago. Anyone could get up while they were in that arbour. And they would have their own personal pipe, and they'd walk around. And it was like they were preaching. They would talk about the things that our fathers and grandfathers told us. And the people would all sit around the arbour, and these elders would get up and talk about singing, how to treat the songs and the drum. And I remember when I was a young, young boy I would listen as they walked around, and the main thing that they would always stress was to never discriminate and say that no one can sing. Everybody's allowed to sing. The men can sing and the women can sing behind the drum and be supportive. That idea was instilled in me as a young boy, and I will always remember that. So when I sing, a lot of young boys come up to me and are really enthusiastic, and they're always wondering what it would be like to be part of a singing group. And they look to me like a role model. I'm not going to discourage them by saying, "You can't sing here." My belief is that everyone has a right to hold that drum stick and sit at that drum. Because I was taught that powwow singing and powwow dancing is a celebration of life. And when people come together for a powwow, everyone who comes there is seeking life and they're celebrating life. I have no right to say, "Hey, you can't be here. You can't sit at this drum," or "you can't sing," or "you can't dance." So, to me, when I hear people say things like that, it's funny. Because deep down, I always think that everyone has a right to sing and to dance. And that's just what I've learned from the elders.

CS: You've mentioned singing competitions a few times now. I'm wondering what your thoughts are on the emergence and popularity of competitions at powwows. Other singers and dancers have told me they worry that competitions lead to a lot of intertribal and intercommunity conflict. It can generate things like jealousy and maybe dishonest behaviour. But on the other hand, competition powwows also really do seem to bring people together. You meet new people, you renew old friendships, you make relatives …

  GABRIEL DESROSIERS AND CHRISTOPHER SCALES

GD: I think there are certain things that you have to like about contest powwows. I really enjoy going to contest powwows because, among other things, it gives me the opportunity to participate as a singer or as a dancer. It also gives me the opportunity, and to have the good fortune, to serve as head staff carrier, or as an arena director, or a singing judge, or a dance judge. I enjoy all of those opportunities. I also like just to dance sometimes. I really enjoy myself just dancing to good, quality music. And when that happens, when you're dancing to a good, quality group, then a lot of things just come out, like the good feeling of being able to dance. What I like is the good, physical workout you get when you dance. It keeps you in shape to dance. And when that happens, you feel good about yourself. You feel good being able to dance to two or three contest songs in a row. It's a very fulfilling feeling for me; it's an energizer, and it brings out the competitive part of me knowing that I am able to dance and keep up with all these young guys. And I don't care if they beat me or not because I'm feeling good about dancing. And when I go to contest powwows, that's what defines me as a dancer. As a singer it's the same thing. You hear other groups and they're sounding really good and it brings out the best in us. I'm thinking, "Hey, we need to compose songs that are going to be able to compete with these other groups." Because these other groups have good songs too, so we want to try and keep up with them. And it just brings out a feeling that you're a part of something – something that's big. Those are some of the good things.

CS: Do you think contests are changing the way people sing?

GD: Absolutely. As an experienced composer, I always try to be innovative in what I do. But this is especially true in the contests. I look at other drums and what they're doing. I don't try to copy them, but I take notice. For example, you have a drum group like Eyabay. They came up with the idea of one lead and no second. One guy leads and everybody just comes in.[5] That was just their way of just trying to be different and innovative. Then there are drum groups, like Eyabay again and Northern Cree, that came up with the idea of using three leads. One guy leads, and then another guy, and then a third guy, and then the whole group joins in for the rest of the song.[6] Groups like that are always doing things differently at contest powwows and that's because of the contest. It's that contest frame of mind.

CS: Trying to be different, trying to be new …

GD: Trying to be different, trying to be new, and trying to keep a step ahead of one another. Because a lot of times groups want to impress people with their singing ability. They want to stand out. And that's all part of the contest. They want to win; they want to make some money. I don't think that's the case all the time. Sometimes you just want to be different for the sake of being different. Not to outdo another, it's just to try something new.

CS: It's really interesting that you mention the role that competition plays in innovation and the development of powwow composition and musical style. In my own writing on this, I've tended to stress elements of competition that generate stylistic homogenization [Scales 2007]. For instance, at many singing competitions you see the same kinds of judging criteria being used, which tends to generate a particular set of stylistic norms. You also see the phenomenon where groups like Eyabay become popular to the point where dozens of younger drum groups try to emulate their style, which again can have a homogenizing effect. So I'm wondering what you think? Is the overall effect of competition making groups sound more similar or making groups sound more unique? Are you seeing greater diversity or greater homogenization?

GD: I think it's a mixture. Again, take Eyabay for an example. They were doing things differently. They had awesome Fancy Dance songs – Trick songs for Fancy Dancers.[7] And people really liked that. And people really liked their style of singing. And so for a while we had all these other really young drum groups that started appearing trying to sound like Eyabay. But there's a mixture of feelings about that. On the one hand, you have young, up-and-coming drum groups trying to sound like a group that is really popular. They're trying to imitate someone else's style so they can open doors and become popular. In a way, that's good for the initial drum group, Eyabay, because they're being idolized and they should feel good about that. But in the powwow sense, maybe Eyabay doesn't like the idea of someone trying to copy them. Maybe they're thinking, "This is our style and we don't want anybody to copy it." So if a drum group tries to sound too much like another group that can be a problem too. So, having said that, a lot of drum groups try to create their own style. Look at Midnite Express. They're a young group. They're really big right now. They created a new style of drumbeat.

They're an Original-style group. Original-style drumming is just
straight style [starts tapping straight beat on arm of chair]. It used to be
just straight and fast, just straight singing. No words. The only time they
used words was for honour songs or maybe ceremonial songs, things like
that. So Midnite Express learned a lot of old-style Ojibwa straight songs.
I think some of them were Dakota straight songs too. But they started
doing this new drumbeat where they all [starts tapping a steady beat
then ends abruptly with one hard beat] come in and they "beat down."
Or they come in real high [starts steadily tapping louder and louder
ending with one hard beat followed by more steady, quiet tapping] and
then they all "beat down."

CS: So they build to intensity through a drum crescendo, and then they
take it back down again.

GD: Yeah, it gets real low and then they build it up again [loud beating followed by one hard beat and subsequent quiet beats] and then
hit down again. You see, that's a contemporary thing. That's not really
Original-style drumming. Even though they enter Original-singing contest categories. That's not really the Original style. So they created this
new style of drumming and it became really popular. Everybody started
noticing what they were doing, and it started catching on with other
groups. Original style is really coming back again. Within the last ten
years, maybe, Original-style singing has really started to come back.

CS: That has been my experience too. When I was on the [powwow] trail
a little bit last summer [2006], a lot of singers were talking about how
the Original style is coming back and was becoming popular again. And
I noticed a lot more young groups singing Original style. Even some
groups that started off singing Contemporary style are switching over to
Original. Is it fair to say that the 1990s was dominated by Contemporary
singing but that now Original-style singing is making a comeback?

GD: I think so. And I think what made that comeback happen was
Schemitzun.[8] That was the first powwow I know of to introduce the dif-
ferent contest categories of singing: Original, Contemporary, Southern.
So when that happened, people heard that kind of singing and thought,
"Wow, Original singing is really good." It just kind of took off from
there.

CS: So before Schemitzun, both styles of singing were judged in one big singing contest and the Original groups would never win?

GD: Right. The Contemporary groups would always win until they started categorizing them into separate contests. And now today, the Original contests have a lot more singing groups entering and competing. So there's a lot more competition in the Original-style contests now. This is also good for Contemporary singing groups because once they started to separate the two styles into different contests at all these powwows, there's less competition in the Contemporary category. There are a lot more groups in the Original contests now.

CS: So it was in the 1990s that powwows started splitting singing contests into Original and Contemporary style. When did that start happening with dancing? Because I've been to a lot of powwows – usually big powwows – where there have been separate "old-style" and "Contemporary-style" dance contests. For instance, you would see separate adult contests for old-style and Contemporary-style Grass Dancing, or old-style and Contemporary-style Jingle Dress Dancing. Did powwow committees start doing this after the singing contests got split up, or was it before, or at the same time?

GD: I think it happened after the singing contests got split up. Schemitzun might have been one of the first powwows to start categorizing dancing that way too. And at Schemitzun, they had a category for old style and they had a category for Contemporary for *all* the dance styles.[9] So right away that categorized each dance style. Because Schemitzun was such a big powwow, I think it influenced a lot of other powwows, and so you saw a lot of other committees doing the same thing, splitting all the contest categories into "Traditional" and "Contemporary."

CS: I'm also wondering about how competitions are affecting the kinds of social conventions surrounding singing and the formation of drum groups. I wonder how that affects the development of powwow singing styles and the degree to which intertribalism is driving new stylistic developments. A lot of the really popular drum groups on the powwow trail today seem to be intertribal groups. I'm thinking about groups like Midnite Express and Mystic River. They have singers from a lot of different communities. Do you think there are more intertribal drum groups now than there used to be?

   GABRIEL DESROSIERS AND CHRISTOPHER SCALES

GD: I think there are some. In Minnesota there's groups like the Boyz, Midnite Express, or Eyabay. Eyabay's mostly Red Lake [Ojibwa] boys, but they have some – or have had some – Ho Chunk and Dakota boys. So they've been mixed right from the beginning. So maybe there are more and more groups that are starting to have different members from different regions or different tribes that come together and sing together.

CS: Do you think that's a function of all the drum hopping that goes on today?[10]

GD: I think there's a lot more of that going on too. A lot of these singers are becoming really well known. Take a look at who the top drums are this summer. A lot of these groups have intertribal members. These groups are filled with really good singers, singers who have the ability to sing with anybody. So they drum hop a lot.

CS: So do you think that with all of these different singers jumping in with different drums, one of the results might be that tribal styles and regional styles of singing are breaking down? If you have all of these different singers singing in intertribal groups, then they're not singing Ojibwa style, or they're not singing Cree style or Lakota style, but they're singing this new kind of blended style.

GD: Well, you can say that drum hopping quite obviously breaks down the sound of the original drum. For instance, everybody in this area pretty much knows how my drum sounds. My group has a distinct style where you can understand the words to the songs. Powwow people can tell how the Whitefish Jrs sound or how Bear Creek sounds. And so you'll know right away if somebody's missing from the group. That group just won't sound the same. Everybody will know that. So if you bring in singers from another community that don't know the language, sure I'd say it's going to break down the style of that drum group to a certain degree. If I brought in four or five Dakota boys to my drum, our sound would certainly be broken down. We just wouldn't sound the same. But I don't think you can ever totally lose the sound of your drum because most drums have a core group of singers that really define the sound of that drum. There are lead singers in every drum group and they're the ones who carry that style of that drum. And so I think the only way you'll break it down is if you lose those lead singers.

CS: I guess I'm thinking more on a community level or regional level rather than thinking about the styles of particular drum groups. Do you think that tribes still have particular and recognizable singing styles when they are singing powwow songs? For example, do you think that a Cree drum group, a drum made up predominantly of Cree singers, sounds different than a Lakota drum group or an Ojibwa drum group? Because what I hear you saying is that powwow people can always identify what Bear Creek sounds like or what Eyabay sounds like, but can you make wider generalizations about musical style? For instance, can you hear a group and say, without even knowing who they are, "that sounds like Cree singing or that sounds like Lakota singing"? Can you tell that?

GD: Well, I think that I could tell. I'm a song maker and so I know right away if a Dakota or Lakota drum was singing because I hear that language in there. Or they are singing a straight song from their region; I'll know where that song came from. I'll know right away if it's a Cree drum. You can tell by their language, their singing style, the words they're using …

CS: Even if there are only vocables being used? Can you tell just by the vocables that they're using?

GD: Sure. I think it's really distinct. Of course, there are more general distinctions you can make too. You can tell if the drum is from the South because those groups sing really low. So that's another distinct feature. Sometimes a drum group will sing really high and that's part of their style. Bear Creek, for instance, sings really high. And it seems like they maintain that level all the time. Northern Cree sings high too; and there was a drum group that was around a while ago called Red Earth, from the Meskwaki nation, who sang incredibly high. Everybody knew who they were. They were practically screaming. Nobody could ever catch those guys. So if you create a style as a drum group, people are going to know who you are and will immediately be able to recognize you. High Noon is another example. They have their own style too. They're always singing really fast straight songs, and they sing really high as well. And that's because of the two singers that are always with the group, Ted Noon and his brother. That drum group always has drum hoppers. Everywhere they go they'll have different guys. But they'll always sound the same because of those two guys.

CS: What about recordings? You seem to be saying that you don't think that drum hopping is really having a significant effect on tribal styles, but what about the widespread availability of recordings. Now that there are so many recordings out there, Lakota groups can listen to Bear Creek and Bear Creek can listen to Northern Cree and so on. I know that singers have always been able to hear other styles of singing from other regions just by going to powwows, especially competition powwows, but do you think that all of these commercially available recordings are having an effect on the development of powwow musical styles? Do recordings have the potential to create more possibilities for the mixing of tribal styles or creating new hybrid styles of powwow singing?

GD: [Long pause.] I don't think so. The recording industry, especially for powwow music, it's always growing, but it's always falling apart too. Lots of recording companies start and then they die out for one reason or another. With the recording industry now, CDs and recordings are available anywhere you go. There are all kinds of vendors at powwows now, and all these vendors sell CDs from top groups. So this music is available to all singers, any tribal nation you go to. But I don't think it's changing the way they sing. I don't think people are buying CDs to try and sound like that drum group. I think a lot of them are just buying them for their own entertainment. They like to collect the CDs of their own favourite drum groups. Or I think a lot of times people buy the recordings just to support that drum, because a lot of these drums are not rich. They need to get some food and gas money. You'll see them walking around the arbour trying to sell recordings. So a lot of these people buy these CDs to help out that drum group because they know how it is on the powwow trail. It's kind of a hard thing. So while a lot of people who buy CDs enjoy the music, it's also about trying to help the drum out financially. And I think that's the main reason that drum groups make CDs. They're trying to make some travel money. That's part of the reason, anyway. For example, in my group, if we have CDs to sell at a powwow, it helps my singers. Sometimes those boys don't have a lot of money, but when they're asked to go to a powwow, they'll jump in without having a cent. So they count on my drum group to help them get through the weekend. If we sell ten or twenty CDs it will feed them for the day. And then we'll try to do the same thing the next day. So part of the reason for making CDs is survival. Another reason, perhaps, is to gain more recognition. Or maybe it's just to keep up with other groups. There's a sense of competition there. You keep track of who is releasing a new one and who's not, or who hasn't put one out in a while.

CS: Do you think it's detrimental to a drum group if they don't release a CD for a few years in a row? Do you have to have a new CD out every year or every couple of years in order to stay popular on the powwow trail? Because I know from talking to powwow record label salesmen that the reverse is true. They have said to me that in order to sell CDs a drum group needs to be out on the powwow trail and needs to be travelling and be visible. Is it a two way street? Is it also the case that travelling to powwows helps a group sell CDs and having CDs to sell helps a group get more hosting gigs and more invitations to sing at powwows?

GD: Well I had some experience with that this past summer. Our group hasn't released a CD in two years. And last year we didn't travel all that much. And that was just my own decision. I wanted to get out to powwows more as an individual and go to more powwows with my family. Plus, as I've mentioned, it was really difficult financially to get my group out there and singing. It takes a lot of work to be a lead singer and the leader of the group and to try to keep a group going every year. So I took a break for a summer. We didn't travel that much; Northern Wind wasn't around at most powwows. I was still going with my family, but not with the drum. And people would come up and say, "Hey, are you guys still going?" or "Hey, where are your boys?" So this summer we came out again and started singing in a few places. And I heard a few comments from dancers and singers saying, "Wow, I haven't heard these guys in a long time. It's good to hear them again." So people notice when a drum group drops out of the circuit. They'll start to wonder whether the group has broken up or whether they're singing anymore. So my experience has been that when you're out of sight for a while, people notice right away. People notice that. And when you come back it revitalizes interest in the group and the good feeling that people used to have when they heard that drum group. And I think coming back out with a new CD is another way to signify that a drum group is still around and singing. But on the other hand, you can't *just* make CDs. Some groups are constantly making CDs but you never see them on the trail. And that doesn't work either. You see, on the powwow circuit you have to justify who you are. And that's the same with dancing too. In order to be known as a dance competitor, you have to show that you are, which means competing every weekend. I think people like that consistency. And the same goes for drum groups; people like to see them travelling and singing at powwows. So with my group, we went out on the trail again and we've been singing here and there and we've had good response. And so that prompted me to think that it was time to do another CD.

CS: What about protocols surrounding recording and song ownership? Has recording changed the way powwow song makers think about ownership? For example, have you ever run across a drum group who was singing your song even though you never gave it to them or you never gave them permission to sing it? Or have you ever heard a drum at a powwow that you've never met before that you see singing one of your songs from a CD?

GD: There was an instance where I had another young group contact me. I think they were from out in the Northwest, the Coeur d'Alene area. They contacted me through e-mail and they said, "We want to apologize because we used one of your songs on our CD that we just recorded." And so they asked, "Is it okay for your song to be on there? Otherwise we'll delete it. If it's okay to be in there we'll give you all the royalties and we'll give you full credit for having your song on our CD. But we just wanted to let you know." I don't know how that happened, but I said, "Well, thank you" [laughs]. And because they asked me in that way I said, "Okay, go ahead you can use the song; just give us credit and make sure you make it known where the song comes from." And they were cool with that.

CS: So they learned the words and everything to the song?

GD: That's right. They were a young group. And as I said earlier, I don't discourage young kids or new drum groups from singing or wanting to learn. So I really don't get too critical about it, unless people are outright trying to do things against your will, after you've told them no for what-ever reason. It's an honour to have other people sing your songs. A lot of people do things for a reason. But generally you need to ask in a good way. I think the right protocol is that you ask that group and you give them tobacco and say, "Is it okay if we do this?" And if you don't do that and you just go ahead and sing someone else's songs, maybe that's not the right thing to do all the time. That can get you into trouble.

CS: But with all the CDs out there now, that must happen a lot. Just like with that young drum group, they learned your song from a CD and re-corded it themselves and then asked your permission afterwards. I had a similar experience when I was singing with Spirit Sands Singers. We were singing at the Onion Lake powwow and we were called on to sing a round dance. Mike Esquash, our lead singer and song maker, hadn't made a lot of round dance songs at that time, so we sang a song made by Art Moosomin, a great Cree round dance singer and song maker. I don't think Mike had ever asked permission to sing it. He had just learned it from a CD. Well we finished singing the song and we looked behind us and there was Mr Moosomin sitting in the stands right behind us. So we all got up and shook his hand, and Mike apologized and thanked him for the song. There were no hard feelings as far as I could tell.

GD: That stuff happens. There are some instances where that happens.

CS: Are there some songs that you think shouldn't be recorded?

GD: I think so. My belief is record your own compositions and just leave the old traditional songs alone. Let them get passed on another way. Traditional songs that belong in ceremonies or belong in the longhouse or roundhouse, leave them there. Leave them at the drum.

CS: What about the argument that recording those traditional songs is a way to preserve them to make sure that they live on so that nobody forgets them. Do you think that's a valid argument?

GD: In a way it is. There is this idea out there that the only way that you preserve your culture is if you put it in archives in some form. That way you can say, "This was written by so and so. Here it is, in a glass case" [laughs]. It's a valid argument. I'm not saying that it shouldn't be done. We know about a lot of old music because of this.

CS: But do you think that putting something in a glass case like that, is that really *preserving* it? You preserve it, but only in a certain way.

GD: I think you're preserving something about the importance of that song. You're preserving how it used to be. That song might have changed through time. Maybe that's what's happened to some old traditional songs. We don't know that.

CS: But don't you think that the danger might be then that you've got this *thing* on record, you've got the song, and so you know how it sounded fifty or sixty or one hundred years ago, but maybe the *meaning* has changed. It's like you were saying earlier, because it wasn't preserved by oral tradition, by learning it from other people, the meanings of it might disappear, and all you have is the song; you don't have the meaning and the context anymore.

GD: Well that's hard to respond to because … I think the *real* value of the song, I don't think that can be lost through time.

CS: You think that resides in the song?

GD: I think it always resides in the song. For myself, I believe that all the songs that I make, I don't make them on my own. I have a gift but that's through the Creator. He gives me that gift. He gives me those songs. They come from somewhere. I absolutely believe that they didn't pop out of the air like that for no reason. They come from the Creator. And so I always take time in my life, when I pray and give tobacco, I always take time to thank Him for all the songs and the ability He gave me to share these songs with the people. I've always believed that's my goal or purpose in life. He's using me to be in the front lines to teach our Indian people. But not only that, I also need to teach non-Indian people about who we are as people. That's what I believe. And these songs are a part of that. They define who I am, because that's been my life. My life is song.

The original intent of this chapter was to reproduce and represent our conversation as faithfully as possible and with minimal interpretation or analysis. There were several reasons for this editorial decision. First and foremost, we wanted the power structure of the collaboration to be as neutral as possible. We both come to the topic of powwow music and culture with differing interests and areas of expertise, and we did not want either of us to dominate or control the nature or content of the conversation, or its interpretation, to an excessive degree. Second, we wanted our words to simply stand as they were, resisting the impulse to have one of us become the "cultural interpreter" for the other. As Keith Negus reminds us, an interview/conversation such as this one is not a context within which knowledge is "revealed" but an instance wherein knowledge is actively *created* (Negus 1999, 10–11; see also Scales 2004, 41–2). As such, the conversation mode is already itself a unique kind of cultural interpretation; in the present case, with its particular conversational context, our individual knowledge about, experiences of, and aesthetic and academic investments in powwow music have been deployed to produce a unique kind of analytic text. Producing a second layer of analysis not only seems superfluous (academic overkill) but could also possibly work to diminish or overshadow what was initially said. In short, because we both worked diligently editing this work and because we both signed off on the final product, we each had the opportunity to make sure that "we said what we meant and meant what we said."

However, the actual process of creating this collaborative work perhaps deserves a few more words and some further reflection. For example, despite our best intentions to keep the social dynamic as collaborative as possible, we found ourselves falling into familiar habits of interaction. Thus Gabe's voice and opinions often dominated the conversation, whereas my tendency was to try to control the direction of the conversation by hammering away at certain topics that were of particular interest to me. The result of this dynamic produced a conversation in which Gabe didn't get to talk as much about what he was interested in talking about, and I didn't get to say as much as I wanted to say about particular topics. In other words, although we had every intention of getting beyond our habitual "informant-ethnographer" social dynamic, we were only partially successful.

Our general points of reference, the result of our differing positions in the powwow social world, also produced interesting moments of conversational tension and sometimes revealed incompatible discursive strategies or analytic frameworks. For example, the more I insisted upon an analysis of musical style at the level of tribe or region, the more Gabe grounded the conversation in the musical choices and social dynamics of individual singers and drum groups. The more I tried to make abstract generalizations, the more Gabe tethered the conversation to real people and lived moments of experience. Indeed, our differing discursive strategies in many ways structured the flow of the entire conversation. For example, three interrelated themes emerged: (1) the relationship between "traditional" and "contemporary/ competition" powwows, (2) the influence of recording technology on musical practice and the development of musical style, and (3) the current protocols governing song ownership and song transmission on the powwow trail, protocols that have been reformulated to accommodate the ubiquity of commercial and personal recordings now available to singers. My own interest in these topics was motivated by my own research goals of uncovering how the twin discourses of "tradition" and "modernity" operate across these broad fields of social practice. How do these discourses absorb and condition the social meaning of recordings or practices that have developed around competition powwows? Gabe, as a teacher, was far more interested in thinking about how "tradition" could be used as a "resource" in educating not only Native youth but the larger non-Native population as well. His engagement with these issues was far more pragmatic and immediate.

Our ongoing challenge, as Gabe and I continue our conversation in other venues and in other media, is to continually push each other to think outside of our own discursive frameworks and culturally and socially conditioned habits of thought and practice as well as to contribute to the constantly growing body of knowledge of powwow song and dance practices in a way that is useful and "truthful" for all parties (Native and non-Native, academic and layman, powwow people and casual observers).[11] In doing so, we hope to construct a vision of powwow song and dance that gives all who are interested a glimpse of the power and beauty of this art form, which has inspired in both of us a life-long dedication and passion.

NOTES

1 At the time of this interview, Gabe taught at the Tiospa Zina Tribal School on the Sisseton-Wahpeton Oyate reservation. At the time of publication, he is a lecturer in Native American culture and history and the Ojibwa language at the University of Minnesota, Morris.
2 Crow Hop songs and Chicken Dance songs have quite different drumbeat patterns and tempos that require significantly different dance steps and body movements from the dancers.
3 "Traditional" and "contemporary/contest" are the two most general "kinds" of powwows found on the northern Plains. Although there are numerous subtle differences in terms of both practice and ideology between these two types of events (see Scales 2007, Albers and Medicine 2005), the most obvious and significant is that "competition" powwows feature regularly scheduled singing and dance competitions for sometimes large cash prizes all weekend long, whereas "traditional" powwows do not.
4 The "arbour" is the physical space where dancing and singing takes place at a powwow.
5 The standard form for the majority of northern-style powwow songs features a phrase structure of either A A¹ B C B C or A A¹ B C D B C D. The A phrase, rendered by a solo singer, is referred to as the "lead" phrase, and its repetition (A¹), performed by all the members of the drum group, is called the "second." Thus the formal innovation found in some of Eyabay's compositions results in a unique (to the powwow world) phrase structure of A B C D B C D.

6 The lead phrase is almost always sung by a single singer. This innovation not only redistributes singing duties within the group in an unusual way but also creates exceptionally long lead phrases that are composed of a number of subphrases.

7 Trick songs are songs that feature unusual stylistic or formal compositional elements, often arranged in a way intended to surprise or confuse dancers.

8 The Schemitzun Powwow and Green Corn Festival, sponsored by the Mashantucket Pequot nation, began in 1993. Almost since its inception, it has been widely acclaimed as one of the largest and most lucrative contest powwows on the east coast of North America.

9 There are six main dance styles found at most northern powwows: Men's Fancy Dance, Men's Grass Dance, Men's Traditional Dance, Women's Fancy Dance, Women's Jingle Dress Dance, and Women's Traditional Dance. At the Schemitzun powwow, other dance styles have become regular competition categories, such as the Women's Eastern Blanket Dance, Men's and Women's Smoke Dance, and Men's Eastern War Dance. These latter dances are generally seen and performed only at eastern powwows and would not typically be found at powwows in the northern Plains or in the North or Southwest.

10 "Drum hopping" is a term that refers to the common practice of singers from one drum group "sitting in," or performing, with other drum groups. Singers could join a group simply for one song or for an entire weekend.

11 This approach is similar to what Choctaw ethnomusicologist and powwow dancer Tara Browner refers to as the "middle way" (Browner 2002, 16).

6

Aboriginal Women and the Powwow Drum: Restrictions, Teachings, and Challenges

ANNA HOEFNAGELS

Aboriginal powwow celebrations increased in popularity and significance throughout the twentieth century in Canada, and now, at the start of the twenty-first century, powwows have developed into annual gatherings with a regular following in most parts of southern Canada. Powwow practices can be traced to warrior societies of the Plains nations of the late nineteenth century and are also considered a product of the forced relocation of American Aboriginal groups to the Oklahoma region;[1] however, in many Canadian Aboriginal communities, powwows as we now know them were launched and grew during the second half of the twentieth century. For example, in First Nation communities in south-western Ontario, contemporary powwows evolved from existing community gatherings that gradually borrowed and adapted music and dance practices from western First Nations and that date back to at least the 1950s (Hoefnagels 2007a). More recently, in eastern Canada, the powwow tradition among the Mi'kmaq began in the early 1980s (Tulk 2008; Tulk 2006, 16). Urban institutions also host annual gatherings, including those held by Aboriginal support organizations and community centres and by universities and colleges. Local constructions of meanings and understandings of powwow activities inform powwow practices, resulting in regional and nation-specific differences at powwows.[2] Teachings around gender restrictions in powwow music performance are also a local consideration, as some regions and communities allow women to participate fully as powwow musicians, whereas others restrict their participation. The issue of women's participation in powwow music making is important, as differing practices illustrate that powwows and powwow traditions are not homogenous and are locally constructed and that the meanings and teachings associated with this celebration are constantly evolving.

I began learning about and attending powwows in south-western Ontario in the fall of 1994, speaking with a number of powwow musicians and organizers about powwow music and traditions and about their meanings.[3] I learned about many of the local powwow teachings, particularly the music and dance practices, as well as about the development and changes to various community powwows in this region over time. When I began investigating the music made at powwows and its associated activities and teachings, the interviewing that I did was exclusively with men since they were the primary music makers in this region. What I learned from these experiences attending powwows in various communities, as well as through interviews about music protocol and "traditions," was also confirmed in the literature that I read about the powwow: powwow music is a male-dominated genre in which men compose songs, strike the drum, and are the principal singers. The role of women in the powwow repertoire is typically restricted to that of backup singers, who stand in a circle behind the male performers and join in singing an octave above the men later in the phrases of each "push-up." Gender role division at powwows is evident in many other ways as well. The master of ceremonies is typically male, as are the arena director and head judges for dance and drum competitions. In the intertribal dancing that takes place at powwows, dancers identify with one of six powwow dance competition categories – Women's Traditional, Women's Jingle Dress, Women's Fancy, Men's Traditional, Men's Grass, and Men's Fancy – and compete with their peers in the same gender and age category. In terms of judging music and dance performances, women do judge competitors in women's dance categories, but they typically do not judge musical performances at powwows. What this results in is gender-specific leadership in musical roles at powwows, as well as an emphasis on male ideologies, aesthetics, and judgments of "good" powwow music.

From my first powwow experience in 1994 until the summer of 2002, I never heard or saw a woman sitting at or striking a powwow drum; women's role, when they were present, was as backup singers to the male drummers. However, in the summer of 2002 at a traditional powwow at the Alexander First Nation in north-central Alberta, I heard, for the first time, women perform with men at a powwow drum, sing the same melody simultaneously, and strike the drum. Since then, I have been intrigued to learn more about the issues surrounding women and powwow music and have begun to discuss these issues and traditional teachings with First Nations male and female musicians in various locations in Canada. This chapter explores various issues and considerations regarding the common practice of limiting women's public music making at powwows. First, I illustrate the historic marginalization of women in academic literature that examines Aboriginal music practices. Following this, I review the literature on powwow music specifically, arguing that the assumptions around women not participating in powwows are geographically bounded and often overstated and simplified. Examining various explanations for limiting women in powwow music performance, I argue that contrary to common teachings women are in fact performing this repertoire (i.e., they do strike the drum and perform independently of men) and are being well received in some regions and communities. Drawing on interviews with First Nations female and male powwow musicians, this chapter explores the traditional teachings around women and powwow music as well as the performance choices and music making of all-female drum groups in terms of where and why they choose to perform. Finally, through a case study of one all-women powwow drum group, I argue that these women often perform in these contested roles not necessarily to be feminists or activists but as a means of empowerment and, in some cases, to "reawaken" their voices as singers and as Aboriginal women.

Women's Roles in Aboriginal Music: Research Trends

In his 1989 introduction to *Women in North American Indian Music: Six Essays*, Richard Keeling summarizes the historical and ongoing assumptions about women's roles in Aboriginal music in North America that had prevailed since the late nineteenth century:

Ever since 1882, when Theodor Baker published his dissertation on American Indian music, it has been widely assumed that males tend to dominate in the performance of music among the indigenous tribes north of Mexico. Basing his observations on a visit among the Senecas in 1880, Baker was the first to suggest in print that Indian females did not share equally in public singing … and this notion has survived even though our view of Indian cultures has changed dramatically over the past one hundred years. In Baker's day, it was assumed that these cultures were quite similar to one another, and thus it was natural for him to interpret his findings quite broadly. Today, even though modern researchers are much more aware of its vast diversity, we continue trying to identify general characteristics of North American Indian music, and male dominance is usually cited among them. (Keeling 1989a, 1)

Citing various sources, Keeling illustrates the commonly held assumption that, historically, Native men played a more prominent role in music making than women did, and he laments "the relatively unknown musical life of American Indian women" (Keeling 1989a, 3). Other academic literature likewise examines the roles of women in Aboriginal music making and the changing status and roles of women as music makers over time. Often scholars have focused on changes in particular performance practices, musical roles, and repertoires as a result of culture change and increasing and varied external pressures. In addition to the essays contained in Keeling's 1989 anthology, various authors demonstrate the important musical roles that Aboriginal women had and continue to have within their diverse communities and cultural practices. Examples include Charlotte Johnson Frisbie's *Kinaaldá: A Study of the Navaho Girl's Puberty Ceremony* (1967), Judith Vander's *Songprints: The Musical Experience of Five Shoshone Women* (1988), Victoria Lindsay Levine's "Arzelie Langley and a Lost Pantribal Tradition" (1991), Judith Ann Jones's "'Women Never Used to Dance': Gender and Music in Nez Perce Culture Change" (1995), Judy Jones and Loran Olsen's "Women and Music in the Plateau" (1996), and Elaine Keillor's "Voices of First Nations Women within Canada: Traditionally and Presently" (1996). Other work emphasizes the activism of female musicians, such as director Annie Fraziér Henry's documentary *Singing Our Stories* (1999), Elizabeth S. Gould and Carol L. Matthews's article "Weavings: Aboriginal Women's Music, Poetry, and Performance as Resistance" (1999), and more recent work by ethnomusicologists, as exemplified in Beverley Diamond's article "Native American Contemporary Music: The Women" (2002). In the 1990s and 2000s scholars and Aboriginal women themselves turned their attention to the music making of Indigenous women throughout North America, examining both traditional and contemporary Aboriginal repertoires (e.g., Diamond 2002, Diamond Cavanagh 1989, Hatton 1986, 1989, Keeling 1989c, Vander 1988, 1989, Vennum 1989a). However, little attention has been dedicated to women and powwow music specifically.

Women and Powwow Music Performance

What has been written about women's roles in powwow music tends to reinforce the historic assumptions about women's marginal roles as music makers in the performance of this repertoire. For example, in William K. Powers's important 1990 monograph *War Dance: Plains Indian Musical Performance*, he offers a description of typical song performance practices in which women stand behind the men at powwows, serving as backup singers to the men (Powers 1990, 32). He writes, "composition and performance of music are still in the purview of men, although women participate much more today, particularly in dance" (Powers 1990, 57). Interestingly, in Bruno Nettl's 1989 monograph *Blackfoot Musical Thought*, he indicates, "In the 1980s, although women's 'drums' were recognized and some women were listed as members of singing groups, the title of 'singer' or 'drummer' was still gender-specific" (Nettl 1989, 83). Furthermore, apart from the recognition of women's role as backup singers in most powwow literature, there have been some references to family drums in which women perform, and, as illustrated in Vander's *Songprints*, women can also assume a leadership role in such ensembles (Vander 1988, 202–5, 207). Orin Hatton was the first ethnomusicologist to focus specifically on women's roles in powwow music, in his 1986 article highlighting the emergence of women performers in mixed-sex drum groups. The lack of ethnomusicological research that acknowledges women's roles as musicians in powwows and addresses the disregard given to women who are performing this repertoire and/or advocating for change to their usual marginalization is evident in Tara Browner's important book *Heartbeat of the People: Music and Dance on the Northern Pow-Wow* (2002). In her description of "common" powwow music making, Browner reiterates the gender roles typically associated with this repertoire: "A Drum is made up of anywhere from three to twelve (or more) men and women who sing together on a regular basis. 'Sitting at the drum' is primarily a male activity, and women, most of the time, stand behind the men and sing the 'women's part' an octave higher than the men and with little or no vocal vibrato. In some all-female Drum groups women sing the 'men's part,' but those groups are rare and, as of this writing, exclusively Northern" (Browner 2002, 73). It is interesting to note the variability in the academic scholarship on the roles of women in powwow music; whereas some authors acknowledge that women have had increasing and variable roles in powwow music, others seem to treat the consideration of women in powwow music as a novelty, despite the assertions by Hatton and Vander over twenty years ago that some women are actively and equally engaged as powwow musicians in some northern communities. It may be time that scholars consider their role in the ongoing perpetuation of contentious assertions about musical practices that are more variable than suggested in academic literature.

Restricting Women as Powwow Musicians: Traditional Teachings
and Explanations

Although there are examples of women performing powwow music independently of men, traditional teachings still permeate powwow rhetoric that limits women's equal and full participation. Various explanations are cited for gender restrictions in music making at powwows, most
of which are predicated on traditional teachings that maintain complementary and equal relations between Aboriginal women and men. Powwow scholar Tara Browner is unusual in that she offers a practical, rather
than a primarily cultural, explanation for restrictions on women in
music making at powwows. Elaborating on the practice of women serving as backup singers, she writes,

> Although gender-based restrictions on female singing at first seem
> arbitrary and perhaps sexist, they are rooted in pragmatic per-
> formance needs and governed in both Northern and Southern
> performance styles by aesthetic preference and acoustics. High
> sounds are directional. If women sit at the drum rather than stand
> behind the men, their contribution to the music – which is con-
> siderable – is buried in the drum's booming tones and by the bodies
> of the men who sit across from them. When women do sit at the
> drum, they sing the same part as the men, something entirely
> possible in Northern singing but almost impossible in Southern
> performance. Almost no woman would be capable of singing the
> full range of Southern style. (Browner 2002, 73)

This description, interestingly, refers only to mixed-sex drums, not to all-
women drums, which have a different sonic quality than mixed and all-
male drums.

Common explanations for prohibiting women from striking the drum
draw from traditional teachings that often emphasize the strength and
power of women's bodies, the historic "gifting" of the drum from a woman
to a man, gender complementarity, and the heteronormative underpin-
nings of much powwow culture. A commonly cited explanation for why
women don't strike the powwow drum is that they have the ability to
bear children; one powwow musician stated,

> Women are already considered sacred. She already has the power.
> The men they have to seek power. And the reason that she has it is

the power to give life. She's the one to give birth. She's the life-giver.
She's the one to suffer; she carries the pain. And she looks after
the children as well. That was the gift that was given to her by the
Creator ... They already have it, and so they don't touch that drum.
(Interview with Kevin Hamlin, May 1986, quoted in Diamond,
Cronk, and von Rosen 1994, 35)

A related teaching was also shared with me by an Anishnabek powwow
organizer:

Well, there's a saying that women had the drum first of all, it's
called the heartbeat of Mother Earth. And the man wasn't able to
give birth like the woman, so the woman, out of respect for the
man, she gave him the right to have that big drum, the powwow
drum. They gave up their right to do that. (Personal communication, 29 July 1997)

The complementary relationship between men and women was also re-
iterated to me by musician Jimmy Dick, who recounted the traditional
teachings about the powwow drum:

[The traditional teachings came] through dreams and visions of
people that [explain] how these drums come to be. The majority say
it's a woman that gave this drum to the man, taught the man, and
today the men, they sing a style high pitch of singing in respect to
that woman. And also the teachings, they promote ... they always
talk about the man-woman relation. (Dick 2004)

The explanation given by Jimmy echoes those offered by other powwow
musicians who have related teachings about a Sioux woman named Tail
Feather Woman receiving the drum in a vision and being instructed to
give it to men to assist in peacemaking at the end of the nineteenth century (Browner 2002, 35; Hoefnagels 2007a, 114–19; Vennum 1982, 44ff). A
summary of this teaching is offered by Rosanna Deerchild:

It is said that long ago there was no drum among our peoples. Then
the spirits gave a vision to a woman. She was gifted with the drum
and told it was the heartbeat of Mother Earth. She returned to her
people with the first drum. They were overjoyed with such a beautiful gift. As part of the vision the spirits told her that, although she

would bring the drum to the people, it was the men who would carry the drumstick. It was the men who would play the heartbeat for the people. Because in that way they would remain connected to Mother Earth and so understand their relationship to women. (Deerchild 2003, 97)

Cree-Métis traditional teacher Myra Laramee likewise emphasizes the teaching quality of the drum in terms of appropriate male-female relationships, explaining why women don't need to sit at the drum:

The big drum was originally given to men to learn about their relationships with women. The drum is the essence of women's spirit. The heartbeat of Mother Earth. How many times have you heard that? But the part that doesn't get taught holistically is that when a man takes a sounder in his hand, and starts that beat in motion, he is giving life to that woman spirit, and he is calling on that woman spirit to come and teach him how to be a man. (Quoted in Anderson 2000, 177)

Within these explanations of why women don't drum, one emergent theme is that for some people the female drum and the male musicians are representative of the "ideal" heterosexual relationship between men and women in Aboriginal society. Indeed, in an interview with musician Jimmy Dick, I was struck by a somewhat heteronormative interpretation of the teachings he recounted about the drum and why women don't strike the powwow drum. He said, "They say that the drum represents a woman, you know? The man ... and then the man and the woman together in a relation. Not a woman-woman type of thing" (Dick 2004).[4] Gender complementarity resounds in many of these traditional teachings, suggesting that "traditional" labour division between the sexes was meant to ensure cultural, and literal, survival.[5]

Many Aboriginal women recognize and respect the traditional teachings around the drum and promote the holistic teaching of these traditions as a means of empowering themselves, as summarized by Kim Anderson: "There is a reason for these distinct roles, and many women will advocate learning about the teachings behind these gender divides in our art and ceremony. Better understanding of these teachings can be empowering for women" (Anderson 2000, 176). It is important to acknowledge the acceptance of these teachings by Aboriginal women and men throughout North America, as many people, both men and women, respect these teachings and expect them to be respected by others. Indeed, the maintenance of male-dominated music making at powwows, both in practice and as described in writings, illustrates the tenacity with which people hold on to these traditions. However, despite common practices at many contemporary powwows that limit women's participation in music making, some women are advocating for a greater musical presence at powwows by forming all-women drum groups and, in some cases, agitating for change to what many Aboriginal women view as their restrictive and marginal treatment at these important cultural events.

Restricting Women as Powwow Musicians: Systemic Marginalization? Internal Colonialism?

Aboriginal artists, writers, activists, and scholars in other areas, particularly Aboriginal women's studies, have also commented on the marginalization of women in powwow music making, usually advocating for change to what are often viewed as oppressive and paternalistic teachings that are indicative of larger social issues in contemporary Aboriginal culture. Often these authors recognize the historically important roles that Aboriginal women had as culture bearers and music makers in their communities, and they agitate for change to musical and cultural practices at many contemporary powwows that limit women's full and equal participation. Indeed, as Cherokee singer and author Zainab Amadahy relates in her article "The Healing Power of Women's Voices," there is often very little space at powwows for music made by women, even women's hand-drumming circles. These drumming circles are comprised of women who sing songs while accompanying themselves on hand drums, and although they may also be met with criticism by some people, they tend to be more commonly accepted than women's powwow drum groups. Drawing on her own experience at powwows and on interviews with other Aboriginal female musicians, Amadahy recounts that various times when women hand-drummers were told they could perform during breaks in regular powwow events, they either were poorly received or were "forgotten" by the programmers, thus waiting and not performing (Amadahy 2003, 151–2).

Some Native women (and others) see the fact that they are not permitted to be full participants in the music making at powwows as a sign of internal colonialism, meaning that Native men have internalized non-Native patriarchal views as a means of negotiating their own displacement through colonization. Related to internal colonialism is the assertion that the government-imposed Indian Act created imbalance and restrictive gender expectations in First Nations communities, which had a tremendous impact on the traditional ways of life and cultural sustenance for individuals and communities.[6] Anishnaabe educator Carl Fernández describes the impact of internal colonization:

> The current state of our people is one of imbalance and uncertainty. The relationship between men and women is unbalanced and men have assumed the dominant position. The poor treatment of women by men affects many areas of their lives. While women are primarily affected by maltreatment, the men are also adversely affected by poisoning their own community. (Fernández 2003, 247)

> Aboriginal women are community leaders who protect the future by transmitting language and culture to their children. Despite the contributions women make, they are commonly excluded from decision-making roles, with far-reaching consequences for them, their families and their communities. As targets of male domination and violence, women and children also bear the brunt of the social disruption that colonization has brought. (Fernández 2003, 242)

The links between internal colonialism and restrictions on female music making have been noted by various authors and musicians, with many people suggesting that restricting women's full participation in music making was introduced as a means to subjugate Aboriginal women. This assertion is evident in an online quotation posted on a discussion board in 2002 on aptn.ca:[7]

> The only reason aboriginal men today have a problem with women drummers is because they have copied the European men's subjugation to their women by distinguishing women and men's social/economic/political and spiritual roles. Hence oppressing their women … Women doing what men do is nothing new; rather, it is a way of reviving true traditional ways.

The impact of internal colonialism and the resultant subjugation of women as musicians at powwows have also been addressed by other Aboriginal women. An example is another comment posted in 2002 on aptn. ca in response to the news that an all-women powwow drum group had been denied the opportunity to perform:

I am astounded that a group of women drummers were turned away from an event. Of course, women should drum. The only "tradition" that is barring women from participating is that which is made up by men and other people who are suffering from internalized sexism. It is time to scrutinize the origins of these so-called "traditions." They are rooted, not in our own traditional practices, but in the colonizer's patriarchal beliefs of women's inferior position in society. The time has come for Aboriginal men and women to reject these imposed attitudes that have nothing to do with our tradition. Our traditions are rooted in respect. Respect means allowing our people – even women – to have voice in council as well as at the drum. To have men sit in a circle and say women are sacred is no longer good enough.

That various Aboriginal women consider their experiences at powwows to be a form of marginalization and silencing is noteworthy, and many Native women have found ways of drawing attention to this issue – through publications, by forming their own drum groups, and, notably, by creating art installations, such as Winnipeg-based Dakota-Anishnaabe artist Lita Fontaine's *A Woman's Drum* (2002).[8] The attention generated around the issue of women's restriction in music making at most powwows parallels the increasingly public calls for equality by Native women more generally, a movement that some people refer to as Indigenous feminism.

Challenging Restrictions, Bridging Discourses: Indigenous Feminism

Although many women are sympathetic to the healing, self-improvement, and sense of community that men gain through their participation in powwow drumming, others are challenging the conventions associated with the powwow celebration and its music by giving voice to their sense of being discriminated against. In many ways, the sense of discrimination associated with women's restriction in powwow music parallels an increasing activism and awareness respecting discriminatory practices in Aboriginal communities more generally. Complementing the increase in research on Aboriginal women and music since the 1980s is a surge in research examining Aboriginal women's oppression both within their own communities and beyond, their historical and ongoing roles and responsibilities in nurturing their families, communities, and culture, and the impact that colonization and forced patriarchy in Aboriginal communities has had on women's lives. Indeed, since the late 1980s various publications have addressed issues of oppression and empowerment efforts of Aboriginal women in North America, creating spaces to challenge assumptions and giving voice to Aboriginal women's experiences and aspirations. Some examples include Paula Gunn Allen's *The Sacred Hoop: Recovering the Feminine in American Indian Traditions* (1986/1992), Lee Maracle's *I Am Woman: An Aboriginal Perspective on Sociology and Feminism* (1996), Kim Anderson's *A Recognition of Being: Reconstructing Native Womanhood* (2000), and Kim Anderson and Bonita Lawrence's collection of essays *Strong Women Stories: Aboriginal Vision and Community Survival* (2003). Although people tend to recognize the role of Aboriginal women as culture bearers, some women are seeking recognition of their experiences of oppression and silencing within their community and acknowledgment of their critical roles in nurturing and sustaining Aboriginal culture. Although this agitation for change and recognition might be viewed as a form of feminist activism, the label "feminist" is problematic for many Aboriginal women, as explained by Aboriginal writer and academic Paula Gunn Allen:

> At the present time, American Indians in general are not comfortable with feminist analysis or action within the reservation or urban Indian enclaves. Many Indian women are uncomfortable with feminism because they perceive it (correctly) as white-dominated. They (not so correctly) believe it is concerned with issues that have little bearing on their own lives. They are also uncomfortable with it because they have been reared in an Anglophobic world that views white society with fear and hostility. But because of their fear of and bitterness toward whites and their consequent unwillingness to examine the dynamics of white socialization, American Indian women often overlook the central areas of damage done to tribal tradition by white Christian and secular patriarchal dominance. (Gunn Allen 1992, 224)

Another key reason why Aboriginal women resist feminist labels is that they see their oppression as Aboriginal people, not as women (Anderson 2000, 275); as Catherine Mattes writes, "Some Aboriginal women are uncomfortable calling themselves feminists. They reiterate that they are Aboriginal first, and have more in common with Aboriginal men than with non-Aboriginal feminists" (Mattes 2002, 10).

"Indigenous feminism" and "tribal feminism" are terms that are increasingly used by Aboriginal women, activists, and academics in reference to contemporary efforts to empower women within Aboriginal society and to recognize the oppressive forces of internal colonialism.[9] As explained by Rosanna Deerchild, Indigenous feminism involves examining Aboriginal "culture, ceremonies and traditions from a feminist perspective" and asking whether gender restrictions in Aboriginal culture are about "tradition" or sexism (Deerchild 2003, 100). Theories and ideas around Indigenous feminism are central to the study of women and Aboriginal music, specifically powwow music, since many female musicians are challenging traditional cultural teachings and might be considered feminists.

Many Aboriginal women resist using the term "feminist" when talking about their positions as musicians and role models for their communities. The resistance and sensitivity of many Aboriginal musicians to the term "feminism" and, among men especially, to the idea of women drumming at powwows were very evident in interviews that I conducted. Among some male musicians with whom I spoke, feminism is viewed very negatively, an attitude often reflected in their insistence that women not drum. For example, on the appropriateness of "feminism" to Aboriginal culture and tradition, one male powwow musician said,

> Things are changing in a way [...] there's feminism you know, but
> feminism doesn't really have anything to do with our culture [...]
> They do that at some ceremonies, say "who here is into feminism?"
> And some lady would put up her hand, and they'd say, "well you can
> leave the camp" ... So that's kind of where some of it's at right now.
> I know that some people are trying to be more tolerant of things
> like that; it's because of that feminism, it doesn't mix with what we
> do, how we do things. That's why [with women and the drum], it's
> really trying to be politically correct and you can't really, I guess, be
> accommodating to something like that. Can't always ... apologize
> for where we live and how we do things. (Dick 2004)

The possibility of facing public chastisement such as that related in this statement may compel many Aboriginal women to resist participating in activities or agitating for change that might result in them being labelled "feminists." Many Aboriginal women may not consider themselves feminist even if they are viewed as such by others. Indeed, from my interviews with powwow musicians, it is clear that the connotations associated with the word "feminist" remain problematic for many of them; indeed, many women who might be perceived as feminist contest the label for themselves. An important consideration, then, particularly vis-à-vis powwow music and all-women drum groups, is what motivates them to perform in a genre that often marginalizes them. Do the connotations associated with the label "feminist" or the potential interpretations of actions as "feminist" prevent women from participating in a male-dominated repertoire in unconventional ways?

All-Women Powwow Groups: "We're singers, the only difference is we're women"[10]

All-women powwow drum groups have been formed in Aboriginal communities since at least the 1970s, with various responses from powwow practitioners and Aboriginal elders. These groups perform the same repertoire as the men, but the sound produced by an all-women drum group contrasts sharply with that of an all-male drum group, as the women start at a higher pitch and no additional voices join in at the ends of phrases. The performance practices of all-female groups mirror those of the men, with the exception of some additional regulations around menstruation and pregnancy. For example, in an all-female drum group, if a group member is menstruating or pregnant, she will refrain from striking the drum, as she is considered particularly strong and her contact with the drum may cause it to break (Fontaine 2003).

All-female drum groups perform at selected powwows and are positively received within some communities in the areas where I have done research. All-female powwow drum groups learn which powwows welcome them as performers and are able to recognize that certain First Nations and certain regions prohibit all-female drum groups at powwows. However, some of these groups have had negative responses to their performance of this repertoire, such as being told they were not welcome to participate in particular events or being criticized in the media. For example, in November 2001 the Sweet Grass Road Drum Group, an all-female powwow drum from Winnipeg, Manitoba, was denied the opportunity to perform at the University of St Thomas Powwow in St Paul, Minnesota, despite having received accolades for their performance at this same event in 2000. Although they easily registered for the 2001 powwow, members of this group were told that "policy" prevented the organizing committee, which cited adherence to "Woodlands tradition," from allowing them to perform. The women were instead offered money and encouraged to leave the powwow. A month later the six members of the drum group filed a lawsuit against the university citing sexual discrimination and violation of their human rights (Allam 2002a, 2002b, Stinson 2002). Eventually, the case was settled out of court, and the annual powwow at the University of St Thomas was cancelled. The media resulting from this lawsuit drew much attention to the plight of this group while forcing people to consider their convictions around the teachings associated with powwow music.

The intensity of the responses to the issue of women performing music that is traditionally in the sole purview of men highlights the currency of this issue and problematizes definitions of "tradition" in contemporary Aboriginal society. Indeed, the experience of the Sweet Grass Road Drum Group provoked a great and varied response from people across North America, ranging from appreciation to disdainful dismissal. The local papers in St Paul closely followed the story, and many of the articles were posted on website discussion boards, such as www.powwows.com and aptn.ca, which were quickly inundated with posts from participants. The following is a sample of letters posted on www.powwows.com in 2002 in response to the question "Should women drum?" Included in these and other online posts are explanations for either restricting or allowing female performance, as well as contrasting interpretations and experiences of the related teachings. The first two responses are clearly opposed to women's drumming:

I am a Lakota woman from the Pine Ridge Indian Reservation in South Dakota. Our way of life, where the drum is concerned, is probably not too entirely different from everyone else's. Wom[e]n play an important role in the drum just as men do. We are called the "Third Circle." The First Circle is the drum itself, it's the heartbeat of the people. People, especially singers are very respectful of the drum and they do not hit the drum needlessly. The drum is usually covered when not being used, and most drum groups have a special case or bag made for the drum. The Second Circle are the Singers. Usually all the singers are men, and they are very respec[t]ful of the drum also. The[y] are the carriers of songs and they make the dancers and people feel happy with their beautiful songs. The Third Circle is the women back up singers, or *wicaglata*. They help the men carry the songs. They stand behind the men. They do not sit at the drum or touch the drumsticks, just because they are that respectful to the drum and the men. In Lakota society, there is no sexual discrimination, but there is a place for everyone and everyone knows their place. I hope that helps!!

I've been dancing and travelling for as long as I can remember ... the powwow life and traditions have been passed down to me from my parents who also have been involved in powwow most of their lives. And this is what I know and have come to believe. Women should not sit or hit the drum like the men do. I was taught women should not even touch or travel in the same vehicle as a drum. But I also think that women back up singers bring their own harmony and spirit when singing behind the men. Women back up singers have been around for a long time and I don't dispute that. But what I don't agree with is women actually sitting at the drum. Women are powerful in their own way especially on their cycle. This is a big no-no! But some women do it anyway [...] When I hear women drum-mers during an intertribal I just leave the dance floor 'til the songs over, cuz no one really dances anyway.

The next two sample responses endorse women's drumming and making of powwow music:

I come from a tribe that allows women to sing on the drum so to me it is acceptable (two of my aunts sing on our drum) ... but in their teaching, they were taught to respect the ways of the host tribe, and when asked by an elder of the host tribe they will not sing on the drum. I will conclude by saying if we did not have open minds and flexibility, we would not have survived the settlement of the white man on our lands. In our history, traditions and customs change with the times. I apologize if I have offended but this is my opinion.

This type of music is [truly] inspirational and I believe that it is ... good for all people, and some of them women out there can "jam" or maybe even "spank" the competition. [He he.] Well times change and things evolve.

Other responses on these discussion forums similarly ranged from hos-tility toward women who drum to the view that prohibitive traditions are old-fashioned, patriarchal, and in need of change. The dynamic and var-ied responses to this issue, with people from many different Aboriginal communities and traditions commenting, illustrate both the divisive na-ture of gender inequities and the variation in regional and nation-specific practices, albeit within a celebration widely recognized as intertribal. Criticisms of internal colonialism and notions of Indigenous feminism inform the views of some female activists and musicians who want to perform powwow music, but others perform, or want to perform, this repertoire for apolitical reasons, usually for the sole purpose of self-expression, healing, and the experience of good feelings.

Keesis Weyabb – Women Making Powwow Music

In the summer of 2003 I had the pleasure of talking about these issues with members of an Ojibway[11] all-women drum group named Keesis Weyabb (Ojibway for "rainbow") from the Sagkeeng First Nation in Manitoba. This group of women, who ranged in age from fourteen to twenty-nine, had been singing together as an exclusively female drum group since 1994, having been encouraged and taught to do so by members of their community. Members of their group assisted in making their drum, which can be sounded only by women. Reflecting on their ten years together, the women recalled only one experience where they were told they could not drum at a powwow. Similar to the case of the Sweet Grass Road Drum Group, this took place in a community in Minnesota. When recounting this experience, the women were not bitter or upset; rather, they matter-of-factly explained that they had asked whether they could set up, were told that in the host community women didn't hit the drum, and were then given $150 to cover the costs of their travel. In addition to this single experience, these women recounted how, when they began publicly performing, they initially received a lukewarm reception from people at powwows. Yet over time they have become very well received as performers at powwows in eastern Manitoba and north-western Ontario. They perform only at traditional powwows, and prior to setting up their drum, they seek permission to perform. They have developed a local reputation and fondly recounted their experiences as musicians. While they perform, people gather around their drum to listen and record, and, perhaps the highest sign of the success of their music making, they have had eagle whistles blown and have been fanned while they sang, gestures from the dancers that they want the song to continue. Members of Keesis Weyabb sing the same songs as local men's drums and similarly learn their songs through oral transmission, either directly from another person or from recordings of other powwow groups.

Usually, when Keesis Weyabb performs at powwows, it is the only all-women drum group in attendance. When I attended the annual powwow at the Sagkeeng First Nation in Manitoba in the summer of 2003, the group performed various songs but was not part of the regular drum rotation since its members were the primary organizers of the powwow.

Keesis Weyabb was called upon to perform at different times in the pow-wow in order to be showcased, and usually when the group performed it was swarmed with listeners. Although I was usually positioned close to the group when it performed, no audience disdain for the group was evident to me. That the group's members were performing in their home community might have influenced their warm reception, although they have also been received similarly in neighbouring communities.

When I was talking with the members of Keesis Weyabb, they shared a variety of perspectives, reactions, and personal histories. They were all very proud that they were empowering themselves through music; each member of the group offered personal reasons for drumming, such as the sense of pride and self-confidence that they derive while performing, the enjoyment of making music, and the knowledge that it helps them to maintain a clean and healthy lifestyle.[12] They stressed that they perform not for attention but for personal satisfaction, as noted by the group's lead singer, Cherie Fontaine:

> It's not for us to show up anybody; it's not for us to say, "hey look at us sing." It's just for ourselves, because when you sing and when you hit that drum, you get a really good sense and a really good feeling, and you just feel it inside, and you get addicted to it! It really gives you this sense of pride and it really gets you inside. And when we're singing, it doesn't really matter what anyone else is thinking, right now because we know we're singing for the right reasons and we know we have the right intentions. It makes us feel good and we know it makes other people feel good too. (Fontaine 2003)

The sense of enthusiasm, camaraderie, and pleasure that emanated from the members of Keesis Weyabb illustrates the importance of this music making to each woman.

In light of the teachings I had received and read about women's musical roles in powwow music, I asked the members of Keesis Weyabb how they felt about the teachings and how they reconciled those with their own experiences and beliefs. When one group member recounted her experience when she started to drum, she related a teaching she had received from a female elder in her community: "An elder told me before, when I started singing, and she was a woman, and I was telling her about me singing, and she said, 'Don't ever stop, because the drum started with a woman and there shouldn't be no reason why a woman can't hit that drum when it started with a woman.' So that was really good to hear"

(Gerard 2003). Cherie Fontaine asserted, "We're singers, the only difference is we're women" (Fontaine 2003). For me, this was an important assertion; initially, I had assumed that since the members of Keesis Weyabb were challenging commonly held traditional rules around powwow music performance, they must have a political or feminist agenda; yet these women, many of whom had completed postsecondary degrees in which they studied feminism, dismissed feminism altogether. They recognized the controversy inherent in their performance of this repertoire, having heard about other groups' experiences and having been turned away at a powwow themselves; yet they insisted that they were not "trailblazers." Cherie Fontaine said, "I guess it kind of seems like we contradict ourselves in that way, but I think it all has to do with how you understand it. Like to some people they may think, 'oh, like they have a feminist attitude about it.' But we try and do everything we can to keep it in balance, by not mixing [men and women at the same drum] and doing everything we can to be respectful of everybody's ways. It's not like anything political or a protest or anything" (Fontaine 2003).

From my interviews with the members of Keesis Weyabb, it became clear to me that even if any of these women are "feminists," most of them would not apply the label to themselves. Yet each woman's pride in her role as a powwow musician was very apparent. Furthermore, the respect they have for powwow traditions was also clear when they described their own guidelines for singing at the drum:

> For us, being women, we're walking on a border almost. We have to
> show the ultimate respect, otherwise we get wicked backlash right
> away, rather than the guys. So we have to try to be a role model
> kind of drum. So usually, for us, we try to wear skirts all the time
> around our drum, just to show our drum that respect. And we
> never use drugs or drink. I don't think any of us do it anyways, but
> not around the drum, we never bring that to the drum. We never
> hit the drum when we're on our time [menstruating], or when we're
> pregnant … And we don't hit the drum with a guy, we don't mix …
> to keep the balance. We don't hit their drum, so they don't hit ours.
> (Fontaine 2003)

Careful negotiation within local traditional teachings and gender restrictions allows members of Keesis Weyabb to openly celebrate their status as members of an all-women drum group and to be recognized as such in their region.

Challenging Tradition or Maintaining the Status Quo? Larger Social Issues?

For many women, it is within the context of the commonly accepted traditional teachings about local practices of powwow music making that they decide whether to perform this repertoire as backup singers to an all-male drum, as full members in a mixed-sex (often family) drum, or as part of an all-women drum.[13] As noted above, many advocates for the prohibition of women striking the powwow drum cite adherence to traditional teachings as the principal reason for limiting women's music making. Indeed, as one female contributor to the online forum on aptn.ca asked, "What is tradition if we keep changing it to suit our own needs?" Others view tradition as a cultural tool to discriminate against certain members of Aboriginal society, as stated by Dakota-Anishnaabe visual artist Lita Fontaine: "They are being rigid and not letting those women be at the drum because 'tradition' says so. To me that is a very subtle patriarchy. I don't think they see it, but it's there" (quoted in Deerchild 2003, 103). Some Aboriginal women are becoming advocates and activists for themselves, their mothers, and their daughters, as they see "tradition" used to justify the subordination of Aboriginal women. This sentiment is apparent in Dawn Martin-Hill's assertion that "In the name of resisting colonial domination, ideologies develop in which a complex multi-layered 'colonial' version of traditionalism justifies the subordination of Indigenous women" (Martin-Hill 2003, 107). Indeed, when one considers the relative newness of the powwow celebration in many Canadian Aboriginal communities, it is clear that "tradition" at the powwow and "traditional teachings" concerning its music may be used by some people as a vehicle for sexual discrimination and the subordination of Aboriginal women.

The issues of regionalism and nation-specific teachings are significant, as they reinforce the fact that powwows and powwow traditions are not homogenous and that the meanings associated with this celebration are constantly evolving and locally constructed. Indeed, from my conversations with powwow musicians, it is clear that many traditional teachings and expectations around women and the drum are culturally constructed and geographically bounded. From their experiences, and from the more public debates about this issue, it appears that women can perform powwow music in certain communities in particular regions, depending on local expectations and performance practices.

As Aboriginal women increasingly draw attention to the challenges they are facing, both in everyday life and in certain music-making contexts, Aboriginals and non-Aboriginals alike are forced to question the relationships between gender restrictions and larger issues of control and power in contemporary Aboriginal society. Many activists see the empowering of Aboriginal women as musicians as an important way to address past injustices and to increase equality in contemporary Aboriginal communities. Aboriginal authors and activists are raising awareness of the power imbalance in Aboriginal communities that resulted from colonialism and the imposition of the Indian Act in Canada, and they are seeking ways of having this imbalance redressed (Anderson 2000, Anderson and Lawrence 2003, Perreault and Vance 1990, Klein and Ackerman 1995, Krosenbrink-Gelissen 1991, Kidwell 1992, Gunn Allen 1992). Similarly, many people recognize the role that Aboriginal women play in community healing, in perpetuating traditions, and in maintaining close relations within their own family and the larger Aboriginal community. In terms of women and powwow music more specifically, it might be suggested that hegemonic and oppressive structures imposed on First Nations communities have been translated and applied to powwows and that emerging all-women drum groups are reclaiming a place in the Aboriginal community that was taken from them. Indeed, some Aboriginal writers, researchers, and musicians contend that women *should* drum and make powwow music as a means of reclaiming their historical positions of power in their communities and as a gesture toward the individual and community healing that needs to occur on reserves and in Aboriginal communities generally.

Clearly, the performance of powwow music by women is a complicated issue on which all people will likely never agree and which needs further investigation. However, all-women drum groups such as Keesis Weyabb are finding success and enjoyment performing powwow music, and the issues around women performing powwow music are being addressed in various venues and forums. Through participation in online discussions, provocative art installations such as Lita Fontaine's *A Woman's Drum*, workshops on traditional teachings, and even the powwows themselves, people are questioning the issues around women's roles in powwow music, and at the start of the twenty-first century, many people are challenging the status quo as a means of empowering themselves and celebrating their cultural heritage.

1 Various explanations about the origins of powwows are offered by ethnomusicologists and powwow musicians. See, for example, Browner (2002, 19–36) and Powers (1990, xvi).

2 Scholars such as Fowler (2005), Hoefnagels (2007a, 2007b), Tulk (2006, 2008), and Warry (1998), among others, have engaged with the issue of tradition and the "histories" of local powwows, asserting that these gatherings do not need a longstanding history to be culturally meaningful, spiritually relevant, and healthy for participants and community members alike.

3 Although southern-style features may be performed by some drum groups and individual dancers throughout Canada, northern-style powwow music and dance predominate. Various authors offer descriptions of the main differences between northern- and southern-style powwow music, including Browner (2000), Cronk, Diamond, and von Rosen (1988), Hoefnagels (2004), Huenemann (1992), Kavanagh (1992), and Powers (1980, 1990).

4 The heteronormativity that is characteristic of most contemporary powwows has not been studied in great detail, although Brian Joseph Gilley (2005) discusses this phenomenon in reference to two-spirited powwows, which Aboriginal gay and lesbian communities are now organizing to create a safe environment in which Aboriginal homosexuals can freely participate in powwows.

5 Interestingly, in various accounts that detail the construction of the powwow drum, male-female symbolism and notions of complementarity are also invoked; see Diamond, Cronk, and von Rosen (1994) for many examples.

6 For a discussion of the impact of colonization on women in Native societies, see, for example, Brodribb (1984), Cannon (1998), Cornet (2001), Etienne and Leacock (1980), Jamieson (1986), Kinsman (1987), La Fromboise, Heyle, and Ozer (1994), and Miller and Chuchryk (1996).

7 Online discussion boards are public sources, and as I am unable to contact the authors, the names by which the authors self-identified and the dates of their postings have been removed in this chapter.

8 See a description and illustration of this installation in Hoefnagels (2007b) and Mattes (2002).

9 See, for example, Anderson (2000), Anderson and Lawrence (2003), Silman (1987), Perreault and Vance (1990), Ouellette (2002), Maracle (1996), and Mihesuah (2003), among others.

10 Fontaine (2003).

11 There are various orthographies for the word "Ojibway," including "Ojibwa" and "Ojibwe," and some communities also use the word "Chippewa" in reference to their nation. I use "Ojibway," as this is how the women with whom I have corresponded refer to themselves, their language, and their culture.

12 Women have expressed other reasons for drumming, including healing as well as fostering a sense of connection with their heritage; see Anderson and Lawrence (2003, 149).

13 The importance of understanding local constructions and associations at powwows is explored in Fowler (2005).

PART TWO
Teaching and Transmission

BEVERLEY DIAMOND AND ANNA HOEFNAGELS

The second section of this anthology addresses important issues in the preservation, teaching, and learning of Aboriginal music in contemporary Canadian contexts. It demonstrates that both Indigenous and non-Indigenous scholars need to engage critically and respectfully with practitioners and culture bearers in order to consider what issues of teaching and transmission require attention and what responsibilities rest with each of us. Teaching and living with a focus on traditional music today are themes that emerge in the first chapter of this section, "The sound of what I hear on earth," a compilation of reflections by Sadie Buck assembled by Beverley Diamond. Drawing from interviews that Buck has done with several different scholars, this text shares stories and experiences that demonstrate how music is very much a lived tradition in Haudenosaunee communities, while also highlighting the new spaces where music is performed, shared, taught, and lived. Buck discusses how she learned traditional Haudenosaunee music and how she has continued to teach and perform within her community and beyond. She highlights creative projects in which she has worked closely with other Indigenous musicians in Canada and in other parts of the world to create exciting new music. Sadie recognizes the importance both of cross-cultural sharing and of maintaining her musical tradition.

Mary Piercey's chapter, "Reflecting on Reflexivity: Teaching and Conducting Research in an Inuit Community," is a careful investigation of a teacher-ethnographer's role and impact in a northern community. She highlights many challenges and issues that confront modern Aboriginal communities and "their" researchers. Piercey reflects on her experience first as a school teacher and then as a researcher in Arviat, a community created through government-enforced resettlement. Drawing on her various roles in the community (i.e., high school music teacher, musical ethnographer, friend), she illustrates changes in her own thinking and positionality, reflecting on how her non-Inuit assumptions were challenged and how she negotiated and reshaped her ideas as a result. Piercey demonstrates the potential of thoughtful autoethnography.

In teaching about the music and cultures of Aboriginal peoples in Canada, educators are often confronted with sparse teaching resources and the Eurocentric biases of materials that do exist. In "*Moose Trails and Buffalo Tracks*: Métis Music and Aboriginal Education in Canada," Annette Chrétien reflects on the lack of adequate teaching resources on Métis peoples and cultures east of Manitoba. With reference to a newly created website for which she developed content, Chrétien describes new resources informed by Ontario Métis concepts and social values with which teachers and students can engage in order to learn about Métis heritage and music making. The site draws on selected songs and narratives, and activities are also recommended to enhance learning opportunities for students. The chapter addresses the marginalization of Métis, particularly those who live in central or eastern Canada, within the curriculum. Through Chrétien's work, pedagogical resources are being created to give voice/place to overlooked Métis histories and cultures.

The final two chapters in this section explore the musical journeys that two musicians have taken, personal journeys in which they learned about their culture, heritage, and music over a period of many years. Beverly Souliere is an Algonquin musician who currently leads all-women hand-drumming circles in various urban institutions in Ottawa, and she is also a member of the award-winning trio Women of Wabano. Souliere discusses the pathways she took to claim her identity as an Aboriginal woman and the various ways that she continued her pathway of learning. Jimmy Dick is a Cree musician who discusses how he came to hold a place of great respect in the Toronto Aboriginal community as a prominent musician and cultural leader. In dialogue with Anna Hoefnagels, he describes how he passes on the teachings and songs that he has learned throughout his journey.

Together, the chapters in this section illustrate the dynamic relations and processes involved in teaching and transmitting Aboriginal music, both within a community and within the academic world. It highlights the conscious decisions of culture bearers to learn about and teach their music to others in their communities while generously sharing with non-Natives some of the musical activities and knowledge of First Peoples in Canada today.

7

The sound of what I hear on earth

SADIE BUCK, WITH A PREFACE
BY BEVERLEY DIAMOND

Preface

Haudenosaunee singer and cultural specialist Sadie Buck was born in the 1950s in the Seneca community of Tonawanda, New York, into a family that was renowned for singing and dancing. As she describes below, she heard traditional Haudenosaunee songs in her childhood from dawn to dusk and had the voice and the memory to become one of the most valued culture bearers of her community. Her family moved to Ohsweken, Ontario, when she was a baby. However, because her father's responsibilities included both the Tonawanda and Six Nations communities, she has memories of a lot of travelling as a child, car rides during which she heard Western swing as well as traditional music. As an adult, she has played numerous roles in the Haudenosaunee Confederacy and Six Nations community, including serving as confederacy clan mother, teacher, culture bearer, and specialist in the arts.

When she was only about six years old, she started singing regularly with a group of her best friends. They became a singing society, one of the many mutual aid societies in her community that raised money for those in need. The group consisted of both girls and boys, but when the boys' voices changed, they tended to drop out, leaving a group of women. Seven of these women decided to take their songs outside the community. They called themselves the Six Nations Women Singers. They are still singing after more than four decades and are now one of the most eagerly sought out Aboriginal performance ensembles, travelling widely in North America and beyond. They have performed at the American Folklife Festival, the New Orleans Jazz Festival, on university campuses all across North America, and in many international venues. Their CD, *We Will All Sing*, was released in 1996, and they participated in the Smithsonian Institution's recording series *Heartbeat: Voices of First Nations Women* (1995, 1998). Sadie performed with Robbie Robertson at the Winter Olympics in Utah in 2002. Some of their children, including Sadie's son George, practise with the group from time to time, learning the tradition in a family context not unlike the one Sadie describes below.

Sadie has long had a larger vision, however, for Haudenosaunee music and for Indigenous music more generally. She started to contemplate this vision when she worked for the Woodland Cultural Centre in the 1980s. Important initiatives by that institution – running a gallery of First Nations art, organizing exhibitions such as *Fluffs and Feathers* (Doxtator 1992), which drew the world's attention to the injustices of stereotypes, and convening conferences such as "Sound of the Drum" (1990), which engendered local pride in the distinctive achievements of the Iroquois nations – have been models for many other Indigenous communities. She and her good friend and cousin Amos Key, who heads the Aboriginal language programs at the Woodland Cultural Centre, have worked with non-Aboriginal scholars to establish new norms of reciprocity in academia.

Then, in 1992, the Banff Centre for the Arts began consulting with Sadie Buck, leading to the formation of a program called Aboriginal Women's Voices, an initiative that was part of a core of Aboriginal programs established there in the 1990s. Shaped by Sadie's vision of respectful exchange and encouragement, this program enabled many Native American women to hone their sonic craft, experiment with new styles, and participate in a unique arts program that respected traditional social values. The CD produced by these women, *Hearts of the Nations* (1997), their "Full Circle" concert,[1] and eventually the Aboriginal dance opera *BONES* (2001), which was not part of Aboriginal Women's Voices but influenced by that experience and inclusive of many of the participants, were each landmark achievements that echoed across the Americas and gave expressive strength to the Indigenous artists of Canada, the United States, and beyond.

Sadie moved back to the Six Nations community in 2002. She was increasingly sought as a teacher. She has taught at York and McMaster Universities and has conducted workshops for Worlds of Music, Toronto. She decided to avail herself of new educational opportunities, taking courses in anthropology and business at McMaster University. She now works for the good of her community in other ways. She spearheads an initiative to gather natural medicines annually and to teach traditional healing practices. She runs a training program for young women, which includes a variety of subjects ranging from prenatal care and birthing to family health. And of course she continues to sing, either on her own, with the Six Nations Women Singers, or with others. Sadie Buck was honoured in 2007 with the Community Spirit Award of the First Peoples Fund in recognition of her outstanding contributions to Aboriginal arts.

Since the late 1980s Sadie Buck has graciously allowed a number of researchers to interview her. Transcripts of six of these interviews have lived together in a file drawer in my home office. Only two have been published.[2] The interviews, cited by date throughout this chapter, are as follows:

- 1990. Sadie Buck and Amos Key in conversation with Sam Cronk. The interview was conducted in conjunction with Sadie and Amos's joint development of the conference "Sound of the Drum" at the Woodland Cultural Centre. This conference led to the publication of the booklet *Sound of the Drum* (Cronk 1990), comprising transcripts from interviews with five non-Haudenosaunee "traditionalists," one brass band member, three "hymners," two fiddlers, two classical performers, and four Haudenosaunee *eskanye* (women's shuffle dance) singers.
- 1994. Sadie Buck in conversation with Anna Hoefnagels on 29 November before Sadie made a guest presentation in a class at York University.
- 1995. Sadie Buck in conversation with Anna Hoefnagels and Anne Lederman in the spring at Sadie's home. Partial transcript. Anne Lederman was in conversation with Sadie Buck around this time about doing a series of workshops for Anne's Worlds of Music program in Toronto.
- 1999. Sadie Buck in telephone conversation with Beverley Diamond in September. Although Buck and Diamond had known each other for over a decade by 1999 and had undertaken a project together (the creation of a course in Iroquois arts at York University, which Buck taught as a visiting professor), they had never tape-recorded a conversation. Diamond asked to do this in conjunction with her research on contemporary women recording artists, which would inform two articles (Diamond 2002, 2005a).
- 2001. Sadie Buck interviewed by composer Elma Miller about the Banff Centre's production of the Aboriginal dance opera *BONES*. The interview was subsequently posted online together with synopses of the scenes.

- 2006. Sadie Buck in conversation with Beverley Diamond at Diamond's home in St John's, Newfoundland, in March. Sadie had agreed to serve on the Aboriginal Advisory Committee for a book Diamond was commissioned to write for the Global Music series of Oxford University Press (Diamond 2008b). They spent several days discussing content for the Haudenosaunee chapter, turning the tape recorder on when it seemed useful to capture parts of their discussion either for general information or for possible citation in the publication.

Sadie's thoughts about themes and issues that are important to her are presented here drawing on these interviews. The resulting text is a composite of a type that academics often shun. It does not reproduce the questions of the interviewer, and, indeed, some paragraphs are composed of statements from different points in an interview or even from different interviews where the same topic was raised repeatedly. This means that we have not enabled the context of the statements to be readily evident in relation to each statement (although we indicate the different contexts for each interview above). The sections are partial transcripts, excluding certain segments of casual conversation and focusing on selected topics that seem central to more than one conversation. On the other hand, the advantages of the composite method used here are several. First, those issues to which Sadie returns in a number of conversations with researchers are usually *her* issues, aspects of the Haudenosaunee experience and worldview that bear repeating, rethinking, or expanding upon. In a number of cases, we see how she has articulated the same point but with slightly different nuances in different parts of a conversation or in relation to a different phase of her life. A second advantage of the composite text is that we were able to use her strongest explanations of some of these key issues. Unedited interviews, as we well know, are filled with the stops and starts, the hesitations and interruptions, of real-time conversation. It is sometimes in the "re-performance" of an idea that it begins to be clarified. Finally, we believe that the composite text is more powerful as a printed text, just as it would be overly formal and contrived as an oral text. The final text has been edited by Sadie Buck herself, who assumed full control over her own words and who helped us to avoid any inaccuracies related to the process just described.

# "Nobody taught me. Everybody taught me": Living and Learning the Haudenosaunee Tradition

We danced, we did it all the time! And we had partners, and you know, we just did the whole thing, social dances in the living room. That amazes me, when I think about it, that we used to do that when we were kids. We were eight, nine, ten, eleven, twelve when we used to dance. I remember the time that my uncle Amos Key Sr came over and said, "Can I have my kids back!" Because my cousins were always over at our house, usually dancing after supper, and our grandfather [George Buck] would sing all the time. I think that's where I learned the "twist" [change of pattern] in the songs; George could do things with a song without changing it somehow. He could always "turn a phrase." And he was really good at it. When we were little, my brother and I, we used to live in Tonawanda [New York] with my grandpa Bill Buck. Every day my mom said he would get up real early in the morning, and we'd get up early too because I was a baby – we only lived there until I was five months old. And he would take us, he would sit us both on his lap, and he would sing from the minute we woke up. Then he'd give us back to our mom and she would bathe us and give us breakfast; then she'd put us back on his lap and he would sing until lunch. And then he'd eat lunch and take a little nap, then right back up. He'd take us again and he would sing until supper; after supper, he'd hold us and sing until it was time for us to go to bed. She said she never needed a babysitter! So it's hard to say whether something like that has an influence … I'm sure it must [1990].

From what my dad tells me, they used to sing a lot more a long time ago. They would always be singing not only because they really enjoyed it, but so they would always be ready to sing for "doings" or for the Long-house. You would never be out of shape to sing. Plus they really enjoyed it. And I think you can tell a singer who really enjoys their music, even when they're young. I remember one time I went to the Allegany Reservation and I stayed over at Dar Dowdy's house. Kyle (Dar's son) wanted to sing and we sang and sang and sang until about noon [1990]. We sang for a good four hours. First I led, then he led, and I led and he led; then he continued to lead because he could remember more songs to lead. That is what we did one morning at his house; we just sang and sang and sang for four hours from eight in the morning until noon [2006]. And he sang just about everything he could think of and he knows a lot of songs. I always remember that. I always thought that was really nice.

When my dad talks about singing, [he tells me that] a lot of old timers would put the drum out where you could see it. What that meant was that when you go there, if you wanted to sing, you could pick the drum up and sing right away. That was kind of like their "hello," their greeting to each other. Instead of having a whole conversation, they would just sit down and sing together. My dad said it could just be neighbours; they'd come over and sing with each other. They'd have their social at night; they'd sing until early in the morning. And be at the Longhouse [for ceremonies] on time. The favourite [longhouse] here for doing that was at Senecas [Longhouse]. I don't know why. [Dad] said that at Gaiwio time [the annual Handsome Lake convention] they'd do that lots when they'd come to Senecas. Even recently, within the last ten years [the 1980s], when Herb [Dowdy] was around, they used to have singing practices after the socials. It's probably because Herb and Dar would have been raised like that [1990].

I learn a lot just sitting around with my dad and gabbing with him, like, not even talking about anything specific, [but] just talking with him. I think that's when you really learn something. You can always learn the procedure for something. People will tell you the procedure but not *why* something's the way it is. I think a lot of times we should just sit around and talk [1990].

Music is everywhere in our community if you're a traditional person. So it's always there and you're just in the middle of it. You just watch and you listen, and then you go and sit on the bench and then you start. I always was a part of singing because my family all did it. I sing all the time. It just kind of happens. A lot of times I'll be singing and won't even notice it, and somebody will say, "Well, what's that song?" and I'll say, "What song?" It's so much a part of what I do and how I do things that I don't even know. It's just always been there [1994].

[In addition to singing,] we always danced with my grandfather George Buck in Hamburg, New York, in the summer and with the Jim Sky Dance Troupe [in the Six Nations community]. We also performed with other dance troupes such as Jake Thomas [2001]. We did a lot of different things, all that travelling, met all those people, and all those people would come to our house. We had more exposure [than some in our community] not only to our own culture but to everything else. When you're riding down the road, you know, we'd play the car radio [1990] ... In the public school system here, we had to learn Western songs and "Every Good Boy Deserves Fudge"[3] and all that stuff. We wrote songs out sometimes. I didn't mind it at all because for me it was music [1995].

[In the late 1980s, Sadie reflected on her hopes for her son.] Now, especially since I've got my own little boy now, little George [who was approximately five at the time of the interview], I always think there is so much I've got to do now so he'll be exposed to it as much as I was. I don't know if he's going to be a singer or a dancer or both or none. But it would be nice that he would have the choice to be any of those things … so that he would appreciate that gift himself, his own gift [1990].

[Years later, she observed,] George sings lots, [along with] my nephews. I don't think you can classify that as learning so much. It's like breathing; it's something you do. We have singing practices and that's really what they are: singing *practices*. It's like everybody's at a certain level, and all you have to do really at a singing practice is put your voices together. Learning has a different connotation here. Once I hear [a song], it's in there. So it's not so much for me to learn it. I already know it. What it is, then, is for me to bring it out. It's not *learning* it. It's like you already know how to make a ham and cheese sandwich, but maybe I can add something that will make it better. You know how to make a ham and cheese sandwich and so do I. Maybe I'll put a different kind of mustard on it than you do. You're trying to sing that song the best that you could sing it, as opposed to learning the song and then doing it the best you can do it. That might be because we've been singing for so long, but even when I look at some of the other groups, it's still the same thing. There's already an understanding of that particular song, even if it's brand new. That might come from the fact that all of our social dance songs are the same [form]. You're not learning how to put the song together; you're learning how to sing as a group [1995].

If you are not familiar with the context that that song should be sung in, then you don't know the boundaries [1995]. Once it is an eskanye song, it belongs to the eskanye genre,[4] and whoever is an eskanye lead [singer] can learn it and sing it. They should always acknowledge whose song it is and where it came from. A lot of people don't do that now, but they should always acknowledge that. My group, we usually don't sing if we don't know where the song comes from. I try to sing only our songs or songs that I can say, "That came from that place or from whoever made the song up." There are ways of honouring or ways of being honorable in singing [2006].

I make up songs anytime, anywhere, mostly when I'm driving – I do lots of driving. Between here [Ohsweken] and Toronto is an hour and fifteen to twenty minutes; so that's an hour and twenty minutes of singing, twice a day, here and home [1994]. [The first song on *We Will All Sing* (Six Nations Women Singers 1996),] I have difficulty even saying that I

wrote it. I sat down one day and that song was there, exactly the way
it was recorded that first night, the first time I sang it. Exactly. It was
like I just plucked it out of the air. It came out in my breath, that song.
[The fourth song on *We Will All Sing*,] I made up that song when I was in
Banff. I was trying to make a song that would fit a woman's voice. The
other thing is, it is very Seneca sounding. I was thinking about how it
was going to sound sung by the whole group of the Six Nations Women
Singers. I really put thought into doing that song and creating sounds
for a woman but also for a "Seneca sound." I was very focused on that.
Usually I don't do that, I just sing – make up songs and sing them [2006].

"Everything has a job": Traditional Knowledge, Values, and Ways of Being

There's no such thing as a bad singer because the whole purpose of
music is its job. The whole point is to dance [1994]. Everything has a
job. Everything has a place. Everything has a context that it's supposed
to be used in [1995]. [Social dance songs] were created to be danced to,
to make you want to feel to dance, and to feel like dancing, you've got
to feel the music. To dance, it has to be a joyous, celebrating feeling.
So you can't take the song out of that context by creating a song about
something that is not good. Even if you are thinking about something
like "cigarettes, taxes and bingo,"[5] that is a social issue mind you, but it's
got to be done in a humorous way so it does not remove itself from the
context of what eskanye and earth songs are all about in the first place.
That is why "Bingo" [recorded on *Heartbeat* (1995)] has to be a funny song
because you don't want to hurt somebody's feelings. When their feelings are hurt, they are not going to dance. So there is a lot of humour.
The song about "Humpty Dumpty": you all know what happened to
him next. It switches into English and he falls off the wall and now he's
scrambled eggs. Beginning the lyrics in Seneca and then switching to
English is the really funny part. Even if you performed that in front of a
non-Aboriginal or non-Haudenosaunee audience, they don't understand
the first part but they hear the words "Humpty Dumpty." All of a sudden
you can hear the audience laugh. It is kind of interesting too sometimes
because they don't laugh right away. It is like [they are thinking], "What
did that song say? They are singing in English." The switching is part of
the comedy [2006].

I continually make up new songs, all the time. I just put things
together and I sing them. When a new song comes and it *stays*, that's

when you got a new song. Sometimes you get a song that just doesn't stay. We were at a Sing[6] in Onondaga one time, and me and my sister were sitting there, gabbing away, and the women were singing a song. The Onondaga women were singing, and right after, between songs, I made up a song. We [my sister and I] both stopped and said, "Gee, that's real pretty. That's a real nice song." And then they started to sing again, and it just went [out of our memories]. It was really, really nice. And we really tried to remember it but we couldn't. So that's just how it is. It's a matter of whether it stays or not. It's a lot of bother for me [to use a tape recorder]. To me, if a song sticks around, it sticks around. If it doesn't, then it will probably come back some time. I just sing and make them up. Only when we need songs do I worry about a song staying around. Because there's so many out there. Not until we get ready for the Sing, then that's when you start worrying [1994].

A lot of people, because they don't see the women or hear the women, they assume that the women don't sing. And that's not true. In the context of our societies, not just Iroquoian society but other [Indigenous] societies as well, women do sing. But mostly in our cultures, it's the male that has public roles and that's why the public only sees that. But it's been a reality that women do sing and have sung and will always sing because that's part of their role. People make it [a Native American women's group] out to be a big thing, but it's not really because it's always been happening within the context of our own life [1999].

The Six Nations Women Singers and the Six Nations Women Singing Society are two separate groups. I'm the lead singer for both, but in terms of decisions for the group, their voices carry just as much weight. I'm the one who decides what we're going to sing, in what order, [but] *only* in terms of the music. As far as the work that we do in the community, the whole group has the say in that. The Six Nations Women Singers (SNWS) is a performance troupe made up of women from the Six Nations Women Singing Society (SNWSS). The singing society has a core group of seven women who have been singing together for a long time – over forty years now. The SNWSS has about twenty women who work doing our fundraising and community work. The SNWS draws from this group to do public national and international performances. That core of seven is in both groups; they and the other women work to maintain the values we were raised with in our community work and in our performance. Like the SNWSS, the SNWS is a fundraising group that channels funds into the SNWSS. In terms of the way we govern – I don't know if that's the right word – we keep them separate so that we're not running into any conflicts. Six Nations Women Singers, we have our own way of deciding what jobs we're going to take or what we're not going to do or whatever. We just get that money and donate it back to Six Nations Women Singing Society. But once it gets over [to them], then it's up to the whole group. They'll decide what will happen with that money. It's no longer just those original seven women. That's always community-oriented; it never goes anywhere else. The singing society's job is to help the community. And even though we're [the Six Nations Women Sing-ers] doing that indirectly, we're not doing it directly. So we can't call ourselves a singing society when we're doing that. So we call ourselves the Six Nations Women Singers. When we go out and perform, that core group just rechannels that [energy]. It's our responsibility to do right by the music in terms of what we're presenting to the public. [Afterward], we can just fall back into that [larger] group and take our regular place among all the twenty other women. So then it goes back [to becoming] a shared responsibility [to help the community] [1994].

When people call me a composer, I would [tend to] say, "No, I don't think so." But then I realized the difference [in our thinking]. "Com-poser" is a noun. It means that is what I am and making up songs is only what I do [1999]. We are doers. I write and compose music, but in our language we do not have a noun for that. We just "do" music. There is a verb that corresponds to "she can write a song." It never becomes a noun like "songwriter" but always remains a verb. In our language one never becomes a composer or an author, but in English you can say that. It is difficult to go from our language to English, as we do not have those concepts. We do not have the term "artist." Our members can carve in stone or out of wood, but these activities are described in the doing. We do not have a "woodcarver" [2001].

Now we get back to how to make a set. For instance, [at] the Sing we just had, we only had three new songs. If we have three new songs, we put them in. If we have four new songs, we put four in. And then we pull from the old songs that we know to round it out. Sometimes we may have too many songs, like we may end up with nine, which means two of them would not be in the set, because we can only use seven songs in a set. In that case, I let the women make the decision and see which ones they do not want in it. It depends on the situation, but sometimes they'll feel like they don't have enough time to learn a new song. Or else they don't want to learn a new song, or they think one song is trickier, or prettier, or whatever. It doesn't really matter to me because I can sing them [all]. Whatever they want to sing is fine with me, because I'll just learn the songs and lead them anyway [1994].

Everything has a job, everything has a place, everything has a context that it's supposed to be used in. If somebody needs help, then I would go and help them, and when I need help, they would help me back, whether I did something for them yesterday or today or a year ago, because of that principle of reciprocity. When you're going to learn something, you demonstrate that willingness [to learn the rules, to learn to live with everybody else], and they [the Haudenosaunee people] reciprocate by giving you the information you need … Everybody has something they can give back to the community, to the people. Whatever your gift is – let's say you can sing – then you have to give that back somehow. They'll help that person who is going to do that. Or they'll help the person who's a good worker, a good organizer. We have to have those people, all of those people [1995].

"It's a cultural thing to be inclusive": Global Vision

[By the late 1990s, Sadie's work was increasingly cross-cultural. She reflects on new challenges that relate to communicating traditional knowledge in culturally diverse contexts.]

Whenever I teach a class where we are going to be looking at Haudenosaunee culture in some way, shape, or form, I always talk to my class about not thinking in English. I start with an explanation of the Cayuga orthography: thirteen consonants, five vowels, and then the A and O, the two extra vowel sounds with a symbol at the bottom which makes it nasalized. I show them the chart and go over the orthography with them. I will write things on the board (in Cayuga orthography) and let them try to read them. I might write "Tai mai shu" [and] then ask, "what does that say?" They will look at it and then look at the chart and try to figure out. Then all of a sudden they are [excited]: "Wow, I get it. [It says] Tie my shoe." It gets them to start thinking that there is another way of thinking about things. That one experience expands their minds in that way [2006].

When I taught at York, that was such an involved course – three months, every Monday and Wednesday night, and there was lots of time. They learned as much as they could about the way we would do it. They had to sit the way we sit. We did a few little things, like working on beating, but that's not traditional. That was just to get them up to a certain level before we could even start to try and teach them to make it more part of them, to immerse them. So they had to be brought to that level first and then immersed. So all we did was sing and then I made tapes. We broke them up into three groups and they each had a set of songs to learn that were totally different from the other groups. They had to learn those songs and then present them, basically. And then they had to set up a social and the whole bit. I explained everything to them, all that business of what had to be done for the social. They had to get the food and organize the singing [to sing and dance] and the whole bit. So it was as much immersed as they could get, doing it our way [1995]. It [Haudenosaunne social dance music] is celebrating; you can't really take it out of the context. It was created to be danced to, to make you want to feel to dance, and [to] make you want to feel to dance, you've got to feel the music [2006].

[Reflecting on the establishment of the Aboriginal Women's Voices program at the Banff Centre for the Arts:] Marjorie Beaucage was working at the Aboriginal Film and Video Art Alliance in Alberta. And they were trying to create a space at the Banff Centre for the Aboriginal arts, our version of the arts. And so they created a partnership. Well, prior to the partnership [in 1994], they had a bunch of artists come in to do public service announcements on self-government, and so that was like the inkling, the physicality of the partnership. And then the next year was the formal partnership and that was when we started Aboriginal Women's Voices. Robert Rosen [Banff Centre] contacted me and he said, "If you had the ability to do a project, what would you like to do?" So I itemized three projects for him that I would like to do, just for the hell of it, I guess, and the one that they really liked and really went for – and it was the biggest one that I had talked about – that was Aboriginal Women's Voices. It was about creating the space where women could sing together and then do a concert and see how the whole thing evolved, being producer for the concert. Each woman was producer for their one-tenth of the performance. So they had to be involved in the whole thing, the whole thing of renewing our arts and making them [1999].

I think it was very difficult in a way because they had to devote ten or twelve weeks of their life to this project. And that meant going to Banff and being there in the wintertime with all the snow and everything, and just relocating for those three months. Whereas that's not a big thing for a lot of people, for Aboriginal people it's a very difficult thing to leave your home. So it was a big step and a great accomplishment for the people that did go there. So we worked and basically what we were doing with that first [program] was really just two things. Just to create a space in the air for the music, and to put it in the air and just have people sing. We sang for twelve weeks. That's like an eight-hour day, six days a week, sometimes seven. It was an awful lot of singing. And [intense] in terms of the atmosphere, because music is all about feeling and all about having people feel. In Haudenosaunee music there's a role for everybody. It's a matter of transposing that atmosphere, that ambience and maintaining that in the actual workshops [1999].

We started out the first year in '95, singing with each other and learning other people's songs, not for the purpose of singing them in public, in concert or on a stage, but just to be able to sing those in the context of your own self. When they sing them, when I sing a song within the context of my own people, and I know that context. I know that sound that's supposed to be there. So we got each other used to knowing those sounds, their sound that they have from their region, and out of that context and those particular songs, we created together as a group. So we jumped out of the context of those songs themselves to a traditional context of learning and being involved and sharing. For me the song context is extremely important. If it's sung at a particular time, or if only certain people sing that, then you maintain that, or if it's only sung with certain instruments, then you maintain that. And the ones who make changes are the singers of that song and the people who are knowledgeable of that song's context. Basically, what we were doing at Banff is creating another context, not [exactly] creating another context, but taking the essence of the context, the feeling of the essence of traditionalism of the music and putting that context [into our minds] and creating new songs. So we sang together as people who were willing to share and people who knew what music can do and what music does, what dance does. We created the travelling song for that first year. I think really it's a song that was created for all those different nations, and it has the voices of all those people in it. It's actually named because that song did travel through all those people. It's within its own context; it has its own life now. I think people should honour that and maintain that. So if they learned that travelling song, they should learn the story that goes with it. So, because there were ten people who knew music, who knew those contexts, we could then take those songs we knew from our own, from those traditions that [had] specific contexts, and just take the essence of that context and work with that, and sing a song that is very powerful and very strong in a different sense. We've created new works in a traditional sense with a public conscience and a public context [1999].

How we did it was we would sit in a circle and we would just sing. We would start with a vocable, any vocable, and we would just sing. Then what happened was, if you're in a room, everybody is impacted in some way by the vocable and people start [to sing]. Usually I start and I'll sing something for a short length of time. Then the next person sings something and the next person and the next person, and what happens is they start to blend together. Not only the lyrics but also the melodies; they blend together. And because all of these individuals come with their own sense of music and their own sense of sound from their land, then all of those things become intertwined and very intrinsic to the actual song that does come out. We just go around until we start hearing [that], and then usually I pull it but there are other individuals who pull melodies. And all you have to do is really listen to what's being sung, and then what you start to hear is a melody that keeps coming out, or else a melody overall that is maintained in the music, and then you just pull that melody out [as well as] the lyric that goes with it. And once you've got it, then you cement it, then you fix it, then you do your second verse. You teach everybody that melody and once everybody has it, in the lyrics, then you can embellish it, or structure it in the way that you want [1999].

The first year was really about creating that sense in people that they had to be fluent in their music traditions. My phone bill was phenomenal. I had to call all over the country. And basically what I did for that first one was that I went by sound alone. I kind of broke the continent up into regions by sound, what the land, what the people, what their general sound was. There's always exceptions within that, but I wanted a land-based, a region-based thing. So I wanted different sounds of different regions [1999].

The CD [*Hearts of the Nations*] was a documentation of our process. I wanted people there who knew our process and were willing to work in it and believed in it so that therefore the CD would be a strong CD so that other people could hear it and realize that this is an opportunity and a way that they can also work. That's why I chose people who were dedicated and committed to the idea and who believed in it. So like Flora Wallace because she's worked her whole life in music. Cornelia [Bowannie], I already knew her sound from having performed at different places and because she was at the first [Aboriginal Women's Voices program]. I always try to have continuity in there. Sharon King was a young singer who had her song [that] she made up in the first Aboriginal Women's Voices. I also wanted her there because of her link to that song for that CD. So she was another form of diversity [but also] continuity. And she is also very committed and dedicated and believed in what we were doing. And then also for Jennifer Kreisberg and Soni Moreno, who [are each] a very good singer, and Olivia Tailfeathers and Jani Lauzon and Elizabeth Hill. I just wanted people who were very dedicated and committed in our process and who were willing to work to create an exceptional product. It would demonstrate what we were trying to do. I wanted the mix of genres (Elizabeth and Jani), the traditional singer part (Flora and Cornelia), the harmony part, the innovativeness of Ulali (Jennifer and Soni), composing (Olivia and I). And also we had an added bonus because Joyce [Fossella] came with her mother [Flora Wallace]. Joyce just would sit in our circle, equal to everybody else, and I realized that she knew what she was doing and she was very good [as a singer] [1999].

We know our sound. We know it. We think the recording process should demonstrate that, should be tuned to that sound. When you just look at the isolated part of it, the recording part, then I think that's coming into another context again. In terms of us, we have to be sure of the recording process before we allow the sound [1999].

I guess the most important thing that I would like to see is if people want to use a song, then the onus should be on them. It should be their responsibility to do the research, to find out the context of that song, then to find the singers who sing that song and ask permission. And ask, "can I use it in this context?" – ask permission to use it. To me appropriation is taking a song out of its context without permission. In order to maintain our music, we have to maintain those contexts as well. So you always have to honour and be true to those, how those songs are sung or why they're sung, in order to pass that knowledge on. And if you can't, then make up your own song [1999].

That's part of Aboriginal Women's Voices [as well]. People think they can't make up songs and part of AWV is saying, "yes, you can." You can do it yourself, or you can do it in a group, whichever way. By doing that whole process, people realize that they can create a song. It's giving people back their voice. They sang with the people. They learned the songs, they learned different ways to use their lungs and their vocal cords, and their ears heard lots of things. So they are just a more involved person because more came into them [1999].

So in terms of Aboriginal Women's Voices, we've come really full circle now. In '95 we did the singing and the concert; in '96 we did workshops and talking about the process; and then in '97 we did [the] *Hearts of the Nations* CD to document the process and push it out even further and to create the opportunity for ideas and things like that. Now in November of '98, we did the Full Circle concert at the Max Bell performing arts complex in Calgary, Alberta, and from that concert we did a live recording. I think now we've cemented our process. Well, not cemented, but we've taken it to the point where we can reproduce it in other [programs] that don't necessarily have to have such a production value [1999].

It's a different context for *We Will All Sing*, because that is raising money for our community. The only reason we are known as we are is because we are true to ourselves. The CD need[ed] to reflect that. It need[ed] to reflect the trueness of the sound, versus innovativeness, or you know, clearly recorded sound or whatever [1999]. We didn't put our best stuff on there though. We want[ed] to see how they're going to treat us and how it's going to be. It's not our best stuff, the songs we really like to put out. We'll put that out when we see how everybody is [1995]. [In the late 1990s], we've been trying to put out a [new] CD but just haven't had the time really or the wherewithal. Because we're a community organization and we try to maintain our money, we don't always have the cash flow to go to a studio. With this next CD, we want to do our own distribution. Maybe not necessarily all, but we want to have control of it, because the dollars from the CD go back to the community. When we sell a CD, part of the money goes into our donations fund, and then it goes back out [into the community]. So we want to maximize that [1990].

In my culture music and dance are the same. Alejandro Ronceria[7] and I talked about the feasibility of creating a fusion of his program, which was dance, and Aboriginal Women's Voices, which was music. We wanted to bring them back together somehow to create something that was culturally closer to the concept of music and dance being one. Over time, this idea melded in [the Aboriginal dance opera] *BONES*. [Our plan was] to bring the two programs back together and do a dance and music show of some kind. So that was how it all started [2001]. It was seventeen Indigenous cultures from around the world because for me it was about being inclusive. For the Haudenosaunee and other Aboriginal peoples, it is a cultural thing to be inclusive. For me to do *BONES*, it was really important that everything be included. For Haudenosaunee people, music and dance go together. All of our songs have a dance to it. There is not one of our songs that does not have a dance through all our ceremonies, including medicine and socials. There is no separation for us [2001]. *BONES* is the sound of what I hear on earth transferred to an actual voiced rendition of it. I think that was the appeal of *BONES*. Aboriginal people understood it at a core level. The [non-Aboriginal part of the] audience had it too but had no vocabulary for it [2006]. [At a jury for arts grants in Toronto, during a discussion of musical fusion,] I realized that fusion to me is this: you hear the music and take it into yourself and it comes out differently. It is at a core level, not a mechanical level [2006].[8]

NOTES

1 "Full Circle" was a concert created, performed, and produced by participants in the Banff Centre's Aboriginal Women's Voices program in the late 1990s. The concert took place in Calgary in 1998.
2 "Amos Key and Sadie Buck," in Cronk (1990, 91–8); interview with Sadie Buck by Elma Miller, http://www.native-dance.ca/index.php/Scholars/Sadie_Buck (accessed 26 July 2011).
3 This common rhyme is used to teach the pitch associated with each line of the staff in Western musical notation.
4 Implicitly, an eskanye song is the cultural property of the Haudenosaunee nation, a point that Sadie has made more directly in classroom contexts. The orthography used in this article is the one used at the time of the interviews; it differs from that used in more recent dictionaries.
5 There is a well-known women's shuffle dance that gently and humorously criticizes "cigarettes, taxes and bingo."
6 A Sing is a biannual event where people from all the Haudenosaunee communities gather to share songs in a day-long celebration. The Sing ends with an evening "social," where everyone dances and, of course, sings some more.
7 Alejandro Ronceria was the director of the Aboriginal Dance project for the Banff Centre and also the choreographer of the opera *BONES*.
8 Because Elma Miller's extensive interview about *BONES* is online, and hence readily accessible, we have not replicated large sections of that interview but refer readers to http://www.native-dance.ca/index.php/Scholars/Sadie_Buck (accessed 26 July 2011).

8

Reflecting on Reflexivity:
Teaching and Conducting Research
in an Inuit Community

MARY PIERCEY

This chapter presents a narrative ethnography made up of my experiences of living, teaching, and conducting research in an Inuit[1] community. Like other ethnomusicologists working today, I am searching for an innovative manner in which to research and write in an ethnographic style. I am also influenced by the insights on methods and Aboriginal voice emerging from postcolonial theory, especially those put forth by Aboriginal researchers themselves,[2] and I recognize the concerns in Aboriginal studies about the way Aboriginal societies tend to be portrayed. In an effort to challenge past anthropological generalizations, I am guided by the work of Michelle Kisliuk (2001) and Anthony Seeger (2004) and have thus decided to explore my own (non-Indigenous) presence in the ethnographic field – my epistemological stance, my relation to the Inuit culture and to the Inuit I encountered, and my relationship to my own culture – to better understand my position in the specific culture of Arviat, Nunavut, and to represent this position in the present ethnography. The chapter is a series of personal narratives and reflections about teaching and researching in an Inuit community, encountering new people, and encountering a new culture. Through reflexive writing, I introduce the people involved in my research, including brief historical, political, ideological, and social (including cultural and musical) contexts, keenly aware of my own personal position in relation to the experience.

Why write in this manner? By telling deeply personal stories about my experiences living, teaching, and researching in an Inuit community, it is my aim to illuminate my relationship to the contexts and individual participants in my research. I hope that through the narration of this lived experience, the reader will get to know the people I encountered as well as see and understand how my motives, goals, habits of mind, and behaviour have shaped my representation of them. As Elizabeth Chiseri-Strater and Bonnie Stone Sunstein have explained, these are things that are "sometimes taken for granted and unexamined in the research process" (Chiseri-Strater and Sunstein 1997, 57). My story ultimately reveals several very important problems and issues pertaining to teaching and conducting research in a culture other than one's own.

First, my narrative about teaching in an Inuit community takes readers through a series of specific situations and how I handled them (not always in the best manner), revealing delicate cultural, social, pedagogical, and ethical issues.[3] Second, the stories I share about conducting research in a culture other than my own disclose research concerns including but not limited to language, translation, interpretation, representation, interviews, cross-cultural understanding and/or misunderstanding, ethics, relationships, and participant observation.

Background – The Big Question

My research explores how the Inuit of Arviat[4] (previously Eskimo Point), Nunavut (figure 8.1), have used their musical practices to negotiate social diversity within the community in response to massive sociocultural changes since three distinctive groups were resettled there in the 1950s. These changes include the loss of their semi-nomadic lifestyle, the enhanced role of colonial institutions in their lives, and political reorganization, including the establishment of Nunavut as Canada's newest territory. Additionally, however, the three distinct Inuit groups – the Padlirmiut, Ahiarmiut, and Tariuqmiut – had to negotiate their differences in language, religion, and life-ways in order to live together. Music has played a significant role in this negotiative process. Through the analysis of musical performance and oral history, I examine the cultural diversity within Arviat, alert to the ways music may reinforce memory and continuity (Shelemay 1998) or constitute a means of innovating or resisting the evolving norms of the community (Averill 1997, Deloria 2004, Bigenho 2002).

I explore continuity and change and how Indigenous identity is negotiated and constructed by examining the song traditions of three musically oriented families in Arviat: the Mamgarks (Tariuqmiut), the Okatsiaks (Padlirmiut), and the Illungiayoks (Ahiarmiut/Padlirmiut intermarriage).

8.1 Map of Nunavut. Used with permission of the Nunavut Department of Education.

These families are recognized as important culture bearers from the three bands who resettled in Arviat. I first noticed diversity among the three groups of Inuit in subtle comments from people. For example, a Tariuqmiut acquaintance has often ascribed certain negative behaviours of an Inuk individual, such as "being bossy" or "attracting too much attention," to that individual's having an Ahiarmiut origin, saying that Tariuqmiut are much "quieter" and thus better behaved. Sarah Anowtalik, an Ahiarmiut, has stated that "Ahiarmiut are the best musicians in Arviat."

I began to wonder whether and/or how these distinct groups developed such a strong sense of identity within the community, whether and/or how music manifests itself in the negotiation of diversity, and whether and/or how it is important for individuals to express their subgroup affiliation.

I found myself becoming extremely attentive to which churches people attended, where and how people sat at church services and community functions, and how people greeted members of different subcultural groups. I focused on which musicians played with whom, in which churches they led services, who went to whose homes for music-making sessions, and what music they chose to sing or play. Gradually, I began to observe that a musician's choice of performance and repertoire options went beyond purely musical criteria to include social considerations related to the value of associating with and performing with members of specific subcultures as well as to age, gender, family, and religious affiliation.

My research investigates the impact of relocation on the negotiation of Indigenous identity formation. It explores the historical relationships and cultural traditions shaping the song repertoire and performance practices of the Ahiarmiut, Tariuqmiut, and Padlirmiut living in Arviat and posits that a better understanding of generational and subcultural diversity through the exploration of music practices and oral histories is useful. By sharing my lived experience – by personally and academically reflecting on this lived experience – I hope to reveal the deep connections between myself and my informants/friends and my relation to contexts in which I lived and worked.

Telling the Story

My ethnography of narratives and music by and about some Inuit living in the small hamlet of Arviat is made up of interviews, conversations, reminiscences, narratives, songs, and musical performances that these Inuit shared with me. During my first stay in this small hamlet on the southwest side of the Hudson Bay, a stay of three years, from 2001 to 2004, I was employed as the high school music teacher with a given mandate to "bring traditional Inuit music into the school." Being from outside the Inuit culture, I was faced with a plethora of cultural, social, pedagogical, and ethical issues, much like the issues addressed in Ted Solís's anthology *Performing Ethnomusicology* (2004). Performing ethnomusicology – the idea of performing music from outside one's culture as distinguished from performing one's own music – is the focus of the anthology. For the most part, the students described in the Solís book are white, middle-class Americans who, in some cases, are taught music by someone from within the culture under study and sometimes not. In contrast, my teaching situation differed in the sense that I, an outsider to the Inuit culture, was given the responsibility of teaching traditional Inuit music to Inuit children. Although my situation is different from that of the authors in Solís's anthology, I encountered problems and considerations similar to those faced by university directors of world music ensembles who contributed to the Solís anthology, issues ranging from representation, reflexivity, hegemony, and aesthetically determined interaction to school administration and pedagogy.

I was uncomfortable with the fact that there was no Nunavut music curriculum and very little Inuit music published for use in the "Western-style" music classroom in which I was accustomed to teaching. I quickly implemented an Inuit elder-youth music mentorship program, collected as much Inuit music as possible from community musicians, and began to build my own music curriculum, which I hoped would meet the needs of my new students. After three years of teaching music in this context, I wrote a paper describing some opportunities and challenges involved in applying and adapting traditional Indigenous knowledge about Inuit music in the social environment in which Inuit now find themselves (see Piercey forthcoming). I tried to present a general analysis of the way contemporary Indigenous youth battle with traditional methods of learning music, with a special focus on tensions between oral and literate educational approaches to the teaching, learning, and performance of the recently revived traditional Inuit drum dances.

However, since I felt that there was much more richness in people's narratives and conversations about music and in their personal musical performances than I had managed to convey in that paper, I was motivated to do further ethnomusicological research. My current research, then, brings together my experiences first as a music teacher (2001–04) and then as a researcher (2006–07) in Arviat and highlights the intimate relationships that I developed with the Inuit of Arviat, particularly the Inuit involved in this study. I have tried to highlight recurrent themes and meanings of music as they emerged in conversations with families in the community in order to convey Inuit views of music making. Writing about the meaning of music for individuals is complicated, especially when those individuals are from a culture different from one's own, and I have accomplished only a partial job. As H.L. Goodall Jr reminds us when writing about ethnography, "Descriptions of the outward world come from deep inside of us. Because each of us has been shaped and informed by different deeply personal experiences, our descriptions of the same scene are likely to be as distinctive as they are personal. Facts are *personal* interpretations. Examined reflexively, they show us not only *how* we see the world, but also *why we interpret it* as we do" (Goodall 2000, 95, original emphasis).

This chapter addresses the organization of ethnographic detail by the ethnomusicologist and the place of that detail in the lives of the people the ethnomusicologist represents. Throughout the writing of this ethnography and certainly even during field research in Arviat, I constantly battled with issues of representation, and I longed to conduct and write research differently from early anthropologists about the experience of living in that particular hamlet in Nunavut. Study of postcolonial theory, specifically Aboriginal perspectives on postcolonial thought, thrust me into a state of reflection and evaluation of my personal role first as a teacher in an Aboriginal community and then as a researcher in that same community. Questions emerged, such as: How and why did I become the music teacher at Qitiqliq High School in Arviat? Why am I pursuing a research project on the effects of resettlement on Inuit expressive culture? Do I qualify as a researcher of aspects of Inuit culture – a culture and tradition of which I am not a member? Although some recent Aboriginal scholarship is supportive of non-Aboriginals studying Aboriginal cultures,[5] most is very critical of non-Aboriginal researchers doing research and writing about Aboriginal history and culture. As I dove deeper and deeper into this literature, I became increasingly aware of my own inadequacies, fears, and personal doubts about conducting research in an Aboriginal community. Non-Aboriginal scholars of history, science, folklore, and anthropology have been criticized for researching from a Eurocentric point of view – a vantage point that neglects to consider Aboriginal worldviews, ignores Aboriginal voices, represents Aboriginal people as exotic "Others" who live in the past before contact with Europeans, and fails to recognize Aboriginal cultures as living and dynamic.[6]

Postcolonial theory plays an important role in the ongoing struggle for the political and economic, as well as cultural, liberation of Aboriginal people and continues to be a valuable tool in the decolonization process. In addition to exposing the complexities of colonialism and its assumptions, postcolonial critique has led to alternative methods of conducting research. These include methods that are not Eurocentric and that address the research initiatives, values, and concepts of Aboriginal people.

As I looked around my student office in the Faculty of Music at the Memorial University of Newfoundland, I saw pictures of an Inuit family in Arviat and pictures of my students dressed in traditional *amoutiks*[7] and headpieces as they performed "traditional" Inuit music at the community hall in Arviat. Are these pictures a nice reminder of my close friends in Arviat or are they an attempt to show off my exotic experience of teaching in an Aboriginal community? Do these pictures display Inuit as romanticized and exotic and as different from my friends and family here in Newfoundland? These are the gut-wrenching, self-reflective types of questions that I have been grappling with over the past few years. Even reflecting on my teaching experience in Arviat, I now wonder whether, by bringing a "traditional" Inuit musical performing group to the International Choral Festival in St John's in 2003, I was (certainly unintentionally) contributing to perpetuating the image of Inuit as different, exotic, and primitive. As I come to terms with perhaps having displayed Eurocentric attitudes and behaviours in the past, I am concerned now with research methods that demonstrate ethical standards by considering Inuit worldviews, allowing Inuit voices to speak for themselves, and foregrounding the privilege that Eurocentric attitudes have enjoyed.

Personal narratives and the examination of music performances (both by the researcher and by informants) address a set of theoretical concerns about representation. I have chosen to write about individual experiences – including verbatim statements as well as my own experiences and thoughts – to examine musical performances from my own perspective, and whenever possible to compare my perspective to Inuit perspectives as I understand them. Collaborative efforts such as these, in research and writing, work against generalizations. Through close collaboration with my informants, I have tried to ward off the troubling aspect of ethnographic description that produces the effects of homogeneity, coherence, and timelessness, which contribute to the creation of "cultures." Furthermore, I have tried to recognize my effect on the field context. I address the fact that I affected and was affected by my social relationships with both the community and the individuals with whom I worked by leaving traces of myself throughout.

In my writing, I describe Inuit music making as I saw it and lived it during my stay in Arviat. Instead of attempting to make formal generalizations about Inuit music, I draw on a series of vignettes of individual Inuit interacting musically with family members, church congregations, and the general public. This line of inquiry is influenced by Lila Abu-Lughod's theory of "writing against culture," which argues that focusing on the particular experiences of individuals works against generalization. Abu-Lughod goes on to argue that "telling stories ... could be a powerful tool for unsettling the culture concept and subverting the process of 'othering' it entails" (Abu-Lughod 1993, 13). Therefore, I have chosen to stress the particularity of individual Inuit experiences with music by building a picture of specific experiences, such as religious worship, from individuals' discussions, recollections, disagreements, and actions.

Constructing a Community

The people of Arviat live in a close community made up of 2,500 people – 98 per cent Inuit and 2 per cent *qablunaaq*.[8] Located on the southwest side of Hudson Bay, Arviat was the resettlement site chosen by the Canadian federal government in 1958 for three distinct groups of Inuit who were living semi-nomadically in nearby areas. The Caribou Inuit in Arviat are an Inuktitut-speaking[9] group comprised of three distinct bands: the Ahiarmiut (Inland Inuit), Padlirmiut (Nomadic Inuit), and Tariuqmiut (Coastal Inuit). Prior to the 1950s, the Ahiarmiut lived in the area of Ennadai Lake and Yathkyed Lake, the Padlirmiut lived in Padlei, and the Tariuqmiut lived in the coastal region between Qamanirjuk and Siurayuk. Today, the Inuit of Arviat call themselves Arviamiut (Arviat Inuit).

Until the mid-1950s, the three distinct Inuit bands were semi-nomadic peoples who travelled seasonally to hunt, gather, and occasionally socialize with each other (Boas 1877, Rasmussen 1927). Scottish and American whalers reached areas in the Kivalliq region[10] in the 1850s, bringing American square dances and Scottish reels to the Inuit throughout the area. In 1913–14, when trading posts were established at Baker Lake and the Kazan River, Inuit began participating in the fur trade and in cultural exchange with European traders. After the 1920s this exchange expanded to include Catholic and Anglican missionaries, government agents, and Hudson's Bay Company employees. Despite these cultural interactions, their life-ways were not radically affected until Arviat was chosen by officials of the Department of Northern Affairs in the 1950s as a resettlement place for Inuit in the surrounding areas. Since this resettlement, Inuit life-ways and culture have undergone rapid change. The three distinct bands, each with its own traditions, language, and history, were forced to settle in a single community and send their children to residential schools. They have incorporated new patterns for hunting and community sustainability and have been heavily influenced by Evangelical Christian missionaries (Tester and Kulchyski 1994). These changes have had serious consequences for both the maintenance of Inuit social networks and the continuing relevance and use of the Inuktitut language. Although the three groups of Inuit still protect customs and practices deeply rooted in their respective cultures, they struggle with concerns about cultural erosion and practical issues related to drug abuse, youth support, employment, education, and community cohesion. Today, Inuit children speak English at school, spend limited time on the land, consume television shows and movies, and create popular music.

My keen interest in the music of the Arviamiut arose partly from personal intrigue and partly out of the sheer need to survive as a qablunaaq music teacher. To have a successful music program, it became evident early on that I would have to learn Inuktitut songs and implement them in the school's music curriculum because, initially, the students were very reluctant to sing songs in English chosen by this new, young qablunaaq. Blank stares and pursed lips were what I received those first few days at school when I asked the students to sing for me. I was under the impression that this was normal because the principal at the time had informed me during my interview for the teaching position that there was no music in Arviat and that I would be the "trailblazer to bring music to the Arctic." He was wrong, as I was soon to discover.

You might wonder how a young music teacher finds herself in the Arctic believing there is no music made among the people living there, considering that there are records dating back to as early as the 1800s of Inuit making music. Franz Boas (1877), a geographer charged with officially mapping the Arctic, but who was also interested in Inuit social life, wrote about customs (including music making) he observed among the Caribou Inuit. Knud Rasmussen (1930), a Greenlandic Danish anthropologist who was fluent in Inuktitut, transcribed and translated the lyrics of hundreds of songs sung by the Inuit he encountered. One of the largest Canadian collections of Inuit music is that of Diamond Jenness, an anthropologist of the southern party (1913–16) of the Canadian Arctic Expedition. He recorded 137 songs mostly of the Copper Inuit at Bernard Harbour, near Dolphin and Union Strait, and Helen Roberts transcribed and analyzed them. Asen Balikci (1970) gives detailed descriptions of the "song duel" and other musical genres practised by the Netsilik Inuit living in Pelly Bay. Throughout the 1970s and 1980s, researchers began to collect and record them. Ethnomusicologists collected primary material to fill in gaps in knowledge concerning specific genres and Inuit groups and conducted research on stability and change.[11] I knew nothing about these geographers, anthropologists, ethnomusicologists, or explorers who wrote about their experiences in the Arctic and did very little to inform myself about the Inuit with whom I would be living. Relying almost solely on the information provided by my new employer, I headed off to the Great White North naive and bursting with excitement at the thought of an adventure.

Teaching in Arviat

My first few days as the new music teacher at Qitiqliq High School were difficult. The piano, which the principal had ordered three months prior, still had not arrived. I spent the first two weeks trying to teach choral music, accompanying myself on an old electronic organ that one of the teachers owned and had graciously loaned the school while we awaited the piano's arrival. My biggest challenge was getting the students to sing. Most just sat there and stared at me when I requested their participation. Furthermore, students refused to answer my questions. I initially saw this as a sign of rejection and disrespect, and it saddened me. I felt like a failure. I eventually learned that many were indeed answering my questions, but through facial expressions rather than by speaking. In general, Inuit in Arviat are very quiet. Most do not like answering questions but will do so when asked. If the question prompts a yes or no answer, this is likely to be delivered by raising the eyebrows for "yes" and crunching the nose for "no."

After a very frustrating first week, I decided to go to the Anglican church on Sunday morning to try to learn a little more about the culture in which I was living. On 26 August 2001 my journal states,

> I went to church this morning; the Anglican Church, and I was the
> only white person there. The two-hour service was spoken entirely
> in Inuktitut and I didn't understand a word. Evidently, you would
> think that I found the service boring … on the contrary. The ser-
> vice was so moving that I cried a number of times. These people
> are so spiritual. There were families with babies and small children
> all singing and praising God. I sat behind Doreen, an Inuk teacher
> from school. She provided me with a service book that had English
> translations and I was able to know a little of what was being said.
> She also gave me a song book so that I could sing along with the
> hymns. The music was great! The band led the service … drums,
> guitar, bass guitar, electric guitar, and a gospel choir. I knew all
> of the hymns … they were oldies that we sing at Fortune United
> Church [in Newfoundland] … but they were sung in Inuktitut.

This is nothing new for those scholars who have written about hym-nody in Aboriginal communities (Cavanagh [Diamond] 1987, 1988, Keil-lor 1986), but for me it was a revelation: music in Arviat! What I thought was good music! I soon discovered, too, that if students enjoyed singing hymns at church, they would also enjoy singing them at school, and that is how the barrier between my students and me was broken down. On 27 August 2001 my journal reads, "My afternoon classes rocked. The students were responsive, they laughed at my jokes. It was like being at camp; everyone was singing and having a good time."

By going to church every Sunday and by participating in events at the community hall, two activities deemed of high importance by Arviamiut, I was soon accepted into Inuit society. At least, from my perspective, I seemed to be more accepted than other qablunaat living in the community who chose not to integrate themselves into the society in which they lived.

I was given full reign over my curriculum. There were only three things required of me by the Arviat District Education Authority: (1) teaching songs in English to encourage better English literary and speaking skills; (2) making music classes "fun" to encourage better overall attendance at the school; and (3) facilitating the teaching and learning of traditional Inuit drum dance songs, a genre that was unfamiliar to most youth at the time.

During the three years I taught music at Qitiqliq High School, these goals were accomplished through a great deal of hard work and dedication. For example, a mentorship program was set up to encourage youth to learn from their elders, and the traditional Inuit drum dance was revived among the youth. I worked closely with the school drama and Inuktitut teachers, Gord Billard and Maggie Mannik respectively, to produce four musicals a year: two at Christmas, one at Easter, and one in the late spring. The musicals were performed in English and Inuktitut: English songs accompanied the English dialogue, and Inuktitut songs accompanied the Inuktitut dialogue. At times, the English text was translated by senior students, and at other times, Inuktitut plays and songs were created by senior students. All of these were well received by the community, and we attracted a "full house" at every performance.

I founded a choir called Arviat Imngitingit (Arviat Singers). This choir is made up of students from Qitiqliq High School and adults from the community, and it specializes in traditional and contemporary Inuit music originating from the Kivalliq region of Nunavut. The Arviat Imngitingit are known for their expertise in traditional Inuit throat singing, "A-ya-ya" singing, and drum dancing, and they enjoy singing contemporary Inuit songs and gospel songs in Inuktitut as well. Several members of Arviat Imngitingit have travelled to Greenland and Alberta to perform for the opening and closing ceremonies of the Arctic Winter Games, and others travelled to Brandon, Manitoba, to perform with the Brandon University Chorale at Rural Forum 2002. All thirty choristers participated in Festival 500: Sharing the Voices, an international choral festival held in Newfoundland in 2003. The choir has been highlighted in television programs on Global Television and the Aboriginal Peoples Television Network and in newspapers such as the *National Post, Evening Telegram, Southern Gazette, Kivalliq News,* and *News North.*

My life as a teacher in Arviat was very rewarding. I often felt proud of what we had accomplished, and I enjoyed my job tremendously. But this is not to say that I did not experience self-doubt, anxiety, and even fear. I questioned daily the impact I was having on my students.

Reflecting on Reflexivity

As I try to position myself in this particular context of Arviat, I wonder whether my writing is a romanticized account of teaching in an "exotic" place. Is it self-indulgent? What really should or should not be included when translating from field experience into ethnography? How much of myself should I include? How do I determine what experiences to relate to help my audience (and me) to better understand my particular context? Is my particular perspective necessary or even interesting? In trying to answer these questions, I keep coming back to Kisliuk's work. As she points out, "Ethnography, like any creative enterprise, is a re-representation, a re-formation of experience, and we need to develop tools that help us sense when and what to include when re-representing a part of life – of our lives" (Kisliuk 1997, 24–5).

Gradually, over the three years I lived and worked in Arviat, shared experiences and defining moments helped me to situate myself. Reflecting on those beginning days, weeks, and years, remembering the naiveté, at times the closed-mindedness, of my firm belief that my way of doing things was the right way and how I projected my beliefs and opinions onto others, and then writing the ethnography about these early experiences have facilitated a process of identity formation and of personal growth. It is surprising to see how much I have learned, how my ideas and opinions have changed, and how these experiences and relationships have impacted my life, just as the lives of my students and friends have been impacted.

Time and experience played a role in shaping me and the field. The relationship I had with my previous experience as a teacher changed how I thought of things theoretically and intellectually and affected how I took in and interpreted new field experiences as a researcher. For example, although teaching religious songs initially bridged a gap between myself and my students and provided me with a warm welcome into the larger community of Arviat, after reading much of the literature on the effects of colonialism on Aboriginal communities, I now wonder whether I contributed to the ongoing act of colonialism. Knowing what I know now of colonial history, I might have approached Christian music differently. Furthermore, by actively sharing my Christian beliefs, participating in Christian ceremonies, and ultimately teaching Christian songs at the high school, I directly illustrated my support of the Christian faith and perhaps indirectly showed my lack of interest in or respect for shamanism or early Inuit beliefs. Viewed this way, I wonder whether this contributed to people's unwillingness to discuss shamanism with me in interviews and their enthusiasm to discuss religious music. Alternatively, one could take the view that by actively practising Christianity in the field, I opened new gates for exploration.

The lesson to be learned here is that this ethnography is particularized by time, place, personality, and social circumstance. I hope to situate readers within the fluctuations and particularities of my informants, myself, and each setting.

Meeting New People

The Mamgark Family (Tariuqmiut)

I first met Gara Siatsiaq Mamgark in August 2001 when she was a grade 10 student at Qitiqliq High School. She was sixteen years old. I remember one particular day after school during that first week of teaching. It had been one of those frustrating days when no one sang and very few students seemed to respond to my many questions. Gara walked into my classroom and said, "huvit." I said, "huh?" She said, "*Huvit* means 'hello' or 'how are you?' in Inuktitut, and your response is *nauk*, and you have to shake your head while you say it." I did as I was instructed and she laughed. It was a genuine, lovely laugh, and I laughed with her. This marked the beginning of a wonderful student-teacher relationship – ironically, one in which I was mostly the student and she was the teacher. Gara became the source of information about Inuit culture that I longed to know. During those first few months in Arviat, she explained little nuances of the culture, such as the fact that Inuit do not respond well to outbursts of anger. She kept me up to date on local community activities, telling me what

8.2 The Mamgark and Piercey families, 2003. Photograph by author.

types of behaviour were considered outrageous in the community and what types of behaviour were acceptable. Gara introduced me to many local musicians. She accompanied me to Catholic church services and square dances, explained family relations, cooked new foods, sang new songs, and taught me basic Inuktitut phrases; all in all, she was the perfect gatekeeper of a culture I knew nothing about.

During the three years I taught at Qitiqliq High School, she participated in all aspects of the music program: she transcribed and translated many Inuktitut songs and travelled with the school choir on many choir trips. Her help to me and to the program was indispensable. In return, I aided Gara with such basic things as her homework. I became her official mentor for the Nunavut Youth Abroad Program, which provides international and national travel and employment opportunities for Inuit youth. With this program, she travelled to Ontario and Botswana, Africa, with other Inuit youth to participate in cultural and employment programs. Successful completion of these programs guarantees a spot in Nunavut Sivuniksavut, a college program located in Ottawa that is designed to teach young Inuit about the Nunavut Land Claims Agreement and other important political, economic, and social issues related to Inuit.

Gara also became my interpreter during my field research. Language barriers between me and my older informants made communication and documentation difficult. Gara's grandmother, Matilda Sulurayok, age sixty-seven, speaks Inuktitut only. Thus our relationship is limited by our dependence on Gara to translate our conversations. Although both of us understand the basics of each other's language, a great deal of detail and feeling is lost when we try to communicate without translation assistance.

I recorded many songs from Matilda. She was passionate about getting the songs on tape so that her children and grandchildren can listen to them after she is gone. She also felt that she was doing the "Creator's work" (*pinguqtitsijiup pilirianga*) or "will of God" (*Gutiup pilirianga*) by recording her favourite religious songs. She believed that sharing her music with others would help to bring the "Holy Spirit" (*anirniq ipjurnaituq*) into their lives. Her reflections, narratives, and reminiscences were told in Inuktitut. Gara provided me with a sketchy recapitulation of her words after each session. I had to wait until much later, when the recordings were translated into English, to learn the vivid and intricate details of her words.

Although Matilda's interviews were conducted in Inuktitut, the gathering of information from Gara and her mother, Rosie, was of a different nature. All of their interviews were in English, and most of our correspondence was in English as well. Rosie was eager to share her musical narratives with me, was happy to allow me to video-record her singing, but was unwilling to have a formal interview taped. She said that she was "shy of her English" and did not want to "sound stupid." Thus, immediately after each formal interview, I had to rush away and write every detail down before I forgot it. Not the best method for recording people's words but one I had to accept because that is what Rosie wanted. If I forgot something or needed clarification, I phoned Rosie and asked her again to make sure that I got her story right.

Matilda and Rosie were especially keen to share their thoughts and music because they were both concerned about the erosion of Inuit musical traditions. Matilda said, "There are many distractions for young people in Arviat, and there is great concern that the younger people are not learning enough of their traditions." She felt that by singing and recording her song repertoire, young people would be able to have access to it, and she hoped that the songs would continue to be passed on from one generation to the next. Matilda's grandchildren were always present during our recording sessions, and they expressed interest in learning many of her songs. This made her very happy, as was evident in her favourite comment, "Quviasuqtunga" (I am happy).

The Illungiayok Family (Ahiarmiut/Padlirmiut)

Ronnie Qahuq Illungiayok (figure 8.3) attended my first Arviat Imngitingit rehearsal. He walked into my classroom, smiled, and sat in the back row of the choir formation I had organized. He said nothing, did nothing, and kind of just sat there detached from the rest of the group. I had noticed that some other Inuit did the same thing in my classes at school, and I began to question my teaching skills and my interpersonal skills.

Perhaps some Inuit felt much trepidation in response to my teaching strategies and manner, but if they did, they never said so. I did learn from Billy Ukutak, the school's Inuit guidance councillor, however, that according to Inuit customs, in an unfamiliar setting an Inuk will likely react by withdrawal, combined with patient observation, until he or she can figure out what the situation is and how to behave. In many cases, withdrawal and nonparticipation in my classes during the early days of my teaching are probably attributable to this "traditional" Inuit custom, which still exists in modern Inuit society.

Ronnie is a drum dancer. He learned how to drum dance from his father, and he performs nationally and internationally as well as throughout the community and territory. Unfortunately, he does not know how to sing any of the songs to which he dances. He can talk about them, telling me who composed them, what they are about, and so on. But when it comes to the text and the melody, he is lost. Although the choir and I could not learn traditional songs from Ronnie, his drum dancing skills proved to be an asset. Later, while the girls learned songs from Eva Aupak or Elizabeth Nibgoarsi or from me via tape recordings, Ronnie worked with the boys on proper drumming technique.

Ronnie (figure 8.4) began to stop by my home to visit. Initially, he would sit on the floor in a corner without talking and observe his surroundings. I found this odd at first, and I found the lack of conversation uncomfortable. As Ronnie became more at ease in my home, he engaged me in conversation about the differences between Inuit and qablunaat. He began, "You are not like other qablunaat … You're more like us Inuit, not expecting us to talk all the time or asking too many questions." He said that most qablunaat "talk too much," are "too bossy," "don't understand Inuit ways," and "don't share what they have, especially food." Possessing and respecting these values contributed to the long-lasting friendships I

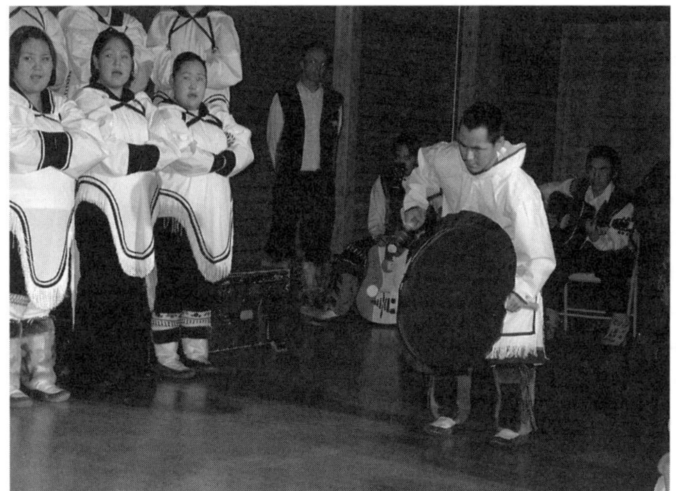

8.3 (left) Ronnie Qahuq Illungiayok and Arviat Imngitingit, performance for commissioner, 2004. Photograph by author; 8.4 (right) Ronnie Qahuq Illungiayok. Photograph by author.

developed with people who later became knowledgeable and eager participants in my research.

The practice of sharing is held to be of the utmost importance in Arviat. Inuit share food, natural resources, labour, and sometimes money. Furthermore, hospitality is considered an essential trait and is almost never refused. Ronnie said that because I opened my home to visitors, people respected and liked me. He said that people knew that I shared my food, instruments, Honda, Skidoo, gas, and so on and that they appreciated it. He also said that this was why people gave me "country food."

Silas Illungiayok, father to fifteen children and the "head" of the Illungiayok family, was born on the land in 1945. A proud Ahiarmiut and one of Arviat's key culture bearers, he is employed by the Arviat District Education Authority to work with students at the schools in order to pass on his traditional Indigenous knowledge, including musical knowledge. He is the vice president of the Sivullinuut (Elders' Society) and is responsible for organizing and performing traditional Inuit drum dances at the Elders' Centre, the Mark Kalluak Community Hall, school functions such as graduations and festivals, and community functions. Drum dancing and passing on traditional knowledge are Silas's trade, for which he receives a comfortable income by teaching at the school and performing for money. Thus, when I phoned his home and asked his daughter, Mariah, about conducting a formal interview with him on the topic of music, he wanted to know how much I would pay him. I told Mariah that I would call her back, and I quickly hung up the phone, a little shocked and somewhat angry that he had requested money in return for the interview. This was the first time anyone had requested anything, and I was under the impression that people did not want anything for their contributions.

I sat in silence for quite some time, first thinking about the audacity of such a request and then wondering whether others were expecting money as well. Silas, a man who works with qablunaat daily at the school, knew that if he wanted me to know that he was expecting payment for his services, he would have to tell me directly. At this point, I began to worry about whether I had offended other interviewees – people whom I had not paid but who probably expected something in return for sharing their knowledge and experiences. I had probably missed hints given by people who needed money to help feed their children, put gas in their vehicles, and so on. My informants were probably thinking that I was another qablunaaq from the outside who would exploit them by taking what information I needed to write my dissertation and that I would soon make lots of money from what I produced about them. I felt ashamed of myself; although my intentions were certainly not to exploit anyone, my failure to take into consideration the historical backdrop of the relationship between whites and Inuit had led me to do precisely that.

In Arviat interracial relations and assumptions about hierarchy and power have been shaped by the history of the region (see Marcus 1995, Mowat 1959, 1952). Part of this history – which includes forced relocation by the Canadian government in the 1950s (with the help of the Royal Canadian Mounted Police and missionaries) – is the infiltration in the 1920s by trading opportunists searching for wealth from fox furs. Methods of acquisition involved low payment to Inuit fox hunters, which, combined with the consequential change in caribou hunting routines, ultimately led to starvation.

As a result of this history (and certainly many other similar historical events), many Inuit tend to assume that anyone coming from the outside will exploit them. Many Inuit with whom I worked believe that all qablunaat are rich, that they get all the good jobs in the community, and that once they have made their fortune, they will leave Arviat, never to return. I thought, at first, that by making long-term and heartfelt connections with people, by gradually becoming an active participant in church services, square dances, and community functions, and by learning the Inuktitut language I could escape being categorized as another exploiter.

But I soon discovered that because I missed subtle nuances of the culture (i.e., the "little hints"), this would be a constant battle.

The way to oppose the lingering effects of the colonial past, I thought, was to grasp the historically defined relationships imposed upon myself and the Inuit with whom I worked and to consciously struggle against that history, reshaping our relationships to fit our respective values and current situation. Thus I immediately phoned Rosie to ask her what her thoughts were on the money situation. Rosie assured me that she did not want any money and that no one in her family expected payment for their time and interviews. She said, "we are friends and we help each other in many ways." She also informed me that others would indeed expect something in return. She suggested $50 per interview, and I set out to correct the wrong I had done.

Accepting a monetary offering in exchange for a discussion about music, members of the Illungiayok family agreed to participate in the current project. Interviews with Silas, his wife Bernadette, and many of their children, including Ronnie, Mariah, John Paddy, and Danny, proved to be indispensable. Silas Illungiayok, father and elder in the Illungiayok family, identifies and discusses the role of the Inuit drum in Inuit educational initiatives and healing processes in his interviews. Ronnie Qahuq Illungiayok emphasizes that drum dancing is an important element in the maintenance and communication of Inuit identity, culture, and pride in the multicultural and international contexts in which he performs. A younger son, Danny Ollie Illungiayok, shows the relation between the use of the Inuit drum in traditional Inuit *pisit* (song) and its employment in newer compositions.

Interviews with the Illungiayok children were all conducted in English. Interviews with Silas, however, were conducted in Inuktitut, with his daughter, Mariah, acting as translator. When information is gathered from informants who speak and understand a language different from the researcher's, there is much room for misunderstanding and misrepresentation. No story can be translated from one language (and thus, inevitably, one culture) to another without some loss of meaning. Many details in the life of Silas are hard to convey in a written text in English. It is not just a matter of what is lost in the transformation from oral to written language. Nor is the problem simply that inevitable shifts of meaning occur when one moves between languages that do not have precise equivalents for each other's expressions and whose words have varying connotations. These problems are compounded by the number of voices involved in the interpretation of the words. In this particular situation, Mariah translated my questions into Inuktitut for her parent, who responded in Inuktitut. Later, Gara Mamgark transcribed these interviews in Inuktitut and then translated them into English. My analysis of the interviews is based on three levels of interpretation: first, Mariah's translations of my words; second, Gara's written translation of Silas's oral narratives; and third, my own interpretation of the translation.

Gara stated many times that it was "extremely difficult" to translate Silas's narratives into English in a manner that would convey meaning to me and other English readers. Furthermore, my understanding, analysis, and writing based on Gara's translations may or may not contain the "truth" in Silas's words. Given all of these compromises of translation, I have struggled to address the great possibility for misunderstanding and misrepresentation by including my informants in the analysis and writing process as much as possible. For this particular situation, I chose to send Mariah Illungiayok copies of the manuscript and asked her to read (i.e., translate into Inuktitut) to Silas the parts about him so that he could offer comments, changes, and/or explanations that would help me to get his stories right or at least as close as possible to the truth.

The Okatsiak Family (Padlirmiut)

When I travelled back to Arviat in January 2007 for my second field research stint, I encountered the Okatsiak family. The Okatsiaks are a Padlirmiut family who lead the musical worship at the Anglican church. In addition to performing songs of a religious nature, many members write their own songs, perform music from a variety of genres at the Mark Kalluak Hall for community functions such as festivals, weddings, and community meetings, and make music in their homes as a popular pastime.

I met Mary Okatsiak (figure 8.5), mother and elder of the Okatsiak family, at the Anglican church during Holy Week. I attended Sunday morning church on 1 April 2007 and learned that there would be services every night throughout the week leading up to Easter. During the service, Mary, who had been playing the organ, walked down to where I was sitting and asked me whether I would like to play. I declined, saying that I did not know the music. She frowned, saying "you know the songs," and asked whether I would play for the service the next night. I accepted on the condition that I could practise with the band before the service. She said that she would arrange it with her husband and son, who were playing the bass guitar and lead guitar respectively.

The next day, Monday, 2 April, I met the Okatsiak family and a few other musicians at the church at 1:00 PM. Mary and her husband, Peter, her son Sandy and his wife, Eva, and Joe Aulatjut, Sarah Anowtalik, and I

8.5 (left) Mary Okatsiak. Photograph by author; 8.6 (right) Sandy Okatsiak. Photograph by author.

practised the music for the service that was to be held later that evening. After the practice, Sandy (figure 8.6) said that he liked my piano playing and asked me whether I would be interested in playing on a CD that he wanted to produce. I agreed, and we planned to get together at my house to practise after Holy Week was over. I told them about my project and asked whether they would like to participate. They were all eager to contribute. I also asked whether I might be permitted to record the church services during Holy Week, and since many people do, they said, "Of course." They told me that I should speak to Rev. Joe Manik and service leader Martha Nutarsungnik for formal permission. I did so, and permission was granted.

Unlike the previous two families mentioned, whom I have known since 2001 – a total of six years of intimate sharing – I spent only two months with the Okatsiak family. I did only one recording session and one formal interview with Mary. Her husband, Peter, who plays the bass in several of my recordings, was unable to do an interview due to his employment as a tour guide for visitors mainly from the United States and Japan. It was Sandy and his wife, Eva, with whom I developed friendships. As we were all the same age, we had many things in common and truly enjoyed spending time together.

For two months, Sandy, Eva, and I played together, recording much of what we played, danced together at square dances and teen dances, played cards and bingo, went on hunting expeditions, and led worship services at the Anglican church. Although we spent a lot of time together during those two months, we did not develop the close relationship that exists between me and certain members of the Mamgark and Illungiayok families, and thus much of our discussion was superficial. They revealed much about their perspectives on music and music making but very little about their personal, social, and economic histories.

Conclusion

This chapter tells the story of how I came to live, work, and do research in an Inuit community. Through reflective research and writing, I have introduced the people involved in the present study, discussed some of the many personal challenges I encountered living and teaching in a culture different from my own, and examined some of the difficulties I faced conducting research in that culture. There were many cultural, social, pedagogical, and ethical issues that arose from my teaching experience that helped to "pave my way" toward conducting better research. The close friendships I developed during those teaching years helped to improve the quality of my work and, more important, made my fieldwork a meaningful experience. Some researchers continue to maintain that, as researchers, we must remain in control of our feelings and emotions at all times in the name of our research objectives. However, it is those feelings and emotions and how we reflect upon them that help us to understand who we are, how we have grown, and how we see the world around us. As Edward Said has explained, "Anthropological representations bear as much on the representer's world as on who or what is represented" (Said 1989, 224). The academic world from which I come is still battling with the illusions of objectivity in social science inquiry. One aim of reflexive fieldwork and writing is to challenge notions of power and "Othering" that exist in colonial scholarship, and it is my goal to work against these notions by sharing my lived experience and by personally and academically reflecting on this lived experience.

Much of the information about me and my informants in this chapter deals very little with music. My intention has been to present as much historical, economic, and social context as possible so that this background can serve as the backdrop for the analysis and description of musical practices in the lives of these individuals. By writing myself into the musical and social context of the experience of the Arviamiut, I aim to provide an opportunity for the reader to interpret the social dynamics and social worlds of all involved.

1 The word "Inuit" means "the people" and is the term by which Inuit refer to themselves. "Inuk" is the singular form of "Inuit." Use of the term "Eskimo" is no longer popular because of its origin. The term is derived from a Cree phrase meaning "eaters of raw meat" and refers to the custom of Inuit eating most of their meat raw, a custom others found to be rather upsetting.

2 See Battiste (2000), Youngblood Henderson (2000), Wilson (1998), Mihesuah (1998), Smith (2000), Fixico (1998), and Champagne (1998) for critiques of Euro-centric research methods in Aboriginal communities.

3 For more information on some pedagogical and ethical issues of teaching in an Inuit community, see Piercey (forthcoming).

4 "Arviat" means "bowhead whale" in Inuktitut. The community got its name from the shape of the peninsula on which is it located.

5 Donald Fixico stresses the importance of incorporating external perspectives: "Combining the external perspective with an understanding of an inner perspective balances the equation, resulting in a proper study of American Indian history. Placing both perspectives within the full context of Indian life in relationship to the natural world is the ultimate goal in analyzing and writing American Indian history" (Fixico 1998, 94–5). In a similar vein, Duane Champagne (1998) argues that an Aboriginal scholar who has access to informants and knows the complexities of his or her own culture can contribute significantly to analysis and interpretation of Aboriginal history and culture. But he also argues that a non-Aboriginal scholar, through vigorous research and a genuinely strong interest in understanding Aboriginal culture, can also bring valuable insight to the analysis and interpretation of Aboriginal history and culture, provided permission has been granted by the Aboriginal community and the researcher follows ethical guidelines intended to alleviate exploitation.

6 See note 2.

7 "Amoutik" is an Inuktitut word for "woman's coat." These women's coats are modelled after traditional Inuit parkas. The woman's traditional caribou-skin parka differed from the man's in certain design elements, reflecting her maternal role in Inuit society. Infants were carried for the first two to three years of their lives in the roomy back pouch. The large hood allowed air to circulate to the child, and the wide shoulders permitted the child to be moved to the front for breastfeeding without leaving the parka's warmth and protection. The women's contemporary amoutiks show resemblance to the traditional style but are made from a cooler cotton-like material called "commander." Women in Arviat today still wear amoutiks to carry their children. There are many new and innovative styles.

8 *Qablunaaq* (also *qallunaat, kabloona,* or *kablukaaq*) is the Inuktitut term for white people. Its origin seems to be an Inuktitut phrase meaning "people who pamper their eyebrows" and can imply that these people pamper or fuss with nature or are of a materialistic nature and greedy.

9 Inuktitut is the Inuit language, although there are many regional dialects that may prevent Inuit of different regions from fully comprehending Inuit from out-

side their region. Inuktitut was an unwritten language until a Christian missionary, Rev. Edmund James Peck, taught many Inuit how to read and write using an Inuktitut syllabics system designed by Rev. James Evans in 1840.

10 The Kivalliq region is an administrative region of Nunavut. It consists of the portion of mainland west of Hudson Bay, together with Southampton Island and Coats Island. The regional seat is Rankin Inlet. Before 1999 the Kivalliq region existed under slightly different boundaries as Keewatin region, Northwest Territories. The hamlets in the Kivalliq region are Arviat, Baker Lake, Chesterfield Inlet, Coral Harbour, Rankin Inlet, Repulse Bay, and Whale Cove. The total population in 2006, as recorded in the Canadian census, was 8,348.

11 See Lutz (1978), Pelinski (1979, 1981), and Cavanagh [Diamond] (1982) for studies about music and stability and change in Inuit communities.

9

Moose Trails and Buffalo Tracks: Métis Music and Aboriginal Education in Canada

ANNETTE CHRÉTIEN

For many years now, I have been accused of being a storyteller by various parties. Whether or not that appellation is favourable seems to depend on the context and the accuser. Regardless, I wear the title of storyteller with pride, even though it does mean I am constantly shifting between what I call my "aca-talk" and storytelling modes in my work, writing, and personal life. The challenge I, and many other Aboriginal scholars, face is what storytelling can offer as a research method, pedagogical practice, and mode of communication as well as the epistemological issues surrounding different ways of knowing.

The website described in this chapter is part of an ongoing struggle to integrate different ways of knowing in educational practice, especially in relation to Aboriginal students in general, and Métis[1] students in particular. It was developed over time through a cumulative process involving various phases of research that I see as inextricably connected in my intellectual and artistic growth. The reasons I developed this website are somewhat more practical.

In the *Ontario First Nation, Métis, and Inuit Education Policy Framework*, the Ontario Ministry of Education cites the following as "overriding issues affecting Aboriginal student achievement": "a lack of awareness among teachers of the particular learning styles of Aboriginal students, and a lack of understanding within schools and school boards of First Nation, Métis, and Inuit cultures, histories, and perspectives" (Ontario Ministry of Education 2007, 5). This chapter and the web-based resource guide it describes address both of these issues with regards to Canada's Métis, particularly those in Ontario and Quebec. First, the learning styles of Aboriginal students are accommodated through the use of storytelling as a framework to explore three different Métis musical traditions, namely *miziksharing*,[2] *mizikcassée*,[3] and music and storytelling. Second, the stories through which these three traditions are presented serve as both teaching and learning strategies, as gateways to information about Métis cultures, histories, and perspectives.

The stories on the website move increasingly from a macro to a micro perspective in their depiction of contemporary Métis identities. The first story, about miziksharing, focuses on Métis histories and how they can differ depending on the community. The second story, featuring mizikcassée, highlights one particular community through this local practice, emphasizing diversity in Métis cultures. Finally, I use music and storytelling to provide some insights into the process of Métis self-identification on an individual and family level.

The title of the website, *Moose Trails and Buffalo Tracks*,[4] is a metaphor for the reality of contemporary Métis existence today, as outlined by the many different pathways Métis people choose to define themselves. It represents both the complexities of Métis identities and my mapping of them, which is to think of "being and becoming" Métis as a process, a journey, rather than an event.[5] I use the notion of trails as a model for mapping the process of self-identification as Métis on collective and individual levels because "trails can represent diversity without disconnection or division" (Chrétien 2005, 7). Throughout my research, trails have become "a useful way for me to analyze and discuss the relationship between music and Métis identities because trails are open-ended. They can move backwards and forward in time, and they can always take new directions. They are connected to, but not limited by, the past" (Chrétien 2005, 8).

Since official recognition of Canadian Métis as Aboriginal in 1982, many individuals and groups of people have self-identified as Métis.[6] Still, official recognition has not resolved the many questions surrounding Métis identities. The boundaries associated with Métis identities are complex and contested along geographical, historical, legal, and political lines, among many others. For example, terms such as the "historical Métis" and the "Riel/Real Métis" are connected to the Métis with Red River ancestry and the military conflicts of the nineteenth century. Other terms, such as "the Métis Nation," draw a political and geographical boundary at the eastern border of Ontario; Quebec Métis are not included. The full repercussions of official recognition of the Métis as Canada's third Aboriginal people are still not clear, even though some twenty-five years have passed since this important constitutional event.

Today, there are still many gaps in available information, ranging from demographic content to educational materials, about Canadian Métis. Existing research tends to focus on western Métis, the nineteenth-century military conflicts led by Louis Riel, and the buffalo hunters of western Canada. These "buffalo tracks" represent the contributions of western Métis to Canadian history, which are undeniable. In this chapter and the web-based resource guide, "moose trails" refer to the pathways that lead to many stories and experiences of Canada's "Other" Métis, those from more easterly places.[7]

Detailed demographic information about Canadian Métis, especially those east of the Manitoba border, has yet to be collected, interpreted, and distributed in a significant way. Indian and Northern Affairs Canada (INAC) cites the following statistics for Métis, based on the 2006 census: "the Aboriginal identity population reached 1,172,785 in 2006 of which 53% are Registered Indians, 30% are Métis, 11% are Non-status Indians and 4% are Inuit."[8] Difficulties in obtaining more nuanced statistics on the languages or national affiliations of the Métis population are partially due to the fact that the process of enumeration has yet to be undertaken in a comprehensive manner. Furthermore, little research has been conducted on Métis communities outside of the western provinces and on how these communities might be defined differently from their western counterparts.[9] As discussed in more detail below, Métis people have only recently been included in developing Aboriginal policies in general and Aboriginal educational policies in particular.

More pertinent to this chapter, there is a dearth of educational materials dealing specifically with Canadian Métis people east of Manitoba. The specific purpose of this chapter and the website is to heighten awareness and deepen current understandings of Métis in Ontario and Quebec, who are not often represented in the predominant narratives of Canadian Métis. The website is not intended to fill the many gaps in information about Métis people as much as to literally guide educators and students alike toward various resources that can foster a deeper understanding of what it means to be Métis in a Canadian context today.

In the first part of this chapter, then, I examine the relevant educational context, focusing on the relationships between Aboriginal education policies and Métis studies and between music education and ethnomusicology. This is followed by a more detailed discussion of how the three musical traditions mentioned above are used on the website.

Finally, in today's world, new media are playing an increasingly important role in negotiating and constructing both contemporary Métis identities[10] and web-based technologies in Aboriginal education. But it is important to note that not all Aboriginal students have access to Internet technologies or the knowledge to use them – or the interest, for that matter. With these caveats in mind, this work can inform anyone who might be interested in Métis cultures, histories, and perspectives east of Manitoba, particularly those of Ontario and Quebec.

The Educational Context

Aboriginal Education and Métis Studies

Aboriginal educational reform in Canada is complicated by the fact that Aboriginal students are educated in a number of different contexts, including federal, provincial (public and separate), and band schools, not to mention issues arising from the damaging legacy of residential schools. Despite the significant challenges posed by these various educational contexts, Aboriginal education and educational policies in Canada have changed substantially in the past forty years or so.

There is a growing body of literature, policies, programs, strategies, and initiatives dealing with Aboriginal education. For example, the literature on Aboriginal education includes historical overviews focused on the development of Aboriginal educational policies,[11] case studies of successful strategies and initiatives,[12] and more recent documents dealing specifically with Aboriginal pedagogy and epistemological issues.[13] It is well beyond the purview of this chapter to provide a detailed analysis of all these materials, but certain benchmarks and recurring issues are relevant to Métis-specific educational issues and challenges.

The development of Aboriginal educational policy began in earnest after the *Indian Control of Indian Education* (*ICIE*) policy was introduced by the National Indian Brotherhood (NIB), now the Assembly of First Nations (AFN), in 1972.[14] As a reaction to the assimilative intent of the Canadian government's 1969 *White Paper on Indian Policy*, the *ICIE* policy identified four major points: (1) responsibility, (2) programs, (3) teachers and counsellors, and (4) facilities. The *ICIE* policy was accepted by Canadian governments and was one factor that helped to successfully prevent the integration attempts of the *White Paper*, but since then progress has been slow in terms of meeting the educational needs of Aboriginal communities. Jurisdictional confusion, lack of adequate funding, and inappropriate legislation continue to inhibit implementation of the major points identified in the *ICIE* policy, most of which are still relevant today. For example, the major reports that followed the policy are remarkably similar in identifying the same major issues around Aboriginal education, including the AFN's *Tradition and Education: Towards a Vision of Our Future* (1989); the accompanying government response, the *MacPherson Report on Tradition and Education: Towards a Vision of Our Future* (MacPherson 1991); and *Gathering Strength*, volume 3 of the *Report of the Royal Commission on Aboriginal Peoples* (1996b). As noted by David Bell, "that the parties most concerned with the education of Aboriginal children in Canada have agreed on what needs to be done for the past thirty years invites the question, 'Why hasn't there been more progress?'" (Bell 2004, 33).

In 2007 the Ontario Ministry of Education released the *Ontario First Nation, Métis, and Inuit Education Policy Framework*. It states, "There is a significant gap between the educational attainment of the Aboriginal population and that of the non-Aboriginal population. Forty-two per cent of the Aboriginal population in Ontario, aged 15 years and over, have less than a high school diploma, and only six per cent have completed a university degree" (Ontario Ministry of Education 2007, 35). As noted in the *Policy Framework*, one of the most pressing issues in addressing these dismal statistics is the urgent need for more appropriate curriculum and educational materials dealing with Aboriginal histories, cultures, and perspectives.

Although recent educational policy shifts seem to point the way to a more balanced and inclusive education framework, much more detailed research and consultation needs to be done before such lofty ideals can be attained, especially when dealing with Métis people. Notably, most of the studies and policies mentioned above do not specifically address Métis issues and perspectives. Since the Métis were recognized as an Aboriginal people only in 1982, early policies did not explicitly include our needs.

Despite recent initiatives in Aboriginal education, a more comprehensive image of Canada's Métis people in their diversity, especially those outside of the western provinces, is still lacking.[15] There are many indications that the educational experiences of First Nations and Métis people are significantly different in some ways and similar in others. For example, European ancestries facilitated the education of some Métis through the fur trade educational systems. Alternately, some Métis people were sent to residential schools.

Detailed research on Métis educational contexts has yet to be conducted, but there is no doubt that the experiences of Métis are further complicated by their multiple ancestries. Furthermore, since Métis students are more likely to be educated in urban mainstream school systems, there is far less support for them to self-identify as Aboriginal. Developing a framework for an Aboriginal educational policy that is effective for Métis people requires a deeper understanding of the specific issues facing Métis people today in defining themselves. The emerging field of Métis studies reflects this urgent need for a deeper understanding of Métis histories, cultures, and perspectives throughout the country.

The burgeoning field of Métis studies faces many challenges, especially in terms of representing Métis people east of Manitoba, who continue to be marginalized in a number of ways. For example, current educational strategies and initiatives in Ontario focus mostly on First Nation communities. As stated in the Métis Nation of Ontario's *Report on Ministry of Education Draft Aboriginal Education Policy Framework*, "it was noted that Métis specific educational issues and the Métis Nation remains largely absent from the overall framework" (Métis Nation of Ontario 2006, 4). The absence of Métis-specific content is evident in the Ontario Ministry of Education's recently implemented "Native Studies program," which is aimed at First Nations communities at the high school level.[16]

Official recognition has also prompted more research about Métis people, but much of this research remains focused on the western Métis, especially the political community known as the Métis Nation. Of particular note are the efforts of the Gabriel Dumont Institute, which has been developing Métis-specific educational resources and curriculum for western Métis for many years.[17] Other Métis studies programs can also be found at various universities, usually as a minor within a First Nations or Aboriginal course of study, but these too focus on the histories and cultures of the western Métis.[18] As noted by Frits Pannekoek, "The real future in Metis studies lies not in Red River, or in the early North West, rather it lies in determining the roots of the new Metis consciousness of today" (Pannekoek 2001, 116).

Finally, Métis music in Ontario has yet to be considered a useful way to learn about Métis cultures, histories, and perspectives, an approach that seems to have been adopted by other provinces in developing and integrating Aboriginal curriculum and educational reform.[19] For example, the Shared Learnings Program in British Columbia incorporates Aboriginal music in the province's K–10 curriculum. Similarly, the Gabriel Dumont Institute has sponsored a number of music-education initiatives focusing on Métis music.

Music Education and Ethnomusicology

In the summer of 2000, I was hired by the Aboriginal Teacher's Education Program (ATEP) at Queen's University to teach prospective Aboriginal educators working in remote communities how to teach music at the elementary school level. I was clearly instructed to teach these students how to meet the criteria established in *Ontario Curriculum, Grades 1–8: The Arts* (Ontario Ministry of Education 1998), *but* I was to teach the music curriculum in a "traditional Aboriginal way." Many of the students came from remote northern Ontario communities. I soon realized that despite the fact that I had learned to play music in a Métis context as a child, had received extensive training in classical music, and had taught music for years at many different levels, there was nothing "traditional" about trying to teach Aboriginal students how to read western European musical notation or to embrace western European values. I even tried "Doe, a deer, a female deer" to teach my students how to write a major scale, only to discover that many of them had never even heard of Julie Andrews or *The Sound of Music*.

This personal anecdote points to the difficulties of integrating Aboriginal ways of knowing and learning styles in an educational system steeped in western European traditions, especially with regards to music education. Another stumbling block I encountered in this educational context was the reluctance that potential teachers from small and remote Aboriginal communities expressed about integrating their local, traditional musical practices in the classroom. Many of the students shared with me that their elders were still influenced by the belief that their Aboriginal traditions were "pagan." I was surprised by the ongoing impact of the Christian Church in these communities. My suggestion that teachers try to include their local elders and musicians in their music programs was met with much resistance, if not outright refusal.

The challenges described in this personal anecdote raise some important questions about the goal of music education and its relationship to ethnomusicology. For example, is the purpose of a cross-cultural music curriculum to teach students how to "make" the music themselves? If so, what kinds of music are they expected to learn? In the case of integrating Aboriginal music forms in the classroom, is the purpose to learn about a musical culture in a broader sense, such as music as social or spiritual practice? Or, if the goal is to learn a particular musical style associated with an Aboriginal culture, are there issues of cultural appropriation that need to be considered?

In recent years, teaching music from a cross-cultural perspective has prompted a move toward integrating the theories and methods of music education and ethnomusicology (Stock 2003, Szego 2002). Since this chapter is not intended as a survey of research trends in music education and ethnomusicology, I limit my comments to the specific initiatives and issues that inform my work and the development of the website, with a particular emphasis on how music education has been used in teaching about Métis-specific subjects.[20]

Until fairly recently, it would seem that "music educators have generally paid much more attention to the ethnomusicological literature than ethnomusicology has to music education" (Szego 2002, 724). The question of how to adapt ethnomusicological work to educational ends has been addressed by a number of scholars in various ways. For example, in her assessment of qualitative research in music education, Kathryn Roulston identifies three areas of research that are relevant to my website design: "life history and autobiography, autoethnography, and narrative inquiry" (Roulston 2006, 158–9). According to Roulston, life histories and autobiography can provide some insights into the perspectives of others, an emic perspective through research that is focused either on the researcher or teacher or on other individuals.[21] Ethnomusicologists have explored musical life stories for similar reasons.[22] Although some life histories and autobiographies of prominent Métis people have been produced, these are not focused on musical life stories.[23]

My use of life histories, autoethnography, and narrative inquiry is somewhat different in that I focus on the individual and personal experiences of the students rather than on those of the teachers or professional performers and musicians. As discussed in more detail below, I encourage students to learn about Métis culture through exploring their own experiences and musical culture. My "inside-out" approach is intended to sensitize students to Métis ways of making music, and to the various meanings associated with these practices, by encouraging them to explore their own values and understandings of how music helps to define them on a personal level. The site is not devoted as much to traditional Métis music as to the many different traditions of making music in Métis communities. This distinction is particularly important since the site is interdisciplinary in its content and educational approach. It can be used as much to teach about history and writing as to teach about musical concepts and multiple perspectives.

Métis musical practices have been used in a tokenistic way to teach about Métis and Canadian history for some time.[24] However, these earlier works were fraught with problematic styles of representation, which tended to homogenize and stereotype Métis people and their musical practices. For example, the publication of Métis songs can be traced back as far as the late nineteenth century.[25] In keeping with the scholarly practices of the day, these early publications included only lyrics without musical transcriptions. Furthermore, the lyrics to Métis songs were corrected to standard French, given that the Métis language of Michif-French was considered an aberration – a corruption of the French language.[26] The web-based resource described below is intended to address the lack of information about Métis histories, cultures, and perspectives through the use of storytelling as a framework to explore eastern Métis musical practices and identities.

Moose Trails and Buffalo Tracks

Moose Trails and Buffalo Tracks is a web-based resource guide that revisits the tradition of using Métis musical practices to teach about Métis histories, cultures, and perspectives. The website represents the journey of past, present, and future Métis identities. The three stories featured on the site guide educators and students along the various pathways of contemporary Métis experiences, which are presented using storytelling as a framework.

My approach is intended to sensitize the readers and listeners to the *process* of being Métis on collective and individual levels. With this in mind, the homepage features a series of images that move from right to left and east to west, thus representing the direction of the early development of Métis communities. The site moves toward understanding contemporary Métis identities by beginning with early Métis histories, then looking at a more localized and regional understanding, and finally ending with an individual and more personalized account of the process of self-identification as Métis. The east to west direction also represents the path of life in many Aboriginal belief systems, including that of many Métis. Figure 9.1 shows what the homepage looks like, with "Home" marking the beginning of the journey.

As a starting point, the "Home" icon provides a brief description of the Métis, how to navigate the website, and how to use it as an educational tool. The next stop on the journey, the "Teachers Guide," gives more specific directions on how to use the site effectively in the classroom. I explain how the links that are embedded in the stories lead to pertinent resources and student activities, some of which can serve as individual lessons about Métis people, and also explain the meanings associated with the musical traditions featured on the site.

My instructional strategy is fairly simple, at least on the surface. I instruct the educators to "pick a link, any link." My open-ended approach is intentional: it reflects the nature of storytelling, which can take many

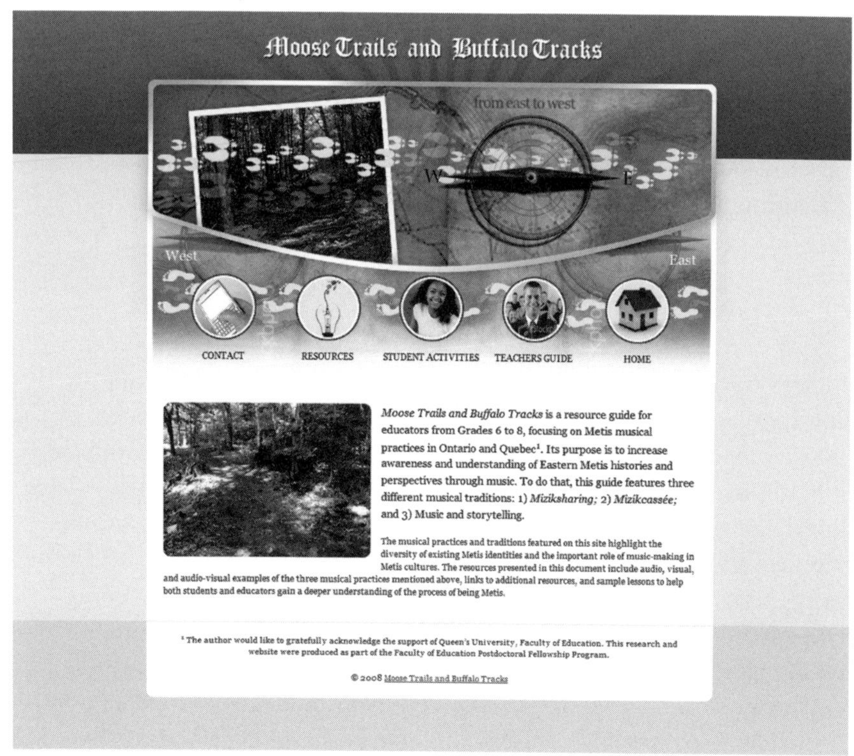

9.1 Homepage of *Moose Trails and Buffalo Tracks* website.

directions, and it provides educators with a broad spectrum of choices so that they can select resources best suited to the needs of their particular class and educational environment. Any word, term, or expression drawn from the stories will guide educators and students to a valuable resource, lesson, or activity about some aspect of Métis histories, cultures, or perspectives. Each of these links can also serve as a lesson in subjects ranging from history to music, storytelling and writing, language, and so on. The permutations are endless, thus enabling the teachers to decide how, or whether, they wish to integrate the materials into their curriculum. Or teachers can let their students surf, choosing what they would like to learn about or study with regard to Métis issues. In today's world, students are far more likely to spend time surfing the Internet, where they can explore new sights and sounds, than reading a book.

The "Student Activities" section features the three stories about mizik-sharing, mizikcassée, and music and storytelling. The first two stories are provided in text and are intended to be read, but they also include audio and audio-visual examples. The last story is aural and needs to be listened to. Each of these stories is described in more detail below. Finally, the resource section on the website provides details and annotations about each of the links used in the stories, as well as many useful links to other resources about Métis people. It also includes a selected annotated discography and bibliography.

Miziksharing and Métis Histories

"Miziksharing" is the term Vic "Chiga" Groulx, a Métis elder from Mattawa, uses to describe one system of Métis music making in this community. He maintains that the music the Métis play is defined by the ongoing *practice* of sharing. Groulx explains the meanings of Métis music making by relating them to various interpretations of sharing, including sharing as gift-giving, as communication, and in the transmission of intellectual, spiritual, and musical knowledge.[27] Furthermore, in Groulx' interpretation, miziksharing is a way of making music that is rooted in, and guided by, the principles and beliefs he associates with being Aboriginal, including sharing, respect, and responsibility.

On one level, miziksharing can be viewed and understood as a local, historical, musical practice. But, on another level, it can also be viewed as a concept that can be more broadly interpreted and applied, which is the way I use it in *Moose Trails and Buffalo Tracks* to explore Métis histories. In keeping with the direction of the early development of Métis communities, the story of miziksharing emphasizes how the sharing of music from different cultures constitutes Métis music making as a historical practice through which diverse Métis histories can be better understood. To demonstrate, I use one example of miziksharing from Quebec in *Moose Trails and Buffalo Tracks*. The story begins like this:[28]

> There's a story that says that the Métis people in Canada started
> about nine months after the first Europeans came to *La Nouvelle*
> *France*. The Aboriginal people who lived here helped the explorers,
> the *coureurs de bois*, and later the *voyageurs*,[29] to find their way, and
> to survive. Usually, it was the Aboriginal women, our *First Nations*[30]
> grandmothers, who helped our European ancestors by teaching
> them how to trap and hunt. Sometimes they even got married *à la*
> *façon du pays*,[31] and that's how the Métis people were born, about
> nine months after the first Europeans came. At least that's what
> some people say.

The example of miziksharing I use on the website is a version of a French folksong called "Ah! Si Mon Moine." This version is still sung in French and Algonquin in the region of Maniwaki, Quebec, where the practice of mixing languages can be traced to the seventeenth century. The historical practice of alternating languages in this Métis community represents the particular relationships that contributed to its early development, the relationships between the French and Algonquin.

In terms of Métis history, the example of "Ah! Si Mon Moine" brings to the forefront the early history of Métis people during the seventeenth century and their connection to the history of Nouvelle France. This approach to understanding Métis histories challenges current narratives in some important ways, which are indicated and further explained in the "Teachers Guide." First, this particular rendition of the song represents the performance practice of mixing French and Algonquin, challenging the myth that such Métis song practices are dying or extinct.

Second, the links provide educators with a broad range of choices in terms of history lessons that can be integrated into their curriculum. In the "Teachers Guide," I provide some context for each link that indicates how current histories and sources of information tend to erase the presence and contributions of Métis people east of Manitoba. Voyageurs, for example, are usually represented as being French Canadian rather than Métis.

The music the Métis make in Quebec and Ontario is shared not in the sense of a fusion of various musics that results in a particular style but in the sense of producing a particular *way* of making music. Music is shared in an ongoing and fluid manner that constantly integrates many different influences, including more traditional practices and contemporary music. However, the underlying beliefs that guide the music making remain consistent. Miziksharing is the active, fluid, and ever-changing "practice of sharing music" rather than a "shared practice," in a fixed sense.

Moose Trails and Buffalo Tracks uses the example discussed above as a way for teachers and students to question their own musical values and associations and to learn how to create their own version of miziksharing. In the "Teachers Guide" I suggest two exercises that can help to guide the students toward a deeper understanding of Métis histories. First, I suggest that the students each keep a musical journal for at least one day. During that time, they are required to describe their musical environment by noting every musical encounter, the function of the music they hear, and the meanings they associate with each instance. Keeping a musical journal prepares the students to conduct further research on their own musical life stories and understandings through ethnography and autoethnography, which are featured in the last two stories.

Second, a sample lesson could consist of asking students to select excerpts of two musical pieces they might wish to integrate in a class performance. In creating their performance, the students could be asked the following questions: What musical values do the students impose on their creations? What musical associations do they make with their chosen selections?

Moving toward an understanding of miziksharing as a social practice can create awareness about how Métis communities develop, and maintain, their relationships according to their own beliefs. Furthermore, students will be more aware of the diversity of Métis people and will understand that local practices reflect local histories and experiences.

The Story of Mizikcassée

In *Moose Trails and Buffalo Tracks*, I use the story of mizikcassée (broken music) to demonstrate how local and regional musical practices can raise awareness and understanding about the specificity of Métis experiences and cultures through local practice. Here's a little bit of the story of mizikcassée drawn from the website:

> This is a story about *mizikcassée*, where it came from, and what it means, like why some Métis people make music this way. The name *mizikcassée* came from a Métis elder from Mattawa. *Mattawa*[32] has a long history going back to the 1600s when Samuel de *Champlain*[33] planted a famous cross there. It's still important in Canada's history. The Aboriginal people who lived there helped the explorers, and voyageurs find their way. The *Algonquin*[34] and Nipissing people were trading furs with the French. They sometimes got married *à la façon du pays* and that's how the Métis people in this area were born. Many Métis still live in Mattawa today. The people in Mattawa still celebrate their history with a big summer festival called "*Voyageur Days*."[35] Anyways, this Métis elder from Mattawa told me that "Métis music is *la mizikcassée, pareil comme not' parler*" (Métis music is broken music just like our language). He was talking about Michif-French, which is one language of the Métis people. There's not a lot of stories about Michif-French except for the stories that talk about how it's used in Michif-Cree. That's the Métis language of Métis people who live in Western Canada. You can even get lessons in *Michif-Cree*[36] online now. But, you can't get lessons in

Michif-French yet 'cause researchers say it's not really a language, it's just a dialect. Either way, lots of people I know in Ontario and Québec still talk Michif-French.

Notably, there is some overlapping and cross-over in the stories of mizik-sharing and mizikcassée. This is intentional, allowing the teachers more choice in selecting the terms they wish the students to address. For example, a lesson about voyageur history can be drawn from either the first or second story. The story of mizikcassée features the relationship of this musical style to the language of Michif as it was recounted to me by a Métis elder from Mattawa. His teachings focus on performance practice, which features spontaneous repetition and the reorganization of musical syntax, and on the inherent characteristics and defining features of both the Michif language and this style of Métis music making.

Many different reasons are given for the "broken" nature of Métis music making.[37] In northern Ontario I have heard some musicians say that one of the reasons the music is so irregular is that they would hear new tunes on the radio but remember only fragments. Since many Métis people were employed in the fur trade and logging industries, they would spend months in the "bush." While the musicians were in remote areas working, they would experiment with the fragments they could remember, thereby creating new versions of well-known tunes. The process of fragmentation, spontaneous repetition, and irregular phrasing allows the musicians to create highly individual versions.

To demonstrate how students can explore the musical characteristics and compositional aspects of mizikcassée, I use a traditional fiddle tune, "St Anne's Reel." I use this example because the story is presented through my own experiences in learning how to make music in this area as a child.[38] "St Anne's Reel" was the first tune I ever learned how to play. My own personal experiences in learning how to make music as a child inform my knowledge of the practice, but it is my training as a classical musician that allows me to see how this musical practice can be regarded as a compositional process rather than a fixed form. As a sample lesson on the website, I include a link to a MIDI (musical instrument digital interface) version of "St Anne's Reel," which is also available in printed form. In the story, I explain how the students can explore the style by creating their own versions of the tune. In doing so, they learn about musical concepts such as phrasing and form while still acknowledging the musical values that Métis players honour in their own traditions.

Finally, my training as an ethnomusicologist informs my use of mizik-cassée as a way of learning about the historical and social associations of this particular style. The fiddle played, and continues to play, an important role in the development of Métis communities and identities. For example, northern Ontario fiddlers were highly prized in the logging camps since they provided the entertainment on Saturday evenings; therefore, being an excellent musician could guarantee work. As one elder has told me, the first people to get hired in the logging camps were the good cooks and the good musicians.

Today, Métis fiddling has become a musical stereotype, often referred to as the "real Métis music," which is usually associated with western Canada. Presenting a local style from another area emphasizes that styles vary depending on the individual, the region, and numerous other factors. More important, in the "Resources" section, I provide educators with a number of links to various Métis organizations through which they can find the appropriate resources in their local or regional community. I encourage them to draw on these resources in order to inform their lessons about Métis people and musical practices in their area.

Finally, as another sample lesson, I suggest that students do an ethnography of their own family's musical heritage. Who are the musicians and songkeepers in their family? What does music mean to them? Are there historical connections in the music they make? What can they learn about other cultures through a deeper understanding of their own? This exercise sensitizes students to their own experiences so that they can understand how music constructs our sense of identity in multiple and profound ways. With this sensitivity, they can move toward understanding that the process of self-identification is complex, which is the focus of the third and last story featured on the website.

Music and Storytelling: Fresh Tracks

Self-identification as Aboriginal is one of the major stumbling blocks to developing effective and appropriate Aboriginal educational policies and curricula. Racism, alienation, and shame are among the many reasons that Aboriginal students may not want to be identified and recognized, especially in mainstream environments. This is particularly so for Métis students but can vary depending on where they are at in their own process of self-identification. Some Métis people have been raised with their culture, but many have been subject to a great deal of shame associated with their heritage, language, and culture. Furthermore, since Ontario and Quebec Métis histories, as well as many others, have yet to be written, Métis students in those provinces are quite likely not to find their own community's history in existing curricula, and they face further challenges in self-identification based on the privileging of western Métis identities. Understanding Métis perspectives requires some understanding of the process of self-identification as Métis in today's world, in different regions, and in various educational contexts.

An excerpt from *Fresh Tracks*, a one-hour radio program about music and Métis identities, is the third story featured on the website. As an educational resource, the show serves three purposes. First, it creates more awareness of Métis perspectives by highlighting the process of self-identification as Métis on an individual, personal, and family level. Second, it provides students and teachers with an example of how autoethnography can serve as a useful strategy for understanding this process. Third, it marks the distinction between writing a story and telling a story, emphasizing the importance of oral traditions in Métis cultures and how storytelling can be used as an effective teaching and learning strategy in the classroom.

Fresh Tracks tells the story of a Métis trapper, called Black Sam, a character based on my grandfather. After his death, Sam returns to earth to find his favourite lost song, a song he has forgotten because his family stopped singing it. He retraces his journey on earth and along the way meets many different Métis musicians who recount their versions of Métis history and share their music. My intention in *Fresh Tracks* is to represent Métis identities as diverse, fluid, and ongoing. To do that, I build on the stereotypes and boundaries often associated with Métis music and people and juxtapose them with the identity constructs presented by the many people whose stories are featured in the show. The show reflects the complexities of the process of self-identification as Métis and the important role music plays in this process.

Only the first segment of *Fresh Tracks* is presented on the website. It serves as an example of how autoethnography can be used to create awareness of how musical choices inform our sense of identity. Since *Fresh Tracks* is based on my own experiences and my family history, it also constitutes a reflexive approach to research, learning, and teaching. One sample lesson on music and storytelling uses my approach in *Fresh Tracks* as a template, a technique, and a methodology, encouraging the students to create their own musical stories based on their individual experiences and cultural backgrounds. It could include writing a short narrative about their favourite song or musical piece with a focus on how and why their music is meaningful to them.

Second, the excerpt from *Fresh Tracks* is presented as an audio file only, meaning students must listen to the story rather than read it, which highlights the difference between telling a story and writing a story. The distinctive storytelling style I use as the narrator serves as an example of this difference. Given the paucity of published materials on the Métis of Ontario and Quebec, it also emphasizes that oral traditions are an important source of knowledge and information about culture, history, and perspectives in these communities.

Finally, the music and storytelling excerpt provides students with an example of how they might construct their own musical stories by drawing on the previous exercises, such as the musical journal and their family ethnography. In doing so, they can appreciate how music constructs their own sense of identity and, by extension, can deepen their understandings of how music shapes the identities of others too. Their own journeys and experiences serve as the vehicle for learning about others – in this case, about Métis cultures, histories, and perspectives.

Final Comments

The website described in this chapter is, like all of us, "a work in progress." It is intended to build connections and to address the issues raised in this chapter about the education of Aboriginal students, such as a lack of awareness of their specific histories, learning styles, and perspectives. Although my focus is Métis people, I believe that integrating traditional ways of knowing with new media and scholarly theories and methods can foster a stronger and healthier relationship between educators and students. My approach is to use storytelling in various ways, including as learning and teaching strategies but also as a research tool and methodology.

The importance of storytelling in Aboriginal cultures is well documented. Stories serve many purposes. For example, stories help to construct personal, family, and local histories. They also have epistemological value as a way of knowing and as part of the process of self-identification as Aboriginal. For Métis in Ontario and Quebec, stories are particularly important since the histories of Métis east of Manitoba are currently being written.[39] Furthermore, narrative inquiry can facilitate self-identification for all students, especially Aboriginal students.

It is impossible to measure all the impacts and repercussions of official recognition of Canada's Métis as an Aboriginal people since this new layer of identity and its accompanying rights are still being negotiated and determined. Nevertheless, there is an urgent need to at least acknowledge the historical erasure of Canada's Métis and to begin to rewrite Métis and Canadian history in a more inclusive way.

Moose Trails and Buffalo Tracks serves a number of purposes. As a resource guide, it begins to address existing gaps with regard to basic knowledge of the existence of Métis people east of Manitoba. As an educational tool, it can help educators and students to find new ways to think about who Métis people are and how some Métis people define themselves. Finally, I hope that by providing some basic information dealing specifically with the "Other" Métis, the website can help us to explore better ways of understanding Métis cultures, histories, and perspectives.

NOTES

This chapter is drawn in part from the author's doctoral dissertation (Chrétien 2005).

1 There is no standardized use of the accent in the word Métis, but I prefer its inclusion, seen throughout this volume, since it reflects my French/Métis background.
2 *Miziksharing* is a Michif word that literally means "music sharing." It also refers to how music is shared as a social and spiritual practice. The deeper meanings of the term are discussed in more detail in a later section.
3 *Mizikcassée* means "broken music" and also refers to a local style of music making.
4 The *Moose Trails and Buffalo Tracks* is at http://resources.educ.queensu.ca/moose_trails_buffalo_tracks. Please note that although this site is live, it is still under construction. Specifically, some audio and audio-visual materials are pending permission of the performers. The author would like to gratefully acknowledge financial support for the development of this site from the E-Learning Incentives Program of the Faculty of Education at Queen's University.
5 The expression "being and becoming" is drawn from Jacqueline Peterson and Jennifer Brown's *The New Peoples: Being and Becoming Metis in North America* (1985). I use it here in a different context. Their work traces various historic paths to Métis identities in western Canada. I am more concerned with how historic paths are connected to contemporary Métis identities.
6 In 1982 the Canadian Constitution was patriated, and the rights of Canada's Aboriginal peoples were enshrined in the *Canadian Charter of Human Rights and Freedoms*. Section 35 of the Constitution Act states, "aboriginal peoples of Canada includes the Indian, Inuit and Metis peoples of Canada."
7 For more details on the various meanings associated with the "Other" Métis, see Chrétien (2008). Métis people in Ontario are connected more closely to moose than to buffalo in many ways. For example, the first Métis Aboriginal right to be defined by the Supreme Court of Canada is found in *Powley vs. Regina*, a moose hunting case involving a man from Sault Ste Marie, Ontario.

8 These statistics are drawn from the INAC website, http://www.ainc-inac.gc.ca/
   pr/info/cad-eng.asp (accessed 24 February 2009).

9 Recent efforts to enumerate Métis have been conducted by the Office of the
   Federal Interlocutor for Metis and Non-Status Indians in the course of its identification of Métis communities. Most of this work has been conducted in the
   past few years and is only now being disseminated more widely. For more information, see http://www.ainc-inac.gc.ca/interloc/ofi/index-eng.asp (accessed 24
   February 2009).

10 Métis websites are growing exponentially. Most political organizations use
   the Internet to increase visibility and to communicate with members and the
   public at large. A few Canadian examples include the Métis Nation of Labrador, La Nation Métisse au Québec, and the Metis National Council. There are
   even some Métis groups in the United States who are claiming Métis identities,
   such as the New England Métis Nation. One site even deals specifically with the
   "Other" Métis. Each of these, and many more sites about the Métis, can be easily
   found through a simple Internet search.

11 See Castellano, Davis, and Lahache (2000) and Neegan (2005).

12 Bell (2004).

13 Binda and Calliou (2001), Friesen and Friesen (2005).

14 For more details on the historical development of Aboriginal education policy in
   Canada, see Kirkness (1999).

15 It should be noted that in recent years Métis perspectives from western Canada
   have been included in some research on Aboriginal education. For example, John
   Friesen and Virginia Friesen include a chapter on Métis education in Canada in
   their book on Aboriginal education (Friesen and Friesen 2002, 119–36).

16 For more details on curriculum development for Native communities, see *Ontario's New Approach to Aboriginal Affairs* (Ontario 2005).

17 For more details, see Dorion and Yang (2000).

18 See, for example, the University of Northern British Columbia,
   http://www.unbc.ca/calendar/certificates/first_nations.html#ms (accessed
   10 February 2009).

19 See, for example, *Shared Learnings: Integrating BC Aboriginal Content K–10* (British
   Columbia Ministry of Education 1998).

20 The author is aware that there are many current initiatives in Aboriginal education that use music and web-based technologies as a vehicle to teach a variety of
   subjects. Of particular note is Buffy Sainte-Marie's "Cradleboard Project,"
   http://www.cradleboard.org (accessed 12 November 2009). However, most initiatives are aimed at First Nations cultures. Alternatively, Métis-specific initiatives,
   such as the educational materials developed by the Gabriel Dumont Institute,
   deal with western Métis cultures, which is why I do not address them in great
   detail here.

21 Examples of the use of life history and autobiography in music education include deVries (2000) and Baker (2006).

22 One example is the "Telling Lives" section in Moisala and Diamond (2000).

23 The classic example is Maria Campbell's *Halfbreed*, which was published in 1973.

24 See, for example, Fowke and Mills (1960, 1984), Cass-Beggs (1967), and Whidden (1993).

25 See Larue (1863), Hargrave (1871), and Tassé (1878).

26 "Michif" is an umbrella term used to refer to the Métis languages. Michif-Cree has received the most attention in terms of linguistic research since it is a rare example of a mixed language, combining Cree verbs and French nouns. For more details, see Bakker (1992). Michif-French is considered a dialect by linguists and has received far less attention from researchers.

27 For more details on the relationships of miziksharing, see Chrétien (2002).

28 Here, and in the second story excerpt, italicized words represent links to other sites, some of which are included in the notes.

29 http://www.thecanadianencyclopedia.com/index.cfm?PgNm=TCE&Params= A1ARTA0008396 (accessed 24 November 2010).

30 Canada's First Nations are very diverse, and each has its own history. You can learn more about them at http://www.ucalgary.ca/applied_history/tutor/ firstnations (accessed 20 March 2010).

31 Excerpt from Sylvia Van Kirk, *Many Tender Ties*, 27–9, http://freepages.genealogy.rootsweb.ancestry.com/~goudied/ a_la_facon_du_pays.html (accessed 10 March 2010).

32 Mattawa history, http://en.wikipedia.org/wiki/Mattawa,_Ontario (accessed 24 November 2010).

33 http://mattawavoyageurcountry.ca/index.php?Itemid=39&id=27&option= com_content&task=blogcategory (accessed 14 February 2010).

34 http://www.kza.qc.ca/alg/AlgFlsh1.htm (accessed 14 February 2010).

35 Mattawa, Voyageur Days, http://www.voyageurdays.com/home.htm (accessed 24 November 2010).

36 Michif lessons, http://www.learnmichif.com/language (accessed 15 March 2010).

37 For example, Anne Lederman (1986) attributes the irregular musical characteristics of Métis fiddling in some Manitoba communities to the influence of the Ojibway language.

38 I was taught how to play the guitar by my uncle Ernie, who was a bush pilot and a hunting and fishing guide in Temagami, which is not far from Mattawa.

39 There are resources for Métis storytelling, but these do not necessarily deal with the "Other" Métis. See, for example, http://www.native-languages.org/ michif-legends.htm (accessed 1 December 2008).

10 

One Strong Woman: Finding Her Voice, Finding Her Heritage

INTERVIEW: BEVERLY SOULIERE WITH ANNA HOEFNAGELS

The following is comprised of excerpts from an interview with Beverly Souliere, Algonquin musician and lead singer of the award-winning women's hand-drumming trio Women of Wabano, based in Ottawa, Ontario. The interview took place on 29 May 2007 and covered a variety of topics, including Beverly's personal journey, her ongoing activism within the Aboriginal community, and her various roles as a musician in Ottawa. This conversation illustrates the vitality of Aboriginal traditions in a modern urban setting in Canada and the important roles that female musicians have in contemporary cultural expressions.

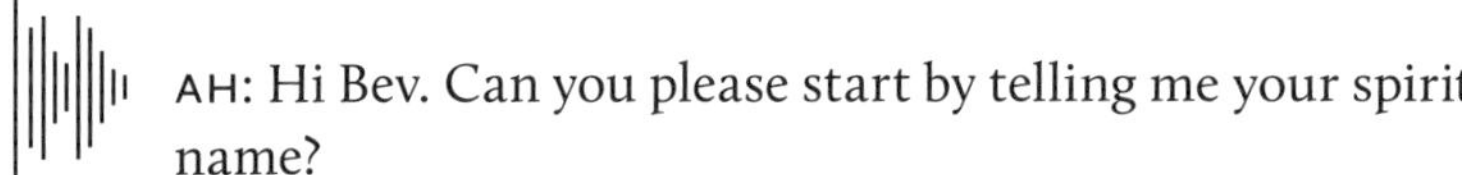 AH: Hi Bev. Can you please start by telling me your spirit name?

BS: My spirit name is Manido Taji Memengwe Kijkwe. Manido (Spirit) Taji (of the) Memengwe (Butterfly) Kijkwe (Honoured Woman). Spirit of the Butterfly Honoured Woman.

AH: How did you learn the repertoire that you perform?

BS: By going to ceremonies. Let me give you a bit of background history on my heritage. My father was ashamed of his heritage, so I was raised believing that I was French. I didn't go to French school, I went to English school, but my father insisted that that's what his heritage was. And

throughout the course of my life, everywhere
I went people would ask me if I was Indian.
And every time it happened, I would go
home and I would ask my dad, "is there any
Indian blood in our family?" And he would
get angry, like literally red-faced angry, in-
sisting that there was no Indian blood in
our family. After a few times of asking this
and seeing his reaction, I just ... as a kid you
don't understand why people are angry ... I
didn't understand why that made him angry.
I believe that ... he was showing me passion
about being convinced that this was the
truth. So I just took it as the truth that there
was no Indian blood in my family. So when
people would ask me, I would just say "no."
But as I got older and I started to understand

10.1 Beverly Souliere.
Photograph courtesy of
Beverly Souliere.

differences in the way people look, I started to realize that I didn't quite
look the way my classmates did ... and I was always darker. And people
would also ask me, when I'd say that I wasn't Indian, they would say, "are
you Italian or Lebanese?" They were trying to connect the golden colour
of my skin. Of course, it was "No, no."

At a certain point I guess I just realized that for whatever reason my
father was ashamed, was covering up, and I decided to just accept that
there was Indian blood and move forward based on that premise. So I
did. I was living in Timmins at the time, going to school, and I was in
my early thirties, I am forty-nine now, and I started to hang around with
Aboriginal people and go to the Friendship Centre that was there, keeping an eye open for ceremonies when they occurred and participating. I
participated in all kinds of things, sweat lodges, spirit feasts, gatherings
of all different kinds. And through the Friendship Centre they would
bring up elders, teachers from all over Canada, and I'd go and listen
to what they had to say. So slowly over the course of the following ten
years, I just educated myself. Initially it was in Timmins and I was learning about Cree culture, but also elders were coming from all over the
place, so I was getting little bits and pieces of Ojibwa, of Cree, of Dene
culture, all different teachings. But there is a thread of similarity that
runs through all of them.

Then I moved here to Ottawa and of course the Archives are here,
so I started to do some more in-depth research and I started to date an

Aboriginal woman. And I brought her home to meet my father, who at that time would have been about eighty-four, and we were not in his house five minutes ... and he said, "I have something that I need to tell you, that your siblings don't know." I said, "What's that?" He said, "my father was a half-blood." So it was eighty-four years before he admitted ... and I at that point was now in my early forties. But he didn't know that I had been doing all this research and all this work, because he would get angry whenever I would mention it to him in childhood, and growing up I just decided that as an adult I had my own path to walk and it was okay if I diversified from what my family was doing, and I just gave myself permission to immerse myself in the culture, which I did. So I went to ceremony, I went to powwows, I went to full-moon ceremonies, I attended sweat lodges, and at all of those things ... At all of those ceremonies, the gatherings, there was always singing. At every single gathering, because at every gathering of First Nations people there is prayer. Sometimes the prayers are verbal, but in conjunction with songs. In the same way that Christians sing hymns, First Nations people's songs are their prayers. And there are certain prayers that are sung at certain ceremonies, so I got to hear them over and over again.

In the early nineties, when I first started to go to ceremony, I attended a winter solstice ceremony. I am a guitar player and a singer, and everybody knew that I sang and I had a good voice ... I put out a CD I think in '96; this would have been before '96, but people knew that I was a singer. So I went to the ceremony and three women came and grabbed me and said, "we want you to drum with us. We want to sing a certain song during the ceremony, and we want you to sing with us." So they grabbed me, and it was at somebody's home. So we went upstairs into one of the bedrooms, closed the door; they stuck a drum in my hand and they taught me this song called "Meegwetch Notowinon." Now it's a very simple song, it's got just those words "Meegwetch Notowinon," which is sung three times, and then there is a bit of a chant. "Meegwetch Notowinon" means "Thank you our father." So they taught me this song very quickly and we sang it a couple of times, and then back down to the ceremony, a pipe ceremony. We did other things, a smudge and prayers. And it came time to sing this song and I couldn't remember it, I mean I had never heard it before I got there, and they sang it to me a couple of times, but I was so nervous. I was just so really frightened to make a mistake, and I had never played a drum before, and I just botched it. I just botched the whole thing and I was so profoundly embarrassed that I swore I would never touch another drum as long as I live. I thought that as a musician I should be able to handle this, and the song was simple: "Meegwetch No-towinon, Meegwetch Notowinon, Meegwetch Meegwetch Meegwetch." Those are the words, and I couldn't get it right. I guess because I was nervous. So over the course of the next twelve, fourteen years, I attended ceremonies and I … you know, you sing the songs and nothing is written down, but you know there is somebody in the circle across from you who knows it, so you watch their mouth and you do your best to sing along with them. But over the course of the years, I guess some of them stuck. But I didn't know that they had.

So now in early 2000 I moved to Ottawa and I was working at Wabano [Centre for Aboriginal Health], and they had a drum-making workshop [one weekend] and I was encouraged to attend as an employee … And I thought, "oh what the heck, why not? I can always hang it on my wall or use it to sing prayers at personal ceremonies." So I went to this drum-making workshop and it was one of the most profoundly spiritual experiences of my life, 'cause I made the drum from scratch. Literally I scraped the hair off of the hide and took the trunk of a tree and cut it with an axe, split it down the middle, and then quartered it, and then took a half-inch segment of that and bent it around by hand. And they offered that if you wanted a really, really round drum they had a tire rim, once you got your piece of wood bent around to meet each other, you could drop it into the tire rim where it would spring back out but dry in that particular round shape. But I didn't want that. Because I wanted to really put myself into it. So I bent it by hand … We had been taught that traditionally it would have been put in the crook of a tree, you would find a "Y" in the branches and just jam it down into there and it would dry like that, and that's what I did. I made this fabulous drum that was not quite perfectly round, a little bit off centre, had a lovely tone … just had the most lovely tone, and I really had to work hard for it. Scraping that hide was just incredibly hard work, took the better part of a day and a half. But also I had to scrape the edge, or round as it's called, because when you cut the round off of the tree you end up with a slat of wood that was really too thick for your purposes, so that had to be shaved and we were using crude tools so it was really hard arm work. But it was so profoundly spiritual because …

AH: You did it with your hands.

BS: And you weren't talking to anybody while you were doing it, so you were kind of immersed in your thoughts and thinking about … what was this drum going to bring into your life, how will my life change as a result of being a drum carrier? I don't know … it is very hard to describe but it was just a very profound experience for me. So I made this drum and there was a woman in town who was hosting a drum circle once a week and I started to go to the drum circle, to sing songs, just a way for women to gather and practise their songs, learn songs. And about a month later I got a call from one of the women in the drum circle. She said, "I've been invited by one of the local big Aboriginal organizations" that was celebrating … probably Aboriginal Awareness Week, "and we're looking for drummers." And I said to this woman, "I can't, I can't come and drum with you." I said, "I've only had my drum for like a month." But she said, "What do you mean? You know the songs." And I said, "No, I don't know any songs." She said, "Well you know the 'Strong Woman's Song.'" And I said, "No I don't know that song," and she started to sing it. And she wasn't half-way through the first line, and I started to sing along with her. She said, "See you know it." And I said, "Well that's one song, I mean we can't just go there and sing one song over and over." She said, "Well, you know the 'Travelling Song.'" And I said, "No, no I never heard of that song." And she started to sing it. And sure enough within half a line I was singing it too. I knew that song too. She said, "See." I said, "That's only two songs." So this went on for another five minutes while she sang another four or five songs, and sure enough, I would identify that I didn't know them. What I realized was I didn't know the names of the songs. So I consented … I was nervous about it and then I consented. I said, "I will go and I will sing with you." When we arrived at this event, we drummed for an hour and a half straight and we did not repeat one song. I had no idea that I knew all these songs; they were embedded in me, I didn't even know their names but I had been sing-ing them for like fourteen years over and over at ceremony. I just didn't know what the name of the song was and so I couldn't start it. I couldn't be the initiator of the song. But I was blown away. I mean I had no idea that I had absorbed all of these songs, an hour and a half worth of music … that I was carrying around in me. I still couldn't start a song though … but I continued to go to this weekly drum circle and over a period of time I started to make the connection 'cause now I knew that I had all these songs. I just didn't know what the titles were, and therefore when I said a title it didn't call up the song in my head.

So I realized that because I had been raised nontraditional, in a non-Native community, in the education system in Canada (without having had any cultural raising – cultural upbringing at all), my brain had been hardwired into a certain way of learning. So I decided that I would write out all the songs that I knew. And it took me some time because they didn't just surface up in my head 'cause I didn't have titles for everything. But I started a little bit at a time with the songs I did know the titles to. And I would go to the drum circle, and sometimes we would sing a song and I would write it down right there. "What was the name of that song?" And I would write down just the first couple of lines to get that trigger, 'cause I knew the whole song but I just had no trigger to get the memory to come out. So when I finally wrote everything down, that's all it took, I didn't have to go back to this repertoire of written music and take that sheet of music and look at it to be able to sing a song, I had them all memorized. But I had to actually write them down for that … to solidify that last piece of information, which was the "Strong Woman Song" sounds like this, the "Travelling Song" sounds like this … all these different songs. And to actually be able to stand up in front of a group of people, name the song, and start to sing it. So I've still done that, I still have this repertoire of songs, and when I learn a new song it is one of the first things I do. I purposefully write it down, not so that I can read off of the [paper, but just] as a cue because that was how I was raised to learn things. I need a visual … it is almost like it brings it into reality for me, I can't explain it better than that … that's what it takes. So that's, in a nutshell, the basic history of how I came into the songs, how as a result of perceiving myself as a First Nations woman, realizing that I needed to learn more about the culture that had been lost to me, and spending … I mean that was in my early thirties, I turned forty-nine this past weekend so …

AH: It's been a journey.

BS: I am closing in on my twentieth year of absorbing teachings and learning songs, and I am now at a time in my life when I am able to impart these things to others [...] Although we delineate ourselves by our cultures – I'm First Nation, you're white, he's Italian, she's Greek, whatever, whatever – we're all tied in to being related to one another. In that vein, we all come from the drum. Whether it be African, Celtic, Aboriginal …

AH: It's a pretty universal instrument

BS: It is a universal instrument, and I think it taps into the spirit of everyone who hears it. I know that when I drum today people are moved by my abilities, but I don't think it's just my ability. I think the drum itself speaks to people at a deeper level, perhaps at a genetic level, as if the genes have retained the memory of the drum from their culture ... whatever that culture is. And it's not just Aboriginal people who are moved by what I do, but people from literally all cultures are moved by the drum. So we'll never really know what that's all about, but it's a reality. People are very strongly impacted by the drum and you see it most strongly in children who feel free to express themselves, who are drawn by it. If I pull out my drum around small children, two and under, they just ...

AH: Come to life.

BS: They flock. They just want to be near it, they want to touch it, they want to hit it. I remember myself as a toddler ... and this is something that I did on a regular basis, almost on a daily basis: I pulled all of the pots out of the cupboard, sat with a wooden spoon and banged on them. I just loved whacking on these pots.

AH: Yeah there is something therapeutic about that motion too, though, right? I think when you're hand-drumming or ... when you're hitting something, or striking something, there is something cathartic about that, kind of cleansing.

BS: Well, shaman[s] traditionally use the drum in ceremony to take themselves into an altered state and there is an energy. I think we don't know everything that there is to know about it because today's society is stuck on what can they see. But there is an unseen world, and our ancestors knew very clearly what that was all about and had very good words to describe it. A lot of our teachings have been lost. The drum is made from living things: the tree was once alive, the animal who provided the skin for the drum was once alive. And we know that everything living has that energy. I've been taught, in terms of traditions, that when you cut a tree down you don't kill the spirit of it ... The spirit of the tree, the spirit of the deer is still in your drum. Maybe those are not the right words to describe what is really happening, but those are the best words that we have. There is an energy about that instrument that draws people, and draws me as a player of the drum. I'll give you an example. There have been days where I worked the full day, eight hours, got off work, and I was absolutely exhausted, and I would go to Wabano to [work, and the other women in Women of Wabano] would beg me to drum with them. "Oh please, please ..."

AH: "Just one song …"

BS: That one song always turned into four or five but … "just one song please, oh please." And I said, "I'm tired, I worked so hard today. I just want to go home and sit in my underwear." But still … "Please just one song." So we would go into the boardroom, and often I didn't even have a drum. I would have to borrow Allison's … "You can use my drum … just sing one song with us." On about the third or fourth song there is a shift that occurs in the body, and I don't know if it is the endorphins that you are putting out because you're singing … I really don't know, I do not have the proper scientific language to explain what happens. But I can tell you that an absolute shift occurred, where I went from being utterly exhausted to fully energized, ready for round two. I would be ready to clean out the garage … like whatever, bring it on, I am ready to go. So I can go from severe exhaustion to absolute euphoria in like fifteen minutes. I have always labelled that as a medicine. I think there is a real medicine in the drum that heals you as a drummer, and when people today thank me, they come to me and say, "it was glorious, it was just amazing," and I always say to them, "Thank you." Then I say to them, "You have no idea what it gives me. You think you received something? I think I got ten times what you did. So I'm glad you liked it." 'Cause they will probably ask me, but again, but I am certain that I am getting ten times what any audience would receive by doing it, by singing the song and playing the drum. It's a phenomenal, phenomenal instrument.

AH: You were telling me earlier about some of your early experiences with women's groups. Is that something that is close to your heart?

BS: Well it's the root from where everything is born for me, my earliest teachings, and those women that I met during that time. They are very fond memories and it was a real bonding experience. Also to have listened to teachings over the course of those ten years that were all so positive. Almost all of the teachers I heard were women and all of their teachings were positive … teachings about children and their role in our lives, their wisdom, the wisdom of children and how they are little elders themselves and to not discount them, and let them be, and let them make noise, and let them be themselves, and not try to hush them and make them sit straight and still and quiet because it is not within their nature. I really received some wonderfully insightful teachings … and I was open, I was ready, I was listening. They transformed me as I was learning […]

AH: I know you perform a lot with different women's groups ... You have
Women of Wabano, but you also participate in some hand-drumming
circles ... what are the main reasons for you and for other women to participate in those music-making experiences.

BS: Well, you know women generally are disenfranchised in our culture, specifically Aboriginal women. And a very large part of the impact
of oppression is the loss of one's voice. And when I say loss of voice, I'm
really talking about, not just about not speaking, although that is certainly part of it, but knowing your place, and being able to say something as simple as "no," if you mean it, or "excuse me, but ..." You know?
We've lost our power, our women who are oppressed, have a tendency
to lose their power to do that. The drum has an amazing healing capacity to unlock that in a woman. To assist her to find her voice, basically, the voice that she's lost. And we do that, through the way the songs
are structured. They have typically a lead line that is sung solo and then
the rest of the group will join in and sing the rest of the verse. Generally
some songs are sung either four or seven times, to honour the directions, either the four directions – north, south, east, west – or the seven
directions, which includes above, below, and within. When a song is
sung, let's say four times, the lead line, the solo line, can be sung by a different woman each time. Now for a woman who's oppressed, who has
not been given permission to say "no," to all of a sudden find herself in a
situation where she's expected to sing a full line of music, solo, by herself, with a group of her peers, standing around her watching her, it is
incredibly intimidating. It's a very scary thing. And I can say that from
personal experience ... I mean, I'm a musician, but I told you about that
very first experience of the drum that caused me to not drum again for
another, something like fourteen years, it was so intimidating. I use myself as a model, to teach. The women come into the circle, so frightened.
They're so afraid of being judged. They're afraid their voice will stand
out amongst everyone else's, and you're singing alone in a group of ten,
twelve, fifteen people who are all looking at you; the thought that you
could make a mistake, that you could not sing it correctly, that your
voice is not as good as the other person's, all of that comes into play, and
works to your disadvantage in silencing you. And many women do, they
come into the circle and they refuse to sing that lead line, they pass it,
they look at the person beside them: "no, you go." And some will do that
for months before they take the risk. But ultimately they do, and that's
why I use myself as an example, to say, "don't let yourself wait fourteen

years to sing that lead line, because it could be yours today." And we all come from the same place, we all come from the same shame background, the same oppression, the same embarrassment, you know? It's okay to take a risk, no one will laugh at you here.

What we're doing here is a form of a prayer. You can't pray wrong! You know, who's going to say, "My prayer is better than your prayer"? What, because I have a better singing voice? The prayer that you're singing is not what's coming out of your mouth. It's what's in your mind, what the intent is in your heart at the moment of doing it. So the prayer is not at all about what's coming out of your mouth. And if you're singing a chant, who cares if you say "way-hay" or "hay-way" or "way-ho" or, you know, it just doesn't matter. It's the intention. And if your intention is pure, then your prayer is heard. And your prayer is the best it can possibly be for you in that moment. So just let yourself go and do it. It's an incredible teaching in letting go. Letting go of your fear, letting go of your worry, letting go of your embarrassment, and just embracing the moment. And we talked about that earlier, about the importance of taking risks. It all ties in. Taking risks, taking one risk here, leads to something else over there, to there, to there. To a whole new way of thinking, to a whole new way of looking at things, and it stems from finding your voice.

AH: So do you see the hand drum and that repertoire ... and performing with other people, with other women ... as a form of empowerment for a lot of women?

BS: Absolutely! Even in the case of the other members of my trio who do not perceive the drum the same way as I do, they still get the benefit. They still get that medicinal ... that turn around.

AH: And when you're talking about healing of others, do you see yourself as a role model for other women? How do you conceive of a role model? Is it kind of a way of showing off what you can do? Or is it a way of saying, "you can do the same thing as I'm doing"?

BS: Yes, I think more of the second. I think ... you know, whenever we see somebody that we look up to, and I think I can probably speak for you when I say this, that there are people in your life that you look up to whom you would aspire to be, but what you don't realize is that they come from the same humble beginnings that you do. And I think the real lesson is that we all can realize our goals. We allow our low self-esteem, we allow the oppression of society, we allow the negativity of the injured people who surround us to impact us in the same way that words impact … We are impacted by what we surround ourselves with and what we see. And if we're spending our day watching movies about criminals, gangsters, hanging out with people who are angry and using drugs, we are not living to our fullest potential. But I would suggest to you that a drug addict, a criminal in the justice system, someone who's in prison, has the same capacity to be a marvelous human being as the next person does. But it's their low self-esteem and everything around them that keeps them down. So we need positive models to inspire us to be greater than we are. Because we all have the capacity to be greater than we are. And we're all born these beautiful, perfect spirits, and we are shaped by the thoughts and words and actions of the culture that surrounds us. But what we don't realize is that we have the choice about how we experience life. Maybe in our formative years not so much, because we need to be fed and clothed by the people who are in power over us, namely our parents or our family units, whether adopted or families of origin. But at a certain point in your life, you can shake anything off and become who, what you want to be and go wherever you want to go and reshape yourself. We have the power to reshape ourselves through choice. And I think that's what I want to emulate in terms of role modelling when I'm up there drumming, because it's a form of prayer; it's something that impacts me physically and mentally and spiritually and emotionally in a positive way. And I can share that with others. Not only can I share it by performing for them, by singing for them, by thereby praying for them, but I can teach them how to do it too. And it transforms you; it takes you to another level, to another set of possibilities where you're stepping outside of your comfort zone, stretching as it were, and thereby growing.

AH: You use the term "strong woman" a lot. How do you define, or how would describe, what constitutes a strong woman?

BS: Well, I think that is probably different for different women […] I think that strong women could be anything from a single mother who raises six children on her own in poverty, to an executive director who provides excellent service to her community in the form of potentials for healing, you know, and everything in between. Doing a good act, doing a positive act, speaking positive words, doing things in a good way, is role modelling, no matter who you are. And I mean people who are not living their lives in a good way can still have moments of gloriousness, as it were, where they can express positive role modelling. A woman who's a drug addict but who truly loves her children and respects her children, in spite of her illness, is still role modelling something good and positive at the same time as she's doing something destructive.

AH: So are you making the correlation between role modelling and strong women? Is a strong woman a good role model?

BS: Yes. I think that what I'm saying is that every woman, regardless of where she comes from, where she is living, how she's living her life, has some spark of positive in her. Whether it's tapped or untapped, it's there. It's just to realize it and act on it.

11

Learning about and Supporting Aboriginal Music and Culture: A Personal Journey

INTERVIEW: JIMMY DICK WITH ANNA HOEFNAGELS

The following is an excerpt of an interview with Jimmy Dick conducted 10 September 2009, which is augmented with his own writings about his background and musical experiences. Jimmy is a Cree musician who has lived for many years in Toronto, Ontario, and who has been highly influential in Native music making in various Aboriginal organizations in Toronto, most notably the Native Canadian Centre of Toronto (NCCT). He is the lead singer of Eagle Heart Singers, a group of musicians that performs powwow music and participates in political rallies and ceremonies in the Toronto area. He has also been a cultural programmer at the NCCT, organizing and hosting workshops, ceremonies, and youth trips and offering cultural and spiritual guidance to many people at the NCCT and beyond. This chapter illustrates the journey of one Native musician who has sought out songs, teachings, and an understanding of Indigenous issues in Canada today and who has had, and continues to have, a profound impact on many Aboriginal people in Toronto.

 AH: I was hoping you could tell me a little bit about your heritage and your background.

JD: I was born and raised in Moose Factory, Ontario, located within the Nishnawbe Aski Nation Territory of James Bay. My mother came from Ontario and my father came from Quebec. And they settled down at the mouth of the bay there, to compromise. Both of my parents were

11.1 Jimmy Dick. Photograph by author.

Cree and we grew up learning the language. My parents had seven children and I was in the middle of them, three older, three younger. When we were growing up, my parents did some hunting and worked various jobs in our community to survive. We grew up a hunting family, and we learned how to live off the land, and we continued that until we were teenagers. And then we were put in school.

AH: Did you have a traditional Cree upbringing?

JD: Yeah, to a certain extent, not ceremonies and stuff like that, but mostly hunting and living off the land, providing for ourselves.

AH: Was music a big part of your upbringing, as a child and as a youth?

JD: Yes, my mother and dad used to sing songs every now and then, to help them along in life. And it wasn't until later on, around the time of high school, that I started to learn about my culture, in the early '70s, when I was exposed to other Indians besides us. [My family was] doing cultural stuff, but then when we got older it was more the spiritual stuff.

AH: And when you went to high school was it in your community or did you have to go somewhere else?

JD: During our younger days we were all put in residential school and my older brothers were in there longer than us younger siblings. We attended school in our community 'til grade 8 and then had to go south to North Bay to attend high school.

AH: Was that a big shock for you?

JD: Yeah, it was different. Because people were always challenging us for how smart we were, how good we were. It was a good and a bad experience. When I went to school in my community, the only person who was non-Native was my teacher. And then when I went to high school it was a whole different thing. I was the only Indian. Everyone else was white and other colours. So it was a bit of a shock.

AH: What did you do after high school?

JD: I ended up travelling around. I started meeting more people who were culturally oriented. My journey started back in 1975, when I was a teenager. Along the way, I experienced many things, which helped me out in my life.

AH: Did that become a goal for you, to learn more about your culture?

JD: Yeah, because that's what they expected of me in school, talking about Indians in Alaska, as if I know everything about them, or in Arizona, or the United States. Even though they weren't from my culture, there were differences, and everyone expected that [knowledge] from me. When I got out of high school, I decided to learn more about my culture and my heritage and that kind of stuff. And also about other Native people, and their stories and legends and music. I associated with people that were doing those things and involved in those things. And that's how I learned, by being around them and listening to them, and watching what they're doing. A lot of people from a lot of different communities were encouraging me and were always there for me.

AH: Can you tell me more about how you learned music? Did you learn some of the music that you perform now when you were a teenager or when you were a kid? Or was it part of this learning journey?

JD: Well, it all evolved from things I did in the past and in my pursuit to learn. And as I went along I met people that taught me drumming music and different languages of music, so that's how I learned.

AH: Now the music that you grew up learning about and that you perform now, is it Cree music, is it intertribal music, or is a bit of both?

JD: Both, because after I moved away from my community, I had to learn the songs from the South, from the West. But then as time went along I tried to retain my roots, and my language and our music. I was learning Lakota, Dene, Plains Cree, but it's different than my area, so I always continued to learn from my area. I always went home every now and then, and when I go back home I try to learn more songs, because some of the songs we've changed the music to. Because some of the songs I learned I shared with them, and the songs they knew they shared with me.

AH: So there's always sharing going on?

JD: Yeah.

AH: Can you tell me about how you got started with powwow singing and drumming?

JD: I was introduced to drumming and singing while I was in Timmins one time during my travels. I had no place to stay and ended up going to Treaty No. 9 offices, as I knew some friends worked there. Anyhow the place was closing up for the day and there was word going around that they'll be having drumming that evening. I waited around and sure enough the guys brought out the drum and began to set up. As they were talking they wanted somebody to get them some refreshments and asked if I can go get some for them. I agreed and rushed back with the drinks. As I walked in I could hear the loudness of the drum and the singing. I waited 'til the song was over, then brought the drinks over to them at the drum. One of the singers asked me if I wanted to join them and I agreed and sat with them. The guys told me just to keep the beat and it was an amazing experience for me. The drum session was two hours long but went by so fast and the next thing we knew it was time to head home. I laughed and told them, I got no place to stay, as I was from out of town. So one of the guys said you can sleep on my couch. So we went to his place and we listened to some powwow tapes before sleeping. The next day I caught the train home and was still feeling happy from being at the drum the night before. I arrived home and it sure was great to see my parents and my family and friends. I went to visit my brother and we hung out at his place. As we caught up on things he told me that they started a drum group on the reserve and that they were going to be drumming within a few days. I was surprised but happy to hear that and looked forward to joining them. My first drum session back home was great and it was good to know the good friends that formed that group from being out at high school down south. I began singing with them and we had fun and we went to some powwows. We formed a group to revive our traditional and spiritual ways of life. I stayed around with them 'til hunting season was over and I headed back to Toronto. I told my dad I was going to check it out for a few weeks. He agreed and supported me and told me to take good care of myself. I arrived back in Toronto and hung out with people I know and stayed with them. We formed a singing group and sang at many rallies and in the Native community. We also sang at prison socials for men and women. We began going to powwows and it was awesome and we had fun.

This is where my journey started and, when I began, many people shared and supported me, which was very helpful. I'm thankful for the many things people shared with me, which shaped me to be who I am today. I can honestly say that it wasn't an easy road to take, as you had to be determined to live life as a singer. There were many challenging times along the way. I suppose when I look back at them now, they were tests about me as a human being and if I really wanted to be a singer and live this kind of life forever. This lifestyle was at times hard to pursue due to surviving in the city with its high costs. At times I had to take jobs working at various places doing different fields of work. During time off work I learned more about the songs and teachings that go along with the drum. The teachings made me proud and made me determined to stay the path too. I started travelling to many places and met many people who were searching for the teachings of our culture. I began learning about the injustices our people faced within the dominant society where they lived. I educated myself about the issues and concerns our people struggled with and began to create awareness about them through drumming and singing. I also learned the many positive things our people contributed to society and I sought to educate them and the dominant society.

AH: How did you end up going from James Bay to end up in Toronto?

JD: Well my friend and I came down here to visit his sister. And so I told my dad I was going to tag along with my buddy to check it for a few weeks. But I ended up coming back and forth, travelling to different places, and then I came back here. My friend and I ended up at a rally at City Hall, and some people we met there, we ended up hanging around with them all winter. The family I stayed with adopted me and I stayed with them 'til springtime. It felt good to be with them, as they followed Native culture and spirituality. I learned a lot being with them and I attended many ceremonies and feasts with them. I also went to drumming socials with them around the city and at the Native Canadian Centre of Toronto. I met a lot of people during my travels. I spent time meeting people and got involved in the American Indian Movement. I learned a lot about our struggle and various issues and concerns our people faced in Indian Country.

AH: Did you get involved in some of the political activism that was going on in Toronto?

JD: Yeah, yeah. Everybody was inviting us to come drum at a rally or a conference – mostly [rallies about] treaty rights, that involved fishing and clear cutting, hydro-electrical projects, and nuclear projects. Things that involved everybody, you know?

AH: Are you still involved in some of these political rallies?

JD: Every now and then we go out and jam it out for people, if they invite us to come out and create awareness.

AH: Now when you say "we" who are you referring to?

JD: Me, sometimes I go alone, or sometimes I bring the whole group.

AH: And that's Eagle Heart, right?

JD: Yes.

AH: Can you tell me a bit about your experience with that group?

JD: We started back twenty-five years ago. And I was the third or fourth person who was invited to come and join. And we did that for a good nine or ten years, and then everybody started taking off to go work here

and there and people started wanting to do their own things in life. So
that left me with a drum. So I just continued it, with family. My kids
grew up around that. So then they learned it too.

AH: So when you started was there a home base for you guys? Like were
you doing that through the Native Canadian Centre?

JD: Well that was our affiliation. We had always gone there every week
to go sing, to take part in activities. So that was somewhat our base, but
mostly it was from home.

AH: Are you guys still performing?

JD: Yes, we are. And we're trying to do another recording. I think we got
about ten of our own songs. And then we'll use songs of other people
who let us use their songs that we've been singing for a few years and
people are identifying us with those songs. And those other songs
that we're going to sing from other groups, it's a tribute, because they
inspired us to continue on.

AH: Has the membership of Eagle Heart changed much over the years?

JD: Yeah, yeah. [Now it's] mostly my kids, younger kids, my nephew,
younger kids in the community.

AH: And is Eagle Heart still affiliated with the Native Centre or are you
guys kind of independent?

JD: We're kind of more independent now. But we still go there and participate in activities, and go drumming there every week at the socials
on Thursday nights. We've been doing that now regularly since '97.

AH: It's before that, wasn't it? Because I met you in '93.

JD: Yeah, before that we went there quite a bit but we've been regulars
since '97. But before then we used to go every now and then.

AH: I know when you worked at the Native Canadian Centre you did
a lot of cultural programming and music workshops. Can you tell me
about that?

JD: Well, when I was there, it was more about community development. My approach was to use our culture. That way people would relate to things we were doing and then start talking about other things that we were in need of. And all of that came together, the different programs that we did there, the drumming, the Gathering of the Drum event, and the programs for kids that they still continue there. And we worked with the elders. We'd invite different elders to come and do things there and they always asked me to help them out. And I worked with them doing different ceremonies, like name-giving ceremonies, or eagle staff ceremonies, or things like that. And then eventually being involved I started to learn more about doing those things and then I started doing those things myself. We used to take [people from the centre] every now and then to do a sweat. Even where I work now, I take them out to a sweat. And other times there'd be things for community members too.

AH: So do you do personal ceremonies for people too?

JD: Yeah, yeah. People like renewing their vows for marriage. I would bring my pipe over to their place and they would renew their vows that way, through the pipe. That's what I do. And one of the things, too, I used to do when I worked at the Native Centre was to take people to a Sun Dance ceremony. We used to drive over to Manitoba.

AH: So that kind of programming that you did, was that part of the Native Centre's mandate?

JD: Yeah, yeah. It was through my program department. And sometimes we took people to the Albuquerque Gathering of Nations Powwow; twice we did that. We had to fundraise, and we had to do that for the Sun Dance ceremony trip too, we had to fundraise.

AH: And why do you think it's important to have these kinds of activities and events for people to go to?

JD: I think that way they'll have an option, what kind of things they'd like to do when they get an education, and skills, to work, doing what they're good at.

AH: And do you think doing programming like that in a place in Toronto is a unique thing that you can do, being in an urban centre?

JD: Yes. I think so, definitely. I agree that you can learn a lot of things here, about culture, about dominant society. And how to work your culture into that.

AH: So how do you see your role in this?

JD: Like an intermediator, I'm the one that guides them along. Showing them what they might like to do, or could do.

AH: So when you teach about your culture, is music a central part of that?

JD: Yeah. That's another thing we try to tell people. This is what music does, it's really a healing thing. It comforts people, along with medicine, things like that.

AH: What kind of music do you perform with people, like where you work now and when you worked at the Native Centre?

JD: Well it's more, like if I do a circle, I'll sing songs that are part of ceremony, like ceremonial songs. And if we do spring unity, we do a social entertainment thing, like we'll do a drum and dance presentation, to create awareness about people and the environment.

AH: What kind of music is it mostly? Like do you use a powwow drum or do you mostly use hand drums?

JD: Both, we use the hand drum and the big drum. Both of them are pretty handy to have.

AH: Thank you very much for talking with me today and sharing your journey with me!

JD: You are welcome.

PART THREE
Cultural Interactions
and Negotiations

ANNA HOEFNAGELS AND BEVERLEY DIAMOND

The third section of this anthology includes texts that consider Aboriginal musicians in interactions with musicians from other (Aboriginal and non-Aboriginal) communities. It is not surprising that it is the longest of the three sections since intercultural contexts are the norm, not the exception, in the late twentieth and early twenty-first centuries, no matter what part of the world one might consider. Noteworthy, however, is the fact that some of the intercultural contexts addressed by authors in this section are often overlooked and underplayed.

This section begins with a reflection by Lil'wat composer Russell Wallace on collaborative processes in which he has been involved – with musicians from a variety of ethnocultural and aesthetic communities. This is a gentle, personal account, not an analytical appraisal. As such, however, it reveals how deeply embedded Native American musical practices are in a larger urban network of musicians. Wallace points to a future in which many issues will be rearticulated and renegotiated.

Dylan Robinson's chapter, "Listening to the Politics of Aesthetics: Contemporary Encounters between First Nations/Inuit and Early Music Traditions," focuses on privileged stage spaces where Aboriginal artists have increasingly been drawn into Baroque-style music events. Using both historical and contemporary examples, he looks at the power-laden relationships of collaborative performance, creating a typology that could usefully inform arts presenters in the future.

Although educators and social workers have written extensively about inner-city residents of Aboriginal descent, the role of music in the poverty-ridden lives of these individuals has rarely been considered. Klisala Harrison worked in one of the most economically depressed communities in Canada – Vancouver's Downtown Eastside – and considers how theatre in particular has been used there to articulate the reality of citizens in this community. She explores how Native musical structures and soundscapes are used alongside such disparate idioms as African American minstrelsy and opera. These theatre productions challenge conventional definitions of theatre genres, transform production processes, and intervene in a cross-cultural dialogue. She resists Homi Bhabha's notion of the "third space" as a "marginalizing" discourse and insists on viewing these theatre productions as part of an expanded mainstream. Segments of interviews that she has conducted with several of the participants in Aboriginal theatre productions are reproduced alongside her study.

A complementary perspective on cultural change from the opposite (east) coast of Canada is provided in an interview that Walter Denny Jr did with Gordon E. Smith. Although the Denny family is esteemed for its role in the revitalization of Mi'kmaw traditions, Walter is equally concerned with cultural interaction – in the Catholic Church, for instance.

Byron Dueck considers the importance of social context in assertions of Métis identity in his chapter, "'No Heartaches in Heaven': A Response to Aboriginal Suicide." He theorizes these spaces in terms of public intimacy, noting how style is a fluid discourse of Métis identity, but his theorization is far from abstract and disengaged. He explores how one artist addresses the tragedy of suicide in his community and his family, using a controversial strategy of offering a hopeful message through song to family members.

The mixing of Aboriginal people and immigrants has been acknowledged more in Canada than in the United States, given the official recognition (since the Canadian Constitution Act of 1982) of the Métis as an Aboriginal people. But many groups of Métis, people of mixed descent affiliated with different Aboriginal languages or life-ways and with varied European (or non-European) cultures, have often been homogenized or ignored. Marcia Ostashewski explores one such lacuna in Métis cultural history – people of Cree and Ukrainian descent. The "Uke-Cree" fiddler who is the focus of this chapter negotiates a fine line between parody and polish to assert a distinctive performative identity in the context of Ukrainian festivals.

Although hip hop cultures have emerged worldwide as a vehicle for articulating social issues, particularly those important to youth, the study of Aboriginal hip hop is still in its infancy. Charity Marsh's exploration of the Saskatchewan hip hop scene and its presentation of "bits and pieces of truth" brings the issues into the space of Aboriginal youth on the Canadian Prairies. She traces the role modelling of emcee Eekwol as well as the impact of projects aimed at social change (e.g., Prairie Roots, Roots of Truth, and various high school programs, one of which she facilitates at the Interactive Media Production Studios at the University of Regina). She demonstrates that the discourses surrounding hip hop culture in Saskatchewan are "incredibly contradictory and tension-filled," pointing to the importance of negotiation in this scene as in those described by Harrison, Ostashewski, Dueck, and Audet.

Véronique Audet also foregrounds social contexts in her consideration of Innu popular music in Quebec. Whereas earlier studies (Grenier and Morrison 1995b) explored how the fame of the duo Kashtin related to the growth of Quebec sovereignty in the 1990s, Audet looks both backward and forward from that decade, exploring an earlier history and a more recent articulation of Aboriginal identity in *la francophonie*. Interviews with key figures in the Innu popular music renaissance – Florent Vollant (co-founder of the superstar duo Kashtin) and Gilles Sioui (Wendat musician and theatre director) – provide a counterpoint to her interpretation.

The chapters in this section illustrate the importance and prevalence of cross-cultural sharing and music making in Canada at the start of the twenty-first century. They highlight the collaboration that is central to intercultural creativity, the careful negotiation of messages and media, and the variable performance modes and reception of Aboriginal music.

12 Intercultural Collaboration

RUSSELL WALLACE

In this chapter, I discuss some of the collaborative projects in which I have participated as a composer and producer of contemporary electronic music and as a traditional Lil'wat singer. I encourage readers to consider what "intercultural collaboration" is, and might be, in terms of sharing music, ideas, and meanings cross-culturally.

"Hey, wanna play?" was all it took on the playgrounds growing up. Most of the time, it worked, and each party played games enthusiastically. Upon growing up, games and play turned into collaborations, co-productions, and many other interactions described by words that have more than one syllable. The terms "intercultural" and "interdisciplinary" have become part of the musical lexicon that is taking shape in Vancouver and elsewhere in Canada. In a pluralistic society, inclusion is key to success and to ensuring that the society can move forward.

How is this inclusiveness taking shape in Vancouver? Many festivals focus on folk music, jazz music, new music, Japanese music, and Aboriginal music. There are also many courses on music from different parts of the world that are taught at the universities and colleges around town, but there are very few places that encourage collaborative intercultural works.

Being Salish myself (more specifically Lil'wat), I wanted to feel like I was a part of this society. My mother, Flora Wallace, always encouraged me to share our songs and to teach them to a wider audience. So I did. I have been working at the Native Education College for six years now and have been teaching Salish forms of music.

I have seen many projects that have embraced "cross-cultural" ideas, but the performances have been a you-show-me-yours-and-we'll-show-you-ours type of collaboration. What is true collaboration? I do not profess that all of my work is truly collaborative. Most of my projects have been negotiations, mediations based on Salish music forms. This is how I play. Mostly, it is because of a limit on time spent together. Really, it is me making a pitch, giving a Salish Music 101 class in ten minutes, and then proceeding to help create a piece in a few hours to perform the same evening.

My first intercultural collaboration was with composer, choral conductor, artistic producer, and community music educator Hussein Janmohamed. The two of us were commissioned by the Westcoast Sacred Arts Society to compose a choral piece for a World Peace Conference in 2004, which featured a visit from the Dalai Lama. Most of our time together was spent meeting and talking over lots of coffee. We talked about community, music structures, our parents, our childhoods, and everything in between. We finally started to improvise together, and eventually we built a structure from the improvisations. Then we layered the voices and put in lyrics for cultural reference.

This collaboration on "Gatherings" was truly intercultural. Each music tradition (Islamic and Aboriginal) was afforded a place in the composition and then given the opportunity to interrelate with the other. Each tradition was equal to the other. The two of us focused on what was similar in each tradition and utilized those elements. Janmohamed explains that the process "Aligns with my own cultural experience of sacred/spiritually inspired music." Elements like repetition, simplicity of tones, melodies, and rhythms were the foundation to the composition. Broader elements like community, spirituality, and connection were also built into the composition. Why are these important to collaboration? Janmohamed says, "Music is built around community, and community is built through and around music. Community participation is important."

Spirituality and connection also refer to the philosophy of Lil'wat music. The Lil'wat creation stories involve the people coming out of the earth and water; this is where we have come from. Therefore, our songs, voices, languages, and dance are rooted in the earth and connected to creation.

At the other end of the spectrum of intercultural collaboration was a composition with the Erato Ensemble. The Erato Ensemble is a chamber ensemble based in North Vancouver. Here was a case of coming into a rehearsal and giving a brief history of Salish music and providing a blueprint for a composition. "Qanimenskan Ku Tmicw" (I Have Heard the Earth) was a communal composition that involved me providing the musicians with four sections that incorporated the four basic song structures of Salish music (mimetic, narrative, expressive, and functional). We improvised music for each section and then assigned certain aspects to different musicians in order to indicate a start or end of a section. William George is one of the co-directors of the ensemble, and his enthusiasm for the collaboration made me feel more comfortable about the process. I did get nervous at first when I was asked for a score because I have a hard time switching to a language of lines and dots. It was necessary, because of time constraints, to establish the four sections and build a composition based on some kind of narrative. The four sections were "Earth" (where the cello established the key for the overall piece, serving the functional aspect of Salish music), "Creation of People" (where the mimetic aspect came into place – the sounds of the earth and water and creation of people bubbled through), "Contact" (where the narrative aspect came through as some of the instruments told the story of contact with Europeans and the gold rush soon after), and "I Have Heard the Earth" (where there was a recognition of the earth as a provider and in need of more respect).

Where did this fit in terms of intercultural collaborations? George says, "As someone outside of the Aboriginal culture, but one who has studied it, I found the experience enriching and satisfying ... in this event all the performers were outside of the culture and were guided by Russell ... we were all a little nervous about authenticity and that we might offend or look silly. But we were all very happy with the outcome, and it was one of the highlights of the [concert] program."

Collaboration can also be viewed from a sociopolitical perspective. Singer and *taiko* performer Linda Uyehara Hoffman has worked with the taiko community for a number of years in Vancouver. Linda and I have worked together on a few projects, and through these projects we have come to recognize the common social displacement of the Japanese and Aboriginal cultural groups in British Columbia and their shared connection to the drum.

Why do the different music traditions of different cultural groups work together so seamlessly sometimes? Hoffman explains,

One interesting realization was that the Japanese and Aboriginal cultures share a basic beat (for us, it reads DONdon, DONdon, DON-

don, DONdon), as well as sharing four-four [time] as the traditional
signature. Those shared musical characteristics allowed us to work
together easily. Also your being able to put one of your vocal songs
together with one of our drum songs was an eye-opener.

So joining with another culture that is also displaced within
the majority is very exciting. Melding our cultural experience with
yours increases our sense of strength in our identity as outsiders.
As well as being an inspiring musical experience, the collaboration
then becomes a political assertion of our cultural bond.

These three collaborations were specific to each project, but each established a connection in friendship, social philosophies, as well as cultural voices. With Janmohamed, the process and core philosophies of
each cultural group were discussed and included in the composition from
the start; with the Erato Ensemble, there was a sketch provided, and the
musicians added colours and dimensions to the final composition; with
Hoffman, each group played a song from its repertoire and found that the
songs meshed well when played together.

There is still segregation in the arts in Vancouver. However, funding
for collaborative exchange is increasing, and different cultural communities are coming together through music. The keys to connecting were
community, identity, participation, and experience. We name ourselves,
we play together, we remember other ways of playing, and we learn new
ways to play.

Wanna play?

13

Listening to the Politics of Aesthetics: Contemporary Encounters between First Nations/Inuit and Early Music Traditions

DYLAN ROBINSON

That Canada inaugurated the turn of the millennium sonically with music that integrated loon calls, Inuit throat singing (each categorized as distinctively "Canadian" sounds), and an organum by Pérotin might give one pause for thought. That such a striking convergence of pre-1750 European art music, often referred to as "early music," and First Nations and Inuit cultural practices has taken place with increasing frequency in Canada in the twenty-first century is yet more unusual.[1] As the following timeline demonstrates, however, these encounters evidence an interest by First Nations, Inuit, and non-Native composers alike to return to the musics of first contact:

- 31 December 1999, a radio broadcast by all members of the European Broadcasting Union. Composer Christos Hatzis's electroacoustic composition *Viderunt Omnes* is heard by an international audience. The work combines a recording of the Toronto Consort performing Pérotin's organum *Viderunt Omnes* with a recording made in Iqaluit, Baffin Island, of Inuit throat singers Angela Atagootak and Pauline Kyak "and other distinctively 'Canadian' sounds, such as the sounds of the loons" (Hatzis 2010).
- 18 March 2001, Sty-wet-tan Longhouse, University of British Columbia; 19 March 2001, Squamish Nation Recreation Centre. The Pacific Baroque Orchestra and baroque dancers Paige Whitley-Bauguess and Thomas Baird share the stage with S'pak'wus Slulum, the Squamish Nation Eagle Song Dancers.

- 2003 to 2007 (various dates), across the United States and Canada, Macau, Hong Kong, and China. The Tafelmusik Baroque Ensemble presents a concert titled *The Four Seasons: A Cycle of the Sun*, a project that adapts Antonio Vivaldi's Concerto No. 4, "L'inverno" from *Four Seasons*, to include Inuit throat singers Sylvia Cloutier and June Shappa of the group Aqsarniit, Jean Lamon playing violin, Aruna Narayan playing the Indian sarangi, and Wen Zhao playing the Chinese pipa.
- 31 March 2005, Canadian Broadcasting Corporation (CBC) Television's *Opening Night* broadcast. The documentary *The Four Seasons Mosaic* premieres. It chronicles the development of Tafelmusik's *The Four Seasons: A Cycle of the Sun* and "takes viewers on a world tour of European, Inuit, Chinese and South Asian music traditions."[2] It is subsequently broadcast internationally on BBC, PBS, TV5, and ARTV and is released commercially as a DVD in 2007 on the Analekta label.
- 13–14 March 2010, Église du Précieux-Sang, Winnipeg. A concert titled *Medieval Inuit* is presented by Camerata Nova, a choral ensemble specializing in the performance of Renaissance music. At this concert throat singers Madeleine Allakariallak and Sylvia Cloutier present songs passed down from elders Elisapie Ootova and the late Minnie Allakariallak, Madeleine's grandmother. The concert brings Nordic folksongs and art music together with Inuit throat singing and drum songs to stage an imagined historical encounter between the Vikings and the Dorset peoples.
- 8–24 April 2010, Theatre Passe Muraille, Toronto. Native Earth Performing Arts Inc. and An Indie(n) Rights Reserve co-produce *Giiwedin*, an opera co-composed by Spy Dénommé-Welch and Catherine Magowan. The opera follows an Anishinabe woman's struggle to protect her ancestral land in the Temiskaming area of north-eastern Ontario from railway expansion. The work is written largely in a neo-Baroque style and integrates Anishinabe singing with references to French Canadian folksong.
- 15 May 2010, Glenn Gould Studio, Toronto. The Aradia Baroque Ensemble and Kwagiulth mezzo-soprano Marion Newman present a concert titled *Thunderbird* that features performances of Kwagiulth songs, dances, and stories in alternation with Baroque works for chamber ensemble based on supernatural themes.

Intercultural projects that draw together Canadian art music and Aboriginal traditions became a standard feature of Canadian music organizations' programming during the late twentieth century. Yet in thinking of the many forms of intercultural music in which First Nations or Inuit traditions constitute one half of the encounter, early music might seem a conspicuous choice of partner. At first listening, these traditions seem to share little common musical ground. Nor do we commonly understand them as having related social functions or addressing similar listening communities. Yet despite their differences, might we understand the re-encounter of these sound worlds in the twenty-first century as a form of symbolic reconciliation? Might we understand the social encounters occurring within the collaborative process and performance event, and the aesthetic encounters taking place within the meeting of musical forms, to model or enact artistic modes of reconciliation and redress?

This chapter examines the differences among the diverse projects in the above list and considers the particular kinds of encounter each concert or work stages. Through their aesthetic structures and forms, the events in the list demonstrate a range of relationships, from the colonizing impulse of integration to agonistic dialogue that aims to make audible the rough edges of difference. While the motivations behind each of these projects are specific to particular synergies between collaborators, I offer several hypotheses by way of conclusion as to why there has been such growth in projects combining art music and early music with First Nations and Inuit cultural practices in the first decade of the twenty-first century.

The Musical Encounters of Early Contact: A Foundation for "Canadian Music's" Unique Musical *Métissage*?

Although the rise in twenty-first century collaboration between early music and First Peoples' traditions may seem a surprising demonstration of interaction between disparate genres, it may more simply be understood as the logical progression of the first musical encounters in what would eventually be named "Canada." We might frame these encounters as the first contact between musical languages and by extension situate them as foundational models of "intercultural music" in Canada. Two of the earliest musical encounters between colonizers and First Peoples in Canada – one on the east coast and one on the west – are of primary significance here: a symbolic encounter (an encounter enacted through the formal and structural elements of a musical work) based upon Marc Lescarbot's adaptation of a Mi'kmaw song; and an embodied encounter (a live encounter between those involved in the performance, including the audience) based upon James Cook's first interactions with the Nuu-chah-nulth upon his arrival at Nootka Sound.

On the east coast of Canada in 1636, Gabriel Sagard-Théodat, in what is considered to be one of the earliest compositions in Canadian music history, adapted Marc Lescarbot's 1606 monophonic transcription of a Mi'kmaw song into a four-voice homophonic setting. Sagard-Théodat's settings, as described by Olivia Bloechl, "represent a more radical process of transformation than [Lescarbot's] earlier monophonic transcriptions. The borrowed melodies quoted in the body of Sagard's *Histoire du Canada* were already twice removed from Mi'kmaq ... performance worlds, and the arrangements in the *Histoire du Canada* further distanced the transcriptions from their sources. The arranger altered the melodies by adding rhythms, and he also changed certain pitches, presumably to accommodate the new harmonies" (Bloechl 2005, 367).

An equally remarkable example of musical first contact took place on the west coast of Canada over a century later. In his journal aboard James Cook's 1778 voyage to Nootka Sound, Lieutenant James King gives an account of "music trading" that exemplifies an instance of musical dialogue that in fact precedes attempts by Cook's crew at verbal communication:

The greatest number of the Canoes remained in a cluster around us til ten O'clock, & as they had no arms, & appeared very friendly, we did not care how long they staid to entertain themselves, & perhaps us: a man repeated a few words in tune, & regulated the meaning by beating against the Canoe sides, after which they all joined in a song, that was by no means unpleasant to the Ear ... A young man with a remarkable soft voice after ward sung by himself, but he ended so suddenly & unexpectedly, which being accompanied by a peculiar gesture, made us all laugh, & he finding that we were not ill pleased repeated his song several times ... As they were now very attentive & quiet in list'ning to their diversions, we judg'd they might like our musick, & we ordered the Fife & drum to lay a tune; these were the only people we had seen that ever paid the smallest attention to those or any of our musical Instruments, if we except the drum, & that only I suppose from its noise & resemblance to their own drums; they observed the profoundest silence, & we were sorry that the dark hindered our seeing the effect of this musick on their countenances. Not to be outdone in politeness they gave us another song, & we then entertained them with French horns, to which they were equally attentive, but have us no more songs in

return, & soon after went away, excepting a few boats that kept pad-
dling around us all that night. (Quoted in Twigg 2004, 123–4)

King's perception of the decorum of the moment, the gestures of "politeness" and light entertainment in the encounter, are here somewhat
amusing. However, the musical encounter is also remarkable for the way
that both parties engage in sustained listening to the other and for the
reciprocity of response in their exchange of gestures and music.

Since these examples of musical contact, encounters between First
Peoples' cultural practices and Western art music have accelerated over
the course of Canadian music history.[3] Such acceleration can be understood as a historical indicator of the increasing interaction between First
Peoples and settlers across Canada. However, might we also consider the
contemporary examples from the opening list – as well as other examples
of that nebulous and heteroglossic entity called "Canadian music" – to be
founded upon, or largely characterized by, a musical *métissage* based in the
originary encounters of first (musical) contact? Might "Canadian Music"
be predicated upon the principle of intercultural encounter? Such an en-
deavour to locate the foundations of Canadian identity is an exercise in
the construction of grand narratives and myths, an exercise in which
Canadian music historians have sometimes participated. And yet such
myth making is not necessarily a thing of the past, as demonstrated by
public intellectual John Ralston Saul's recent sweeping and unsupported
assertion that there is an "Aboriginal cadence to much of our popular
music, and Aboriginal art fits us like a glove … these are the marks of our
reality" (Ralston Saul 2008, 40).

In his book *A Fair Country: Telling Truths about Canada* (2008), Ralston
Saul declares that Canada's national identity and multicultural values are
founded upon First Nations principles of intersubjectivity and ideals for
governance, and he claims that Canadians have internalized such principles over centuries of interaction with First Peoples. He redefines Canada's founding multicultural principles as based upon First Nations concepts of inclusion and the "ever-widening circle." When he "digs around
in the roots of how we [Canadians] imagine ourselves," what he finds is
"deeply aboriginal" (3). Continuing his litany of claims to the essential
"Métissage" of Canadian identity, Ralston Saul cites celebrated Canadian
novelist Guy Vanderhaeghe, who states, "We have a subconscious Métis
mind" (9). Most emphatically, Ralston Saul declares in the very first sentence of *A Fair Country*, "We are a Métis civilization" (3).

Although the words "we" and "our" in these instances refer to all Canadians, Ralston Saul's use of "Métis" co-opts the distinct cultural identity

of the Métis as shorthand for "multicultural." *A Fair Country* thus celebrates First Peoples and positions their cultural values at the centre – the centre, that is, of what it means to be Canadian. Ultimately, Ralston Saul claims, "the fundamental influence of Aboriginals on our civilization is revealed in the ease with which we have adopted their art as an expression of ourselves" (16). But should we not feel some uneasiness with this ease? What are the ethics of coding Canadian values as the internalization of First Nations values? To what degree does Ralston Saul's argument smooth over the complex encounters of past and present between First Peoples and Canada by claiming that "we" are a Métis society because we daily perform "their" (the "Other's") values?

Ralston's Saul's argument is, of course, an index of the present moment in Canadian and First Nations history. The first decade of the twenty-first century in Canada has witnessed Prime Minister Stephen Harper's residential school apology and the recognition of First Peoples on the international stage exemplified by the four host First Nations' involvement in the 2010 Olympics. Such events are central to the process of redressing the history of colonization and its impact on First Peoples in Canada. However, it is equally important to question how the nation-state acknowledges egregious wrongdoings while at the same time nominating the history of colonization, First Peoples' stories, and the general inclusion of First Peoples as contributions to the ongoing development of the Canadian nation-state itself. Ralston Saul's *A Fair Country* is a contribution to the emerging dialogue of reconciliation that is at once forward-thinking for its recognition of the historical elision of the roles First Peoples have played in Canada's history yet troubling in its insistence upon the use of First Nations principles to reconceptualize *Canadian* identity. I do not dispute Ralston Saul's claim that Canadian culture has, as stated throughout *A Fair Country*, been deeply *influenced* by First Nations principles. Yet although Ralston Saul references principles such as the Mohawk concept of *tewatutowie* ("sovereignty as harmony through balanced relationships") and the Cree concepts of *witaskewin* ("people of different nations living together") and *miyo-wicaytowin* ("happy, respectful relationships"), his words (or rather the Mohawk and Cree words he uses) speak instead to the ease with which such concepts might be mobilized for Canadian nation building under the sign of inclusionary multiculturalism.

Ralston Saul's remythologizing of Aboriginal culture as the foundation of Canadian identity takes part in a larger initiative to claim Aboriginal culture as essentially Canadian, a claim long employed by the tourism industry at home and abroad. I have critiqued Ralston Saul's rhetoric at some length to contextualize how it acts as a backdrop to the musical encounters taking place in the concerts and music listed at the outset of the chapter. In relation to Ralston Saul's inclusionary framework, it is important to examine such First Nations intercultural performances not simply as the successful products of Canadian multiculturalism, for such a reading would conscript the works as contributions to Canada's cultural identity and to the development of the Canadian nation-state. Instead, it is important to understand the encounters between musical traditions as reflecting a more diverse range of models that reveal the continuing processes of negotiation, misunderstanding or mistranslation, and agonistic dialogue between First Nations across Canada and the Canadian nation-state. Although my interpretations of many of the works in this list present criticisms similar to those articulated in my reading of Ralston Saul's mobilization of Aboriginal culture in *A Fair Country*, my intent in this chapter is neither to praise nor to condemn the aesthetic choices made by the performers and composers involved. Rather, my hope is that this critique raises questions as to the ethical and political implications of aesthetic choices in the ongoing development of intercultural art music projects between First Nations, Inuit, and art music performers and composers in Canada.

What Kinds of Musical Encounter?

Drawing upon the previous critical reading of Ralston Saul's redescription of First Nations culture within a framework of Canadian multiculturalism, I will examine the *symbolic* and *embodied* aspects of musical encounter that take place in the performances from the opening list. By symbolic aspects, I refer to the kinds of semiotic encounter taking place between the sonic, visual, spatial, and textual forms present in the concerts and individual pieces of music. By embodied aspects of encounter, I refer to the kinds of physical encounter that occur between the agents in these collaborations: the performers, composers, and members of the listening communities.

To further guide this examination of musical encounters, I employ a model that classifies the mode of encounter in three ways. Indeed, the first musical encounters – the example of *integration* in Gabriel Sagard-Théodat's *Haloet* on the east coast and the *music trading and presentation* on the west – offer useful models by which to distinguish forms of interaction between early music and First Nations/Inuit cultural practices in the twenty-first century. In the case of Sagard-Théodat's integration of Mi'kmaw song within Renaissance chant, the first model can be considered a model of *integration* wherein such musical languages enter into dialogue, speaking over top of each other or with one another. The second model, drawing upon Lieutenant James King's account of musical communication with the Nuu-chah-nulth, can be considered a form of *musical trading or presentation.* In this encounter, early music and First Nations/Inuit traditions alternate as a form of cultural presentation or trading of traditions. The final model *combines* these two modes of encounter and enacts a progression that begins with extended musical trading and concludes with a single composition that demonstrates musical integration. Each of these three modes of musical encounter questions what might be termed the sonic positionality of encounter. By sonic positionality, I want to suggest that we might listen to the spatial organization of First Nations and Inuit voices in these works to hear how such voices claim sovereign aural space or find themselves situated as supportive background.

Using the three categories of musical encounter outlined above, I begin by examining two works that present an integrated approach to early music and First Nations/Inuit traditions: *Giiwedin* and *Viderunt Omnes.* I follow this by addressing the example that represents most fully the category of musical trading/presentation: the collaboration between the Pacific Baroque Orchestra and S'pak'wus Slulum. To conclude, I examine how the remaining concerts bridge these two models to enact a progression from presentation toward integration. Camerata Nova's concert *Medieval Inuit*, Marion Newman and the Aradia Ensemble's concert *Thunderbird*, and Tafelmusik's DVD *The Four Seasons Mosaic* each, with varying degrees of success, aim to combine the presentational and integrative models.

The Challenges of Integration: *Giiwedin* and *Viderunt Omnes*

Both *Giiwedin* and *Viderunt Omnes* demonstrate the integrative mode of musical encounter, an integration that merits consideration for the symbolic relationships taking place in the musical worlds they bring together and for the relationships their musical aesthetics have with their intended audiences. As I will illustrate in detail, the composers of these works make aesthetic choices based upon the particular audience they seek to address. Whereas Christos Hatzis's *Viderunt Omnes* speaks as a millennial proclamation of Canadian identity to a global radio audience, Spy Dénommé-Welch and Catherine Magowan's *Giiwedin* addresses a local community of largely non-opera specialists by employing a musical language largely devoid of "high opera" values and the dissonance often associated with contemporary art music.

In the choice of an early music aesthetic for *Giiwedin*, issues of audience engagement and musical alienation were central. In addition to Magowan's training as a Baroque music specialist, the early music sound world was chosen in large part as an attempt to engage an audience with less tolerance for dissonance than one might encounter in a contemporary opera. In conversation with Joseph So, Dénommé-Welch and Magowan describe their choice of a musical style that would not alienate the audience: "we choose to write accessibly in a way that pleases us, and others. We've listened to everything – from Gilbert and Sullivan to Hildegard von Bingen to madrigals, early music, rock 'n' roll and jazz" (So 2010, 5). Of interest here is how such a choice might be valued differently by "art-music specialist" and "nonspecialist" listening communities. As Joseph So observes in response to Dénommé-Welch and Magowan, "There is some snobbery in classical music circles about music that is very accessible, for example, music with hummable melodies " (So 2010, 5). Conversely, the choice for accessibility might be understood within an ethical framework of responsibility to the Native community, a community with whom atonal musical languages do not resonate. The critique of how the language of postcolonial theory subjugates Indigenous voices is here similarly pertinent for questioning the degree to which atonal musical languages hold relevance for expressing Indigenous worldviews.[4]

And yet this choice for musical accessibility is also revealing as an indicator of how the creators understand *Giiwedin*'s audience's tolerance for visual and verbal dissonance to be higher than their tolerance for musical dissonance. *Giiwedin*'s story focuses on particularly violent events that include the lobotomy of the opera's protagonist, Noodin-Kwe, and the brutal killing of Noodin-Kwe's allies. The brutality of these events is represented in strikingly dissonant ways both verbally and visually in *Giiwedin*'s libretto and staging. In contrast, the accessibility of the music, rather than balancing the brutality represented visually and verbally, and thus drawing the audience in, seems instead to elide and undermine the power of those moments. The wider semiotic implications of using an early music style – that is, what this particular sound world signifies in relation to *Giiwedin*'s story – seem strangely ignored. The choice to use early music as a "pleasing" musical style that avoids alienating the audience in effect contradicts the political efficacy held in the dramatic and symbolic encounters taking place within *Giiwedin*.

That the wider signifying aspects of the early music aesthetic were overlooked is particularly strange given that Dénommé-Welch and Magowan are in fact keenly aware of the connotations of musical genre. For example, in their musical characterization of the French Indian Agent, Jean, they use a flippantly stereotypical "French Canadian"–sounding jig. As Magowan notes in an interview, this genre quotation represents "this whole of idea of ridiculous, fun themes, and turning the convention on its head and sort of flipping it. Everyone else has serious, beautiful, lush themes, and these colonizers enter with music that is evocative of a completely different place, which, although [it] is completely appropriate to the character, seems really silly set in northern Ontario in the 1890s" (Dénommé-Welch and Magowan 2009). Although Dénommé-Welch and Magowan pointedly invert the gaze of musical stereotypes and quote musical styles for other characters and historical contexts (notably the "girl group" sound of the 1950s in reference to the Dionne quintuplets), their more general use of an early music style remains particularly unusual. Given the importance Dénommé-Welch and Magowan place on the semiotics of musical genre, it is similarly relevant to question what the choice of early music might express. Moreover, what does the tradition and sound of early music connote for the "nonspecialist" audience or, more specifically, for the audience that attends Theatre Passe Muraille and for those of the Native community who attend work by Native Earth Performing Arts?[5] By way of answering these questions, we might turn to contemporary reception studies of Baroque music that examine the mood-regulating function of such music since the rise of "easy listening" Baroccoco beginning in the 1950s and continuing into the present.[6] In this context, I question the ramifications of making *Giiwedin* "accessible" through the use of both a predominantly early music aesthetic and the associations with such an aesthetic. Historically, Baroque music's frequent function as *Tafelmusik* (literally "table music" or background music at social gatherings) and its contemporary function in an everyday context as "easy listening" or, worse, as muzak should be considered, particularly given the specific audience of "nonspecialist" listeners in attendance. For those audience members who do not engage with early music primarily in concert situations, early music is perhaps most often encountered as background music, where it codes the atmosphere as pleasant or calming. Let me make clear that it is not my intention to deride the quality of composition by associating it with background music. Rather, my aim is to draw attention to the symbolic implications of musical accessibility and to question how such musical accessibility in *Giiwedin* might inadvertently smooth over the more dissonant political aspects of the opera instead of allowing such violence to be heard as well as seen. In this instance, *Giiwedin*'s early music sound world, with its ties to calming mood regulation in the contemporary situation of everyday listening, makes overly palatable the very history of resistance that Dénommé-Welch and Magowan seek to portray.

A much different audience is addressed in Christos Hatzis's *Viderunt Omnes*, specifically an international audience listening to a radio broadcast. Hatzis was commissioned by the CBC to compose the Canadian contribution to the multinational Millennium Project, a radio project of the European Broadcasting Union. The project guidelines stipulated that all national entries were to be based on the organum *Viderunt Omnes* by Pérotin. Hatzis's resulting composition manipulates samples from a recording of the Toronto Consort performing Pérotin's organum and recordings Hatzis made of *katajjait* (throat games) and a song by two Inuit throat singers (Atagootak and Kyak). Hatzis describes the piece as

> the bringing together of the colonial and native elements, the primary building blocks of Canada's culture, into a celebration of the 2000th birthday of Jesus of Nazareth ([represented by] 'Viderunt Omnes', a Christmas chant ...). Imagine a nativity scene in which the chanting angels are the singers of the chronologically and geographically distant 12th century Notre Dame Cathedral, while the shepherds are the natives of arctic Canada, the Inuit. This is the image which has inspired *Viderunt Omnes*, a utopian image perhaps, but then the historical interaction between the Europeans and the arctic natives of North America has been for the most part one of cooperation, not confrontation, unlike the relationship between the Europeans and the more southern natives of the American continent. Furthermore, present day Inuit culture is deeply Christian, in spite of its animistic origins. So this representation of the nativity scene as a virtual meeting place between two musical worlds that have not actually "met" yet, is not as inappropriate as one might originally imagine. (Hatzis 2010)

Hatzis's *Viderunt Omnes*, as the Canadian contribution to an international project, explicitly represents a millennial vision for the future of Canadian identity to an international audience. Thus Hatzis frames the work within the Canadian myth of peaceful encounter between First Peoples and settler-invader, a myth that understands Canadian history as a history of nonaggressive settlement and tolerance for First Peoples in contrast with the more violent history of First Peoples' forced migration in the United States. It is here important to disentangle the history of contact from the myth of white-settler innocence in Canada, a myth that includes Hatzis's understanding of "the historical interaction between the Europeans and the arctic natives" as "for the most part one of cooperation, not confrontation." Speaking to this myth of white-settler innocence in Canada, Eva Mackey notes how "from the early days of Canadian historical writing, historians liked to portray the colonizers of Canada as more generous than those of the USA. According to these histories, while the Americans violently and brutally conquered their 'Indians,' the Native peoples of Canada never suffered similar horrors of conquest … these claims … indicate a push to construct a settler national identity perceived as innocent of racism" (Mackey 2002, 25). Moreover, although it is true that the Inuit are now deeply influenced by Christianity, this influence was often the result of, as throat singer Sylvia Cloutier candidly explains in *The Four Seasons Mosaic*, the efforts of missionaries to "crush" her people's spirituality. Cloutier's description does much to redress the myth that portrays the settlers and missionaries as generous, tolerant, and "cooperative," as Hatzis puts it in his program notes, in their treatment of First Peoples.

Hatzis ends his description of *Viderunt Omnes* by noting that the piece "is dedicated to all those who view contemporary culture as the reflection of a borderless global human identity; a culture whose elements are constantly cross-referenced, but are never dominated or usurped by any particular contributor" (Hatzis 2010). This position is consistent with Hatzis's [illegible] the cultural pluralism of a postmodern musical aest[illegible] New Snow: Postmodernism or Cultural Approp[illegible]zis outlines in this article, such a "borderless gl[illegible] positions those musical materials from Inuit [illegible] now "willing players and contributors" to the gl[illegible]ailable resources for composers who wish to make [illegible]d that they are used in "(genuine) postmodern [illegible] Throughout the article, Hatzis articulates an ethical dist[illegible]n an unethical use of cultural material that is "parasitical" and an ethical use of such material to innovate new meaning. This is to say, any musical composition that "recontexualizes the borrowed material in ways in which it reveals a startlingly new meaning and significance in its re-articulated state" exists outside of the frame of cultural appropriation (Hatzis 1999). Hatzis's views are in sharp contrast with the perspectives of many First Peoples regarding the need for cultural autonomy and with the view of many Inuit that such work is part of an intangible cultural heritage that is not simply useable as an artistic resource. Although Inuit throat singers have expanded the range of Inuit throat singing through the years, in many communities elders believe it inappropriate for those outside of Inuit communities to manipulate throat songs. Even if a composer is to travel to the North to understand the harshness of the landscape, spend time in a community, and consult with a cultural "representative" for permission to use a throat song or other song, there remains the question of who is able to speak for the community and give permission.[7]

Although the majority of the throat singing included in the piece is layered together with Pérotin's organum to add a regular rhythmic pulse, at the 3:30 mark a four-second song fragment emerges that is striking as the first instance of melodic singing not from throat song practice. The fragment is also conspicuous for its melodic contour and use of Inuktitut. In an e-mail correspondence, Hatzis noted that "Most of our recordings were of ayaya songs and throat songs, but this particular one is neither. The reason I used it was because it confirmed rhythmically and tonally the *Viderunt Omnes* section against which it sings."[8]

Hatzis's separation of the sonic qualities from the cultural significance of the fragment's text is significant. Although Hatzis acknowledges in the program notes that Atagootak and Kyak are the singers of the throat songs he uses in *Viderunt Omnes* (Hatzis 2010), he gives no indication of the cultural significance of the recorded material nor any translation for the text or meaning of the song. The fragment, used because "it confirmed rhythmically and tonally," evidences the value of musical composition over cultural context. In this compositional paradigm, cultural significance is decoupled from musical/aesthetic significance.

Although it is expected that a writer be held responsible for the ways that he or she represents other cultures, to what degree should we hold composers responsible for the ways that formal musical choices made in their manipulation of source material represent cultural identity? That is, to what degree should composers engage with or be held responsible for the politics of their *aesthetic* choices, the semiotics of musical inclusion, and the structures of cultural encounter their works enact? Composers, by nature of their artistic practice, are concerned primarily with the sonic musical characteristics of their sources and with the aesthetic interweaving of musical materials. The manipulation of musical form is precisely what composers devote their training to. They are trained to craft sound, to find innovative musical resources, and to stretch the possibilities for how different sources might be uniquely combined. The near-exclusive focus on the formal qualities of music – with the effect that composers are not given adequate opportunity to question the ethical ramifications of the "postmodern aesthetics of cultural pluralism" and, more generally, the cultural and social significance of the musical languages they use – is a significant shortcoming of compositional training. Thus academic programs in composition might benefit from a rethinking of how the curricula might expand outward to consider the ethical and political implications in intercultural music composition. Such consideration might focus on how incorporating music from other cultures expresses cultural and political significance through the semiotics of compositional form. Similar consideration might be given to how extramusical choices – how musicians are positioned on stage, how musicians are attired, or how the performance is contextualized by program notes or in pre-concert talk – articulate cultural and political meaning. Both the Pacific Baroque Orchestra's collaboration with S'pak'wus Slulum and the Aradia Baroque Ensemble's collaboration with Marion Newman are unique in this regard, each giving explicit consideration to the intercultural semiotics of the stage.

Reciprocal Presentation: The Pacific Baroque Orchestra and S'pak'wus Slulum as "Visiting Nations"

In contrast to the integrative model enacted in *Giiwedin* and *Viderunt Omnes*, the presentational model employed in the Pacific Baroque Orchestra's (PBO) collaboration with S'pak'wus Slulum alternates between musical performance by each group and situates the ensembles as equal partners in a meeting that has as its aim a sharing of traditions. Marc Destrubé, the principal organizer of the event, noted that "the idea wasn't in any way to meld the two things, it was simply to say here are two ancient traditions ... existing at pretty much the same time" (*First Story* 2001). In turn, Bob Baker, the leader of the S'pak'wus Slulum dancers, described the dances that S'pak'wus Slulum presented as those "that would be given to visiting nations at a potlatch" (*First Story* 2001). By introducing the metaphor of the concert as a site for visiting nations (here with the PBO and S'pak'wus Slulum representing those "visiting nations") to present their cultural practices to each other, Baker situates early music and Squamish cultural practices on shared ground.

As a consequence, the concert takes a comparative approach to the music and dance presented by each group. S'pak'wus Slulum begins with a welcome song, a "Canoe Journey Song," in which the dancers arrive from behind the audience. The PBO, along with Baroque dancers Thomas Baird and Paige Whitley-Bauguess, in turn presents "Fête Marine." As Baird describes, the piece begins on a boat caught in a tempest, which strands Prince Acis on an island where he meets and falls in love with Galatea the sea-nymph. Completing the love triangle is the Cyclops Polyphemus, who regularly eats those visitors unfortunate enough to land upon his shores and who is also enamoured with Galetea. In response to the introduction of Polyphemus, S'pak'wus Slulum presents the story of Qalqalil (or Kalkalilh), the wild cannibal woman of the forest who steals children in her basket. The alternation of these dissimilar musical languages – the agile counterpoint of the PBO's strings against the intensity and solidity of the Squamish voices and drumming – are linked together by their shared focus on myth and legend but also by their focus on ceremony. Whitley-Bauguess describes the focus on protocol in seventeenth-century balls taking place at the European courts as another link between the two traditions that emphasizes the importance of protocol in ceremonial dance.

This equality of "visiting nations" was made further apparent in the choice of venues at which the concerts were presented: Sty-wet-tan Longhouse at the University of British Columbia and the Squamish Nation Recreation Centre. At the former, the audience consisted primarily of the Pacific Baroque Orchestra's patrons, many of whom would not regularly see Coast Salish dancing. In the latter venue, the audience was to a greater degree composed of members of the Squamish Nation, who were not as likely to regularly see Baroque dancing or hear live Baroque music. Thus we might additionally apply the theme of reciprocal presentation to Bob Baker's metaphor of "visiting nations," wherein each visiting ensemble/nation presents its music to a different community/nation.

Developing Trust: From Reciprocal Presentation to Integration in Camerata Nova's *Medieval Inuit* and Marion Newman and the Aradia Baroque Ensemble's *Thunderbird*

The concerts discussed with reference to the theme of "developing trust" fall into the third category of musical encounter, which incorporates elements from both the presentational and integrative models. This form entails a progression from the presentation of musical languages to a single composition within which both languages occupy the same sonic space. Although I discuss each concert individually, I would like to characterize the group of concerts homologically as demonstrating the development of trust between Indigenous and non-Indigenous communities over time.

The works presented in Camerata Nova's *Medieval Inuit* alternate between Nordic folksong and Inuit throat singing or drum songs. In the program notes, Cree composer Andrew Balfour describes the premise for the concert:

> to explore musically the mystery of the first contact between the Vikings or Norse and the indigenous people of Canada's Arctic. Historically, the Saga of the Greenlanders tells that Leifur Eiríksson set out in 1002, heading northwest from Greenland. The first land he encountered was called Helluland, the Land of Flat Stones. This was possibly Baffin Island. Although there is no firm evidence that these early Norse encountered the indigenous people of the region, this concert and composition, in an abstract, musical way, imagine this happening. I also realize that, if the Norse did encounter indigenous people, they would have been from the now-extinct Dorset culture, rather than the Inuit. I hope people will forgive my license. (*Medieval Inuit* 2010)

The concert concludes with a new composition by Balfour, itself titled "Inuit." Of interest in this composition and the concert as a whole are the ways by which inclusion is inverted and recuperated. In her critique of the inclusionary nature of multiculturalism in Canadian society, Eva Mackey notes that the word "inclusion" reinforces the dominance of those in power that decide who and *who not* to include (Mackey 2002). The word "inclusion" by its very nature expresses a hegemonic position. Similarly, when this model of inclusion is applied to intercultural music making in Canadian art music genres, the issue of power is once more at stake. In the case of *Viderunt Omnes* – and Mychael Danna's *Winter*, discussed in the next section – we see how even composers with the best of intentions inadvertently reinforce the hierarchy of music practices that maintain the dominance of art music as the genre to which one must conform. Inuit and First Nations performers are asked to present themselves as part of the choir or ensemble by taking the postures of its members and by following the musical time set out by the composer. Improvisational play, so fundamental to First Nations and Inuit cultural practices, is infrequently encountered in Canadian art music that incorporates First Nations and Inuit performers, despite the wealth of aleatoric methods at the composer's disposal. Here the relative degree to which Canadian art music composers are asked or expected to change their habitual methods of working in intercultural projects is small. Rarely do we find an orchestra asked to play an entire work from memory, as in Indigenous oral traditions of performance. Instead, First Peoples and their cultural practices are included in art music as long as composers can find ways to script those musicians (who frequently do not read Western music notation) into the art music genres within which the composers work. Here the scripting of only the musical aspects of a cultural practice enacts a form of symbolic violence upon that cultural practice itself.

This paradigm of musical inclusion through conformity to Western art music is avoided in several ways in Balfour's *Medieval Inuit*, which displaces the traditional sound of an early music choir by asking the singers to adopt "uncomfortable" techniques foreign to the practice of early music singing. First, Balfour has trained some of the singers in the art of overtone singing, which they engage in at various points throughout the piece. Second, in the third movement, "Into the Cold," Balfour has women in the choir sing a repetitive flat-tone "eee-eeeee" in head voice for the majority of the movement, which lends their performance an otherworldly quality. More important, this technique inverts the common position of throat singing as background to art music and limits the choir's material so that it supports the throat songs as the focus. The most significant inversion of inclusion, however, takes place following the performance itself. Returning to the stage for what the audience believes will be an encore presentation, singer Madeleine Allakariallak proceeds to teach the audience the refrain to a drum song. Once she has led the audience through the tune several times, she leads them in a sing-along where she conducts them in a performance of the full Inuit song.

The second concert that falls within the category of combined presentation and integration is Marion Newman and the Aradia Baroque Ensemble's *Thunderbird*, which presents traditional Kwagiulth stories and dances with her family in Toronto alongside Baroque works for chamber ensemble. As with the Pacific Baroque Orchestra's collaboration with S'pak'wus Slulum, Newman has expressed the importance of not integrating her family's traditional songs and dances with the Baroque music that Aradia performs. In the concert's program notes, Newman expresses how she feels First Nations cultural practices are still too frequently used to "enliven" old works or, worse, how "First Nations performers [are] paraded out for special effect" (*Thunderbird* 2010).

In *Thunderbird* members of Marion Newman's family, including George Taylor (singer-drummer) and Jason Taylor (dancer), performed traditional

Kwagiulth songs and dances using masks carved by Newman's father, Victor Newman. These pieces included Raven, Bukwus (wild man), and Sap'a (echo) dances, a chief's peace dance, and a Thunderbird dance. In alternation with these performances, the Aradia Baroque Ensemble, drawing on the story of the Thunderbird, who by beating his wings causes thunder, stirs the wind, and pulls clouds together, performed Baroque music "that similarly depicted the molding of the natural world through supernatural forces" (*Thunderbird* 2010).

Notably, in both *Thunderbird* and *Medieval Inuit* an inversion of inclusion takes place whereby the spirit of the space is altered. Through ceremony and welcoming entrances, the audience is made aware that this is a shared space and that the performers have chosen to include this audience as part of the event. In *Medieval Inuit* this is achieved by projecting images on a scrim of thirty by forty feet from the Ford Family Archives, photographs of Inuit men, women, and children taken between 1910 and 1930 by Henry Thomas Ford. Additionally, at the beginning of the concert the space takes on a heightened sense of sacredness through the ceremonial lighting of the *qulliq* (oil lamp) by elder Lavinia Brown. *Thunderbird* opens with the Aradia Baroque Ensemble arriving from backstage to the customary welcome of audience applause. In contrast, the Kwagiulth performers then enter from behind the audience and between the aisles, and the movement of their song – the heartbeat of the drums and low tones of their voices – seems to deepen the sense of space around the audience members. Their song moves toward us and beside us, entering and physically transforming the space through its embodied presence. In their entrance, Marion Newman, Victor Newman, and Jason Taylor indeed seem to bring a different sense of space with them into the hall, a depth of space familiar to the forests of Vancouver Island.

Each concert also subtly shifts the context of the event from aesthetic engagement to a focus upon historical and present challenges facing the First Nations and Inuit performers' respective communities. During the *Thunderbird* concert, George Taylor described the importance of the potlatch in Kwagiulth and Coast Salish traditions, how the Canadian government outlawed it from 1884 to 1951 and by doing so "forbade us to be who we are." In *Medieval Inuit* Madeline Allakariallak, both in the preconcert discussion and in the concert itself, related her community's struggle to rebuild St Jude's Cathedral in Iqaluit, which was destroyed by arson in 2005. In the program notes to the concert, Allakariallak describes the cathedral as "more than a building. It was a nerve centre for the community … a precious part of the heritage of the Inuit people" (*Medieval Inuit* 2010).

The presentational models employed in each of these concerts address the importance of educating the audience about First Nations and Inuit cultural practices by not dismembering and redeploying elements of the cultural practice simply as musical colour. The story, dance, and song in these First Nations and Inuit traditions are tied to the cultural practices themselves. Additionally, the *combined* model of encounter employed in these concerts acknowledges that integrating Western art music and First Nations traditions involves a lengthy process of questioning, dialogue, and learning about each other's traditions, considering protocol, developing trust, and having time to let ideas fail and be readdressed.

Tafelmusik's *The Four Seasons Mosaic*, Featuring Aqsaarnit

The presentation of the concert *The Four Seasons: A Cycle of the Sun*, of which Mychael Danna's Vivaldi-adaptation *Winter* was a part, took place in a variety of locations across North America and Asia. In the present chapter, however, I confine my analysis to the film documentary of *The Four Seasons Mosaic*, which in large part recreates the format of the concert. As with the other concerts I have considered within the third category of combined presentation and integration, the *Four Seasons* concert and documentary provided a forum for the musicians to present their music and to contextualize it by discussing their cultural traditions. At the conclusion of the concert and documentary, the musicians present Danna's *Winter*, an adaptation of Vivaldi's Concerto No. 4, "L'inverno" from his *Four Seasons*, in which all of the participants take part. Perhaps the greatest strength of the documentary is how it features the musicians travelling to their "homes" and how they describe the process of learning their musical traditions from their mentors/elders. Yet, although the documentary allows the musicians to contextualize their music as part of a larger cultural tradition, such traditions are unfortunately elided in Danna's final adaptation of Vivaldi's "L'inverno."[9] Despite the documentary's rich explorations of East Indian musical traditions, as related by Aruna Narayan, and of Chinese musical traditions, as described by Wen Zhao, I largely confine my remarks here to the section of the documentary that focuses on throat singers Sylvia Cloutier and June Shappa and on their involvement in Danna's adaptation of Vivaldi's "L'inverno."

Of central importance in Cloutier and Shappa's segment of the documentary are the history of throat singing and the wider expressions of Inuit spirituality. As with Narayan and Zhao, Cloutier tells stories about the important role that Inuit cultural practices play in her community and explains her community's desire to pass its knowledge on to younger generations. Cloutier discusses both the nature of throat singing as play and the way environmental sounds are imitated in the songs. As noted, Cloutier also candidly discusses the effects of colonization on Inuit cultural traditions: "Unfortunately, missionaries came up and banned many things in our culture, and our spirituality was sort of [pause] crushed in many ways, and throat singing was part of that. My mother's generation didn't learn how to do that because people stopped having pride in throat singing in those days, so they didn't pass that on to their kids" (Tafelmusik 2007a). Moreover, Cloutier notes the value she feels that throat singing has in empowering young people in Inuit communities:

> It's something that I can't be selfish with because these songs really don't belong to me; they belong to our people. Young people feel so powerless and they feel so … troubled and they don't realize that their problems are just temporary and they take their own lives. It's *so* hard because everyone's been affected by suicide. Every single person living in the North has been affected by suicide. What I really try to work hard at is trying to work with young people and trying to find ways to empower them through the arts. I'm going to teach those songs. I'm not just going to keep them to myself. I'm not just going to share them with my audience, but I'm going to share them with young people that want to learn. (Tafelmusik 2007a)

Cloutier's presentation highlights the relationships between the singers and the elders as well as the continuance of Inuit cultural practices through teaching the younger generation. Despite the emphasis on Inuit culture in the interview portion of *The Four Seasons Mosaic*, the cultural significance of throat singing is exscribed in Mychael Danna's *Winter*.

The first movement of Danna's *Winter* opens with an extended two-minute solo passage for the sarangi, demonstrating the unique pitch-bending capabilities of the instrument and Aruna Narayan's intricate technique, in which her fingernails control the subtle glides and embellishments that are characteristic of Hindustani music. This opening transitions into "L'inverno" proper, in which the violin, pipa, and sarangi exchange solo passages, and shows Cloutier and Shappa looking on from the background in anticipation. Finally, three minutes into the performance, Cloutier and Shappa enter for the first time, singing a remarkably metered throat song that is unaccompanied for three seconds, and then are joined by the string section for a total of twenty-one seconds. It is clear from this initial introduction that Cloutier and Shappa's relationship is with the orchestral, rather than the soloist, parts. The first movement continues with soloistic exchanges between the violin, sarangi, and pipa, with Cloutier and Shappa coming in one final time to sing the same throat song as before for twenty seconds. This formula is repeated in the second movement of *Winter*, in which the violin, pipa, and sarangi again exchange virtuosic phrases with one another. In this movement, Cloutier and Shappa perform only twice, from between ten to twenty seconds, in contrast to the almost complete soloistic presence of the sarangi and pipa parts. Moreover, although the throat song that is included is different from the one presented in the first movement, it is again repeated in the same way as in the first movement, expressing a decided lack of transformational potential. Visually, in its focus on the aesthetic finger dexterity of the violinist, sarangi player, and pipa player, the documentary reinforces the high degree of virtuosity evident in string instrument capability against the aesthetic limitations of throat singing.

One might argue that the throat singing and its performers are equally conscripted to the background, the former sonically and the latter spatially, thus marginalizing the throat singers' virtuosity. However, this would be a specious argument, for it misrepresents the orchestral part of Vivaldi's "L'inverno" as somehow being of less importance than are the solo parts in the work as a whole. Instead, I argue that Danna's inclusion of the throat singers in *Winter* neglects the wide variety of forms that throat singing often takes and thus the extent of the virtuosity it requires. Throat songs demonstrate both extreme diversity and virtuosity in their incorporation of meaningless syllables, names of ancestors or elders, animal names, terms designating an object seen while playing the game, animal cries (often goose calls), sounds from nature, the melody of an *aqausiq* (an affectionate song composed for an infant), or the tune of a drum dance song or religious hymn. Moreover, in the competitive and ludic aspects of throat singing, the singers demonstrate an improvisational vocal virtuosity when exchanging vocal motives. The omission of these aspects of throat song virtuosity in *Winter* is ironic, for the same basic features expressed in Vivaldi's *Four Seasons* – namely call and response, fluidity of response, and even the virtuosity of improvisation – are also features of throat singing. Danna's adaptation of "L'inverno" ultimately uses the singers' traditions more for colour than for the cultural tradition of throat singing itself.

I do not suggest that Inuit cultural practice is intentionally marginalized either by Tafelmusik or by Mychael Danna (or, for that matter, by

Hatzis in *Viderunt Omnes*) but want rather to foreground how a question of primary significance in any intercultural work must be how the semiotics of inclusion function in the formal encounters between musical languages. In *Winter* it is important to question how the level of audio and visual virtuosity may unwittingly be framed as the singers' lack of ability to integrate or as an aesthetic limitation of throat singing and thus as an aesthetic devaluation of that cultural practice. Such a reading is only further reinforced by a statement of Jean Lamon in the interview portion of the documentary: "In the case of the Inuit throat singers, they said they just needed to 'feel it in their gut.' At first I thought they're never going to feel it in their gut, they're so far off ... [but eventually] they got from being totally off to being completely on and totally reliable and perfect every time." The language of Lamon's statement is revealing, for to expect any Inuit or First Nations performer to acclimatize to the highly controlled and literally "measured" language of much Western art music is to curtail the inclusion of the cultural practice itself. To expect Inuit throat singers to be "completely on and totally reliable and perfect every time" is to overlook the very nature of throat singing as play and the flexibility of time in play.

Accounting for Encounters between First Nations/Inuit Practices and Early Music

I would like to conclude this chapter as I began, with a list. Here, I provide hypothetical answers (of varying lengths) to the question with which I opened this chapter: *why* was there such a striking increase in encounters between First Nations/Inuit practices and early music in the first decade of the twenty-first century?

- One could argue that some of these events place early music side by side with First Nations and Inuit traditions in order to redress historical misconceptions of Indigenous cultural practices as unsophisticated. Although early writings on First Nations/Inuit characterize their song practices as existing at an earlier stage of musical development, ethnomusicologists, musicologists, and First Nations scholars have, as demonstrated in this volume, expanded both the historical knowledge of these practices and the intricate ways that cultural practices have continued to change throughout the twentieth and twenty-first centuries. However, despite this deepening of our knowledge, the internalized history of colonization remains a force with which many First Peoples struggle on a daily basis in their personal and professional lives. As a result, the memory of the Indian Act's banning of "uncivilized" music in potlatches and sun dances from 1885 to 1951 has an enduring presence in the consciousness of many First Peoples. The aftershocks of colonization have not abated with symbolic acts of reconciliation, such as Stephen Harper's 2009 residential school apology.

Additionally, in looking at the placement of these musical languages side by side, we might question the ways that distinctions are made between the appropriate stages for the presentation of art music and First Nations/Inuit traditions. As one example, the mezzo-soprano Marion Newman spoke to me of her desire for opportunities to present both forms of her artistic practice (Kwagiulth traditions and operatic repertoire) in equally professional contexts. Newman's statement speaks to the all too frequent use of First Nations traditions for "festival display." The "festival multiculturalism" of such display ultimately casts First Peoples as Canadian citizens content to contribute to the celebration of Canadian identity in civic events and other government-sponsored celebrations of inclusion, events through which struggles for sovereignty and cultural autonomy are subtly elided.

- One could also argue, in tandem with Ralston Saul that, from the vantage point of the Canadian composer, the rise in intercultural musical encounters indicates the degree of First Nations influence on (or constitution of) Canada's musical heritage. That is, this increase might be seen to express and celebrate an innate Canadian métissage. On the international stage, such a message seems to be increasingly cultivated by the drive of globalization toward marketing "unique" (as a modality of the exotic) national identity. Ironically, what makes Canada's national identity unique, it seems, are the cultural "contributions" made by First Peoples. Yet, as many First Peoples continue to assert, the songs, stories, and dances that are so valued by the Canadian nation-state as part of "our" Canadian heritage do not, in fact, represent Canada at all. They are first and foremost expressions of cultural identity for the many nations that exist within Canada, which are distinct from the Canadian nation-state itself.
- Undoubtedly, intercultural performances have seen a sharp increase because national and federal funding bodies reward musical institutions in Canada for demonstrating their commitment to multiculturalism. Under the aegis of "multicultural relevance," one might question how many intercultural compositions are funded regardless of whether, or to what degree, a composer articulates an ethically sound

model for collaboration. It is also important to note that whereas the Social Sciences and Humanities Research Council of Canada has implemented guidelines for ethical research for scholars who work with First Nations and Inuit communities, no such guidelines and review exist at the Canada Council or other regional funding agencies for composers who wish to collaborate with First Nations and Inuit performers.

- One might finally explain this increase as a sign of Canada's having entered an age of reconciliation. Less optimistically, one might claim that we have entered an era that privileges the discourse, images, and perhaps even sounds of reconciliation over the actual challenges of dialogue and substantive change for which many First Nations and Inuit communities continue to call.

To look cynically at the discourse of reconciliation's effect on intercultural collaborative work, I wonder whether we might see the de rigueur response of standing ovations to intercultural performances with First Peoples as a demonstration of support for "getting along" or at least as the staging of "togethering." Are such ovations a demonstration of support for the Canadian ideal of multiculturalism in the image of these performers sharing the same stage, a demonstration of support that occurs *regardless* of the degree to which First Nations and Inuit cultural practices are respected as more than just "musical material" in these works? Although the musicality, virtuosity, and diverse grain of vocality in First Nations and Inuit song are important features to be valued, the near-exclusive focus upon the aesthetic aspects of such practices in a composition reduces these traditions to what Veit Erlmann (1996) has called an aesthetics of pastiche.

And yet, thinking more positively of reconciliation, one might also see reconciliation realized through what Beverley Diamond (2011) has referred to as the decolonization of the audience. Along with the rise in intercultural collaboration between First Peoples and early music, there has been a rise in educating non-Native audiences about the history of colonization, the role and vibrancy of story, song, and dance in different nations across Canada, the challenges that First Peoples face in their communities, and their hopes for the future. Indeed, since the majority of these works take the third approach I mentioned earlier, that of combining presentation and integration, and thus follow a homological model, they might structurally seem to enact the progression of interaction between First Nations/Inuit and settler worldviews. This approach enacts a model for a reciprocal presentation of cultural traditions and repeated encounters between musical languages that then, over time, allows for a shared language to emerge.

To use the model of reconciliation as a frame by which to hear the musical encounters taking place in these works is to question the degree to which each party in the encounter, and each artistic form, is changed through the collaborative process. Although the inclusionary strategy of fitting First Nations and Inuit musicians into Canadian art music compositions and concerts may allow organizations to demonstrate on paper their commitment to diversity, more elusive are the challenging processes of collaboration that result in demonstrations of *bi-directional* change in the concert or composition that is produced. Institutions that would claim to address imbalances of power are limited by the very power that they retain if the subjugating power remains unaltered. With intercultural music projects, we must note that a unidirectional attempt to "fit" First Nations musicians, singers, and artists into an art music paradigm of performance precision and accuracy, as well as into a concert venue and the embodiment of an "art music ensemble," forces change upon the terms of art music production. The colonizing impulse of assimilation is here enacted under the aegis of inclusion. First Nations/Inuit musicians become simply part of the ensemble or are added to the composition as another musical colour in the composer's palette. As discussed earlier, Tafelmusik's *The Four Seasons Mosaic* is an unfortunate and unintended example of this. In contrast, the collaborations between Marion Newman and the Aradia Baroque Ensemble, between the Pacific Baroque Orchestra and S'pak'wus Slulum, and between Camerata Nova and Allakariallak and Cloutier each incorporate welcoming dances or ceremonies that work to destabilize the order of art music hegemony. A final way that such change can be enacted bidirectionally is in the choice of location, which can be a choice both to move art music out of the sanctity of the concert hall and to engage with a different community, such as in Marc Destrubé's decision to present one performance of the Baroque Orchestra's collaboration with S'pak'wus Slulum at the Squamish Nation Community Recreation Centre.

- Of course, the above answers, although they address the many reasons for intercultural collaboration between First Nations/Inuit musicians and Canadian art music ensembles, do not exactly address any specific affiliation between First Nations/Inuit and early music traditions. To answer this question of affiliation, we might look to what Newman notes is the commonality between the beat and dance forms of each. Newman notes that, for her, "The biggest thread that ties together Baroque and Aboriginal culture would be the beat that music provides. It starts with the heartbeat, it moves to the drum, the instruments strike up, people's feet begin to twitch and dance is born. It may seem like a crazy thing to be combining such forces, but in my heart and mind it makes perfect sense" (*Thunderbird* 2010). Indeed, the majority of the works that both Aradia and the Kwagiulth performers presented were works intended for dance.

Although First Nations, Inuit, and Western art music composers alike continue to be drawn to intercultural creation, continue to refine mutually respectful models for collaboration, and continue to present and learn from the diversity of traditions encompassed in early music and First Nations and Inuit cultural practices, such intercultural work must not fall short of addressing the politics of aesthetics enacted symbolically in the encounters taking place in musical works and concerts. Although ethnomusicologists have sought to understand the myriad aesthetic choices in First Peoples cultural practices in order not to ascribe to them a purely functional significance,[10] equal effort must be made to understand the structures and political choices of creative practices that bring art music together with First Nations and Inuit performers and their cultural practices.

NOTES

1 The terms "early music" and "First Nations and Inuit cultural practices" are admittedly nebulous as categories that denote any particular kind of music. They are employed throughout this chapter to refer to the encounter between two different sound worlds and to the diverse variety of music brought together in the list of works examined here.
2 Tafelmusik, press release, October 2007, http://www.tafelmusik.org/media/presspdfs/Tafelmusik_CD_L'estro_armoinco.pdf (accessed 28 June 2011).
3 For a thorough bibliography of works by Canadian composers who use First Nations and Inuit song and story, see Strachan (2005). When published, this guide listed nearly three hundred compositions, and since then the number has steadily increased with compositions that include First Nations and Inuit song, reference cultural practices, and feature First Nations and Inuit performers themselves. For a detailed description of Canadian art music based on First Nations and Inuit song, see Keillor (1995b).
4 For more information regarding Native nationalism and First Nations–centred criticism, see Womack (1999), Fagan (2004), and Weaver, Womack, and Warrior (2006).

5 This formulation of the "nonspecialist" audience takes into account that audience composition dramatically changes the recognition of musical signs. My intention is not to construct the audience as a unified mass whose members perceive the work in the same manner but merely to note that some generalizations regarding the different communities that attend music performance are useful for conceptualizing the ways that aesthetic choices are perceived.

6 For an excellent examination of the rise in Baroccoco easy listening in the 1950s, see Fink (2005, ch. 4).

7 These are some of the justifications Hatzis (2009) offers for his use of Inuit throat singing in his composition.

8 E-mail correspondence with author, 11 June 2010.

9 The documentary contains the first and final movements of *Winter*, both of which I analyze here.

10 Kofi Agawu, in particular, challenges the myth that distinguishes between non-Western music forms as essentially functionalist (i.e., as part of a ritual, work, or any other circumstance that gives songs a direct purpose) and Western art music as essentially contemplative, or "functionless," since "it demands nothing of its hearers save contemplation" (Agawu 2003, 98). Such a myth works to elide the aesthetic qualities of non-Western music forms and elides the fact that there are clear functions that Western art music plays in contemporary Western societies.

14

Musical Form as Theatrical Form in Native Canadian Stage Plays: Moving through the Third Space

KLISALA HARRISON

In Canada, stage plays written by Aboriginals developed along a musical trajectory after Tomson Highway (Cree) became a renowned First Nations playwright in the mid-1980s. Highway trained as a classical pianist in England[1] and fused music styles of opera, serialism, blues, and Cree lullabies with characters from Greek and Eastern Woodlands Aboriginal myth. Subsequently, eastern Canadian playwright Drew Hayden Taylor (Ojibway)[2] evolved blues structure as theatre structure, and Daniel David Moses (Delaware/Tuscarora) adapted forms of minstrelsy to contemporary theatre about Saskatchewan. Marie Humber Clements (Métis) in British Columbia borrowed operatic form, and an extensive list of Native Canadian playwrights and theatre groups based plays on traditional Aboriginal music and ritual forms and functions: Floyd Favel Starr, Margo Kane, Maria Campbell, Lisa C. Ravensbergen, Injun'Nuity Theatre Company, Tunooniq Theatre, and the Igloolik Dance and Drama Group, among many others.

This chapter is the first survey of music in First Nations, Métis, and Inuit theatre throughout Canada. I document several overarching trends in the uses that Native Canadian playwrights have made of diverse Native and non-Native musical genres and sonic structures as bases for theatre forms. My focus is stage plays penned partly or solely by Native Canadians, in English, from 1986 to 2007. These Native Canadian plays are primarily performed for intercultural Canadian audiences yet, importantly, are staged in Aboriginal communities. Here, I am interested in how the authors, producers, and performers of the musical stage plays have evoked instances of cultural and social marginalization by drawing attention to differences between Native and non-Native expressions, histories, and relationships. I highlight (re)makings and (re)readings of relevant culturally and socially engaged meanings that evolve as musical genres and structures are adopted in Aboriginal Canadian theatre.

My thinking is inspired by Homi Bhabha's ideas about the third space and a "third area." Bhabha articulated his third area idea in an interview on the visual art work of Brian Jungen (Dane-ẕaa/Swiss Canadian). The notion names a space of social interpretation that may emerge when different ideas that are culturally iconic and rooted in distinct meaning systems interact with one another in a human expression or object so as to engage power relations of social, ethnical, and cultural difference (Bhabha in Jungen 2006, 15–16). His related third space idea, in its most classic sense, focuses on active social negotiating of such difference and power around a specific structure of symbolization – for example, a book or a performance – that occurs within one cultural group but in ways that engage different cultures abutting on one another (Bhabha in Rutherford 1990, Bhabha 1994). I also am interested in other sorts of intercultural negotiations – the juxtaposition of cultural ideas and the creating of hybrid expressions, for example – that are at play as Aboriginal Canadian theatre adapts musical forms and structures.

This chapter is informed by fieldwork in Toronto, Ontario, from 2000 to 2002 on stage plays produced by Native Earth Performing Arts and the Centre for Indigenous Theatre, by archival research at the University of Guelph's L.W. Conolly Theatre Archives, by secondary source research, and by fieldwork from 2000 to 2006 on Native theatre in Vancouver, British Columbia. In Vancouver my theatre study included stage plays at the Vancouver Aboriginal Friendship Centre but centred on both live and archived productions at the Firehall Arts Centre. Under founding director Donna Spencer, Firehall Theatre Society Productions has staged many plays written and performed by First Nations people: Ian Ross's *fareWel* (in 1999), Gummerson's *Wawatay* (in 2002), and Drew Hayden Taylor's *Someday* (in 1995), *Only Drunks and Children Tell the Truth* (in 1997 and 1998), *alterNative(s)* (in 1999), and *The Buz'gem Blues* (in 2004). The Firehall Arts Centre enjoyed a collaborative relationship with Marie Clements, premiering her *Age of Iron* (in 1993) and *The Unnatural and Accidental Women* (in 2000). Different theatre companies have premiered plays by Aboriginal writers at, and sometimes in association with, the Firehall. Examples include Michael Lawrenchuk's *The Trial of Kicking Bear* (in 1991), Marie Clements's *Burning Vision* (in 2002), the collaborative venture initiated and directed by Marie Clements *Rare Earth Arias* (in

2002), Lisa C. Ravensbergen and Michelle Olson's *The Place Between* (in 2004), Tasha Faye Evans's *She Stands Still* (in 2004), and Margo Kane's *The River—Home* (in 2005).

First, I discuss Native Canadian play forms that are inspired by art music forms, spotlighting opera in *Rare Earth Arias* (Clements 2002), which portrays marginalization through vocal style and sonority. *Rare Earth Arias* introduces the useful theoretical concept of the rare voice. Second, I consider stage play adaptations of popular music forms of Native Canadians and African Americans, like minstrelsy and the blues. Third, musical activism and ritual are revealed as integral to forms of Indigenous stage plays for Indigenous communities. Fourth, I explain how music, ritual, and sound have contributed to the forms of nonlinear stage plays in the "third wave" style (Gunn Allen 1996).

Art Music Forms: Opera

I am watching the 2002 premiere of *Rare Earth Arias* at Vancouver's Firehall Arts Centre Studio. The Red Dress Singer character, played by red-haired and white-skinned Katherine Harris, wears glistening red lipstick, sparkling green eye shadow, brilliant red finger and toenails, and a tight-fitting red gown. Standing on a table, the highest point of the set, she sings lyrics by Leith Harris (Anglo Canadian) about the explosive rare earth element lanthanum. The Red Dress Singer sings, ethereally and operatically,

Lanthanum, the hidden one

Found most reactive, rare earth element
Reactive and highly explosive

Lanthanum
Metal, silvery white, soft
Malleable, ductile and buried in mother earth's crust
Lanthanum, the hidden one

Watch for the silvery spark igniting into flame
From too much heat, too much heart
Turn away, escape
Care must be taken handling or the flame explodes into a fiery
   bombing
A starburst and gone

Lanthanum, the hidden one

Lanthanum, the hidden one
Rare earth element
Mad mother walking time-bomb about to go off
Do this do this do this do that hu-ree hu-ree hurry
You don't know how

Lanthanum, the hidden one
Masquerading as normal, spy from the underworld
Listening to ugly insults against skid row scum
Lazy bums, junkies, dirty hookers, whores
Lanthanum, the hidden one
(Field note, October 2002, lyrics by Leith Harris)

In 2002 Marie Clements's theatre company, Urban Ink Productions, commissioned six women in Clements's Downtown Eastside Women's Writing Group, which ran from 2000 to 2002, to each write a "spoken-word aria," or monologue, that used metaphors of opera. These writers were from Vancouver's inner city, the Downtown Eastside, and were each mentored by a female director. The six writer-director duos workshopped the monologues with six professional female actors who performed the works.

Urban Ink is a Native Canadian production company that seeks to bring together diverse cultural and artistic perspectives via interracial experiences. As such, the company extended the *Rare Earth Arias* project to all ethnicities. Two of the writer-mentor-actor teams were First Nations, with the exception of one woman, two teams were Anglo Canadian, one trio was African Canadian, and one group was Asian Canadian. Opera singer Katherine Harris (Anglo Canadian) arranged, composed, and performed vocal music; writers Leith Harris (Anglo Canadian) and Muriel Williams (English/Tsimshian) created lyrics. Marie Clements (Métis) and Maiko Bae Yamamoto (Japanese Canadian) oversaw artistic direction. The intercultural cast and crew, Yamamoto commented, reflected the interethnic makeup of the Downtown Eastside writing group and community (Yamamoto 2002). It also seemed to enable specific ethnic and cultural affiliations in stories and characters created by the writers.

Leith Harris's lanthanum lyrics are interwoven with *Rare Earth Arias'* narrative through-line, which is a monologue also by Harris that is interspersed with the other "spoken-word arias." Harris's story shows a single white mother's struggle and volatility as she lives and raises boys in

Vancouver's Downtown Eastside. Amid homelessness, prostitution, and gang warfare, the mother tries to cope with the murder of a First Nations friend (L. Harris 2002). Harris's monologue and two other monologues by Aboriginal writers Muriel Williams and Rosemary Georgeson emphasize First Nations female experience, and three other spoken-word arias convey Asian, African, and Anglo Canadian women's experiences. The "operatic" style of the Red Dress Singer singing "Lanthanum" in between monologues inspired by the aria format is supported by dramatized, popular notions of the red dress[3] and the diva. Playing with the diva label has precedents in other theatrical works like Tina Mason's *Diva Ojibway*. Written in 1990, *Diva Ojibway* premiered in 1994 in the Ojibway language with a score that Native Earth Performing Arts commissioned from Jerod Impichchaachaaha' Tate (Chickasaw).

In such ways, *Rare Earth Arias* takes up Tomson Highway's idea to use concepts of opera and opera arias to structure Native Canadian stage plays, as he had done in his one-woman show *Aria*.[4] Similar to *Rare Earth Arias*, Highway's *Aria* unfolds within a formal and narrative framework reminiscent of opera. An instrumental piece introduces and closes *Aria*, which consists of twelve song-flecked monologues and twelve female characters and was premiered by Greenlander Makka Kleist in March 1987. Melding expressions of indigeneity and Western high art, however, has been a colonial and postcolonial trend internationally – for example, in art music, including opera, chamber works, symphonic compositions, and music for ballet, and in Indigenous visual art.

Rare Earth Arias is an example of what Diane Debenham (1988) calls "co-op plays," theatre written by Natives working together with non-Natives. Other examples include *The Book of Jessica* (1989), co-written by non-Native Linda Griffiths and Maria Campbell (Métis), and *NO'XYA'* (*Our Footprints*) (Diamond et al. 2001), which was authored by David Diamond, director of Vancouver's Headlines Theatre, in conjunction with three members of the Gitxan-Wet'suwet'en First Nation. Co-op plays are defined by the co-authorship of Native and non-Native writers.

The Rare Voice

Rare Earth Arias is centred on Marie Clements's notion of the rare voice. Although the authors, performers, and directors of the play expressed different views on what the rare voice meant to them individually, they agreed that *Rare Earth Arias* gives voice to inner-city women, who are rarely heard in Canadian public expressions. The "rare voice" expressed by the stage play is, as writer Leith Harris said, "all the precious, precious voices that are just 'ground into the dirt'" (L. Harris 2002). Harris's image evokes inner-city women's experiences of the intersecting oppressions of low gender, race, or class status, for example, and their sufferings of premature death due to addictions and violence, including serial murder.[5] "In terms of the idea of the [opera] aria," mentor Adrienne Wong said, the rare voice is of "the fallen women or the women who fall in between the cracks; the women who don't belong; the women who are outsiders in some way, which I think makes it so much more poignant that their voices are heard" (Wong 2002). Mentor Kathleen Flaherty, a producer of the Canadian Broadcasting Corporation's *Ideas* and *Dead Dog Café* programs, mused, "I thought of the monologues as each [inner-city writer's] song, as their aria" (Flaherty 2002).

At the same time, *Rare Earth Arias* explores and performs a cause of the rare voice: the fact that when people find themselves between cultures, subcultures, or social contexts that involve specific communities, often their voices are not heard in those communities. I would like to propose the rare voice as a concept that is useful for subaltern studies. It importantly evokes a discursive implication of social marginalization.

What did it feel like to experience conditions that could produce a rare voice? In *Rare Earth Arias* the operatic Red Dress Singer coalesces repeatedly with dramatic action in the monologues so as to enact a subjective in-between space: a felt experience of ambivalence, destruction, and possibility created when one belongs neither to one identity or another, one community or another, one social space or another.

For example, "Hollow," a monologue by Muriel Williams, shows a First Nations Downtown Eastside woman who is between cultural and ethnic communities: a prostitute with few or no connections to the Aboriginal community and with business but no friendships in seamy Anglo circles. The prostitute, Hollow, is a composite of the Indigenous missing and street women Williams knew. In the premiere, her monologue ended as the Red Dress Singer sang a First Nations and Catholic version of the lullaby "Mary Had a Little Baby." The lullaby appears on gospel recordings popular among Inuit in northern Canada and among First Nations and Métis in western Canada and in the United States. However, Katherine Harris, who sang the lullaby, identified it as Anglo and from the southern United States (K. Harris 2002). The protagonist turns to prostitution after being sexually abused by a Caucasian church reverend, and spiritually unfulfilled, she slits her wrists. However, Hollow does not die. A combination of her Christian faith and a vision of an eagle, a memory of her Native roots, inspires her to quit the sex trade, despite a lack of community support. For the end of "Mary Had a Little Baby," Harris created new lyrics and a melodic tag in consultation with Williams. The words, provided below, are reminiscent of the eagle, a bird sacred to many First Nations, and the Catholic hymn "On Eagles Wings" from Isaiah 40:31:

> She shall rise up with wings
> She shall rise up with wings
> Wings of an eagle
> Rise up
> All rise up.

This music reflects the "split" nature of Native and non-Native cultural affiliations in Hollow's self, which forms a focus in Muriel Williams's spoken-word aria.

Similarly, through various "iconic" expressions, African and Asian music and monologues in *Rare Earth Arias* narrate characters' "in-betweenness" due to conflicts with different ethnicities and cultures. In this way, the characters negotiate third areas. For example, "The Girl in the Red Dress," a monologue by Wendy Chew, and Katherine Harris's performance therein of "Geo Xian Qing," which in Vancouver is a "repre-sentatively" Taiwanese folksong, convey the experience of a girl who re-locates from a tribal Chinese town to urban Asia but never feels at home in inter-ethnic, westernized city circles. Like the iconic Native prostitute and eagle of Harris's new lyrics for the end of "Mary Had a Little Baby," this song evoked power relations of displacement and race.

The concept of the rare voice, as performed in *Rare Earth Arias*, extends beyond interactions between Indigenous and non-Indigenous people to encompass the following problem: some socially dislocated people may not have a voice in the space between social groups, including diverse ethnicities and cultures. In *Rare Earth Arias* Muriel Williams's and Leith Harris's monologues voice such rarely heard experiences, namely those of missing and murdered Aboriginal street women whom the authors knew from Vancouver's Downtown Eastside (Collins 2002, L. Harris 2002).

Popular Musical Forms of African Americans and Native Canadians: Minstrelsy and the Blues

Often in contemporary Aboriginal Canadian theatre, the articulation of social marginalization results in crisis and then a transformation that recognizes uneven (post)colonial realities. Such transcendence of suffering was linked to music by Jerry Wasserman, who named Tomson Highway's play *Dry Lips Oughta Move to Kapuskasing* blues-like because its ending involves a narrative transformation with "unresolved ironies, the embrace of contradiction and the resistance to closure so characteristic of the blues" (Wasserman 1998, 71). For Wasserman, this aspect evokes expectations of narrative outcomes in blues lyrics, where in Richard Wright's words, "burden and woe is dialectically redeemed" (quoted in Wasserman 1998, 60).

Numerous Canadian plays use blues music, including Highway's *Dry Lips Oughta Move to Kapuskasing* (Wasserman 1998). In *Dry Lips'* 1989 premiere, Zachary, played by Gary Farmer, performed twelve-bar blues on harmonica each time the Cree trickster Nanabush appeared so that, in Roberta Imboden's words, the audience "can more easily follow the laugh of the trickster" (Imboden 1995, 121). As well, blues is a music genre that Aboriginals in audiences can immediately connect with. The performance of blues music is immensely popular in Aboriginal communities across Canada, especially but not exclusively in recordings by musicians and bands whose careers are centred, at the time of writing, in urban areas in Ontario (e.g., Derek Miller, Harrison Kennedy, Brock Stonefish, Mark Laforme, Robbie Antone, the Pappy Johns Band, and Jacques and the Shakey Boys), Manitoba (e.g., Isaac Mandamin and Billy Joe Green), Alberta (e.g., Jared Sowan), and British Columbia (e.g., Shakti Hayes, Helene Duguay, Jason Burnstick, and Murray Porter). Native Canadian blues may incorporate localized, Aboriginal perspectives and non-Native blues styles (Beaudry et al. 1992) but also traditional and regional Aboriginal music elements. Like African American blues styles such as the classic blues, 1930s urban blues in Harlem and Chicago (Oliver 1990), and country or early down-home blues (Titon 1994), lyrics of Aboriginal Canadian blues address social complaints, including racism (of whites), but often do so within the context of an affirmation of life, love, sex, movement, and hope (Wright, quoted in Wasserman 1998, 72).

By the 1990s and 2000s, Drew Hayden Taylor, a self-proclaimed "blue-eyed Ojibway" from Ontario, exploited blues music, narrative expectations of the blues, and blues lyric structure when writing theatre. These multiple blues influences appear in his four-play series *The Blues Quartet*, which includes *The Bootlegger Blues* (1991), *The Baby Blues* (2007a [1999]), *The Buz'gem Blues* (2002a), and *The Berlin Blues* (2007b).

In fact, Drew Hayden Taylor refers to *The Blues Quartet* plays as blues songs in theatrical form. Each play features one or more blues songs with lyrics and/or music by Taylor. The plays' narratives focus on characters feeling "blue" about, respectively, bootlegging, babies, lovers (or *buz'gem* in Ojibway), and a German conglomerate. Some plays in *The Blues Quartet* also flow through blues narrative structure, particularly the A A B stanza recognizable across lyrics of many blues styles.

The Baby Blues, for instance, has two acts, the first of which has three scenes and the second of which has five. Scenes 1 to 3 of act 1 and scenes 1 to 3 of act 2 show characters feeling blue about different meanings of the word "baby": a child, someone who pouts, and a ravishing woman, among other definitions. Pashik is a beautiful, intelligent, and kind seventeen-year-old who wants to see the world. Jenny, her controlling mother, is upset because her "baby" has trouble focusing on school and occasionally wants to run away with teenage crushes. Noble, a thirty-eight-year-old powwow dancer, has promised to drive Pashik to a powwow in Connecticut. Neither Noble nor Pashik knows that they are father and daughter. Jenny suddenly recognizes Noble, who promptly disappeared after contributing to Pashik's conception. Jenny demands $40,800 in retroactive child support. This makes Noble pout, or "act like a baby." Noble does not work but prefers to drink beer and womanize. He and fellow dancer Skunk compete to score "live ones," or attractive women, at a powwow, the setting for this play. One "babe," Summer, is an anthropology student who claims to be one-sixty-fourth Aboriginal, but she does not know which tribe. Not getting sexual action makes the men "blue." Scenes 4 and 5 of act 2 relate an ironic narrative resolution involving Aboriginal father-daughter interactions. Pashik admiringly accepts Noble as her father. In Jenny's words, "the ironic thing is, [he does not] deserve a daughter like her" (Taylor 2007a [1999], 102). In this way, the narrative structure of *Baby Blues* has two "A" sections of similar scene lengths followed by a narrative resolution in a "B" section.

Taylor writes that he adapted blues music structures in an attempt to parody depressing histories of First Nations oppression: "In our zeal as writers, some of us have tended to explore the darker side of First Nations existence, to illustrate and document the tragedies and their continuing repercussions in our communities. When an oppressed people get their voice back, they tend to write about being oppressed. But, a Blood Elder was once quoted as saying, 'Humour is the WD-40 of healing'" (Taylor 2002a, 7–8). Integrating "blues" as a metaphor for an Aboriginal discursive approach, Taylor says, is "part of [his] constant attempt to highlight and celebrate the fabulous Aboriginal sense of humour" (Taylor 2002a, 7).

Thus Taylor plays with sensitivities of race and power between Natives and non-Natives, which Aboriginals engage in the creation of plays and blues. In *The Blues Quartet* the playwright negotiates a third area of power and difference surrounding theatre and blues music. He seems to want to generate third spaces in the reception of said issues by audiences of his plays.

By contrast, playwright Daniel David Moses used generic expectations of blackface minstrelsy to shape the narrative of *Almighty Voice and His Wife* (2001). This use of minstrelsy, most often performed by whites, is a First Nations appropriation of a white appropriation of black expressions that plays with race in the colonial era. In Aboriginal Canadian stage plays, many uses of musical expressions have become third area negotiations in their performance and have inspired third spaces outside of their performance. The play tells and then retells the story of Almighty Voice, who as Rob Appleford observes, was "a nineteenth-century Saskatchewan Cree folk hero ... whose initial poaching of a settler's cow [led] to the killing of a Mountie and an eventual stand-off involving Almighty Voice, two of his companions and one hundred officers and civilian volunteers" (Appleford 1993, 22). Act 1 tells the story as a tragedy. Almighty Voice's death devastates his wife, whose existence becomes precarious. She has just had a baby, and Almighty Voice provided their family with food.

Act 2 re-examines this outcome as a minstrel show, with Almighty Voice, in death, playing the character Ghost and his wife playing Interlocutor, a stock minstrel character.[6] Both Ghost and Interlocuter appear in whiteface and reference other stock minstrel characters like Tambo and Bones, who are personifications of the tambourine and bones, primary rhythm instruments in some minstrel show music (see Winans 1996, 142). Various scenes in act 2 take their titles from vocal music solos. Examples of these scene titles are "Baritone Solo," "Tenor Solo," and "Duet." It is relevant here that opera was an important part of the nineteenth-century minstrel repertoire (Mahar 1999, 101–56). Other scenes borrow names that may evoke, among other performances, "Ethiopian" sketches (the code word for "black" in this period), which were common in minstrel shows after 1847 (Mahar 1999, 162). Still other scenes use titles of dances of African American slaves, like the cakewalk, which originally parodied Anglo American ballroom dance, and the walkaround.[7] Daniel David Moses explains why he borrowed the minstrel show format:

> I looked into the history and conventions of the minstrel show
> and discovered that troupes performing these entertainments
> had traveled across much of North America in the 1800s not
> far behind the settlers ... I knew it was important that minstrel
> shows had still existed at the time Almighty Voice had died. It
> allowed me to suppose that it would not have been impossible that

many of the people who gathered to watch the standoff had also watched and enjoyed a minstrel show, that their attitudes had been partly formed or at least encouraged by the minstrel show's racist stereotypes. (Moses 1998, 140)

When writing, Moses imagined his network of actors playing the Mounties, soldiers, and settlers:

It then crossed my mind that if I were going to create all those white characters, then the Native actors I usually worked with would get to play them and that maybe they'd have to wear white-face. The idea amused me … I found myself … turning over in my mind that image of my Native actors in Whiteface. What I found on its other side was the image of white actors in black face. (Moses 1998, 139–40)

Like Taylor, Moses wanted to write a healing and humorous text by engaging a racialized musical form:

White as a color exists only because some of us get told that we're black or yellow or Indians. I think my ghosts [in whiteface] exist to probe the white problem, this tonal confusion, to spook its metaphors. Maybe my ghosts are like mirrors but from a fun house. (Moses 1998, 147)[8]

Other Native Canadian stage plays incorporate whiteface minstrel performance when critiquing race issues – for instance, *The Scrubbing Project* (2002), a vaudevillian fantasia by the Toronto-based Turtle Gals Performance Ensemble of Jani Lauzon (Métis), Monique Mojica (Kuna/Rappahannock), and Michelle St John. As Helen Gilbert argues, "By stressing the performativity of race alongside the enormous power (still) invested in skin color as a categorizing and stratifying tool [such] indigenous whiteface acts directly address the racial hierarchies that have undergirded the settler/invader cultures in which they are staged" (H. Gilbert 2003, 680).

Musical Activism and Ritual in Indigenous Theatre for Indigenous Communities

Indigenous theatre for Indigenous audiences is part of an international trend; Ross Kidd writes, "from within [the Native] culture, [there are projects] to revive theatre as part of communal life, as something organically related to the struggles of the [Native] community, with active participation, collective expression, and little separation between actors and audience" (Kidd 1984, 112). In Canada a main aim of Indigenous community-centred theatre is to work through Native-Native interactions for the benefit of Aboriginal artists and audiences and sometimes as a means of addressing relationships between Natives and non-Natives, my focus here.

In theatre by and for Inuit produced in Nunavut and the Northwest Territories, musical expressions are central to the process by which stage plays and dance theatre[9] are created. Frequently, Inuit playwrights embed music into a soundscape on which dramatic action is constructed. A structural basis of a soundscape is layered over with movement, dialogue, costumes, and lighting. Soundscapes typically include live presentations of Inuit drum dance songs, throat singing, and songs for northern games (see Tunooniq Theatre 1992, 17) but sometimes incorporate recordings of popular or classical music.

Some Inuit theatre artists use theatre creation to revive the performance of traditional Inuit song and dance genres, which declined following cultural-assimilation efforts initiated by non-Native Christian missions and residential schools in Canada.[10] Tunooniq Theatre actor Pakak Innuksuk explains that "Inuit drum dancing has been slowly fading since Christianity was started in the North. This is because the drum was sometimes used to call the Spirits" (Innuksuk 1992, 22). Tunooniq Theatre spends most of its theatre creation and rehearsal time practising and reviving suppressed song and dance expressions (Innuksuk 1992; Qamaniq and Cowan 1992, 18). This musical process of revival is common in both professional and amateur Inuit stage plays for Inuit communities, Tunooniq Theatre's *Changes* (1986) being an example of the former and the Igloolik Dance and Drama Group's *Uvanga* (*Me*) (Ott, Robinson, and MacDonald 1992) being an example of the latter. It is also present in one-act plays workshopped at the Baffin Summer School of the Dramatic Arts (Hall 1988). Through musical expressions, the Inuit plays negotiate the third space via activist gestures that engage Indigenous performers, characters, and audiences. Music and dance revival outside of the theatre but inspired by the theatre performances is one point of the works. Cultural revitalization also happens in the process of creating the performances.

Parallel examples exist in Aboriginal communities in southern Canada, where First Nations, Métis, and urban Aboriginals view stage plays created and performed by, for example, Native theatre-artists-in-training. Institutes like the Centre for Indigenous Theatre in Toronto, the

Saskatchewan Native Theatre Company's Circle of Voices Aboriginal Youth Theatre Program, and Full Circle: First Nations Performance, run by Margo Kane in Vancouver, train Indigenous theatre professionals. Grassroots theatre groups, like Injun'Nuity Theatre Company in Vancouver, may be forums for aspiring actors and directors to practise skills of play writing and performance, sometimes with non-Native involvement. Injun'Nuity received mentorship from Jay Hamburger (non-Native), director of Vancouver's Theatre in the Raw, for premieres of Curtis Ahenakew's *All My Relationships* (in 2002), Curtis Ahenakew, Jerilynn Webster, and Duane Howard's *The Lost One* (in 2003), and Curtis Ahenakew and Jerilynn Webster's *Eastside* (in 2003).

In such student theatre productions, diverse Native and non-Native music genres often interpolate plots' narratives or lived experiences of audiences. These interventions tend to initiate or promote restitution and well-being, sometimes concerning destructive aspects of living, which the rare voice concept also addresses. Especially when they incorporate traditional Aboriginal values or songs, the interventions intensify the ritualistic aspects of staged performance and blur the boundaries between theatre performance and Native musical ritual. In this way, instances of musical "healing," traditionally negotiated through structured performances of Indigenous ritual and ceremony, may be transported into theatre. For instance, song allows the largest narrative transformation in Injun'Nuity's *The Lost One*. It is only memories and spirits evoked by a rattle gifted to a homeless and culturally alienated Chilcotin (Interior Salish) man living in Vancouver's intercultural Downtown Eastside with addictions, and his subsequent singing of a traditional song, that make him want to continue living.

Another example is *Eastside*, about a clique of First Nations youth negotiating multiple cultural worlds and identities in East Vancouver. A rap battle in scene 1 contrasts values of First Nations traditions and hip hop subcultures. Kenny arrogantly snorts to Sonya, "Rhyme is the shit, girl. I never heard you rap before," to which Sonya replies:

> You tell me our culture is nothing
> But really, you know, it is something.
> Okay, first of all, stop judging.
> It's not your place,
> So don't you dare come up in my face
> With that disgrace, that attitude.
> What the fuck happened to you?

> It's like all of a sudden you're running from your problems [by
> abusing alcohol].
> But really, honey, you know you've got to solve them.

Kenny rhymes that he should rape the "bitch" in a "surgical" manner, where he works her over "like a doctor should." But the girl titters "maybe not," releasing further critique:

> So, Kenny, you think you're alert
> But all you act is like a pervert.
> I always hear you talk lies
> Ain't nothing but complete lies.
> I don't even know why I try
> Because you ain't nothing but a french fry.

When young actors performed *Eastside* at the Vancouver Aboriginal Friendship Centre in 2003, cheers burst from an enthusiastic, youth-filled audience after the girl's first rhyme, groans erupted after Kenny's comeback, and groans, claps, and laughs intermingled following the girl's second rhyme. The lyrics elicited youth engagement with the practice of "dissing" (put downs) in hip hop subcultures, including the misogynistic verbal insults that captivate media critics. A co-author of *Eastside*, Jerilynn Webster (Mohawk/Cayuaga/Nuxalk), said the scene was based on performance practices of "Red" hip hop by Native youth in Vancouver (Webster 2003).

Eastside ends up critically examining possible relationships between disconnection from First Nations traditional values and behaviours of substance misuse and misogyny. The character Jason dies from alcohol misuse, which prompts the other teenagers to seek counselling at Young Bear's Lodge, an addictions treatment program rooted in Indigenous traditions. Drawing on Theatre in the Raw's previous work with First Nations, Injun'Nuity included talking circles after the show.[11] Audiences and actors discussed substance misuse and the treatment of women in Aboriginal communities.

Interventions of music that draw on Native traditional values are important to transformations depicted in the narratives of Indigenous plays across Canada. One can make this argument for the plots of almost all of the Native plays already mentioned, from Tomson Highway's *Aria* to Drew Hayden Taylor's *The Baby Blues*, Inuit theatre, and plays at the Firehall Arts Centre in Vancouver. Such plot transformations may reflect the unresolved ironies, presence of contradiction, and resistance to closure characteristic of the narrative flow of blues lyrics, perhaps within larger forms of classical music or African American music. In the final scene of *Aria*, a First Nations woman appears drugged and dying but finds a drum at her feet. She beats it, sings a First Nations song, then yells, "I knew she was alive," intimating that part of her knew that she would find again her Native heritage. Her solution to feeling threateningly suspended between the Western and Indigenous is to revive Native tradition inside herself.

Aboriginal Musical Forms in Third Wave Plays

As Native North American theatre methodology has matured, Native Canadian and American playwrights increasingly have moved away from linear forms. Jaye T. Darby, Bruce King, and Drew Hayden Taylor note that much of Western theatre follows a linear progression of conflict, climax, and resolution (Darby 2000; King 2000; Taylor 2000, 260–2). However, in what Paula Gunn Allen calls the third wave of Native North American (play)writing, contemporary issues and stylistic aspects are fused with "the oldest First Nations traditions" of "inclusion, incorporation, and transformation of alien elements into elements of ceremonial significance" (Gunn Allen 1996, 13). This approach – which began in the 1990s – is nonlinear, a characteristic typically attributed to storytelling, whereby stage plays "possess a circular structure, incorporating event within event, piling meaning upon meaning, until the accretion finally results in a story" (Gunn Allen 1996, quoted in Darby 2000, x). Deserving of further exploration is the role of Aboriginal music, dance, and ritual in the creation of such artistic structures. Canadian Aboriginal theatre artists whom I interviewed for this research beginning in 2000 associated the "circular and episodic" structure (Darby 2000, x) with ceremonies' episodic inclusion of music and dance and with First Nations and Inuit traditional songs in which melodies are repeated again and again, often with subtle variation.

A simultaneous striving for nonlinearity and inclusion of traditional Aboriginal music, dance, and ritual is shown in the artistic development of Edmonton/Vancouver playwright Margo Kane (Cree/Saulteaux). Kane's stage plays *Moonlodge* (1994; first draft 1990), *Confessions of an Indian Cowboy* (2001), and *The River—Home* (premiere 2005) progressively integrate episodic structures and music in a ritualistic way. *Moonlodge* starts and ends with a dream and consists of multiple memory flashes of how the protagonist Agnes came into womanhood through a hitchhiking road trip, her first powwow experience, and forced sex. The play, metaphorically, is a ceremony of Native womanhood. Yet its narrative is linear except for the dreams. Fourteen instances of Christian, popular mainstream, and Indigenous traditional song do not connote ritual structure but underscore and comment on the dramatic action (Kane 1994).

In *Confessions of an Indian Cowboy* and *The River—Home*, prolific use of music facilitates transitions between memories and visions. Kane's writing consists almost entirely of fragments of memory – comprising disparate subject matter and rich historical snippets – that are so nonlinear they are reminiscent of poems staged back to back. *Confessions* includes round dance songs, some "chanting," and various country rock songs. Having begun as a performance art work, *The River—Home* is a stage play whose 2005 performance featured songs in a Kwakwa̲ka̲'wakw traditional style (see Halpern 1981, Harrison 2000, 2002) that were commissioned from George Taylor. Three songs marked transitions between three sections of the play, the first about precontact fishing in relation to myths of the Pacific Northwest Coast salmon people, the second about the impact of industrialization on rivers and First Nations life-ways, and the third about a desire to return to past fishing lifestyles. *The River—Home* culminates in a danced ritual, which in the performance mentioned featured four Kwakwa̲ka̲'wakw songs, a number sacred to numerous First Nations. Many plays by Kane's students are also nonlinear, poetic, music-oriented, and ritualistic: for instance, Lisa C. Ravensbergen and Michelle Olson's *The Place Between* (premiere 2004). Other Vancouver productions that resist linearity may not incorporate traditional music and ritual so intensely. An example is Tasha Faye Evans's first mainstage play, *She Stands Still* (premiere 2004), which modernizes a "manufactured" myth about a cedar tree woman, was written under the mentorship of Muriel Miguel (Kuna/Rappahannock) of Spiderwoman Theater in New York City, and was inspired by Evans's activism around saving old-growth forest on Vancouver Island, British Columbia.

Some third wave Aboriginal plays negotiate relationships between Natives and non-Natives in activist ways that involve theatrical form and music yet reach far beyond play scripts themselves. Third wave plays, such as co-op plays, are intended primarily for intercultural audiences and may engage inter-ethnic and intercultural disputes and issues involving Natives and non-Natives while using theatre as a means to contribute to national political discourses and negotiations. Marie Clements's *The Unnatural and Accidental Women* (2005) is one example that engages an inter-ethnic space in the public arena of theatre reception in Canada.

Here, the cultural debate of Bhabha's third space idea is framed in national and societal terms.

The Unnatural and Accidental Women has a sound-inspired form and plot, which have historical precedent in Aboriginal plays like Daniel David Moses's *Almighty Voice and His Wife* and Drew Hayden Taylor's *The Blues Quartet* series. This play takes on the problem of Indigenous women being murdered or going missing, particularly from Canada's inner cities. This topic has been important to some Canadian political discourses, which have debated the harmfulness of racist and sexist stereotypes of Native women to perceptions of their dignity and worth, Canadian government policies that may leave Aboriginal women and girls vulnerable to attack, and racial attitudes of police forces if they privilege non-Aboriginals.

The two-act *The Unnatural and Accidental Women* dramatizes convicted killer Gilbert Paul Jordan's encounters with women in Vancouver's Downtown Eastside. The non-Native man, called Gilbert or the Barber for legal reasons in the play, forces eight Native and two non-Native women to drink to their deaths. Act 1 barrages the audience with Gilbert's murder of each of the eight women. An actor in the play's 2000 premiere, Christine Willes, adds: "Punctuating the [eight] deaths is Rebecca's search through Skid Row for the mother who abandoned her twenty years ago – Aunt Shadie – and Aunt Shadie's spirit's efforts to protect her daughter" (Willes 2000, 3). In Act 2 the "dead women's spirits protect Rebecca, and offer a hilarious and moving critique of the sexist, racist, and classist institutions and attitudes that have helped kill them. Their rage, strength, and determined collaboration move Gilbert to justice at Rebecca's hands" (Willes 2000, 3).

Dialogue, sound effects, slide projections, and music convey the story within a highly nonlinear structure that emerges through brief scenes in which one swirls with the women through their life memories. In an interview with me, Marie Clements said the form of *The Unnatural and Accidental Women* was inspired by "what we hear [and see] in the last few minutes of life. When things are so quiet, what do you really hear? Do you hear your past – past conversations or ideas that come into your head, the animation of your life, memories?" She thought to fictionalize the women's stories because media reportage on the Gilbert Paul Jordan case focused a lot of attention on him but very little on the women themselves (Clements 2000).

At the end of act 1, two languages in one song's lyrics, English and Cree, draw attention to cultural and ethnic differences involved in the missing women issue. These lyrics may be understood to mirror Clements's sonic and activist impetus in forming the play because they describe the women's experiences of hearing and seeing each other in life and death and of "drowning" in alcohol.[12] The lyrics are interspersed with episodes about six of the women's deaths, highlighting the nonlinearity of the play. At the 2000 premiere, dance and singing were used to make a ritual of welcoming each woman into death. Jennifer Kreisberg and Soni Moreno, of the Native American a cappella trio Ulali, created a melody for Clements's lyrics, which they called "The Calling Song" (Kreisberg 2000). The accompanying dance blended Coast Salish, Odawa, and East Indian movements (Bobb and Merasty 2000, Eshkibok 2000).

In such ways, *The Unnatural and Accidental Women* extended activism (R. Gilbert 2003) on violence against Aboriginal women from a sound-inspired play structure to a song and musical ritual. Media activism was associated with the 2000 premiere of this play. In a promotional newspaper article in the *Vancouver Sun* on 4 November 2000, journalist Jim Beatty wrote extensively on Gilbert Paul Jordan's crime history and female victims in cooperation with Marie Clements. A reader of the article, whose comments appeared in the *Vancouver Sun* on 25 November, noticed that Jordan, who was on parole, was violating conditions of a court order, which resulted in his rearrest. Clements's awareness-raising play lives on in a feature film adaptation, *Unnatural and Accidental*, released in 2006, starring Tantoo Cardinal, Sophie Merasty, Marie Clements, and Margo Kane.

Conclusion

This chapter has explored how the adoption of musical forms as theatrical forms in Native Canadian stage plays has engaged issues of relations between Natives and non-Natives in Canada. In my analysis of African American, Indigenous, and art music expressions, I found that musical genres and structures with identifiable Native or non-Native meanings are often juxtaposed with theatrical content that is oppositely non-Native or Native in ways that might reasonably draw audience attention to intercultural power differences. The plays discussed here accomplish this process of drawing attention by evoking the metaphoric poetry of their narratives – which may be connoted through diverse musical genres and structures or through sounds in the example of *The Unnatural and Accidental Women* – and by creating a rich and complex field of meanings for possible narrative resonance in audiences. In other cases, musical expressions are placed in stage plays in ways that might evoke ritual forms involving song. Injun'Nuity Theatre Company's productions of *The Lost One* and *Eastside* mixed Aboriginal and non-Native elements in a single song in this way, and Margo Kane's *The River—Home* uses a pastiche of a series of music expressions that culminate in a dance ritual addressing the politics of relations between Natives and non-Natives. Not limited to audience "readings" and "listenings," the creative process of making Aboriginal Canadian theatre, through incorporating musical forms in playwriting or performance preparation, has negotiated intercultural relations.

I have considered the intentions of Aboriginal Canadian playwrights and performers in adapting musical genres and structures as bases for theatre. As in the cases of Drew Hayden Taylor's use of the blues and Daniel David Moses's use of minstrelsy, one intention has been to critique oppressive culture and race relations, either historical or contemporary, including in discourse, as per Taylor's parodic *The Blues Quartet*. A second intention has been to take social action on problems of relations between Natives and non-Natives in Canada. Tunooniq Theatre has countered the cultural assimilation of the colonial period by nurturing a revival of Inuit throat singing and drum dancing among its performers when creating soundscapes as bases for theatre forms. Whereas action in Aboriginal communities is an important goal of Native theatre for Native Canadian audiences, intercultural activism is more typical of third wave and co-op plays for cross-cultural audiences. A third goal of using musical forms has been to propose new ways of understanding the marginalization that may occur in intercultural contact and exchange. With the co-op play *Rare Earth Arias*, Marie Clements offered her co-writers and performers a structure that was roughly inspired by opera and a monologue format that evoked the aria in order to introduce a critical concept of cultural in-betweenness: the rare voice. Clements's rare voice idea is a new framework for understanding discursive marginalization, particularly in situations where one's voice may be rarely heard if one finds oneself to be culturally dislocated and thus in between social or cultural groups. Across such diverse approaches to music and form, Native Canadian stage plays have enacted a variety of attempts to move through the third area and the third space.

Many thanks to Muriel Miguel, conversations with whom started all of this. I would also like to thank Marie Clements, Columpa Bobb, Sophie Merasty, Gloria May Eshkibok, Jennifer Kreisberg, Kathleen Flaherty, Jay Hamburger, Jerilynn Webster, Adrienne Wong, Maiko Bae Yamamoto, Katherine Harris, and Leith Harris for taking the time to talk with me about their theatrical and musical artistry. Pirkko Moisala, Beverley Diamond, Judith Rudakoff, and an anonymous reviewer offered insightful comments. Research for this chapter was funded by the Social Sciences and Humanities Research Council of Canada and by the Ontario Ministry of Training, Colleges and Universities.

1 For biographical discussions of Highway's art music training, see Filewod (1992, 18), Knowles (1999, 62), and Sherrin (1990).
2 In this chapter, "Ojibway" refers to Drew Hayden Taylor's (2002b) ethnic identification. I use Taylor's spelling of the term.
3 In popular media, a woman wearing a red dress has become a metaphor for sexual vitality, as articulated in rock songs such as Lightnin' Hopkins's "Put Your Red Dress On," Paul McCartney's "High Heel Sneakers," Georgia Satellites' "Sheila," the Charlie Daniels Band's "Fais Do Do," Richard Norton's "Run with Me," Hannah Fury's "Meathook," and Love/Hate's "Cream." Such red dress associations have been mapped onto the vitality of self-expression in Indigenous Canadian discourse both outside and within *Rare Earth Arias*. These assimilated ideas have begun to suffuse Canadian artistic discourse on social oppression, violence, and cultural hybridity, as seen in Anna Camilleri's book *I Am a Red Dress* (2004) and in her 2005 touring spoken-word performance *Sounds Siren Red*.
4 Basing theatre on opera forms has precedents in non-Native Canadian theatre – for example, famously in Michel Tremblay's *Sainte Carmen de la Main* (1976).
5 In this quotation and her monologue, Leith Harris meant to reference a specific case of serial murder (L. Harris 2002). By October 2002, the largest forensic search in Canadian history – of the dirt of a Vancouver-area pig farm operated by Robert Pickton – had produced the remains of numerous women (*Vancouver Sun*, 4 December 2008). Many were from the Downtown Eastside and from First Nations. Pickton had been charged with fifteen counts of first-degree murder by October 2002 (*Canadian Press Newswire*, 3 October 2002), and he was charged with eight additional murders as the farm investigation continued. By December 2007, Pickton had been convicted of six counts of second-degree murder (*CanWest News*, 10 December 2007). Legal proceedings are ongoing at the time of writing.
6 Like Highway's *Dry Lips Oughta Move to Kapuskasing*, Moses's *Almighty Voice and His Wife* is a play whose ending embraces the unresolved ironies, contradictions, and resistance to closure characteristic of blues lyric narratives (Wasserman 1998). By the end of act 2, titled "Ghost Dance," characters in whiteface called Ghost and Interlocutor have unmasked, showing that they are Almighty Voice and his wife. Ghost, who dies in the folk story, speaks his traditional language

and dances. He evokes the ultimately unsuccessful Ghost Dance movement, which as Ross Kidd writes, "provided a powerful revitalizing and unifying ideology for the Sioux in trying to overcome their spiritual debasement and oppression" in the colonial context (Kidd 1984, 112).

7 Although there is robust scholarly documentation of minstrelsy in the United States, a comprehensive history of minstrelsy in Canada has yet to be written. See Best (2008) and Elliot (2008) for initial work on Canadian minstrelsy.

8 For example, through music, Moses also takes on "Indian" and misogynist characterizations that existed in nineteenth-century minstrel performance (Mahar 1999, 157, 268–328). In act 2, scene 2, the "Baritone Solo," Ghost starts to sing "Lament to a Redskin Lover" – "Oh! Susanna" sung to new lyrics – in which he parodies his grief at death separating him from his wife. Daniel David Moses's lyrics begin,

> I track the winter prairie for the little squaw I lost.
> I'm missing all the kissing I had afore the frost.
> I'm moping, oh I'm hoping oh, to hold her hand in mine.
> My flower of Saskatchewan, oh we were doing fine. (Moses 2001, 38)

This racist, "Indian" characterization becomes increasingly misogynistic: one verse ends, "My little squaw was shaking, the wind was standing still," and the next verse starts, "The banic bread was in her mouth, the blood was in her eye" (Moses 2001, 38).

In act 2, scene 7, the "Duet," Ghost and Interlocuter sing – to the melody of "God Save the Queen" – lyrics that show respect for First Nations traditional beliefs involving women:

> The Moon's an old woman
> A very wise woman.
> She's made of light!
> She watches over us,
> Over the children.
> Each of us is a child again
> In the coldest night.
>
> The Moon's a young woman
> A very new woman
> Made out of dark.
> She's waiting for the light
> Just as a child might
> Wrapped warmly in a blanket and
> Not at all afraid. (Moses 2001, 58–9)

In such ways, Moses's use of light and dark races, blackface and whiteface, extends to sung musical texts in *Almighty Voice and His Wife*.

9 One example is Sylvia Ipirautaq Cloutier's scene in *Chinook Winds*, a dance theatre production created by various Aboriginal artists at Alberta's Banff Centre
for the Arts in 1996 (see Ronceria 1998).

10 From 1879 to 1986, Canadian Inuit and First Nations children were forcibly removed from their families and sent to often distant residential schools, where
they were forbidden to practise their Native cultures, including music making
and dancing (see Milloy 1999). The schools were loci of emotional, physical, sexual, and spiritual abuse (Assembly of First Nations 1994, 2). Residential schooling
was a heavy-handed attempt by Canada's federal government and various Christian churches to "civilize" Aboriginals by assimilating them into Euro-Canadian
society. The Christian denominations involved were Catholic, Anglican, United,
and Presbyterian (Milloy 1999, xii).

11 Theatre in the Raw (TITR) had used "talking circles" that were panel discussions
modelled on South Africa's Truth and Reconciliation Commission. The talking
circles followed performances of TITR's 2002 touring production of *Medicine*, by
LaVerne Adams (non-Native). *Medicine* tells a true story of five First Nations girls
who attended Canada's controversial residential schools. TITR's *Medicine* visited
Native and non-Native communities throughout British Columbia, where few
public discussions on the topic between Natives and non-Natives had occurred
(Hamburger 2002).

12 In the script, a Cree translation follows each of these English lines of the song:

> Do I hear you sister like yesterday today
> Do I hear you sister like yesterday today
> Under water – under time
> Do I hear you sister like yesterday today
> Hear your words right next to mine
> Do I hear you sister like yesterday today
> You are not speaking and yet I touch your words
> So the river says to me drink me feel better
> Like the river must've said to you first
> Drink me – feel better
> There is no sadness just the war of a great thirst
> Do I see you sisters like yesterday today
> See you as if you were sitting right here next to me
> Under the water – under the earth
> My body's floating where all the days are the same
> Long and flowing like a river
> My root – my heart
> My hair drifts behind me (Excerpted from Clements 2005, 58–65)

15

Music and Narrative in *The Unnatural and Accidental Women*

INTERVIEW EXCERPTS: MARIE CLEMENTS, SOPHIE MERASTY, AND COLUMPA BOBB WITH KLISALA HARRISON

This chapter draws on interviews that I conducted with artists involved in the production of the stage play *The Unnatural and Accidental Women*, which premiered at Vancouver's Firehall Arts Centre in 2000. *The Unnatural and Accidental Women* fictionalizes the drinking deaths of eight Aboriginal and two non-Native women who were associated with convicted killer Gilbert Paul Jordan in Vancouver's inner city. Conversations with the artists featured here offer insights into their creative processes, musical and dramatic choices, and narrative strategies as they negotiated socially and politically charged topics.

Marie Clements wrote *The Unnatural and Accidental Women* but also co-directed the premiere with Donna Spencer. In her interview, Clements discusses the inspiration for *The Unnatural and Accidental Women* and the ways that she used music in her creative process. In a second conversation, two actors in the premiere, Sophie Merasty and Columpa Bobb, share their understandings of the social roles of musical sound in Native Canadian theatre and in Aboriginal expressive culture more generally.

These interviews speak to "The Calling Song" melody by Jennifer Kreisberg and Soni Moreno of the Native American a cappella trio Ulali. This two-sectioned melody was used at the ends of acts 1 and 2 in the premiere. The first part, "Aunt Shadie's Call," was sung solo by the character Aunt Shadie (played by Muriel Miguel), who welcomes into death the ten women who are murdered in the play. As described in the synopsis of the play in chapter 14, a character representing Jordan, named the Barber or Gilbert, forces the women to drink to their deaths. As the victims joined

Shadie in the premiere, they sang the second part of the song together but left their performance unfinished. Unlike in the 2005 published script, which features song lyrics in English and Cree, the 2000 rendition of "The Calling Song" was comprised of mostly vocables created by Jennifer Kreisberg and Michelle St John, who premiered the character Rebecca. Only some lines of the published English and Cree lyrics were used. The murdered women perform the second part of "The Calling Song" when they take revenge on their killer at the end of act 2.

 Marie Clements

KH: How did your idea to create the play come about?

MC: I had been following the story [about Gilbert Paul Jordan] for quite a while through the newspapers. People had been giving me clippings about the story also. Then I had read the huge four-page spread in the *Vancouver Sun* about Jordan in 1988 [22 October]. I was struck by the fact that so much was said about him and very, very little on the women themselves. So I started taking [down] whatever details [there were] – and there weren't a lot – of the last few days of their lives, their situations, and started building their stories mostly from imagery and images, and went from there … Images I drew from the facts, mostly. Whatever pictures those conjured up, dealing with themes of isolation and loneliness, vulnerability, those kinds of things. I tried to find what would make it possible for him to get away with it. He found something vulnerable in each and every one of them, and was able to get them through that.

KH: When you were developing the stage play, did you focus on music a bit?

MC: I think, in the beginning, mostly sound – trying to create each room and each world, not only on a text level but on a visceral level.

KH: So you worked with the ambiance of the text?

MC: Yes. What we see, what we hear in the last few minutes of life. When things are so quiet, what do you really hear? Do you hear your past – past conversations or ideas that come into your head, the animation of your life, memories? Originally, I had constructed three scenes called the barbershop scenes [with] barbershop quartets. I had written lyrics and had them translated in[to] Cree and [Coast] Salish to be sung as part of the scene, because of the connection between barbershops and quartets and singing, those themes, and those women's stories, I was trying to cross them together culturally. It started out with that. When I got into the actual production, it didn't seem to flow well structurally. So what evolved was one song at the end of act I, [which was] translated and sung in harmonies. [For the play's premiere, a melody] was composed by Ulali and the women picked it up.

KH: Why did you make the decision to have "The Calling Song" text partly in Cree?

MC: In the research that I'd done, [I learned that] probably three of the women were Cree but had moved to Vancouver. So some of the main characters came from the Prairies. I was trying to get back to the authentic language after death because I believe that we go back to our authentic selves. That was part of them reclaiming that language. A lot of people say that [Cree] is the language of the heart. [I wanted] for them to go back and speak to each other from that place. Most of the [Cree words] came from [English] lyrics that I have in the play. A lot of it was a call or an honouring of each other. They call to each other: one of the main lines [is] "do I hear you sister, like yesterday today?" They go on into different verses. It is like being under water and under time and under the earth. They use it to hear each other finally. [The women] completed the first act and their journey within that [song]. So, different branches but the same tree. Trying to bring it all together.

KH: I was really struck by the audiences' responses to "The Calling Song." I saw the play a couple of times, but it seemed like that was a point where peoples' perceptions about Native women or women and violence switched in quality. I heard comments from audience members like, "That's the first time I have been able to feel empathy towards people in that position."

MC: Basically, it was trying to get the effect of being submerged in and out of water, in and out of liquid, and in and out of reality. [In] the last few scenes of the first act, you're flowing. You are with the women in a river. The visceral feeling of being able to float, submerging, coming in and out of realities. Then, joining the swirl, joining the rhythm of the river in different ways. In some ways, you are drowning and then you come up. Their dying and drowning being a metaphor for a lot of their deaths because of their drowning by alcohol. [In theatre,] sound and music [are] always dependent on the world you are creating. With this piece, there are so many places where it was surreal or memory or imagination. That gave us a lot of leeway to go into each room and different thoughts, and surface that up.

KH: I noticed that you didn't use drums for "The Calling Song" or the play. How did that decision come about?

MC: We felt that percussion was a different sound, and I think that we were trying to tap into the journeys of the women through their voices. That gave enough emotion to it. It seemed more organic. It came to the point where the women's voices were like a drum. They were the heartbeat of the piece, really.

 Sophie Merasty and Columpa Bobb

KH: The relationship between music and narrative is complicated in *The Unnatural and Accidental Women*. In the premiere, I especially noticed how different female characters came out in song, in between dialogue, at the end of act 1. Yet "The Calling Song" is not finished then.

SM: Yes, part of the reason that we did it that way [is that] the directors didn't want to complete the song because ...

CB: ... the journey itself wasn't complete. The journey that they go through isn't complete until Gilbert gets it in the end. [We were] trying to find varying degrees of their own community dealing with it. It starts individually and becomes somehow communal.

SM: The end of the play is the only time that the whole song gets sung fully [in the premiere]. It was amazing because Ulali just came in. They had a concert in town and they had just arrived into Vancouver. One of the actresses in the play was Michelle St John, a good friend of theirs, so they agreed to compose the song at her request, which they did very quickly.

CB: It was very sentient in terms of communicating through music, communicating with others. I think part of the struggle we had, when we finally got it as an ensemble, was: "How do I hear you and you?" At first, it was the mechanics of let's all sing the same note, let's all sing it at the same time, let's start and stop at the same time. After the mechanics of it, it was totally into feeling. I remember one show, every one of us, at different times during the song, broke down. It was bound to happen sooner or later. The emotion was so overwhelming, the emotional realization of what we were doing and the power of what we were doing. All of us were like [gasps], still keeping the integrity of the piece alive and what we were doing with it. It was sort of that dichotomous death is pain, death is beauty, death is final, death is rebirth. We all felt that. Everybody, one by one, was affected by that vocally.

SM: It was really very profound.

CB: And we got a standing ovation that night.

SM: Closing night was very powerful, too, because of the way we sang the song, the way we played it, the honour and respect that we wanted to give to these women and all women. We had a ceremony before the preview, during rehearsals, to honour the women, to invoke and invite them to come. I believe it too. I think it was important that we did that because it really helped us in some way on a spiritual level.

CB: For me, it helped [me] to realize that this was for them, on behalf of them. We were vessels for them. It helped in keeping our sanity offstage without having to disassociate or disconnect, which is usually what actors do. Drop it and go. But with this, we were able to become a part of something bigger than just a show, which allowed me to feel empathy instead of getting caught in feeling that pain, which is really interesting. I think the song was a big part of that, in releasing that.

SM: It was really powerful. There are a lot of Native songs out there. A lot of them are powerful, but [there are] certain songs that are really moving, one [of] which is from the West Coast, a song by Columpa's late great-grandfather Chief Dan George. When I first heard it, I thought,

"Oh my God. It is so beautiful." I could feel the power and meaning of it resonate in my being, and I knew a little bit about the history of it. It had been passed on a few generations prior. It was an old song. It is one of their honour songs. And then we have another song, which is the AIM [American Indian Movement] song [explained below], also an honour song and every time I hear that, I have that same feeling. The reason I think that happens is that the songs are imbued with spirit. They come from that spirit that is ancient, powerful, and intact, and no matter what has happened to us as Native people over the centuries, colonization and attempted genocide, we have been able to retain our culture. I think that is what makes certain songs so memorable. For me, I feel that this is one of those songs, simply because we asked the spirits to be with us, simply because we included them. That is what made it what it was.

KH: Yes. It is amazing how the audience responded to "The Calling Song" by Jennifer Kreisberg and Soni Moreno of Ulali. So many people said [in Q&A sessions with the actors that followed shows] that this performance was the point when they could feel empathy and identify with the characters. It seemed to switch people's mentality towards these women, towards women, towards Native people.

SM: Absolutely.

CB: In trying to create an energy where community comes together, especially for these women it was after life, there is a sadness to that, but it is all-inclusive. We just don't invite the spirit plane in. We consciously include the audience. We all are part of a community together, whether we like it or not, regardless of cultural differences, race, gender, age. We are part of the same community. I think what brings us together as human beings is spirit or soul or whatever you want to call it, the life-force. There is an energy, a physical energy that we have. [It] sonically alters all these different kinds of sound, what they do, how they affect us, how they move us, what they do molecularly to us. We use sound as part of a way to be one on an energy level, which is higher or more significant than just the tangible.

SM: It is universal at that point.

CB: It's like, when you hear that really hard bass music in clubs and you can feel it going through you: it's literally scrambling your energy. A lot of the songs on the West Coast are about realigning energy or reconnecting collectively. If it's about one person, it's a power song. It's that person's personal power song. It lifts them and lifts their energy out and forward. It makes them big, big enough to find their own. I think things like the AIM song, it's an honour song, but the purpose of that song, for me, on a feeling level, is to bring us together as a nation, as allied nations, to come together. It's totally not a pan-Indian song, but it calls to all Native peoples. For lack of a better word, it's like an anthem, sort of an international anthem. The thing I find powerful about Chief Dan George's song: it is all about family. So it brings up all of those feelings – even without knowing it – feelings of family: the sad feelings, the angry feelings, the happy feelings, the need for family. Whether we are with them or not, we are part of a family. This family just keeps growing and extending and extending because family to us is not nuclear. So it, too, in its own way, is inclusive because people will always fit into it. You don't have to be from his personal family to feel the effects of family. I think Chief Dan George's song is endowed with that spirit vocally.

SM: One of the things that came up in our rehearsal process was kind of funny. When [a non-Native musician] first came in to compose the music, naturally, we were all excited about it. We had these Cree words that were translated. The poetry that Marie Clements wrote was translated into Cree by James Nicholas. So we were going to sing the Cree verses. The first day of the workshop, we just sat around; then we got to the music bit. Then we started to talk about, well, how are we going to do this? [The non-Native musician] came in and he's listening to us. We grabbed drums and started fooling around. He came back the next day and he had melody, some type of a little ballad. It sounded very European. It sounded almost like one of those Gregorian chants!

CB: Yes, it had that quality to it. The thing that I heard was the stereotypical Hollywood Sioux. It was subtle, but I kept imagining eleven women singing in four-four metre, overemphasizing beats one and three: "Do I hear you sister like yesterday today. Boom-diddy-boom-boom boom." Other people were trying to sing the song and I just had this weird smile on my face. I was sitting right beside [the musician] and I didn't want to be rude, but it was almost stereotypically what happens when a non-Native person tries to compose Native music. Maybe because I grew up with it, I think it's so simple. We don't have that many beats, but different rhythmic schemes. I was looking around the room at all of these women singing. I caught Sophie's eye. I don't know how long she was staring at me, but she mouthed, "Say it!" After everybody stopped, I talked to him. Not being a musician, I was trying to explain to him musically the difference between what he was doing and what we'd do. I said, "The typical explanation from a Native person would be: It's like a heartbeat. You're stressing on the one. We stress on the two. It's not two-four time, it's almost iambic." That's the closest I could get to explaining it from a European-derived point of view. When you are doing a round dance rhythm, it's not a straight four-four time in terms of one-two-three-four.

SM: It's more natural. It follows the rhythm of the heartbeat, which a lot of our songs do. It works much better for us. I was feeling the same way about the song, but I just couldn't figure out how to say it. Singing Ulali's song was neat, too, because of one of the things that Gloria May Eshkibok [another actor in the premiere] said: "We have our own voices. We all have distinct voices when we are singing our songs, especially when we are singing in our own languages." If you were to do it or some other non-Native person who doesn't have that sound tried to do it, it wouldn't be the same. You could really hear the difference, sense it and feel it. Whereas to us, it just comes naturally.

KH: When you First Nations actresses sang and then Christine Willes [a non-Native actor] sang, it was so noticeably different.

CB: It was. It's funny because when we are sitting around singing "Me and Bobby McGee" or whatever, we all meld. She doesn't seem that distinct. But again, when we are singing the Native song, you could just hear the cultural difference. I kind of like it actually because …

KH: … it is the whole point of "The Calling Song" scenes.

CB: Yes. The inclusiveness. Christine was wondering in the beginning whether she should sing or not. She was saying, "I don't want to take away from these women." Especially because she is physically on a higher level, she didn't want any assumptions of the English woman [being] higher up and therefore … I said, "Do you know what? The song is all about community, about finding a community for these women. You are one of these women, so regardless of race or age it has to be all of us singing. It can't just be us and you. It can't be like that because that is how the audience is going to feel. Then the spirit of it is not inclusive. It's not community. It's Native women, which is not bad, but it is a different play. It is a different story." She was like, "Hmm."

KH: Why was the song in Cree?

CB: Initially, it was supposed to be several different languages. It was supposed to be English, Cree, and Salish. They couldn't get anybody from the West Coast to contribute to the translation. So everything became Cree. That is how it happened because of lack of time, resources.

SM: It would have been wonderful if we could have had some in Salish because, really, this business takes place in Vancouver, where there are a lot of Salish people. For me, I would have had a problem trying to sing [in Salish]. My character is supposed to be Salish, right? Because of the time frame, we changed her into a Cree. She would have had to sing in Salish and I don't know Salish.

CB: It's vocally very different from Cree.

SM: Yes, to me it is very guttural, in some ways. A lot of words are at the back of your throat. How do I sing like that?

CB: Yes, it is very different. Different parts of the throat. Salish is more back here and Cree, for me anyway, seems to roll up off the tongue.

SM: It's more fluid, Cree, whereas Salish I find choppy in some ways, but I love it.

CB: You can almost hear the difference in terms of where people live. Cree to me, when I hear it, it is very up. You see the prairie grasses flowing. That is kind of the feeling of it. On the West Coast, everything is very rooted, very deep.

SM: Which is like the dances, too. The dances are very grounded, whereas powwow dancing is up there, right?

CB: Yes. Touch the sky. So again, environmentally, where we are situated, informs our art.

SM: I think that would have given the song a whole different feel in a big way. I think it would have because of the extreme differences between the Cree and the Salish. But you know, this is very challenging and exciting because this is the kind of stuff we have been doing for a long time with European music, mainstream types of music, incorporating, borrowing. Now, when we borrow within our own nations, that's a whole new thing. Even the style of drumming is different.

SM: What I really like about this is that all we had were our voices.

KH: No drums. Did the actors decide that?

CB: Yeah, we decided that. Technically, where are we going to get the drums? I think [actor] Delores [Dallas] brought it up. She said, "You know, Indians drum in every show. Let's not do it." We all kind of went, "Why shouldn't we drum?" I would like to hear the sound of a drum. But at the same time, what she said made sense. So we jammed about that. "Really, it's the women's voices that need to rise up. So, in a sense, it's bigger than just a music number, bigger than just that." So having a drum or a rattle there would make it more about a musical number as opposed to voices rising up. Just aurally, when you hear the piano intro to *O Canada*, everybody rises. There is a recognition that this is what we're doing. Whereas if people just got the spirit to sing their national anthem because of a situation, it's different. The drum for us becomes a typical "We're going to sing you a song now," like the grade school intro to *O Canada*.

SM: You know what the main thing was: a few people told me after the show that when we did sing the song complete at the end of the show, they wanted to stand because that is acknowledging, honouring the spirits of these women. Some of the people who knew that wanted to stand, which is something we just do anytime anyway in funerals when honouring someone or singing certain songs.

KH: Once when I attended, one guy behind me was singing along. I thought that was his way of honouring the women.

CB: To be a part of it.

KH: That is what he knew.

16

Music, Religion, and Healing
in a Mi'kmaw Community

INTERVIEW: WALTER DENNY JR
WITH GORDON E. SMITH

The following is a collaborative narrative based on three extended conversations between myself, Gordon E. Smith (Kingston, Ontario), and Walter Denny Jr (Eskasoni, Cape Breton Island, Nova Scotia). These conversations took place on 6 December 2008, 9 May 2009, and 15 August 2009 at Walter's home in Eskasoni. We emphasize the collaborative aspect of this text, as our conversations were free-flowing and informal. We have tried to maintain this spirit here.[1] By way of introduction, I first present some contextual information on Eskasoni and on my research in Eskasoni, which led to these conversations with Walter Denny Jr. The goal in this introduction is to help illuminate the various themes that emerge in the interview narrative.

My research in Eskasoni dates back to the late 1980s, when I lived and worked for five years in Sydney, Cape Breton Island. During that period, I taught music courses at Cape Breton University (known then as the University College of Cape Breton), where I encountered Mi'kmaw students from Eskasoni in my classes. Eskasoni is the largest Mi'kmaw reserve in Atlantic Canada with a population of approximately 3,000. The total estimated Mi'kmaw population is 20,000. Located on the shores of the Bras d'Or Lakes, fifty kilometres west of the nearest city of Sydney, Eskasoni became a reserve as part of the centralization program established by the Canadian federal government in the 1940s. The Eskasoni reserve is the only Roman Catholic parish in Nova Scotia, the other reserves being served by the Catholic mission system. Eskasoni residents are predominantly Roman Catholic. This does not mean, however, that the relationship is a close one. Of those who are baptized into Catholicism, many are nominally Catholic and participate in church activities, such as funerals and christenings. Anthropologist Angela Robinson (2005, 12) has noted that although many Eskasoni residents use the term "traditionalist" to refer to specific persons or groups of people within the community who follow what are considered to be authentic or pre-Christian religious practices exclusive of Catholicism, for many Mi'kmaq, a person can be identified a traditionalist by upholding Mi'kmaw culture and tradition while accepting Catholicism as a primary religious orientation.

My encounter with Mi'kmaw students in my classes at Cape Breton University in the 1980s led to research at Eskasoni, which focused primarily on individual musicians and traditionalists, including Lee Cremo, Sarah Denny, Rita Joe, and Wilfred Prosper. Over the course of the past ten years, each of these elders has passed away. A conversation I had with fiddler, chanter, and Mi'kmaw scholar Wilfred Prosper in February 2004 is a point of departure for the following narrative and links to my conversations with Walter Denny Jr. In conversations with Wilfred, he always asked the same question when we started to talk about music, one that fieldworkers frequently hear: "Why do you want to know this?" I can't recall my exact response, other than that it was general and was along the lines of wanting to learn about Mi'kmaw music and culture (e.g., fiddling, hymn singing, popular music, etc.). In that February 2004 conversation, Wilfred responded: "One of the best places where you'll see all kinds of music working together is the church. Actually, if I think about it, a funeral is where there's a real mixing of music. Traditional, modern, and the two going together. It's best if you go to a funeral, and see for yourself. Why not go to my funeral if you're around [laughs]. If you can't make it, maybe someone will make a movie of it [still laughing]" (Wilfred Prosper, field notes, February 2004). Sadly, just over a year later, Wilfred passed away. I didn't get to his funeral, but someone did make a "movie" of it. I remembered his comment to me about funerals, and the next time I visited the Prosper family, Wilfred's wife, Bessie, kindly gave me a copy of the funeral video.

Inspired by Wilfred's advice and my research at Holy Family Roman Catholic Church in Eskasoni, recently my work has been focused on music making and funeral practices. Aspects of the video of Wilfred's funeral that stand out, at least for me, are the participation of the fiddlers (twenty from the Cape Breton Fiddlers Association, of which Wilfred was a member), the readings and prayers in Mi'kmaq, and the hymns in English and Mi'kmaq. One of the readers at Wilfred's funeral was Walter

Denny Jr; Walter also chanted in Mi'kmaq at the graveside ceremony immediately following the funeral Mass (the graveside ceremony is not on the video). In subsequent conversation with Elizabeth Cremo, daughter of the late legendary Mi'kmaw fiddler Lee Cremo, Elizabeth recommended that I meet Walter Denny Jr, whom she described to me as a singer and a chanter continuing in the tradition of Wilfred Prosper, who, like Wilfred, was committed to knowing and passing on Mi'kmaw traditions through music and language. "A must meet guy," Elizabeth told me. "I guarantee you'll see what I mean when you meet him." Elizabeth was right. In addition to his exceptional musical skill as a singer and a chanter, Walter is a fervent believer in traditional Mi'kmaw practices, as well as being a practicing Roman Catholic. Walter is committed to facilitating learning and maintaining the Mi'kmaw language and traditions, and he believes that music can be a powerful means to enact processes of healing and to sustain and enhance traditional values.

This narrative is presented in four sections, revolving around Walter's life experience, his musical experience, the experience of his father's death and funeral, and the difficult challenges around the recent spate of suicides in Eskasoni. In various ways, this narrative focuses on aspects of history, Mi'kmaw traditions, music, religion, community, and social issues. Significantly, Walter's words focus on healing and his helping to facilitate a positive outlook. Thus, as much as this narrative reaches back into the stories of history, it is rooted in the realities of the present and in the processes of hope that can shape the future for Eskasoni and the Mi'kmaw people.

 Life Experience

GS: Maybe we can begin by you talking about your own life stories, and then move to talking about your work and experiences as a chanter, music, religion, and so on. Does that sound okay?

WD: Sure. I'll start at the beginning. Stop me whenever you want ... I was born November 23, 1968, here in Eskasoni. I was brought up on 74th Street. It's a very famous street in Eskasoni ... 74th Street was a really nice place growing up. I grew up there near the church and we moved here [Denny family land] when I was young. This has always been our land. We're not allowed to possess our own land, because it's federal land, but they gave us a deed for our family. I still have the deed for this area here. It was given to me by my grandfather when he passed. My grandfather and my dad ran a store here for about twenty-five years. And then when my grandfather passed, my father had it going for a few years, then he gave it up. Sold the building ... again, you can't sell the land, but he sold the building. It was a big store. Sort of like a trading post. It was one of the biggest of all the stores here. I grew up in that store. We had a grill there, I used to eat there every day. My grandfather, he died in '78, but I lived with my grandparents from about age four. I was sort of like a jolly of the family. And jollies are like the favourite of the family. So I lived with them and I grew up with them. I grew up at the store. It was a very beautiful store, they had all kinds of groceries, hardware, they sold clothes, they had an arcade on the right; it was a beautiful store. I lived here, and then when my grandfather died, my family moved here. We moved in to the old house, from 74th Street to here, when I was about five years old. We built a house for my grandmother, which is not far from here. You can probably see it from here ... my dad moved into the old house.

GS: Did you go to school here?

WD: Ya I went to school here. We had elementary school here. It was next door to the church. It used to be run by the nuns, sort of like an Indian day school. Not a residential school, but it was run by nuns. I went to elementary school there, and then they built the big school, the new school. They still call it "the new school" but it's not that new.

GS: When you were going to elementary was there anything in Mi'kmaq or was it in English?

WD: No we didn't have Mi'kmaw class, it was all in English. But my parents spoke Mi'kmaq and my family spoke Mi'kmaq, so once school was over, I'd be speaking Mi'kmaq.

GS: So when you went home, it was Mi'kmaq.

WD: My language is first Mi'kmaq, and then English.

GS: Would you say that's typical of people of your generation from Eskasoni?

WD: I would say that it is.

GS: School was in English, but home was in Mi'kmaq.

WD: ... in Mi'kmaq ya. But today, it has changed; my children go to school in Mi'kmaq. The youngest one, she just started kindergarten in [Mi'kmaw] immersion, and she'll be in there until grade 3. The other ones weren't in immersion, but they do teach Mi'kmaq at the school. Back then they didn't ... I also went to junior high here, the new school had kindergarten to grade 9. Then after grade 9 we would go to Sydney. I should say that my wife of sixteen years is Nicole, and we have three beautiful children, Walter (16 years), Jaylynn (9 years), Kelly (5 years), and foster son, Cody (15 years).

GS: You went to high school in Sydney?

WD: Ya we went to Riverview High School in Sydney.

GS: What was that like?

WD: It was different because it was more of a culture shock than any-thing. You'd be going to another school where it's totally different. There was quite a bit of discrimination against Mi'kmaw students. Calling us names ... they'd be making gestures. It was hard, but I made some friends there, non-Native friends there, that I'm very close with. I took a kind of Christian leadership course ... it was called "boy's challenge." There was a mixture of students at that challenge. It was at Riverview. But it was held at an old convent near the school. It was more of a reli-gious weekend, where you learn about God. With that I broke some bar-riers and then met some friends, then went back to school and was able to converse with them, but it was tough. We went three years to high school, so I graduated in '87, and after that I went to school to CBU [Cape Breton University, known then as the University College of Cape Breton] and went there for two years, and after that I was offered a job here, so I started working [as a youth worker] in addictions.

GS: What kind of courses did you take at CBU?

WD: Just a regular BA course – psychology, sociology ... Back then they didn't have any Native courses yet, no Mi'kmaw studies. They have it now. In fact, it's pretty good now. Big. And there are also a lot of outreach courses. And they have a lot of Mi'kmaw professors there, which we've never had before.

GS: That's good … So you were an addictions counsellor here?

WD: Yeah. I went into addictions, and then … as part of the work at the treatment centre, I took a certificate program in social work with Dalhousie … they didn't offer us the social work [degree] program, but they offered us a certificate program. And I went to school for three years, one week of each month. Then you'd go back and work in your community. As soon as I graduated in May, I didn't even go to my graduation at Dalhousie. I got offered a job with the police, and that's when I joined. I was sent to Regina for seven months. I got out of there in '95. When I got sent back I was posted in Baddeck. From Baddeck I went to Whycogomagh; from Whycogomagh I worked in St Peters. After St Peters, I worked in Sydney, and then back to Eskasoni … And then about three, four years ago I left Eskasoni and went to North Sydney, where I was offered a community police position for the five reserves on the island. When my dad died [December 2008] I took a month's leave, and during that time I got a call … and they offered me [the position of] domestic violence officer … I would be reviewing files, reviewing files in all twelve First Nations in Nova Scotia … I review the files that come to us as domestic violence. And then make sure that they are properly investigated, that they're following the protocol.

GS: So that work is in addition to your regular job? Or is that your job?

WD: That is my job. It's out of here now. It's plain clothes.

GS: So you're not in the car or anything either?

WD: No. I'm not in uniform in this job. The job is different from my previous one. I like it though, and it's important work.

GS: And you're on the Band Council?

WD: Yes, I've been on the Mi'kmaw Grand Council since '98. The Mi'kmaw Grand Council, known as Sante' Mawio'mi in Mi'kmaq, is our traditional government. Actually I'm a keptin [captain] on the council. This is a life-long position and was passed down to me from my father, Walter Sr, who was passed the position from his brother, Leonard Peter, who died suddenly from a trucking accident when he was thirty-two years old. The position was passed onto him after the death of my grandfather, Levi R. Denny, who passed away from a heart attack back on June 16, 1978. We have had these positions of keptin on the Mi'kmaw Grand Council and represent Unama'ki, one of the seven districts in Mi'kma'ki [traditional lands of the Mi'kmaq]. As I think I told you, my dad passed away last year [2008] and his anniversary date is coming up [17 December]. My mother, Annie Marie (Piero), is living at home with my nephews. I have two brothers, Leroy, who is a Band councillor and educator, and Dion, a supervisor for the Eskasoni Crisis Centre, and one sister, Shelley, who is a teacher aid for the Eskasoni School Board. We are a close-knit family and live amongst each other on our family land and compound. My siblings work very hard to continue my family's legacy of volunteering and helping people in our community. We work hard to continue our Mi'kmaw language, customs, and traditions with our families and our community.

Musical Experience

GS: I want to ask you about your experiences with music when you were growing up. How did you learn music – school, church, elders, groups …?

WD: We had music in school, but it was contemporary music, the ukulele and guitar …

GS: But it was nothing to do with the Native stuff …

WD: No.

GS: Did you learn anything about reading music at school.

WD: Nope, not even that. It was just basically from visiting with Wilfred [Prosper] and on my own.

GS: What about at church, did you always go to Mass?

WD: Yes, I always went to Mass, I'm one of those that go to Mass every Sunday in a suit. I guess that's because I was brought up that way. My grandfather Levi went to Mass every Sunday in a suit, and I remember him getting me a suit and he said that "Sunday is a dress-up day." You

dress your best on Sunday. I always dress my best on Sundays. I wear a
suit every Sunday when I go to Mass. My wife thinks differently [laughter]. She says, "Walter, I'm in jogging pants and you're in a suit." Well it's
how I was brought up and how I'm bringing up my kids.

GS: When did you get going with the chanting?

WD: I grew up with my grandparents, and my great-grandmother was
the one that did all of the chanting. Her name was Jesse, Jesse Gould. In
the Grand Council, they called her Queen of Prayers, and that's my title
now, King of Prayers. Wilfred was the King of Prayers, and after Wilfred
passed I took over Wilfred's position. If it hadn't been for the [Prosper]
family, I wouldn't have had that position. But the family, they offered
a lot of help. They gave me some of the work that Wilfred had done.
Also there's another gentleman I'm fond of, that's Peter Joe Augustine.
He's another Band Council captain that sings old hymns. He's out in
Big Cove [New Brunswick]. He's older than I am. He would be at least
seventy-seven. He's one of the elders I call, and we sing on the phone. I
would have some problems with some of those hymns, and he would say,
"take your book out," and then we would sing hymns on the phone. And
he has a daughter that lives here, married to a fellow from Eskasoni, a
Mountie, and every time he comes for a visit, he would come here and
we would sing. He's a very good singer.

GS: One of the things I find interesting talking with you is there aren't
very many young people, people your age, who do this [chanting].

WD: I know. I think just growing up with it for one thing … with my
great-grandmother … every day she prayed at three o'clock in the afternoon and she'd sing hymns. And it made an impression on me, even
when starting out. In my sobriety I always wanted to have something
to do. When you're stuck with an addiction, afterwards you want to do
something that you like, and that's something that I really enjoyed. Also,
just visiting elders … I took one of those pictures that I was showing you
there. We would get together on Sundays. We haven't done that since
she passed away, Mary Catherine Stevens. She was from Crane Cove.
We would get together on Sundays a lot and sing old hymns. And Sarah
Denny was another one. They [Sarah Denny's family] have a Christmas
party every year … they would invite me to their Christmas parties and
they'd be singing all of these old hymns.

GS: So would you say that your family and ancestors were on the traditionalist side?

WD: I would say so because we are very traditional. "Traditional" meaning [that] we are very attached to our culture, we are very attached to nature, and we are very attached to Catholicism, even though we only had it for 400 years. And this is something I've had a lot of discussions with different people about, and I always tell them that … I really believe that.

GS: So you were pretty young when you started learning the old songs?

WD: Oh yeah, I'd say nine or ten. Maybe even younger … it's difficult to remember, but I do remember that we prayed and sang every day.

GS: So that was important?

WD: That was important for sure, and we would have rosaries in the evening. Sometimes we'd have rosaries at my other grandma's, which was Noel's mother. And we still have rosaries here, with the kids; every day we have rosaries.

GS: And you say them in Mi'kmaq?

WD: We say it in Mi'kmaq, and we have this Mi'kmaw satellite channel [EWTN] … It's great … we listen to it, you know, Mass and other things in Mi'kmaq … So we did that every day. And then when she passed on, my [other] grandmother said, "Walter, your grandmother left some literature for you." I said, "What do you mean literature?" They were her books. I said, "You're kidding me." She said, "No." I said, "God, really?" She said, "Yep … it's a sign, I think she wants you to keep this going." I said, "Sure." So I did, and so these [books] are old. They've been in my family, well, it'd be almost a hundred years. This is the instructional one. I'm able to read it … I'm able to read Father Pacifique. We have different writing systems, so for me it's a lot easier reading Pacifique than Bernie Francis [language systems]. I guess just from growing up with it … So my grandmother would open this book and say, "Well we're going to say this prayer."

[Looking at an old book.]

GS: These are prayers …?

WD: Yep. These are all prayers and here are hymns. This one here has hymns at the back. See the hymns? They start over here. That word means "hymns." It's funny how long the word is but it only means hymns.

GS: How does it work for the tunes?

WD: When I started learning these, I'd have a hard time picking up the tune from my grandma, my great-grandmother because she was eighty-nine when she passed away. So I went to Wilfred … I said, "Wilfred, I'm having problems with the airs." Wilfred called the tunes "airs." He said, "But Walter, you know a lot of our songs. They are old songs, some are at least a hundred years old." Like this one here. This was written in 1913. Wilfred used to say that a lot of our music was like opera and operas have "airs." He always told me to try this song and then another, and "You'll know what I mean … you need to practise" … And he always used the "Song of St Anne" for starters. It's the same thing with the Christmas songs. Even though some are written in English [and] then translated to Mi'kmaq … they're not as similar as the original songs when you sing them.

GS: So when you were learning these songs, did Wilfred sing them or your great-grandmother sing them, and you picked them up from them?

WD: Ya it was basically picking it up from them, Wilfred and my great-grandmother, who was also my great aunt, Annie Cremo, who was Lee Cremo's mother. I also went to her a lot. She said, "Walter, if anyone ever tells you that you're singing this song wrong, give them your book and tell them, 'you sing it'" [laughter]. That's what she always told me. "'Cause you're not singing it wrong … at least you're singing it …"

GS: We mentioned earlier about reading music …

WD: Wilfred was good at reading music. He learned it from the sisters [at church] and taught himself. But though I don't really read music, I used to look at the music Wilfred had written down and printed music … and when you look at the air in the music, the symbols there, you can see a lot about how the music works … you can get a lot from the symbols ... notes or signs ... So I guess you could say that's where a lot of this music comes from ... different ways of writing it down or not ... A lot of these old hymns don't have written-down music, and some of these hymns are English hymns, like Roman Catholic hymns translated, but some are not.

GS: Some are like prayers in Mi'kmaq that are sung?

WD: Ya that's hard. To me that was harder because you had to sort of memorize it and the air. This [book of prayers] was rebound, a friend of mine rebound it for me, 'cause it was just breaking apart ... It's from 1912, too, so it's almost one hundred years old.

GS: These [books] are from Restigouche [Mi'kmaw reserve in eastern Quebec]. This one too?

WD: Yes, they come from Restigouche.

GS: Do you use them very much?

WD: Ya I use them practically every day. Every day in different places. Funerals, wakes, peoples' homes ... Nancy May, she died this summer. Last Christmas she called me and asked, "Walter, my family is having a little party for me ... can you come over and sing some prayers for me? Sing some hymns?" She was going to dialysis three times a week. And the family got together and I went over. I knew I should be staying at home on Christmas, but I thought that it was important for me to help like this. I sang some Christmas songs, and I only sang Christmas songs because it was Christmas. I sang about a good ten songs, and oh was she ever happy, and the family was happy because she was happy, because she always talked about how important these prayers are and how they should be continued.

As I think I said earlier, when Wilfred passed away the council didn't have anyone to continue with the prayers, and I was already on the council, and they said, "Why can't we have Walter continue the prayers even though he's captain?" I told you earlier I'm also captain. So I got the blessing to be the prayer leader as well.

GS: In the church at the Mass, is there much traditional, let's say drumming or burning sweetgrass ...?

WD: From the recollection of elders, I guess there used to be a lot of drumming. But when we had the residential schools, a lot of that stuff was taken. So the generation that we have now wouldn't remember that with the dancing. Sarah [Denny] was one of them that tried to bring that back. She had drumming at her funeral. But that was unusual for today. But, when you look at the Concordat [treaty] and the wampum belt, there's a sign there of a church, and on the church, there's a door, and the door looks like it's open … Elders would always say, "it's open because we were always able to bring in our culture."

GS: I understand what you're saying, but do other people of your generation agree with that?

WD: Some do, some don't … Even when I do my workshops, I say that I practise traditionalism … fifteen or so years ago some thought it [traditionalism] was all like voodoo or something. "Oh no, you do sweats?" somebody would say. But it's starting to come round, even with the Band Council. At a couple of meetings we had, I mentioned that we should have a sweat lodge on the island, and it didn't go well … some of the members said, "good idea," and some of the elders got up and said, "I've been coming here this many years and we never had that." But when you look at Nicholas Denny's writings, he talks about sweat lodges and the Mi'kmaw people. I think it's more like influence … if I can influence as a Mi'kmaw person, as a prayer leader … and if I mention, "okay we should have a sweat," that can mean something positive to other people. Part of my work as a police officer … [involves] a cultural component, where RCMP [Royal Canadian Mounted Police] in Nova Scotia are supposed to be culturally sensitized. So I run a program once or twice a month. I have [non-Native] members [of the RCMP] come here. We talk about our traditions, we introduce our literature, I take them to an elder to speak to. There are two or three elders I take them to … Suzie Marshall and Murdena and Albert [Marshall]. And then we would have a sweat. I'll explain the sweat. In the sweat we pray, I pray, and I say some of these prayers. So it's coming, I think it's coming. Again, it's by example. They can ask, "Why is Walter going to a sweat?" But if they see me as a very Catholic, spiritual person doing it, then they might say, "Well it must be good. He's going." And on sweetgrass … Eugene [Denny] and I used to have sweetgrass ceremonies in the morning before the sun goes up and we would offer prayers to our higher power. Eugene would always explain that even before Catholicism, we always still had prayers … We always believed that something was higher than us. We always prayed to someone – something.

GS: So the idea of prayer is not new with you, before you were Catholic?

WD: No and I always say that, and that's why I think that my ancestors thought that this was a really good religion. We're starting to plan the 400-year anniversary [2010] of [Mi'kmaw chief] Membertou [baptized Christian in 1610]. It's quite an undertaking because an invitation has been offered to the pope. So we've been writing back and forth through our bishop in Antigonish. And he [the bishop] is positive about this, and he's hoping that the visit will work out … They [the Vatican] won't be in a position to make a decision about coming until about six months prior.

GS: What's the response like to the invitation? A celebration of 400 years? Are some people saying, "Why are we doing this?"

WD: I know! Especially with what's been happening with the residential schools … The Catholic Church is the one church that hasn't come out and offered an apology. They say they will get involved after the Independent Assessment process. They'll be releasing some of their documents, and they'll be releasing some of the documents to the Truth and Reconciliation Commission. But that's after the fact.
   It's difficult because other churches have come forward with their apologies. And the best record recorders in time are supposed to have been the Roman Catholics. They recorded everything. They have our treaties. We lost this one [important] treaty with the Vatican, the Concordat, and then we found it. It's there. We have one council member who's a consulate to the Vatican … I don't know if you know him, Stephen Augustine, he's from Big Cove and lives in Ottawa. So we'll see what happens with all of this.

Walter's Father's Funeral

GS: We've been talking about you singing at funerals. Did you sing at your father's funeral last December [2008]?

WD: I did.

GS: That must have been hard.

wD: Ya it was.

GS: Did you sing at the grave?

wD: I did sing at the grave. I sang at the hospital, in the church, and at
the grave site. It was hard, but yet we were so happy when my dad died.
It's difficult to explain. When he died, we came out of the hospital room
laughing because we were very happy, happy for him and happy that
he died on the anniversary date of the death of my grandmother. So I
sang in the hospital room after he passed ... we did the rosary and some
prayers too.

GS: And did you have the wake out here in Eskasoni?

wD: Well we had a wake here, but prior to that he was waked for one day
at Curry's [funeral home in Sydney]. My dad wanted to be waked at the
funeral home in Sydney because he was old friends with the Currys for
thirty-five or forty years. So I said to Bill [Curry, funeral director] ... his
father [Leo Curry], my dad's old friend, is not working there anymore ...
I said, "My dad had asked for you, and that he'd like to be waked here for
the first day in the funeral home, in honour of your dad [Leo]." Bill was
just stunned.
    It was very unusual [to have part of the wake at the funeral home], but
it's what my dad wanted. And we've never had a wake for anyone from
Eskasoni at Curry's. So we did. It was nice ... We had a wake there during the day from about twelve to around five. Then we took him home
and brought him to Eskasoni, to his house, for a traditional wake.

GS: Was there much Mi'kmaw tradition at the funeral?

wD: All Mi'kmaq. We wanted all the prayers in Mi'kmaq, we wanted
all the readings in Mi'kmaq, and all the songs were in Mi'kmaq. I had
asked if I could sing, and the choir allowed it. So it was really a beautiful
funeral, it really was a beautiful funeral. We had wanted to have a video
made, and then the person that was going to make the video had a death
in his family the same day as the funeral. So we weren't able to do the
video. It would have been nice to have. I really wanted a videotape, but
we couldn't do that ... but that was fine.

GS: But then you had the burial in the graveyard there [at the church].

16.1 Annual trip to Sainte-Anne de Beaupré, first week of June 2004. Walter is in his RCMP uniform. Photograph courtesy of Walter Denny Jr.

16.2 Walter (left) with choir members at St Anne mission, Chapel Island, July 1998. Photograph courtesy of Walter Denny Jr.

wd: Yep, yep we had the burial there. My father was buried where his families are. He's next to his brother, my godfather … he died when he was only thirty-two years old, crushed by an eighteen-wheeler. Then of course, right behind my dad is his mother and father. So it just worked out good. As I said already, I sang at the graveside … it was the hymn to St Anne.

gs: Then you had an auction?

wd: Yep we had a nice auction [called *salite*]. We celebrated a last feast for my dad, in his honour. Salite [Mi'kmaw feast and auction tradition following funerals] is a very unique gathering, very unique, where you hear all kinds of stories about the one who has passed. The best way to understand salite is as a celebration of life. Then, after the feast, of course you have the bidding, that's always fun for everyone. People bidding and out-bidding themselves and out-bidding others. Trying to help the family.

gs: A lot of this process seems to be about healing.

wd: Absolutely it's about healing. I should say that healing is a major part of my work in the community. I think I already mentioned about going to Sainte-Anne de Beaupré (Quebec) every year in May or June with a group from Eskasoni. That trip is kind of like a pilgrimage. It's about physical and spiritual healing. St Anne is the mother [saint] of the Mi'kmaq nation and we celebrate her at our annual mission at Chapel Island [Cape Breton] at the end of every July. That's [the annual St Anne mission] also about healing and renewal. I have some photos on these celebrations you might be interested in.

Healing and Recent Events in Eskasoni

[In the fall and winter of 2008 the community of Eskasoni experienced a tragic series of suicides of young people. In our May conversation, Walter spoke about these events, and the healing processes that were initiated by himself and others to help address the serious social problems facing many of the youth living in Eskasoni and in other Aboriginal communities.]

wd: Since last fall we've had eight suicides, young people.

GS: That was on the news too. I heard about it.

WD: Ya. We made it on the national [news]. It's sad when you help your community, [to see it made into] a very public thing. The RCMP was very vocal, the community leaders were very vocal. We tried to come up with some strategies. We've had a crisis intervention team here for about fifteen, twenty years, and we tried to build on their work by calling on the help of different groups of people ... let's say young people, women, men, children, frontline workers. So we started gathering what we can do and we had a vacant building that was there for at least four or five years [before] the money ran out. So we said, "Let's build on that [earlier work] and use that vacant building." It's a building right behind the health centre. It used to be used for some kind of adolescent program. But we've turned it into a crisis centre. We've mobilized the crisis team and in two weeks, we moved into the centre. But since then we've had eight [suicides] and all young people. There are a lot of factors here. So we tried to come up with some different strategies, and we came up with the idea of having a very positive youth rally. We wanted to rally all the youth. We had Waneek Horn-Miller come down. She was an Olympian, world Olympian and Mohawk. We had Lorne Cardinal come down. We had Lisa Robinson from CBC [Canadian Broadcasting Corporation]. She's also Mohawk I believe. Then of course we had [the former member of Parliament] Elijah Harper. And we had a very good weekend and we were all lifted ... so were the kids.

GS: So all of those people came on the same weekend?

WD: The same weekend. We had a day where they all had the chance to speak. We gave them an hour, an hour and a half, two hours and then we showed the video of Elijah Harper in the evening.[2] And then Elijah spoke. When Elijah spoke he had a very interesting story. I didn't know that Elijah's son had committed suicide and he spoke of that. And Lisa Robinson, she also spoke of a suicide in her family. It was a very good weekend. We had a nice gathering at the end. And we said, "How are we gonna top this?" And we weren't going to top it ... it was just about how we were going to be able to follow it up ... And then we got a phone call from this music production company in Halifax named Drum, and they said, "We're looking for a venue to bring in your community ... we felt that you needed something." They said, "We've seen Elijah there, we've seen all of these actors there." Adam Beach had a video conference with the youth ... he started it off on Friday, at the school. So Adam spoke about an hour, and he spoke about how he was suicidal when he was young, and he challenged the youth. He said, "I'm starting something soon," and he bought a big Aboriginal production company where they have access to a satellite. And he said, "I want to share this with your community, I want to challenge your youth to do something. Whatever it is and I'll help you. I'll get you on this satellite network." The kids loved him; they went with it and they're still going with it. They made a short video [see below], I'll show you the short video. It's a very moving video. And they've been doing a lot of stuff, speaking to elders, going back to the root level, finding out about their culture. They said that our language is the most important aspect of our lives. We have to speak, in order for us to be a strong nation. We have to speak the language, keep speaking the language ... And the language which is so old ... We're one of the few reserves across Canada that can say, "We speak Mi'kmaq." We used to have 100,000 people strong, but with the diseases that we had, the smallpox, that went down. But we're still here and we still speak Mi'kmaq. I'm on the education board here in Eskasoni and we've been working at ways of building our language programs in the schools. We want to strengthen our immersion program. We have a Mi'kmaw immersion program here, from kindergarten to grade 3, total immersion. Everything in Mi'kmaq. So we're going to build on that. We're going to extend it to maybe grade 5, and then to grade 6. We started this program ten years ago, and the teachers followed the students and their academic abilities. And they're doing very well. It's much better than a Mi'kmaw student going into the mainstream education system.

So we had this production company, Drum, come and help us out. We participated in a production ... The production is based on those losing their talk [language]. In fact, they used Rita [Joe]'s poem "I lost my talk" at the end with Rita saying the poem. So what it is is four nationalities, four colours: Mi'kmaq, French, black, and Acadian. Four of them. They each talk about their history. We talk about our drums and Mi'kmaw dancing and chanting. And how even the French had a relationship with the Mi'kmaw people. When the French were expelled by the English, the Mi'kmaw people took them in ... because they were expelled by the English. The blacks spoke about their hard times when the English came here and they weren't allowed to speak their language. And how they used language – song – down by the bay, and they were singing in codes ... it's very interesting. They said, "The English didn't know. When we were slaving, we were always singing and there was a code behind that singing." Same thing with the Gaelic and them losing their traditions and fighting to get them back. It's a very good production.

I don't have the Drum documentary here, but I'll show you the video of the kid's production I was talking about. It's all done by the students themselves, about twenty-six of them. They wanted to do something on their own … they did all their own shooting of the video. In fact they just received a cheque, a $60,000 cheque to buy some video equipment and some computers. They're buying six very nice cameras. Those big ones. So they've been doing this and they have a consulting agency from Halifax sponsoring them. Hopefully this video I'm going to show you will be the beginning of more to come. The video is called "Art of Resilience" (Eskasoni youth production) and it's available on Youtube at http://www.youtube.com/watch?v=ngxV6b-49vo.

[After watching the video …]

GS: Thanks for showing me that. It's very powerful. I love the visuals of the kids and their lines.

WD: Same here. The images of the kids and their words are strong … healing, turning away from drugs, reaching out, not judging others, teaching, never losing hope, staying positive, and never giving up … Those are important things to remember and they kind of sum up all of this.

NOTES

1 This text is published here with the permission of Mi'kmaw Ethics Watch, Cape Breton University, Sydney, Nova Scotia. Editorial notes: (1) in keeping with current practice, *Mi'kmaq* is used as the plural form and as referring to the Mi'kmaw people and the Mi'kmaw language. *Mi'kmaw* is the singular and is also used for adjectival and adverbial forms; (2) we have used ellipses to reflect where there is a pause in the spoken text; (3) square brackets appear around brief explanatory comments; (4) Gordon is grateful to Adam Gaudry (recent master of arts student in sociology at Queen's University) for his assistance with transcribing the December and May interviews.
2 A video of the session in which Elijah Harper blocked the Manitoba Legislature from voting on the Meech Lake Accord, effectively defeating it.

17

"No Heartaches in Heaven": A Response to Aboriginal Suicide

BYRON DUECK

"No Heartaches in Heaven," a song by Chris Beach, an Ojibwe Métis songwriter and playwright from Manitoba, does not celebrate suicide, but it does present the reasoning of its suicidal protagonist in a sympathetic light.[1] It has angered some listeners and comforted others; still others probably find its sympathetic tone perplexing. A consideration of how the song relates to its context of origin suggests some interpretations. On the one hand, "No Heartaches" reflects the songwriter's personal experiences, as well as the all-too-frequent occurrences of suicide in Manitoban Aboriginal communities. On the other hand, the song is more than a mirror of its circumstances: it is also a socially consequential response. It extends comfort to those who are bereaved, it challenges theological conceptions of death and judgment, and in doing so, it affirms and elaborates certain longstanding Aboriginal cultural practices. In this chapter, "No Heartaches in Heaven" is considered alongside a number of dramatic works by Beach, the *Indian Joe Blow* plays. These provide additional perspectives on Aboriginal suicide and the social and historical conditions that contribute to its prevalence. Although Beach's songs and plays highlight the social difficulties that Indigenous people face, they do not suggest a terminally troubled culture. Rather, they demonstrate the continued expression of valued modalities of Manitoban Algonquian selfhood and collectivity, even in the unhappiest of circumstances.

Chris Beach

I first met Chris Beach in 2002, at a moment when Manitoba's Aboriginal public was beginning to validate his efforts as a musician. That year his

No Heartaches in Heaven

17.1 "No Heartaches in Heaven," first verse and chorus. Only the melody and basic harmonic progression are shown. Transcription by author.

country song "My Soap Opera Woman" held the number one position for several weeks on NCI FM's Aboriginal top-thirty list (NCI is a radio station that broadcasts to Indigenous communities across Manitoba). In the months and years that followed, he was regularly invited to perform for appreciative audiences in Aboriginal communities around the province. The first time I spoke with Beach, he told me that three kinds of music were special to him: country music, gospel singing, and traditional drum songs. Accordingly, it was not surprising that when he recorded and released two CDs in 2004, one of them was a country album called *Maano*, consisting mostly of secular songs about love and family, and the other was a gospel album entitled *A New Life with Jesus*, whose songs, as the title suggests, dealt mostly with spiritual transformation (Beach 2004a, 2004b).

Something else was surprising, however, namely "No Heartaches in Heaven"[2] and its inclusion on both albums. Although the song fit in with

17.2 Chris Beach. Photograph by author.

the material on *Maano*, it was considerably more provocative alongside the gospel songs on *A New Life with Jesus*. The song presents a dialogue between a narrator and a heartbroken, suicidal protagonist. In the first verse, the narrator meets the protagonist wandering in anguish by the lakeshore. She asks him to leave her to die alone in peace.[3] The reason for her distress becomes apparent in the second verse: her lover has abandoned her and she has swallowed a bottle of pills. The narrator protests that what she is doing is wrong but is answered by the words of the chorus: "There's no heartaches in heaven / And no tears to cry."

Thus "No Heartaches" traces a trajectory from despair to hope, with heaven the protagonist's escape from pain and suicide the means of achieving it. This unexpectedly positive perspective is not evident in other popular songs about suicide (or at least those I know best, which typically focus on the despair or trauma that precede the act and do not point to a happier future).[4] It seems even more remarkable in an instance of gospel song. "No Heartaches" appears to endorse the idea that suicide will allow those who are suffering to find solace in heaven. But suicide is considered a grievous offence in many Christian traditions, and in Catholic theology some suicides are deemed mortally sinful. In fact, Beach told me that he had grown up believing that those who ended their own lives were damned for eternity.[5]

Beach was born in 1958 and spent the first seven years of his life in a two-room shack without running water in the town of Vogar, a Métis[6] community in the Manitoban Interlake.[7] In his later childhood he moved several times between that community and Winnipeg. His father worked for the Canadian National Railway as a chef and later went into business with his brother as co-proprietor of a gas station. His mother, Anne Beach, raised six daughters and four sons (a fifth son was raised by his grandmother). In Winnipeg, Anne started drinking heavily, frequenting the bars on the city's Main Street strip. When she didn't have enough money for the bar, she would buy anything with alcohol in it: rubbing alcohol, vanilla, Chinese wine, Lysol. At her lowest point, Chris told me, she was "ragged." As a boy, he sometimes wondered whether his own death might shock her enough to stop her from drinking. He explored this idea in one of his earliest songs, "The Devil's Blood," in which a young boy begs his alcoholic mother to put away the bottle. She laughs off his plea, with tragic consequences:

> She wouldn't listen to her son;
> She thought it was one big joke.
> But then when she came home drunk
> She found him hanging from a rope.[8]

Happily and to the relief of her family, Anne Beach eventually stopped drinking. When I met her in 2002, she had been sober for decades.

Suicide has affected Chris's life and those of many he loves, as has untimely death by other causes.[9] He told me that when he was young he used to go drinking with a group of friends and that all but one of them had since died, most having committed suicide. One relative, a close friend, overdosed on pills when the man she loved left her; another had come close to killing herself while drinking, Chris believed. In 1981 his sister-in-law, nine months pregnant, was killed by a drunk driver.[10] Her husband (Chris's brother) began to drink heavily and take pills after her death, and six weeks later he drowned in a gravel pit.

Beach got married in 1986. That year, he dreamed his deceased brother shook him as he had done when he was still alive. "Chris," his brother told him, "I want you to take care of my boys for me." Chris and his wife took the three children into their home to raise them. Later, they also took in a number of foster children, including two First Nations boys they eventually adopted and another with whom they remained on close terms. Shortly after they had adopted the two boys, a daughter was born to them. The household sadly did not stay together for long: Beach and his wife separated in the late 1980s, and Beach went through a period of depression during which he himself considered suicide. Things got better with the passing of time, and Beach eventually took custody of the children. In the mid-2000s, however, another series of crises occurred in quick succession. In March 2005 Chris's former foster son committed suicide. In September of that year, his mother passed away after a battle with cancer. And in 2006 someone close to him and his family became distraught for a time and made a number of unsuccessful suicide attempts.

These events led to a breakdown of sorts for Beach, who took leave from his elementary school job. They also initiated a creative outpouring, and in 2006 and 2007 he wrote a set of plays: the *Indian Joe Blow* trilogy, consisting of *Peshikii (Indian Joe Blow)*, *Kigeet*, and *Black Eagle Thunderbird Man*.[11] The dramas centre on the life of Joe, a young man who struggles with suicidal impulses. A series of flashbacks revisit key moments in Joe's life, including his mother's heavy drinking while pregnant, the mistreatment and sexual abuse he encounters in foster homes, the beating he receives at the hands of a group of strangers, and the suicide of a friend. A number of these scenes recall stories that Chris told me about his own friends and family. In particular, they bring to mind the life, and death by suicide, of one of Beach's former foster sons, of whom he has written: "[My former foster son] told me that when he turned eighteen, he was pushed out the door by the [child welfare] system and forgotten about. He had gone to Toronto with a promise of a new life and a good paying job. That didn't happen, and he ended up getting hooked on street drugs and living the street life. He shared with me some of the sexual, physical, emotional, and verbal abuse he had endured all the years he was in foster care" (Beach 2006b, 16).

There is something overwhelming about the implacable succession of unfortunate occurrences in Beach's plays. But their incessantness is not melodramatic overstatement; it is in many respects representative of the author's experiences. Beach has lived through periods when one heartache followed another, and he has seen sorrows, insults, and abuses compounded in the lives of those he loves. This biography has said all too little about the love and happiness I observed in Beach's interactions with family, friends, and fellow musicians, but it does give some idea of how life experiences sometimes weighed upon him and upon others I met while doing fieldwork. It was never a single tragedy or a sole sad memory but many all at once. Of the origin of "No Heartaches in Heaven," Chris told me, "the story … was a true story. I wrote it for [a relative] who committed suicide.[12] She was a good friend of mine. She OD'ed on pills because her boyfriend had left. But it's more than that … People might think it's just that but it's more … She had a lot of abuse in her life, and alcoholism and stuff."

The Social Context of Chris Beach's Artworks

Chris Beach's biography is not anomalous: statistics reveal a disproportionately high rate of suicide for Manitoba's Aboriginal population. A study of all instances of suicide in the province between 1988 and 1994 revealed that the rate was 2.3 times higher for Aboriginal people than for non-Aboriginal people (Malchy et al. 1997, 1135). The figures were particularly divergent in the case of young people: the suicide rate for Aboriginal youth aged fifteen to nineteen was almost 7 times higher than that of non-Aboriginal youth of the same age (and 23.4 times higher in this age range for Aboriginal girls) (Malchy et al. 1997, 1137). These rates raise urgent questions about the causes of Aboriginal suicide; both scholarly and vernacular discourses seek answers.

Contemporary psychiatrists, social workers, and scholars of medicine have identified risk factors thought to have an immediate connection with Aboriginal suicide and suicidality[13] (see Angell, Kurz, and Gottfried 1997, Chandler and Lalonde 1998, or Grossman, Milligan, and Deyo 1991). These include alienation from family and community; exposure to suicide completions and attempts by friends and family; heavy consumption of intoxicants; the perception of poor health; poverty; physical and sexual abuse; and cultural discontinuities resulting from government interventions.[14] Chris Beach's works and interviews suggest another set of potential determinants, with considerable overlap. The similarities between the two lists should not be surprising given that Beach, like many Aboriginal people, is aware of the factors that counsellors and social workers associate with suicide. Thus his music, plays, and stories present an accounting for suicide that is vernacular and hybrid, drawing not only upon personal experiences but upon circulating clinical discourses as well.[15]

Beach has related Aboriginal suicide to a number of potential causes: physical and sexual abuse, drinking and drug use, urban violence and the sex trade, foster care, and heartache. In a 2007 interview, he described a friend's suicide as the end result of traumatic abuse: "My friend ... lived through all this abuse in his life and really suffered at the hands of other people. And he didn't do anything. And then in the end, because he was so traumatized by it all ... he took his life."

Beach secondly connected suicide to misuse of intoxicants. In interviews he suggested that alcoholism was a factor in one relative's suicide and in the temporary suicidality of another. In the latter case, he suspected that at a particularly low point, under the influence of drink, the relative had tried to commit suicide, surviving only by miraculous accident. Beach thirdly connected suicide to urban prostitution and the dangers of life on the street. In *Peshikii*, Joe's suicide attempt is linked in part to the low sense of self-worth he has as a sex worker. In such contexts, violence is particularly damaging to dignity and self-worth. Thus in *Black Eagle Thunderbird Man*, while reflecting upon a brutal beating he suffered as a street kid, Joe remarks, "You know, before that night, when those boys beat me up, I thought everything that could be taken from me had already been tooken. But those five youth took something even deeper than that" (Beach 2007, 38).

In Beach's plays, problems associated with the child welfare system are a fourth and central contributing factor. The experiences Joe encounters within that system initiate a spiral of negative events. Beach knew a number of people who had been in care. The stories he told me about their experiences suggested that it often failed those it tried to help, sometimes tragically. All the same, there were occasions when it improved the situation of vulnerable children. Beach related one case that exemplified both flaws and benefits. He knew of two siblings born to a mother who drank heavily and used drugs; the children acquired what he described as fetal alcohol syndrome in the womb. The older one lived in six different foster homes during his first two years and was abused in one of them. The younger child lived with a relative for several months but was neglected owing to the heavy drinking of the latter. It was through foster care that these siblings eventually found a permanent, caring home.

The foregoing fictional and real-life accounts reflect the recent history of the social welfare system in Manitoba and in Canada more generally. In the 1960s Canadian provinces initiated a major extension of child welfare services to First Nations communities; this marked the beginning of an era that continued until the early 1980s, sometimes called the "sixties scoop," during which provincial organizations seized an unprecedented number of Aboriginal children from their birth families (Johnston 1983, 23–4).[16] These interventions were ostensibly carried out with the best intentions, but they tore apart families and alienated younger generations from Indigenous languages and traditions.

And so Beach's artworks and personal narratives connect suicide to sexual and physical abuse, intoxicant misuse, the sex trade, the dangers of life on the street, and, especially, aggressive social service interventions. However, they suggest that other factors are more immediate triggers of suicide, namely personal losses and break-ups. When Beach commented on an earlier version of this chapter in 2008, he told me that suicide was at root a response to pain. He said that he had lived through six months of seemingly unending suffering when his marriage fell apart. He told me that his former foster son had felt such anguish before he committed suicide and that his brother had felt something similar when his wife died. And he explained that he had tried to convey this feeling in "No Heartaches in Heaven." Beach's interpretation accords with my own observations during fieldwork and with what other Algonquian Manitobans have told me: a deep and sometimes self-destructive melancholy often follows a break-up or the death of a loved one.[17] But again, it's more than that: in many cases the pain of loss follows other traumatic experiences.

Anomie, Agency, and Cultural Practice

Although the study of risk factors offers insight into the immediate reasons for Indigenous suicide and suicidality, it does not address their deeper structural causes. Here, Emile Durkheim's theory of suicide (1951 [1897]) has frequently been brought to bear. His comparative study suggested that the rapid social transformations associated with European modernization were responsible for an increase in suicides. He argued that modernization reduced social integration, resulting in what he called egoistic suicide, and that it decreased social regulation, contributing to what he called anomistic suicide.[18] In North American Aboriginal contexts, state interventions and attempts at acculturation have often disrupted the integrity of Indigenous families, communities, and governing structures, with severe consequences for Indigenous social regulation. Accordingly, scholarship and mainstream discourse have often characterized Aboriginal suicide as an anomistic phenomenon (see Angell, Kurz, and Gottfried 1997; compare Levy and Kunitz 1971). These Durkheimian interpretations seem convincing, but they also present potential problems.

On the one hand, there is a danger that they will mesh too easily with discourses that characterize postcontact and postcolonial Indigenous cultures as decadent or corrupted (see, for instance, Hickerson 1967). On the other hand, when too direct a connection between state intervention and suicide is presumed, cultural practice and social agency tend to fall out of the picture.[19] This is not to say that a middle road cannot be found, one that acknowledges the impact of state interference without discounting Aboriginal social or cultural practice. For instance, Brent Angell and colleagues (1997, 21) connect high contemporary rates of Ojibwe suicide to the devastating effects of attempts to acculturate Indigenous people, thus perpetuating the Durkheimian connection between suicide and social anomie.[20] But they also suggest that suicide is culturally specific and that pressures such as the demand to acculturate have been inflected by uniquely Ojibwe cultural elements – for instance, a "low-integration" social structure.[21]

Still, discussions of suicide could focus more upon strategy and agency and upon contemporary Indigenous cultural practice, which is what this chapter seeks to do, hopefully without downplaying the difficulties Manitoban Aboriginal people face. As far as agency is concerned, the musical and dramatic works of Chris Beach do not simply reflect suicide in a particular social context; they also seek to transform it. In some cases this strategy is explicit: Beach himself characterizes his works as interventions of a particular kind. For instance, in a 2008 magazine article, he wrote that his plays had originated in a desire to prevent other Indigenous young people from killing themselves following the death of his former foster son (Beach 2008, 16). And indeed performances of his *Kigeet* have targeted audiences of young Aboriginal people.

Beach's songs and plays, however, do other kinds of social labour that are neither explicit nor obvious: for instance, they engage the stylistic conventions of country music and Algonquian funerary traditions and in doing so enact Algonquian ways of expressing personhood and affirming community. This is especially evident in the case of "No Heartaches in Heaven," which addresses its cultural context in both overt and subtle ways, contesting certain aspects of it while affirming others. Culture is here understood as "cultural practice" (compare Appadurai 1996, 11–13) – that is, as something dynamic and performative. Beach's song not only acknowledges its social circumstances; it also effects (or attempts to effect) consequences within them. Its repercussions are evident at more than one level, for even as it produces local and immediate social effects, it also plays a part in the larger task of producing "culture" (see Silverstein 1998) – that is, in affirming, contesting, and elaborating aspects of northern Algonquian ideology and practice.

Individuation and Resistance to Musical Norms

The 2004 recording of "No Heartaches in Heaven" affirms a number of musical conventions associated with what many Manitoban Aboriginal musicians would call "classic country" music: it makes use of antecedent-consequent phrasing, a limited harmonic palette structured by tonic-dominant polarity, and a straightforward strophic structure (see table 17.1). Yet certain aspects of the recording stray from contemporary norms in this style, including in the areas of tuning and musical form.[22] Beach's intonation is imprecise, and there does not seem to have been a great deal of effort made to repeat it into exactness during the recording process or to bring it into line afterward using pitch-correcting software. Moreover, the phrase structure of the song departs from what is typical in contemporary country music in a classic style, where phrase lengths tend to stay the same from verse to verse. Table 17.1 breaks the song into its component parts, listing the lengths of phrases and subphrases so that they can be compared from one iteration to another. In contrast to most recent mass-mediated country music, the phrases and subphrases in "No

Table 17.1
Phrase structure in "No Heartaches in Heaven"

Section	Phrase group	Harmonic progression in subphrase	Subphrase length (bars)	Phrase group length (bars)	Cadence (at end of phrase group)[a]
Instrumental introduction		I-V-I	5	5	PAC (implied)
Verse 1	Antecedent	I-V	5	10	IAC
		V-I	5		
	Consequent	I-IV	5	10	PAC
		IV-I-V-I	5		
Chorus	Antecedent	IV-I	4	9	HC
		I-V	5		
	Consequent	I-IV	4	9	PAC
		I-V-I	5		
Instrumental solo section[b]	Antecedent	I-V	4	10	IAC (implied)
		V-I	6		
	Consequent	I-IV	4	9	PAC (implied)
		I-V-I	5		
Verse 2	Antecedent	I-V	5	10	IAC
		V-I	5		
	Consequent	I-IV	4	9	PAC
		I-V-I	5		
Chorus	Antecedent	IV-I	4	9	HC
		I-V	5		
	Consequent	I-IV	4	9	PAC
		I-V-I	5		
Tag/coda	Consequent	I-V-I	5	5	PAC

a The abbreviations in the "cadence" column are as follows: PAC indicates a perfect authentic cadence, IAC an imperfect authentic cadence, and HC a half cadence. Repertories like gospel song tend to organize phrases in pairs, with the first phrase ending on a "weak" cadence and the second on a "strong" cadence: IAC then PAC or HC then PAC.

b Played over harmonic changes from verse.

Heartaches in Heaven" vary capriciously in length from verse to verse.[23] This is evident to a moderate degree when verse 1 and verse 2 are compared: the third subphrase in verse 2 is a bar shorter than the analogous subphrase in verse 1. It is even more apparent in the instrumental solo section, which moves through the same harmonic changes as the verses. Here, the four subphrases are four, six, four, and six bars in length, compared to five, five, five, and five in the first verse.

"No Heartaches in Heaven" and other songs on *Maano* and *A New Life with Jesus* exhibit a number of characteristics of the Manitoban Aboriginal approach to country music that I came to know while doing fieldwork in Winnipeg. Many of the performances I heard took a loose, in-the-moment approach to rhythmic organization and phrase structure: they strayed from regular metrical patterns and sometimes seemed to do without them entirely. Some performers varied the length of phrases and other formal units from one verse or performance to the next (compare Lederman 1988, 215, on Indigenous fiddle music in western Manitoba). Beach seemed to appreciate having freedom in the areas of rhythm and form. In a 2007 interview he told me,

> I don't worry about being perfect. I don't worry about making mistakes, and sometimes I make them. I just laugh it off, just showing the real me ... Stan [Cook, another well-known Winnipeg singer] complains about that sometimes, when we're together. He says, "You know," he says, "You're doing that, that song a bit too *fast*" [laughs]. And I'm saying, "I'm doing it the way I feel like doing it *today*." The words are the same, and people still –. But I don't want to *click-track* my music, you know?

The click track Beach mentioned is an electronic metronome that keeps performers in time during studio recording sessions. In the interview he used the term as a metaphor for predictable or fastidious approaches to music that detract from its immediacy and expressivity.[24] His deployment of this metaphor suggests that he felt that personal aspects of his music were threatened by certain corrective aspects of the recording process. Other parts of the same interview bore this out. I mentioned to Beach that I had noticed a great deal more rhythmic freedom on the two albums he recorded in 2004 than on his 2002 album; I was referring, among other things, to phrasing of the kind identified in table 17.1. Beach told me that he had wanted the music he recorded in 2004 to convey the "real," personal character of the songs:

[T]he first [2002] album I did was very mechanical. It was done in a studio [where the producer] does a lot of things mechanically. He's got a click track and the drums weren't real drums. They were from a machine and a lot of that stuff he did on keyboard. So ... most of it was mechanical ... which was ok; it had a good sound and a good quality.

But when I went to do the *second* album [i.e., one of the 2004 albums], I wanted a more *realistic* sound, something that wasn't so mechanical. Just something maybe like a live performance or something like that: I wanted that kind of a sound. Because some of the songs were very personal. And I wanted people to kind of get that *difference* in those two sounds ... I wanted it to be more *real* than mechanical.

For Beach, then, the rhythmic and structural freedom that made its way onto the 2004 recordings conveyed something of himself.

Beach's effectiveness as a social actor, however, was not only evident in his realization of a personal aesthetic: it was also apparent in his affirmation of a particular northern Algonquian manner of performing selfhood. During the course of the interview just cited, Beach and I discussed how one of the songs on the *Maano* album frequently moved away from a particular "pattern." Beach's use of the word "pattern" in this context referred to the regularization of phrase structure and metre in a song. He used the same word with a similar kind of valence later in the interview, when discussing his desire to be musically and lyrically unique. Hence the following quotation sheds light not only on the lyrics he writes but also on the metrical irregularities that appear in his recorded performances:

And sometimes I want to be different. I don't want to be a person who follows a *pattern* all the time. I think in order to kind of stand out, you have to be different in some sense. And even words: like sometimes I'll throw in a word that's not really *correct*, eh, and just leave it there ... Well, it's like that song ["The River Runs Red," in which appears the word] "Christianate." It's "Christia*nize*" [laughs]. And even [our mutual friend] Adria said, "That's got to be a Chris Beach word" [laughs].

In short, occasional "errors" in the lyrics and phrase structure not only have expressive potential; they are also manifestations of musical personhood.

Evident here is a way of relating to others that I frequently observed in interactions with Manitoban Cree and Ojibwe people and that accorded with the observations of earlier ethnographers.[25] My consultants valued individualism, charisma, and nonconformity. This was particularly evident in music making: in the way performers distinguished themselves from one another by means of rhythmic idiosyncrasies, in the way that some musicians evidenced a confident disinclination toward orthodoxy, and in the way that others accommodated and tolerated such irregularities. These rhythmic and stylistic peculiarities did not simply represent a performer's difference; on the contrary, they *produced* it as a social and musical fact for which others had to compensate. And thus Beach's 2004 recording sessions were socially effective not only as an instantiation of his musical personality but also as an affirmation of a certain music-cultural way of performing, and producing, selfhood.[26]

Individuation and the Comforting Community

A similar kind of individuation was evident in how Beach navigated the world of ideas. As explained above, Beach grew up believing that people who committed suicide went to hell. This eschatology – that is, this theology of death and judgment – weighed heavily upon him, especially since he knew many people who had killed themselves. He eventually became convinced that it was wrong. He explained,

> I had a lot of friends, relatives who – the suicide rate was really high when I was young ...
>
> One of the big issues I had was [this:] my mind had this vision of heaven where I would like to be someday, this beautiful place. And these people weren't going to be there. They were going to be in a bad place. And I couldn't figure that one out because every person I'd known who's committed suicide were good people. They were kind, maybe a bit too kind, and I've loved them. It was a really hard thing for me to even think. I believed at one time that they were going to hell, also, because I was told that. But I didn't want them there. And I kept thinking, "What kind of God do we have, that would do something like [that]?"

Here, he related two stories, one about a friend and one about a relative, both of whom had suffered abuse and subsequently committed suicide. Speaking of his relative (the same one who inspired "No Heartaches") he said,

I think what she wanted was something better. She wanted to be
happy … And whether she believed there was a greater existence
out there, her thing was that, "It's got to be better than here." And
… I didn't write [the song] to encourage people to use [suicide] as an
option. I wrote it as a reality. And maybe to make the suggestion, at
least for people to think about, that because somebody's committed
suicide, I really don't think that they're going to burn for eternity.
That they're even going to burn at *all*.

   … Some people don't like that, but anybody who's had a loved one
who's committed suicide has listened to that song and kind of made
peace. I've been asked to sing that song a few times because people
can relate to it and understand and kind of change their view on,
"Well, maybe there's a chance that my child, my sister, my brother,
isn't in a bad place like that." Because we all need to think those
good things and have that hope.

   … I don't have a right to judge anybody, you know, and I don't
think anybody else should. And if anybody's had a child of their
own that's committed suicide, I think it'd be really devastating if
somebody were to come up and say, "No, your kid's in hell" … I don't
want to tell people that.

So, "No Heartaches in Heaven" is a personal response to a belief Beach
found increasingly problematic, but it is also a socially oriented intervention. Beach performed the song for people he knew whose family members had committed suicide, and he released it on recordings for a wider
public. His intimate-oriented performances and stranger-orientated publications (see Warner 2002, 73–6) shared similar aims: on the one hand,
to instil hope that deceased loved ones were happy and in a better place
and, on the other, to transform religious ideas about the spiritual consequences of suicide.

   Beach's inclusion of "No Heartaches in Heaven" on *A New Life with
Jesus* provoked negative reactions from listeners with more traditional
views. Beach told me,

The Christian community, I think, could be helping bring down the
suicide rate in a good way. And sometimes … I became *angry* when
I would hear stuff like my friend … was in hell. It made me angry.
And I want the Christian community to stir enough inside them
that they should take another look at how they deal with people
who have committed suicide and become more sympathetic to the
cause, and stop being so harsh.

And if I've upset them, that's exactly what I wanted to do [laughs].
I want to create controversy. I want people to start talking about it.
And there are some people who have said, who would never buy an-
other Chris Beach album because of that, so …

… I put that song on both albums, you know. For a purpose. And
I remember somebody saying, "You're going to have problems selling your CD unless you get rid of that song, 'cause people are getting
mad." And I'm saying, "Well, that's why I put it there" … It's a pur-
poseful thing. I could have just put it on the *Maano* CD and probably
would have had no problem with it. But I wanted it to be on the
gospel [album], and then I've sang it at gospel places also …

And in a sense if you really believe in the afterlife, I mean, I think
it does speak the truth on some level.

So, despite some negative reactions, Beach believed his song could change
how Christians conceptualized suicide. Perhaps just as significantly, he
felt that he was presenting a truer perspective on the afterlife. The way
Beach oriented himself to the eschatology he found wanting is important. He did not engage theological discourse, appeal to the Bible, or cite
Catholic catechism. He advanced his argument apparently unconcerned
that some listeners might consider his ideas about suicide and the afterlife to have less validity than statements on the subject made by ordained
clergy persons or religious scholars; in effect, he placed his own interpretation on par with what he understood to be the orthodox Catholic
position.

It is certainly the case that many people feel freer than they did three or
four decades ago to express resistance to theologies they do not like and
to assemble ones that are more amenable to them. Mainstream churches
have lost authority since the child sexual abuse scandals of the late twentieth century, not least in the Canadian Aboriginal context, where many
people suffered abuse at church-run residential schools. But Beach's op-
position to orthodoxy is more than vernacular theology filling a vacuum
left by ecclesiastical authority. Again, his protest affirms longstanding
northern Algonquian cultural practices, elaborated below: certain ways
of approaching sacred observance, performing selfhood, and mobilizing
community. Hence the effectiveness of Beach's song can be understood
and evaluated in more than one way. On the one hand, it is an explicit,
public-oriented intervention that advocates an alternative theological
position. On the other hand, and less obviously, it is an instantiation of
certain kinds of northern Algonquian practice and sociability.

My Cree and Ojibwe consultants, whether traditional people or Christians (and some are both), tend to be oriented toward practice rather than belief and toward action rather than concepts so far as spiritual life is concerned. They are not particularly anxious about theology and tend not to debate fine points of belief (compare Rogers 1962, D36–41). They are however serious about leading moral lives, about singing and praying, and about acting in the proper way.[27] Such a practical orientation seems to have informed Chris Beach's decision to record and release "No Heartaches in Heaven." For Beach, the act of comforting was paramount. People who had lost a loved one to suicide needed to be consoled, and it was useless for the community to extend solace while simultaneously asserting that the deceased had gone to hell. As Beach remarked in an interview I conducted with him in 2007, "what about the people who are left behind? I don't want them to be traumatized even further by people telling them that there's no hope for them, they're in a bad place. Because that's just going to create more, it's going to create a ripple effect … and more hopelessness and more despair." In short, social necessity took precedence over eschatology.

The Manitoban Algonquian people I know (again, traditionalists and Christians alike) are in many ways individualists when it comes to spiritual matters.[28] Like Beach, they tend to have their own opinions about theology and protocol, and these often differ from orthodox and authoritative ones. Nor do they set great stock in institutions. Individuation is well documented in the ethnographic literature on northern Algonquian sacred life, which attests to the importance of personal dreams and one-to-one relationships with other-than-human dream visitors (for a concise account, see Hallowell 1992, 80–98). A similar emphasis is evident in contemporary Cree and Ojibwe approaches to Christianity. Beach's decision to include "No Heartaches" on a gospel album, his defiant attitude toward those who have found this inclusion problematic, and his faith in the eschatology he believes to be true are acts and professed attitudes that sharply delineate him. In doing so, they also affirm a cultural precedent of nonconforming personhood.

It could even be said that a particular emphasis on, and respect for, the self is also evident in how Beach represents suicide in his artworks and interviews. The suicide in "No Heartaches in Heaven" is not represented as senseless. On the contrary, the protagonist is portrayed as a thinking agent who makes a choice and defends her action. It is in part for this reason, I think, that the song is perplexing to those who have some cultural distance from it. Beach remarked in one of the interviews cited above

that he did not feel that he or anyone else had the right to judge someone for a decision to commit suicide. He asserted a person's sovereignty
in matters concerning his or her own life. Thus Joe, at the opening of
Beach's play *Peshikii*, a dog leash around his neck, preparing to hang himself from the floor joists in a basement, warns the audience against con-
demning his decision: "I know what [you're] thinking, but I'll tell you one
thing: you have no right to judge me, you don't even know me. You don't
know what I've been through." Unwillingness to pass judgment is perhaps also evident in the lyrical structure of "No Heartaches in Heaven,"
where the narrator's protests in the second verse are answered by the assured words of the protagonist in the closing chorus. It is as though the
narrator gives her the last word – and in doing so acknowledges her right
to choose her own way.

The importance of individualism in Manitoban Algonquian social and
musical life should not obscure the importance of broader social orien-
tations. Indeed, individualism is a way of relating to others. Thus A.I.
Hallowell has suggested that individuality in northern Ojibwe cultural
practice is bound in a close, reciprocating relationship to community. In
his discussion of the traditional dream fast practised by the Saulteaux
of Berens River, he explains that the special blessings imparted to individual dreamers were in fact gifts that assisted the broader community:
"It was in the prepuberty fast [a period of self-imposed abstinence during which dreams and blessings were sought] that boys, besides receiving
personal benefits, were invested with power and skills that, when exercised in their mature years, benefited their community" (Hallowell 1992,
88). Similarly, the idiosyncratic aspects of Chris Beach's music and lyrics
should not obscure their broader social orientation: "No Heartaches in
Heaven" addresses an audience. On the one hand, it seeks to comfort the
bereaved and curtail despair. On the other hand, it asserts what Beach
sees as a truer picture of the afterlife: a state that is inclusive of persons
who have taken their own lives. Here, an even broader social orientation may be evident – one in which communities are comprised of persons both living and dead.[29] Relegating suicides to hell erases the hope
of future mutuality and of one day re-encountering the dead in a happier place. In contrast, Beach's song renders communities, in the broadest
sense of the word, complete.

For Manitoban Ojibwe and Cree people, the occasion of death is often
a moment when a community comes together, united by music and by a
common eschatological hope; it is traditional to hold a wake for one or
more nights. At such events it is common for musicians and groups from a

range of denominations to sing Christian songs throughout the night (see Dueck 2005, 279–87; compare McNally 2000, 3–5, 167–71, on Minnesota Ojibwe practices). They perform hymns from various denominational traditions in Cree, Ojibwe, and English. They also sing "country gospel" music – ecumenically popular country-style songs on sacred themes. Particular favourites include "In the Sweet Bye and Bye," "How Beautiful Heaven Must Be," and "Will the Circle Be Unbroken?" – all of which offer comfort to bereaved family members and the hope that their loved ones are happier and in a better place. Certainly, gospel songs are sung in church services and at informal gatherings, but they are associated in an especially close way with funerary observances, where they are the beloved medium through which the community conveys its support.

"No Heartaches in Heaven" stands in dialogue with this gospel tradition. Like other such songs, it makes use of the stylistic characteristics of classic country music, including a limited harmonic palette, straightforward strophic structures, guitar accompaniment, and country-style vocal production and ornamentation. It also makes use of familiar lyrical tropes. The chorus, for instance (see figure 17.1), faintly echoes the following lines from "In the Sweet By and By":

> We shall sing on that beautiful shore
> The melodious songs of the blest,
> And our spirits shall sorrow no more
> Not a sigh for the blessing of rest.[30]

In both songs, heaven is a respite from sadness: from tears in one and from sighs in the other. Thus Beach frames his narrative of suicide and release using a musical and poetic language that is closely associated with gospel music and, consequently, the wake. In doing so, he symbolically extends the comfort of this genre to a group that has not always benefited from it. Those who mourn suicide victims have in some cases been inconsolable because they fear that those victims are damned. To those mourners, "No Heartaches" extends the hope of heaven.

In summary, the effectiveness of "No Heartaches in Heaven" can be understood in a number of senses. On the one hand, its author has explicitly characterized it as an intervention into the way that Aboriginal Christians conceptualize suicide. On the other hand, and less obviously, the song affirms certain northern Algonquian ways of observing ritual passages, performing valued selfhood, and mobilizing community comfort. Effective social action in this case does not simply involve the reproduction of existing cultural practices; it also involves reinventing them. "No Heartaches in Heaven" does just this: it draws upon a tradition of funerary song to extend comfort to a constituency whose members were previously unconsoled.

Conclusion

Beach's songs and plays bear witness to a particular social context: to the songwriter's personal encounters with suicide and suicidality, to a broader Manitoban environment in which suicide is all too common, and to the theological and clinical discourses that address those deaths. His works identify a number of reasons for Indigenous suicide: physical and sexual abuse, misuse of intoxicants, urban violence and the sex trade, and problems associated with the interventions of government child welfare organizations. They also suggest that suicide is a response to pain, especially the pain that takes some people over when a loved one dies or a relationship fails. Beach's works, however, do more than represent their circumstances: they also strive to effect change within them. Beach conceived his plays as pieces that might help to keep young Aboriginal people from committing suicide, and he placed "No Heartaches" on a gospel album in the hope of transforming listeners' beliefs about suicides. These works also move toward less obvious outcomes, as a consideration of "No Heartaches in Heaven" suggests. In eschewing musical norms and theological orthodoxy, Beach's recorded performance produces individuality and, beyond this, affirms a northern Algonquian way of expressing personhood. Perhaps more significantly, these particularities have implications for community practice. In combining controversial theology and the country-gospel idiom, Beach's song extends and elaborates the communal musical practice by which Manitoban Algonquian people observe the passing of loved ones and soothe those who mourn them.

When non-Aboriginal writers discuss Aboriginal suicide, there is sometimes a valedictory tendency to bid farewell to Indigenous cultures. But the songs and dramatic works discussed here point to the life, rather than the death, of Manitoban Algonquian culture – even as they point to the difficulty of achieving life in its fullest. Although they press a critique of the social, political, and historical circumstances that contribute to despair, they do not suggest that Indigenous culture is disintegrating or fighting a losing battle with anomie; rather, they point to its ongoing creative elaboration.

1 My spelling of "Ojibwe" follows that used by my Ojibwe language teacher at the University of Manitoba, Roger Roulette.

2 I first heard Beach perform the song live in 2002 or 2003, at which time I was already struck by its lyrics.

3 I presume it is the shore of a lake, not another body of water. Vogar and the neighbouring Lake Manitoba First Nation are located beside Lake Manitoba.

4 Two songs come to mind in particular: (1) "Whiskey Lullaby," popularized by Brad Paisley and Alison Krauss: "She put that bottle to her head and pulled the trigger / And finally drank away his memory. / Life is short but this time it was bigger / Than the strength she had to get up off her knees"; and (2) "Fade to Black" by Metallica: "Life, it seems, will fade away, / Drifting farther every day. / Getting lost within myself; / Nothing matters, no one else. / I have lost the will to live, / Simply nothing more to give. / There is nothing more for me; / Need the end to set me free."

5 There may be some interpretive flexibility in the Catholic theology on suicide, but it does not seem like its moderating aspects were emphasized in Beach's upbringing.

6 The term "Métis" obscures many complexities of genealogy and cultural affiliation so far as Chris Beach's family history is concerned. On his mother's side, Chris's grandmother was an Ojibwe woman from the Cody reserve in Saskatchewan and his grandfather was a Métis man from St Laurent in Manitoba. They spoke Michif, a mixed French and Cree language, at home. Chris's mother, Anne, spoke Ojibwe and English. On his father's side, his grandmother was an Icelandic woman and his grandfather was English Canadian. His father spoke English. Chris Beach's parents lived in Vogar during his younger years and from time to time afterward. Vogar, although it has an Icelandic name, has a large and perhaps predominantly Métis population and is located on the outskirts of the Lake Manitoba First Nation. Many Manitoban reserves have such neighbouring Métis communities, often inhabited by people who have a strong sense of Indigenous identity, who speak Indigenous languages, and who associate closely with the First Nations people on the neighbouring reserve. This is the case in Chris Beach's family, which has strong connections to First Nations roots: three of his ten siblings speak Ojibwe, and five of them married Status Indians, as did Chris. Consequently, all of Chris's seven children are Status Indians (as I relate in the main body of the text, Beach adopted two foster children and three of his brother and sister-in-law's children).

7 The biographical material presented here and elsewhere draws upon an interview I conducted with Beach in 2003 and is supplemented by information drawn from another interview conducted in 2007. I took handwritten notes during the 2003 interview and recorded the 2007 interview. Additional information, including corrections of inaccuracies present in an earlier draft of this chapter, was attained in an August 2008 discussion.

8 Beach quoted this verse to me in a 2003 interview; it appears here with his permission. To my knowledge, it remains otherwise unpublished. A newer version of "Devil's Blood," without the material quoted here, can be heard on *A New Life with Jesus*.

9 In Beach's play *Kigeet*, Indian Joe Blow's final monologue includes the following lines: "You know, suicide is a spirit who will come and whisper in your ear, usually when you are at your lowest point in life" (Beach 2006b, 54).

10 Beach's sister-in-law was walking by the side of the road in Lake Manitoba First Nation when a drunk driver hit her. She sustained severe injuries, and eventually she and her unborn child died. She might have survived, Chris told me, if a white ambulance driver, complaining that someone on the reserve owed him money, had not refused to come to pick her up. There was a long delay before another driver could be found, and Sally Ann passed away.

11 These plays have recently been published as a collection (Beach 2011). References to the plays in this chapter are to drafts of the plays rather than to the published book. The middle play, *Kigeet*, has had a number of well-received public performances, most notably one in spring 2008 at the Winnipeg Convention Centre with Chris's son, the actor Adam Beach, in the lead role (other performances have been given in Phoenix and Oklahoma City).

12 I have omitted names and other identifying information at several points in this chapter where suicide, suicidal behaviour, or sexual abuse is alleged.

13 The term "suicidality" refers to "suicide ideation and suicide attempts" (see Thorlindsson and Bjarnason 1998, 95).

14 On what they call cultural continuity and discontinuity, and the effects of these on youth suicidality, see Chandler and Lalonde (1998). On the remaining risk factors listed, see Angell, Kurz, and Gottfried (1997, 3–4), and Grossman, Milligan, and Deyo (1991, esp. 872), who focus on youth suicide among Navajo adolescents. Note that "extreme alienation from family and community" closely corresponds to the Durkheimian category of egoism, or lack of integration.

15 This hybrid explanation hints at the increasingly reflexive consciousness of culture and society (see Hannerz 1996, 17). People know that they have a culture and that it is susceptible to social problems, and they sing, speak, and write about the latter. Social-scientific discourse shapes self-conception.

16 In 1983 Patrick Johnston estimated that around 4.6 per cent of Status Indian children in Canada had been placed in the child welfare system, compared to around 0.96 per cent of all Canadian children (Johnston 1983, 57). As for Manitoba, Johnston quoted an estimate that suggested that up to 60 per cent of the children in care in the province were Aboriginal, a figure far out of proportion to the actual population of Aboriginal children (40). In the majority of Manitoban cases, it appears, Indigenous children were placed in white foster homes or adopted out to white families (57–9; see also Manitoba 1991).

17 On the melancholy that sometimes follows a death, compare Rogers (1962, B60–1). Probably as a warning against this kind of state, a well-loved Cree funerary hymn ("Kē Kē Pā Sakihitin") urges those who are bereaved, "Do not be lazy," warning them against falling into despondency. Thanks to Nelson Menow for translating this song and explaining it to me in a summer 2008 interview.

18 Durkheim (1951) conceived of four different types of suicide, grouped in pairs: altruistic and egoistic suicide, on the one hand, and fatalistic and anomic suicide, on the other. Altruistic suicides happen frequently in cultures where social integration is high; in such cases, suicide victims are unhesitant to sacrifice their lives because they do not regard individual existence as particularly significant when viewed in relation to the larger group or to its values. In contrast, egoistic suicides happen where integration is low; these are suicides in which victims are not closely connected to the feelings, experiences, and activities of others within their society and consequently do not feel inhibited about taking their lives. Anomic suicides happen in situations when social regulation is weak and particularly where there has been a collapse of socially mandated norms and constraints on behaviour. In contrast, fatalistic suicides happen in cultures where social regulation is high, perhaps unbearably high, and where victims feel that they are trapped by excessively strict norms and rules.

19 This is less likely to be the case in scholarly literature since Durkheim, which has emphasized how suicide is inflected by culture. Durkheim suggested that certain cultural particularities, including differences in religious belief and variations in the prevalence of divorce, mediated the suicide-inducing effects of European modernities (Durkheim 1951, 152–70, 259–76).

20 Angell and colleagues analyze their case study as one that manifests not only anomie but egoism and altruism as well (Angell, Kurz, and Gottfried 1997, 9–11, 13–14). For a contrary view of the relationship between European contact and suicide, see Levy and Kunitz (1971).

21 Other scholarly literature on suicide and Indigenous cultures provides additional evidence that culture shapes the forms that suicide takes. For instance, Robert Brightman describes how, in the nineteenth century and earlier, northern Algonquians sometimes believed themselves to be degenerating into windigos: powerful, icy-hearted monsters who ate human flesh (Brightman 1998). Convinced that past misdeeds or fate had predestined them to become cannibals, they exhibited behaviour – for instance, rejection of regular food and hunger for human flesh – that invited execution at the hands of their fellow community members. Apparently, some who believed themselves to be in the process of transformation even begged others to put them to death (Brightman 1998, 350–1); such transformations occurred with much less frequency after the nineteenth century.

22 A performative theory of genre suggests that norms (1) exist in musical grammars and genres, (2) are determined through social praxis and authorized by those with the social power to do so, and (3) are subject to negotiation and contestation. Put another way, genre norms are presumed and brought into being through acts of composition, performance, and recording, through critical discourses commenting upon such practices, and through choices about listening and consuming undertaken by audiences. Emerging as they do through the variegated and sometimes contradictory practices of many actors, norms are in no way uniform or fixed; they do however have social and aesthetic authority.

Beach occasionally encountered persons who attempted to bring the authority of stylistic norms to bear. Such encounters reveal at once their social power and contested status. For instance, Beach told me that one Aboriginal radio announcer was disinclined to broadcast songs from the 2004 *Maano* album because he felt that the recording was not up to professional standards. Nevertheless, songs from the album were eventually broadcast on the station, perhaps as a result of Beach's advocacy.

23 Some mainstream country musicians also stray from dominant practice and approach phrasing and rhythm capriciously; Willie Nelson is perhaps the best known example.

24 Beach's perspective is reminiscent of a remark Bruno Nettl makes about the aesthetics of good singing in Blackfoot music-cultural practice (Nettl, of course, examines the traditional singing of a Plains group, whereas I focus on country gospel music performed by northern Algonquian musicians). The Blackfoot people Nettl worked with did not emphasize perfection or excellence but rather getting things basically right. He remarks, "The Blackfoot people thought there were a good many who 'had it right,' and thought I could learn their musical culture properly with any of them" (Nettl 2005, 145). This is *not* to say that "excellence," "virtuosity," and "professionalism" are never demonstrated in Manitoban Ojibwe, Cree, or Métis performances. It is the case, rather, that democratic participation is valued and that performers tend not to let musical details become more important than musical participation.

25 See Hallowell (1955, 1992), Landes (1968), Dunning (1959), and Mason (1967). Compare, however, Hickerson (1967).

26 Thus Beach's emphasis on uniqueness should be distinguished from the standard Western ideology of the innovative artist, although Beach did draw upon such tropes during the interview. Similarly, the individualism explored here is not the same thing as "Western liberal individualism," although in the context of centuries of European-Indigenous contact, the two have borrowed from one another.

27 Michael D. McNally has also noted this focus on praxis. In a hermeneutic passage focusing on the Ojibwe term for "Christian," McNally observes that Ojibwe Christians call themselves *"Anami'aajig,"* which he translates as "those who pray," "that which we pray," or "how we pray." He notes that the stress is "on the practice of prayer – not on its content, its object, or the system to which it refers." He goes on to remark, "Christianity is not marked as a system or even a body of beliefs. In Ojibwe idiom, Christianity itself is a practice, a way of praying" (McNally 2000, 15–16).

28 To join this point to the preceding one, it is not simply that they are oriented to practice; it is that particular persons find certain practices amenable to them.

29 On the traditional Ojibwe conceptions of the spirits of the dead, or *djibaiyak*, and the land of the dead, or *djibaiaking*, see Hallowell (1955, 151–71; 1992, 74–9).

30 These lyrics are quoted from the fifteenth page of the song binder of Kendra and Mary Sinclair, two of my Winnipeg consultants; I photocopied the contents of the binder in 2003. The Cyberhymnal website gives the author and date of the lyrics as Sanford F. Bennett, 1868; see http://www.cyberhymnal.org (accessed 16 June 2008).

18

Arnie Strynadka,
"The Uke-Cree Fiddler"

MARCIA OSTASHEWSKI

I met Arnie Strynadka, who billed himself as the "The Uke-Cree Fiddler," while conducting field research at the Vegreville Ukrainian Pysanka Festival in Alberta in 2002. When I stopped at Arnie's booth to chat, he told me that he was the child of a marriage between a Cree woman and a man born of Ukrainian immigrants. I had already spent almost a decade researching and writing about Ukrainian music, culture, and identity, and I had spent my entire lifetime as a Ukrainian cultural, music, and dance performer and enthusiast. This was the first I had ever heard of family relations between Aboriginal people and Ukrainian immigrant families, even though histories and experiences of Ukrainian immigrants and their descendants in Canada are extensively addressed in popular and scholarly literature by storytellers, journalists, historians, sociologists, religious scholars, folklorists, filmmakers, visual artists, dancers, and musicians. Because of this evident lacuna, I decided to explore the circumstances that led families of Cree-Ukrainian descent to make specific types of music or to use music in their lives in localized ways. Arnie's is one such story.

Arnie's musical life and personal history provide examples of ways that one person negotiated his joint Aboriginal and Ukrainian Canadian heritage in late twentieth- and early twenty-first-century Canada. Born in 1940 in northeast-central Alberta, Arnie spent most of his childhood on the Goodfish Lake reserve and in the nearby Ukrainian settlement community of Two Lakes. As a young adult, Arnie spent many years working in logging camps in British Columbia; he later worked for the Alberta

18.1 Arnie Strynadka with his plunger-fiddle. Photograph courtesy of Arnie Strynadka.

government as a consultant for resources development and as an activist and educator in regard to Aboriginal issues, before devoting his energies to music performance and production. Arnie's most active years as a professional musician were from the early 1980s to the early 2000s. During these years, Arnie spent most of his days travelling between venues across western Canada and into the United States. This included country music centres like Nashville and Branson, Missouri, where he was awarded "Star in Residence" status, an accolade he proudly mentioned on many of his album covers. In his performances, Arnie made much of a comedic persona (as is evident in figure 18.1). His repertoire, as recorded first on cassette tapes and more recently on CDs and DVDs, is primarily composed of old-time American country music, gospel tunes, and waltzes. From about 2005, Arnie's sometimes failing health kept him in one place: with family in and around central Alberta. This was until his death on 28 May 2011. Arnie's wake and funeral were held a few days later on the Goodfish Lake Reserve. I offer this information as an introduction to Arnie Strynadka and address a few aspects of his musical life in more detail later in this chapter.

Since Arnie was not performing during his final years, the period during which I met and conducted several interviews with him, the investigation of Arnie's music and life that I have begun is conducted primarily through his recordings, conversations, and formal interviews. In this chapter, I draw on different resources, including Arnie's life story as he told it to me and what I have learned from Arnie's recordings about his repertoire and style choices or identity constructs. In my analysis of these data, I consider historical and statistical information about the Ukrainian and Aboriginal communities of Two Lakes and Goodfish Lake as a means of providing a broader perspective on both Native and European immigrant groups living in the geographical region of northeast-central Alberta that is the focus of this study. I engage scholarship that addresses the politics of American Indianness, especially in relation to what is widely referred to as "mixed-blood" identity, and Philip Deloria's discussion of expectations and anomalies in his book *Indians in Unexpected Places* (2004). Also, since Arnie Strynadka chose to ally himself, at least partly, with a Ukrainian Canadian ethnocultural identity, throughout this work I consider ways that people choose to perform (and sometimes transform) a Ukrainian ethnic heritage and identity in modern Canada, particularly through expressive cultural practices like music.

This chapter, which focuses on the music of Arnie Strynadka, provides insight into specific music cultures that is not normally possible (as do Smith 1994, Levine 1991, and Waterman 1991) in generalized ethnographic approaches. Works like this one present a "plurality of interpretations" (Smith 1994, 541) as regards individual experience and agency in relation to music, culture, and identity. Like the scholarship of other authors who have written in this way, especially Gordon E. Smith (1994) in his essay about Mi'kmaw fiddler Lee Cremo, this chapter is woven with historical, cultural, and political aspects of Native and non-Native life, all intertwined with the "individual experience and creativity" (Smith 1994, 541) of Arnie Strynadka the musician.

I occasionally use the term "Indian" to refer to Arnie Strynadka in this chapter since this is the term that he used when he referred to himself, his family, and his community. In a conversation on this point, he explained that he used this term because it meant something – both to him and in wider contexts. "Indian" had a history in his experience. "First Nation" and "Aboriginal," Arnie said, being much more recent terms, were not as familiar to him. He signalled his awareness of the importance of the new terminology by noting that "everything is done for some political gain" (personal communication, 27 April 2009).[1]

Histories of Settlement and Interaction: Aboriginal and Ukrainian Communities in Alberta

The centre of Ukrainian experience and history in Canada is situated on prairie land and in the very region that is the focus of this study. A farming population, most of whose members left their eastern European rural homes in search of farmland and prosperity in Canada, the first wave of Ukrainian immigrants was encouraged by the Canadian government to settle the Prairies in the late nineteenth century. The government offered an incentive to immigrant settlers in the form of a "free" homestead of 160 acres of land on the Prairies.[2] Historian Orest Martynowych, who has focused his research on Ukrainian Canadians, describes the Dominion government's political and economic goals, the interests of central Canadian industrial capitalists and political elites, and the development of Canadian industry as factors behind the immigration policies that sought to increase continental European immigration to Canada and, specifically, to settle the Prairies (Martynowych 1991, 37–41).

Tensions between Aboriginal groups and Euro-Canadians on the Prairies led both groups toward the negotiation of treaties during the late 1800s.[3] Aboriginal groups hoped to mitigate the incursion of Euro-Canadians; Euro-Canadians wanted to secure the land for development. The Canadian government had both financial and political interests in signing treaties with First Nations on the Prairies. Subsequent to the signing of treaties, First Nations were generally moved to land set aside for reserves. This left the land open for the Dominion government, which enticed central Europeans to immigrate to the Prairies and develop the land for agriculture, something the government hoped to do to ensure Canadian instead of American control of it (Martynowych 1991, 37-41). Martynowych notes the presence of "Indian" and Métis groups and the resolution of land title issues only briefly, and he vaguely refers to a context of racial conflicts between Aboriginal people and white settlers on the Prairies. He is one of the few recent historians of Ukrainian immigration in Canada to address the topic at all (Martynowych 1991, 45-6). Yet, in my view, these conflicts also need to be integrated into the broader history of the region, including the fact that the signing of the treaties made it possible for the Dominion government to develop the aforementioned immigration policies and to offer land titles to Europeans if they would come and farm the land.[4]

An initial wave of large-scale Ukrainian immigration to Canada began in the 1890s and continued to 1914 (Martynowych 1991). Among these early immigrants was a group of Ukrainians who settled near what is now Star, in east-central Alberta, northeast of what is now the provincial capital of Edmonton (Lehr 1991, 34). This settlement and the many other Ukrainian settlements subsequently established in surrounding areas on the Canadian Prairies are commonly referred to as northeast-central Alberta in Ukrainian Canadian scholarship and wider public discourse.

This settlement region includes hubs of Ukrainian Canadian cultural activity such as the city of Edmonton and the towns of Vegreville (where I first met Arnie at the Ukrainian festival), Smokey Lake, Lamont, and Star-Edna. In proximity to these communities is the reserve community of Goodfish Lake, where Arnie Strynadka spent his early years. These early Ukrainian settlements and the Goodfish Lake community all fall within the boundaries of Treaty 6, signed in 1876 at Forts Carleton and Pitt (Taylor 1985, Alberta Aboriginal Affairs 1996).

In community publications and government documents today, what Arnie referred to as his home community of Goodfish Lake is called Whitefish (Goodfish) Lake First Nation No. 128. This reserve community is part of a larger Saddle Lake First Nation community,[5] where Cree is the dominant Aboriginal language (Statistics Canada n.d., appendix D). Historical studies show that the geographical area of northeast-central Alberta has been inhabited mainly by Plains and Woodland Cree nations (Dempsey 1997, 104).

There is a history of encounters and relations between Ukrainian immigrant families and Aboriginal people in northeast-central Alberta. Yet, except for the present study, I am aware of only one other academic publication that addresses relations of any kind between Aboriginal people and Ukrainian Canadians. Two stories of meetings between Ukrainian immigrants and Native peoples are recounted in a book of first-person accounts by "Ukrainian Pioneers, 1891–1914" (Piniuta 1978, 79–84). The events in these stories occurred in and around the Smokey Lake area, northeast of Edmonton. One of these events occurred near Hamlin, which is a little more than ten kilometres away from Saddle Lake First Nation No. 125; the other occurred near the town of Smokey Lake, which is about seventy kilometres from both the Whitefish Lake No. 128 and Saddle Lake No. 125 reserve communities. In each of these cases, Ukrainian immigrants benefited from the life-saving aid and hospitality of Aboriginal people. According to Arnie Strynadka, his Ukrainian immigrant ancestors likewise benefited from his Cree grandfather's employment and care, as I describe later in this chapter.

Mixed Ancestry: Complicated Cultural Values and Affiliations

Although there is certainly evidence of relations between Aboriginal people and Ukrainians, little attention has been paid to this matter in scholarship or public memory. Given the discrimination against Aboriginal people in Canada, and a broader social context in which Ukrainian immigrants and their descendants worked to be accepted in mainstream Euro-Canadian society, early twentieth-century generations of Ukrainians in Canada may well have been concerned about a stigma of Aboriginal roots. From a mainstream perspective, a double stigma existed regarding both an Aboriginal and Ukrainian immigrant identity. Stories I heard while conducting ethnographic research for this study have led me to believe this has been the case.

For those who would research relations between Aboriginal people and Ukrainian settlers, another challenge exists in the lack of a clear historical record. When I asked a colleague who has worked for several years as a historical researcher for the Alberta government about why it might be that we have so little information and scholarship about people of mixed Aboriginal and Ukrainian ancestry, she replied that they fall under the category of Métis. The concept and definition of the term "Métis" has been variable through the past century, as historians of Métis history have described (Peterson and Brown 1985).[6] There have been people of mixed Aboriginal and European ancestry from the beginning of the time of the meeting of these peoples. However, it has only been in certain places and at certain times that people of mixed ancestry have chosen to self-identify as neither "Indian" nor "white" but as "an 'in-between people' – neither Indian nor non-Indian" (Frideres and Gadacz 2008, 40). The most spectacular politicization of Métis self-consciousness was in the 1860s at Red River, during the resistance to Canadian takeover of Rupert's Land. Even this had earlier roots, namely in the idea of a "New Nation" that was part of a Métis resistance to the colonization of Red River in the 1810s (Dickason and McNab 2009, 232).

In contrast, at the time Ukrainian immigration was beginning in the 1890s, the Métis had been militarily defeated and marginalized – most notably during the North-West Rebellion of 1885 in the province of Saskatchewan (Beal and MacLeod 2009). At the time of treaty signing with First Nations in the Canadian West, the Dominion government had not included Métis as signatories but instead had offered them scrip.[7] In the emerging agricultural economy of the new territories that had once been Rupert's Land, there was no place for people who were "in-between"; there were only "whites" and "Indians" (Dickason and McNab 2009, 282–7). Only in the last half of the twentieth century would there be a political resurgence of Métis identity (Dickason and McNab 2009, 282), and official recognition of Métis in the 1982 Constitution was especially significant.

Sociologists and historians alike write that little is known about the identity and culture of people of mixed ancestry in Canada, aside from the Red River (French-speaking, Catholic) and Rupert's Land (English-speaking, Protestant) Métis, largely on account of inconsistent government approaches to this topic (Frideres and Gadacz 2008, Peterson and Brown 1985). As an old French adjective meaning "mixed," the term "Métis" was being used already in the late-1700s "to refer to a population of French-Indian descent which was noticed as culturally and socially distinct from its parents' communities on either side" (Brown 1993, 20). However, the matter of identity of children of mixed Aboriginal and non-Aboriginal heritage is far more complex, as John Foster and others have argued (Foster 2007, Brown 1980, Devine 2004, Peterson and Brown 1985). Nonetheless, detailed information about individuals and families of mixed ancestry is limited. For example, from the way the census data are reported, it is impossible to ascertain whether Ukrainian is spoken in Aboriginal households.[8] Recent data on languages spoken by Aboriginal people specifically in Alberta tabulate numbers of people who speak languages other than Aboriginal languages, English, or French but do not note what these languages are (for example, the data do not state whether the other languages might include Ukrainian).[9] In one case, that of Whitefish Lake First Nation No. 128, the focus of the present study, identification of Aboriginal "heritage"[10] is described in terms of North American Indian or Métis identity; no further details are provided (Statistics Canada n.d., 12).

Further, as Arnie described of his childhood on the reserve, it was not uncommon for children of Euro-Canadian ancestry born "out of wedlock" to grow up on the reserve with their Aboriginal mothers, a fact supported by recent census data as well (personal communication, 27 April 2009); European ancestry, in such cases, might not be known or acknowledged. The statistics I cite above are compiled from a census that relies upon a process of self-identification. How a person chooses to self-identify can change over time depending on a variety of factors; the number of Aboriginal people has increased in recent years partly because more people are choosing to self-identify in this way.[11] For all of the reasons discussed above, it has not been possible to determine statistics or to find much historical information regarding Aboriginal-Ukrainian personal relationships and/or marriages in Canada.

Arnie Strynadka: A Personal Life History

I now turn my focus to musician Arnie Strynadka, reviewing what he told me about his personal history and musical influences. Considering that self-identification may signal ways that cultural values are played out in the lives of individuals, I reflect on Arnie's life-history narrative as a means by which he performed his identity. For instance, one major aspect of his character, both onstage and off, was humour. Arnie said he was always somewhat goofy, so a funny act on stage was a natural extension of his personality. He also said that he was inspired to build his plunger-fiddle after working with a country music performer who had turned a toilet seat into a guitar. Arnie's "goofy" comedian-fiddler act also plays readily into an oft-storied aspect of Aboriginal North American identity; as Arnie pointed out to me, more than once during our interview sessions, Indian people are often known as jokesters.

That Indians are jokesters may be something of a familiar notion we have all heard many times,[12] but Arnie also had experience growing up in a First Nation community and among Cree families. Arnie (Arnold) Strynadka was born in 1940 on the Goodfish Lake reserve near Vilna, Alberta, to a Cree mother, Dora Bull, and a father of Ukrainian immigrant descent, Nick Strynadka. The families of Dora and Nick had come together in the 1920s when Arnie's Cree grandfather – a wealthy farmer, trapper, and trading post owner/operator named Sam Bull[13] – hired the destitute Ukrainian immigrant Strynadka family to work on his 1,200-acre farm. Nick and Dora, children of these Cree and Ukrainian families, married in 1933. Arnie had three older siblings, but he told me that he was the last child to be born to his parents since his father died in a farm accident when Arnie was little more than a month old. Arnie's Cree and Ukrainian grandparents all contributed significantly to helping Arnie's mother raise him and his older siblings. Arnie liked to say that he "grew up with bannock in one hand and kobassa[14] [Ukrainian garlic sausage] in the other" (interview, February 2009) – speaking Cree with one grandmother, Ukrainian with the other, and English at school and with various folks on the reserve and around home.

During Arnie's childhood, his life appears to have involved a rather seamless synthesis of aspects of both Cree and Ukrainian-immigrant-pioneer life; he was nonetheless aware of differences between the ancestry of his parents and some implications of these differences. Since his mother had married a non-Native man, Arnie's family lived off the reserve and he attended the school in the nearby Ukrainian settlement community of Two Lakes, not the school on the reserve. Arnie noted that Indian Agents were known, among those who lived on the reserve, to have a strong hand in ensuring only treaty Indians lived on the reserve and went to school there.[15] Although Arnie had positive memories of Ukrainian Canadians and Cree people working together in rural Alberta where he grew up, he did not suggest that such good relations were necessarily the norm in other places. In fact, he said it was commonly known among Aboriginal people in his community that "you don't go to 'so and so's' farm because they don't hire Indians." Arnie also experienced, first-hand, severe racism when he moved to the city of Edmonton at the age of twelve, which led to his dropping out of school and leaving town to begin working in a lumber camp by the age of fifteen. Arnie's memories of the Goodfish Lake reserve community remained strong nonetheless. Although he did not live directly on the Goodfish Lake reserve in his early years, Arnie often spent time there, playing with other children, working on his grandfather's farm, and meeting with local folks at his grandfather's home in the evenings and on weekends to listen to the radio, make music, dance, and sing.

Musical Influences in Arnie Strynadka's Early Years

Arnie cited three major musical influences from this early part of his life, sources that strongly contributed to his musical tastes and style. First among these was the gospel music that was common on the reserve community of his Cree family. Second was radio, particularly country music stations. And third was music and musicians local to the Goodfish Lake area, including Aboriginal musicians in and near the reserve community and also those in the Ukrainian settlement. Here, I look at the impact and different roles of each of these influences in Arnie's life and music.

Although hymns and Christianity are obviously a recent part of Indigenous expression, Christian hymn singing has become integral to the identity of many Native Americans, woven into their lives with both personal and cultural significance (see, for example, Lassiter, Ellis, and Kotay 2002, Diamond 2008b). Arnie remembered vividly that his Cree grandfather, Sam Bull, who was a preacher, loved singing gospel hymns along with whatever he was doing. Arnie also remembered pumping the organ that was in his grandfather's home while his mother played hymns on it.

The second major source of music in Arnie's life both on and off the reserve was the radio – he remembered spending countless hours listening to country music stations CKUA and CFCW. Arnie's favourite artists included Mother Maybelle Carter, Hank Williams, and bluegrass musicians like Bill Munro. Picking out the tunes he heard on the radio by ear, Arnie eventually learned to play old-time country and bluegrass songs on a fiddle that Sam Bull had purchased second-hand at a furniture store in 1903. Sam Bull, says Arnie, owned several instruments – although he could not play a single one. Instead, he displayed them in his home and strongly encouraged the children to learn to play. "Respect them," Arnie remembered his grandfather saying, "for they will be with you in good times and in tough times. And if you're too lazy to work, they'll help you make a living" (interview, February 2009). Arnie's radio interest signalled a cultural experience that is much wider than the reserve. He also emphasized the primacy of his Cree grandfather's wisdom as a guiding influence in his personal and musical development – something he spoke about even in his last days when I visited him at the hospital. Although country music and radio tunes might not, on their own, be readily connected to Aboriginal culture, Arnie called attention to the fact that he often engaged this music at his grandfather's house, stressing, once more, the importance of his Cree family connections.

Arnie learned to play by ear, learning much about both style and repertoire from musicians local to the communities in which he grew up – the third major influence in Arnie's young years and musical education. One of two key musicians local to the reserve community was Arnie's uncle, a man named Washington Howse. Arnie said that Washington lived off but near the reserve. Washington played the fiddle only a very little, and he played left-handed, but "he knew all the fiddle tunes" and would hum them to teach melodies and aspects of performance style to Arnie. Another local musician, fiddler Paul Memnook, "lived up on the hill" on the Goodfish Lake reserve. Arnie remembered both Paul and Washington teaching him tunes and also teaching him *how* to play, getting him to stop and repeat until they were satisfied he was playing it right, playing it "the old Indian way." "The old Indian way," Arnie explained, results directly from playing to the dancers. Sometimes dancers miss a step or skip a beat, and the musicians must follow along and adjust to the dancers (personal communication, 27 April 2009). Measures are sometimes truncated or lengthened by a beat or two, and phrasing is sometimes asymmetrical.

Arnie told me that, whether he was playing for dancers or not, he still played music "the old Indian way." He sometimes referred to this way of playing, in which the rhythmic regularity of the piece is disrupted, as "broken timing."[16] Upon review of Arnie's recordings – of which there are about a dozen, each with twelve to twenty songs – I found no evidence of broken timing among them. Arnie explained that it was necessary for him to adapt his style to recording and performing along with the preset, rhythmically regular tracks of electronically generated music. He added that, when he first began to play with machines, he used a synthesizer and a few times played with broken timing; this worked fine except that he had some trouble dealing with the bass, which he explained "went backwards." More recently, he played with rhythm machines, which did not allow him to play broken timing at all. Yet, importantly, Arnie described "the old Indian way" as a main aspect of his style. Indeed, all three of Arnie's musical influences, as he described them to me, highlight connections to his Cree ancestry (personal communication, 27 April 2009). There is also evidence of other musical influences in Arnie's musical practice and memories, including music of the Ukrainian settlement. In the next section, I take up this discussion in relation to a more nuanced analysis of his sound.

Other Aspects of Arnie Strynadka's Style and Repertoire: The Recordings

Although "the old Indian way" of playing may not have been a significant part of Arnie's actual performance practice (in his most recent years of performing, at least), I note here three other important aspects of his musical practice. One aspect concerns timbre and tuning, another is a description of how Arnie chose to depict himself on his album covers, and a third is repertoire. My earlier discussion of Arnie's music is based primarily on his telling of his life story, and it emphasizes his Cree family connections. This part of my analysis nuances the story of Arnie's music in a way that suggests multiple and complex locations of his music practice.

When I played a recording of Arnie's music for Sherry Johnson, a colleague who specializes in Canadian old-time fiddling (Johnson 2006), her initial reaction was that Arnie's fiddling sounds much like that of many western Canadian Métis fiddlers. My own description of Arnie's sound includes a specific description of aspects of timbre and tuning; Arnie's fiddling is characterized by occasional slides up to, in, and around notes and by a sometimes less-than-crisp articulation of individual pitches in the melody. One might be tempted to consider attributing Arnie's sound to the somewhat arbitrary fact that he played on a plunger, but I would dispute this argument. Arnie's plunger-fiddle is a very carefully crafted fiddle, the twelfth version of Arnie's construction efforts, and he told me he made significant efforts (and invested considerable funds in state-of-the-art technologies) to get it sounding just right. Instead, I believe his musical style had more to do with how he learned to play music or, more to the point, where he learned to play and from whom.

One way of describing Arnie's music may be that it sounds like that of a western Canadian Métis fiddler, and we know that Arnie did learn to play from at least one Métis fiddler. My own description of Arnie's fiddling indicates aspects of style that are typical of many western Canadian fiddlers of the mid-twentieth century who are of Ukrainian descent; a prime example of this is musician Metro Radomsky, who, like Arnie, grew up and learned to play music in northeast-central Alberta. Therefore, some aspects of Arnie's music may be characteristic of "the old Indian way" of playing. His tuning and timbre also suggest the importance of shared historical and cultural experiences of different groups of people who lived in proximity to one another in a specific geographic, regional location.

Arnie's cover art also suggests that his musical practice was connected to a variety of genres and scenes. Of the eleven albums Arnie had available for me to purchase, all but two covers include mention of Arnie's honour as a "Star in Residence" in the major country music centre of Branson, Missouri. He noted this honour very proudly when I met with him (interview, February 2009). Five of eleven albums mention "country" music in their titles, and four more depict Arnie wearing a cowboy hat and boots. From this, it appears that Arnie felt strongly about his affiliation with old-time American country music. Also, four albums depict Arnie wearing items of clothing that are readily associated with a kind of pan-"Indianness," such as a beaded necklace and a beaded vest, although the vest, with its flowered pattern and fringes, might readily be associated specifically with western Canadian Métis culture (Brasser 1985). Or, as in one cartoon image in which Arnie bows his fiddle with an arrow, Arnie is directly described as "an Indian [with a plunger]." However, aside from Arnie's surname and his handle as "The Uke-Cree Fiddler" (sometimes in very small print on the album covers), nothing on the album art directly connects Arnie to a visually identifiable Ukrainian ancestry.

Arnie's repertoire choices further inform my understanding of his music and identity. He made over a dozen recordings, but, he told me, he did not record any "Ukrainian songs" or any "Indian songs." When asked what these pieces might be, he provided a little more explanation. As for "Indian songs," Arnie said these are especially like square dance songs, played as a triple set beginning with a slow six-eight time and moving to a little faster tempo in two-four time. "Ukrainian songs" are "bouncy, and much faster"; he mentioned the specific dance type *kolomyika*, a well-known Ukrainian social dance form in Canada, which he did play at weddings and social dances in the Ukrainian settlement where he grew up (interview, February 2009).

Arnie recalled playing for Ukrainian social dances held in the Ukrainian settlement near the reserve in the 1950s, where he played kolomyikas, polkas, and waltzes, among other social dances. He described the kolomyika as being danced in the following manner: a man and woman would dance as a couple much as they might for a polka, and the couples would dance in the formation of a large circle around the room.[17] Arnie also noted that the musicians would play a kolomyika once per set, or once every hour and a half or so (whereas it is currently played once per evening, right around midnight). Arnie suggested it was a rather straightforward form and recognized that this early kolomyika was different from kolomyikas that are typically danced nowadays at Ukrainian social dance concert parties in Alberta (with more elaborate dance movements being performed in turns in the centre and very little dancing in the outer circle).[18] Arnie speculated that, since non-Ukrainians would often join in these social dance parties, including Aboriginal people, who might not be as familiar with Ukrainian dances, the kolomyikas may have been simplified to be more inclusive (interview, February 2009).

I asked Arnie why he chose not to record what he called Ukrainian or Indian songs. "[B]ecause no one will buy them," he answered. "Indians don't want to buy that stuff from me," he said (a signal that he felt his music and other accomplishments were not always appreciated in the reserve community of his early years). He went on to say, "if somebody wants to buy 'Ukrainian music,' they go out to the Vegreville [festival marketplace] or the Ukrainian store in Edmonton and buy recordings by [Metro] Radomsky or bands like the Ukrainian Old-Timers"[19] (interview, February 2009).

It has occurred to me, however, that Arnie *was* playing both "Ukrainian songs" and "Indian songs" in a way. Upon review of the repertoire on Arnie's recordings, I note that most of his albums are a composite of covers of Hank Williams and other country musicians, bluegrass music, old-time fiddle music, and gospel hymns. Arnie told me that gospel tunes and country music were what he learned on the reserve and from his Cree family. Old-time fiddle tunes are typical of Métis repertoire; they are also, as I found in my earlier research, a core part of the repertoire of mid-twentieth-century descendants of Ukrainian immigrant prairie pioneers (Ostashewski 2009b). Furthermore, although Arnie's albums are not heavily laden with songs that might be strongly symbolic of either "Indian" or "Ukrainian" culture (as the kolomyika is of Ukrainian culture in Canada), his recordings do contain a small sampling of each. For instance, he included a few tunes that, he said, would be suitable for square dances, which he identified as specifically "Indian," and he recorded one social dance tune that is regularly played at Ukrainian Canadian social dance concert parties, a "heel & toe polka."

The heel and toe polka appears on one of Arnie's albums among his regular assortment of old-time, country, and gospel tunes. After reading an early version of this chapter, Arnie pointed out that the heel and toe polka is not a Ukrainian song and that it is commonly played as part of American old-time fiddle and country music, although he was aware that it is typically played at Ukrainian Canadian social dance concert parties. Like much of the music Arnie grew up playing at social dances both on and off the reserve, he believed he learned the heel and toe polka on the reserve. A quick Internet search brings up hits that link the heel and toe polka with American country music star Bill Munro and other artists of his era.[20] An online archive of a Vancouver newspaper from 1939 mentions it was performed in that city as well. Yet, based on ethnographic research conducted mainly in Swan Plain, Saskatchewan, folklorist Andriy Nahachewsky writes that a heel-toe polka was among the social dances that Ukrainians brought with them to Canada (Nahachewsky 2003, 32; Nahachewsky 1985).[21] And Arnie's recording is very much like other Ukrainian Canadian recordings of this dance tune, not the American ones that I have come across. Although it is unclear whether Ukrainian immigrants where Arnie grew up learned this from or taught this to people living in Canada, the heel and toe polka clearly has multiple cultural locations when it comes to repertoire and communities. The heel and toe polka may, by some, be understood as a marker of "Ukrainian" culture and identity in Canada, but this ethnically bounded classification only begins to describe the complex histories of this dance tune type and its multiple significances in a variety of contexts of musical, ethnically defined, and otherwise localized communities – and in the lives and repertoires of individual musicians like Arnie Strynadka. I am left wondering, however, whether part of the reluctance Arnie perceived among both Native and Ukrainian Canadian audiences to celebrate Arnie and his music is related to a lingering reluctance to accept that the blending of traditions is an integral aspect of culture – Native, Ukrainian Canadian, or otherwise (see Smith 1994, 550).

The heel and toe polka and other aspects of music in Arnie's repertoire can be understood as particular nexuses of styles and repertoires, much like those seen in the music of the late Mi'kmaw fiddler Lee Cremo, who competed and performed in the Maritimes, Ontario, Manitoba, and Nashville (Smith 1994, 546). Cremo played a repertoire that Smith says "represent[s] fascinating syncretic combinations of Micmac [sic] and Scottish traditions" (Smith 1994, 548). Like Cremo, Strynadka played music that he grew up with, music that is not specifically associated with Aboriginal culture and music, and made it very much his own. He played mostly country fiddle tunes he heard on the radio and in American country centres and gospel music he learned from his Cree grandfather; for him, his occasional performance of music for Ukrainian social dances spoke more to his past than to his recent identity and musical locations, a heritage he continued to value nonetheless. All of these musical genres made up the distinctive repertoire of Arnie Strynadka, "The Uke-Cree Fiddler."

Georgina Born and David Hesmondalgh (2000b, 32) and others have written that sociocultural identities are not simply constructed in music; rather, there are "prior" identities that come to be embodied dynamically in musical cultures, which then also form the reproduction of those identities. This is neither passive reflection nor solely transformation of identities through music; it is simultaneously layers of both. Arnie remade these prior music forms and identities in a fashion that was all his own. He also used the music of a colonized identity and experience, reflected in his performance of music that has Anglo-American (and Ukrainian Canadian) roots, music played by a man who, born of a history of colonization and settlement, was Cree and also Ukrainian and Canadian. In Arnie's case, music was both involved in the construction of a new identity and reflected pre-existing ones.

Another point of interest is that both Cremo and Strynadka learned much of their musical practice in social dance contexts. In earlier research, I found it was in social dance contexts that norms of behaviour were most directly challenged (Ostashewski 2009b, 429–32). To me, this suggests that less formalized music and dance performance contexts may be important sites in which to observe the transformation of practices and powerful negotiations of identities and cultures. As in the case of the kolomyikas that Arnie remembered playing in the 1950s, in which Ukrainian settlers and Aboriginal people danced together, it may be that in less formalized sites of performance individuals are more inclusive and accommodating of people who have different experiences – they have more "room to move."

Expectations, Anomalies, and Arnie Strynadka's Story

Prior to meeting Arnie, I had not heard about familial relations between Aboriginal people and Ukrainian immigrants or their descendants. Clearly, such expectations are not mine alone – in talking with colleagues and friends in various disciplines across the country about my research on Canada's Aboriginal Ukrainians, I am regularly met with comments such as, *are* there actually any?!" But Arnie's family history is a part of the histories of many families in Canada today, although this fact has not been addressed in any scholarship or public memory.[22] A fundamental aspect of my work in this research project, then, is a challenge to expectations regarding histories, ethnicities, and identities in modern Canada. For, as Philip Deloria (2004) has argued, anomalies and expectations are mutually constitutive, particularly when it comes to norms and categories.

I am also struck by the fact that, as Arnie told me, most people were surprised to hear that his musical skills came from his Cree family culture; he said people generally expected that it came from a Ukrainian immigrant musical culture. This tells me something about how North Americans still tend to imagine Native Americans – namely, as Deloria (2004, 5) describes the familiar stereotype, as primitive, technologically incompetent, physically distant, and culturally different. This is surely part of why Arnie was so proud to tell me that he was among the first people around to begin making and distributing his own recordings. Arnie's story offers a challenge to a number of paradigms, or sets of expectations, regarding Native American culture and identity – including the fact that, contrary to conventional stereotypes, in Arnie's family history the Indian is the wealthy and successful man, whereas the European immigrant is the one in need.

The documentation of encounters between Indigenous people and Ukrainian Canadians is, in itself, a project of social historical importance – my work addresses an empirical gap in the literature. From a historical point of view, it is valuable to make a record of these encounters and relations and to ensure that people of mixed Aboriginal and Ukrainian descent are counted in order to ensure their experiences are acknowledged and remembered as part of what characterizes Canadian, Ukrainian, and Aboriginal experiences in Canada today. Arnie's story also demonstrates that the nature of these encounters and relations is complex. As other scholars who study Aboriginal musics have written, music embodies many different kinds of responses to encounter, including cultural resistance, incorporation, syncretism, and maintenance. Arnie's musical life story alone provides evidence of all of these dynamics.

The music and expressive cultures engendered by colonial encounter between Ukrainian settlers and Aboriginal groups in western Canada, I am finding, represent a variety of historical experiences and expressions of oppression and difference within colonizing formations. Born and Hesmondalgh (2000b, 5) offer a discussion on such combined destructive and productive impacts of imperialism (in which they make reference to Gayatri Spivak's general arguments). In studies of Mi'kmaw music, Janice

Tulk (2009) has also written that postcolonial narratives of contact and colonial encounter are often described in terms of assimilation and cultural loss; she notes that Julie Cruikshank warns against a denial of the potential for "transfers of knowledge ... on both sides" (Cruikshank 2005, 9). My research compels me to consider how colonial encounter has been experienced, remembered (Tulk 2009), and represented in a variety of ways through music. Certainly, Arnie Strynadka's musical life story is one that speaks to a heterogeneity of colonizing experiences.

Deloria writes that a "rich cluster of meaning surrounds cultural expectation and its visible manifestation in images, acts, sounds, and texts, to be sure" (Deloria 2004, 5) – a cluster of meaning that I have only begun to understand, as described in this chapter. Are the complicated history and contemporary performance of musical forms like the heel and toe polka – which intersects with American country, old-time, "Indian," and Ukrainian Canadian music – just an anomaly? I suggest that identity, music, and culture are far more complex than ethnic and/or racial categorizations imply.

There are also ways that Arnie's story represents common experiences of "mixed-blood" Native Americans. For instance, Arnie's feeling of being undervalued by his Aboriginal community is typical of many people of mixed Native and non-Native ancestry (Nagel 1995, Krouse 1999). Like many "urban Indians" described in these studies, who claim both Aboriginal and non-Aboriginal identity, Arnie lived for many years in the city; he worked as a professional for the government, taught seminars in universities and colleges, was involved in Aboriginal activism, and participated in scholarly conferences where he recalled engaging with highly respected scholars like Vine Deloria. He was sad to note, however, that his achievements were not valued in the rurally based First Nation community where he grew up.

Other factors weigh heavily in Arnie's self-identification through his music and related performance. One of these is physical traits, brown skin in particular, which is all too often unproblematically assumed to be a marker of Aboriginal identity in Canada. Arnie, in his typically joking manner, on more than one occasion referred to the brown colour of his skin in conversations (see Krouse 1999, 78), once engaging in a joke about a "tan" he got while on a coastal holiday. Arnie's Aboriginal identity also came into play in the marketing of his music. He told me that around the time he started playing more in the 1980s, he was approached by an American fellow who was an "Indian art promoter" and interested in promoting Arnie along with other Native artists in the United States. Arnie benefited from this relationship. Arnie also stressed that he was most successful in the United States, where, I would argue, Euro-Canadian identities may be part of an American melting-pot identity, whereas Aboriginal identity has remained more distinctive.

This resonates with Joane Nagel's argument that "ethnic identity is both optional and mandatory, as individual choices are circumscribed by the ethnic categories available at a particular time and place" (Nagel 1995, 156). This is to underscore the idea that identity is mutable and involves choice, at least to some degree. As other case studies show, often people with mixed Native and non-Native ancestry emphasize their Aboriginal identity by means of calling attention to their Aboriginal lineage (Krouse 1999). As discussed earlier in this chapter, during the late twentieth and early twenty-first centuries, a wide resurgence and proud claiming of Aboriginal identity in North America led to official recognition of Aboriginal identities – Métis, specifically – in important legal and political ways (see Deloria 1974, Johnson 1996).[23] In this context, through the proud telling of stories of his Cree grandfather, Arnie Strynadka laid claim to his Aboriginal culture and identity.

Conclusion

In personal narratives and in his musical production, Arnie Strynadka emphasized his Aboriginal identity, although he firmly underscored the importance of both Cree and Ukrainian ancestral and cultural ties in his life. As Roger Abrahams notes, "one's identity emerges from the stories one tells on oneself" (Abrahams 2003, 198) – whether the narrative is told in words, or in music, or in pictures, or as in Arnie's case, using all of these means and media. Arnie's choices in this matter, in his individual life, coincided with a resurgence in Native American "consciousness," particularly Métis identity, in Canada in the second half of the twentieth century (Frideres and Gadacz 2008, 22–55). Various factors were involved in Arnie's self-identification as a "Uke-Cree," from physical traits to personal experiences, all within broader historical, social, and cultural contexts. As Karlie King states, in her analysis of the maintenance of "mixed" identities by Aboriginal individuals in Newfoundland, "the issue of self-identification is crucial" (King 2007, 67). Perhaps it is partly *because* Arnie's Aboriginal identity was "under siege" by discrimination, and took shape amid the political and social tensions of a resurgence, that he made an extra effort to defend it (see King 2007, 78). Just as Arnie did, the research participants in King's study articulate that they are of Aboriginal and of Euro-Canadian descent simultaneously. Multiple identities co-mingle, literally, in their individual, whole (not fragmented) bodies.

All too often, individuals and groups of people, particularly Native peoples in the Americas, have been ascribed an identity. One reason it is important to tell Arnie's story as I have done in this chapter is that it privileges his own telling of his story and himself. Arnie had agency in these matters, and he chose to exercise this agency in sophisticated ways. Further, throughout our interviews and meetings, Arnie repeatedly stressed the importance of Native peoples learning about their histories and telling their own stories of themselves. The Dominion government at the end of the 1800s and the Canadian government of the twentieth century made significant efforts to restrict the mobility and agency of Aboriginal peoples to reserves in order to control and assimilate them. Historians have shown that, in fact, such restriction was enforceable only intermittently (Miller 1990). Arnie's identity was shaped in the context of wider, changing historical, social, and cultural pressures, but he was not simply "caught" in signifying processes. He actively and adeptly negotiated and navigated them. He exercised choice, refusing to be "fenced in," actually or metaphorically, with regard to his identity and music performance. Considering that Strynadka's performance career was spent largely on the road and crossing the border between Canada and the United States, his musical life story provides an opportunity to consider how mobility and migrancy, as well as hybridity, enable and constrain musical performance and agency in different ways. Studies such as this one, then, begin to make evident the complexity with which locations of identity are played out in the lives and music of individuals like Arnie Strynadka, "The Uke-Cree Fiddler."

Arnie greatly valued the individual autonomy and agency he had within broader cultural frameworks as well. He worked for many years as a public servant, many of those years with universities and colleges, and he finally left that work due to what he called "administrivia" – which had him, in his own words, "boxed in so tight," *too* tight for his comfort (interview, February 2009). It occurs to me that an assessment of his music according to categories of identity that might have him "boxed in too tight" would also be a disservice to him, his family, and his music. If Arnie's story is any indication of the character of music and other expressive culture created by people of Aboriginal Ukrainian ancestry, we are clearly in need of some new paradigms for thinking about music, culture, and identity.

1   The matter of nomenclature as regards Aboriginal groups is complex. Section 35 of the Constitution Act of 1982 states that Aboriginal peoples include Indians, Inuit, and Métis. These three terms represent over one hundred different groups of people, literally hundreds of communities, with over fifty different Aboriginal languages spoken among them. "Some ... groups are known by multiple names, some older or newer, some invented by outsiders or community members" (Diamond 2008b, 4). Terms commonly used in public discourse (depending on time period and location), include "Aboriginal," "Indian," and "First Nations"; there are also names that individual groups have for themselves and/or that others also use for them, such as "Cree." "First Nations" was first promoted by the National Indian Brotherhood (NIB), a pan-Canadian political organization. In 1982 the NIB was reorganized as the Assembly of First Nations (AFN). It promoted the use of "First Nations" in the context of constitutional negotiations in which non-Aboriginal political elites emphasized the importance of Canada's two "founding nations," England and France (Frideres and Gadacz 2008, 22–53). Terms such as "Indian" have widely varying meanings. The terms "Indian" and "Aboriginal" also have legal and constitutional meaning; in these contexts they may or may not include Inuit and Métis in specific instances. In Canada today, out of respect for Native peoples generally and for the representation of the AFN, the term "Indian" is not normally used; however, some people, as did Arnie, use it quite frequently.

    Politics of nomenclature are not unique to Aboriginal groups, of course. The name for groups of people now generally referred to as Ukrainians in Canada is laden with its own cultural values. For example, John Lehr notes that the term "Ukrainians" was not initially used to name the earliest Ukrainian immigrants; many people who today identify as Ukrainians in Canada are descendants of those who were from multi-ethnic empires (Austria-Hungary or Russia) at the time of their immigration. The earliest Ukrainian immigrants to Canada were in fact described according to their national or provincial origins: Austrian, Russian, Ruthenian, Galician, and Bukowinian. "Ukrainian" was not an officially recognized term in Canada until the 1930s (Lehr 1991, 31n1). In spite of this fact and the political realities during the time of immigration, most people who currently identify as Ukrainians in Canada think of their ancestors' homeland as something called "Ukraine" (Magocsi 1991, xii). This matter directs attention to the importance of nomenclature in the history and memory of identity, as well as in its construction, performance, and perception – all of which come into play as regards the politics and cultural values related to Aboriginal and Ukrainian identity in Canada.

2   These homesteads were "free" after payment of a ten-dollar registration fee, residence on the land for a minimum of six months each year for three consecutive years, and the cultivation of thirty acres of prairie (or less if the land was heavily forested) (Martynowych 1991, 80).

3   For the Plains people, the situation was exacerbated by a subsistence crisis after the demise of the bison in the 1870s (Miller 2000).

4 One of the results of a long-time failure, on the part of historians of Ukrainians in Canada, to acknowledge this aspect of the sociopolitical context of late nineteenth-century Canadian prairie life is the perpetuation of the idea that Ukrainian pioneers settled on "virgin land" ("A Home away from Home," pamphlet published by the University of Saskatchewan, n.d., 3), "sparsely populated … [with] vast tracts of uninhabited terrain" (Martynowych 1991, 34–5). Writing Native peoples out of the history of agricultural development is a problem of North American historiography, one that ongoing research for this project begins to address. The notion that the New World was "terra nullius" (Richardson 1993) is not specific to the histories of Ukrainians in North America, but it lingers there even as mainstream Canadian historiography has already begun to integrate Native experiences into its narratives. It certainly appears that concerns over the land becoming property of the United States were real (Daugherty 1983), a detail that is also a part of popular discourse on the subject. However, dialogue with historians has taught me that the matter was far more complicated in ways that counter the popular notion that the Prairies were a wide-open, undeveloped, and unused space.

5 Both the current website of the Goodfish Lake community and government documents refer to this community as Whitefish (Goodfish) Lake First Nations No. 128; see http://www.wfl128.ca/index.php (accessed 6 May 2009) and Statistics Canada (n.d.). Whitefish (Goodfish) Lake First Nation falls under the administration of Saddle Lake No. 125 Aboriginal Communities; see http://www.aboriginalcanada.gc.ca/acp/community/site.nsf/en/fn462.html (accessed 7 May 2009). Patricia Bartko, who has worked as a historical researcher for Alberta Aboriginal Affairs and Northern Development in the past, brought to my attention that this is a different community than Whitefish Lake First Nation No. 459.

6 In ethnomusicology, too, the tendency has been to understand Métis as referring to "those of mixed French and Native ancestry" (Lederman 2001, 404) – although there has also been recognition that "there are still large gaps in our current knowledge" (Lederman 2001, 405).

7 Métis scrip was a one-time offer, a coupon that was intended for redemption for land allotment. "[The Métis] dilemma was that if they took treaty, they became legally Amerindian; if they took scrip, they moved into the non-Amerindian camp" (Dickason and McNab 2009, 285).

8 For instance, 2001 census interpretations report the "mother tongue" of individuals in terms of choices of various First Nations and/or either French or English. All "other" languages fall under the categories of "other multiple responses" (Statistics Canada n.d., appendix D), but no further details are provided.

9 See profile information on these communities at http://pse5-esd5.ainc-inac.gc.ca/FNP/Main/Search/FNLanguage.aspx?BAND_NUMBER=462&lang=eng (accessed 7 May 2009).

10 "The concept of aboriginal identity was first used in the 1991 Aboriginal Peoples Survey (APS) and differs slightly from the concept used in the 1996 Census. The APS question asked 'With which Aboriginal group do *you* identify?,' while the

census question asks 'Is this person an Aboriginal person, that is, a North American Indian, Métis or Inuit (Eskimo)?'"; see http://www12.statcan.ca/english/census01/Products/Reference/dict/pop001.htm, original emphasis (accessed 7 May 2009).

11 For further discussion, see the interpretation of census data on the Statistics Canada website, http://www12.statcan.ca/english/census01/Products/Reference/dict/pop001.htm (accessed 7 May 2009).

12 The idea of "Indians" as jokesters is explored by Drew Hayden Taylor and others in *Me Funny* (2005). I have begun to address Arnie's use of humour in a recent publication (Ostashewski 2009a).

13 Arnie told me that his grandfather Sam Bull is an older relative of famed Sam Bull the chief, lawyer, and activist of the Goodfish Lake reserve, who is mentioned in Olive Dickason's *Canada's First Nations* (1992, 403–5). Arnie further mentioned that, in 1955, his grandfather wrote "The Sam Bull Story"; Arnie gave the manuscript to "an anthropologist" who had come to the reserve and who promised to get it published. However, Arnie neither saw it again nor heard from that anthropologist. I recently came across another document written by Sam Bull (1955), which includes descriptions of life on the reserve and in the region. Finally, more recent ethnographic data suggest that Sam's wife (Arnie's grandmother) may have, in fact, been the owner of the trading post, or "store."

14 Arnie pronounced the word "kobassa" like his older generation of Ukrainian prairie immigrant descendants – something between the original Ukrainian "kovbassa" and the contemporary popular term "kubassa." This signifies a language experience similar to that of other Ukrainian immigrant descendants of his age and generation and of the prairie region where he grew up; indeed, Arnie spoke Ukrainian in a way that is familiar among this group.

15 Prior to the introduction of Bill C-31 in 1985, Arnie's mother's marriage to a non-Native man had resulted in her loss of treaty status (see Frideres and Gadacz 2008, 32–6).

16 Anne Lederman notes that a "distinctive feature of older Northwest Métis fiddle repertoire" (Lederman 2001, 406) is irregular or asymmetric phrasing, although she speculates this characteristic may somehow relate to the Aboriginal languages spoken by the communities she studied.

17 This kolomyika of Arnie's early years, as he described from memory, seems not unlike kolomyikas danced in other parts of the Prairies during that era, which ethnochoreologist Andriy Nahachewsky refers to as "some combination of circle and couple dance forms" (Nahachewsky 2002, 186). Further research is required as regards the details of kolomyika history and practice in this region, specifically in the time period discussed by Arnie.

18 I discuss the contemporary kolomyika in my dissertation (Ostashewski 2009b); this description of its contemporary form resonates with Nahachewsky's (2002) description of its current form.

19 The Ukrainian Old-Timers is a dance band popular on the Prairies today, one that parodies and caters especially to an audience of older and rural Ukrainian Canadians.

20 My thanks to Sharon Graff who, at the 2009 meeting in Denver of the Society for American Music, brought to my attention that she came across this tune while conducting research on old-time American fiddle music. In personal communications, Canadian fiddle scholar Sherry Johnson has also noted that heel and toe polkas are a familiar part of fiddling repertoires in various parts of Canada (see Perlman 1996, 153). Further, ethnomusicologist Robert Witmer has pointed out that online sites such as answers.com include a number of pertinent entries, including ones on a Bill Munroe tune identified as a heel and toe polka. The Southeastern Louisiana University Collection of the Department of Music apparently also holds a recording of the heel and toe polka; see http://www.selu.edu/acad_research/programs/ csls/historical_collections/archival_collections/r_s/southeastern_archiva/ slu_music_dept.html (accessed 8 May 2009). Johnson went on to say that there was frequent interchange between western Canadian and American fiddlers during the mid-twentieth century due to the Grand Ole Opry and other musicians' tours, which took them through many parts of western Canada.

21 The research of musicologist William Noll bears out this possibility. Noll writes that urban polkas – as well as other trendy urban dances of the time, including the tango, foxtrot, rumba, and schottische – were played around the turn of the twentieth century by musicians in parts of what is now western Ukraine or southern Poland (Noll 1991, 369; Noll 1993, 148). These are regions from which many Ukrainians immigrated to western Canada at the end of the nineteenth and beginning of the twentieth centuries.

22 This chapter focuses on the groups who interacted on the Prairies, but I have also heard from people who talk about growing up "Oji-Ukrainian" in north-western Ontario; and a colleague recently informed me of Judge Rose Toodick Boyko, whose "mother was from the Tsek'ehne First Nation at McLeod Lake, B.C. and her father was a Ukrainian immigrant" (Black n.d.). In future research, I plan to follow up on these and other stories of Aboriginal Ukrainian relations in Canada.

23 My thanks to ethnomusicologist Christopher Scales for providing these references and for sharing a paper he presented at the Society for American Music's 2009 conference, in which he discusses Native American activism in the late twentieth century. An expanded version of the conference paper was published as "Plight of the Redman: XIT, Red Power, and the Refashioning of American Indian Ethnicity" (Scales 2011).

19

Bits and Pieces of Truth: Storytelling, Identity, and Hip Hop in Saskatchewan

CHARITY MARSH

It's time for you to listen for a minute
Cause this is where I share bits and pieces of my truth
What I know and don't know about life
It's time to think back
To remember who we were
Whoever that may be
Take back what we dream
And say what we mean
I want to know more
You want to know more
But I always feel like obstacles are stopping me
And could it be that I'm trying not to see
Creating diversions convenient to me
Running away hurting my people, my family
And those most important to me
Well I can't do that anymore
Because I'm guessing through experiences and lessons
And I'm stopping the cycle and sending the message
And I'm trying every day I walk this earth
To stay away from what's bad for me
And the only way I can do that
is by recognizing the strengths we have
Power in numbers
We got … power in spirit
I got … power in music
I got … power in my voice
Hear it[1]

The Canadian landscape is shaped by its colonial past and present (Mackey 1999, Young 1990), its global identity as a multicultural nation (Bannerji 2000, Day 2000), and its proximity to the United States (Théberge 1997, Krims 2000, Pegley 2008). So too are the contemporary Indigenous youth music cultures within Canada's borders influenced by the effects of these discourses and the processes by which they are mapped onto the geographical, social, cultural, and political landscape. For local music cultures across Canada, globalization continues to have a profound impact on the way that cultural forms and practices – both those forms and practices signifying the "traditional" and those understood as "contemporary" – are adopted, adapted, and developed, particularly in regions that are isolated from major urban "cultural" centres.[2] Despite the fact that the consequences of globalization and its impact on local music cultures are often complex and contradictory at best (King 1997, Guilbault 1993, Taylor 2001), the globalization of popular music cultures such as hip hop contributes to provocative ideas of hybridity (Bhabha 1994), to the cosmopolitan citizen (Kristeva 1991, Derrida 2001), as well as to the bleeding of identities and cross-cultural identifications (Diamond and Witmer 1994, Mitchell 2001, Bennett and Peterson 2004). The emergence and continuing rapid growth of a vibrant Indigenous hip hop scene in the prairie provinces, specifically in Saskatchewan, illustrate these very things. And if hip hop is a "vehicle for global youth affiliations and a tool for reworking local identity all over the world" (Mitchell 2001), we need to think about why and how hip hop culture created by Indigenous youth living in Saskatchewan is an important cultural site for new dialogues concerning complex issues of identity, community, politics, and citizenship within the context of Canada.[3]

In contemporary Saskatchewan many unique, rich, and complicated narratives of "traditional" Indigenous musics are represented – narratives that have developed out of, or in spite of, the horrific circumstances associated with colonization, settlement, and a federal policy of assimilation. These narratives can be differentiated from those of other regions within the context of present-day life in the prairie provinces. Today, music and cultural practices represented as "traditional" (e.g., drumming, round dance singing styles, powwow dancing, etc.) continue to play a primary role in the preservation of identity, culture, and resistance for Indigenous peoples. And yet many Indigenous youth living in Saskatchewan are turning toward the arts practices of hip hop culture (rapping/emceeing, DJing/beat making, break/hip hop dancing, and graffiti arts) as a way to express and make sense of present-day lived experiences, including the ongoing legacies of state enforced residential school programs and other practices of colonization, the current climate of contentious government initiated truth and reconciliation processes, and systemic issues of racism, poverty, and violence faced by young people today. These expressions are, as suggested in the title of this chapter, "bits and pieces of truth," a phrase that reworks the second line of Saskatchewan emcee Eekwol's lyrics to her song "Apprento," presented above.

One outcome has been the emergence of a different and arguably "new" style of hip hop. Similar to other musical genres that have been borrowed by Indigenous artists, this style of hip hop combines local, cultural, and regional elements with current global hip hop forms and stylistic traits; but what makes it so interesting and provocative is that this new style of hip hop allows for a rethinking of everyday life for young Indigenous people living in Saskatchewan today.

Taking into account the relevance of hip hop culture on both a local and global scale, in this chapter I address the significant impact of hip hop culture created and practised by Indigenous youth living in Saskatchewan. To shape this discussion, I begin with the following questions: How does hip hop play an integral role in narrating colonialism (as experienced today) in Saskatchewan? How does hip hop as it is created, produced, and consumed by Indigenous youth challenge contemporary Canada to think about "Aboriginal" politics currently and in the future rather than think of colonialism as relevant only to the past? In what ways does hip hop contribute to the struggle for decolonization in Saskatchewan?

Through a contextualization of the places and spaces in Saskatchewan where hip hop culture thrives,[4] interviews with artists, organizers, and young people participating in hip hop, and an analysis of musical examples from Saskatchewan emcee Eekwol, I argue that hip hop is a contemporary example of a culture of sublimation through which Indigenous youth living in Saskatchewan convey the contradictions, struggles, resistances, and celebrations of their current lived experiences while simultaneously attempting to acknowledge and respect the (hi)stories of their ancestors.

The Many Spaces, Places, and Faces of Hip Hop Culture in Saskatchewan

Contrary to its mythic identity as a ubiquitous flat prairie landscape used solely for agriculture, Saskatchewan is geographically diverse with a topography of partial desert conditions south in the badlands, ocean-like fields of wheat, barley, and flax, rolling hills and numerous fresh-water lakes, heavy forests, and dense and unwieldy bush and rocky mining terrain in the northern part of the province. For such a great and diverse landmass, the province's population is small, just over the million mark with almost half of the population living in the cities of Regina, the capital of the province, and Saskatoon, the corporate big business centre of the province. Smaller cities, towns, and reserves dot the vast amounts of highway and grid roads running north and south or east and west. And yet one can travel for hours only to come across a signpost, a cluster of vacant buildings, or the remains of an old house or barn. The remaining evidence of once thriving settler communities amounts to abandoned, decrepit, and boarded-up buildings, which followed the amalgamation of schools, post offices, and other services, along with mass purchases of farm land by large agri-businesses and the decline in the use of the railway. The uncertainty of crops, the rise in farming costs, and the depressed markets for wheat, barley, flax, canola, and other crops have created difficult socioeconomic conditions for independent farmers, and this has led to a growing pattern of relocation – from the rural to the urban.

Saskatchewan is home to numerous rural reserves[5] (some of the poorest in Canada) and twenty-eight urban reserves.[6] The provincial borders cross through Cree, Saulteaux, Sioux, Anisnawbe, and Dene territories, and the communities are divided into Treaty Areas 4, 5, 6, 8, and 10.[7] Approximately 142,000 Indigenous people live in Saskatchewan, and in the 2006 census collected by Statistics Canada, approximately 12 per cent of Canada's Indigenous peoples were living in Saskatchewan,[8] which at the time equalled about 14 per cent of Saskatchewan's total population.[9] By 2045 it is predicted that the number of Indigenous people (including First Nations, Métis, and Inuit peoples) will increase to 33 per cent of Saskatchewan's total population.[10] These kinds of statistics are important for a couple of reasons: first, following the reports about the trend toward a rise in "Aboriginal" populations, we are witnessing a variety of responses illustrating what one could interpret as white-settler anxiety; second, the landscape – social, cultural, geographical, economic, and political – has historically had a considerable influence on cultural and arts practices.[11] Today, its effects are clearly evident in how the culture of hip hop has developed and is understood throughout the province.

Hip Hop in the (Neighbour)hood

Hip hop culture seems to be everywhere one turns these days in Saskatchewan. Over the past five years, many hip hop–related community-based arts projects, school projects, public awareness events, performances, and hip hop–affiliated businesses have sprung up in the major cities of Regina and Saskatoon, in smaller cities and towns, including Prince Albert and Moose Jaw, as well as in some rural communities.[12] In Regina and Saskatoon there are hip hop events (often break battles or rap "warz") held at cultural exchange centres, restaurants (like Selam, an Ethiopian restaurant in Regina), or community halls, which bring artists, listeners, and dancers together on a monthly basis. Other smaller communities (Prince Albert) and some of the reserves (White Buffalo) also organize and present hip hop events, although these are not scheduled quite as regularly. There are many hip hop shows presenting local, national, and international talent throughout the province. Online, there are many list-serves, websites, social network sites, and forums dedicated to hip hop culture in Saskatchewan and its connections with hip hop in Canada and around the globe.

Over the past few years, there has been a significant increase in the number of free public workshops focusing on one or more of the four primary hip hop elements (DJing, rap, break dancing, and graffiti). Many of these workshops are geared toward Indigenous youth and/or young people living in the inner cities and are sponsored by arts organizations such as Paved Arts (in Saskatoon)[13] or Common Weal (in Regina and Prince Albert). Other workshops are spearheaded by community neighbourhood organizations that hold weekly or monthly sessions on the hip hop elements as a way to support the interests of young people specifically from their neighbourhood. One of the most important pioneering community projects in Saskatchewan was the Prairie Roots Project: A Provincial Youth Hip-Hop Community Collaboration (PRP). The PRP was created under the umbrella arts organization Common Weal. Common Weal's vision and mandate is "to engage communities and professional artists to come together and create art … [to] inspire ideas for social change through art … [and to] empower people – and their communities – to tell their stories in their own voices."[14]

For the PRP, the primary goal was to organize hands-on workshops of the hip hop creative elements as a way to promote social change and foster connections between established and emerging hip hop artists and youth, offering access to arts practices that may not otherwise be available.[15] In the liner notes of the first PRP CD, the initial project coordinator, Oin Nicholson, provides the parameters for the project: "The 'hands-on' collaborations between established and emerging artists and youth provided a forum for skill development and voice, while promoting access, diversity and inclusion. The project covers a broad spectrum of content:

the social-political history and creative process of hip-hop, production, recording, performance and product development" (Nicholson 2005). The sites for the project were in three locations: Regina, Saskatoon, and Prince Albert. The programming included workshops, mentoring, access to equipment and materials, facilitators, and recording a compilation CD presented as part of the Saskatchewan Centennial Celebrations with the Saskatchewan Jazz Festival. In Nicholson's words, "the project was successful in that it connected youth from across the province in a meaningful experience, and provided a forum for the voice of youth and Saskatchewan hip hop, promoting understanding of their unique culture amongst each other and with other Saskatchewan communities" (Nicholson 2005).

When I spoke with Nicholson at the Regina site about the PRP, he maintained a positive, almost idealist vision of the project. And yet, when I asked about issues of sustainability and gender representation, his responses became vague and he offered a comment about some young women who had been into the space the day before participating in some hip hop dance.[16] When I asked whether these women were also break dancing, the answer was no, they were practising hip hop dance. His response spoke volumes about the ongoing gendering practices often associated with hip hop culture and its arts practices. Hip hop dance is a complex dance form that demands competence, skill, strong cardio vascular fitness, creativity, and rhythm. Yet, because of certain break styles, which demand specific acrobatic and strength movements, break is a form that is often gendered as masculine, whereas hip hop dance is often represented as the feminine dance in a culture that generally offers very little space for women's participation.

Nicholson opened up more about some of the issues concerning access to the project as our conversation continued. Some of these issues were about gender and the importance of drawing on women artists to facilitate workshops and to act as role models, as well as about other concerns such as access to the project sites. Although the PRP held workshops around the province and the three project sites were established in cities geographically located in the southern, central, and northern parts of the province, it was not always easy for young people living in smaller communities or on reserves to travel to the sites. Different events and workshops do travel to more remote locations, but an important aspect of the PRP was its mandate to enable access to the sites and equipment and to facilitate participation both within and outside of specifically designated and organized sessions. Another consideration was that each site did not necessarily contain the same type of physical space or technological equipment; one location may have had a concentration on graffiti arts, whereas another location focused on recording and production.

For Nicholson, and many of the other artists and youth who participated, the project "created a spark of creative, positive and conscious energy that has already started to have a residual effect" (Nicholson 2005). In response to a paper presented in June 2008 at a conference held at the University of Saskatchewan in Saskatoon, hip hop emcee Eekwol spoke about the significance of the PRP and the positive impacts it had on Saskatchewan communities:

> [W]ithin the last maybe four or five years, we've really started to see these programs popping up everywhere, and it's really nice to be consulted when these [programs] are coming up in youth facilities and schools ... When I started eleven years ago, there was absolutely nothing like this. Hip hop and rap were considered a horrible, horrible genre, negative, gangsta'. So I've been spending all these years trying to prove that it is a positive form of expression that young people relate to because of the oral practice ... the storytelling that's involved in it and the way we can relate our experiences through it.

Hip hop projects/workshops help artists like Eekwol and organizers like Nicholson to demonstrate that hip hop can be a positive and socially conscious cultural expression rather than tied only to media representations of gangs and violence. For Eekwol, hip hop also allows Indigenous youth to connect with each other and their Indigenous cultures through the practice of storytelling, which is so much a part of her Cree culture.

"Keep It Simple": A Hip Hop Education

Hip hop is also becoming more visible in Saskatchewan in some of the high schools, not only because of the commercial success of the hip hop fashion that many students are wearing but more so because of the implementation of hip hop programs in the curriculum or extracurricular activities. Some Saskatchewan schools are welcoming hip hop projects or clubs as a way to create and/or hold students' interest in subjects such as English, poetry, music, arts, and social studies. Hip hop is also being used, however problematically, to offer incentives to keep students in school, as well as to provide an alternative for students who do not necessarily identify with or participate in conventional extracurricular activities like soccer, band, or basketball. Robert Usher Collegiate was one of the first schools to initiate hip hop programming in Regina (2005–06).[17] By introducing hip hop and creating a break-dance crew as an extra-curricular activity, vice principal Corrine Miller had greater success in keeping students in school and working on their studies. Her rules were simple: participation in the club was open to all students who maintained passing grades and attended classes. What she saw was an improvement of about 20 per cent in achievement and a significant rise in regular attendance.

In March 2006 I presented a community talk on Indigenous hip hop in Canada as part of the Nourishing Food Bank lunchtime community series, and prior to the event I was invited to speak on the Canadian Broadcasting Corporation's (CBC) Saskatchewan morning show to discuss hip hop and respond to the aired CBC radio documentary on the Usher Collegiate hip hop club.[18] During this segment, radio host Sheila Coles explained that most of the students who participated in the club were Indigenous youth, and then she asked why I thought Aboriginal youth in Saskatchewan are drawn to hip hop culture? In my response, I offered four thoughts. First, there is a productive (and perhaps innovative) aspect in allowing young people agency around how they connect to school, politics, culture, social relations, and the various artistic practices they enjoy. Second, hip hop culture offers a wide variety of entry points that are fairly accessible (physically and economically) – a person can participate by rapping (or writing rhymes), dancing (break or hip hop), painting (graffiti arts), DJing, or creating music or beats in other ways – for example, by beat-boxing or by using free downloadable software programs – or one can engage in the role of audience (giving "props" and appreciating other's attempts or skills).[19] Third, it is not surprising that marginalized communities from all over the world identify with and adopt the socially conscious politics of hip hop and the mythologies surrounding its origins. Hip hop is a culture that has a context – it comes from a specific time and place and has evolved out of many cultural practices that came before it, practices that also have histories. Early hip hop represented a new form of cultural and political expression for disenfranchised African American and Latino youth living in the South Bronx (and then elsewhere in the United States) during the late 1970s and early 1980s. For Indigenous youth living in Saskatchewan, there are identifications with these roots/routes of hip hop culture, including similar stories of marginalization, segregation, poverty, and racism, as well as strong identifications with stories concerning the importance of community ties, acts of resistance, and empowerment through creativity and music.[20] Finally, I made the suggestion that Indigenous youth living in Saskatchewan need a voice – not necessarily a voice tied to words but a voice rooted in more of a presence – and that these young people need to be heard by an audience who will listen to their stories and engage with them in dynamic and respectful conversation. Hip hop programs found in Saskatchewan schools seemingly have the power to offer a fulfilment of these needs while also offering a critical injection of arts programming into an arts curriculum devastated by ongoing budget cuts.

For these reasons, the Scott Collegiate/IMP Labs Hip Hop Project was launched in the fall of 2008. The project is a collaborative initiative between the high school and the Interactive Media and Performance (IMP) Labs, which are housed in the Faculty of Fine Arts at the University of Regina.[21] Scott Collegiate is the only high school located in the North Central neighbourhood of Regina, made familiar to the nation as one of Canada's most notorious 'hoods in a controversial issue of *Maclean's* magazine published on 15 January 2007. The majority of the school's student population are Indigenous and live in North Central.[22] Scott Collegiate offers students project-based learning as a way to manage and reduce problems associated with regular attendance and with students completing work in the classroom or at home, achieving (and maintaining) passing grades, and acquiring hands-on skills. These projects also aim to assist students in their understandings of self-preservation, self-esteem, and "positive" life choices.[23]

Given that one of the primary mandates of the IMP Labs is to build bridges between the surrounding communities and the University of Regina, the partnership with Scott Collegiate (both teachers and students) was an exciting opportunity. As part of the project, it was decided that the students would come and work in the IMP Labs at the university two days a week for three hours each day during the fall 2008 and winter 2009 semesters.[24] During these sessions, the students had the opportunity to work with and were mentored by local, national, and internationally recognized hip hop artists, as well as with the IMP Labs' research assistants, and had full access to the technologies required for the creative practices of hip hop culture.[25] And although there are myriad tensions and contradictions within such programs, this new hip hop–"positive" curriculum has enabled the students (and the school) to work against stereotypes and generalizations mapped onto hip hop culture, the neighbourhood, and Indigenous youth.[26] The project has also become a blueprint for similar projects that are being developed in other high schools and elementary schools around the province.

"The People / The People / It's all about the People"[27]

A number of successful Indigenous artists living in Saskatchewan create, produce, and perform hip hop regularly, either independently or as part of a larger group. As expressed previously, many of these up-and-coming and established artists, including emcee Eekwol, producer Mils, and rapper InfoRed, participated in the PRP and continue to act as role models in their communities and across the region. These artists are often invited to cities, towns, and reserves to facilitate workshops on the arts practices associated with hip hop, to perform, to host events, and most important, to mentor young Indigenous people through music.[28] Since moving to Saskatchewan in 2004, what I have observed from some of these artists is the emergence of an arguably new, provocative, and hybrid music culture – one that combines aspects of music, dance, language, stories, and performance practices that signify local "indigineity" with elements of global hip hop culture.

For some, the burgeoning Indigenous hip hop scene in Canada represents the globalization (read Americanization) of Indigenous youth. And yet Tony Mitchell, along with many other scholars,[29] challenges such simplistic readings of the impact of globalization on new local hip hop cultures, arguing against "the prevailing colonialist view that global hip-hop is an exotic and derivative outgrowth of an African-American owned idiom subject to assessment in terms of American norms and standards" (Mitchell 2001, 1–2). Rather than view the appropriation of hip hop aesthetics, styles, and artistic elements as diminishing cultural identity, it is critical to recognize that "the commercial packaging of hip hop as a global commodity has facilitated its easy access by young people in many different parts of the world" (Bennett 2004, 180), and as cultural theorist Andy Bennett has also noted, "such appropriations have in each case involved a reworking of hip hop in ways that engage with local circumstances. In every respect hip hop is both a global and a local form" (Bennett 2004, 180). Young people from all around the world with diverse cultural, social, economic, and political backgrounds are drawn to hip hop because the culture allows for a confluence of a multitude of national, regional, and cultural sensibilities with its aesthetics, styles, and pleasures.

For media theorist Murray Forman, "Youths who adhere to the styles, images, and values of hip-hop culture ... have demonstrated unique capacities to construct different spaces, and, simultaneously, to construct spaces differently" (Forman 2002, 3). Although Forman's study on hip hop focuses primarily on the politics of place, race, culture, and identity in the United States, his statement challenges the notion that hip hop culture, and the spaces within which it exists or is constructed, is only about appropriation or mimicry. Rather, the adaptations of hip hop culture by young people to include local cultural practices, sounds, vernacular, landscape, politics, etcetera demonstrate an interconnectivity between local and global discourses. What has become apparent is that "hip hop is culturally mobile" and that "the definition of hip hop culture and its attendant notions of authenticity are constantly being 'remade' as hip hop is appropriated by different groups of young people in cities and regions around the world" (Bennett 2004, 177). Indigenous hip hop artists, audiences, or participants living in Saskatchewan may at times draw on and adopt hip hop aesthetics, styles, and performance practices found within America, Australia, the United Kingdom, Germany, Japan, New Zealand, Turkey, or other regions of Canada; there are, however, elements that are distinctive, being generated from the local vernacular, landscape, cultural practices, politics, and place.

The combining of culturally (and locally) specific elements with mainstream styles is not a new practice. In her research on Indigenous women and music, ethnomusicologist Beverley Diamond states, "Contemporary First Nations, Inuit, and Métis women may choose to be primarily classical or folk musicians, reggae or blues artists, or rappers. But many – in fact most in some part of their work – draw upon a combination of culturally specific elements and mainstream styles, creating syntheses or stark juxtapositions in some cases that are unique in feel and in message, while contributing to a redefinition of the genres in which they work" (Diamond 2002, 12–13). This redefinition of genres that Diamond refers to is what interests me. This "redefined" hip hop, which I am arguing is a new style, represents a dramatic shift in the way that young Indigenous people living in Saskatchewan are telling their stories – stories that are steeped in a colonial history and a colonial present as well as stories that offer counter-resistance to the national discourse on Aboriginal youth living in Canada today. The discourses associated with global hip hop offer young Indigenous people living in Saskatchewan a relatively new oral culture (building on older cultures) and encourage the articulations of both unique and shared sensibilities.

For an excellent (and innovative) example of what this redefined hip hop sounds, looks, and feels like, I want to shift the focus away from a broad contextualization of hip hop in Saskatchewan and look at hip hop emcee Lindsay Knight (a.k.a. Eekwol) and at some specific examples from her 2004 album *Apprentice to the Mystery* and from lyrics on her 2007 album *The List*, which she recorded with her brother Justin Knight (a.k.a. Mils).

"Keepin' It Real": Eekwol Redefining Hip Hop Culture

Eekwol's family is from the Muskoday First Nation in northern Saskatchewan, near Prince Albert, the small city where she grew up. Currently, however, she resides in Saskatoon, and her brother Mils, with whom she works closely and performs regularly, lives in Prince Albert, 134 kilometres away. As a young teenager, Eekwol listened to "old-school" hip hop emcees on mixed tapes shared between friends: "around here [...] we didn't have much access because Internet wasn't around and when it was available ten, fifteen years ago, it was limited. If some kid in the hip hop scene went to Calgary or somewhere and picked up a cool underground tape, we'd dub it like thirty times just to listen ... So I still have a lot of my old dub mix tapes" (interview, 18 June 2008). For Eekwol, being able to access rap and hip hop music is key, and she and her friends found ways to access and then share the music, even though it often meant having to listen to recordings dubbed multiple times, resulting in a dramatically reduced quality of sound. There was something in rap that compelled her; as a teenager, Eekwol identified with some of the stories, but she also respected the skills it took to create a flow. "Since I was twelve or thirteen and started listening to all these emcees, I was [...] amazed by the way that they could throw words together and [...] create this imagery and these stories, and talk about issues [... The] very first CD I bought was Public Enemy, *Fear of a Black Planet*, 1990." These musical experiences had a substantial impact on the creation and shape of her earlier music, as they do on her music today. She explains, "You can just sort of feed off the rebelliousness and social and political issues of the African American movement, because that's where hip hop originates. I drew on that quite a bit as well as underground hip hop, the kind that never made it to the mainstream, because of those issues and the discussions that went on within the lyrics."

Eekwol's early relationship with hip hop culture, however, is filled with contradictions. When I asked her why she thought Indigenous youth living in Saskatchewan have such an intense relationship with hip hop culture, and whether it was a result of the many workshops, role models, and mentors like her, Eekwol quickly sidestepped taking any credit. Rather than drawing a route back to the underground hip hop scene as I expected, Eekwol suggested that the embodiment of hip hop among

Indigenous youth in Saskatchewan is to some extent an outcome of the success of commercial hip hop: "A lot of times the commercial is really negative, but at the same time, it's relatable. When I was a teenager I listened to Tupac. That's what I loved. Tupac. I related [...] Hip hop is a relatable genre because a lot of the people who are doing hip hop are in the same sort of social struggle, whether or not they're recognizing it or doing anything to change it." And yet an ongoing concern for Eekwol is youth who identify with the stereotypical and overly romanticized experiences represented in much of commercial rap and hip hop today. Whether young people can consciously recognize these identifications while also seeing the potential for transformation, rather than just glamorizing the violence, is crucial. Given her status as an emcee and a role model in Saskatchewan, Eekwol feels a sense of responsibility to convey something more positive. "When I see inner-city kids, Indigenous or not, doing positive for the underground conscious hip hop, that's when I feel, okay maybe they are getting a little bit of what we tried to do back in the day or what we do now. I can only hope that's where that is coming from."

Taking her responsibilities as a role model seriously, Eekwol incorporates socially conscious elements in her music and her everyday living. Along with the emcees she listened to in her youth (underground and commercial), she is "inspired by people who stand up and take action for what they believe in for the good of their people, like Leonard Pelletier, Malcolm X, Vine Deloria Sr. and Jr., Alfred Taiake and so many young people who are starting to speak about correcting and creating an awareness of history" (interviewed in Sealy 2007, 29). Rapping into a microphone while on a stage or recording an album has become a critical place from where Eekwol feels comfortable to speak out:

> It doesn't take a genius
> to see the situation
> Oppression class systems
> control of the nation
> We want to be equal
> but it just don't cut it
> All my good people
> it's time to rise above it ...[30]

For Eekwol and other young Indigenous people living in Saskatchewan, hip hop is a "safe" place to talk about politics and all of the other issues that people are afraid or unwilling to discuss openly. In an interview with freelance journalist David Sealy, Eekwol explains, "I'm all about honesty.

I grew up in an environment where people didn't talk about the problems even though there were huge elephants in the room. I grew up around addictions. To survive that you have to be honest with yourself" (Sealy 2007, 29). Eekwol's albums focus on a number of these elephants in the room – issues that are difficult, painful, and challenging to take on – while also including moments of celebration and reclamation.

Creating a Place: On Being a "Girl" in Hip Hop

As a woman who writes, produces, and performs in hip hop both as a solo artist and in collaboration with male artists, Eekwol works against the grain and the stereotypes associated with the genre. Her identity as an Indigenous woman in a music culture that is still dominated by men has been at times both liberating and frustrating, as she explains:

> I get endless requests to drop a verse, requests from all over. And I used to find that very rewarding. But a lot of the times I'd be doing it for free. Now I've got this huge stack of CDs that I'm on, but I started to realize why I'm asked. Because I'm well known, but also because of my novelty status as a female emcee. A lot of times that's the only reason they want me on their track. When I started coming to that realization, I was like, oh, okay – that's not what I want. (Interview, 18 June 2008)

Although Eekwol is considered by many of her peers to be a "dope," or highly skilled, emcee, hip hop culture continues to be harsh to women (in Saskatchewan), representing women who participate as novelty figures, objectifying them or treating them differently from their male counterparts, offering less opportunity for them to perform or gig, and devaluing their skills. She vocalizes her frustrations with these sexist attitudes when she asks, "Is it because I write good lyrics or is it because I'm female and Indigenous, filling a category no one else is occupying at the moment?" (interviewed in Sealy 2007, 29). The difficulty for Eekwol – and for many other women who create and perform within musical genres that are represented as masculine arenas and that are heavily guarded by industry gatekeepers who continue to perpetuate normative standards – comes down to issues of access, opportunity, networking, and collaborative partnerships.

When questioned about how her gender influences or plays a role in the creation of her music and what it means in relation to how she is treated in the scene, Eekwol's discomfort with normative ideas of gender categorizations and behaviours is evident: "There is no escaping it. I mean, I grew up my whole life hanging out with guys, and even that term 'tom boy' I don't like, because then you're saying I'm more like a guy." When pressed for more on the subject, Eekwol is able to quickly articulate the contradictions in attitudes, behaviours, and expectations that are informed by gender norms. At the same time, she also speaks about her ability to avoid being completely overwhelmed by such oppressive frameworks:

> It's totally there. There's no getting around it. But when I write lyrics, I'm not consciously thinking from a "woman's perspective." I'm not trying to be, "I am woman, hear me roar" type of thing. To me, the issues don't have gender. Like, I guess, "Let's Move"[31] for example. We all have to move and my music's always reflected just that. All of us, we can all do this; we can all work together. Or else the stories reflect people, not men and women. Unless … One of my more recent songs is the "men" song that stems from a more personal place. There are a lot of guys that rap about their girlfriend or their mom [...] But at the same time that doesn't really pigeonhole the guys [...] If they're talking about a woman, people aren't saying, you know, that's a guy rapping.[32]

The contradiction that Eekwol highlights is typical of the normative gender roles that are prominent in rap and hip hop narratives. Why is it still that when a man raps about a woman he cares for, he is represented as a compassionate and upstanding guy, in spite of rap's prevalent narrative of objectification and sexualization of that woman, but when a woman raps about a man, it tends to be read as sentimental, emotional, or a manhunt?[33]

On 2 April 2008, during the launch of the IMP Labs, Eekwol was one of ten hip hop artists who participated in the roundtable discussion on hip hop in Saskatchewan (and the only woman).[34] Her initial comments concerned gender and some of the issues she faced because she is a woman who likes to rap and because there are so few women who participate in the scene living in Saskatchewan:

> [T]he thing about hip hop here is that there aren't many girls who are doing it. It's kind of a lonely thing, because whenever I'm somewhere else where there are girls that are rapping or break dancing or whatever, it's always just this automatic connection. It's like this vibe, like we're doing this, and you know it would be nice to have more.

The loneliness that Eekwol discussed openly during the roundtable is something I asked her about in a follow-up interview. Here she reflects on the reasons why so few women participate in the scene:

> [I]t is lonely because there's really very few and it's just cool that I have a little cousin who's taking that on. But to say "taking that on," [...] well, why does it have to be that? She loves the music. She loves to create lyrics. She loves to put them to a beat. Why does she have to also take that on? It's not really fair. It's just not fair! [She laughs.] You know?

The hip hop scene constantly reminds Eekwol (and other women who participate) that she is a woman, that she is different and not like everybody else. "I get a lot of respect to my face from all these guys [...] but their true feelings come out in different ways: 'you're pretty good for a girl.'" Eekwol openly challenges this sexist myth, offering yet another example of why she is sought out as a mentor and role model.

Contradictions and Tensions in (Saskatchewan) Hip Hop Culture

The contradictions surrounding hip hop culture are highlighted in Eekwol's experience. Clearly, some hip hop in Saskatchewan is being created in order to critique colonialism, and yet predictable and depressing patterns concerning gender norms and constraints continue to exist. To avoid being identified within this category of "woman," early on in her career Eekwol changed her style and donned hip hop fashions that hid her shape:

> I'd rock the baggy clothes – baggy jeans and big hoodies and I'd do that so I wouldn't get placed in the "hoochie" category, like I have to hide my body in order to get respect. Then you learn to question these things as you get older: Why are we doing all this? Why are we working so damn hard to, you know, be accepted? And now I don't give a shit.

This is the attitude – self-reflection, a critical engagement with her surroundings, and a genuine appreciation for those who respect the people around them – that comes through clearly in Eekwol's lyrics:

> from the roots/to the trunks/to the branches/to the leaves
> the change I want to see is the change I got be

from the roots/to the trunks/to the branches/to the leaves
all in together we're just planting the seeds[35]

In 2004 Eekwol released *Apprentice to the Mystery*, her first full-length solo album. The album, which was co-produced by Eekwol and Mils (by Mils's production company), won the award for best rap and hip hop album at the 2004 Canadian Aboriginal Music Awards. The co-production and the development of Mils's own production company conveys the importance of the DIY (do-it-yourself) aesthetics of hip hop culture. It also speaks to the significance of having access to technologies used to create hip hop tracks today. "We have industry-standard recording equipment that can be used anywhere. We've recorded in hotel rooms. Thanks to technology, it's easier for broke artists to collaborate and create high quality music. We produce albums on a small budget that are comparable to what you hear on the radio" (Eekwol, interviewed in Sealy 2007, 31). Taking into account this comment, I asked Eekwol about the technologies of production and how much easier it seems for young people to create hip hop tracks today. In her response, Eekwol speaks out against what she feels is a common misconception:

People say nowadays there's no real hip hop anymore and that the young generation they have no idea what real hip hop is. But I like to argue against that idea. [Hip hop] comes from passion, it comes from within, and either you're good at it or you're not. Technology has always been advancing ever since the beginning of time, right? So I don't think it's fair to these young kids […] yeah sure, they can make a beat a lot easier than my brother could've made a beat ten years ago, but they're still using the talents and the passion that comes with hip hop.

The DIY component of hip hop is also indicative of Eekwol's political ideology concerning the commercialization and "selling out" of hip hop and the representations of hip hop in the mainstream. And although she argues against the problematic misconception that all mainstream hip hop is "bad" and "a sell-out" and that all underground hip hop is "good" and "socially conscious," Eekwol admires and respects originality and thoughtfulness in other hip hop artists' work. "Everything comes from somewhere right? So a lot of times we have outside influences and we end up utilizing them in our own way and that's what is happening with hip hop, with the different cultures within the culture of hip hop." For Eekwol, the artists who have something original to say are the ones drawing on their histories, culture, and local politics:

> [This music] sounds different from something coming out of the Bronx, and that works as long as you continue to have that respect for where the music comes from. I always push that idea everywhere I go. It's always one of the first things I say about hip hop. I do hip hop but I know where it comes from. It doesn't come from my history, my background. But I can relate to it because of its oral history, my oral culture, the oral storytelling traditions, the social politics and stuff like that.

Hip hop is an oral culture, having developed out of a long history of oral traditions. This orality, in Eekwol's opinion, is one of the forces drawing Indigenous youth to hip hop culture. It is also a sign of understanding for some elders and other community members that Indigenous youth are not turning from their cultural history but incorporating the past with the present and future:

> I have this notion in the back of my mind that our ancestral history runs through our blood and our spirits, and I think a lot of the times youth relate to the storytelling aspect [of hip hop] because of the storytelling traditions. And maybe they have it in their ancestral knowledge and maybe it comes out, and maybe that's an attraction that they can't fully comprehend yet. I like to think that.

From the title of the album *Apprentice to the Mystery* to the lyrics, the metaphors, and the sounds, Eekwol embraces the culture of storytelling. Throughout the thirteen tracks, she tells stories, some autobiographical and others fictional representations of other peoples' lives. In the track titled "Apprento," Eekwol begins using a spoken-word style rather than a straight-up rap. Accompanying her voice is a strong bass line that feels as though it is breathing with each movement as well as synthesized keyboard sounds. At various points throughout the introductory section, rattle sounds fade in and out. As Eekwol speaks the lines, "Because I'm guessing through experience and lessons," the keyboard becomes more present, increasing in volume, introducing additional melodic sounds, building the tension through dynamics and an ascent in pitch. Eekwol's voice becomes stronger and fuller as she drops to the lower part of her vocal range, participating in the building of tension. When she arrives at the phrase "We got power in numbers," she is joined by another voice, that of award-winning round dance singer Marc Longjohn. His vocalizations give weight to the meaning of the line. Eekwol is speaking both literally and metaphorically.

Eekwol continues with the line "We got … power in spirit" and then shifts from "we" to "I" in the lines "I got … power in music/I got … power in my voice." Literally, her voice sounds as though it is becoming more powerful as additional effects and filters are added, along with a slight echo. Her enunciation of "I got" in each phrase becomes crisper, and she holds onto the last word of each phrase ("music," "voice," or "it"), extending the length of the sound and emphasizing the lyric. When she gives out the last line, "Hear it," there is a slight pause, followed by a heavy bass beat dropping on the first count of the next measure as she begins to rap the verse.

These changes in her vocal style cause a renewed sense of urgency, and her rap demands the listener's attention. The melody, played by a synthesized keyboard, moves up and down the scale, contributing to a continual forward rhythm that complements Eekwol's style of vocal delivery. The bass beats remain heavy and fat as she offers narratives of the complexities of identity, loss of culture, responsibility to one's culture, anxiety, the seduction of power, money, confusion, and the possibilities of empowerment that come with the passing of wisdom down through the generations from the elders to the rest of the community. For Eekwol, these are her "truths," bound by what she knows, what she does not know, and what she hopes to come to know – the mystery.

As she arrives at the chorus, Eekwol implicates herself in the stories and then goes on to explain how she makes herself accountable:

> So what I'm doing is
> Observing the mystery
> Understanding the mystery
> Following the mystery
> Becoming the mystery
>
> I'm nothing without the mystery
> I know nothing about the mystery
> A tiny source of the force of this universal history

Here, her vocal style changes again. The chorus is sung in a lyrical style, the syllables becoming more fluid, which gives a sense of inward reflection. The bass lessens and the melodic synthesized sounds that had a strong presence at the beginning of the tune return. As she builds to the second section of the chorus, her intense rapping voice, clear enunciation, and rapid delivery style return. It is at this moment that Longjohn's round dance singing builds in volume. Longjohn's voice is present at various moments throughout the track, sometimes barely audible, but at points of intensity his vocalizations are strong, offering an integration of narratives – an interconnection of "traditional" and "contemporary" Indigenous cultures. There is a synergy between past, present, and future, and Eekwol needs/wants/hopes to understand the mystery in order to embrace/challenge/resist past and present – and most important, to create change for the present and future.

In the remaining tracks of *Apprentice*, Eekwol interrogates, confronts, and seeks to transform. She continues to tell complicated stories concerning renewed spirituality, community crisis, sickness, healing, apologies, loneliness, strength, alcoholism, love, suicide, nurturance, death, celebration, and mourning. In the track "Too Sick," her emphasis is on breaking free from cycles of violence:

> too sick to stop this cycle
> hammer this nail into my head
> living in the cost of a culture loss
> some say I'm better off dead[36]

"Too Sick" is literally about domestic violence, and metaphorically, it can be understood as representing cultural abuse and hatred. It is a familiar story of violence toward women perpetuated by men who claim to care. This narrative calls attention to the devaluing of Indigenous women from outside and within. "Too Sick" is a song of crisis – a song that challenges the listener to remember the hundreds of Indigenous women, the missing women, the lost women, the dead women, who have disappeared from their homes and communities across Canada.[37] Eekwol deconstructs these conventionally gendered narratives as a method for (re)shaping different narratives for herself, other young Indigenous women, and the rest of the community.

The politics of place and combining of cultures is prevalent in *Apprentice*, as Eekwol incorporates new hybrids of musical genres and soundscapes, namely hip hop combinations of rap and R&B singing styles as well as Indigenous vocalizations and aspects of Cree language.[38] There is also an inclusion of instrumentation that is not usually found in commercial North American mainstream (or underground) hip hop. In addition to more conventional-sounding hip hop beats, the listener also hears an organ, a flute, a guitar, rattles, and traditional drums, many of these digitally sampled or synthesized. The listener is reminded of both Eekwol's roots and routes in all of her lyrics. She challenges the listener to really hear her stories and to embody the affects of the storytelling act and the storyteller's meaning. Eekwol puts herself, and her contradictions, out there, simultaneously becoming vulnerable and powerful as she dares the listener to reflect and to move.

Hip hop is the genre that enables Eekwol to convey the contradictions and burdens of the current colonial situation in Saskatchewan. From within hip hop culture, she has begun to think about decolonization and the possibilities of what this might look like: "I can only speak for myself, but I do try to use music as a tool to try to comprehend exactly what needs to happen to decolonize, to decolonize myself and to try to talk about it, to try to get that discourse going [...] whether it be music or not, maybe ceremonies, a resurgence of the ceremonies and the desire to learn and relearn the ceremonies and revitalize the language. That's starting to happen quite a bit." Decolonizing actions are subjective; they are social but also personal and psychic. For Eekwol, hip hop culture presents many possibilities for reflection, speaking out, and returning to a place outside of colonial history. In her music, she fights against a reified identity bound to a historical past and represented through a colonial lens. She breaks out of this narrative. But at the same time, she is compelled not by music alone, nor does she believe that hip hop culture holds all the answers: "Music itself is obviously a good tool. But it's not enough. We still need the action because we speak it. I can speak it to death, and I will, but the action has to be there. We have to live it too."

Conclusion

Clearly, from the examples provided throughout this chapter, contemporary hip hop practices in Saskatchewan contribute to a current dialogue on colonialism as it is experienced today. Indigenous hip hop artists living, producing, and performing in Saskatchewan, like Eekwol and Mils, complicate the discourse on Indigenous youth in Canada – so much so that during past Canada Day celebrations outside the provincial Legislature Building in Saskatchewan, hip hop artists have performed alongside Indigenous "traditional" drummers and powwow dancers. Indigenous youth are adopting a culture and adapting this culture to represent their lives. They are constructing spaces differently and in so doing telling new stories. Cultural anthropologist Julie Cruikshank suggests, "Stories allow listeners to embellish events, to reinterpret them, to mull over what they hear and to learn something new each time, providing raw material for developing philosophy" (Cruikshank 2002, 154). The stories being told in the hip hop scenes in Saskatchewan are diverse, contradictory, political, and at times, fantastical.

The discourses surrounding hip hop culture in Saskatchewan are incredibly contradictory and tension-filled. As I argue in other works, hip hop programs in Saskatchewan are successfully used as incentives to keep young people in school, while at the same time, hip hop is represented by the media through a lens of racism that draws connections between hip hop, gang culture, and Indigenous youth.[39] Hip hop is used to critique colonialism by some artists, participants, and community members, but the culture also holds strong to gender norms and constraints, promoting male dominance, marginalizing women in the scene, and devaluing women's contributions. Thus the question of mimicry – and whether or not hip hop in Saskatchewan is just caught up in the sensationalized and romanticized "bling," "booty," and violent images of American mainstream hip hop – cannot be answered with a simple yes or no.

As I have demonstrated, there is a new, "redefined" style of hip hop that has developed in Saskatchewan, and this hip hop is what Tony Mitchell (2001) describes as an example of "glocal" culture, a culture that represents a dynamic relationship between the local and global, a culture that is in flux. In a keynote talk given at the "Critical Race" conference, held at the University of Regina in May 2006, Indigenous studies scholar Emma LaRoque argued that Indigenous youth need to embrace cultural styles that speak to current lived experiences. She was not suggesting that historical practices be abandoned, but her argument takes into account the understanding that culture, arts practices, and communities are not static. Indigenous hip hop is a relatively new form of popular culture, which offers the potential to challenge the reified identities and cultures that liberalism within a multicultural framework invites. In the music discussed throughout this chapter, for example, it is evident that Eekwol's (and Mils's) hip hop does not solely focus on the preservation of past traditions but also attempts to explore the complex experiences of Indigenous youth living in Saskatchewan today, which include community workshops based on the hip hop arts, hip hop programs and projects in schools, hip hop–affiliated media and businesses, and hip hop performances. Eekwol tells stories, and these stories and performances are informed by her surroundings – her community, her experiences, and her history. Eekwol's music is politically, socially, culturally, and ethically relevant to today.

However, because the possibilities for identifications on an international scale are extraordinary and vast, it is essential to understand, as

Andy Bennett has determined, that "the localization of hip hop, rather than being a smooth and consensual transition, is fraught with tensions and contradictions as young people attempt to reconcile issues of musical and stylistic authenticity with those of locality, identity and everyday life" (Bennett 2004, 180). It is essential that we understand the complexities of what this may mean in relation to the social, political, economic, cultural, and geographical landscape of Saskatchewan. Even the few examples offered here for analysis show the soundness of the argument that hip hop culture in Saskatchewan is a possible strategy for decolonization. Hip hop culture has been redefined in Saskatchewan – adopted and adapted – to reflect local Indigenous culture, politics, and experience, as well as other hip hop cultures from around the world. Within this new style of hip hop, there are some intelligent, thought-provoking, critical, and complicated narratives being conveyed. Old stories are being retold through innovative and new hybrid forms, and current experiences are being (re)shaped and expressed as new stories ready to be told and to be heard.

NOTES

The stories told within this chapter are only glimpses into the diverse and evolving hip hop cultures in Saskatchewan. I want to express my deep gratitude to all the hip hop artists and enthusiasts who shared their stories with me and gave me permission to interpret these stories and contextualize them within this collection of music narratives. To convey these stories ethically, I must acknowledge that I write as both insider and outsider. I am an insider because I am a long-time lover of hip hop, as well as a facilitator of hip hop workshops and a producer of hip hop shows in Regina, Saskatchewan. And yet I am an outsider because I moved to Saskatchewan in 2004 and because I am someone who speaks from a place of privilege, a trained popular music scholar working in one of the three universities in Saskatchewan, and a non-Indigenous woman. Knowing these things, many people shared their stories with me, granting me permission to retell their stories in academic-speak, a form of language that is for the most part foreign to the culture of hip hop and to many of the young people who participate in this culture. I have a deep appreciation for these stories (the "truths," the "fictions," the "in-betweens"), and I have a profound respect for these storytellers and the roles they carve out for themselves.

1   "Apprento," from Eekwol's *Apprentice to the Mystery* (2004).
2   Generally, the cities in Canada that are represented as major urban cultural centres are Toronto, Montreal, Vancouver, Calgary, Winnipeg, and Edmonton. Cities such as Saskatoon, Regina, Halifax, Victoria, St John's, and Quebec City, although large and unique, tend to fall outside of such categorization.

3 I contextualize Canada both as a liberal pluralist nation-state with a contested state-initiated policy on multiculturalism and as a neocolonial state still in the process of decolonizing (psychically, geographically, culturally, and socially).

4 These include grassroots community arts-based projects in urban centres and on reserves, education-oriented hip hop projects in inner-city schools, dance academies, music festivals, businesses affiliated with the hip hop scene, home production studios, online forums, and live concerts.

5 For a complete list of the reserves found in Saskatchewan, refer to *The Encyclopedia of Saskatchewan* at http://esask.uregina.ca/home.html (accessed 21 June 2011), to the First Nations Bands of Saskatchewan website at http://www.sicc.sk.ca/bands (accessed 21 June 2011), or to the Government of Saskatchewan website at http://www.gov.sk.ca (accessed 21 June 2011).

6 An urban reserve is defined as "land that has received official Indian Reserve status from the Federal Government and is located within a municipality or a Northern Administration District" (Lorne A. Sully and Mark D. Emmons, *Urban Reserves: The City of Saskatoon's Partnership with First Nations*, 6, quoted in Western Economic Diversification Canada – Saskatchewan Region 1999). For more information on urban reserves in Saskatchewan, refer to http://www.wd.gc.ca/ rpts/research/urban_reserves (accessed 21 June 2011).

7 Ocean Man First Nation, Pheasant Rump Nakota Nation, and White Bear First Nation are all located within the area of Treaty 2 but are signatories of Treaty 4. Similarly, Red Earth First Nation and Shell Lake First Nation are in Treaty 6 but adhere to Treaty 5; see http://www.sicc.sk.ca/bands (accessed 21 June 2011).

8 For more information concerning the percentages in other provinces and territories, refer to http://www12.statcan.ca/english/census06/analysis/aboriginal/ tables/table2.htm (accessed 21 June 2011).

9 For more information about the concentration of Aboriginal peoples living in Canada, refer to http://www12.statcan.ca/english/census01/Products/Analytic/ companion/abor/canada.cfm#5 (accessed 21 June 2011).

10 For more information, refer to "Aboriginal Population Trends," in *The Encyclopedia of Saskatchewan* at http://esask.uregina.ca/entry/ aboriginal_population_trends.html (accessed 21 June 2011).

11 For examples and theoretical analyses of how these have influenced culture and arts practices in Saskatchewan, refer to Rogers and Ramsay (forthcoming).

12 The businesses range from beat making and production studios to graphic design and record stores, skate shops, clothing stores, live music venues, and dance and performance companies committed specifically to the styles of hip hop. For a complete list of current businesses, refer to the "Friends and Affiliates" section of the IMP Labs website, http://www.interactivemediaandperformance.com (accessed 21 June 2011).

13 An example is the K-Beez Cook-Out hip hop events that were held at the White Buffalo Youth Lodge and sponsored by Paved Arts.

14 http://www.commonweal-arts.com (accessed 21 June 2011).

15 Some of the artists who participated in the initial Prairie Roots Project were Def 3, Aries, Truth, Merky Waters, Cappo, Lok-1, Eekwol, Tallisman, and osho.

16 I asked Nicholson about gender representation because of the glaring absence of women each time I visited the Regina site.

17 Usher was a high school located near one of Regina's industrial neighbourhoods and drew a student population from diverse socioeconomic backgrounds and cultures; however, due to budget cutbacks, Usher Collegiate was one of three schools to close in Regina in 2008.

18 Produced by Jennifer Canal for CBC Saskatchewan.

19 By making this suggestion, I am not in any way downplaying the importance of the rituals and expertise that go along with being an audience member of a music culture. At the same time, insider knowledge does not always preclude young people from actively participating as audience members.

20 The new global hip hop culture is indeed an integral part of what Paul Gilroy (1993a) has referred to in his work on the "Black Atlantic" as the "routes" of African-derived hip hop. For another current example of how hip hop culture is being appropriated as a strategy of resistance, see my paper with Sheila Petty on the Hip Hop Parliament, which was initiated in Nairobi, Kenya (Marsh and Petty 2010).

21 For more detailed information, refer to http://www.interactivemediaandperformance.com (accessed 21 June 2011).

22 For the full article, "Canada's Worst Neighbourhood," see http://www.macleans.ca/article.jsp?content=20070115_139375_139375 (accessed 21 June 2011), and for the follow-up article, published 29 January 2007, see http://www.macleans.ca/article.jsp?content=20070129_139986_139986 (accessed 21 June 2011). To read the article "Article Stirs Hot Debate," in the *Regina Leader Post*, see http://www.canada.com/reginaleaderpost/news/viewpoints/story.html?id=35fdce10-1c28-4c8b-9b3f-b10592a83158 (accessed 21 June 2011). One year later, on 17 January 2008, *Maclean's* published the article "Regina One-Year Later: Residents and Local Leaders Have Done Much to Improve Life in North Central"; see http://www.macleans.ca/canada/opinions/article.jsp?content=20080117_95971_95971 (accessed 21 June 2011). In my article "Keepin' It Real?: Masculinity, Indigeneity, and Media Representations of Gangsta' Rap in Regina, Canada" (Marsh 2011), I analyze the original *Maclean's* article within the context of place making and also discuss the racialization of urban ghettos in relation to Indigenous bodies.

23 The Albert Scott Community Centre, attached to the high school, houses daycare facilities and a police detachment, speaking to a number of other social and systemic issues that these young people face in their daily lives. During my first visit to Scott Collegiate, I asked about the needs for both the daycare and the highly visible police presence on school property. One of the teachers suggested that the daycare services were used mostly by members of the community and that the police presence was overstated and then completely absent by the middle of the day. And yet, while visiting the school at various times during the past two years, I have seen and worked with a number of pregnant students and/or young mothers, and I have witnessed a strong police presence – police officers detaining young men in the parking lot for a variety of reasons.

24 A third version of the Scott Collegiate/IMP Labs Hip Hop Project occurred in the winter of 2010, and a fourth segment of the project took place in March 2011.

25 For a critical analysis of the Scott Collegiate/IMP Labs Hip Hop Project, along with a theoretical discussion of the complexities and contradictions of integrating hip hop programs into innercity schools in Canada, see Marsh (2010).

26 For a detailed discussion of how the media constructs narratives concerning Indigenous bodies and hip hop in Regina, see Marsh (2011).

27 "The People," featuring Def3, from Eekwol and Mils's *The List* (2007).

28 Giving back to one's own community and the surrounding communities is indeed an essential component of the musical careers of most of the Indigenous artists with whom I have had the privilege of working within Saskatchewan. This aspect of Indigenous music culture is not unique to the artists working in hip hop but is evident in most genres of popular music.

29 Other scholars who contribute to this dialogue in Mitchell's *Global Noise* (2001) are André J.M. Prévos, Ted Sedenburg, David Hesmondhalgh, Caspar Melville, Mark Pennay, Claire Levy, Mir Wermuth, Jacqueline Urla, Ian Condry, Sarah Morelli, Ian Maxwell, and Roger Chamberland.

30 "That's Just Me," from Eekwol's *Apprentice to the Mystery* (2004).

31 "Let's Move," from Eekwol and Mils's *The List* (2007).

32 To read more of this interview, refer to my "Interview with Saskatchewan Hip Hop Artist Lindsay Knight" (Marsh 2009).

33 For more in-depth discussions of this argument, refer to Shaviro (2005) and Rose (1994).

34 "Roundtable Discussion on Hip Hop in Saskatchewan," at launch of IMP Labs, University of Regina, 2 April 2008, organized and facilitated by Dr Charity Marsh. The participating artists were Eekwol, Mils, DJ Quartz, Etea, Aries, Truth, Merky Waters, and Def3.

35 "The Tree," from Eekwol and Mils's *The List* (2007).

36 "Too Sick," from Eekwol's *Apprentice to the Mystery* (2004).

37 For more information and a list of women who are missing, see http://www.missingnativewomen.ca/alert.html (accessed 21 June 2011), http://www.amnesty.ca/campaigns/sisters_overview.php (accessed 21 June 2011), and http://missingwomen.blogspot.com (accessed 21 June 2011).

38 Supported by the Saskatchewan Arts Board, Eekwol is currently working on a new hip hop album entirely in the Cree language.

39 See Marsh (2011).

20

Why Do the Innu Sing Popular Music? Reflections on Cultural Assertion and Identity Movements in Music

VÉRONIQUE AUDET

We are currently witnessing a renewal and a recognition of an Aboriginal movement in Quebec, in Canada, and in the world. Internationally, this movement falls under a political climate of decolonization, of recognition of cultural diversity, and of increased rights of minorities, all of which have, over the course of the twentieth century, allowed for a recognition of Aboriginal peoples' rights to self-determination. This is most evident in the 2007 United Nations Declaration on the Rights of Indigenous People. These contemporary movements are complemented by cultural revitalization and by revalorizing social healing processes,[1] in which Aboriginal people turn to their roots, their traditions, and their elders to build a unique Indigenous place in the world, transcending past experiences to live fully in the present and the future (Frisbie 2001, 492). New forms of Aboriginal music are an integral part of this process (Diamond, Cronk, and von Rosen 1994, 12). They are used as cultural emblems, as instruments of resistance, and as a means to assert contemporary concerns, and they reinforce a distinct identity vis-à-vis dominant societies (Nettl 1992). These music forms combine Aboriginal and Euro-American elements, the traditional and the modern, the local and the global. Aboriginal popular music is a particularly interesting example of appropriation and indigenization processes (Friedman 1994, Appadurai 2001). In this music, we see the importance of revitalization and identity as well as the potential for action and transformation through personal and collective expressions and through voiced criticism of social problems. This music contributes dynamically to movements of identity and cultural assertion as well as to healing in Aboriginal circles.

The Aboriginal popular music movement is very strong in Quebec, particularly among the Innu,[2] a people that boasts great musical vitality, musicians, events, and important productions. Innu popular music is a social movement to which the majority of Innu, in one way or another, are tied and with which they identify themselves either as artistic creator, composer, singer, listener, dancer, consumer, producer, friend, and/or relative, and so on. Innu music is widespread and significant for contemporary Innu. For example, to give an idea of the magnitude of this music, we may count about one hundred locally produced albums (between circa 1975 and 2011) and more than one thousand original songs in the language of the Innu, Innu-aimun, not all of which have been recorded (see the Innu discography). Innu popular music reveals the great vitality and creative adaptation of the Innu in their contemporary lives. The change from a nomadic to (semi)sedentary people in the 1950s marked a rupture with the ancestral way of life and inflicted many wounds upon the Innu, wounds that require healing in a context where the pain of loss often gives way to feelings of powerlessness (Samson 2004, Tanner 2004, Vincent 2004). These realities are often expressed in the songs, and by these expressions, Innu revitalize their personal and collective lives in a movement of cultural continuity and transcultural newness.

In this chapter, I argue that Innu popular music is a movement that asserts Innu identity and culture. The questions that I raise include: Why do the Innu sing popular music? And why are these pop songs so popular in the Innu world? The answers to these questions help to highlight relatively unknown repertoires, artists, and practices, and they locate these musical movements and their creators in their own world, while seeking greater understanding of these repertoires and movements by non-Innu people. In this chapter, I explore Innu popular music – its significance, dynamism, and power – in a contemporary Innu context. I loosely draw on the features of Innu music, illustrated by examples from some influential artists, interviews conducted with these artists, and an examination of some particularly popular and significant songs.[3] I focus specifically on the relation between cultural continuity and transcultural awareness and on the Innu sense of music, which, despite borrowings and transformations, survives and is constantly renewed.

What is Innu Popular Music?

I define Innu popular music as songs in Innu-aimun, generally sung with guitar accompaniment using typical rock 'n' roll, country, or folk music instruments and styles. The group Kashtin (Tornado) popularized this style of Indigenous popular music on a Québécois, Canadian, and international scale at the beginning of the 1990s, the period that saw the rise of commercial "world music" more generally. With the exception of Florent Vollant and Claude McKenzie, the artists who formed Kashtin, and Philippe McKenzie, who recorded with the Canadian Broadcasting Corporation (CBC) in circa 1975 and 1982, Innu popular music remains relatively unknown to non-Natives. This music is, however, omnipresent within Innu communities. The Innu popular music world is very dynamic, abounding in musicians, singers, and composer-songwriters, and is supported by an avid and proud public. Although this repertoire has the potential for intercultural communication and integration within the Québécois and world music scenes, the contemporary Innu musical scene largely remains local in scale and impact. This music is primarily addressed to the Innu people, through its messages in Innu-aimun, and it is an important part of the daily life of Innu communities. The musicians perform together and with their loved ones informally and in shows and festivals (such as Innu Nikamu)[4] in various communities, produce albums in local recording studios,[5] sell their albums within the Indigenous Innu network, and share their music through community radio programs of the SOCAM network.[6] The Innu are also connecting more and more with the world via the Internet by introducing their music and video clips on websites such as Youtube, Facebook, and MySpace.[7]

Through music sung in their Native language, the Innu express what they live and what they think, putting their concerns and feelings about their personal and collective history and visions into words and music. There are many common themes in the songs, including identity; the appeal to solidarity, an assumption of responsibility, awakening; traditional life in the woods, the bond with the earth, the animals and entities of the land; the respect, attention, and transmission of the elders' words; alcoholism, problems of drug addiction and dependence; family violence and negligence; love, friendship, sorrows of love, adultery; praise and love for the family, parents, children; illness, death, suicide, the loss of loved ones; and sedentary life in the community or urban centres. For Kim Fontaine, from Mani-utenam, a musician, sound technician, and producer at Studio Makusham, the topics of Innu songs express culture as lived today, in all its forms:

> There are songs which speak as much about the land as what
> occurs in our community, of language difficulties, or other things
> [...] I would say that it is the same as with French. Often, there are
> songs of love, or the sorrows of love, family difficulties ... There is

also, in our area, many songs that speak about drugs, and of the difficulties with drink, or all those things. You know, people that are
in misery, financially and emotionally. It's pretty much what the
youth speak about today. (Interview with Kim Fontaine, 2003)

These musical expressions draw upon traditional Innu relationships and
associations between sound and the world around them, and they are
also inspired by other musical genres, including Christian songs in Innuaimun, fiddle music, country, folk, rock 'n' roll, pan-Aboriginal music, and
more contemporary genres such as reggae and hip hop. In spite of these
multiple influences, Innu pop music maintains continuity with the ancestral world, where songs confer power on individuals and their surroundings (Speck 1977, Preston 2002).

Innu Nikamu, Teueikan, and *Makushan*: The Meaning of Innu Music

Innu popular musicians and the music they create continue the historic
borrowing and sharing that characterized earlier encounters; hence this
music is inspired by ancient Innu traditions. In this section, I explore the
meaning of traditional Innu music, the Innu sound universe, and the use
of environmental sound to illustrate the continuity of Innu traditions in
popular musical expressions of the contemporary world.

The term "Innu Nikamu" is used today to describe all ancient and contemporary Innu songs and music. "Innu Nikamu" literally means "the
Innu sings" or "he/she sings the song of the Innu." "Innu" means "human
being." For the Innu, the term indicates their nation first but also any
Aboriginal person who has a particular relation with the earth and who
likewise has experienced oppression historically and today. "Nikamu"
makes reference to power and voice through song and music. "Nikamu"
evokes the existence of a power given to sound and transmitted through
sound. This spiritual power brings personal, social, economic, and political power to the recipient, who becomes a guide and messenger. It is interesting to note that traditionally *nikamu* refers first to a powerful drum
(*teueikan*) song, which is performed with a strong voice, sung by nonhuman spirits during dreams, and tied to power and maturity acquisition
(see Cavanagh [Diamond] 1985, 10–11; Audet 2005a; Audet forthcoming).

Ancient Innu musical expression is especially evident in songs performed on a teueikan, a circular-shaped Innu drum made of caribou
skin and crossed with a snare with resonators (see Diamond 2008b, 63–7;
Audet 2005a, 37–62; Audet forthcoming). We can hear two teueikan
drumming styles: a more meditative, rumbling rhythm for the spiritual

communication; and a more punching, punctuated short-long rhythm for the *makushan* dances. These teueikan songs are first and foremost personal, private, secret, and shamanic, favouring exchange between good Innu hunters and nonhuman spirits, generally masters of animals. These songs send, receive, and transmit wishes and messages about the course of life and make it possible for the Innu to be nourished, to be cured, and to live. Only certain people have the right to strike a teueikan; the songs themselves are acquired through dreams of experienced hunters who are respectful of the value that the Innu place on the land and animals. Permission to sing teueikan songs is granted by spirits recognizing the singers' experience, wisdom, and maturity:

> When they sing, […] the elders sing their masters' message that was sent [with respect to animals, food]; then they transmit that to people who hunt. This is what I hear, today, that we continue or perpetuate what the elders explained, what they left as a heritage for the youth. (Interview with Jean-Charles Piétacho, chief of Ekuanitshit, 2003)

> Even if [the elders are] not there anymore, you must ensure that the message they give to you is heard. When you do it, you will have dreams. But you need to have three dreams about the drum. If you dream these three dreams, you will then be able to sing with the drum what we transmitted to you, so it is never lost. Say it, do it, that is the elders' message. (Interview with the late Pinip Piétacho, elder singer on the teueikan and former chief of Ekuanitshit, simultaneous translation by his son Jean-Charles Piétacho, 2003)

Pinip Piétacho went as far as saying that "the Innu culture will cease to exist the day when all our drums will be stored in the museums" (Piétacho et al. 2000).

During family and community gatherings, the singers of teueikan songs are animators and interpreters, transmitting values, maintaining relations, and expressing communion between humans and the world in which they live; they beat the rhythm for the collective and circular makushan dances, where participants stand up and form a walking circle (see Audet 2005a, 58–60; Audet forthcoming). The term "makushan"[8] names a festive gathering, a shared meal during these occasions,[9] and the traditional Innu dance evoking the nomadic hunters' walk, which affirms their presence on and with the earth. These ancient makushan are still performed today, particularly during elders' gatherings.

20.1 Ben McKenzie sings with the teueikan while children of the group Mashkussat of Nutashkuan perform the makushan dance at the Innu Nikamu festival, 2003. Photograph by author.

Since the 1970s, the teueikan has been played on stage, and it has been recorded on albums, albeit with respect for certain restrictions due to its spiritual associations. The majority of youth refrain from playing it because they have not received a dream allowing them to play or because they do not feel ready to assume this responsibility in the contemporary world. Several elders have recorded songs with the teueikan for albums, so this repertoire is not lost, and they sing on stage during festivities, yet the teueikan is seldom used in contemporary popular styles. However, the makushan rhythm is reproduced in this music with other percussion instruments in order to evoke pride in Innu identity.[10]

The makushan is often danced during Innu popular music shows. There are three types of contemporary songs directly inspired by makushan songs or by the dream processes of the teueikan songs. First, certain songs are specifically evocative of Innu identity and have a marked makushan short-long rhythm. These songs almost inevitably involve the spectators in the makushan dance; examples include "Tshinanu"[11] (Kashtin 1989) and "Ekuan Pua"[12] (P. Mckenzie 1982, C. McKenzie 1996), songs that are like national anthems for the Innu. Second, certain teueikan songs that were popularized and remade with the guitar, such as "Uisha,

20.2 The makushan is danced to the song "Uisha, uishama," sung by Alexandre McKenzie of Matimekush (a descendant of the late Alexandre McKenzie), closing of the Innu Nikamu festival, 2003. Photograph by author.

uishama"[13] (Kashtin 1991) and "Uapan Nuta" (Tshimun n.d., Rock 2007, Youtube/Kathia Rock/"Quand le jour se lève"), also encourage the makushan dance during contemporary shows (see Audet 2005a; Audet forthcoming). Third, we find popular contemporary songs tied to the dream world; they were dreamed of or given through a dream. For example, some Innu do not feel comfortable striking the teueikan and instead sing their songs with the guitar, like the singer Bryan André, from Mani-utenam and Matimekush, in his song "Teueikan" (André 2002).

> "Teueikan" (Innu Drum)
> Bryan André, album *Anisheniu* (2002)
> Translation from Innu-aimun
>
> *There I will sing to you my dream*
> *So you can know what I've seen*
> *My grandfather who struck his drum*
> *That's what I saw in my dream*
> *My grandfather invited me near the woods*
> *Then I saw animals pass by*

Resonance, Manifestation, and Assertion of an Existence in the World

In an ancestral Innu context, similar to several Aboriginal peoples, musical expressions are above all spiritual acts of communication and communion in the world. Frances Densmore has stressed this eminently spiritual, metaphysical, and cosmological sense of Aboriginal music and its ability to connect to and communicate with the forces of the world (Densmore 1968, 78–9, cited in Wickwire 1985, 199–200). Tim Ingold suggests a similar understanding of the meaning of sound expressions among the Ojibwa,[14] for whom sound is the manifestation and assertion of an existence in the world, an engaging poetic act tied to the poetics of dwelling (Ingold 1996, 2004), and a contribution to life's movement:

> The rumbling of thunder is the manifestation of its presence in the world, just as the sounds of humans speaking, singing, clapping or drumming are the manifestations of ours. Indeed, the world is full of such sounds, each one the signature of a particular mode of life. As people move through their environment, they constantly listen to the speech of these manifold life-forms, revealing each for what it is, and respond with speech of their own. Both non-human sounds, like thunder, and human speech have the power to move those who hear them, and both kinds of sound take their meaning from the context in which they are heard. (Ingold 2004, 47)

Through its dynamic, energetic, vibrant, penetrating, intimate, and sub-jective qualities, sound establishes a resonance and a connection between the human being and the invisible world:

> [I]n hearing, … the world seems to flow "from-out-there-toward-me-and-through-me" … There are some hints, in Hallowell's account, that the Ojibwa might make a similar kind of distinction. Thus he tells us that under no circumstances can the inner essence of the person, the soul, be a direct object of *visual* perception. "… The only sensory mode under which it is possible to directly perceive the presence of souls … is the auditory one" … And this

sound, as we have seen, is of the essence of being rather than its outward expression. (Ingold 2004, 47–8, original emphasis)

What is seen is external, whereas sound crosses space and borders impermeable to sight. Sound reveals the lived essence of beings, their own identity. For the Innu, a sound that is heard but not seen is considered very powerful and is associated with messages from the spirit world (Cavanagh [Diamond] 1985, Speck 1977; on the Cree and Ojibwa, respectively, see also Preston 2002 and Hallowell 1960, 1971).

A great power is granted to sound and musical action, and drum and rattle songs have an essential role in Innu spiritual practices:

> As adjuncts to the execution of the will in matters directed toward securing a successful hunt, or in concerns of a more personal nature, the influence of the human voice and the tympanic vibrations of the drum and rattle are considered indispensable. The ordinary process is this: When an individual has begun to concentrate his thoughts upon securing animals, or upon some other objective he desires to accomplish, he will sing and at the same time, if an instrument is available, accompany himself with the drum or rattle. It depends on the occasion. The more frequently a hunter has occasion to resort to the power of sound in arousing his soul-spirit to activity on his behalf, the more likely he is to make for himself a drum ... Musical action is, in short, regarded as a means of strengthening the Great Man[15] of the individual. (Speck 1977, 174)

An extract from Kashtin's (1989) first album cover corroborates these remarks. Although this is a marketing tool used to promote the group in the exotic niche of world music, it significantly evokes the Innu's conception/experience of music, their relation to the world through sound, and their ties to a lifestyle of nomadic hunters:

> The [Innu-aimun] language has no equivalent for the word "music." To us, music is everywhere; it vibrates through every living thing. Our forefathers sought oneness with nature through sound. They used the *teueikan* (the Innu caribou-skin drum) as a means of communicating with nature. Our definition of "traditional music" is reminiscent of a time when the knowledge and mastery of the various sounds of nature were the keys to the power of survival. To Kashtin, music still holds the same power, transcending the lyrics,

to pass on the traditional spirit. By traditional spirit, we mean the values our people live by, such as tolerance, sharing, generosity and respect for nature. (Kashtin 1994b)[16]

According to Richard Preston (2002), for the Cree, and by extension the Innu and other Algonquians as well, songs express very strong positive feelings of willingness and "deep hope" about what one desires to see happen (207–8). Songs received through dreams by men relate mainly to hunting and reveal animals as partners that give themselves to the hunter in a symbolic loving, sensual, and seducing relationship or in a playful relation that is akin to interactions with tricksters; they recognize the reciprocity of the human-animal and human-nonhuman relation. These songs are sung with the goal of making real the meaning of the song; they send messages and have a real effect on the animals and their generosity toward humans (208). The best hunters are those who have received the most songs in dreams. The songs heard in a dream reveal what must be done to have a good hunt or to thank the animals that willingly gave themselves (199–208). In difficult times, such as a famine, the Cree often sang to receive sympathy from nonhumans and to transform their difficulties into fullness and abundance (202). These songs play a central, and even vital, social and spiritual role in the survival of Algonquian people.

We have seen that Innu consider traditional Innu music to be human (Innu) interactions and resonances within the world. According to my research and understanding, it is the same for their contemporary popular music. In spite of great transformations, the Innu musical tradition and meaning are uniquely maintained. This Innu meaning of music is based on a way of being in the world directed by orality, the powers of sound expression, and an active engagement in the world through personal experience and expression (see Preston 2002, Cavanagh [Diamond] 1985, Diamond, Cronk, and von Rosen 1994). As Florent Vollant has said, "For young aboriginals, art – sculpture, painting or art in any other form – is a way of existing" (Vollant 2002). Their engagement in music is related to life and survival; they live it, and they often allow others to experience music as a form of renewal and as a personal, cultural, and social healing process:

It keeps me alive. It gives us the will to continue living. Making music, it's what we like the most. (Mathieu McKenzie, of the group Maten, in Meney 2002)

It's a type of therapy, music. (Germain Hervieux, of the group
Maten, in Meney 2002)

What I like in the music is the fact that one is appreciated, that
people appreciate my songs. If people tell me, "Hey, I recognize
myself in this song," that pleases me! When I touch someone, you
know, when someone says, "Hey, whose song is this?" "Who did you
write it for?" [...] "Why did you say that in the lyrics?" These things,
I like! [... I sing] to send messages. If the message is not appreciated,
or [if it] is, at least it is heard! By everyone. It will touch someone
like that, and another like this [...] All Natives here see themselves
in Innu music, because we live what we live here [...] We have several social problems. In the songs that we sing, we try to touch
people [...] These are beautiful tunes, and for people, it speaks to
them [...] It's what you live, and what almost everyone lives here. It's
still fun, and we try to compose tunes, to use beautiful lyrics that
will touch, we try to play with that, it's in our language, and everyone understands us here. (Interview with Samuel "Pudu" Pinette, of
the group Maten, 2003)

As Samuel "Pudu" Pinette explains, several singer-musicians notice the
emotional and direct effect of their music and messages. Similar to the
way that elders tell stories and sing their dreams for the continuation of
the Innu way of life, the singer-musicians tell stories that are often personal, delivering messages that affect the emotions, actions, and lives of
listeners as much as themselves. They are messengers (*katipatshimusht*),
mediators, narrating various experiences of the world.

A Short History of Musical Encounters by the Innu

Innu popular music is a product of the Innu musical trajectory, which is
influenced by the Innu way of life and being in the traditional world and
by social and cultural encounters and transformations. It evokes and is
anchored in an Innu "reduction" process (Simard 2003), an encouraged or
forced evangelization, acculturation, and sedentarization. In the spirit of
resistance, survival, or continuity of experience, Innu show great artistic
vitality, creativity, and an ability to adapt in a world that places challenging burdens on them.

Christian songs translated into the Innu-aimun language were, as of
the seventeenth century, a unique mixture of Innu and Euro-Canadian
traditions. Chants, hymns, and cantiques were the Catholic mission-

aries' tools for fascination and conversion (see Dubois 1997a; Gagnon 2003; Audet 2005a, 65–9; Audet forthcoming). Missionaries recognized the Innu passion for songs and the effect of the songs on the Innu. As the Jesuit François Le Mercier said, writing in 1655, "when these songs travel from the ear to the heart, it is salvation, an intervention by God stating that He wants to be the Master" (quoted in Dubois 1997a, 9); "Without song, no savage missions," wrote the Oblate Jean-Marie Nédelec in the nineteenth century (quoted in Gag-non 2003, 153); and, according to the Oblate Thomas Clément, "singing is for them the most important thing, they cannot withhold from singing" (quoted in Gagnon 2003, 154). Similar to the teueikan songs, these songs are used to communicate and connect with spiritual forces in order to acquire power over one's life. It was thus easy to integrate them into the Innu world and way of life, and today they are still part of a strong Innu identity and part of the ancestral heritage of the Innu (Cavanagh [Diamond] 1988, Diamond, Cronk, and von Rosen 1994).[17]

The teaching of musical instruments of European origin to Innu seems to have occurred much later (Dubois 1997a). Pinip Piétacho once told me that in his most distant memories, he did not know of musical instruments other than those belonging to the Innu. It was around 1940 when he first saw foreign instruments "of all forms, with funny sounds" in the North Coast villages of the Gulf of St Lawrence where Acadian fishermen had been established (interview with Pinip Piétacho, simultaneous translation by Jean-Charles Piétacho, 2003). The Innu who occupied the south-western regions, which were nearer to the activity hub of Euro-Canadians and for which reserves had been established earlier, were able to learn and appropriate these instruments (i.e., violin, accordion, and harmonica) and their associated music as early as the nineteenth century (see Audet 2005a, 62–5).[18] In the middle of the twentieth century, when country, folk, and rock 'n' roll music were expanding, the guitar became the main instrument of choice, and its popularity eclipsed the other European instruments adopted by the Innu.

To his knowledge, as of the 1950s, Émile Grégoire was the first Innu of the Sept-Îles region to play guitar, to sing country songs, and to perform in shows (interview with Émile Grégoire, 2003; see also Audet 2005a, 65–73; Audet forthcoming). It was during his young years, while his family was living in a log cabin in Clarke City, close to the St Marguerite Dam, that he first heard country music on the radio. Like other Innu of his generation, he was fascinated by the radio and spent his nights listening to these sounds – lyrics and music that came from another world. He dreamed of owning a guitar as he perused catalogues, and eventually

20.3 Innu Elvis. Émile
Grégoire in the 1950s
in Uashat. Photograph
courtesy of Émile
Grégoire.

his father was able to buy him one, which he learned to play by listening to the radio host. Little by little, he started to appear in shows in the region of Sept-Îles, then in Schefferville, in Quebec City, and in several Aboriginal communities. Grégoire was then recognized as the Innu Elvis, the King. He passed on his taste for commercial Euro-American music and showmanship, all the while affirming his goal of reinterpreting songs in an Innu style. He translated and adapted many songs from the country and rock 'n' roll repertoires into his language, and he composed his own songs. He produced many albums on cassette locally (Grégoire n.d., 1997), which he afterward made into a compilation on CDs (Grégoire 2000a, 2000b).

During the 1960s and 1970s, the new music of postwar Western youth fully entered the musical customs and tastes of Innu youth.

Music was increasingly used for leisure and entertainment. In the 1970s the Innu fully adopted country, rock, and folk music. Like Philippe McKenzie, from Mani-utenam, they aligned their musical creations with the identity, cultural, and political assertion movement that was gaining momentum at this time. This music then became a means of cultural expression, nation building, identity assertion, and intercultural communication (see Audet 2005a, 73–86; Audet forthcoming).

Philippe McKenzie is recognized by many Innu as the pioneer of their popular music, as the one who created a distinctive style of music by singing in Innu-aimun with his own melodies and by amalgamating traditional and folk-country-rock styles. In the middle of the 1970s, inspired by his friend Cree folksinger Morley Loon (see Loon c. 1975, 1981), McKenzie created and produced the first Innu popular music broadcast with the CBC in Montreal (three short-play albums circa 1975, circa 1976, and circa 1977, edited as a long-play album in 1982). He initially used the teueikan in his music but gave it up after an elder told him that he should not use it in this context. In his music, however, he still keeps the long-short rhythm of the makushan, traditionally played on the teueikan.

Although his long-play album *Mistashipu* (1982) has been broadcast nationally, his albums (c. 1975, c. 1976, c. 1977, c. 1982, c. 2000) have

20.4 CD cover for *Philippe McKenzie* (2000), by Philippe McKenzie of Mani-utenam, pioneer of Innu popular music. Left: Alexandre McKenzie I (Innu Scottish ancestor of the Innu named McKenzie), Philippe McKenzie (background), and Jean-Marie McKenzie (foreground, Philippe's uncle, who sang with the teueikan). Right: Philippe McKenzie and his son Mishta-Shipu McKenzie in the 1980s. Courtesy of Philippe McKenzie.

rarely aired outside of Aboriginal circles. His songs have been popularized within non-Native audiences by the Québécois singer Chloé Sainte-Marie, who interpreted three of his songs on her album *Je marche à toi* (2002) and fifteen of his songs on an entire album in tribute to him, *Nitshisseniten E Tshissenitamin* (I Know that You Know) (2009).

"Mistashipu" (The Great River) is the first song he composed. It speaks about the Moisie River,[19] which was like a motorway for the Innu to travel around the land. The song tells about misery but also about the strength and pride felt by the Innu who travelled on the river, as well as about difficulties of the youth, who are unable to live today as elders did in the past. Indeed, there is a certain degree of fatalism about the loss of traditions, of the *Innu-aitun* (Innu folk knowledge), and of the things the elders were once able to do, as well as about the loss of the land that allowed these practices. The river is, like the song "Mistashipu," a strong symbolic image of the elders' strength and the reality of ancestral nomadism on this land. The song "Mistashipu" was one of elder Pinip Piétacho's favourites, and he acknowledged McKenzie's role in preserving Innu knowledge through his lyrics: "Philippe McKenzie, it was really him who thought of these words, which are very strong, about the government ... It's good! He was a pioneer. It's been a while, and his words, his lyrics, they are very captivating, very informative. It appeals to me a lot [...] *Mistashipu*, the great river, the words are very true" (interview with Pinip Piétacho, simultaneous translation by Jean-Charles Piétacho, 2003).

> "Mistashipu" (The Great River, Moisie River)
> Philippe McKenzie, album *Mistashipu* (1982, first recorded
>   with CBC circa 1975)
> Translation from Innu-aimun
>
> *Mistashipu*
> *Mistashipu*
> *Mistashipu*
> *When the Innu used to go up in the land*
> *and when they went back down to the coast*
> *They used the river*
> *and had a hard time there*
> *We, the young*
> *we'll never be able to do that*
> *Like the Innu did before*
> *we will never be able to do that*

Other songs highlight despair, akin to shouting without being heard, of a great dream lost. These songs reflect negotiations, politics, and land claims that originated in a spirit of optimism and, despite several positive developments, have dragged on for more than thirty years. McKenzie's song "Mamitunenitamun" (Meditation) (c. 1975, 1982, 2000) speaks about the search for strength to live as an Innu, as well as about the bitterness and despair of not knowing what the future will bring for generations to come. It speaks about the loss of freedom, culture, and land.

> "Mamitunenitamun" (Meditation)
> Philippe McKenzie, albums *Philippe McKenzie* (2000),
>   *Mistashipu* (1982, first recorded with CBC c. 1975)
> Translation from Innu-aimun[20]
>
> *Sitting, I meditate*
> *About what I will do tomorrow*
> *Looking for the strength to live*
> *As a human being (Innu)*
> *What will I do?*

In 1985 the Innu Nikamu festival was founded, providing a stage for Aboriginal music, dance, and art of Quebec, of Canada, and of the world (see Cavanagh [Diamond], Cronk, and von Rosen 1988; Audet 2005a, 86–90; Audet forthcoming; http://www.innunikamu.net). Every August, thousands of Innu, other Aboriginals, and some non-Aboriginals gather for a few days in the Mani-utenam community close to the town of Sept-Îles. The local Innu radio station, CKAU FM Kushapatshikan of the SOCAM network, along with the festival organizers, plays a major part in its organization, financing, and promotion. The festival serves as a platform for new groups to emerge and to contribute to the Innu musical scene. It thus offers beginners or inexperienced stage performers a chance to express themselves, to be known, and to be heard publicly, next to recognized Aboriginal stars. Innu popular music has acquired an important place in the Innu world, while serving as a magnet for the gathering, social cohesion, and pride in identity of the Innu.

Born from this pioneering period of the 1980s, the group Kashtin popularized Innu popular music on a national and international scale, particularly from 1989 to 1995, a peak moment in the commercial rise of world music. After having started performing music within their families and communities, Florent Vollant and Claude McKenzie played together, accompanying Philippe McKenzie. They then formed the duo Kashtin around 1984 and quickly became very popular with the Innu, and Aboriginals more broadly, by becoming the Kings of the North Coast. In 1988 they were filmed by Radio-Canada during the Innu Nikamu festival (V. Morrison 1996), and they were then discovered by producer Guy Trépanier, who recorded and produced their debut commercial album, *Kashtin*, in 1989 (Kashtin 1989, 1994b). It was at this point that their solo "E uassiuian" invaded Québécois radiowaves, and they sold 150,000 albums in four months! Their subsequent unexpected international success made them a major musical influence as leaders of Aboriginal music in Canada, contributing indirectly to the creation of the "Aboriginal music" category for the Juno Awards in 1994 (see V. Morrison 1996; Scales 1999; Diamond 2008b, 142–5; Leblanc 1994). They produced two other albums, *Innu* (Kashtin 1991) and *Akua tuta* (Kashtin 1994a), before pursuing solo careers since 1995. Their musical style continues to influence Innu and Aboriginal musicians in general, who identify with it, interpret their songs, and create new ones.

"Tshinanu" (Us, Our People, or What We Are), by Florent Vollant and popularized by Kashtin, serves as a national anthem for the Innu, suggesting a strong feeling of pride in and identification with the Innu nation and culture. It stresses the importance of the connection with the land by strongly evoking the traditional way of life and relation with the land. It is regularly played on the radio, and it is often covered by performing groups during shows, inciting people to dance the makushan. On 24 May 2008, during the *Mishta Amun* show, which brought Aboriginal artists together at the Palais Montcalm in Quebec City, Florent Vollant and Claude McKenzie performed together on stage for the first time in a long while, having rarely played together since Kashtin's separation, and excited the mainly Indigenous crowd by performing "Tshinanu," to which a great makushan dance was performed (see YouTube/Kashtin/ "Tshinanu").[21] The liner notes to the album *Kashtin* explain the significance of the song: "With time, it became a national anthem, 'Tshinanu' symbolizes the new generation of Innuat. Tshinanu names without giving names, our grandfathers, our rivers, our children and our bearings. Tshinanu also names land. Tshinanu is as if we saw our country in front of us. It is so much of all that, by listening to this song our people start to dance the makusham, the traditional celebration dance" (Kashtin 1994b).

 "Tshinanu" (Us, Our People, or What We Are)
 Kashtin, album *Kashtin* (1989)
 Translation from Innu-aimun

It's for us to know it
It's us, it's us
It's for us to see it
It's us, our path
It's us, our children
It's us, our grandfathers
It's for us to know it
It's us, it's us
It's for us to see it
It's us, our path
It's us, our river
It's us, our land
Ai ai! Ai ai! Ai ai! Ai ai! Ai ai! Ai! ...
It's us, we tell the truth and we are right

Beyond events, shows, and recordings, Innu popular music today is above all part of the creative, expressive, and artistic acts lived and experienced every day in Innu communities. It is within the context of everyday life that Innu music is created. Informal contemporary practices correspond and connect with ancient musical forms, evident in the formation of a circle around the guitar and in the messages expressed in the lyrics. Gatherings of friends and/or family often include collective musical practice and creation, where each performer takes a turn at the guitar and sings. One Innu from Sheshatshit speaks about these occasions as a form of therapy, making reference to the circle of expression and sharing:

> For me, my therapy is ... to sing. That's how I get through the days, sometimes. Just singing and having fun with it. For me, it is just being there and ... what we call the circle, with your friends, passing along the guitar, listening to every singer. If somebody is a good singer, you can just feel them, at their heart. I think for me that's what we call a circle. You hear everyone and they hear you. Some singers talk about getting through, and some singers just play. And some singers need some help to get through the song. Everybody is helping them to sing. It's what we call a group, a group party. (Interview with Frederick Penashue, of the group Innutin, 2003)

Although largely inspired by popular Euro-American currents, Innu popular music and its scene are also unique in their perpetuation of Innu ancestral heritage. A selection of influential singer-musicians and their particularly significant songs are discussed here to illustrate the uniqueness of Innu music.

Claude McKenzie

Claude McKenzie is originally from Matimekush (next to Schefferville), but he also lived in Montreal, and for a long time he has been rooted in Mani-utenam. A member of the former duo Kashtin, he has also produced three solo albums, *Innu Town* (1996), *Pishimuss* (2004), and *Inniu* (2009). He sings and composes romantic and festive songs, often addressing relationships among people and between people and their surroundings. His performance style oscillates between behaving like a rocker, performing fully and without constraint, and being able to express emotion and problems of the "dangerous" pleasures of life in more painful songs. Several of his songs address major difficulties experienced by the Innu and the desire to heal from them. His albums have encouraged several Innu to reflect, to awaken to their problems, and to work toward healing. His personal life serves as a strong example to others.

The song "Nutaui" (My Father), also known as "Putai" (The Bottle), is one song that is highly valued by the Innu public. It has a strong impact on listeners, addressing the misery of alcoholism and the desire to quit the habit.[22] It is often requested or dedicated to someone on the radio. Throughout the morning of Father's Day 2003, this new single was broadcast repeatedly on Radio CKAU of Uashat mak Mani-utenam. During Claude McKenzie's outdoor show for a celebration in Pessamit on 15 August 2004,[23] the song drove the crowd wild. The partygoers raised their drinks during the song as a sign of understanding and compassion, showing that the lyrics resonated with them and that they shared the misery caused by alcoholism. In this context, the "therapeutic" song took the form of an "alcoholics' anthem," manifesting an irrepressible but suffering intoxication, lived and shared collectively. Claude McKenzie tells us that when he sings this song for an Innu audience, he feels that he gives them a moment of happiness, that he is in communication with the audience, that he touches them, and this makes him happy (interview with Claude McKenzie, 2008). On the album, in the song's introduction, we hear Claude's father, Paul-Arthur McKenzie (nicknamed Mitshapeu), a respected elder, who delivers a message to the youth (see Youtube/ Claude McKenzie/"Nutaui").

"Nutaui" (My Father), or "Putai" (The Bottle)
Claude McKenzie, album *Pishimuss* (2004)
Translation from Innu-aimun

Introduction by Paul-Arthur McKenzie:
You, the youth
Be aware of the values of your parents
And pay attention to the value of your life, all along your life.

Lyrics:
The bottle, it gives me pain.
I could not sleep without first having a drink.
Many times I stop, but it's stronger than me.
I must stop before I die.
My father often tells
He helped many people to feel better [by stopping their
   drinking].
Me my friends
Really I like them.
When I am drunk
I give myself pain
Alone.
Only my father comes again
To tell me that he loves me, in my home.
It harms myself
Me, before I die.

Chantal Bellefleur

Chantal Bellefleur, from Unaman-shipu and Mani-utenam, is one of the first female Innu popular music singers. Innu women are an integral part of the Innu musical world, yet they are not very prominent as writer-composers nor as studio or stage performers. In recent years, however, it seems that there are increasing numbers of young women in Innu popular music, like Kathia Rock and Alek-Sandra Vollant-Cormier.[24] For nearly twenty years, Chantal Bellefleur has composed beautiful songs; she sings for the lover who left her, for women who have been beaten, and for her father, who goes to the woods while her mother remains working for the community. She told me what inspires her to compose her songs:

I like to compose a lot for women. How a woman feels inside. Opposite a man, or life. What occurs in the life of a woman. It is mostly for the women that I sing [...] Sure, the song is composed with a man in mind, so that he may catch on! [...] We need to help them sometimes. [Audet: Help them understand women?] To reflect, yes that's it, to understand women [...] If it can help Aboriginal women, then it's worth composing the songs. [Audet: Do you think that your songs touch men?] In my view yes, because, one time, I had dedicated one of my songs to two women [who were beaten], and the men who had beaten them, when they heard the song, they stopped. They calmed down and stopped drinking. They caught on. I think that it is worth sometimes to say what we think inside. (Interview with Chantal Bellefleur, 2003)

Like several Innu song writers-composers and performers, Bellefleur sings informally in her social circle, but she seldom performs in a show. She has not recorded an album of her songs, but her song "Ashtam uitshi" (Come Help Me) is one of the songs in an Aboriginal language that the Québécois singer Chloé Sainte-Marie chose to interpret. By recording it on her album *Je pleures, tu pleures* (I Cry, You Cry) (1999) and by performing it at several shows, Sainte-Marie made it known to a large audience outside of the Innu world. This song is a call for help. It expresses current and striking realities of life in the community: problems of love, loneliness, suffering, drinking, and drugs. It is the first song that Bellefleur composed, when she was in her early twenties, at a time when she was learning how to play the guitar. Her boyfriend at the time had left for several days on a binge, leaving her on her own. This experience gave her the emotion and inspiration to create this lament-style song that several Innu still like today. She succeeded in calming her boyfriend by singing to him; he said he was intimidated that a woman would sing that way for him. "Ashtam uitshi" is also used during healing sessions. Several people have thanked Bellefleur for this song that helped them to understand how they were living and helped them to see their problems and their behaviours.

> "Ashtam uitshi" (Come Help Me)
> Chantal Bellefleur
> Translation from Innu-aimun[25]
>
> *I walk around the reserve*
> *I visit my friends.*

They are always drinking
Always smoking.
So that I'm not bored
I go with my friends.
It's then that I drink alcohol
So I don't have to think anymore.

So that I'm not bored
So that I'm not sad.
To not suffer anymore
I go with my friends.
That's why we smoke
So I can be at ease with myself.
I feel lost.
Where am I?
I know when I go back home
I'll be alone.

Come help me
Come help me
Come help me
Come help me

So that we'll be both of us
So that we'll be together
Like before
When we were seeing each other.
You know what I think of you
How I love you.
I can't live well
When you're not with me.
Come help me.
I can't do anything.
Come help me.
I'm all alone.
Come help me.
I'm waiting for you
Here in our home.
Me too there are many things I think about
When I see you.
I really miss you.

Truly I cry a lot.
It doesn't matter how you are.
I'd like to see you
To squeeze you in my arms
To hold you so tight.
I walk around the reserve
In case I'm able to meet you.
I would say
That I love you.
The truth, I love you

Shauit

Shauit Aster is a rising Innu singer in his thirties, who demonstrates the Innu ability to adapt and personalize new musical styles while promoting the language, as was done by his predecessors. His album *Shapatesh Nuna* (2004) was distributed locally in Innu communities, and he's now in the studio in Montreal to make an album for a broader audience. He collaborates with the young Anishnabe rapper Samian (2007, 2010), who is a rising hip hop star and young Aboriginal spokesperson in Quebec. As Samian always says, Shauit is the only reggae man in the world who has ever sung in Innu-aimun. Shauit's background is particularly interesting because it was by interpreting Innu songs on the guitar that he learned the language of his relatives, in which he composes today. Shauit integrates reggae and rap/hip hop with the style of Innu popular music. We hear the Innu language folded into the rhythm and melody of Shauit's songs, which are very popular among young Innu. By performing in this style, Shauit inscribes the Innu youth within the global reggae and hip hop movement. His originality and talent have been noticed beyond Innu borders. Since 2007 he has travelled with Samian across Quebec, elsewhere in Canada, in Cuba, and in Europe and has been on stage with him during well-known shows such as the Fête nationale québécoise in Montreal and the Francofolies and at the Canada Day celebrations in Ottawa in front of Queen Elizabeth II. Together, they composed and proudly sing the song "Les Nomades" (Samian 2007). This trilingual song (Anishnabe, Innu-aimun, and French) speaks about realities that are experienced and shared by people of various First Nations. The video clip of the song climbed the charts on the Top 5 Franco list on Musique Plus (the French version of Much Music) during July 2008, paralleling the fall 2007 success of the song "La Paix des braves," which Samian composed with the Québécois group Loco Locass (see http://www.samian.ca; Youtube/Samian and Shauit/"Les Nomades"). They also composed and sing together the song "So Much" (Samian 2010), which plays on the radio, and did a video clip in Cuba in May 2011 of that lovely song in French, English, and Innu-aimun.[26]

Shauit's 2004 song "Nui kushpen" (I Want to Go to the Woods) evokes the contemporary worlds of the "reserve" and the "woods." It illustrates a strong desire to go to the woods, and it explores the motivation of people to live the life of a hunter in order to avoid boredom, social problems, and materialism in the community. It is similar to other songs that use the themes of the land and the traditional Innu way of life. Such songs express the contemporary experiences of people who go to the woods for new reasons and with new technology and transportation modes while continuing a way of life in keeping with the Innu world. They talk about the train, the hydroplane, the snowmobile, and CB communications (short-wave radios) rather than the rivers, portages, canoes, and teueikan, for example. "Nui kushpen" calls to those whose lives are based in the villages. It values their connection with the land and incites people to live the experience instead of succumbing to the problems identified with life on the reserve.

> "Nui Kushpen" (I Want to Go to the Woods)
> Shauit, album *Shapatesh Nuna* (2004)
> Translation from Innu-aimun
>
> *Ah-an-an-an-an-an*
> *I wake up before the sun.*
> *I dress warmly so I'm not cold.*
> *I start up my ski-doo to warm it up.*
> *I prepare my tea in advance.*
> *I will draw my water and eat.*
> *Before I go to kill the caribou.*
> *I look for life, like these hunters.*
> *I like to see that.*
> *Never give up.*
> *Each day I see*
> *The caribou getting up, there in the woods, there we walk.*
> *I like going to the woods.*
> *Whenever I have the time*
> *I prepare myself.*

And I wait again so I can get on the train.
Each time that I get on, I can't wait to get off.
And I see myself there. I'll be happy to hunt the caribou.
I'll do it as I think it.
That's how I like it.
That's what I want to do today.

I allow myself to go to the woods
In order to learn how to hunt well.
It's so beautiful here in the forest.
I look forward to that …
Why again, am I bothered by always sitting at home?
Why do I sing?
There will not be anyone.

REFRAIN:
Already there I find things here that I love.
I want to do something in order to go often to the woods.
It's been a longtime since I looked for this life I'm talking about.
Yo yo[27]
You don't worry about anything when you're there.
You know?[28]
You don't exhaust yourself with your worries.
You know?
Just to go searching for your wood and your water.
You know?
Just to go searching for something essential to life.
You know?

Sometimes I've been bothered with life.
I'm bored, I want to die, I talk to myself.
Shauit! I say to myself
What have you done, why do you worry yourself?
You're just sitting there
Just there drinking.
For nothing you harm yourself, for nothing you mistreat yourself.
A little bit of time you'd go up to the woods.
It's been a long time since you saw it.
What you're waiting for, you'd like to go see before you're more
    depressed.

Maten

The group Maten, very popular at the beginning of the 2000s, is comprised of young Innu singers and musicians from Mani-utenam. They have made two albums, *Akua Tutu* (2001) and *Tshi Metuatshen* (2003), and they have performed many shows in Aboriginal and non-Aboriginal circles. They are celebrated for their lyrical themes and musical innovation by a young public as well as by all Innu generations. They have participated in large-scale shows outside the Innu world, particularly during the commemoration of the Great Peace of Montreal 1701–2001. They have also taken part in television broadcasts and are involved in their communities, especially through the community radio station CKAU FM Kushapatshikan and Studio Makusham in Mani-utenam. Their songs, like those of other young musicians, speak about realities of modern life, problems of love, competition, materialism, alcohol and drug abuse, loneliness, and the joy of being among friends. Some of their texts stress the importance of prayer and paying respect to Tshishe-Manitu (God, Creator), from whom they request help and strength to live and achieve their dreams in a world that is not always easy.

The song "Tshe shatshiek[u]" (You Will Love Him), on the album *Tshi metuatshen* (2003), is sung in duet by Mathieu McKenzie and Alek-Sandra Vollant-Cormier. Addressing a healing journey, it is very popular and holds great emotional power for listeners, even making some cry. Vollant-Cormier's performance, recorded when she was sixteen years old, greatly contributes to the impact of this song, as it is a rare public performance of music by a talented young girl. The narrator of the song expresses his problems and his desire to change and have a better life; he wishes to be loved and cherished by his loved ones in spite of his bad behaviour. The song encourages forgiveness, love, and the support and acceptance of friends, relatives, and members of the community, as well as taking responsibility for oneself to find a better path in life. Many Innu songs express the same topics, regularly evoking the symbol of the personal path of life that one must create and follow. The word *meshkanau*, which is used in "Tshe shatshiekᵘ," means the road, the way, the path traditionally taken to get around the land. In its current use, it often refers to personal growth. By its emotional and suggestive qualities, this song has a therapeutic effect on many listeners.

> "Tshe shatshiekᵘ" (You Will Love Him)
> Maten (words and music by Uapush Vollant; sung by
>   Mathieu McKenzie and Alek-Sandra Vollant-Cormier),
>   album *Tshi metuatshen* (2003)
> Translation from Innu-aimun

> *You will love him*
> *You will cherish him*
> *In spite of how he behaves in his life.*
> *He, too, had misery in his life.*
> *He is not conscious of his bad character.*

> *It's very difficult, for him too, his path.*
> *He doesn't want to know.*
> *What should I do, in order to be well?*
> *So that I, too, feel well?*
> *I'm trying to think how I am.*
> *Okay, it's time that I pray.*
> *Okay, me too, it's time that I let go*[29]
> *So that I, too, feel comfortable with myself*
> *To never lose hope*
> *So that I can follow a good path in life.*

> *My friends are with me*
> *To know how I feel.*
> *Everybody is looking*
> *To love him, to accept him as he is.*

Conclusion

In this chapter, I hope to have contributed to an understanding of Innu popular music and why the Innu sing a great deal, particularly popular music compositions in Innu-aimun. According to my interpretation, they sing first and foremost as a means of "being alive well" (Adelson 2000) and to take part in the world in an original way. For the Innu, music continues to explore a human/Innu way of being in the world. By creating and singing popular music in their language, Innu singer-messengers express and affirm their existence in the world, engage in it, and thus give themselves the power to take part in and change it. In the past (and still today, although rarely) Innu used teueikan songs to address and participate in the spiritual world of nonhuman beings and their land. Today, through the medium of popular music, they address and take part in the human/Innu and globalized worlds. The study of Innu pop songs and their history, meanings, power, and potential for action reveals how the Innu live and revitalize their contemporary world in order to exist in harmony within their contemporary environment, seeking acceptance for what they are. This popular music is an expressive and dynamic product of Innu life and a privileged expression of Innu identity today. These songs resonate everywhere in the Innu world and beyond, whether through the nearly constant sound of the local radio, on the Internet, in shows, or in gatherings of friends, families, and communities.

INNU DISCOGRAPHY

Aishkat. 2007. *Ueshkat*. CD. Self-produced. Chute-aux-Outardes: Studio Concept-Plus.

André, Bryan. 2002. *Anisheniu*. CD. Produced by Bryan André, Gilles Sioui and Mario J. Teixeira. Quebec: Studio Le Loft.

- 2009. *Nipeteti*. CD. Self-produced. Mani-utenam: Studio Makusham.

Ashini, Benoît, Pierre Courtois, Michel Grégoire, André-Charles Ishpatao, Jean-Marie Mackenzie, Étienne Mark, Simon Mestenapeo, Pierre Z. Mestekosho, Damien Mestokosho, André Poker, and Pierre Tobis. 1982. *Puamuna/Rêves de chasse montagnais/Montagnais Hunting Songs*. LP. SQN 100. Boot Records.

Ashukan. 2008. *Le pont entre les peuples*. CD. Les productions SAG.

Aster, François, Georges Gabriel, and Uldéric McKenzie. 1999. *Ka utamuat teueikana: Matimekush*. CD. Mani-utenam: Studio Makusham.

Aster, Goeffrey. 2009. *Minuatakanu*. CD. Self-produced. Uashat: Studio Inniun.

Aylestock, Guillaume. 1990. "Tshin Innu." *La Côte Nord*. Cassette. Alma: Studio Cégep d'Alma. Self-produced.

Bacon, Delvina. 2010. *Delvina Bacon*. CD. Self-produced. Chute-aux-Outardes: Studio Concept-Plus.

Bellefleur, Charles-Api. 2008. *Tshekashkassiunnu*. CD. Self-produced. Mani-utenam: Studio Makusham.

Blacksmith, Alcide. N.d. Title unknown. Cassette. Self-produced.

– 2009. *Unikamuna*. CD. Tribute to Alcide Blacksmith with various artists. Mani-utenam: Studio Makusham.

Canapé, Michel. 2008. *Mille après mille*. CD. Self-produced. Chute-aux-Outardes: Studio Concept-Plus.

– 2009. *Celle que je cherchais*. CD. Self-produced. Chute-aux-Outardes: Studio Concept-Plus.

Couture, Bobby. 2008. *Ninan*. CD. Self-produced. Uashat: Studio Inniun.

Déry, Marc. 1999. "Ninanu." *Marc Déry*. CD. Les éditions Audiogramme, Les productions Anacrouse.

Einish, Ben, Jr. 2005. *Nikaui*. CD. Self-produced. Uashat: Studio Inniun.

Fontaine, Bernard, Cyrille Fontaine, and Philippe Piétacho. 1982. *Utakushit mak kashikat nakamun/Chansons montagnaises d'hier et d'aujourd'hui/Montagnais Songs of Yesterday and Today*. LP. SQN 101. Boot Records.

Fontaine, Shaushiss. 2009. *Amélya*. CD. Self-produced. Mani-utenam: Studio Makusham.

Goliath. 2008. *Mamitunenita*. CD. Self-produced. Uashat: Studio Inniun.

Grégoire, Émile. N.d. *J'ai perdu mon amie Annie*. Cassette. Self-produced.

– N.d. *7 sur 10: Sans être instruit quelqu'un quelque part*. Cassette. Self-produced.

– N.d. *Stranger (Nutetuk nete manteu)*. Cassette. Self-produced. Studio Circuit.

– 1997. *Maiken Kachiuelet: Les loups affamés*. Vol. 6. Cassette. Self-produced.

– 2000a. *Capteur de rêves: Tekshaman (24 succès country)*. CD. Self-produced.

– 2000b. *J'ai rêvé à Tshchémanitu (11ième)*. CD. Self-produced.

Grégoire, Tintin. 2011. *Tintin*. CD. Self-produced. Uashat: Studio Inniun.

Iniun. N.d. *Namash*. CD. Self-produced.

Innu Auassat (Benjamin Fontaine, Matthew Jourdain, Spencer St-Onge, Shaushiss Fontaine, John Ambroise, Tshishapeu Vachon). 2007. *Innu Auassat*. CD. Mani-utenam: Studio Makusham.

Innu Pacific. 1997. *Innu Pacific*. CD. Produced by Clément Rock. Quebec: Studio DBX.

Innutin. 2005. *Inniun*. CD. Self-produced. Uashat: Studio Sonoluc 'boot' La Chapelle.

Jourdain, Sol. 2008. *Napeu*. CD. Self-produced. Uashat: Studio Inniun.

Kashkun. N.d. *Menuatetau*. Cassette. Uashat: Les Studios Inniun.

Kashtin. N.d. *Kashtin*. Demo cassette. Self-produced with Marcel Néron.

– 1989. *Kashtin*. Cassette and LP. Éditions Groupe Concept Musique.

– 1991. *Innu*. CD. Éditions Groupe Concept Musique.

– 1994a. *Akua tuta*. CD. Productions Tshinuau and Éditions Groupe Concept Musique / Uapukun Music.

– 1994b. *Kashtin*. CD. 1989. Reissue, Productions Tshinuau and Éditions Groupe Concept Musique.

Kuanutin. c. 1993. Title unknown. CD. Self-produced.

Les Frères Grégoire (Eshkan). N.d. *Innu Nekemun*. Cassette. Innu Tekenep Enr.

– 2004. *Uapet*. CD. Self-produced. Lac-Beauport: Les Studios New Rock.

Mamit Innu Nikamu (Mamit Innut, Pakua Shipu Band, Charles Api Bellefleur, Tradition, Rod Pilot, Keshken). 1990. *Mamit Innu Nikamu*. Vol. 1, *Première édition La Romaine Mars 1990*. Cassette. Studio F.E. Promotions Innu Nikamu.

Mark, Kenikuen. 2011. *Tshimueshtaton*. CD. Mani-utenam: Studio Makusham.

Maten. 2001. *Akua tutu*. CD. Mani-utenam: Studio Makusham.

– 2003. *Tshi metuatshen*. CD. Mani-utenam: Studio Makusham.

McKenzie, Claude. 1989. *Claude McKenzie*. Demo cassette. Self-produced with Marcel Néron.

– 1996. *Innu Town*. CD. Groupe Concept Productions and Éditions Groupe Concept Musique.

– 2004. *Pishimuss*. CD. L-A Be.

– 2009. *Inniu*. CD. Hello Musique.

McKenzie, Laurent. 2009. *Kanuelim*. CD. Self-produced. Quebec: Studio Sismique.

McKenzie, Paul-Arthur. N.d. *Aiamieun Nikamun*. Vols 1–5. Cassettes. Mani-utenam: Studio Les Productions A.B. and Aiamieun Nikamun/Productions Religieuses.

– N.d. *Shuk ka shatshishk tiu*. 2 CDs. Uashat: ICEM.

McKenzie, Philippe. c. 1975. *Indian Songs in Folk Rock Tradition*. Self-produced. QCS – 1422. Montreal: CBC Northern Service Broadcast Recording.

– c. 1976. *Innu*. Self-produced. SRC – 006. Montreal: CBC Northern Service Broadcast Recording.

– c. 1977. *Groupe folklorique montagnais* (with Bernard Fontaine and Florent Vollant). Self-produced. QCS – 1466. Montreal: CBC Northern Service Broadcast Recording.

– 1982. *Mistashipu/La Grande Rivière/Great River*. LP. SQN 103. Boot Records.

– 2000. *Philippe McKenzie*. CD. Mani-utenam: Studio Makusham and Éditions Uapan Nuta.

Menutan. 1990. *Menutan*. Cassette. Produced by Michel Jourdain and Mario Paradis. Pointe-Bleue: Production Son-Art.

Meshikamau. N.d. *Nitassinan*. Cassette. Self-produced.

– 1996. *Meshikamau*. CD. Produced by Robert Moore. Goose Bay: Eagle Studios.

– 1998. *Nika*. CD. Produced by Mathieu McKenzie and Kim Fontaine. Mani-utenam: Studio Makusham.

– 2009. *Best of Meshikamau*. CD. Produced by Andrew Penashue. Mani-utenam: Studio Makusham.

– with Sharon Grégoire. 2006. *Niman Niteit*. CD. Produced by Andrew Penashue. Happy Valley: Studio Mukluk.

Meshikamau – Andrew Penashue. 2004. *Utaishimau*. CD. Produced by Luc Charest and Mathieu McKenzie. Mani-utenam: Studio Makusham.

– 2011. *Nussim*. CD. Self-produced. Chute-aux-Outardes: Studio Concept-Plus.

Mestokosho, Sylvester (SLY). 2008. *Tepeshkat*. CD. Self-produced.

Nimuk. N.d. *Nuitsheuakan*. CD. Self-produced. Chute-aux-Outardes: Studio Concept-Plus.

Nipateu. c. 2006. *Nteut Shakastuet*. CD. Produced by Etienne Rich. Goose Bay: PH Balance Studio.

Nitatshun. N.d. *Numushum*. CD. Self-produced. Goose Bay: Eagle Studios.

– 2004. *Ishkueu Tipatshimu*. CD. Produced by Tunker Campbell and Nitatshun. Happy Valley: Mukluk Studios.

O'Cleary, Mike. 2008. *Kassinu auenitshe ute assitsh/Tous les êtres vivants sur cette terre/All Living Beings on This Earth*. CD. Trois-Rivières: Studio Radicart and Ilnu Spectacle Production.

Petapan. N.d. *Shash*. Cassette. Self-produced.

– N.d. *Pessamishkuess*. CD. Self-produced.

– 2004. *Kanatuut*. CD. Self-produced. Chute-aux-Outardes: Studio Concept-Plus.

– 2006. *Anutshish kashikat*. CD. Self-produced. Chute-aux-Outardes: Studio Concept-Plus.

– 2011. *Petapan*. CD. Self-produced. Mani-utenam: Studio Makusham.

Picard, Raphaël. 1986. *Eka ma malianne*. Cassette. Self-produced.

– 1998. *Epeikussenanut*. CD. Self-produced.

Piétacho, P., J. Mollen, A. Poker, F. Bellefleur, J. Bellefleur, and W.M. Mark. 2000. *Mamit Puamuna: Ekuanitshit, Nutashkuan, Unamen-Shipi, Pakua Shipi*. CD. Mani-utenam: Studio Makusham.

Pilot, Rod. 1990. *Uitamunan*. CD. Self-produced.

– 1998. *Nukum*. CD. Self-produced. Studio TSA.

– and Robert Pilot. 2000. *Eka ashuapatetau Nitassinan Innu*. CD. Mani-utenam: Studio Makusham and Édition Eka ashuapatetau Nitassinan.

Pinette, Jean-François (Patof). N.d. Title unknown. CD. Produced by Moïse Jourdain. Uashat: Studio Inniun.

Puamun. N.d. *Innu*. CD. Self-produced. Pakua Shipu: Studio Puamun.

Richard, Zachary, composed with Florent Vollant. 2007. "Ekuan Ishpesh." *Lumière dans le noir*. CD. Zach Rich and Musicor.

Rock, Kathia. 2006. *Uitshinan*. Demo CD. Self-produced with Jacques Roy. Montreal: Studio de Jack and Shawn.

– 2007. "Quand le jour se lève." *Deviens-tu c'que tas voulu? L'année Daniel Boucher*. CD. Festival en chanson de la Petite-Vallée édition.

Sainte-Marie, Chloé. 1999. "Tshin nikaui" and "Ashtam uitshi." *Je pleures, tu pleures*. CD. Les Films Gilles Carle and Productions DOC.

– 2002. "Mishapan Nitassinan" and "E pamuteian e peikussian – Innu." *Je marche à toi*. CD. Octant Musique.

– 2005. "Ashuapimushuan." *Parle-moi*. CD. FGC Disques.

– 2009. *Nitshisseniten e tshissenitamin/Je sais que tu sais*. CD. GSI Musique.

Saint-Onge, Bill. 2004. *Maikan*. CD. Self-produced. Mani-utenam: Studio Makus-ham.

Set Léo. N.d. Cassette. *Ishkuess*. Self-produced.

Shaman Boyz (Josélito Fontaine). 2006. *Nishutetau*. CD. Self-produced. Mani-utenam: Studio Makusham.

Shanipiap (Geneviève McKenzie-Sioui). 1999. *La lune du Labrador*. Cassette and CD. Quebec: Studios Séquence, Simon Carpentier Musique et Son, and Les Disques Ishkueu.

Shauit. 2004. *Shapatesh Nuna*. CD. Self-produced. Mani-utenam: Studio Makusham.

– with Samian. 2007. "Les Nomades." Samian, *Face à soi-même*. CD. 7ième Ciel Records.

– with Samian. 2010. "Les Mots," "Délivrez les jeunes," and "So Much." Samian, *Face à la musique*. CD. 7ième Ciel Records.

Tepentamun. N.d. *Tepentamun*. Cassette. Recorded and mixed by Léonard McKenzie.

– N.d. *Nishapet*. CD. Self-produced.

Teueikan. N.d. *Teueikan*. Cassette. Self-produced.

– N.d. [Untitled]. CD. Pakua Shipu: Studio Puamun.

– 2000. *Nimushum*. CD. Self-produced. Mani-utenam: Studio Makusham.

Tipatshimun. 1999. *Pishum*. CD. Produced by David Penashue and Bob Moore. Goose Bay: Eagle Studios.

– 2004. *Tshenut*. CD. Self-produced. Happy Valley: Mukluk Studios.

Tremblay, Jean-François. 2005. "Tanite etuteiak." *Roches et racines*. CD. Self-produced. Quebec: Studio RSF, Studio 43, and Groupe Sismique.

Tshimun. N.d. *Nitanish*. Cassette. Self-produced.

Uashau Stone. 1994. *Menteta*. CD. Self-produced.

Uasheskun. 2007. *Ninan*. CD. Self-produced. Mani-utenam: Studio Makusham.

Ussinniun. N.d. *Metshu*. Cassette and CD. Winnipeg: Maddock Studio; Village-des-Hurons, Quebec: Musique Premières Nations.

Vollant, Florent. 1999. *Nipaiamianan*. CD. Studio Montana, Productions 44.1, and Productions Makusham.

– c. 2001. *Sheueu. Échos du passé des Innuatsh*. CD. Studio Montana, Productions 44.1, and Productions Makusham.

– 2003. *Katak^u*. CD. Enregistrements D7/DEP.

– 2008a. "Nitshiuenan" (2003). *Québec*. CD. Putamayo World Music.

– 2008b. "Viens avec moi." *Hommage à Ronald Bourgeois: J'ai trouvé dans une chanson … v. À l'infini communications.

– 2009. *Eku Mamu*. CD. Studio Montana and Disques Tempête.

– with Innu professors and children. 2002. *Nikamunissa: Innu-auass nikamu*. CD. Uashat mak Mani-utenam: Studio Makusham and ICEM.

– with Claire Pelletier. 2005. "Le Picbois." *Beau Dommage: Hommage*. CD. Spectra Musique.

– with Samian. 2007. "Sur le dos d'une tortue." Samian, *Face à soi-même*. CD. 7ième Ciel Records.

– with Samian. 2010. "Tshinanu." Samian, *Face à la musique*. CD. 7ième Ciel Records.

– with Gilles Vigneault. 2010. "Jack Monoloy." Gilles Vigneault, *Retrouvailles*. CD. Productions Tandem.

Wapikoni Mobile (various artists). 2006. *Compilation musicale, Uashat mak Mani-utenam 2007*. Demo CD. Wapikoni Mobile.

– 2007a. *Compilation musicale, Lac-John-Matimekosh 2007*. Demo CD. Wapikoni Mobile.

- 2007b. *Compilation musicale, Uashat mak Mani-utenam 2007.* Demo CD. Wapikoni Mobile.
- 2008a. *Compilation musicale, Pessamit 2008.* Demo CD. Wapikoni Mobile.
- 2008b. *Compilation musicale, Uashat mak Mani-utenam 2008.* Demo CD. Wapikoni Mobile.
- 2009. *Compilation musicale, Uashat mak Mani-utenam 2009.* Demo CD. Wapikoni Mobile.
- 2010. *Compilation musicale, Uashat mak Mani-utenam 2010.* Demo CD. Wapikoni Mobile.
- 2011. *Compilation musicale, Uashat mak Mani-utenam 2011.* Demo CD. Wapikoni Mobile.

NOTES

1   This revalorization has been described as a "process of healing and renewal" (see Diamond, Cronk, and von Rosen 1994, 12).
2   There are approximately 15,000 Innu living in thirteen communities (eleven Band Councils) in Quebec and Labrador, as well as in urban centres. Eight of these communities are found on the North Coast of the St Lawrence River and the Gulf of St Lawrence, and the other communities are found around Lake St Jean, near Schefferville, as well as along Labrador's Atlantic Coast. The Innu are also known by the name Montagnais, given by colonials. Innu (or Ilnu) is the name they give themselves and the one by which they wish to be referred; they are part of the Algonquian cultural and linguistic group.
3   The information presented comes chiefly from my master's research in anthropology (Audet 2005a) and from my current doctoral research (2006–12) and has been updated until the time of publication. The Innu have been a part of my life since 1997. During my academic training, I strengthened my relations with the Innu and my knowledge of this area of research by completing an ethnographic study of Innu popular music in the Ekuanitshit, Uashat mak Mani-utenam, and Pessamit communities. I engaged in intensive fieldwork during the summer and fall of 2003 and 2009. Since 2003 I have been in ongoing collaboration with the Innu from Quebec City up to the North Coast. I am currently undertaking doctoral studies on Aboriginal popular music in Quebec and its relational dynamics. Transcriptions and translations of the songs presented here were done by Simon Mollen, Jimmy McKenzie, and Sonny Hervieux and were revised by Caroline Malek and Yvette Mollen. Some of these songs are also taken from the album covers when available. I would like to thank the Social Sciences and Humanities Research Council of Canada for awarding me with master's (2003–04) and doctoral (2006–10) fellowships. For more information on my theoretical approach and methodology, see Audet (2005a, 1–36; 2010). Some information mentioned here is also published in French in an article and a book that emerged from the same research (Audet 2005b, Audet forthcoming).
4   The Innu Nikamu festival was founded in Mani-utenam in 1985.

5 Examples are Studio Makusham in Mani-utenam, the Inniun Studio in Uashat, and many other home or school studios.

6 The SOCAM (Société de communication Atikamek-Montagnaise) is a broadcasting network in the Innu and Atikamekw communities. It was founded in 1983 and celebrated its twenty-fifth birthday in October 2008. It was implemented within the framework of the Conseil Attikamek-Montagnais (CAM), by which the Innu and Atikamekw had collaborated to claim their rights from various governments (see http://www.socam.net).

7 Examples can be found in the list of Internet sites. Also, search "Innu" at http://www.youtube.com for a good selection of Innu music and videos. A site called Innutube was created in June 2008 by Innu Jérôme Labbé from Pessamit but was closed down in July 2009.

8 In *Dictionnaire montagnais-français*, we find *makushan* [*mukušan*] defined as a "festin de graisse suivi de danse, banquet rituel" [feast of animal fat followed by dance, a ritual banquet] (Drapeau 1999, 243). Today, on the North Coast of the St Lawrence, the Innu also commonly refer to the traditional dance as *makusham*. According to Frank Gouldsmith Speck, feasts with drum songs and collective dances are the only ceremonial events that take the form of festivals among the north-eastern Algonquians. These types of hunting feasts are known in Algonquian literature as all-you-can-eat feasts. Speck also refers to these feasts by the name *cabetowan* (*shaputuan*) (passage lodge) (Speck 1977, 103–4, 207), which also names the large gathering tent in which these feasts take place (103–7, 206–10). He specifies that the ceremony accompanied by dance is named *magucan* (Naskapis) or *muk^Wcan* (Montagnais). The direction of the dance can be clockwise or counterclockwise, but in my experience it is most generally clockwise. However, as Speck writes, it can take the shape of a figure-eight, thereby alternating the direction between the hoops of the eight (104).

9 This meal is generally prepared using the hunted meat, bannock (Innu bread without yeast), and caribou fat (made of crushed and boiled caribou bones).

10 For example, Florent Vollant now plays an Indigenous hand drum during shows, but this drum is not a traditional Innu teueikan; it is a hand drum given to him by an Algonquin friend (interview with Florent Vollant, 2009). Philippe McKenzie completely abandoned the teueikan when an elder singer on the teueikan told him not to play with it. He then played the beat with other instruments and musicians, such as bongo drummers (interview with Philippe McKenzie, 2003). In the videoclip of the song "Ashtam Nashu" by Kashtin (see Youtube/Kashtin/"Ashtam Nashu"), we can see Innu women and Florent Vollant dancing the makushan and Claude McKenzie playing the teueikan, but it is probably the only time he has played it, having made an exception for the purpose of the video (interview with Claude McKenzie 2009). Also, to beat the rhythm, some Innu play the guitar while striking the case. Innu guitar playing is also characterized by a beating style of picking. Some women are also appropriating the teueikan practice to express themselves and accompany their songs. This is a complex subject, which I address briefly in my master's thesis (see Audet 2005a, 54, 61, 108–9; Audet forthcoming).

11 This song is analyzed later in this chapter.

12 The song "Ekuan pua," composed by Philippe McKenzie (titled "Tshekuan ma kie tshe tutaman" on his circa 1977 and 1982 albums) and popularized by Claude McKenzie (1996) and by the Québécois singer Chloé Sainte-Marie (2009), expresses an identity that is strongly shared and lived by many Innu. It is the song of the nomad Innu of yesterday and today, who live their lives seeking food, seeking their way, seeking their reason for living, seeking balance in mobility, and seeking their place in a world in which they do not always feel familiar and welcome (see Audet 2005a, 123–4; Audet forthcoming).

13 "Uisha, uishama" (Invite Me, or Yes Really) is a song credited to Alexandre McKenzie III, Claude McKenzie's grandfather; it is sung to the women to accommodate them, honour them, and thank them (Kashtin 1991). Speck (1977, 92, 184–5) mentions an old drum song that is possibly an earlier version of the song known today as "Uisha, uishama." It was sung to him in Sept-Îles by Alexandre Mackenzie of the Michikamau band in 1925, who would have learned it from his grandfather, who would have learned it from his father, Jérôme Antoine, who would have received it in dream and then transmitted it to the following generations. The song's lyrics are "uca' uca'm kabetci' eminona'gonewatega" (because of him [the caribou] who comes, it looks fine) (Speck 1977, 184–5).

14 He bases his reflection on ethnographic information provided by Hallowell (1960).

15 "Great Man" is a translation of *Mishtapeu*, a powerful and clairvoyant spirit guide akin to and connected with a human soul, a messenger between humans and nonhumans. This spirit guide is associated with humans who have a connection with him by means of wilful concentration, singing and drumming, works of visual art, looking into a mirror, into water, or into the eyes of an animal, and the shaking tent ritual (see Speck 1977, Vincent 1973, Preston 2002, and Tanner 1979).

16 This description was written by Danielle Descent, a psychologist married to an Innu of Mani-utenam and residing there, to describe Innu music in a grant application for the third edition of the Innu Nikamu festival in 1987.

17 The Innu elder Paul-Arthur McKenzie (father of the popular singer Claude McKenzie) is a teueikan singer and a great singer of the Catholic songs in Innu-aimun. See Paul-Arthur McKenzie's recordings *Aiamieun Nikamun* (n.d.) and *Shuk ka shatshishk tiu* (n.d.).

18 It is possible that they also learned how to play some European instruments with trading post agents, as was the case for the Inuit, Cree, Métis, and many other Aboriginals (see Preston 1985, Lederman 1990, Whidden 1990, 2007).

19 Today, this river and part of its drainage basin are completely protected by the 2003 Preservation of Natural Heritage Law, making it the first aquatic reserve of Quebec (Ministère du développement durable, environnement et parcs du Québec 2003).

20 This song is transcribed in Innu-aimun and translated in French and English on the album cover (P. McKenzie 2000).

21 On his second album, Samian (2010) also does a cover of "Tshinanu" with Florent Vollant that includes extracts from Kashtin and a rap text in French that

underlies the power of the song. See http://www.youtube.com/watch?v=ab83J2_
AfuQ (accessed 15 November 2010).

22 It has to be noted that since the beginning of 2008, Claude McKenzie has given
up alcohol.

23 The Assumption of the Virgin and the Feast of Our Lady of Pessamit are celebrated on 15 August. In Pessamit this is like a national festival, celebrated as the
Fête des Innus, similar to St Jean Baptist Day for the Québécois. For the Innu,
15 August is characterized by a religious procession and great festivities, uniting
Innu of various communities. In nomadic times in Pessamit, it coincided with
the departure of the Innu families upon their great journey by canoe to their
hunting land.

24 Some are songwriter-composer-singers, like Kathia Rock, who have been performing for many years; these women have been joined recently by artists such
as Alek-Sandra Vollant-Cormier, Wendy Moar, and Jennifer Bellefleur. Several
other female Innu sing with groups, including Sharon Grégoire Penashue, Annie
Hervieux, Delvina Bacon, Uapukun Mestokosho, and Shanice Mollen-Picard.

25 Sung in Innu-aimun by Chantal Bellefleur in a 2003 interview. The song was
translated from Innu-aimun into French by Chantal Bellefleur and then translated into English for this chapter.

26 See http://www.samian.ca (accessed 9 June 2011); and
http://www.musiqueplus.com/samian/so-much (accessed 9 June 2011).

27 "Yo" can be understood to mean *iu* (he says) (McNulty and Basile 1981, 16). However, Shauit did not consciously intend this significance (interview with Shauit
Aster, 2005).

28 The Innu expression used here, *tsin a*, is an abbreviation of *tshitshisseniten a* (you
know?) in the current language.

29 *Patshitinaman* (to give). In this case, *patshitinaman* means to let go of bad emotions in order to improve one's state of mind.

21

Aboriginal Popular Music in Quebec: Influences, Issues, and Rewards

INTERVIEW: FLORENT VOLLANT WITH VÉRONIQUE AUDET

Florent Vollant is Innu, from Mani-utenam, Quebec, and a member of the former duo Kashtin. An inspired artist, spirit seeker, proud defender of his culture, songwriter, composer, and performer of folk-country-rock/pop music in the Innu-aimun language, he is an important figure in the Québécois and Aboriginal popular music scene in Quebec. The first music he was exposed to was traditional song accompanied by the *teueikan* (the traditional Innu drum) that he heard as a child in Labrador. Growing up, he also listened to folk music and to American and Québécois country music on the radio, and he was also influenced by his family, who sang and played various instruments. In Mani-utenam he also immersed himself in the Gregorian chants he heard in residential school, as well as the Beatles, Eagles, and the folk/protest music of Bob Dylan, Richard Séguin, and Native artists such as Buffy Sainte-Marie, Willie Dunn, Willy Mitchell, and Morley Loon. For nine years he accompanied prominent Innu musician Philippe McKenzie, most notably on his album *Mistashipu* (1982). In 1984 he formed the group Kashtin (Tornado) with Claude McKenzie, and from 1989 to 1995 they achieved national and international success, issuing three albums that were awarded four Felix awards: *Kashtin* (1989), *Innu* (1991), and *Akua Tuta* (1994).

In 1985 he co-founded Innu Nikamu, an Aboriginal music festival in Mani-utenam, and in 1998 he founded Studio Makusham. He has also produced three solo albums, *Nipaiamianan* (1999), which won a Juno award in 2001, *Katak^u* (2003), and *Eku Mamu* (2009). With *Katak^u*, he won the Guy Bel Award for the best male performance in 2008 at the Pully Lavaux festival in Switzerland. He has also collaborated with artists such as Zachary Richard, Gilles Vigneault, Marc Déry, Richard Séguin, Éric Lapointe, Claire Pelletier, Jeff Smallwood, Robbie Robertson, Gilles Sioui, and Samian. He created the soundtracks for various Innu and Aboriginal films, such as *Mesnak* (Sioui-Durand and Vollant 2011), and for television series, such as *Le monde perdu* (VRAK TV), and he is the host of the television music series *Makusham* (APTN). Spokesperson for many causes, he was honoured in 1994 with the title Artist for Peace.

During my study in Mani-utenam for my master's research, I met Florent Vollant at the community radio station, CKAU FM Kushapatshikan, for the first of many interviews with him. At that time he was finalizing his album *Katak^u*, and he had just received the album cover and was very happy with it. What follows is the edited interview that I conducted with Vollant on 17 September 2003, in which we talk about his musical influences, creativity, and the challenges that contemporary musicians face in promoting and finding support for their musical careers.

VA: Kuei, Florent Vollant. Could you please start by telling me about your journey in music?

FV: Kuei! I was born in Labrador, and I grew up in a place where all the family on my father's side lived by hunting and fishing. At that time we didn't have electricity or running water, but we had a small transistor radio. I think it was on the radio that I first heard music [other than Innu traditional music]. I was probably four or five years old. It was English music from Labrador, and mostly country. There was Hank Williams, all that kind of music, and I liked it a lot. I continued to like it, and I played it as well. Of course, my parents sang country songs, and it was natural to have this type of influence. We also had traditional music at home, because there were songs and dances, for celebrations and for making a *makusham*[1] when the hunt was good. I kept these images. I was young, four or five years old. My parents were very musical and there was a lot of music at our home. There were also the lullabies used to put babies to sleep. Peu, peu, peu [pronounced bew or bow], all using [vocables]. Often we remember the gestures in these lullabies. I remember all that; it has marked me. When there was a traditional dance, or a traditional chant, I was there, I was very impressed, I stood next to the dancers. I was fascinated by that and I thought that my parents were giants, I saw them like ... Wow! On top of that, there was a sense of celebration; it was strong, intense. I lived through their gestures, their dances, all that ... From there, at that point, I saw and heard a guitar, because there was a singer who had a knack for western songs: Émile Grégoire. You will surely be hearing about him. He really did something new. My uncles also played the guitar. My father [Thomas Vollant] played the harmonica in an extraordinary fashion, and he didn't even know it. My parents were people who really loved music. But my father didn't really play in public. He played for himself, for us, for the family. My uncles played the violin. If you think about it, these are all instruments which are transportable. We didn't often see guitars with these people, as they were nomads. Harmonicas transport well, a violin, perhaps, an accordion as well, you can transport these instruments; it's not too complicated. A guitar, that's a little complicated. These instruments all had a spirit that they transported with them. And a teueikan transports well. It's in the spirit; these instruments fit within the nomadic life of the Innu. The Innu exchanged these things amongst themselves. In view of the fact that they were isolated, they often expressed their distance with instruments or with singing, and with dances, all this ... I grew up with this.

Émile Grégoire came to our place. The first time I played a guitar, it was his guitar. He sang Hank Williams tunes, and I found that extraordinary! When the party was finished, and everyone left, all that remained was the guitar. That appealed to me! I had observed him, what he was doing, and I wanted to do the same thing. At that time I was seven, eight, nine, ten, twelve years old. I was in residential school. At residential school I learned and I heard religious chants. But I always enjoyed all kinds of music. In residential school, I found Gregorian chants were fascinating – I really liked them. Around thirteen, fourteen, fifteen years old, after I left residential school, I learned that there were other kinds of music you could play. I started playing music when I was fourteen or fifteen years old. I started here, learning music at Mani-utenam, playing the guitar, and then accompanying. I played for many years with Philippe McKenzie, who had a talent for writing songs and for making music. I was the accompanist in the group, and I sometimes sang as well. During my teenage years, I was listening to the Beatles, Bob Dylan. I listened throughout this period to folk, protest songs, everything that would lead to an identity and to a day of action, a claim, to all these types of activities. It was very influential. I also listened to Native folksingers, and with Morley Loon, that was the first time I heard a folksinger who sang in Innu, in Cree. And there were others, Willie Dunn, Willy Mitchell, Philippe McKenzie, a whole movement. During that period, there was a return. When we went to residential school, we lost a lot, a whole generation, where we were completely withdrawn from our parents, from our culture, our pride. For two generations, we were separated from our identity, and an identity was imposed on us with people saying to us, "You are not going to sing any more traditional songs; you are not going to dance the makusham any more; you are going to sing church hymns!" I withdrew from music for several years. When I came back there was that whole era of protest, and musically I became involved in it. I went back to the traditional drum, to the teueikan, I heard singing, and I started to dance the makusham, with pride. All this is to say that there was a whole movement, a time for Indigenous people everywhere in America. There was a period of action, a movement, an awareness, which was saying, "That's not us. This is us." Music at that time worked to influence us; we were greatly influenced by folksingers. We really identified with Neil Young, Bob Dylan, and then there were also Indigenous folksingers, Buffy Sainte-Marie, among others. During that period our sense of pride was very strong. We were definitely influenced by all these movements. The music became a way of telling the world, "We also exist. We also have an opinion, a culture, a language, rhythms, and a soul which is capable of reaching and uniting people. We, too, have an openness because we were influenced by country music, by the Beatles, the Eagles, Cat Stevens." That period was very important and it was very influential. Musically, this influenced me greatly, and it continues to influence me. Again it's the Beatles; I think everyone who makes music has to listen to and appreciate what these musicians did.

VA: It was revolutionary!

FV: Revolutionary, absolutely! In another way, the whole phenomenon of traditional music has always attracted me. Whether it's Cree, Ojibwa, Dene, or the Navajo of the United States, I've always been attracted to traditional song. I was definitely influenced by these kinds of music. This music appeals to me enormously, because I grew up within this. Actually, I make music that is more current. I did an entire period with Kashtin that was much more folk, more acoustic. This was an extraordinary experience, to share rhythms around the world! We were heard everywhere! We were even not aware of what we had done. It's extraordinary. When I go for a walk and someone says, "he has made it there because of your influence ..." It wasn't our aim or mission with Kashtin, to do what we did, to be so influential in bringing awareness to Aboriginal music. That was not our goal. Our goal was to be on stage, sharing and performing our best, and at the time it was a matter of survival for us. When we talk about music, when I say that music heals, it's at this level. It healed us, and we wanted it to heal those who listened to us. When I speak of music which heals, I speak of the roots of traditional music; it's music that heals. It's done for that [healing]. Whether it is Hurons, Mohawks, traditional music is a medicine. It's like that across America, from what I've seen. Native music, it's a music which was originally a medicine. It's spiritual, that's for certain; it's not a performance. It's a spiritual communication. Myself, I guard this spirit, even today, in the music that I make. If it doesn't make me feel good, I can't see how it would make someone else feel good. You know, I'm convinced that music heals. In any case it has helped me enormously. Without music, I don't know how I would stay healthy. At the foundation, Indigenous music is a music of medicine. That's what brings your consciousness to the spiritual level. It is the path to spirituality. For me that's it.

VA: Spirituality, is that broadly defined?

FV: Yes. Broad enough. Me, I don't have a problem with that. And the word that captures that idea is "inspiration." It is a derivative of the word spiritual. Things inspired, these are things that are from another world. It begins in a dream; in my conscience, it is there. That's my reference. For me, when there's no inspiration, it doesn't feel right for me. I don't say that I'm better off than anyone else. This is my way. If it works and if I can reach out to people with that, I'm happy. I have no intention other than to be good at what I do.

VA: How does this music come to you? How are you inspired?

FV: For me it's a slow affair. I don't sit down and do incantations and then this happens. It's not that at all! Sometimes it involves others. In the project that I just completed [*Katak^u* album] music was suggested to me, which came via other musicians who eventually joined me. This was natural, for me, to become involved and to then be inspired for the texts, because I had a music that came from someone else, from another creator. That's what he had proposed, and it was very cool. Sometimes I'll be walking, then, wow! We must do that! It was Zachary Richard who said, "We just have to know how to present ourselves, to be there at the right time." That's right. When inspiration comes, you have to be there, to be available. That's inspiration. It can happen almost anytime. But you must be there, be conscious of it; there must be an opening. That's it, for me, that's the gesture you have to make. Sometimes, it is a sacrifice to be available and open. Afterwards, there is a whole process. The thought, the light, which will become a song … I liken it to a fire. To be available, it's to have the spark that starts the fire, then inspiration is the wind that will start making the fire. That's it for me. Then the fire, you have to look after it as well. One blow and it's out … There, you have to pay attention, because a fire also burns, and it can be dangerous! This trade is also dangerous, because you become popular, and people see you in another manner. That's what's difficult to deal with, because artists who are creators, like sculptors, painters, probably also comedians, these are people who are tortured, I would say. When one is at a certain level, it can be easy to be available and to have this sensibility that is very difficult to deal with. Because you see and you hear things that other people probably do not hear, everywhere, in life. That's what inspires you. It's very, very, special. I say this without pretension. I've seen that there are some people more affected than me at this level. Musicians and artists have this sensitivity. For me, sometimes a word – clack! – that brings me to an extraordinary universe. One word, just one that I find resonates for me. You have music in that word. Sometimes it's a sentence I heard from someone, then I tell myself I'll finish my tune with that. I just end there. I have nothing else. With that context, I say look, I must finish my song with this phrase that I had heard. Everything else, I must work to bring myself there, the music too. It's not like I'm there and sit down and write for three months. I never do that. I would be incapable of doing that. Sit myself down and search for music; it's not like that at all for me. Sometimes I'm sitting, then I find two, three harmonies that go well together. Then whoup! I have the ending of a song that I found a long time ago. Whoup! I'll put it together, tak! I never force it. That's why it takes time. That's how I do things myself. I am very influenced by Indigenous rhythms. I love it, but I am also very open to other music as well. I'll listen to a Ray Charles song, and I find it extraordinary. Ben Harper, I think he has a wonderful voice, he has everything in his voice! I love music, that's it!

VA: That's interesting. Would you like to talk to me a little about the festival [Innu Nikamu]? Is the festival really important in Innu music?

FV: During the first years of the festival, I was one of the people who started things. We wanted a gathering – music is something that brings people together. We knew the musicians, and at the time, there were few Indigenous musicians we knew who had recorded. Very few. No one knew what we were doing, I think. It was just us who didn't think it was impossible. There was a desire there that you can still feel twenty years later, because we did it with heart and soul. If we had no spirit, we would have done it for three years and then, bye-bye! It's over. It is a gathering that has grown because it was done initially with a beautiful spirit. It's still there! It still lasts! And I hope it will continue. It's certainly very important, because first of all, it's the biggest Indigenous gathering in Quebec. There's no other event in Quebec which brings together as many Indigenous people in the same place at the same time. That's the spirit of the festival. The music, it is the pretext to gather people. We see that people here, they are in contact with Atikamekw. They are in contact with Innu of Labrador. They are in contact with Naskapis and with the whole Lower North Coast. It's a large gathering! There are the Huron, there are the Cree, you know. It's as enormous an exchange as one can have at the community level. At that level there's much pride. It helps to maintain pride. That's what the festival is to me. A youngster starting off, who is more or less comfortable playing music, that doesn't bother me at all. Everyone has the right to speak. We don't discriminate. Sure there are others that perform more, they have their albums; all that, it's also good. It influenced everybody. It's unpretentious. It's organized like that; it has its stamp. I always liked that. Years ago I did the programming, and there are other years that I've had other things to do. But I'm involved. I did the programming this year. I worked a lot, I spent the entire summer working on that project.

VA: There are many groups that pass through during the four days.

FV: Very much so. We could have done yet another weekend, and then there would have been even more. Music is very important among Indigenous peoples.

VA: That's why I want to do something about it. I find that there is really so much to discover. It's also unknown!

FV: It's really not well known! Totally unknown, I would say, even excluded. On the industry level, that's for certain. But presently, for example, you go to the Juno Awards, there is a Native category. There's also a Native category at the American Music Awards. Myself, I won a Juno award. That gave me nothing! You don't have the support.[2]

VA: It's how to get there as well, I imagine?

FV: Yes, but not as much as that. No, you can get there. Maten[3] could get there. Because they need to make it there. They need it, they must listen; they must have stuff. But the industry as such, forget it, you don't really ... I have a chance, because I've already been there. They're familiar with me now. That's true. But the others, I don't know. Besides, it's a huge investment. Before getting to a level where you're recognized, it's enormous, the time and money. There's a lot of money before you go in front of the microphone and sing. At that level, there's so much money.

VA: I imagine you also have to have mentors? Or someone who can show you the way ...

FV: Yes, yes, but the music must be inspiring as well. It's not always like that but in my case it is.

VA: In any case, I find that it would be good if it could be more widely known.

FV: Yes, but while it's good to be known, are you sure it's something you need?

VA: Because it has to work at home, inside, and in the communities?

FV: That's right. It has to work at home. If you go out there, there is no credible support for Aboriginal music. No help. Zero. You know! That's right, there is no help. It's embarrassing, what they give. But young people they will play in bars. It's the ones who help you to finally continue. They're the ones who buy your CDs too, this network. Artists work like that. They travel and they sell after the shows; so that's it, in the communities. But there is no level of support for Indigenous music from the government. And the young people, many artists, do not want to apply for grants, because the paperwork is so complicated! Besides, are they going to give it to you? I'll do all the paperwork, if you can tell me that it will work, that I'll not receive a reply, "Oh, you were not far off!"

I put in three months doing that. The next time you're not going to do that again! You'll see the little bar owner, he'll deal with you, he'll say, "Look, I'll give you this rate. You play this hour to this hour." That's concrete. He won't say to you after the show, "You were great, I think we'll give you this payment." It's regulated up front. Aboriginal artists don't want to take too many risks, and it requires too much, for an answer of which you are not sure. There are programs for Aboriginals. But most Aboriginals don't profit. It's those who have time to do so, who specialize in these kinds of things. It works for them. They make money. That's what they do. But in any case, that's me, just trying to find the balance with it all. And to encourage and support young people starting. I have a recording studio [Makusham]. It took me three years to assemble the studio. As well, it was the community that built it, the youth in the community built it for me. I say to myself, it's as much for them. They go there, and they try to find the money that allows them to dream of having an album. It is a way of being known across the circuit, finally to make the circuit. We made two albums for children. We had Philippe McKenzie, Meshikamau, a group from Labrador, we had Maten two times … We did music documentaries, Zachary Richard,[4] Marc Déry,[5] and eventually it was full of people.[6]

va: Can you talk about what you say through your music?

fv: Ah! What I realize with the last project I did, I always spoke of the North. A lot. I speak about the North, about people who live in the North, I talk about the space. In the last project I talked a lot about nomads. I'm always moving. *Katak*ᵘ is the title of the album: "Away." We come from afar, and hopefully we will go far. That's me, my world. I speak about the nomads, their gestures, their dreams, their movements, their displacement; I speak about their past and where they came from. The Innu. I also do prayers. That's what I sing.

va: Do you have political ambitions? In the sense of, for example, to say who the Innu are or to encourage listeners to experience another lifestyle?

fv: I am very disappointed with politics in general. I admire those who can work within a system like that. I'm talking about politicians. I have some admiration for them. For me, to live in that type of spirit, I'd never be capable of it. I find that there is no Aboriginal policy. There is no intention, I would say, of gathering, truly. One thing which we once had very strong, and now become weaker, is solidarity. They succeeded in dividing us. It's very serious. The system imposed on us has led us to be divided. And, at the same time, they idealized us as people who are able to be independent and in solidarity with one another. Then we are asked to be supportive and to be together! We wonder what others are capable of doing, in a system like this! Aboriginals, being asked to be together. Otherwise, it's not worth discussing! And Quebecers are not even able to be together! Neither are the others. I say Quebecers, but other nations there, the current president of the United States [Bush at that time] – a judge appointed him! This is not the people! The people are divided. Then we are accused of being divided. What's that? Don't ask us to do things in a system that you yourselves aren't even able to do! That's what I say. Then they ask us not to be bankrupt, when everyone else is bankrupt. It's just been fifty years since we've had that system! Not three hundred years! People want to warm themselves around a fire. Okay, that keeps us there for thousands of years. But at the same time, they are bent on turning it off. Because there is no support. You want to warm yourself around my fire! Come on, don't put water on my fire! Then at the same time, you will send the world to me to warm everyone! I must maintain my fire too. My kids, they need it! Then you are interested in my fire? Bring your fire, bring your wood. We will make things together. Not just for my children, for your children too. That's how I see myself. There is no support on the language level. There isn't! Music, forget that! There isn't anything! But the world, they want us to sing in Innu! But they won't support us. That's when I tell you that they want our fire, but they do not want to deal with it.

VA: It's in effect about being Innu and succeeding in the "modern" system at the same time?

FV: At the same time. You have to be strong in everything, you know? The social problems that we know, and all that, it's not there for nothing!

VA: We talked about music that heals, but does singing in Innu, and telling stories of Innu life, help you to continue, to live?

FV: It helps me to continue. I also hope for others, that with the music that I do, I keep the fire. If there are others who want to maintain that –

sculptors, painters, professors, doctors, surgeons, lawyers, politicians –
let's do it! Whether it's whites, nonwhites, whatever. Myself, that's what
I think I do. I hope that it helps. It helps me anyway. This is what I think
about things and I am very proud of my project [*Katak^u* album]!

VA: Great. I'd like to thank you for speaking with me.

FV: You're welcome!

NOTES

1 The *makusham* (as pronounced by Florent Vollant), or *makushan*, is an Innu
traditional feast where people gather around a meal of hunted food, involving
teueikan songs and the Innu traditional round dance, also called *makusham*. See
also chapter 20 in this volume.

2 Even if there is an Aboriginal category at the Juno Awards, as well as organizations like Canadian Aboriginal Music Awards and Aboriginal Peoples Choice
Music Awards, there is no Aboriginal category at the Gala de l'ADISQ, the Québécois gala that presents the Félix Awards. Aboriginal artists from Quebec are
listed mostly in the category "Québécois artist of the year – Interpretation in
other languages," along with artists singing in English, Spanish, and so on. To
overcome these situations, in 2011 the Société de communication Atikamekw-
Montagnais founded the Gala of Music Teweikan, which honours and awards
Aboriginal music and artists from Quebec and Labrador
(see http://www.teweikan.com).

3 Maten is a music group from Mani-utenam comprised of young Innu in their
twenties and thirties, which was very popular in the Innu communities at the
beginning of the 2000s.

4 Zachary Richard is a well-known Cajun songwriter-composer-performer from
Louisiana and a good friend and collaborator of Florent Vollant. Among others,
they have done the song "Ekuan Ishpesh" together (Richard 2007, Vollant 2009).

5 Marc Déry is a Québécois songwriter-composer-performer and a friend and collaborator of Florent Vollant. He came to Studio Makusham in Mani-utenam,
where he created and recorded the song "Ninanu" (Déry 1999) with the help of
Vollant.

6 Since this interview, more than ten new Innu albums have been produced at
Studio Makusham.

22

Gilles Sioui: Supporting and Performing with Aboriginal Artists in Quebec

INTERVIEW: GILLES SIOUI WITH VÉRONIQUE AUDET AND DONNA LARIVIÈRE

Gilles Sioui is a well-known Huron-Wendat musician, born in Wendake (Huron Village), and the son of the late Wendat grand chief Claude Sioui.[1] A professional musician since 1974, Sioui is a singer-songwriter, a talented and inspired guitar soloist and accompanist, a self-taught musical director and arranger, and a special education teacher. He performs contemporary Aboriginal music, as well as Québécois and Canadian blues-folk-rock, and he is highly regarded on the Quebec music scene. Sioui started his career as a bassist and then drummer in his brother Bruno's band Ook Pik. In the late 1970s, he developed his unique style as a guitarist, performing the music of Jimmy Hendrix and Neil Young in Quebec City bars and eventually performing with a variety of musicians and bands. He joined the Stephen Barry Band, which supported tours of Big Mama Thornton and Big Moose Walkers in the 1980s. He also created the trio Storm/Soft Rain in the 1980s, a group that divided its time between the south of France and Quebec. During the 1980s he was invited by Florent Vollant and Claude McKenzie to join their group Kashtin (Tornado), and he toured with Kashtin during their North American tour. In the mid-1990s he also accompanied the Québécois singer Kevin Parent. In 1997 he formed a new group, the Midnight Riders, and they produced their first album.

Sioui has performed on over fifty albums and in many concerts. Known for his mastery of the guitar as much as for his musical inspiration, he has worked with many notable musicians, including Bob Walsh, Stephen Barry, Richard Séguin, Chloé Sainte-Marie, Marc Déry, Wilfred LeBouthillier, Georges Langford, Guy Bélanger, Steve Hill, Breen Leboeuf, John McGale, Dan Bigras, Shawn Phillips, Carl Tremblay, Roy Robi, Vincent Vallières, Mishka, Jay Sewall, Andrée Dupré, Jean-Pierre Cyr, Gaétan Racine, and Kanu, as well as with a number of Indigenous artists or groups, such as Kashtin, Florent Vollant, Claude McKenzie, Bryan André, Ussinniun, Taima/Elisapie Isaac, Sakay Ottawa, Pascal Ottawa, Arthur Petiquay, Laura Niquay, Wendy Moar, Stéfanie Morin-Roy, Patrick Gros-Louis, and Christian Shondak8a Laveau. Sioui has also participated in a number of events and projects that spotlight Native artists, including La Tournée Soleil Levant in 2005, *Tshenu, Gilles Sioui sur six cordes* at the Impérial in Quebec City, the Marché des Trois Sœurs/Fête des récoltes in Wendake, the Innu Nikamu festival in Mani-utenam, the show *Mishta Amun* at the Montcalm Palace in Quebec City in 2008, Canada Day celebrations in Ottawa in 2008, and the 475th anniversary of Gaspé in 2009. Since 2008 Sioui has been the official spokesperson for Centre de développement de la formation et de la main-d'œuvre Huron-Wendat. In this position, he regularly meets with Aboriginal youth to share his experiences as a singer-musician.[2]

The material presented here comments on Sioui's musical training, influences, and experiences while positioning him as an important contemporary Aboriginal musician in the Quebec popular music scene. The material was edited and assembled by Véronique Audet from two interviews conducted by her and Donna Larivière (Algonquin). The first interview took place on 20 May 2008 on the *Voix autochtones* (Indigenous Voices) radio program, on CKIA FM 88.3, Quebec City, with Donna Larivière and Véronique Audet. The second interview was conducted by Véronique Audet on 23 January 2009 in Quebec City.

DL: Hello, Gilles Sioui, and thank you for talking with us today.

VA: To start, as a well-known Indigenous Huron-Wendat musician, perhaps you could introduce yourself?

GS: Certainly. My name is Gilles Sioui, son of Claude Sioui, a furniture salesman. I was born in the community of Wendake, band number 777, and I am the luckiest human in the world! [Laughter.] For those who do not know, the community of Wendake is located approximately twenty kilometres north of Quebec [City]. It's a very assimilated community; a mixture of whites and Aboriginals.

I am a mixture of Huron on my father's side and Acadian and Irish on my mother's side. I discovered music through my brother and through the music itself, I think, which came to find me before I began to play. There are two ways I would say to dig the music: to be a fan of music, and I am firstly that; and the other, is to play the music, and that I do secondly. But I am always a fan. I listen to music to relax me. I listen to music to move me, to make me cry, to make me laugh, so I have all sorts of motivations.

VA: How would you describe the music that you play?

GS: Folk-rock with an Indigenous flavour. I learned how to play the guitar by [listening to] black bluesmen, B.B. King, Albert King, and Freddie King, and then some English guitarists like Eric Clapton, Peter Green, and Santana. I really like country, blues, folk, rock, metal, early rock; it's not really one precise style but a mix of everything.

VA: You are well known as a bluesman, is that right?

GS: Yes, yes. Basically I'm a bluesman. I like to think of myself in that way. I like to say that the blues is a lifestyle and not a style of music. In the blues, one would say that you are not entitled to happiness; there is something inside blocking you from reaching what is called happiness. Therefore, the music is the therapy for that, and the blues is the way of executing it.

VA: Do you make a link between your life, your Indigenous personal experience and your interest in the blues?

GS: Yes, because the blacks, in the United States, it was their style, their therapy. They began this style of music in the cotton fields, and it finished in completely shabby-looking clubs. And then when whites understood that they could make money from the blacks, that's when they put them in the market to make money on their backs. So this is to say that Indigenous music is twofold. For me, true Indigenous music is the traditional songs. But in the twentieth century there are many Indigenous groups playing many different styles of music. I'd rather see it like that than to believe that by buying a drum, we could play the same things as 5,000 years ago. That would be completely untrue.

But what is really thrilling for me is to see a man of a certain age sing with his drum, like the father of Claude McKenzie. For me that is stronger than all the groups in the world! And in today's world we have electricity, there are keyboards, lots of things, so we are certainly far from pure tradition, but I think as long as you put your heart into what you think, what you write, wherever you play, I think that's the Aboriginal way.

VA: In your lyrics or in your music, along with what is done with the heart, what comes most from your Aboriginal heritage?

GS: Often it's like a cry from the heart … I have many pieces about family, I did one about my father, one about my brother, about my sister, my mother, I'm doing another about my brother. My favourite subjects are the quest for love, lost love, and the environment. These are my subjects that I figure are not very white, not so modern. These are common old themes, but it will always be like that, always in the same vein.

VA: Does your song "Wendat Land" have an explicitly Wendat theme?

GS: Yes. My father was a chief. He died in 1987. During the time that I had a house in Huron Village, I just wanted to let it be known that his spirit would always be present over the village. And I wanted to speak about my house as well, I wanted to speak about how I felt each time I was there, because it's still like that when I go there. Right away when I go back, my heart starts to race, and that will never change. It's very special. Music is funny: you spend time working on a piece, and then sometimes it just falls, comes out of nowhere like that. Bing! Often at my house, when I start working, taking up the guitar, I'll never know what's going to come out. Often something works, sometimes it doesn't. It can't be forced. For the theme of "Wendat Land," I was sitting in my home in Huron Village, and when I picked up my guitar, I turned on the amp and that's what came out – *pang*! Like that, the first time, I never revised it. There are songs like that, that just appear out of nowhere. These are not the most brilliant songs in the world, but I am proud that they came out like that. There are people, pretty *grounded* at Huron Village, who are interested in translating "Wendat Land" into the Wendat language [which is not currently spoken anymore], and I'm certainly in favour of that. On the other hand, I wouldn't want to put it on disc, because there are already two versions on disc. I don't want to annoy the world with that. But I will give copies, perhaps for the radio and to those who want the single. I myself am curious to see the text, because those involved are concerned with translating word for word, so I'm intrigued!

VA: There are not many songs like that which speak of being Huron-Wendat, from Wendake!

GS: To us, this is the national hymn. So, perhaps if it is translated into Wendat, it will take another direction. They might make use of it in the church before Mass or before bingo games!

DL: Your songs are all in English. Is this a choice you've made?

GS: It's not a choice. My love of music in English came in high school when they began to show us how to speak in English. They had us learn English through Simon and Garfunkel, Bob Dylan, Neil Young, Cat Stevens. So for me, that was my first exposure to this sort of music. After that, my parents listened to Santana, Doobie Brothers, Pink Floyd, so I was pretty much on the English side when I was growing up instead of being on the side of Harmonium, Beau Dommage, or Les Séguin.[3] I think it's pure coincidence! Then I continued in English because I grew up in that! On the other hand, there is the eternal promise of a future album mostly in French.

DL: And why folk?

GS: Folk, country, blues, I find these sorts of music are all very accessible for musicians and for people as well. I find that the simpler musics are the ones that touch people's hearts. Take jazz, though it's more complicated or more intellectual for people, it touches only 10 per cent of people. I don't play folk music to reach the most people possible, but for me it is conducive to my personality. I'm a *folk-boy*, a *folk-man.*

VA: And you mainly play with electric guitar?

GS: Yes. At home it's very rare that I'll branch out, because I find it's a heck of an instrument! In the production studio I'm often invited to play the electric guitar. But like The Perls and The Band, they were formed with an electric guitar and still made good folk-rock.

DL: How long have you been playing guitar?

GS: The guitar, I would say it's my third accident in music. I started with the bass. Then, when I was younger, my parents wanted to pay for music lessons. My sister took classical piano lessons, and my brother took classical guitar, but I said I didn't want to because nothing interested me. Then at age sixteen, my brother had a group and he needed a bassist. He asked if I would be interested. Then we went and bought a bass, and without knowing how to play the bass, I quietly practised so I could join the group. Later, another group, they were missing a drummer. Thinking nothing of it, I went out and bought a drum set. I played drums for four years, then I discovered the guitar in my last year in CÉGEP [College of General and Vocational Education in the Quebec education system] when I was twenty-one years old. I didn't touch the guitar until I was twenty-one years old.

VA: I'd like to know what other things influenced your music before that?

GS: There are many other kinds of influences on the music as well. Before I was sixteen, at my house when my mother was doing her housework, she played records to pass the time. So I got caught up in it. On the other hand, at that time there was Gilbert Bécaud, [Salvatore] Adamo, Mireille Mathieu, whom I have nothing against at all! I was hooked at the age of thirteen in my father's car during a fishing trip; it was a song by Michel Pagliaro, I remember, which was playing on the radio. From that moment on, I realized my life would be lost without music in it. The flashback I have of that day! I arrived at school and I said to the teacher, "There's nothing much that interests me anymore." He said, "Go talk to the counsellor!" Lo and behold, I made an appointment with the guidance counsellor. I was thirteen then, and I said, "I just have music in my head. When the teacher is in front, I don't hear him, I hear music." Then he said, "It's simple, you're going to go into music." I said, "Wow! That's extraordinary, it's as simple as that!" When I arrived home and told my father, I'd prefer not to say what he said to me. So I didn't jump into music right away. That was a five-minute flash, I was really crazy. The other moment was similar. It was a recording by Donald Lautrec. My parents bought it for me when I was sick, to cheer me up. After listening to it fifty times, I thought I was possessed! I listened to that and then I sang the songs, then I did the guitar sounds with my mouth. That was an early influence. On the other hand, it was a long time after that before touching anything.

VA: [When you began with the guitar], was it to learn the guitar or to become part of a group?

GS: At the time I played drums, I earned my living with my brother. Then one crazy evening in Gaspésie when we were playing with the group, he showed me three chords, and then I practised these three chords – all night! Then the next morning before everyone woke up, I turned on the sound system. I put a mike in front of the guitar and when I listened to the sound that made in the loudspeakers, I turned up the sound system, I woke everybody up. I said, "That's it, I'm not play-ing drums anymore. From now on I'm playing the guitar!" When we got back to Quebec [City], I exchanged my drums for a guitar. It wasn't a very smart move but that's how it happened.

VA: This really led you where you are today!

GS: Yes, but the first six months, the time when you only know how to play one tune, the reality is that you've decided that you play, but you don't know how to play! I worked at it since I had plunged myself into it – I played sixteen hours a day for the first two years before achieving any satisfaction …

About my band Ook Pik: "Ook pik" is an Inuit word meaning "snowy owl." My sister often wore a fur coat with really big sunglasses, then when I saw her from afar, I thought she looked like that, so I nicknamed her Ook Pik. So in her honour, the group was named Ook Pik, and besides we wanted a word with an Aboriginal sound.

VA: You interpreted Aboriginal songs?

GS: Not at all! We were into disco! In those days, when you wanted to work, you had to know the Top 40 and at that time, it was the disco explosion, and there were groups like K.C. and the Sunshine Band, André Gagnon, the Quebec pianist, who at the time did disco hits.

VA: Did you compose anything?

GS: Not at all. My brother did a composition, very guitaristic, rhythmic, disco, and he asked me to write the words. I called it "Danse, danse, danse!" It was totally naive and insignificant but good; it was the first in a long series!

VA: For some time you've been collaborating with many musicians, sometimes Aboriginal and non-Aboriginal, some widely known and recognized such as Stephen Barry, Bob Walsh, Kevin Parent …

GS: Yes. This is by chance. I don't sell myself well. But this group came to search me out at home; they called me. Perhaps what they liked was the quality of the music. What the singers search for in a guitarist is somebody who won't crush them, instrumentally speaking. They want someone who is able to say much with little. Perhaps that's why people want me for collaborations. I've always said that it's about integrity. I only know one way of doing things and it's like that, with the heart. So maybe that's the basis of collaboration.

VA: Yes. What are your biggest collaborations, those that you are most proud of?

GS: Me, what I'm most proud of, was that, when I was young, I saw my idols in Quebec, in the clubs. And I thought to myself, they are as good as Eric Clapton, John Mayall, and Santana. That was Bob Walsh, Stephen Barry. Then I was asked to work with them. For me, it's as if I had worked with the greatest bluesmen in the world! Their style is very original, very strong, and their style is their own.

VA: They come from an anglophone environment in Quebec?

GS: Yes, Bob is Quebec-Irish, and Stephen Barry was born not far from Montreal. They are two Quebec anglophones.

VA: And they are very active in the Montreal scene?

GS: Yes, I think they are hands-down the best bluesmen.

VA: And they like to play with you!

GS: It's reciprocated!

DL: Let's talk a little bit about the show that will take place May 29 [2008] at the Impérial. You have many guests who will be present.

GS: Yes! We had carte blanche. It's been thirty-five years since I got the bug, and today it hasn't decreased in intensity or intent. We are celebrating the thirty-fifth anniversary of my career! We could have done a full show of my music, but I quickly get fed up with that idea. I thought of inviting the people who have been major influences for me. I will always remember the day Kashtin called me to be a part of the group; I will always remember when Bob Walsh called me; when Stephen Barry called me. Those were the best days of my life! Then I thought that for the public as well, it would be interesting. These are people that I have accompanied for most of my life. Of the newcomers there is Bryan André, who I love, and there are others who are farther away. In any case, I thought it was important to invite Bryan, because I find him very talented and he deserves to be shown there.

DL: It will be broadcast on SOCAM[4] in the Aboriginal communities Atikamekw and Innu [and later on the Aboriginal Peoples Television Network]. And you are also going to be with your band, Midnight Riders.

GS: Unfortunately, without my little brother. This show is being done for him actually. He belonged to that group, and then we decided not to replace him as guitarist, because it's unthinkable! So we work the two remaining guitarists a little harder, David Cardey and myself.

DL: It's a tribute.

GS: It is a tribute, yes, exactly. On that evening, I'm playing for him. I'm playing for everyone there, but I mean … I've always said that had my brother not played guitar, I would have missed out …

VA: On the Indigenous side, in the beginning you weren't identified as an Aboriginal musician apart from the name of your group Ook Pik?

GS: Aboriginal music came later, in a way, because at home in the village, we lost most of the oral traditions of music. Then, maybe in 1985, it started. I was invited to Innu Nikamu.

VA: Ah! This had to be the first edition, in 1985?

GS: Yes. Then right, that's where it started. I met Florent, Claude, we chatted. I did my little songs, which they reminded me of many years after.

VA: They had already heard about you as a musician?

GS: Yes. It was well known that I was a blues guitarist, that I was from Huron Village, and so forth. It started there. Then the day they invited me to join the band, Kashtin, was the beginning of playing on the reserves; then other performances came.

VA: Was this before Kashtin recorded their first disc?

GS: Ah yes!

VA: Were they called Kashtin at that time?

GS: Not at all! Claude was on bass, Florent was on guitar, and I found myself playing solo. We were playing the Beatles; we weren't doing much in Innu. The first year at Innu Nikamu, I played alone. When I was playing alone in those years it was a little bit of Bob Dylan, Neil Young. I had started writing, but nothing to perform publicly.

VA: Was the reception good?

GS: Yes. What was the greatest fun was the last evening. It was a holiday, and everybody there took out their guitar and their amp, everything, and it turned into a wild jam session. It was closed off, it was in a small room next to the stage, there were perhaps forty musicians teaching little tricks and jamming. It was perhaps there that they saw who I was.

VA: Who were some of these forty musicians?

GS: Everyone. Philippe McKenzie, Florent, Claude, people whose names I forget. Almost all the "who's who" in those days, on the Aboriginal side. In effect, all the artists who had played during the three days of the festival. They had a huge jam session. I went back to the festival almost every year, to accompany groups and under my own name.

VA: Were you a musician on Kashtin's first album?

GS: No, I arrived on the third one, *Akua tuta* [1994]. The third album was with Sony; it was a huge production, with fifty musicians. It was an enormous project! It's there that I came on the scene for them. Afterwards, I also played on Claude's feature sets, solo [*Innu Town*], then also the solo album of Florent [*Katak^u*, 2003].

VA: Were you picked up for their big North American tour with *Akua tuta*?

GS: That's right, yes. I caught the tail end of the tour, the end of their last tour, because they had a problem with a guitarist; he backed out of the tour. That's when I got a call at home – I had twenty-four hours to learn twenty-four tunes. I went to Toronto, played on stage the next day with lots of projectors, and some twenty new songs to play! I finished their tour, which was nearly completed elsewhere. And after that we did festivals and powwows in New Mexico, Arizona, and casinos as well, in western Canada and a few in the United States, Ontario ...

DL: With all these years and all of your performances, all your involvement with other artists, including the *Tournée Soleil Levant 2005* [*Rising Sun*] tour, do you find that you are a mentor, a model for Aboriginal artists?

GS: Myself, I don't really think that, but I am told that I am a mentor, yes. An idol, even, by whites as well as Natives. Personally, I find that quite funny but that's what I have been told! I don't work with that goal in mind.

VA: You've helped many artists produce their albums, to get themselves known.

GS: I helped out as best as I could with the knowledge that I have about the arrangements. It didn't cost them a fortune either.

VA: Wendy Moar[5] recently said that you were her mentor and that you had helped her with many things.

GS: This, I find this extraordinary. When I see somebody who deserves a good thing – I am always ready to help the men and women who have drive.

DL: I find that you are very generous with Indigenous artists. Especially when they need somebody to play the guitar, you're always present.

GS: You know, I go on the principle that if I didn't like the tunes, or the guys, I wouldn't do that. I'm still stubborn; I can say no quite easily, in fact. If I become involved it's because I really appreciate what they do, and I think they need a helping hand. I have had lots of help in my life. I do it to bring them out of the shadows a bit.

VA: Did you go to many Aboriginal events, apart from Innu Nikamu, and the Wendake powwow? Did you travel anywhere?

GS: Yes, oh yes. On a bunch of reservations, Pointe-Bleue, the Atika-mekw Wemotaci, and Manawan reserves … We went to Labrador, and American reservations as well. I've travelled quite a bit! I was called, just last week to go to France, three different visits. I left CDs there with someone, and Yvon's DVD [Lemieux 2004, 2005, 2008; Lemieux and Drolet 2007], so I'd say that's what started it. In 1987, '88, '89, we escaped the winter; we left on November 4 and returned home on May 4. It was with a trio called Storm/Soft Rain, with Daniel Gaudreault and Steve Tremblay. We developed a taste for spending the winter in the south of France, playing music. After that, I went back to France quite often, with Kevin Parent, in Switzerland, and in Belgium, regularly. Also with Kashtin, and then with Florent Vollant, and with Guy Bélanger this year. Let's say Europe, North America, at the moment. I have already had an invitation to New Zealand. I haven't gone yet. Perhaps one day. Because as I've always said, I'm going to give up this gig when I turn fifty [already passed]. I try to live more in the moment, take the chance to live in the present. Therefore, less looking into the future with expectations. We're less disappointed in life when things don't happen.

VA: Thank you very much, Gilles, for sharing so much about your life and music!

GS: You are very welcome.

NOTES

1 The Wendat are also known as Huron, and their only reserve in Quebec, Wen-dake, is also known as Huron Village. Other Wendat, known as Wyandot, live in the United States.
2 Biographical information on Sioui is drawn from his Myspace site (http://www.myspace.com/gillessioui) and was adapted by Véronique Audet.
3 These are important groups in the chansonnier movement of Quebec.
4 SOCAM (Société de communication Atikamekw-Montagnais) is a broadcasting network in the Innu and Atikamekw communities.
5 Wendy Moar is a Cree Innu songwriter-composer-performer from Mashteuiatsh (Pointe-Bleue). She participated in the television show *Tshenu* (Lemieux and Drolet 2007).

Abel, Kerry. 1993. *Drum Songs: Glimpses of Dene History.* Montreal and Kingston: McGill-Queen's University Press.

Abrahams, Roger. 2003. "Identity." In *Eight Words for the Study of Expressive Culture*, ed. Burt Feintuch, 198–222. Urbana: University of Illinois Press.

Abu-Lughod, Lila. 1993. *Writing Women's Worlds: Bedouin Stories.* California: University of California Press.

Adelson, Naomi. 2000. *"Being Alive Well": Health and the Politics of Cree Well-Being.* Toronto: University of Toronto Press.

Agawu, Kofi. 2003. *Representing African Music: Postcolonial Notes, Queries, Positions.* New York: Routledge.

Albers, Patricia C., and Beatrice Medicine. 2005. "Some Reflections on Nearly Forty Years on the Northern Plains Powwow Circuit." In *Powwow*, ed. Clyde Ellis, Luke Eric Lassiter, and Gary H. Dunham, 26–45. Lincoln: University of Nebraska Press.

Alberta Aboriginal Affairs. 1996. *Indian Reserves.* Map. Alberta: Resource Data Division, Alberta Environmental Protection.

Alfred, Taiaiake. 1999. *Peace Power Righteousness: An Indigenous Manifesto.* Don Mills, ON: Oxford University Press.

Allam, Hannah. 2002a, 10 May. "St. Paul: Lawsuit Ends Fall Powwow at St. Thomas." *Pioneer Press*, B1.

– 2002b, 15 October. "Powwow Suit Dropped after Dispute with Women, St. Thomas to Cancel Event." *Pioneer Press*, B1.

Alstrup, Kevin. 2003. "'The song – that's the monument': Eskasoni Mi'kmaq Tribal Culture in the Music-Making of Rita Joe and Thomas George Poulette." PhD diss., Brown University.

– 2004. "Mi'kmaq Atukwaqann and Aural Symbolism in the Music-Making of Thomas George Poulette." *Papers of the Thirty-Fifth Algonquian Conference* 35: 1–12.

Amadahy, Zainab. 2003. "The Healing Power of Women's Voices." In *Strong Women Stories: Native Vision and Community Survival*, ed. Kim Anderson and Bonita Lawrence, 144–55. Toronto: Sumach.

Anderson, Benedict. 1991. *Imagined Communities: Reflections on the Origin and Spread of Nationalism.* Rev. ed. London: Verso.

Anderson, Kim. 2000. *A Recognition of Being: Reconstructing Native Womanhood.* Toronto: Second Story.

– and Bonita Lawrence, eds. 2003. *Strong Women Stories: Aboriginal Vision and Community Survival.* Toronto: Sumach.

Anderson, Margaret, and Marjorie Halpern. 2000. *Potlatch at Gitsegukla: William Beynon's 1945 Notebooks.* Vancouver: University of British Columbia Press.

Angell, G. Brent, Brenda J. Kurz, and George M. Gottfried. 1997. "Suicide and North American Indians: A Social Constructivist Perspective." *Journal of Multicultural Social Work* 6, nos 3–4: 1–26.

Antane Kapesh, Anne. 1976. *Je Suis une Maudite Sauvagesse/Eukuan Nin Matshi-manitu Innu-Iskueu.* Ottawa: Lemeac.

Appadurai, Arjun. 1996. *Modernity at Large: Cultural Dimensions of Globalization.* Minneapolis: University of Minnesota Press.

– 2001. *Après le colonialisme: Les conséquences culturelles de la globalisation.* Paris: Payot.

Appleford, Rob. 1993. "The Desire to Crunch Bone: Daniel David Moses and the 'True Real Indian.'" *Canadian Theatre Review* 77: 21–6.

"Article Stirs Up Hot Debate." 2007. *Leader Post,* 17 January. http://www.canada.com/reginaleaderpost/news/viewpoints/story.html?id=35fdce10-1c28-4c8b-9b3f-b10592a83158 (accessed 26 May 2009).

Asch, Michael. 1988. *Kinship and the Drum Dance in a Northern Dene Community.* N.p.: Boreal Institute for Northern Studies.

Assembly of First Nations. 1989. *Tradition and Education: Towards a Vision of Our Future.* Vol. 3, *National Review of First Nations Education.* Summerstown, ON: National Indian Brotherhood and Assembly of First Nations.

– 1994. *Breaking the Silence: An Interpretive Study of Residential School Impact and Healing as Illustrated by the Stories of First Nations Individuals.* Ottawa: First Nations Health Commission.

Audet, Véronique. 2005a. "Innu Nikamu: Expression musicale populaire, affirmation identitaire et guérison sociale en milieu innu contemporain." MA thesis, Université Laval.

– 2005b. "Les chansons populaires innues: Contexte, signification et pouvoir dans les expériences sociales de jeunes Innus." *Recherches amérindiennes au Québec* 35, no. 3: 31–8. http://classiques.uqac.ca/contemporains/jerome_laurent/jeunes_autochtones/RAQ_35_3_Jeunes_autochtones.pdf (accessed 5 May 2009).

– 2009–2010. "Hip hop autochtone au Québec: Oralités contemporaines au gré des ondes politiques et médiatiques." *Indiens/Indians/Indios,* special issue of *Inter, art actuel,* no. 104 (Winter): 34–7.

– 2010. "Entre l'étranger et le familier, le personnel et le professionnel: L'engagement personnel et émotif dans nos rapports humains en milieu autochtone. *Les Cahiers du CIÉRA,* no. 6: 27–45.

– Forthcoming. *Innu Nikamu – L'Innu chante: Pouvoir des chants, identité et guérison chez les Innus.* Quebec City: Presses de l'Université Laval.

Averill, Gage. 1997. *A Day for the Hunter, A Day for the Prey: Popular Music and Power in Haiti*. Chicago: University of Chicago Press.

Baker, David. 2006. "Life Histories of Music Service Teachers: The Past in Inductees' Present." *British Journal of Music Education* 23, no. 1: 39–50.

Bakker, Peter. 1992. *The Genesis of Michif, the Mixed Cree-French Language of the Canadian Métis*. Amsterdam: University of Amsterdam.

Balikci, Asen. 1970. *The Netsilik Eskimo*. Garden City, NY: Natural History Press for the American Museum of Natural History.

Balme, Christopher. 1999. *Decolonizing the Stage: Theatrical Syncretism and Post-Colonial Drama*. Oxford: Clarendon.

Bannerji, Himani. 2000. *The Dark Side of the Nation: Essays on Multiculturalism, Nationalism, and Gender*. Toronto: Canadian Scholar's Press.

Barkwell, Lawrence J., Leah Dorion, and Darren R. Préfontaine. 1999. *Resources for Metis Researchers*. Saskatoon: Gabriel Dumont Institute.

Battiste, Marie. 2000. "Introduction: Unfolding the Lessons of Colonization." In *Reclaiming Indigenous Voice and Vision*, ed. Marie Battiste, xvi–xxx. Vancouver: University of British Columbia Press.

– 2008. "The Decolonization of Aboriginal Education: Dialogue, Reflection, and Action in Canada." In *Educational Theories and Practices from the Majority World*, ed. P.R. Dasen and A. Akkari, 168–95. New Delhi: Sage.

– and J.Y. Henderson. 2000. *Protecting Indigenous Knowledge and Heritage: A Global Challenge*. Saskatoon: Purich.

– and Helen Semeganis. 2002. "First Thoughts on First Nations Citizenship: Issues in Education." In *Citizenship in Transformation in Canada*, ed. Yvonne Hébert, 93–111. Toronto: University of Toronto Press.

Baxter-Moore, Nick. 2000–01. "'Making a Noise in This World': New Sounds from Canada's First Peoples." *London Journal of Canadian Studies* 16: 22–47.

Beach, Chris. 2006a, 11 March. "Peshikii (Indian Joe Blow)." Unpublished draft.

– 2006b, 23 October. "Kigeet." Unpublished final draft.

– 2007, 17 August. "Joe Blow Part 3: Black Eagle Thunderbird Man." Unpublished first draft.

– 2008. "Kigeet." *Say Magazine,* US ed., 16–17.

– 2011. *Indian Joe Blow: Pishikii – Kigeet – Black Eagle Thunderbird Man*. Bloomington, IN: AuthorHouse.

Beal, Bob, and Rod MacLeod. 2009. "North-West Rebellion." In *The Canadian Encyclopedia*. http://www.thecanadianencyclopedia.com (accessed 26 June 2009).

Bealle, John. 1993. "Self-Involvement in Musical Performance: Stage Talk and Interpretive Control at a Bluegrass Festival." *Ethnomusicology* 37, no. 1: 63–86.

Beaudry, Nicole. 1978. "Toward Transcription and Anlysis of Inuit Throat-Games: Macro-structure." *Ethnomusicology* 22, no. 2: 261–74.

– 1988a. "Review of Michael Asch, *Kinship and the Drum Dance in a Northern Dene Community* (Boreal Institute for Northern Studies, 1988)." *Canadian Journal of Native Studies* 8, no. 2: 304–8.

– 1988b. "La danse à tambour yupik: Une analyse de sa performance." *Recherches amérindiennes au Québec* 18, no. 4: 23–35.

- 1988c. "Singing, Laughing and Playing: Three Examples from the Inuit, Dene and Yupik Traditions." *Canadian Journal of Native Studies* 8, no. 2: 275–90.
- 1992a. "The Language of Dreams: Songs of the Dene Indians (Canada)." *World of Music* 34, no. 2: 72–90.
- 1992b. "Rêves, chants et prières Dènès: Une confluence de spiritualités." *Recherches amérindiennes au Québec* 21, no. 4: 21–36.
- 1997. "The Challenges of Human Relations in Ethnographic Inquiry: Examples from Arctic and Subarctic Fieldwork." In *Shadows in the Field,* ed. Gregory F. Barz and Timothy J. Cooley, 63–86. New York: Oxford University Press.
- 1999. "Le 'dynamism' d'une tradition: La danse à tambour chez les Dènès." *Canadian University Music Review* 19, no. 2: 79–93.
- et al. 1992. "Native North Americans in Canada." In *The Encyclopedia of Music in Canada*, 2nd ed., ed. Helmut Kallmann et al., 923–35. Toronto: University of Toronto Press.
Beck, Mary. 1993. *Potlatch: Native Ceremony and Myth on the Northwest Coast.* Anchorage: Alaska Northwest Books.
Bell, David. 2004. *Sharing Our Success: Ten Case Studies in Aboriginal Schooling.* Kelowna, BC: Society for the Advancement of Excellence in Education.
Belsey, William. 1985. "The Ennadai Project." *Inuktitut Magazine* 62: 6–23.
Bennett, A., and R. Peterson, eds. 2004. *Music Scenes: Local, Trans-local and Virtual.* Nashville, TN: Vanderbilt University Press.
Berbaum, Sylvie. 2000. *Ojibwa Powwow World.* Ed. and trans. Michael M. Pomedli. Thunder Bay, ON: Lakehead University Centre for Northern Studies.
Berger, Harris, and Michael Thomas Carroll, eds. 2003. *Global Pop, Local Language.* Jackson: University Press of Mississippi.
Best, Kelly. 2008. "'Making Cool Things Hot Again': Blackface and Newfoundland Mummering." *Ethnologies* 30, no. 2: 215–48.
Bhabha, Homi K. 1994. *The Location of Culture.* New York: Routledge.
Bigenho, Michelle. 2002. *Sounding Indigenous: Authenticity in Bolivian Music Performance.* New York: Palgrave.
Binda, K.P., and Sharilyn Calliou. 2001. *Aboriginal Education in Canada: A Study in Decolonization.* Mississauga, ON: Canadian Educators' Press.
Black, Joan. N.d. "Judge Rose Toodick Boyko: Nursing Aspirations Put on Hold for Career in Law." *Windspeaker.* http://www.ammsa.com/achieve/ AA99-R.Boyko.html (accessed 11 January 2010).
Bloechl, Olivia A. 2005. "The Pedagogy of Polyphony in Gabriel Sagard's 'Histoire du Canada.'" *Journal of Musicology – A Quarterly Review of Music History, Criticism, Analysis, and Performance Practice* 22, no. 3: 365–411.
- 2008. *Native American Song at the Frontiers of Early Modern Music.* Los Angeles: University of California Press.
Boas, Franz. 1877. *The Central Eskimo.* Lincoln: University of Nebraska Press.
Born, Georgina, and David Hesmondalgh, eds. 2000a. *Western Music and Its Others: Difference, Representation and Appropriation in Music.* Berkeley: University of California Press.
- and David Hesmondalgh. 2000b. "Introduction: On Difference, Representation, and Appropriation in Music." In *Western Music and Its Others: Difference,*

Representation, and Appropriation in Music, ed. Georgina Born and David Hesmondhalgh, 1–58. Berkeley: University of California Press.

Brant, Beth, and Sandra Laronde, eds. 1996. *Sweetgrass Grows All Around Her.* Toronto: Native Women in the Arts.

Brasser, Ted J. 1985. "In Search of Métis Art." In *The New Peoples: Being and Becoming Métis in North America*, ed. J. Petersen and J.S.H. Brown, 221–30. Winnipeg: University of Manitoba Press.

Briggs, Jean L. 1970. *Never in Anger: Portrait of an Eskimo Family.* Cambridge: Harvard University Press.

Brightman, Robert A. 1998. "The Windigo in the Material World." *Ethnohistory* 35, no. 4: 337–79.

British Columbia Ministry of Education. 1998. *Shared Learnings: Integrating BC Aboriginal Content K–10.* Victoria: British Columbia Ministry of Education.

Brodribb, Somer. 1984. "The Traditional Roles of Aboriginal Women in Canada and the Impact of Colonization." *Canadian Journal of Aboriginal Studies* 4, no. 1: 85–103.

Brody, Hugh. 1981. *Maps and Dreams: Indians and the British Columbia Frontier.* Vancouver: Douglas and McIntyre.

Brown, Jennifer. 1980. *Strangers in Blood: Fur Trade Company Families in Indian Country.* Vancouver: University of British Columbia Press.

– 1993. "Métis, Half-Breeds and Other Real People: Challenging Cultures and Categories." *History Teacher* 27, no. 1: 19–26.

Browner, Tara. 2000. "Making and Singing Pow-Wow Songs: Text, Form and the Significance of Culture-Based Analysis." *Ethnomusicology* 44, no. 2: 214–33.

– 2002. *Heartbeat of the People: Music and Dance of the Northern Powwow.* Urbana: University of Illinois Press.

– ed. 2009. *Music of the First Nations: Collected Essays on Native North American Music.* Urbana: University of Illinois Press.

Buddle, Kathleen. 2004. "Media, Markets and Powwows: Matrices of Aboriginal Cultural Mediation in Canada." *Cultural Dynamics* 16, no. 1: 29–69.

Bull, Sam. 1955. *100 Years at Whitefish Lake.* Calgary: Glenbow Museum.

Burleson, Richard. 2004. "The Time-Pitch Axis in Traditional Music of the First Nations." *Papers of the Algonquian Conference* 35: 35–44.

– 2006. "Encountering Changing Currents in the Music of the First Nations." *Actes du 37e Congrès des Algonquinistes* 37: 37–47.

Burley, David, Scott Hamilton, and Knut Fladmark. 1996. *Prophecy of the Swan: Fur Trade History of the Upper Peace River Valley, 1794–1823.* Vancouver: University of British Columbia Press.

Butler, Judith, and Gayatri Spivak. 2007. *Who Sings the Nation-State? Language, Politics, Belonging.* Oxford: Seagull Books.

Cain, Celia. 2006. "Red, Black and Blues: Race, Nation and Recognition for the Bluez." *Canadian Journal of Traditional Music* 33: 1–14.

Caldwell, E.K. 1999. *Dreaming the Dawn: Conversations with Native Artists and Activists.* Lincoln: University of Nebraska Press.

Camilleri, Anna. 2004. *I Am a Red Dress: Incantations on a Grandmother, a Mother, and a Daughter.* Vancouver: Arsenal Pulp Press.

Campbell, Maria. 1973. *Halfbreed*. Toronto: McLelland and Stewart.

Cannon, Martin. 1998. "The Regulation of First Nations Sexuality." *Canadian Journal of Aboriginal Studies* 18, no. 1: 1–18.

Cass-Beggs, Barbara. 1967. *Seven Metis Songs from Saskatchewan*. Don Mills, ON: BMI Canada.

Castellano, Marlene Brant, Lynne Davis, and Louise Lahache, eds. 2000. *Aboriginal Education Fulfilling the Promise*. Vancouver: University of British Columbia Press.

Castleman, Craig. 1982. "The Politics of Graffiti." In *Getting Up: Subway Graffiti in New York*, 135–57. Cambridge, MA: MIT Press.

Cavanagh [Diamond], Beverley. 1982. *Music of the Netsilik Eskimo: A Study of Stability and Change*. Ottawa: National Museums of Canada.

– 1985. "Les mythes et la musique naskapis." *Chants et tambours: Le pouvoir des sons*, special issue of *Recherches amérindiennes au Québec* 15, no. 4: 5–18.

– 1987. "The Performance of Hymns in Eastern Woodlands Indian Communities." In *Sing Out the Glad News: Hymn Tunes in Canada*, ed. John Beckwith, 45–56. Toronto: Institute for Canadian Music.

– 1988. "The Transmission of Algonkian Indian Hymns: Between Orality and Literacy." In *Musical Canada: Words and Music Honouring Helmut Kallmann*, ed. J. Beckwith and F.A. Hall, 3–28. Toronto: University of Toronto Press.

– M. Sam Cronk, and Franziska von Rosen. 1988. "Vivre ses traditions: Fêtes intertribales chez les Amérindiens de l'est du Canada." *Recherches amérindiennes au Québec* 18, no. 4: 5–21.

Cebula, Larry. 2003. *Plateau Indians and the Quest for Spiritual Power, 1700–1850*. Lincoln: University of Nebraska Press.

Chamberland, Roger. 2001. "Rap in Canada: Bilingual and Multicultural." In *Global Noise: Rap and Hip-Hop outside the USA*, ed. Tony Mitchell, 306–26. Middletown, CT: Wesleyan University Press.

Champagne, Duane. 1994. *Native America: Portrait of the Peoples*. Detroit: Visible Ink.

– 1998. "American Indian Studies Is for Everyone." In *Natives and Academics: Researching and Writing about American Indians*, ed. Devon A. Mihesuah, 181–89. Lincoln: University of Nebraska Press.

Chandler, Michael J., and Christopher Lalonde. 1998. "Cultural Continuity as a Hedge against Suicide in Canada's First Nations." *Transcultural Psychiatry* 35, no. 2: 191–219.

Charron, Claude. 1978. "Toward Transcription and Anlysis of Inuit Throat-Games: Micro-structure." *Ethnomusicology* 22, no. 2: 245–60.

Chiseri-Strater, Elizabeth, and Bonnie Stone Sunstein. 1997. *Fieldworking: Reading and Writing Research*. Upper Saddle River, NJ: Blair Press and Prentice Hall.

Chrétien, Annette. 1996. "Mattawa, Where the Waters Meet: The Question of Identity in Métis Culture." MA thesis, University of Ottawa.

– 2002. "Under the Double Eagle: From Military March to Métis Miziksharing." *World of Music* 44, no. 1: 95–114.

– 2005. "'Fresh Tracks in Dead Air': Mediating Contemporary Métis Identities through Music and Storytelling." PhD diss., York University.

- 2008. "From the Other Natives to the Other Metis." *Canadian Journal of Native Studies* 28, no. 1: 89–118.
- and R. Papen. 2010. "Le voyage de la 'Chanson de la Gornouillère' de Pierre Falcon, barde métis." In *(Se) Raconter des H/histoires? Histoire et histoires dans les littératures francophones du Canada*, ed. L. Hotte et al., 35–69. Ottawa: Éditions Prise de parole.
- and B.L. Murphy. 2009. "'Duty to Consult': Environmental Impacts and Métis Indigenous Knowledge." Policy brief. Ottawa: Institute on Governance. http://www.iog.ca/sites/iog/files/content_files/ DutytoConsultPB-ChretienMurphy.pdf (accessed 24 February 2011).
Chute, Elizabeth. 1992. "Ceremony, Social Revitalization and Change: Micmac Leadership in the Annual Festival of Ste. Anne." *Papers of the Twenty-Third Algonquian Conference* 23: 45–61.
Clements, Marie. 2002. *Rare Earth Arias*. Theme sheet. Vancouver: Urban Ink Productions.
- 2005. *The Unnatural and Accidental Women*. Vancouver: Talonbooks.
Clifford, James. 1988. *The Predicament of Culture.* Cambridge, MA: Harvard University Press.
Cole, Douglas, and I. Chaikin. 1990. *An Iron Hand upon the People.* Seattle: University of Washington Press.
Coleman, William S.E. 2000. *Voices of Wounded Knee.* Lincoln: University of Nebraska Press.
Confederacy of Mainland Mi'kmaq. 2002. Mi'kmaq–Nova Scotia–Canada Tripartite Forum. http://www.cmmns.com/pdf/tri.pdf (accessed 21 November 2003).
Conlon, Paula Thistle. 1992. "Drum-Dance Songs of the Iglulik Inuit in the Northern Baffin Island Area: A Study of Their Structures." PhD diss., University of Montreal.
- 2009. "Iglulik Inuit Drum-Dance Songs." In *Music of the First Nations: Collected Essays on Native North American Music*, ed. Tara Browner, 7–20. Urbana: University of Illinois Press.
Corbett, John. 2000. "Experimental Oriental: New Music and Other Others." In *Western Music and Its Others: Difference, Representation, and Appropriation in Music*, ed. Georgina Born and David Hesmondhalgh, 163–86. Berkeley: University of California Press.
Cornet, Wendy. 2001. "First Nations Governance, The *Indian Act* and Women's Equality Rights." In *First Nations Women, Governance and the Indian Act: A Collection of Policy Research Reports*, ed. Judith F. Sayers et al., 117–66. Ottawa: Status of Women Canada.
Cronk, Michael Sam. 1988. "Writing While They're Singing: A Conversation about Longhouse Social Dance Songs." *New York Folklore* 14, nos 3–4: 49–60.
- comp. 1990. *Sound of the Drum.* Brantford: Woodland Cultural Centre.
- Beverley Diamond, and Franziska von Rosen. 1988. "Celebration: Native Events in Eastern Canada." In *Folklife Annual 1987*, ed. Alan Jabbour and James Hardin, 70–85. Washington, DC: Library of Congress.
Cruikshank, Julie. 1990. *Life Lived Like a Story: Life Stories of Three Yukon Elders.* Lincoln: University of Nebraska Press.

– 1998a. "Claiming Legitimacy: Prophecy Narratives from Northern Aboriginal Women." In *The Social Life of Stories: Narrative and Knowledge in the Yukon Territory*, 116–37. Lincoln: University of Nebraska Press.

– 1998b. "'Pete's Song': Establishing Meanings through Story and Song." In *The Social Life of Stories: Narrative and Knowledge in the Yukon Territory*, 25–44. Lincoln: University of Nebraska Press.

– 2002. "Oral History, Narrative Strategies, and Native American Historiography: Perspectives from the Yukon Territory, Canada." In *Clearing a Path: Theorizing the Past in Native American Studies*, ed. Nancy Shoemaker, 3–28. New York and London: Routledge.

– 2005. *Do Glaciers Listen? Local Knowledge, Colonial Encounters, and Social Imagination.* Vancouver: University of British Columbia Press.

Darby, Jaye T. 2000. "Introduction: A Talking Circle on Native Theatre." In *American Indian Theater in Performance: A Reader*, ed. Hanay Geiogamah and Jaye T. Darby, iii–xvi. Los Angeles: UCLA American Indian Studies Center.

Daugherty, Wayne. 1983. *Treaty Research Report: Treaty One and Treaty Two (1871)*. Ottawa: Treaties and Historical Research Centre, Indian and Northern Affairs Canada.

Davis, Stephen A. 1997. *The Micmac*. Halifax: Nimbus.

Day, Richard J.F. 2000. *Multiculturalism and the History of Canadian Diversity*. Toronto: University of Toronto Press.

Debenham, Diane. 1988. "Native People in Contemporary Canadian Drama." *Canadian Drama* 14, no. 2: 137–58.

Deerchild, Rosanna. 2003. "Tribal Feminism Is a Drum Song." In *Strong Women Stories: Native Vision and Community Survival*, ed. Kim Anderson and Bonita Lawrence, 97–105. Toronto: Sumach.

Deloria, Philip. 2004. *Indians in Unexpected Places*. Lawrence: University Press of Kansas.

Deloria, Vine, Jr. 1974. "The Rise of Indian Activism." In *The Social Reality of Ethnic America*, ed. R. Gomez, C. Collingham, R. Endo, and K. Jackson, 179–87. Lexington, MA: Heath.

Dempsey, Hugh A. 1997. *Indian Tribes of Alberta*. Calgary: Glenbow Museum.

Derrida, Jacques. 2001. *Cosmopolitanism and Forgiveness*. London and New York: Routledge.

De Shane, Nina. 1988. "Danses de pouvoir 'Ksan." *Recherches amérindiennes au Québec* 18, no. 4: 49–57.

– 1991. "Powwow Dancing and the Warrior Tradition." *Studia Musicologica Academiae Scientiarum Hungaricae* 33, nos 3–4: 375–99.

Devine, Heather. 2004. *The People Who Own Themselves: Aboriginal Ethnogenesis in a Canadian Family, 1660–1900*. Calgary: University of Calgary Press.

deVries, P. 2000. "Learning How to Be a Music Teacher: An Autobiographical Case Study." *Music Education Research* 2, no. 2: 165–79.

Diamond, Beverley. 1988. "The Transmission of Algonkian Indian Hymns: Between Orality and Literacy." In *Musical Canada: Words and Music Honouring Helmut Kallmann*, ed. John Beckwith and Frederick Hall, 3–28, 325–26. Toronto: University of Toronto Press.

- 1992. "Christian Hymns in Eastern Woodlands Communities: Performance Contexts." In *Musical Repercussions of 1492: Explorations, Encounters, and Identities*, ed. Carol E. Robertson, 381–94. Washington, DC: Smithsonian Institution.
- 1998. "When Spirits Sing and Singers Have a Voice." In *Sharing the Voices: The Phenomenon of Singing*, ed. Brian Roberts, 75–88. St John's: Memorial University of Newfoundland.
- 1999–2000. "First Nations Popular Music in Canada: From Practice to Theory." *Repercussions* 8–9, special double issue, ed. J. Shepherd, J. Guilbault, and M. Dineen: 397–431.
- 2001. "Re/placing Performance: A Case Study of the Yukon Music Scene in the Canadian North." *Journal of Intercultural Studies* 22, no. 1: 211–24.
- 2002. "Native American Contemporary Music: The Women." *World of Music* 44, no. 1: 9–35.
- 2005a. "Media as Social Action: Native American Musicians in the Recording Studio." In *Wired for Sound: Engineering and Technology in Sonic Cultures*, ed. Paul Greene and Thomas Porcello, 118–37. Middletown, CT: Wesleyan University Press.
- 2005b. "The Soundtracks of Indigenous Film." In *From Bean Blossom to Bannerman: Festschrift for Neil Rosenberg*, ed. Diane Tye, Martin Lovelace, and Peter Narvaez, 125–54. St John's, NF: MUN Folklore.
- 2008a. "Deadly or Not: Aboriginal Music Awards in Canada and Australia." In *Post-Colonial Distances: The Study of Popular Music in Canada and Australia*, ed. Beverley Diamond, Denis Crowdy, and Daniel Downes, 175–90. Newcastle upon Tyne, UK: Cambridge Scholars.
- 2008b. *Native American Music in Eastern North America*. New York: Oxford University Press.
- 2008c. "Native American Music of the Northeast: An Ethnography of Copyright." Unpublished manuscript.
- 2011. "De-centering Opera: Early Twenty-First-Century Indigenous Production." In *Opera Indigene: Re/presenting First Nations and Indigenous Cultures*, ed. Pamela Karantonis and Dylan Robinson, 31–56. Farnham, UK: Ashgate.
- and James Robbins. 1992. "Ethnomusicology." In *Encyclopedia of Music in Canada*, 2nd ed., ed. Helmut Kalmann et al., 422–31. Toronto: University of Toronto Press.
- with M. Sam Cronk and Franziska von Rosen. 1994. *Visions of Sound: Musical Instruments of First Nations Communities in Northeastern America*. Waterloo, ON: Wilfrid Laurier University Press; Chicago: University of Chicago Press.
- and R. Witmer, eds. 1994. *Canadian Music: Issues of Hegemony and Identity*. Toronto: Canadian Scholars Press.
Diamond Cavanagh, Beverley. 1989. "Music and Gender in the Sub-Arctic Algonkian Area." In *Women in North American Indian Music: Six Essays*, ed. Richard Keeling, 55–66. Bloomington, IN: Society for Ethnomusicology.
Diamond, David, with Hal B. Blackwater, Lois G. Shannon, and Marie Wilson. 2001. "NO'XYA' (Our Footprints)." In *Playing the Pacific Province: An Anthology*

of British Columbia Plays, 1967–2000, ed. Ginny Ratsoy and James Hoffman, 397–418. Toronto: Playwrights Canada Press.

Dickason, Olive. 1992. *Canada's First Nations: A History of Founding Peoples from Earliest Times*. Toronto: McClelland and Stewart.

– and D.P. McNab. 2009. *Canada's First Nations: A History of Founding Peoples from Earliest Times*. 4th ed. Don Mills, ON: Oxford University Press.

Doig River First Nation. 2004. *Hadaa ka naadzet: The Dane-zaa Moose Hunt*. Virtual exhibit. Doig River First Nation: Canada's Digital Collection and Industry Canada. http://www.moosehunt.doigriverfn.com (accessed 1 January 2006).

– 2007. *Dane Wajich – Dane-ẕaa Stories and Songs: Dreamers and the Land*. Virtual exhibit. Doig River First Nation: Virtual Museum of Canada. http://www.virtualmuseum.ca/Exhibitions/Danewajich (accessed 19 April 2011).

Dorion, John, and Kwan R. Yang. 2000. "Métis Post-Secondary Education: A Case Study of the Gabriel Dumont Institute." In *Aboriginal Education Fulfilling the Promise*, ed. Marlene Brant Castellano, Lynne Davis, and Louise Lahache, 176–98. Vancouver: University of British Columbia Press.

Dorion-Paquin, Leah, coordinator. 2002. *Drops of Brandy: An Anthology of Métis Music*. Saskatoon: Gabriel Dumont Institute.

Doxtator, Deborah. 1992. *Fluffs and Feathers: An Exhibit on the Symbols of Indianness*. Brantford, ON: Woodland Cultural Centre.

Drapeau, Lynn. 1999. *Dictionnaire montagnais-français*. Sainte-Foy: Presses de l'Université du Québec.

Dubois, Paul-André. 1997a. *De l'oreille au coeur: Naissance et évolution du chant religieux en langues amérindiennes dans les missions de Nouvelle-France au cours de la première moitié du XVIIe siècle*. Sillery, QC: Septentrion.

– 1997b. "Naissance du cantique en langue vernaculaire dans les missions de Nouvelle-France et conquête des langues amérindiennes: une relation." *Recherches amérindiennes au Québec* 27, no. 2: 19–31.

– 2001. "Des mondes religieux parallèles, un espace commun? Amérindiens et musique vocale européenne sous le Régime français." *Études d'histoire religieuse* 67: 105–15.

– 2002. "Innovation et langue vulgaire: Les chants mobiles du Propre de la Messe dans les missions de Nouvelle-France." In *L'espace missionnaire, lieu d'innovations et de rencontres interculturelles*, ed. Gilles Routhier and Frédéric Laugrand, 141–56. Paris: Karthala.

– 2003. "Les Amérindiens, les missionnaires et la musique européenne." In *La vie musicale en Nouvelle-France*, ed. Jean-Pierre Pinson and E. Gallat-Morin, 255–80. Sillery, QC: Septentrion.

Dueck, Byron. 2005. "Festival of Nations: First Nations and Metis Dance Music in Public Performance." PhD diss., University of Chicago.

– 2006. "'Suddenly a Sense of Being a Community': Aboriginal Square Dancing and the Experience of Collectivity." *Music and Ritual*, themed issue of *Musiké* 1: 41–58.

– 2007. "Public and Intimate Sociability in First Nations and Métis Fiddling." *Ethnomusicology* 51, no. 1: 30–63.

Dueck, Jonathan. 2001. "From Whom Is the Voice Coming? Mennonites, First Nations People, and Appropriation of Voice." *Journal of Mennonite Studies* 19: 144–57.

Dunning, R.W. 1959. *Social and Economic Change among the Northern Ojibwa*. Toronto: University of Toronto Press.

Durkheim, Emile. 1951. *Suicide: A Study in Sociology*. Trans. John A. Spaulding and George Simpson. Ed. with an introduction by George Simpson. First French ed. 1897. New York: Free Press.

Dyck, Noel, and James B. Waldram. 1993. *Anthropology, Public Policy and Native Peoples in Canada*. Montreal and Kingston: McGill-Queen's University Press.

Easterson, Mary. 1992. *Potlatch: The Southern Tutchone Way*. Burwash Landing, YT: Kluane First Nation.

Elliot, Robin. 2008. "Ragtime Spasms – Anxieties over the Rise of Popular Music in Toronto." *Post-Colonial Distances: The Study of Popular Music in Canada and Australia*, ed. Beverley Diamond, Denis Crowdy, and Daniel Downes, 67–90. Newcastle upon Tyne, UK: Cambridge Scholars.

Ellis, Clyde, Luke Eric Lassiter, and Gary H. Dunham, eds. 2005. *Powwow*. Lincoln: University of Nebraska Press.

Enrico, John, and Wendy Bross Stuart. 1996. *Northern Haida Songs*. Lincoln: University of Nebraska Press.

Erlmann, Veit. 1996. "The Aesthetics of the Global Imagination: Reflections on World Music in the 1990s." *Public Culture* : 467–87.

Etienne, Mona, and Eleanor Leacock, eds. 1980. *Women and Colonization: Anthropological Perspectives*. New York: Bergin and Garvey.

Fagan, Kristina. 2004. "*Tewatatha:wi*: Aboriginal Nationalism in Alfred's *Peace, Power, Righteousness: An Indigenous Manifesto*." *American Indian Quarterly* 28, nos 1–2 (Winter–Spring): 12–29.

Favel Starr, Floyd. 1997. "The Artificial Tree: Native Performance Culture Research, 1991–1996." *Canadian Theatre Review*: 83–5.

Fernández, Carl. 2003. "Coming Full Circle: A Young Man's Perspective on Building Gender Equity in Aboriginal Communities." In *Strong Women Stories: Aboriginal Vision and Community Survival*, ed. Kim Anderson and Bonita Lawrence, 242–54. Toronto: Sumach.

Filewod, Alan. 1992. "Averting the Colonizing Gaze: Notes on Watching Native Theatre." In *Aboriginal Voices: Amerindian, Inuit and Sami Theater*, ed. Per Brask and William Morgan, 17–28. Baltimore, MD, and London: Johns Hopkins University Press.

Fink, Robert. 2005. *Repeating Ourselves: American Minimal Music as Cultural Practice*. Berkeley: University of California Press.

Fixico, Donald L. 1998. "Ethics and Responsibilities in Writing American Indian History." In *Natives and Academics: Researching and Writing about American Indians*, ed. Devon A. Mihesuah, 84–99. Lincoln: University of Nebraska Press.

Forman, Murray. 2002. *The 'Hood Comes First: Race, Space, and Place in Rap and Hip-Hop*. Middletown, CT: Wesleyan University Press.

"For Regina, Anger Is No Substitute for Action." 2007, 29 January. *Maclean's*. http://www.macleans.ca/article.jsp?content=20070129_139986_139986 (accessed 26 May 2009).

Foster, John. 2007. "Wintering: The Outsider Adult Male and the Ethnogenesis of the Western Plains Métis." In *The Western Métis: Profile of a People*, ed. P. Douad, 91-103. Regina: University of Regina, Canadian Plains Research Centre. http://hdl.handle.net/10294/24 (accessed 26 June 2009).

Fowke, Edith, and Alan Mills. 1960. *Canada's Story in Song*. Toronto: W.H. Gage.

– and Alan Mills. 1984. *Singing Our History*. Toronto: Doubleday Canada.

Fowler, Loretta. 2005. "Local Contexts of Powwow Ritual." In *Powwow*, ed. Clyde Ellis, Luke Eric Lassiter, and Gary H. Dunham, 68-84. Lincoln: University of Nebraska Press.

Frideres, James, and René Gadacz. 2008. *Aboriginal Peoples in Canada*. Toronto: Pearson and Prentice Hall.

Friedman, Jonathan. 1994. *Cultural Identity and Global Process*. London: Sage.

Friesen, John W., and Virginia Lyons Friesen. 2002. *Aboriginal Education in Canada: A Plea for Integration*. Calgary: Detselig.

– and Virginia Lyons Friesen. 2005. *First Nations in the Twenty-First Century: Contemporary Educational Frontiers*. Calgary: Detsilig.

Frisbie, Charlotte Johnson. 1967. *Kinaaldá: A Study of the Navaho Girl's Puberty Ceremony*. Middletown, CT: Wesleyan University Press.

– 1980. "Vocables in Navajo Ceremonial Music." *Ethnomusicology* 24, no. 3: 347-92.

– 2001. "American Indian Musical Repatriation." In *The Garland Encyclopedia of World Music*, vol. 3, *The United States and Canada*, ed. Ellen Koskoff, 491-501. New York: Garland.

Fulford, George. 1989. "A Structural Analysis of Mide Song Scrolls." *Papers of the Twentieth Algonquian Conference* 20: 132-53.

– 1990. "A Structural Analysis of Mide Chants." *Papers of the Twenty-first Algonquian Conference* 21: 126-58.

Gagnon, Denis. 2003. "Deux cents ans de pèlerinages: Les Mamit Innuat à Musquaro, Saint-Anne-de-Beaupré et Saint-Anne-d'Unamen-Shipu (1800-2000)." PhD diss., Université Laval.

Gatehouse, Jonathan. 2007, 15 January. "Canada's Worst Neighbourhood." *Maclean's*. http://www.macleans.ca/article.jsp?content=20070115_139375_139375 (accessed 26 May 2009).

Gilbert, Helen. 2003. "Black and White and Re(a)d All Over Again: Indigenous Minstrelsy in Contemporary Canadian and Australian Theatre." *Theatre Journal* 55: 679-98.

Gilbert, Reid. 2003. "Marie Clements's *The Unnatural and Accidental Women*: 'Denaturalizing Genre.'" *Theatre Research in Canada/Recherches théâtrales au Canada* 24, nos. 1-2: 125-46.

Gilley, Brian Joseph. 2005. "Two-Spirited Powwows and the Search for Social Acceptance in Indian Country." In *Powwow*, ed. Clyde Ellis, Luke Eric Lassiter, and Gary H. Dunham, 224-40. Lincoln: University of Nebraska Press.

Gilroy, Paul. 1993a. *The Black Atlantic: Modernity and Double-Consciousness.* Cambridge, MA: Harvard University Press.

- 1993b. *Small Acts: Thoughts on the Politics of Black Cultures.* New York and London: Serpent's Tale.

Goertzen, Chris. 2005. "Purposes of North Carolina Powwows." In *Powwow*, ed. Clyde Ellis, Luke Eric Lassiter, and Gary H. Dunham, 275–302. Lincoln: University of Nebraska Press.

Goodall, H.L., Jr. 2000. *Writing the New Ethnography.* New York: AltaMira.

Gorbman, Claudia. 2000. "Scoring the Indian: Music in the Liberal Western." In *Western Music and Its Others*, ed. Georgina Born and David Hesmondhalgh, 234–53. Berkeley: University of California Press.

Gordon, Tom. 2007. "Found in Translation: The Inuit Voice in Moravian Music." *Newfoundland and Labrador Studies* 22, no. 1: 287–314.

Gould, Elizabeth S., and Carol L. Matthews. 1999. "Weavings: Aboriginal Women's Music, Poetry, and Performance as Resistance." *Women and Music* 3: 70–8.

Goulet, Jean-Guy. 1996. "A Christian Dene Tha Shaman? Aboriginal Experiences among a Missionized Aboriginal People." In *Shamanism and Northern Ecology*, ed. Juha Pentikainen, 349–64. Berlin: Walter de Gruyter.

- 1998. *Ways of Knowing: Experience, Knowledge, and Power among the Dene Tha.* Lincoln: University of Nebraska Press.

- 2000. "Cérémonies, prières et medias: Perspectives autochtones." *Recherches amérindiennes au Québec* 30, no. 1: 59–70.

Grant, John Webster. 1984. *Moon of Wintertime: Missionaries and Indians of Canada in Encounter since 1534.* Toronto: University of Toronto Press.

Green, Rayna. 1989. "The Image of the Indian in American Popular Culture." In *The Handbook of North American Indians*, vol. 4, ed. Wilcomb Washburn, 587–606. Washington, DC: Smithsonian Institution.

- 1992. "Mythologizing Pocahontas." In *Musical Repercussions of 1492: Encounters in Text and Performance*, ed. Carol E. Robertson, 289–97. Washington, DC: Smithsonian Institution.

- ed. 1999. *The British Museum Encyclopedia of Native North America.* London: British Museum.

- and John Troutman. 1999. "By the Waters of the Minnehaha: Music, Pageants and Princesses in the Indian Boarding Schools." In *Away from Home: American Indian Boarding Schools*, ed. M. Archuleta, T. Lomawaima, and B. Child, 60–83. Phoenix, AZ: Heard Museum.

Grenier, Line, and Val Morrison. 1995a. "Le terrain socio-musical populaire au Québec: 'Et dire qu'on ne comprend pas toujours les paroles …'" *Études littéraires* 27, no. 3: 75–98.

- and Val Morrison. 1995b. "Quebec Sings 'E Uassiuian': The Coming of Age of a Local Music Industry." In *Popular Music – Style and Identity*, ed. Will Straw et al., 127–36. Montreal: Centre for Research on Canadian Cultural Industries.

Griffiths, Linda, and Maria Campbell. 1989. *The Book of Jessica: A Theatrical Transformation.* Toronto: Coach House.

Grossman, David C., Carol Milligan, and Richard A. Deyo. 1991. "Risk Factors for Suicide Attempts among Navajo Adolescents." *American Journal of Public Health* 81, no. 7: 870–4.

Guilbault, Jocelyne. 1993. "On Redefining the 'Local' through World Music." *World of Music* 35, no. 2: 33–47.

Gunn Allen, Paula. 1992. *The Sacred Hoop: Recovering the Feminine in American Indian Traditions.* 1986. Reprint, Boston: Beacon.

– 1996. "Introduction." In *Song of the Turtle: American Indian Literature, 1974– 1994*, ed. Paula Gunn Allen, 3–17. New York: Ballantine Books.

Hall, Stuart. 1997a. "The Local and the Global: Globalizations and Ethnicity." In *Culture, Globalization and the World-System: Contemporary Conditions for the Representation of Identity*, ed. Anthony D. King, 19–40. Minneapolis: University of Minnesota Press.

– 1997b. "Old and New Identities, Old and New Ethnicities." In *Culture, Globalization and the World-System: Contemporary Conditions for the Representation of Identity*, ed. Anthony D. King, 41–68. Minneapolis: University of Minnesota Press.

Hallowell, Alfred Irving. 1955. *Culture and Experience.* Philadelphia: Pennsylvania University Press.

– 1960. "Ojibwa Ontology, Behavior and World View." In *Culture in History: Essays in Honor of Paul Radin*, ed. S. Diamond, 19–52. New York: Columbia University Press.

– 1971. *The Role of Conjuring in Saulteaux Society.* 1942. Reprint, New York: Octagon Books.

– 1992. *The Ojibwa of Berens River: Ethnography into History.* Ed. with preface and afterword by Jennifer S.H. Brown. Fort Worth, TX: Harcourt Brace Jovanovich.

Hannerz, Ulf. 1996. *Transnational Connections: Culture, People, Places.* London: Routledge.

Hargrave, Joseph J. 1871. *Red River.* Montreal: John Lovell.

Harrison, Klisala. 2000. "Victoria's First Peoples Festival: Embodying Kwakwaka:wakw History in Presentation of Music and Dance in Public Spaces." MA thesis, York University.

– 2002. "The Kwagiulth Dancers: Addressing Intellectual Property Issues at Victoria's First Peoples Festival." *World of Music* 44, no. 1: 137–51.

– 2008. "Heart of the City: Music of Community Change in Vancouver, British Columbia's Eastside." PhD diss., York University.

Hatton, Orin T. 1986. "In the Tradition: Grass Dance Musical Style and Female Pow-Wow Singers." *Ethnomusicology* 30, no. 2: 197–221.

– 1989. "Gender and Musical Style in Gros Ventre War Expedition Songs." In *Women in North American Indian Music: Six Essays*, ed. Richard Keeling, 39–54. Bloomington, IN: Society for Ethnomusicology.

– 1990. *Power and Performance in Gros Ventre War Expedition Songs.* Ottawa: National Museums of Canada.

Hatzis, Christos. 1999, November. "Footprints in New Snow: Postmodernism or Cultural Appropriation?" http://www.chass.utoronto.ca/~chatzis/

footpaper.htm (accessed 6 June 2010).

– 2010. Program notes to *Viderunt Omnes*. http://www.chass.utoronto.ca/
~chatzis (accessed 6 June 2010).

Hennessy, Kate. 2010. "Repatriation, Digital Technology, and Culture in a Northern Athapaskan Community." PhD diss., University of British Columbia.

Herzog, George. 1928. "Musical Styles in North America." In *Proceedings of the 23rd International Congress of Americanists*, 455–8. New York: N.p.

Heth, Charlotte, ed. 1992. *Native American Dance: Ceremonies and Social Traditions.* Washington, DC: Smithsonian Institution.

Hewson, John, and Beverley Diamond. 2007. "Santu's Song." *Newfoundland and Labrador Studies* 22, 1: 227–58.

Hickerson, Harold. 1967. "Some Implications of the Theory of the Particularity, or 'Atomism,' of Northern Algonkians." With comments by several respondents and a reply by the author. *Current Anthropology* 8, no. 4: 313–43.

Hoefnagels, Anna. 2001a. "Powwows in Southwestern Ontario: Relationships, Influences and Musical Style." PhD diss., York University.

– 2001b. "Remembering Canada's Forgotten Soldiers at Contemporary Powwows." *Canadian Journal for Traditional Music* 28: 24–32.

– 2002. "Powwow Songs: Traveling Songs and Changing Protocol." *World of Music* 44, no. 1: 227–36.

– 2004. "Northern Style Powwow Music: Musical Features and Meanings." *Canadian Journal for Traditional Music* 31: 10–23.

– 2007a. "The Dynamism and Transformation of 'Tradition': Factors Affecting the Development of Powwows in Southwestern Ontario." *Ethnographies* 29, nos 1–2: 107–42.

– 2007b. "'What is tradition if we keep changing it to suit our own needs?' 'Tradition' and Gender Politics at Powwows in Southwestern Ontario." In *Folk music, Traditional Music, Ethnomusicology: Canadian Perspectives, Past and Present*, ed. Anna Hoefnagels and Gordon E. Smith, 187–200. Newcastle upon Tyne, UK: Cambridge Scholars.

– and Gordon E. Smith, eds. 2007. *Folk Music, Traditional Music, Ethnomusicology: Canadian Perspectives, Past and Present.* Newcastle upon Tyne, UK: Cambridge Scholars.

Hornborg, Anne-Christine. 2002. "St. Anne's Day – A Time to 'Turn Home' for the Canadian Mi'kmaq Indians." *International Review of Mission* 91, no. 361: 237–55.

Houston North Gallery. N.d. "Mi'kmaq Petroglyphs from Barry Stevens." http://www.houston-north-gallery.ns.ca/petroglyph_art.htm (accessed 21 November 2003).

Howard, James. 1955. "Pan-Indian Culture of Oklahoma." *Scientific Monthly* 81, no. 5: 215–20.

Howard, James H. 1965. *The St. Anne's Day Celebration of the Micmac Indians, 1962. Museum News* (South Dakota Museum) 26, nos 3–4: 5–14.

Huenemann, Lynn F. 1992. "Northern Plains Dance." In *Native American Dance: Ceremonies and Social Traditions*, ed. Charlotte Heth, 125–47. Washington, DC: National Museum of the American Indian.

Imboden, Roberta. 1995. "On the Road with Tomson Highway's Blues Harmonica in 'Dry Lips Oughta Move to Kapuskasing.'" *Canadian Literature* 144: 113–24.

Ingold, Tim. 1996. "Hunting and Gathering as Ways of Perceiving the Environment." In *Redefining Nature: Ecology, Culture and Domestification*, ed. R. Ellen and K. Fukui, 117–55. Oxford: Berg.

– 2004. "A Circumpolar Night's Dream." In *Figured Worlds: Ontological Obstacles in Intercultural Relations*, ed. J. Clammer, S. Poirier, and E. Schwimmer, 25–57. Toronto: University of Toronto Press.

Innuksuk, Pakak. 1992. "Carrying on the Song." *Canadian Theatre Review* 73: 22–3.

Invitation Project. N.d. "Invitation: The Quilt of Belonging." http://www.invitationproject.ca/cgi- win/quilt.exe?LISTING=1210 (accessed 21 November 2003).

Jamieson, Kathleen. 1986. "Sex Discrimination and the Indian Act." In *Arduous Journey: Canadian Indians and Decolonization*, ed. J. Rick Ponting, 112–36. Toronto: McClelland and Stewart.

Janke, Daniel. 1992. "Music up Here – Presenting Musical Life on Television: A Pilot Project on Issues of Representation and Identity." MA thesis, York University.

Jerôme, Laurent. 2005. "Musique, tradition et parcours identitaire de jeunes Atikamekw: La pratique du *tewehikan* dans un processus de convocation culturelle." *Recherches amérindiennes au Québec* 35, no. 3: 19–30.

Jessup, Lynda. 2002. "Moving Pictures and Costume Songs at the 1927 'Exhibition of Canadian West Coast Art, Native and Modern.'" *Canadian Journal of Film Studies* 11, no. 1: 2–39.

– 2008. "Marius Barbeau and Early Ethnographic Cinema." In *Around and about Marius Barbeau: Modelling Twentieth-Century Culture*, ed. Lynda Jessup et al., 269–304. Ottawa: Canadian Museum of Civilization.

Joe, Rita. 1997. "The Honour Song of the Micmac: An Autobiography." In *The Mi'kmaq Anthology*, ed. Rita Joe and Lesley Choyce, 239–79. Lawrencetown, NS: Pottersfield.

Johansen, Bruce E. 2006. *The Native Peoples of North America: A History*. Piscataway, NJ: Rutgers University Press.

Johnson, Sherry A. 2006. "Negotiating Tradition in Ontario Fiddle Contests." PhD diss., York University.

Johnson, Troy. 1996. "Roots of Contemporary Native American Activism." *American Indian Culture and Research Journal* 20, no. 2: 127–54.

Johnston, Patrick. 1983. *Native Children and the Child Welfare System*. Toronto: Canadian Council on Social Development in association with James Lorimer.

Johnston, Thomas. 1990. "The Northwest Coast Tlingit Indian Musical Potlatch." *South African Journal of Musicology* 10: 77–99.

Jonaitis, Aldona. 1991. *Chiefly Feasts: The Enduring Kwakiutl Potlatch*. Seattle: University of Washington Press.

Jones, Judith Ann. 1995. "'Women Never Used to Dance': Gender and Music in Nez Perce Culture Change." PhD diss., Washington State University.

Jones, Judy, and Loran Olsen. 1996. "Women and Music in the Plateau." In *A Song to the Creator: Traditional Arts of Native American Women of the Plateau*, ed. Lillian A. Ackerman, 142–55. Norman: University of Oklahoma Press.

Jungen, Brian. 2006. "Interview with Homi K. Bhabha." In *Witte de With Source Book 1/2006: Brian Jungen*, ed. Solange de Boer and Zoë Gray, 11–25. Rotterdam: Witte de With Center for Contemporary Art.

Kaczmarek, Josephine. 1998. "The Ojibwe Dream Dance." *Papers of the Twenty-Ninth Algonquian Conference* 29: 169–81.

– 1999. "The Dream Dance: An Examination of Its Music and Practice among Woodlands and Central Subarctic Indians." MA thesis, University of Manitoba.

Kallmann, Helmut, et al., eds. 1992. *The Encyclopedia of Music in Canada*. 2nd ed. Toronto: University of Toronto Press.

Kan, Sergei. 1989. *Symbolic Immortality: The Tlingit Potlatch of the Nineteenth Century*. Washington, DC: Smithsonian Institution.

– 1990. "The Sacred and the Secular: Tlingit Potlatch Songs outside the Potlatch." *American Indian Quarterly* 14, no. 4: 355–66.

Kane, Margo. 1994. "Moonlodge." In *Singular Voices: Plays in Monologue Form*, ed. Tony Hamill, 77–108. Toronto: Playwrights Canada Press.

– 2001. "Confessions of an Indian Cowboy." In *DraMétis: Three Métis Plays*, ed. Greg Daniels, Marie Clements, and Margo Kane, 274–309. Penticton, BC: Theytus Books.

Karantonis, Pamela, and Dylan Robinson, eds. 2011. *Opera Indigene: Re/presenting First Nations and Indigenous Cultures*. Farnham, UK: Ashgate.

Kavanagh, Thomas W. 1992. "Southern Plains Dance: Tradition and Dynamism." In *Native American Dance: Ceremonies and Social Traditions*, ed. Charlotte Heth, 105–23. Washington, DC: National Museum of the American Indian.

Keeling, Richard. 1989a. "Introduction." In *Women in North American Indian Music: Six Essays*, ed. Richard Keeling, 1–4. Bloomington, IN: Society for Ethnomusicology.

– 1989b. "Epilogue." In *Women in North American Indian Music: Six Essays*, ed. Richard Keeling, 79–87. Bloomington, IN: Society for Ethnomusicology.

– 1997. *North American Indian Music: A Guide to Published Sources and Selected Recordings*. Lincoln: University of Nebraska Press.

– ed. 1989c. *Women in North American Indian Music: Six Essays*. Bloomington, IN: Society for Ethnomusicology.

Keillor, Elaine. 1986. "The Role of Youth in the Continuation of Dogrib Musical Traditions." *Yearbook for Traditional Music* 18: 61–75.

– 1987. "Hymn-Singing among the Dogrib Indians." In *Sing out the Glad News*, ed. John Beckwith, 33–44. Toronto: Institute for Canadian Music.

– 1988. "La naissance d'un genre musical nouveau: Fusion du traditionnel et du country." *Recherches amérindiennes au Québec* 18, no. 4: 65–74.

– 1995a. "The Emergence of Postcolonial Musical Expressions of Aboriginal Peoples within Canada." *Cultural Studies* 9, no. 1: 106–24.

– 1995b. "Indigenous Music as a Compositional Source: Parallels and Contrasts in Canadian and American Music." In *Taking a Stand: Essays in Honour of John Beckwith*, ed. Timothy McGee, 185–218. Toronto: University of Toronto Press.

– 1996. "Voices of First Nations Women within Canada: Traditionally and Presently." *Australian-Canadian Studies* 14, nos 1–2: 33–9.

– 2002. "Amerindians at the Rodeos and Their Music." *World of Music* 44, no. 1: 75–94.

– 2004. "Marius Barbeau and His Performers." *Canadian Journal for Traditional Music* 31: 24–38.

– 2006. *Music in Canada: Capturing Landscape and Diversity.* Montreal and Kingston: McGill-Queen's University Press.

"Kē Kē Pā Sakihitin." 2003. Song. In "Sinclair Binder." Unpublished song binder owned by Kendra Sinclair and Mary Sinclair of Winnipeg. Photocopied by Byron Dueck in 2003.

Kidd, Ross. 1984. "Reclaiming Culture: Indigenous Performers Take Back Their Show." *Canadian Journal of Native Studies* 4, no. 1: 105–20.

Kidwell, Clara Sue. 1992. "Indian Women as Cultural Mediators." *Ethnohistory* 39, no. 2: 97–107.

King, Anthony D., ed. 1997. *Culture, Globalization and the World-System: Contemporary Conditions for the Representation of Identity.* Minneapolis: University of Minnesota Press.

King, Bruce. 2000. "Emergence and Discovery: Native American Theater Comes of Age." In *American Indian Theater in Performance: A Reader*, ed. Hanay Geiogamah and Jaye T. Darby, 165–8. Los Angeles: UCLA American Indian Studies Center.

King, Karlie. 2007. "Maintaining a 'Mixed' Identity." *Culture and Tradition* 29: 66–80.

King, Thomas. 2003. *The Truth about Stories: A Native Narrative.* Toronto: House of Anansi.

Kinsman, Gary. 1987. "Sexual Colonization of the Aboriginal Peoples." In *The Regulation of Desire: Sexuality in Canada*, ed. Gary Kinsman, 71–4. Montreal: Black Rose Books.

Kirkness, Verna J. 1999. "Aboriginal Education in Canada: A Retrospective and a Prospective." *Journal of American Indian Education* 39, no. 1: 14–30.

Kisliuk, Michelle. 1997. "(Un)doing Fieldwork: Sharing Songs, Sharing Lives." In *Shadows in the Field: New Perspectives for Fieldwork in Ethnomusicology*, ed. Gregory F. Barz and Timothy J. Cooley, 23–44. New York: Oxford University Press.

– 2001. *Seize the Dance: BaAka Musical Life and the Ethnography of Performance.* New York: Oxford University Press.

Klein, Laura F., and Lillian A. Ackerman, eds. 1995. *Women and Power in Native North America.* Norman: University of Oklahoma Press.

Knowles, Ric. 1999. *The Theatre of Form and the Production of Meaning: Contemporary Canadian Dramaturgies.* Toronto: ECW Press.

Kolstee, Anton. 1988. "The Historical and Musical Significance of Northwest Coast Indian Hámáca Songs." *Canadian Journal of Native Studies* 8, no. 2: 173–82.

Koskoff, Ellen, ed. 2001. *The Garland Encyclopedia of World Music*, vol. 3, *The United States and Canada.* New York: Garland.

Krims, Adam. 2000. *Rap Music and the Poetics of Identity.* New York: Cambridge University Press.

Kristeva, Julia. 1984. *Revolution in Poetic Language.* New York: Columbia University Press.

– 1991. *Strangers to Ourselves.* Trans. Leon S. Roudiez. New York: Columbia Press.

Krosenbrink-Gelissen, Lilianne Ernestine. 1991. *Sexual Equality as an Aboriginal Right.* Saarbrücken: Verlag breitenbach.

Krouse, Susan Applegate. 1999. "Kinship and Identity: Mixed Bloods in Urban Indian Communities." *American Indian Culture and Research Journal* 23, no. 2: 73–89.

– 2001. "Traditional Iroquois Socials: Maintaining Identity in the City." *American Indian Quarterly* 25, no. 3: 400–8.

Kulchyski, Peter, et al., eds. 1999. *In the Words of Elders: Aboriginal Cultures in Transition.* Toronto: University of Toronto Press.

Lafferty, Lucy, and Elaine Keillor. 2009. "Musical Expressions of the Dene: Dogrib Love and Land Songs." In *Music of the First Nations: Collected Essays on Native North American Music*, ed. Tara Browner, 21–33. Urbana: University of Illinois Press.

LaFrance, Ron. 1992. "Inside the Longhouse: Dances of the Haudenosaunee." In *Native American Dance*, ed. Charlotte Heth, 19–31. Washington, DC: National Museum of the American Indian.

La Fromboise, Teresa D., Anneliese M. Heyle, and Emily J. Ozer. 1994. "Changing and Diverse Roles of Women in American Indian Cultures." In *Native American Resurgence and Renewal: A Reader and Bibliography*, ed. Robert N. Wells Jr, 463–94. Lanham, MD: Scarecrow.

Lamb, Roberta, Lori-Anne Dolloff, and Sondra Wieland Howe. 2002. "Feminism, Feminist Research, and Gender Research in Music Education." In *The New Handbook of Research on Music Teaching and Learning*, ed. Richard Colwell and Carol Richardson, 648–74. New York: Oxford University Press.

Landes, Ruth. 1968. *Ojibwa Religion and the Midéwiwin.* Madison: University of Wisconsin Press.

LaRoque, Emma. 2007. "Métis and Feminist: Ethical Reflections on Feminism, Human Rights and Decolonization." In *Making Spaces for Indigenous Feminism*, ed. Joyce Green, 53–69. Halifax: Fernwood.

Larue, F.A.H. 1863. *Le Foyer Canadien.* Quebec City: Bureau du Foyer Canadien.

Lashua, Brett. D. 2005. "Making Music, Remaking Leisure in 'The Beat of Boyle Street.'" PhD diss., University of Alberta.

– 2006a. "The Arts of the Remix: Ethnography and Rap." *Anthropology Matters Journal* 8, no. 2: 1–10.

– 2006b. "'Just Another Native?' Soundscapes, Chorasters, and Borderlands in Edmonton, Alberta, Canada." *Cultural Studies/Critical Methodologies* 6, no. 3: 391–410.

– and Karen Fox. 2006. "Rec Needs a New Rhythm Cuz Rap Is Where We're Living." *Leisure Sciences* 28, no. 3: 267–83.

– and Karen Fox. 2007. "Defining the Groove: From Research to Remix in 'The Beat of Boyle Street.'" *Leisure Sciences* 29, no. 2: 143–58.

Lassiter, Luke Eric. 2005. *The Chicago Guide to Collaborative Ethnography.* Chicago: University of Chicago Press.

– with Clyde Ellis and Ralph Kotay. 2002. *The Jesus Road: Kiowas, Christianity, and Indian Hymns.* Lincoln: University of Nebraska Press.

Lawrence, Bonita. 2004. *"Real" Indians and Others: Mixed-Blood Urban Native Peoples and Indigenous Nationhood.* Lincoln: University of Nebraska Press.

Leacock, Eleanor, with Mona Etienne. 1980. *Women and Colonization.* New York: Praeger.

Leblanc, Larry. 1994, 3 September. "Canada's Aboriginal Musicians Seek Mainstream Recognition." *Billboard.*

Lederman, Anne. 1986. "Old Native and Metis Fiddling in Two Manitoba Communities: Camperville and Ebb and Flow." MA thesis, York University.

– 1988. "Old Indian and Métis Fiddling in Manitoba: Origins, Structure and Questions of Syncretism." *Canadian Journal of Native Studies* 8, no. 2: 205–30.

– 1990. "The Drops of Brandy: Several Versions of a Métis Fiddler Tune." *Canadian Folk Music Bulletin/Bulletin de musique folklorique canadienne* 24, no. 1: 3–11.

– 2001. "Métis." In *The Garland Encyclopedia of World Music*, vol. 3, *The United States and Canada*, ed. Ellen Koskoff, 404–11. New York: Garland.

Lefebvre, Henri. 1984. *The Production of Space.* Trans. Donald Nicholson-Smith. Oxford and Cambridge, UK: Blackwell.

Lehr, John. 1991. "Peopling the Prairies with Ukrainians." In *Canada's Ukrainians – Negotiating an Identity*, ed. L. Luciuk and Stella Hryniuk, 30–52. Toronto: University of Toronto Press in association with the Ukrainian Canadian Centennial Committee.

Leroux, Jacques. 1992. "Le tambour d'Edmond." *Recherches amérindiennes au Québec* 22, nos 2–3: 30–43.

Levine, Victoria Lindsay. 1991. "Arzelie Langley and a Lost Pantribal Tradition." In *Ethnomusicology and Modern Music History*, ed. Stephen Blum, Philip V. Bohlman, and Daniel M. Neuman, 190–206. Urbana: University of Illinois Press.

– ed. 2002. *Writing American Indian Music: Historic Transcriptions, Notations, and Arrangements.* Middleton, WI: A-R Editions for the American Musicological Society.

Levy, Jerrold E., and Stephen J. Kunitz. 1971. "Indian Reservations, Anomie, and Social Pathologies." *Southwestern Journal of Anthropology* 27, no. 2: 97–128.

Lillos, Brian. 1977. "Selective Studies in Musical Analysis of Beaver Indian Dreamer Songs: A Structuralistic Approach in Ethnomusicology." MA thesis, University of British Columbia.

Longboat, Jan Kahehti:io. 2010. *Idawadadi: Coming Home: Stories of Residential School Survivors with Contributions by Aboriginal Women.* Ed. Dawn Kawenno:ta's Avery. N.p.: Aboriginal Healing Foundation.

Louisbourg Institute. N.d. "Parks Canada: Fortress of Louisbourg." http://fortress.uccb.ns.ca/ parks/mik_e.html (accessed 21 November 2003).

Lutz, Maija M. 1978. *The Effects of Acculturation on Eskimo Music of Cumberland Peninsula.* Ottawa: National Museums of Canada.

Mackey, Eva. 2002. *The House of Difference: Cultural Politics and National Identity in Canada.* London and New York: Routledge.

MacPherson, James. 1991. *MacPherson Report on Tradition and Education: Towards a Vision of Our Future.* Ottawa: Department of Indian Affairs and Northern Development.

Magocsi, Paul R. 1991. "Preface." In *Canada's Ukrainians – Negotiating an Identity,* ed. L. Luciuk and Stella Hryniuk, xi–xv. Toronto: University of Toronto Press.

Mahar, William J. 1999. *Behind the Burnt Cork Mask: Early Blackface Minstrelsy and Antebellum American Popular Culture.* Urbana and Chicago: University of Illinois Press.

Malchy, Brian, Murray W. Enns, T. Kue Young, and Brian J. Cox. 1997. "Suicide among Manitoba's Aboriginal People, 1988 to 1994." *Canadian Medical Association Journal* 156, no. 8: 1133–8. http://www.cmaj.ca/cgi/reprint/156/8/ 1133?ck=nck (accessed 24 February 2008).

Maligne, Olivier. 2006. *Les nouveaux Indiens: Un ethnographie du mouvement indianophile.* Quebec City: Les Presses de l'Université Laval.

Manitoba. 1991. *Report of the Aboriginal Justice Inquiry of Manitoba.* http://www.ajic.mb.ca/volumel/chapter14.html#6 (accessed 26 February 2008).

Maracle, Lee. 1996. *I Am Woman: An Aboriginal Perspective on Sociology and Feminism.* Vancouver: Press Gang.

Marcus, Alan Rudolph. 1995. *Relocating Eden: The Image and Politics of Inuit Exile in the Canadian Arctic.* New England: University Press of New England.

Marsh, Charity. 2006. "Understand Us before You End Us: Regulation, Governmentality, and the Confessional Practices of Raving Bodies." *Popular Music* 25, no. 3: 415–30.

– 2009. "Interview with Saskatchewan Hip Hop Artist Lindsay Knight." *Canadian Folk Music* 43, no. 1 (Spring): 11–14.

– 2010. "It's about Action, Not Reaction: The Scott Collegiate/IMP Labs Hip Hop Project." Keynote address presented at the "(E)merging Professionalism Conference: Interrelated Issues in Education." University of Regina, January.

– 2011. "Keepin' It Real?: Masculinity, Indigeneity, and Media Representations of Gangsta' Rap in Regina, Canada." In *Making It Like a Man,* ed. Christine Ramsay, 149–70. Waterloo, ON: Wilfred Laurier University Press.

– and Sheila Petty. 2010. "Globalization, Identity, and Youth Resistance: Kenya's Hip Hop Parliament." Paper presented at the conference "Spaces of Violence, Sites of Resistance: Music, Media and Performance," a joint meeting of IASPM-Canada and the Canadian Society for Traditional Music. Regina, University of Saskatchewan, 3–6 June.

Martin, Lee-Ann, and Bob Boyer. 2001. *The Powwow: An Art History.* Regina: MacKenzie Art Gallery.

Martin-Hill, Dawn. 2003. "She No Speaks and Other Colonial Constructs of 'The Traditional Woman.'" In *Strong Women Stories: Native Vision and Community Survival,* ed. Kim Anderson and Bonita Lawrence, 106–20. Toronto: Sumach.

Martynowych, Orest. 1991. *Ukrainians in Canada: The Formative Period, 1891–1924.* Edmonton: Canadian Institute of Ukrainian Studies Press.

Mason, Kaley. 2004. "Sound and Meaning in Aboriginal Tourism." *Annals of Tourism Research* 31, no. 4: 837–54.

Mason, Leonard. 1967. *The Swampy Cree: A Study in Acculturation.* Ottawa: National Museums of Canada and Department of the Secretary of State.

Mattes, Catherine. 2002. *Lita Fontaine: Without Reservation.* Winnipeg: Winnipeg Art Gallery.

Matthews, Maureen, and Roger Roulette. 1996. "Fair Wind's Dream: *Naamiwan Obawaajigewin.*" In *Reading beyond Words: Contexts for Native History,* ed. Jennifer S.H. Brown and Elizabeth Vibert, 330–60. Peterborough, ON: Broadview.

McBride, Bunny. 1995. *Molly Spotted Elk: A Penobscot in Paris.* Norman: University of Oklahoma Press.

– 1999. *Women of the Dawn.* Lincoln: University of Nebraska Press.

– 2001. "Lucy Nicolar: The Artful Activism of a Penobscot Performer." In *Sifters: Native American Women's Lives,* ed. Theda Purdue, 141–59. New York: Oxford University Press.

McGee, Timothy. 1985. *The Music of Canada.* New York: Norton.

McMillan, Alan D. 1988. *Native Peoples and Cultures of Canada.* Vancouver: Douglas and McIntyre.

McNally, Michael D. 2000. *Ojibwe Singers: Hymns, Grief, and a Native Culture in Motion.* New York: Oxford University Press.

McNulty, Gerry E., and Marie-Jeanne Basile. 1981. *Lexique montagnais-français du parler de Mingan.* Quebec: Centre d'études nordiques, Université Laval.

Medieval Inuit. 2010, 13–14 March. Program notes. Camerata Nova, Winnipeg.

Métis Nation of Ontario. 2006, 1 November. *Report on Ministry of Education Draft Aboriginal Education Policy Framework.* Ottawa: Métis Nation of Ontario.

Mihesuah, Devon Abbott. 1998. "Introduction." In *Natives and Academics: Researching and Writing about American Indians,* ed. Devon Abbott Mihesuah, 1–22. Lincoln: University of Nebraska Press.

– 2003. *Indigenous American Women: Decolonization, Empowerment, Activism.* Lincoln: University of Nebraska Press.

Miller, Christina, and Patricia Chuchryk. 1996. *Women of the First Nations: Power, Wisdom and Strength.* Winnipeg: University of Manitoba Press.

Miller, J.R. 1990. "Owen Glendower, Hotspur, and Canadian Indian Policy." *Ethnohistory* 37, no. 4: 386–415.

– 2000. *Skyscrapers Hide the Heavens: A History of Indian-White Relations.* 3rd ed. Toronto: University of Toronto Press.

Milliea, Mildred. 1989. "Micmac Catholicism in My Community *Miigemeoei Alsotmagan Nemetgig.*" In *Papers of the Twenty-First Algonquian Conference* 20: 262–6.

Milloy, John S. 1999. *A National Crime: The Canadian Government and the Residential School System, 1879 to 1986.* Winnipeg: University of Manitoba Press.

Mills, Antonia C. 1982. "The Beaver Indian Prophet Dance and Related Movements among North American Indians." PhD diss., Harvard University.

– 2004. "The Ghost Dance and Prophet Dance." In *Shamanism: An Encyclopedia of World Beliefs, Practices, and Culture,* ed. Maria Walter and Eva Friedman, 287–92. Santa Barbara, CA: ABC-CLIO Press.

Ministère du développement durable, environnement et parcs du Québec. 2003, 8 February. *Stratégie québécoise sur les aires protégées: La majestueuse rivière Moisie: Un joyau patrimonial dorénavant protégé.* Press release. http://www.mddep.gouv.qc.ca/infuseur/communique.asp?no=318 (accessed 7 February 2007).

Mishler, Craig. 1993. *The Crooked Stovepipe: Athapaskan Fiddle Music and Square Dancing in Northeast Alaska and Northwest Canada.* Urbana: University of Illinois Press.

Mitchell, Tony. 2003. "Doin' Damage in My Native Language: The Use of 'Resistance Vernaculars' in Hip Hop in France, Italy, and Aoteroa/New Zealand." In *Global Pop, Local Language,* ed. Harris Berger and Michael Thomas Carroll, 3–18. Jackson: University Press of Mississippi.

– ed. 2001. *Global Noise: Rap and Hip Hop outside the USA.* Middletown, CT: Wesleyan University Press.

Moisala, Pirkko, and Beverley Diamond, eds. 2000. *Music and Gender.* Urbana and Chicago: University of Illinois Press.

Moore, Patrick, and Angela Wheelock. 1990. *Wolverine Myths and Visions.* Lincoln and London: University of Nebraska Press.

Moores, Sylvia. 2003, 31 July. "Silvia Moores' Journal of Her Journey throughout Canada." http://southwest.ednet.ns.ca/sylvia/julyjournal.htm (accessed 21 November 2003).

Morel, Leo. 1980. *"Mattawa" Meeting of the Waters.* Mattawa, ON: Société Historique de Mattawa Historical Society.

Morrison, Ann. 1996. "Christians, Kyries, and *Kci niwesq*: Passamaquoddy Catholic Songs in Historical Perspective." *Native American Studies* 10, no. 2: 15–21.

Morrison, R. Bruce, and C. Roderick Wilson, eds. 1986. *Native Peoples: The Canadian Experience.* Toronto: McClelland and Stewart.

Morrison, Val. 1996. "Mediating Identity: Kashtin, the Media, and the Oka Crisis." In *Resituating Identities: The Politics of Race, Ethnicity and Culture,* ed. Vered Amit-Talai and Caroline Knowles, 115–36. Peterborough, ON: Broadview.

Moses, Daniel David. 1998. "How My Ghosts Got Pale Faces." In *Speaking for the Generations: Native Writers on Writing,* ed. Simon J. Ortiz, 118–47. Tucson: University of Arizona Press.

– 2001. *Almighty Voice and His Wife.* Toronto: Playwrights Canada Press.

Mowat, Farley. 1952. *People of the Deer.* Boston: Little, Brown.

– 1959. *The Desperate People.* Boston: Little, Brown.

Nagel, Joane. 1995. "American Indian Ethnic Renewal: Politics and the Resurgence of Identity." *American Sociological Review* 60: 947–65.

Nahachewsky, Andriy. 1985. "First Existence Folk Dance Forms among Ukrainians in Smokey Lake, Alberta, and Swan Plain, Saskatchewan." MA thesis, University of Alberta.

– 2002. "New Ethnicity and Ukrainian Canadian Social Dances." *Journal of American Folklore Studies* 115, no. 456: 175–90.

– 2003. "Avramenko and the Paradigm of National Culture." *Journal of Ukrainian Studies* 28, no. 2: 31–50.

Nattiez, Jean-Jacques. 1999. "Inuit Throat Games and Siberian Throat Singing: A Comparative, Historical, and Semiological Approach." *Ethnomusicology* 43, no. 3: 399–418.

Neegan, Erica. 2005. "Excuse Me, Who Are the First Peoples of Canada? A Historical Analysis of Aboriginal Education in Canada Then and Now." *International Journal of Inclusive Education* 9, no. 1: 3–15.

Negus, Keith. 1999. *Music Genres and Corporate Cultures*. New York: Routledge.

Nettl, Bruno. 1954. "North American Indian Musical Styles." *Journal of American Folklore* 67, no. 266: 351–68.

– 1989. *Blackfoot Musical Thought: Comparative Perspectives*. Kent, OH: Kent State University Press.

– 1992. "Recent Directions in Ethnomusicology." In *Ethnomusicology: An Introduction*, ed. H. Myers, 375–99. New York: Norton.

– 2005. *The Study of Ethnomusicology: Thirty-One Issues and Concepts*. 2nd ed. Urbana: University of Illinois Press.

Neuenfeldt, Karl. 1996. "Songs of Survival: Ethno-Pop Music as Ethnographic Indigenous Media." *Australian-Canadian Studies* 14, nos 1–2: 15–31.

– 2002a. "An Overview of Case Studies of Contemporary Native American Music in Canada, the United States of America and on the Web." *World of Music* 44, no. 1: 7–10.

– 2002b. "www.nativeamericanmusic.com: Marketing Recordings in an Interconnected World." *World of Music* 44, no. 1: 93–102.

Nicholson, Oin. 2005. Liner notes to the CD *PRP 05*. Regina: Prairie Roots Project: A Provincial Youth Hip-Hop Community Collaboration.

Nicks, Trudy. 1999. "Indian Villages and Entertainments: Setting the Stage for Tourist Souvenir Sales." In *Unpacking Culture: Art and Commodity in Colonial and Post-Colonial Worlds*, ed. Ruth B. Phillips and Christopher Steiner. Berkeley: University of California Press.

Noll, William. 1991. "Economics of Music Patronage among Polish and Ukrainian Peasants to 1939." *Ethnomusicology* 35, no. 3: 349–79.

– 1991. "Music Institutions and National Consciousness among Polish and Ukrainian Peasants." In *Ethnomusicology and Modern Music History*, ed. Stephen Blum, Philip Vilas Bohlman, and Daniel M. Neuman, 139–58. Urbana: University of Illinois Press.

Nova Scotia Museum. 1997. *The Mi'kmaq Portraits Collection*. http://museum.gov.ns.ca/ mikmaq/mp0001.htm (accessed 21 November 2003).

Nurse, Andrew. 1997. "Tradition and Modernity: The Cultural Work of Marius Barbeau." PhD diss., Queen's University.

Nyce, Allison. 2008. "Transforming Knowledge: The Nisga'a and the Marius Barbeau Collection." In *Around and about Marius Barbeau: Modelling Twentieth-Century Culture*, ed. Lynda Jessup et al., 257–68. Ottawa: Canadian Museum of Civilization.

Ogg, Arden C. 1988. "Four Cree Love Songs: The Interaction of Text and Music." *Canadian Journal of Native Studies* 8, no. 2: 231–50.

Oliver, Paul. 1990. *Blues Fell This Morning: Meaning in the Blues*. Second ed. Cambridge and New York: Cambridge University Press.

Ontario. 2005. *Ontario's New Approach to Aboriginal Affairs*. Toronto: Queen's Printer for Ontario.

Ontario Ministry of Education. 1998. *The Ontario Curriculum, Grades 1–8: The Arts*. Toronto: Ministry of Training and Education.

– 2007. *Ontario First Nation, Métis, and Inuit Education Policy Framework*. Toronto: Queen's Printer for Ontario.

Ostashewski, Marcia. 2009a. "A Fully-Fledged and Finely Functioning Fiddle: Humour and 'The Uke-Cree Fiddler.'" *Canadian Folk Music* 43, no. 1: 1–5.

– 2009b. "Performing Heritage: Ukrainian Festival, Dance and Music in Vegreville, Alberta." PhD diss., York University.

Ott, Alison, with Qajaq Robinson and Lucy MacDonald. 1992. "Forging Their Own Modernity: The Igloolik Dance and Drama Group." *Canadian Theatre Review* 73: 10–14.

Ouellette, Grace J.M.W. 2002. *The Fourth World: An Indigenous Perspective on Feminism and Aboriginal Women's Activism*. Halifax: Fernwood.

Padfield, Marsha. 1991. "Cannibal Dancer in the Kwakiutl World." *Canadian Folk Music Journal* 19: 14–19.

Pannekoek, Frits. 2001. "Metis Studies: The Development of a Field and New Directions." http://auspace.athabascau.ca:8080/dspace/bitstream/2149/81/4/f09.pdf (accessed 18 August 2008).

Patterson, Michael. 1996a. "Native Music in Canada: The Age of the Seventh Fire." *Australian-Canadian Studies* 14, nos 1–2: 41–54.

– 1996b. "Native Music in Canada: Through the Seven Fires." MA thesis, Carleton University.

Paul, Daniel. 2000. *We Were Not the Savages: A Mi'kmaq Perspective on the Collision between European and Native American Civilizations*. Halifax: Fernwood.

Paul, Margaret. 1999. "'Every song you sing just keeps getting better and better.'" In *In the Words of Elders: Aboriginal Cultures in Transition*, ed. Peter Kulchyski et al., 3–36. Toronto: University of Toronto Press.

Pegley, Kip. 2008. *Coming to You Wherever You Are: MuchMusic, MTV, and Youth Identities*. Middletown, CT: Wesleyan University Press.

– and Susan Fast. 2010. "Music, Violence and Geopolitics: Towards a Theoretical Framework." Paper presented at the conference "Spaces of Violence, Sites of Resistance: Music, Media and Performance," a joint meeting of IASPM-Canada and the Canadian Society for Traditional Music. University of Regina, 3–6 June.

Pelinski, Ramon. 1979. *Inuit Songs from Eskimo Point*. Ottawa: National Museums of Canada.

– 1981. *La musique des Inuit du Caribou: Cinq perspectives methodologiques.* Montreal: University of Montreal Press.

Perdue, Theda, ed. 2001. *Sifters: Native American Women's Lives.* New York: Oxford University Press.

Perlman, Ken. 1996. *Mel Bay Presents the Fiddle Music of Prince Edward Island: Celtic and Acadian Tunes in Living Tradition.* Pacific, MO: Mel Bay.

Perreault, Jeanne, and Sylvia Vance, eds. 1990. *Writing the Circle: Aboriginal Women of Western Canada: An Anthology.* Edmonton: NeWest.

Peterson, Jacqueline, and Jennifer Brown, eds. 1985. *The New Peoples: Being and Becoming Metis in North America.* Winnipeg: University of Manitoba Press.

Piercey, Mary. 2005. "Gender Relations in Inuit Drum Dance." *Canadian Journal for Traditional Music* 39: 4–27.

– Forthcoming. "Traditional Indigenous Knowledge: An Ethnographic Study of Its Application in the Teaching and Learning of Traditional Inuit Drum Dances in Arviat, Nunavut." In *Critical Perspectives in Canadian Music Education*, ed. K.K. Veblen and C.A. Beynon. Waterloo, ON: Wilfrid Laurier University Press.

Piniuta, Harry. 1978. *Land of Pain, Land of Promise: First Person Accounts by Ukrainian Pioneers, 1891–1914.* Saskatoon: Western Producer Prairie Books.

Pisani, Michael. 2005. *Imagining Native America in Music.* New Haven, CT: Yale University Press.

Powers, William K. 1980. "Plains Indian Music and Dance." In *Anthropology on the Great Plains*, ed. W. Raymond Wood and Margot Liberty, 212–29. Lincoln: University of Nebraska Press.

– 1987. *Beyond the Vision: Essays on American Indian Culture.* Norman: University of Oklahoma Press.

– 1990. *War Dance: Plains Indians Musical Performance.* Tucson: University of Arizona Press.

Pratt, Mary Louise. 1991. "Arts of the Contact Zone." *Profession* 91 (MLA): 33–40.

Preston, Richard J. 1985. "Transformations musicales et culturelles chez les Cris de l'Est." *Chants et tambours: Le pouvoir des sons*, special issue of *Recherches amérindiennes au Québec* 15, no. 4: 19–28.

– 2002. *Cree Narrative: Expressing the Personal Meanings of Events.* 1975. Reprint, Montreal and Kingston: McGill-Queen's University Press.

Prince of Wales Northern Heritage Centre. 2008. *The Dogrib Tea Dance Sound Room.* http://pwnhc.learnnet.nt.ca/exhibits/teadance/teadance.html (accessed 5 June 2008).

Prins, Harald. 1994. "Neo-Traditions in Native Communities: Sweat Lodge and Sun Dance among the Micmac Today." *Papers of the Twenty-Sixth Algonquian Conference* 25: 383–94.

– 1996. *The Mi'kmaq Resistance, Accommodation, and Cultural Survival.* Fort Worth, TX: Harcourt Brace Jovanovich.

Qamaniq, David, and Cindy Cowan. 1992. "On Independence and Survival." *Canadian Theatre Review* 73: 18–21.

Quick, Sarah. 2008a. "Performing Heritage: Métis Music, Dance and Identity in a Multicultural State." PhD diss., Indiana University.

– 2008b. "The Social Poetics of the Red River Jig in Alberta and Beyond: Meaningful Heritage and Emerging Performance." *Ethnologies* 30, no. 1: 77–101.

Ralston Saul, John. 2008. *A Fair Country: Telling Truths about Canada.* Toronto: Penguin.

Rasmussen, Knud. 1927. *Across Arctic America: Narrative of the Fifth Thule Expedition.* New York: Greenwood.

– 1930. *Observations on the Intellectual Culture of the Caribou Eskimos.* New York: AMS Press.

"Regina One Year Later: Residents and Local Leaders Have Done Much to Improve Life in North Central." 2008, 17 January. *Maclean's.* http://www.macleans.ca/canada/opinions/article.jsp?content= 20080117_95971_95971 (accessed 26 May 2009).

Report of the Royal Commission on Aboriginal Peoples. 1996a. Vols 1–5. Ottawa: Canada Communication Group.

– 1996b. Vol. 3, *Gathering Strength.* Ottawa: Canada Communication Group.

Richardson, Boyce. 1993. *People of Terra Nullius: Betrayal and Rebirth in Aboriginal Canada.* Vancouver: Douglas and McIntyre.

Ridington, Amber, and Kate Hennessy. 2008. "Building Indigenous Agency through Web-Based Exhibition: Dane Wajich – Dane-ẕaa Stories and Songs: Dreamers and the Land." In *Museums and the Web 2008: Proceedings,* ed. J. Trant and D. Bearman. Toronto: Archives and Museum Informatics. http://www.archimuse.com/mw2008/papers/ridington/ridington.html (accessed 19 April 2011).

– and Robin Ridington. 2011. "Performative Translation and Oral Curation: Ti-Jean/Chezan in Beaverland." In *Born in the Blood: On Native American Translation,* ed. Brian Swann, 138–67. Lincoln: University of Nebraska Press.

Ridington, Robin. 1966. Unpublished field notes in the personal archive of Robin Ridington.

– 1968. "The Environmental Context of Beaver Indian Behavior." PhD diss., Harvard University.

– 1978. *Swan People: A Study of the Dunne-za Prophet Dance.* Ottawa: National Museum of Man.

– 1988a. *Trail to Heaven: Knowledge and Narrative in a Northern Native Community.* Vancouver: Douglas and McIntyre.

– 1988b. "Why Baby Why: Howard Broomfield's Documentation of the Dunne-Za Soundscape." *Canadian Journal of Native Studies* 8, no. 2: 251–74.

– 1990. *Little Bit Know Something: Stories in a Language of Anthropology.* Vancouver: Douglas and McIntyre.

– 1996. "Voice, Representation, and Dialogue: The Poetics of Native American Spiritual Traditions." *American Indian Quarterly* 20, nos 3–4: 467–88.

– 2006a. "That Is How They Grab It: Celestial Discourse in Dane-zaa Music and Dance." In *When You Sing It Now, Just Like New: First Nations Poetics, Voices, and Representations,* ed. Robin Ridington and Jillian Ridington, 171–87. Lincoln: University of Nebraska Press.

– 2006b. "Tools in the Mind: Northern Athapaskan Ecology, Religion and Technology." In *When You Sing It Now, Just Like New: First Nations Poetics, Voices, and Representations*, ed. Robin Ridington and Jillian Ridington, 207–20. Lincoln: University of Nebraska Press.

– Jillian Ridington, and Doig River First Nation. 2003. *The Ridington/Dane-zaa Digital Archive – Dane-zaa Archive Catalogue*. Doig River First Nation. http://fishability.biz/Doig (accessed 19 April 2011).

– and Jillian Ridington. 2003. "Archiving Actualities: Sharing Authority with Dane-zaa First Nations." *Comma: International Journal on Archives*, no. 1: 61–8.

– Dennis Hastings, and Tommy Attachie. 2005. "The Songs of Our Elders: Performance and Cultural Survival in Omaha and Dane-zaa Traditions." In *Powwow*, ed. Clyde Ellis, Luke Eric Lassiter, and Gary H. Dunham, 110–29. Lincoln: University of Nebraska Press.

– Jillian Ridington, Patrick Moore, Kate Hennessy, and Amber Ridington. 2011. "Ethnopoetic Translation in Relation to Audio, Video, and New Media Representations." In *Born in the Blood: On Native American Translation*, ed. B. Swann, 211–41. Lincoln: University of Nebraska Press.

– and Jillian Ridington, eds. 2006. *When You Sing It Now, Just Like New: First Nations Poetics, Voices, and Representations*. Lincoln: University of Nebraska Press.

Robbins, James. 1993. "Canada." In *Ethnomusicology: Historical and Regional Studies*, ed. Helen Myers, 63–76. New York: Norton.

Roberts, Helen H. 1970. *Musical Areas in Aboriginal North America*. 1936. Reprint, New Haven, CT: Human Relations Area Files Press and Yale University Press.

– and Diamond Jenness. 1925. "Songs of the Copper Eskimo." In *Report of the Canadian Arctic Expedition of 1913–1918*. Ottawa: F.A. Ackland.

Robinson, Angela. 2005. *Ta'n Teli-ktlamsitasit (Ways of Believing): Mi'kmaw Religion in Eskasoni, Nova Scotia*. Toronto: Pearson.

Roe, Steve. 2003. "'If the Story Could Be Heard': Colonial Discourse and the Surrender of Indian Reserve 172." *BC Studies*, nos 138–9: 115–36.

Rogers, Edward S. 1962. *The Round Lake Ojibwa*. Toronto: Ontario Department of Lands and Forests for the Royal Ontario Museum.

Rogers, Randal, and Christine Ramsay, eds. Forthcoming. *Mind the Gap: Saskatchewan's Cultural Spaces*. Regina: Canadian Plains Research Press.

Rose, Tricia. 1994. *Black Noise: Rap Music and Black Culture in Contemporary America*. Middletown, CT: Wesleyan University Press.

Roulston, Kathryn. 2006. "Mapping the Possibilities of Qualitative Research in Music Education: A Primer." *Music Education Research* 8, no. 2 (July): 153–73.

Ruml, Mark F. 2000. "The De-sacralization of the Powwow? Some Initial Observations." *Papers of the Thirty-First Algonquian Conference* 31: 333–8.

Rutherford, Jonathan. 1990. "The Third Space: Interview with Homi Bhabha." In *Identity: Community, Culture, Difference*, ed. Jonathan Rutherford, 207–21. London: Lawrence and Wishart.

Sable, Trudy. 1996. "Another Look in the Mirror: Research into the Foundations for Developing Alternative Science Curriculum for Mi'kmaw Children." MA thesis, St Mary's University.

– 1998. "The Serpent Dance: The Multiple Layers of Meaning in a Mi'kmaw Dance." In *Papers of the Thirtieth Algonquian Conference* 30: 329–40.

– and Julia Sable. 2007. "The Mi'kmaq of Eastern Canada – Why We Dance." *Nativedance.ca*. http://nativedance.ca/index.php/Mi%27kmaq/ Why_We_Dance (accessed 1 November 2008).

Said, Edward. 1989. "Representing the Colonized: Anthropology's Interlocutors." *Critical Inquiry* 15: 205–25.

Saladin D'Anglure, Bernard, ed. 2001. *Interviewing Elders: Cosmology and Shamanism*. Iqaluit, NU: Nunavut Arctic College.

Samson, Colin. 2004. "'We Live This Experience': Ontological Insecurity and the Colonial Domination of the Innu People of Northern Labrador." In *Figured Worlds: Ontological Obstacles in Intercultural Relations*, ed. J. Clammer, S. Poirier, and E. Schwimmer, 151–88. Toronto: University of Toronto Press.

Samuels, David William. 2004a. *Putting a Song on Top of It: Expression and Identity on the San Carlos Apache Reservation*. Tucson: University of Arizona Press.

– 2004b. "The Rap on Rap: The 'Black Music' that Isn't Either." In *That's the Joint! The Hip-Hop Studies Reader*, ed. Murray Forman and Mark Anthony Neal, 147–54. New York: Routledge.

Sarkissian, Margaret. 2000. *D'Albuquerque's Children: Performing Tradition in Malaysia's Portuguese Settlement*. Chicago: University Chicago Press.

Scales, Christopher A. 1996. "First Nations Popular Music in Canada: Identity, Politics and Musical Meaning." MA thesis, University of British Columbia.

– 1999. "First Nations Popular Music in Canada: Musical Meaning and the Politics of Identity." *Canadian University Music Review* 19, no. 2: 94–101.

– 2002. "The Politics and Aesthetics of Recording: A Comparative Canadian Case Study of Powwow and Contemporary Native American Music." *World of Music* 44, no. 1: 41–60.

– 2004. "Powwow Music and the Aboriginal Recording Industry on the Northern Plains: Media, Technology, and Native American Music in the Late Twentieth Century." PhD diss., University of Illinois at Urbana-Champaign.

– 2007. "Powwows, Intertribalism, and the Value of Competition." *Ethnomusicology* 51, no. 1: 1–29.

– 2011. "Plight of the Redman: XIT, Red Power, and the Refashioning of American Indian Ethnicity." In *Popular Music and Human Rights*, vol. 1, *British and American Music*, ed. Ian Peddie, 127–41. Burlington: Ashgate Press.

– Forthcoming. *Recording Culture: Powwow Music and the Aboriginal Recording Industry on the Northern Plains*. Raleigh, NC: Duke University Press.

Schilling, Vincent. 2009. *Native Musicians in the Groove*. Summertown, TN: Native Voices.

Schmidt, David L., and Murdena Marshall. 1995. *Mi'kmaq Hierogyphic Prayers: Readings in North America's First Indigenous Script*. Halifax: Nimbus.

Schulman, Sandra Hale. 2002. *From Kokopellis to Electric Warriors: The Native American Culture of Music*. Bloomington, IN: 1st Books Library.

Sealy, David. 2007. "Eekwol Opportunity." In *Degrees: The University of Regina Magazine* 19, 2 (Fall): 26–31.

Seeger, Anthony. 2004. *Why Suyá Sing: A Musical Anthropology of an Amazonian People*. Urbana and Chicago: University of Illinois Press.

Shaviro, Steven. 2005. "Supa Dupa Fly: Black Women as Cyborgs in Hip Hop Videos." *Quarterly Review of Film and Video* 22: 169–79.

Shea Murphy, Jacqueline. 2007. *The People Have Never Stopped Dancing: Native American Modern Dance Histories.* Minneapolis: University of Minnesota Press.

Shelemay, Kay Kaufman. 1998. *Let Jasmine Rain Down: Song and Remembrance among Syrian Jews.* Chicago: University of Chicago Press.

Shepherd, John, et al., eds. 2005. *Continuum Encyclopedia of Popular Music of the World.* 7 vols. London: Routledge.

Silman, Janet. 1987. *Enough Is Enough: Aboriginal Women Speak Out.* Toronto: Women's Press.

Silverstein, Michael. 1998. "The Improvisational Performance of 'Culture' in Realtime Discursive Practice." In *Creativity in Performance*, ed. Keith R. Sawyer. Greenwich, CT: Ablex.

Simard, Jean-Jacques. 2003. *La réduction: L'Autochtone inventé et les Amérindiens d'aujourd'hui.* Quebec City: Septentrion.

"Sinclair Binder." 2003. Unpublished song binder owned by Kendra Sinclair and Mary Sinclair of Winnipeg. Photocopied by Byron Dueck in 2003.

Slobin, Mark. 1993. *Subcultural Sounds: Micromusics of the West.* London: University Press of England.

Smith, Gordon E. 1989. "Ernest Gagnon on Nationalism and Canadian Music: Folk and Native Sources." *Canadian Folk Music Journal* 17: 32–9.

– 1994. "Lee Cremo: Narratives about a Micmac Fiddler." In *Canadian Music: Issues of Hegemony and Identity*, ed. B. Diamond and R. Witmer, 541–56. Toronto: Canadian Scholars Press.

– 1996. "Appendix 1: Six Songs of Rita Joe." Transcriptions with commentary by Rita Joe. In Rita Joe, *Songs of Rita Joe: Autobiography of a Mi'kmaq Poet*, 173–85. Charlottetown: Ragweed.

– 2006. "Learning about North American Native Music: A Case Study." *Institute for Canadian Music Newsletter* 4, no. 2 (May): 2–7. http://www.utoronto.ca/icm/0402.pdf (accessed 20 April 2011).

– 2008. "Ethnomusicological Modelling and Marius Barbeau's 1927 Nass River Field Trip." In *Around and about Marius Barbeau: Modelling Twentieth-Century Culture*, ed. Lynda Jessup et al., 213–40. Ottawa: Canadian Museum of Civilization.

– and Kevin Alstrup. 1995. "Words and Music by Rita Joe: Dialogic Ethnomusicology." *Canadian Folk Music Journal* 23: 35–53.

Smith, Linda Tuhiwai Te Rina. 1999. *Decolonizing Methodologies: Research and Indigenous Peoples.* Oxford: Oxford University Press; Dunedin: University of Otago Press.

– 2000. "Kaupapa Maori Research." *Reclaiming Indigenous Voice and Vision*, ed. Marie Battiste, 225–47. Vancouver and Toronto: University of British Columbia Press.

Smith, Nicholas. 1996. "The Wabanaki Trading Dance." In *Papers of the Twenty-Seventh Algonquian Conference* 27: 238–47.

– 2004. "Wabanaki Chief-Making and Cultural Change." In *Papers of the Thirty-Fifth Algonquian Conference* 35: 389–405.

So, Joseph. 2010. "Interview with Spy Dénommé-Welch and Catherine Mago-wan." *Music Scene* 8, no. 2 (Spring): 4–5.

Solís, Ted, ed. 2004. *Performing Ethnomusicology: Teaching and Representation in World Music Ensembles.* Berkeley: University of California Press.

Speck, Frank Gouldsmith. 1914. *The Double-Curve Motive in Northeastern Algonkian Art.* Ottawa: Government Printing Office.

– 1977. *Naskapi: The Savage Hunters of the Labrador Peninsula.* 1935. Reprint, Norman: University of Oklahoma Press.

Spier, Leslie. 1935. *The Prophet Dance of the Northwest and Its Derivatives: The Source of the Ghost Dance.* Menasha, WI: George Banta.

Spinney, Ann Morrison. 1991. "Voces Cantantes in Vestro: History of Research on Music among the Wabenaki." *Papers of the Twenty-Second Algonquian Conference* 22: 246–63.

– 1996. "Christians, Kyries, and *Kci niwesq*: Passamaquoddy Catholic Songs in Historical Perspective." *Native American Studies* 10, no. 2: 15–21.

– 1997. "Music that Moves between Worlds: Passamaquoddy Songs in the Cultural History of the Northeast." PhD diss., Harvard University.

– 1999. "Dance Songs and Questions of Intercultural Influence in Wabanaki Ceremonial Life." *Papers of the Thirtieth Algonquian Conference* 30: 334–50.

– 2006. "Medeolinuwok, Music, and Missionaries in Maine." In *Music in American Religious Experience*, ed. Philip V. Bohlman et al., 57–82. New York: Oxford University Press.

– 2009. *Passamaquoddy Ceremonial Songs: Aesthetics and Survival.* Boston: University of Massachusetts Press.

Statistics Canada. N.d. *Aboriginal Community Data Initiative: Whitefish Lake 128.* Ottawa: Statistics Canada.

Steenhoven, Geert van den. 1962. *Leadership and Law among the Eskimos of the Keewatin District, Northwest Territories.* The Hague: Uitgeverij Excelsior.

Steltzer, Ulli. 1984. *A Haida Potlatch.* Vancouver: Douglas and McIntyre.

Stinson, Daune. 2002. "Redefining 'Tradition': A Women's Drum Group Files Civil Complaint for Sexual Discrimination." *The Circle: Aboriginal American News and Arts* 23, no. 2 (February). http://www.thecirclenews.org/022002/cover.html (accessed 29 October 2002).

Stock, Jonathan J. 2003. "Music Education: Perspectives from Current Ethnomusicology." *British Journal of Music Education* 20, no. 2: 235–45.

Strachan, Jeremy. 2005. *Music Inspired by Aboriginal Sources at the Canadian Music Centre.* http://www.musiccentre.ca/media/downloads/en/CMC_Rep_Guide_Aboriginal.pdf (accessed 30 June 2010).

Surmont, Jean-Nicolas de. 2004. "Le destin des pratiques vocales autochtones entre protoethnographie, modernité et antimodernité." *Canadian Journal for Traditional Music* 31: 39–49.

Szego, C.K. 2002. "A Conspectus of Ethnographic Research in Ethnomusicology and Music Education." In *The New Handbook of Research on Music Teaching and Learning*, ed. Richard Colwell and Carol Richardson, 707–29. New York: Oxford University Press.

Tafelmusik. 2007b, October. Press release. http://www.tafelmusik.org/media/ presspdfs/Tafelmusik_CD_L'estro_armoinco.pdf (accessed 9 June 2011).

Tanner, Adrian. 1979. *Bringing Home Animals: Religious Ideology and Mode of Production of the Mistassini Cree Hunters*. London: C. Hurst.

– 2004. "The Cosmology of Nature, Cultural Divergence, and the Metaphysics of Community Healing." In *Figured Worlds: Ontological Obstacles in Intercultural Relations*, ed. J. Clammer, S. Poirier, and E. Schwimmer, 189–222. Toronto: University of Toronto Press.

Tassé, Joseph. 1878. *Les Canadiens de l'Ouest*. Vol. 2. Montreal: Cie d'imprimerie canadienne.

Taylor, Drew Hayden. 1991. *The Bootlegger Blues*. Saskatoon: Fifth House.

– 2000. "Alive and Well: Native Theatre in Canada." In *American Indian Theater in Performance: A Reader*, ed. Hanay Geiogamah and Jaye T. Darby, 256–64. Los Angeles: UCLA American Indian Studies Center.

– 2002a. *The Buz'Gem Blues*. Vancouver: Talonbooks.

– 2002b. *Furious Observations of a Blue-Eyed Ojibway*. Penticton, BC: Theytus Books.

– 2004. "Rhythm of Nations: Families Meet up on the Powwow Trail under the Spell of Drum and Dance." *Canadian Geographic* (July–August): 54–9.

– 2005. *Me Funny*. Vancouver: Douglas and McIntyre.

– 2007a. *The Baby Blues*. 1st online ed. 1999. Reprint, Alexandria, VA: Alexander Street Press. http://solomon.indr.alexanderstreet.com.ezproxy.library.ubc.ca/ cgi-bin/asp/philo/navigate.pl?indr.65 (accessed 19 June 2011).

– 2007b. *The Berlin Blues*. Vancouver: Talonbooks.

Taylor, John L. 1985. *Treaty Research Report – Treaty Six (1876)*. Ottawa: Treaties and Historical Research Centre, Indian and Northern Affairs Canada.

Taylor, Timothy. 2001. *Strange Sounds: Music, Technology, and Culture*. New York: Routledge.

Teskey, Nancy, and Gordon Brock. 1995. "Elements of Continuity in Kwakiutl Traditions." *American Music Research Center Journal* 5: 37–56.

Tester, Frank James, and Peter Kulchyski. 1994. *Tammarniit (Mistakes): Inuit Relocation in the Eastern Arctic, 1939–63*. Vancouver: University of British Columbia Press.

Théberge, Paul. 1997. *Any Sound You Can Imagine: Making Music/Consuming Technology*. Hanover, NH, and London: Wesleyan University Press.

Thompson, Judy. 2007. *Recording Their Story: James Teit and the Tahltan*. Vancouver: Douglas and McIntyre.

Thomson, Alex. 1995. "Inner Journey: An Actor's Diary." *Aboriginal Voices* 2, no. 5: 8–9.

Thorlindsson, Thorolfur, and Thoroddur Bjarnason. 1998. "Modeling Durkheim on the Micro Level: A Study of Youth Suicidality." *American Sociological Review* 63, no. 1: 94–110.

Thunderbird. 2010, 15 May. Program notes. Baroque Ensemble, Toronto.

Titon, Jeff Todd. 1994. "Formulaic Structure and Meaning in Early Downhome Blues Lyrics." 1977. In *Early Downhome Blues: A Musical and Cultural Analysis*, 2nd ed., 175–89. Chapel Hill: University of North Carolina Press.

Tremblay, Michel. 1976. *Sainte Carmen de la Main*. Montreal: Leméac.

Tremblay-Matte, Cécile, and Sylvain Rivard. 2001. *Archéologie sonore: Chants amérindiens*. Laval: Trois.

Trigger, Bruce. 1985. *Natives and Newcomers*. Montreal and Kingston: McGill-Queen's University Press.

– Wilcomb E. Washburn, Frank Salomon, Richard E.W. Adams, Stuart B. Schwartz, and Murdo J. MacLeod. 2000. *The Cambridge History of the Native Peoples of the Americas*. 3 vols. Cambridge and New York: Cambridge University Press.

Trott, Christopher G. 2000. "Structure into Practice: A Theory of Inuit Music." In *Indigenous Religious Musics*, ed. Karen Ralls-MacLeod and Graham Harvey, 183–97. Aldershot, UK: Ashgate.

Tulk, Janice Esther. 2003. "Medicine Dream: Contemporary Native Music and Issues of Identity." MA thesis, University of Alberta.

– 2006. "Traditional, Contest, or Something In-between: A Case Study of Two Mi'kmaq Powwows." *Canadian Journal of Traditional Music* 33: 15–32.

– 2007a. "Cultural Revitalization and the Language of Tradition: Mi'kmaq Music in Miawpukek, Newfoundland." In *Folk Music, Traditional Music, Ethnomusicology: Canadian Perspectives, Past and Present*, ed. Anna Hoefnagels and Gordon E. Smith, 201–11. Cambridge, UK: Cambridge Scholars.

– 2007b. "Cultural Revitalization and Mi'kmaq Music-Making: Three Newfoundland Drum Groups." *Newfoundland and Labrador Studies* 22, no. 1: 259–86.

– 2008. "'Our strength is ourselves': Identity, Status, and Cultural Revitalization among the Mi'kmaq in Newfoundland." PhD diss., Memorial University of Newfoundland.

– 2009. "Postdoctoral Pathways: From Powwow to Gregorian Chant Research with One Document Request Form." *Canadian Folk Music* 43, no. 1: 15–20.

– 2010. "An Aesthetic of Ambiguity: Musical Representation of Indigenous Peoples in Walt Disney's *Brother Bear*." In *Drawn to Sound: Animation Film Music and Sonicity*, ed. Rebecca Coyle, 120–37. London: Equinox.

Tunooniq Theatre. 1992. "Tunooniq." *Canadian Theatre Review* 73: 15–17.

Twigg, Alan. 2004. *First Invaders: The Literary Origins of British Columbia*. Vancouver: Ronsdale.

Ullestad, Neal. 1999. "American Indian Rap and Reggae: Dancing 'To the Beat of a Different Drummer.' *Popular Music and Society* 23, no. 2: 63–91.

Valentine, Lisa Philips. 1995. *Making It Their Own: Severn Ojibwe Communicative Practices*. Toronto: University of Toronto Press.

– 2003. "Song of Transformation: Performing Iroquoian Identity through Non-traditional Song." *Ethnologies* 25, no. 2: 131–44.

Vander, Judith. 1988. *Songprints: The Musical Experience of Five Shoshone Women*. Urbana and Chicago: University of Illinois Press.

– 1989. "From the Musical Experience of Five Shoshone Women." In *Women in North American Indian Music: Six Essays*, ed. Richard Keeling, 5–12. Bloomington, IN: Society for Ethnomusicology.

– 1997. *Shoshone Ghost Dance Religion: Poetry, Songs and Great Basin Context.* Chicago: University of Illinois Press.

Vascotto, Norma Kritsch. 2001. "Transmission of Drum Songs in Pelly Bay, Nunavut, and the Contributions of Composers and Singers to Musical Norms." PhD diss., University of Toronto.

Vennum, Thomas, Jr. 1982. *The Ojibwa Dance Drum: Its History and Construction.* Washington, DC: Smithsonian Folklife Studies.

– 1989a. "The Changing Role of Women in Ojibwa Music History." In *Women in North American Indian Music,* ed. Richard Keeling, 13–21. Bloomington, IN: Society for Ethnomusicology.

– 1989b. *Ojibwe Music from Minnesota.* Minneapolis: Minnesota Historical Society.

Vincent, Sylvie. 1973. "Structure du rituel: La tente tremblante et le concept de *Mista.pe.w." Recherches amérindiennes au Québec* 3, nos 1–2: 69–83.

– 2004. "Apparent Compatibility, Real Incompatibility: Native and Western Versions of History – The Innu Example." In *Figured Worlds: Ontological Obstacles in Intercultural Relations,* ed. J. Clammer, S. Poirier, and E. Schwimmer, 132–47. Toronto: University of Toronto Press.

Vollant, Florent. 2002. "Entretenir le feu." In Patrimoine canadien, *Rassemblement national sur l'expression artistique autochtone.* http://.wwwexpressions.gc.ca/vollant_f.htm (accessed 15 January 2003).

von Rosen, Franziska. 1994. "Thunder, that's our ancestors drumming." In *Canadian Music: Issues of Hegemony and Identity,* ed. B. Diamond and R. Witmer, 557–79. Toronto: Canadian Scholars Press.

– 1998. "Music, Visual Art, Stories: Conversations with a Community of Micmac Artists." PhD diss., Brown University.

– 2009. "Drum, Songs, Vibrations: Conversations with a Passamaquoddy Traditional Singer." In *Music of the First Nations: Collected Essays on Native North American Music,* ed. Tara Browner, 54–66. Urbana: University of Illinois Press.

Vosen, E.C. 2001. "Fire Children: Gender, Embodiment, and Musical Performances of Decolonization by Anishnaabe Youth." PhD diss., University of Pennsylvania.

Warner, Michael. 2002. *Publics and Counterpublics.* New York: Zone Books.

Warrior, Robert Allan. 2005. "Intellectual Trade Routes." In *The People and the Word: Reading Native Non-fiction,* 181–88. Minneapolis: University of Minnesota Press.

Warry, Wayne. 1998. *Unfinished Dreams: Community Healing and the Reality of Aboriginal Self-Government.* Toronto: University of Toronto Press.

Wasserman, Jerry. 1998. "Where the Soul Still Dances: The Blues and Canadian Drama." *Essays on Canadian Writing* 65: 56–75.

Waterman, Christopher. 1991. "Juju History: Toward a Theory of Sociomusical Practice." In *Ethnomusicology and Modern Music History,* ed. Stephen Blum, Philip V. Bohlman, and Daniel M. Neuman, 49–67. Urbana: University of Illinois Press.

Weaver, Jace, Craig S. Womack, and Robert Warrior. 2006. *American Indian Literary Nationalism.* Albuquerque: University of New Mexico Press.

Wenger, Etienne. 1998. *Communities of Practice: Learning, Meaning and Identity.* New York: Cambridge University Press.

Western Economic Diversification Canada – Saskatchewan Region. 1999. *Urban Reserves in Saskatchewan.* Saskatoon, SK: Purich.

Whidden, Lynn. 1985. "Les hymnes, une anomalie parmi les chants traditionnels des Cris du Nord." *Chants et tambours: Le pouvoir des sons,* special issue of *Recherches amérindiennes au Québec* 15, no. 4: 29–36.

– 1990. "A Note on Métis Music." *Canadian Folk Music Bulletin/Bulletin de musique folklorique canadienne* 24, no. 1: 12–15.

– 1992. "Global Restructuring: Is the Powwow Becoming a World Music?" *Canadian Issues* 16: 97–108.

– 1993. *Métis Songs: Visiting Was the Métis Way.* Saskatoon: Gabriel Dumont Institute.

– 1998. "Rethinking Native Music Scholarship." *Canadian Journal of Native Studies* 18, no. 1: 135–40.

– 2000. "Métis Music." *A Métis Historiography and Annotated Bibliography.* Winnipeg: Pemmican.

– 2003a. "'Gnaah' and the Trout Song." *Proceedings of the Eighth Workshop on the Structure and Constituency of Languages of America (WSCLA).* Vancouver: University of British Columbia, Department of Linguistics.

– 2003b. "The Songs of Their Fathers." *Ethnologies* 25, no. 2: 107–30.

– 2007. *Essential Song: Three Decades of Northern Cree Music.* Waterloo, ON: Wilfrid Laurier University Press.

Whitehead, Ruth Holmes. 1982. *Micmac Quillwork: Micmac Indian Techniques of Porcupine Decoration, 1600–1950.* Halifax: Nova Scotia Museum.

Wickwire, Wendy C. 1985. "Theories of Ethnomusicology and the North American Indian: Retrospective and Critique." *Canadian University Music Review* 6: 186–221.

– 1988. "James A. Teit: His Contributions to Canadian Ethnomusicology." *Canadian Journal of Native Studies* 8, no. 2: 183–205.

– 2001. "'The Grizzly Gave Them the Song': James Teit and Franz Boas Interpret Twin Ritual in Aboriginal British Columbia, 1897–1920." *American Indian Quarterly* 25, no. 3: 431–52.

Willes, Christine. 2000. "The Case of 'The Unnatural and Accidental Women': A Feminist Theoretical Analysis of the Play by Marie Clements." Unpublished manuscript.

Williams, Maria P. 1996. "The Wolf and Man/Bear: Public and Personal Symbols in a Tlingit Drum." *Pacific Review of Ethnomusicology* 7: 79–92.

Wilson, Angela Cavender. 1998. "American Indian History or Non-Indian Perceptions of American Indian History?" *Natives and Academics: Researching and Writing about American Indians,* ed. Devon A. Mihesuah, 23–6. Lincoln: University of Nebraska Press.

Witmer, Robert. 1991. "Stability in Blackfoot Songs, 1909–1968." In *Ethnomusicology and Modern Music History,* ed. Stephen Blum, Philip V. Bohlman, and Daniel M. Neuman, 242–53. Urbana: University of Illinois Press.

Winans, Robert B. 1996. "Early Minstrel Show Music, 1843–1852." In *Inside the Minstrel Mask: Readings in Nineteenth-Century Black Minstrelsy*, ed. Annemarie Bean, James V. Hatch, and Brooks McNamara, 141–62. Hanover, NH, and London: Wesleyan University Press.

Womack, Craig. 1999. *Red on Red: Native American Literary Separatism*. Minneapolis: University of Minnesota Press.

Wright-McLeod, Brian. 1996. "Bury My Heart: A Brief History of Resistance and Protest in Contemporary Native Music." *Aboriginal Voices* 5, no. 2: 36–9, 49.

– 2005. *The Encyclopedia of Native Music: More Than a Century of Recordings from Wax Cylinder to the Internet*. Tucson: University of Arizona Press.

Young, Alannah Earl, and Denise Nadeau. 2005. "Decolonising the Body: Restoring Sacred Vitality." *Atlantis* 29, no. 2: 1–13.

Young, Robert. 1990. *White Mythologies: Writing History and the West*. New York and London: Routledge.

Youngblood Henderson, James (Sákéj). 2000. "Postcolonial Ghost Dancing: Diagnosing European Colonialism." In *Reclaiming Indigenous Voice and Vision*, ed. Marie Battiste, 57–76. Vancouver: University of British Columbia Press.

Žižek, Slavoj. 2008. *Violence: Six Sideways Reflections*. New York: Picador.

Zwick, Jim. 2006. *Inuit Entertainers in the United States: From the Chicago World's Fair through the Birth of Hollywood*. Conchohocken, PA: Infinity.

Acko, Brian. 2007. Recorded interview with Amber Ridington. Catalogue no. ARDZMD#6-2007-07-30 GP003-1. Digital audio file and transcript archived with Amber Ridington as well as the Whatcom Museum, Bellingham, Washington.

Acko, Leo. 2007. Recorded interview with Amber Ridington. Catalogue no. #11-2007-10-07 GP9-4. Digital audio file and transcript archived with Amber Ridington as well as the Whatcom Museum, Bellingham, Washington.

Acko, Sam. 2007. Recorded interview with Amber Ridington. Catalogue no. ARDZMD#9-2007-08-11 GP8-1. Digital audio file and transcript archived with Amber Ridington as well as the Whatcom Museum, Bellingham, Washington.

Askoty, Freddy. 2007. Recorded interview with Amber Ridington. Catalogue no. ARDZMD#6-2007-07-30 GP002-1&2-2. Digital audio file and transcript archived with Amber Ridington as well as the Whatcom Museum, Bellingham, Washington.

Askoty, Johnny. 2007. Recorded interview with Amber Ridington. Catalogue no. ARDZMD#8-2007-08-06 GP002-1. Digital audio file and transcript archived with Amber Ridington as well as the Whatcom Museum, Bellingham, Washington.

Attachie, Tommy. 2007. Recorded interview with Amber Ridington. Catalogue no. ARDZMD#3-2007-07-24 GP003. Digital audio file and transcript archived with Amber Ridington as well as the Whatcom Museum, Bellingham, Washington.

Bobb, Columpa, and Sophie Merasty. 2000, 12 December. Interview with Klisala Harrison.

Clements, Marie. 2000, 13 December. Interview with Klisala Harrison.

Davis, Madeleine. 2007. Recorded interview with Amber Ridington. Catalogue no. ARDZMD#5-2007-07-29 GP004-2. Digital audio file and transcript archived with Amber Ridington as well as the Whatcom Museum, Bellingham, Washington.

Dénommé-Welch, Spy, and Catherine Magowan. 2009, 29 November. Interview with Dylan Robinson.

Dick, Jimmy. 2004, 17 February. Interview with Anna Hoefnagels.

Eekwol. 2008, 2 April, 18 June. Interviews with Charity Marsh.

Eshkibok, Gloria May. 2000, 19 November. Interview with Klisala Harrison.

Flaherty, Kathleen. 2002, 6 November. Interview with Klisala Harrison.

Fontaine, Cherie. 2003, 22 May. Interview with Anna Hoefnagels.

Gerard, Andrea. 2003, 22 May. Interview with Anna Hoefnagels.

Hamburger, Jay. 2002, 7 July. Interview with Klisala Harrison.

Harris, Katherine. 2002, 8 November. Interview with Klisala Harrison.

Harris, Leith. 2002, 15 November. Interview with Klisala Harrison.

Kreisberg, Jennifer. 2000, 9 December. Interview with Klisala Harrison.

Makadahay, Rita. 2007. Recorded interview with Amber Ridington. Catalogue no. ARDZMD#6-2007-07-31 GP004-1. Digital audio file and transcript archived with Amber Ridington as well as the Whatcom Museum, Bellingham, Washington.

May, Aleyna. 2008, 19 June. Interview with Charity Marsh.

Nicholson, Oin. 2006, Fall. Interview with Charity Marsh.

Oker, Garry. 2007. Recorded interview with Amber Ridington. Catalogue no. ARDZMD#4-2007-07-25 GP4. Digital audio file and transcript archived with Amber Ridington as well as the Whatcom Museum, Bellingham, Washington.

– 2008b. Recorded interview with Amber Ridington. Catalogue no. ARDZMD#14-2008-01-14 GP3-1. Digital audio file and transcript archived with Amber Ridington as well as the Whatcom Museum, Bellingham, Washington.

Skookum, Emma (Ak'ize). 1966. Audio Recording by Robin Ridington. Ridington/Dane-ẕaa Digital Archive, catalogue no. OT19-1. http://fishability.biz/Doig (accessed 19 April 2011). Translation by Doig River First Nation community member Madeline Oker, 2003, in the personal archive of Madeline Oker.

Spencer, Donna. 2000, 20 December. Interview with Klisala Harrison.

Strynadka, Arnie. 2009. Interviews with Marcia Ostashewski.

Van Berkel, Harris. 2008. Recorded interview with Amber Ridington. Catalogue no. ARDZMD#14-2008-07-03 GP4-1. Digital audio file and transcript archived with Amber Ridington as well as the Whatcom Museum, Bellingham, Washington.

Webster, Jerilynn. 2003, 25 June. Interview with Klisala Harrison.

Wong, Adrienne. 2002, 15 November. Interview with Klisala Harrison.

Yamamoto, Maiko Bae. 2002, 19 November. Interview with Klisala Harrison.

Claude McKenzie. http://www.myspace.com/claudemckenzie.

Common Weal. http://www.commonweal-arts.com.

Cyberhymnal. http://www.cyberhymnal.org (accessed 16 June 2008).

Dane Wajich – Dane-ẕaa Stories and Songs: Dreamers and the Land. Virtual exhibit created by the Doig River Dane-ẕaa community in collaboration with curators Amber Ridington and Kate Hennessy and other ethnographic specialists. http://www.virtualmuseum.ca/Exhibitions/Danewajich (accessed 19 April 2011).

The Encyclopedia of Saskatchewan. http://esask.uregina.cahome.html.

Florent Vollant. http://florentvollant.michelinesarrazin.com.

Gala of Music Teweikan. http://www.teweikan.com.

Gilles Sioui. http://www.myspace.com/gillessioui.

Government of Saskatchewan. http://www.gov.sk.ca.

Graffiti in Saskatchewan. http://graffitiregina.tripod.com; http://ie.youtube.com/watch?v=CiEA-a531B8&feature=related; http://ie.youtube.com/watch?v=9Fj__BwFdk4&feature=related.

Graffiti Regina. http://graffitiregina.tripod.com.

IMP Labs. http://www.interactivemediaandperformance.com.

Innu Nikamu festival. http://www.innunikamu.net.

Innutube. http://www.innutube.com.

Kathia Rock. http://www.myspace.com/kathiarock.

Missing Aboriginal Women. http://www.amnesty.ca/campaigns/sisters_overview.php; http://missingwomen.blogspot.com.

Moose Trails and Buffalo Tracks. Website created by Annette Chrétien with financial support from the E-Learning Incentives Program of the Faculty of Education at Queen's University. http://educ.queensu.ca/project/moose_trails_buffalo_tracks.

Native Dance. http://native-dance.ca.

Native Drums. http://native-drums.ca.

Paved Arts. http://www.pavedarts.ca.

Radio CKAU Kushapatshikan. http://www.ckau.com.

Samian. http://www.samian.ca; http://www.myspace.com/samianmusic.
Samian and Shauit. "So Much." http://musiqueplus.com/samian/so-much.
Saskatchewan Arts Board. http://www.artsboard.sk.ca.
Saskatchewan Hip Hop Forum. http://saskhiphop.com.
Saskatoon Police Service.
   http://www.police.saskatoon.sk.ca/index.php?loc=programs/graffiti.php;
   http://www12.statcan.ca/english/census01/Products/Analytic/companion/
   abor/canada.cfm#5.
Sask Music. http://www.saskrecording.ca.
Shauit. http://shauit.weebly.com.
– http://www.myspace.com/shauit.
Société de communication Atikamekw-Montagnais (SOCAM).
   http://www.socam.net.
Studio Makusham. http://www.makusham.com.
YouTube. http://www.youtube.com.
– Alek-Sandra Vollant-Cormier. 2010. *Mamituenitetau*. Wapikoni Mobile
   (Uashat mak Mani-utenam) in collaboration with Les Productions des beaux
   jours and Office national du film Canada.
   http://www.youtube.com/watch?v=T8Td-noLkdk.
– Bryan André.
   http://www.youtube.com/watch?v=k1WDRsgocFs&feature=related.
– Claude McKenzie. "Ekuan Pua."
   http://www.youtube.com/watch?v=iCRnnS5W1Xo&feature=related.
– Claude McKenzie. "Nutaui."
   http://www.youtube.com/watch?v=k_2s_XgkhgA.
– Kashtin. "Ashtam Nashu."
   http://www.youtube.com/watch?v=aGGCiqQ4RoE&feature=related.
– Kashtin. "E Uassiuian."
   http://www.youtube.com/watch?v=DK3hOAyln8c&feature=related.
– Kashtin. "Tshinanu."
   http://www.youtube.com/watch?v=YZf1Nfef-38&feature=related.
– Kathia Rock. "Quand le jour se lève."
   http://www.youtube.com/watch?v=4MjrueJSSqM.
– Kathia Rock. "Shatshitun." http://www.youtube.com/watch?v=hHyhyVtljWU.
– Samian. "Tshinanu" (featuring Kashtin).
   http://www.youtube.com/watch?v=ab83J2-A fuQ.
– Samian and Shauit. "Les Nomades."
   http://www.youtube.com/watch?v=V_aHeokb4IY&feature=related;
   http://www.youtube.com/watch?v=BYEszMWKfwI&feature=related.

André, Bryan. 2002. *Anisheniu*. CD. Produced by Bryan André, Gilles Sioui, and Mario J. Teixeira. Quebec: Studio Le Loft.

Beach, Chris. 2004a. *Maano*. Privately distributed CD. CB2004CD2. Published by Man-U-Sun. Winnipeg: Apple Blossom Studios.

– 2004b. *A New Life with Jesus: A Special Christmas Edition*. Privately distributed CD. Unnumbered. Published by Man-U-Sun. Winnipeg: Apple Blossom Studios.

Déry, Marc. 1999. *Marc Déry*. CD. Les éditions Audiogramme, Les productions Anacrouse.

Eekwol. *Apprentice to the Mystery*. CD. 2004. Mils Productions.

– and Mils. *The List*. CD. 2007. Mils Productions.

Grégoire, Émile. N.d. *J'ai perdu mon amie Annie*. Cassette. Self-produced.

– N.d. *7 sur 10: Sans être instruit quelqu'un quelque part*. Cassette. Self-produced.

– N.d. *Stranger (Nutetuk nete manteu)*. Cassette. Self-produced. Studio Circuit.

– 2000a. *Capteur de rêves: Tekshaman (24 succès country)*. CD. Self-produced.

– 2000b. *J'ai rêvé à Tshchémanitu (11ième)*. CD. Self-produced.

Halpern, Ida. 1981. *Kwakiutl Indian Music of the Pacific Northwest Coast*. Double LP. FE 4122. Folkways Records.

Heartbeat: Voices of First Nations Women. 1995. SFW 40415. Washington: Smithsonian Folkways.

Heartbeat 2: More Voices of First Nations Women. 1998. SFW 40455. Washington: Smithsonian Folkways.

Hearts of the Nations: Aboriginal Women's Voices in the Studio. 1997. Banff, AB: Banff Centre for the Arts.

Kashtin. N.d. *Kashtin*. Demo cassette. Self-produced with Marcel Néron.

– 1989. *Kashtin*. Cassette and LP. Éditions Groupe Concept Musique.

– 1991. *Innu*. CD. Éditions Groupe Concept Musique.

– 1994a. *Akua tuta*. CD. Productions Tshinuau and Éditions Groupe Concept Musique/Uapukun Music.

– 1994b. *Kashtin*. CD. 1989. Reissue, Productions Tshinuau and Éditions Groupe Concept Musique.

Kwakiutl Indian Music of the Pacific Northwest Coast. Double LP. FE 4122. Folkways Records.

Loon, Morley. c. 1975. *Songs in Cree Composed and Sung by Morley Loon*. LP. QC 1271. CBC Northern Service Broadcast Recording.

– 1981. *Northland, My Land/Cette terre du Nord qui est mienne*. LP. NCB 503. Boot Records.

Maten. 2001. *Akua tutu*. CD. Mani-utenam: Studio Makusham.

– 2003. *Tshi metuatshen*. CD. Mani-utenam: Studio Makusham.

McKenzie, Claude. 1989. *Claude McKenzie*. Demo cassette. Self-produced with Marcel Néron.

– 1996. *Innu Town*. CD. Groupe concept Productions and Éditions Groupe Concept Musique.

– 2004. *Pishimuss*. CD. L-A Be.

– 2009. *Inniu*. CD. Hello Musique.

McKenzie, Paul-Arthur. N.d. *Aiamieun Nikamun*. Vols 1–5. Cassettes. Mani-utenam: Studio Les Productions A.B., Aiamieun Nikamun, and Productions Religieuses.

– N.d. *Shuk ka shatshishk tiu*. 2 CDs. Uashat: ICEM.

McKenzie, Philippe. c. 1975. *Innu*. LP. SRC-006. Service du Québec nordique and Société Radio-Canada.

– 1982. *Mistashipu/La Grande Rivière/Great River*. LP. SQN 103. Boot Records.

– 2000. *Philippe McKenzie*. CD. Mani-utenam: Studio Makusham and Éditions Uapan Nuta.

Medicine Dream. 1998. *Identity*. CD. Wasilla, AK: Medicine Dream.

– 2000. *Mawio'Mi*. CD. CR-7039. Canyon Records.

Metallica. 1984. "Fade to Black." *Ride the Lightening*. Metallica.

Northern Wind Singers. 2000. *Ikwe Nagamonan: Women's Songs*. CD. AR-11282. Winnipeg: Arbor Records.

Oker, Garry. 2005a. *Symbols Lodge Prayer Songs*. Enhanced audio CD-ROM. Doig River First Nation: Eagle Vision Video Productions.

– 2005b. *Tea Dances*. Enhanced audio CD-ROM. Doig River First Nation: Eagle Vision Video Productions.

– 2005c. *"They Dream": The Soundtrack Remixed*. Enhanced audio CD-ROM. Doig River First Nation: Eagle Vision Video Productions.

– 2005d. *Trail Dreamers Songs*. Enhanced audio CD-ROM. Doig River First Nation: Eagle Vision Video Productions.

– 2008a. *Dane-zaa Dreamer's Melodies*. CD. Doig River First Nation.

– Robin Ridington, and Stacy Shaak. 2000. *Dane-zaa Dreamers' Songs, 1966–2000*. Vol. 1, *Suu Na chii K'chi ge, "The Place Where Happiness Dwells."* CD. Doig River First Nation.

Paisley, Brad, featuring Alison Krauss. 2003. "Whiskey Lullaby." *Mud on the Tires*. BMG Music.

Piétacho, P., J. Mollen, A. Poker, F. Bellefleur, J. Bellefleru, and W.M. Mark. 2000. *Mamit Puamuna: Ekuanitshit, Nutashkuan, Unamen-Shipi, Pakua Shipi*. CD. Mani-utenam: Studio Makusham.

Public Enemy. 1990. *Fear of a Black Planet.* CD. Def Jam Recordings.

Richard, Zachary. 2007. *Lumière dans le noir.* CD. Zach Rich and Musicor.

Rock, Kathia. 2006. *Uitshinan.* Demo CD. Self-produced with Jacques Roy. Studio de Jack and Shawn.

– 2007. "Quand le jour se lève." *Deviens-tu c'que tas voulu? L'année Daniel Boucher.* CD. Festival en chanson de la Petite-Vallée édition.

Sainte-Marie, Chloé. 1999. *Je pleures, tu pleures.* CD. Les Films Gilles Carle and Productions DOC.

– 2002. *Je marche à toi.* CD. Octant Musique.

– 2005. *Parle-moi.* CD. FGC Disques.

– 2009. *Nitshisseniten e tshissenitamin/Je sais que tu sais.* CD. GSI Musique.

Samian. 2007. *Face à soi-même.* CD. 7ième Ciel Records.

– featuring Shauit and Florent Vollant. 2010. *Face à la musique.* CD. 7ième Ciel Records.

Shauit. 2004. *Shapatesh Nuna.* CD. Self-produced. Mani-utenam: Studio Makusham.

Sioui, Gilles C. 1997. *Gilles C. Sioui and the Midnight Riders.* CD. Les Disques Kalamoss Records.

– 2000. *Rising Sun.* CD. BYC.

– 2004. *Old Fool.* CD. Les Disques Kalamoss Records.

Six Nations Women Singers. 1996. *We Will All Sing.* CD. Albuquerque, NM: SOAR Records.

Thomason, Dovie, and Ulali. 1996. *Lessons from the Animal People.* CD. Yellow Moon Press and Corn, Beans and Squash Music.

Tshimun. N.d. *Nitanish.* Cassette. Self-produced.

Tzo'kam. 2000. *It'em – To sing.* CD. Red Planet Records.

– 2004. *Journeys.* CD. Red Planet Records.

Vollant, Florent. 1999. *Nipaiamianan.* CD. Studio Montana, Productions 44.1, and Studio Makusham.

– 2003. *Katak^u.* CD. Enregistrements D7/DEP.

– 2009. *Eku Mamu.* CD. Studio Montana and Disques Tempête.

We Are Full Circle: An Aboriginal Women's Voice Concert. 2001. Banff, AB: Banff Centre Records.

Beat of the Drum. 2004. DVD. Vancouver: First Nations Films.

Collins, Patricia J., dir. 2002. *Rare Earth Arias*. Student project. VHS. Vancouver: School for the Contemporary Arts, Simon Fraser University.

First Story. 2001, 23 March. Episode 422. Television series. CTV.

Hall, Dan, dir. 1988. *1988 Baffin Summer School of Dramatic Arts*. VHS. Iqaluit, Nunavut. Copy in Canadian Museum of Civilization Archives.

Henry, Annie Fraziér, dir. 1999. *Singing Our Stories*. VHS. Ottawa: National Film Board of Canada.

Lemieux, Yvon, prod. and dir. 2004. *Gilles Sioui: Wendat Land Blues*. Television show and DVD. Quebec: Productions A Priori with Global Television Network.

– prod. and dir. 2005. *La Tournée Soleil Levant*. Television show and DVD. Quebec: Productions A Priori with APTN and Télé-Québec.

– prod. and dir. 2008. *Gilles Sioui sur six cordes*. Television show and DVD. Quebec: Productions A Priori with APTN.

– prod., and Y. Drolet, dir. 2007. *Tshenu*. Television show and DVD. Quebec: Productions A Priori with APTN.

Malenfant, Eddy, dir. 2004. *Innu Nikamu: L'Indien chante – The Native Sings: 20 ans de musique autochtone!* DVD. Mani-Utenam: Production Manitu.

Meney, Florence, dir. 2002, February. "La fin d'un long silence: Les jeunes autochtones du Québec." Television show in the series *Émission Enjeux*. Société Radio-Canada.

Oker, Garry, Robin Ridington, Jillian Ridington, and Stacy Shaak, dirs. 2001. *Contact the People: Dane-zaa Continuity and Change*. DVD. 24 mins. Doig River First Nation.

– and elders of the Dane-ẕaa First Nation, dirs. 2005. *They Dream about Everything*. DVD. Doig River First Nation and Eagle Vision Video Productions.

Powwow Trail. 2004. DVD. Eleven-part series. Winnipeg: Arbor Records.

Prowse, Joan, dir. 2006. *Buffy Sainte-Marie: A Multimedia Life*. DVD. CineFocus Canada.

Ronceria, Alejandro, dir. 1998. *Chinook Winds: The First Aboriginal Dance Project*. VHS. Banff, AB: Banff Centre for the Arts.

Sherrin, Robert, dir. 1990. "Highway, Native Voice." In the series *Adrienne Clarkson Presents*. VHS. Canadian Broadcasting Corporation.

Samian, featuring Shauit. 2011. "So Much." Videoclip. Co-directed by Martin Gendron and Steve Jolin. 7ième Ciel Records.

Sioui-Durand, Yves, and Réginald Vollant. 2011. *Mesnak*. Montreal and Mani-utenam: Les Films de l'Isle and Kunakan Productions.

Tafelmusik, dir. 2007a. *The Four Seasons Mosaic*. DVD. Analekta.

Vincent-Savard, Luc, dir. 2009. *TAM (Talents autochtones musicaux)*. Television show. 1st season. Wendake: Production TAM with APTN.

– dir. 2010. *TAM (Talents autochtones musicaux)*. Television show. 2nd season. Wendake: Production TAM with APTN.

Vollant, Réginald, and François Savoie, dirs. 2010. *Makusham*. Television show. 1st season. Kunakan Productions, Mani-utenam, and Connections Productions, Moncton, APTN and TFO.

– dirs. 2010. *Makusham*. Television show. 2nd season. Kunakan Productions, Mani-utenam, and Connections Productions, Moncton, APTN and TFO.

VÉRONIQUE AUDET is an anthropologist working with Aboriginal peoples in Quebec. She is the author of *Innu Nikamu – L'Innu chante* (forthcoming), drawn from her master's research (Audet 2005a), which examines Innu popular music, identity affirmation, power, and healing. Currently, she is a doctoral candidate in anthropology at the Université de Montréal, completing her dissertation on the Aboriginal popular music scene in Quebec. She is a member of the Centre interuniversitaire d'études et de recherche autochtones, Canadian Society for Traditional Music, International Council for Traditional Music, and Critical World. She has published in the journals *Recherches amérindiennes au Québec*, *Les Cahiers du CIÉRA*, and *Inter, Art actuel*, and, with Amélie Courchesne, she has worked on the project Diaspason (1996–2001), which examines the stories and music in Burkina Faso. Audet is engaged in various Aboriginal, university, and cultural environments. Since 2004 she has participated in the *Voix autochtones* (Indigenous Voices) program on the radio station CKIA FM 88.3 in Quebec as co-host and producer, and she has co-organized the annual colloquium of CIÉRA and the Association étudiante autochtone de l'université Laval and its Aboriginal show in Quebec City. In 2011 she co-organized with the Société de communication Atikamekw-Montagnais the first edition of the Gala of Music Teweikan in Quebec City, which honours and awards Aboriginal music and artists from Quebec and Labrador.

COLUMPA BOBB is the head instructor and program director of the Aboriginal Arts Training and Mentorship Program at the Manitoba Theatre for Young People. Ms Bobb is of Tsleil Waututh and Nlaka'pamux First Nations heritage and has been in the acting world for twenty-two years as a performer, writer, director, and teacher. She is a Jessie Richardson

Theatre Award winner and has been nominated for several more Jessies as well as for several Dora Mavor Moore Awards in the categories of performance in a lead role, writer, and production. She was also nominated for an award in recognition of her "Contribution to North American Native Writing" by the Returning the Gift Writer's Gathering in Norman, Oklahoma. She has taught at universities and elementary and secondary schools as well as at the grassroots community level as both an artist and an Empowerment through the Arts facilitator. Ms Bobb is a co-founder of Empowerment through the Arts and the creator of the Aboriginal Arts Program 2002 at the Manitoba Theatre for Young People. For the past eleven years, she has also been a clown and drama instructor for the Circus and Magic Partnership Camps organized by the Winnipeg International Children's Festival in northern Manitoba and Winnipeg. With Ian Ross, Ms Bobb co-wrote the 2008 *Aboriginal Day Live 08* show for the Aboriginal Peoples Television Network and the 2008 *Aboriginal People's Choice Awards*.

SADIE BUCK is a Haudenosaunee musician and cultural specialist living in the Six Nations community in Ontario. She leads the Six Nations Women Singers, a group that has performed at numerous festivals, on university campuses all across North America, and in many international concerts. The group's CD, *We Will All Sing*, was released in 1996. In the late 1990s at the Banff Centre for the Arts, she directed Aboriginal Women's Voices, an innovative program that enabled many leading North American artists to hone their craft and experiment with new styles while respecting traditional social values. She also co-created the Aboriginal dance opera *BONES* (2001). She has taught at several universities and in her own community. Sadie Buck was honoured in 2007 with the Community Spirit Award of the First Peoples Fund in recognition of her outstanding contributions to Aboriginal arts.

ANNETTE CHRÉTIEN is a Métis from Sudbury, Ontario. She obtained her doctorate in ethnomusicology from York University. She has held postdoctoral fellowships from the Canadian Museum of Civilization, the Faculty of Education at Queen's University, Wilfrid Laurier University, and the University of Ottawa. Her research is focused on contemporary Métis identities and on Métis Indigenous Knowledge (MIK).

MARIE CLEMENTS is a Métis Dene award-winning performer, playwright, director, producer, and screenwriter. As a writer, Ms Clements has worked in a variety of media, including theatre, film, new media, radio, and television. Her film *Unnatural and Accidental*, directed by Carl Bessai and starring Tantoo Cardinal and Callum Keith Rennie, was invited to premiere in New York at the Museum of Modern Art and went on to screen at sixteen film festivals across the Americas, including the Toronto International Film Festival and Vancouver International Film Festival, winning six awards and seven nominations at the Genie and Leo Awards. As a writer, Ms Clements has garnered numerous awards for her theatrical work, including the 2004 Canada-Japan Literary Award (*Burning Vision*) and a Jessie Richardson Theatre Award (*The Unnatural and Accidental Women*), as well as nominations for the 2004 Governor General's Literary Award (*Burning Vision*), the 2008 Governor General's Literary Award (*Copper Thunderbird*), and the Leo Awards (*Unnatural and Accidental*). In theatre, she has produced and toured twelve original productions to national and international showcases, directed ten original productions, written twelve original plays, acted in over fifty productions, receiving twenty-one award nominations and four awards, and produced eighteen publications. As a writer and director, Ms Clements premiered both *The Edward Curtis Project* and *The Road Forward*, commissioned by the Vancouver Organizing Committee for the 2010 Olympic and Paralympic Winter Games. She has been in residence at Playwright Workshop Montreal's Tadoussac translation lab, and her play *Burning Vision* is being translated into Catalan. She is currently working on a short film, a feature with her newly formed film company Frog Girl Films.

WALTER DENNY JR was born in Eskasoni, Cape Breton Island, Nova Scotia, where he grew up and where he now lives and works. A member of the Royal Canadian Mounted Police, his work has involved his participation in various projects related to social and political issues in his local community of Eskasoni and in the wider Mi'kmaw community.

GABRIEL DESROSIERS is a highly respected and well-recognized Ojibwa singer, dancer, songmaker, and educator. Born into the Bear Clan, he was raised in Lake of the Woods, Ontario, and was taught the ancient life-ways and language of his Ojibwa ancestors. Having come to prominence singing and composing songs with the popular powwow group the Whitefish Bay Singers, Mr Desrosiers left the group in 1991 to lead his own group, Wind, one of the most requested and respected drum groups on the North American powwow circuit. He is a well-known grass dancer, performing throughout North America and eastern and western Europe, and he has won many powwow competitions across North America. He has also served as a head man dancer, arena director, and head singing/dance judge for many contest powwows throughout Indian Country. After teaching for several years at the Tiospa Zina Tribal School on the Sisseton-Wahpeton Oyate Reservation in South Dakota, Mr Desrosiers is currently a lecturer and Ojibwa language instructor at the University of Minnesota, Morris.

BEVERLEY DIAMOND is the Canada Research Chair in ethnomusicology at Memorial University of Newfoundland, where she established and directs the Research Centre for the Study of Music, Media, and Place. Among other projects, the centre produces an archival CD series featuring diverse traditional music from the province of Newfoundland and Labrador. She has worked for several decades with Inuit, First Nations, and Sami elders, musicians, and other culture bearers. Her recent articles focus on aspects of Indigenous modernity, addressing recording studio practices, Indigenous awards, film soundtracks, intellectual property, and Indigenous opera. Her newest book, *Native American Music in Eastern North America* (2008) is part of Oxford University Press's Global Music series. She was named a Trudeau Fellow in 2009.

JIMMY DICK is a Cree musician who comes from Moose Factory, Ontario, located within the Nishnawbe Aski Nation Territory of James Bay. He has lived for many years in Toronto with his wife and children, where he has served as a cultural programmer and advocate for Native health and healing with various Native organizations in Toronto, including the Native Canadian Centre of Toronto (NCCT). He is the lead singer of Eagle Heart Singers, a group of musicians that performs powwow music and participates in political rallies and ceremonies in the Toronto area. He has also been a cultural programmer at the NCCT, organizing and hosting workshops, ceremonies, and youth trips and offering cultural and spiritual guidance to many people. Mr Dick currently works at St Christopher's House in Toronto, where he supports the needs and spiritual health of disadvantaged people in Toronto through Native ceremonies, music sharing, and conversation.

BYRON DUECK is a lecturer in music at the Open University. He studied ethnomusicology at the University of Chicago, where he received his doctorate in 2005. His research interests include First Nations and Métis music and dance in western Canada, popular music in Cameroon, and jazz in the United Kingdom. His current work focuses on connections between rhythm, metre, musical intimacy, and public culture.

KLISALA HARRISON is an ethnomusicologist whose areas of academic interest include: Native North American music, especially Northwest Coast First Nations traditional music forms; music of Native Canadian theatre; applied ethnomusicology theory, method, and praxis; and the roles of music in urban poverty situations, Aboriginal well-being, and intellectual property debates. Dr Harrison is the chairperson of the Study Group on Applied Ethnomusicology of the International Council for Traditional Music. She has worked in research and teaching capacities at the University of British Columbia, Vancouver Island University, and Columbia University and is currently the research fellow for the Ethnomusicology of Indigenous Modernities project at the University of Helsinki. Her recent publications include "'Singing My Spirit of Identity': Aboriginal Music for Well-Being in a Canadian Inner City," *MUSICultures* (2009): 1–21, and the edited volume *Applied Ethnomusicology: Historical and Contemporary Approaches* (2010).

ANNA HOEFNAGELS is an assistant professor of music at Carleton University, and she is also a past president of the Canadian Society for Traditional Music. Her teaching and research specialize in First Nations music, the music of Canada, and music and gender. She has presented papers at the British Forum for Ethnomusicology, the Society for Ethnomusicology, the Folklore Studies Association of Canada, the Canadian University Music Society, the Canadian Society for Traditional Music, the International Council for Traditional Music, and the Society for American Music, among others. She has also published in the *Canadian Journal for Traditional Music*, *Ethnologies*, and *World of Music*, and with Gordon E. Smith she co-edited *Folk Music, Traditional Music, Ethnomusicology: Canadian Perspectives, Past and Present* (2007).

DONNA LARIVIÈRE is an Algonquin (Anishnabe) from Abitibi-Témiscamingue. She has lived in Quebec City for more than twenty-seven years. She is a member of Quebec Native Women/Femmes Autochtones du Québec, and she is the assistant director in the urban area for that organization. She is also a member of the Board of Directors of the Maison communautaire Missinak in Quebec City. Since 2005 Ms Larivière has been hosting the radio show *Voix autochtones* (Indigenous Voices) on CKIA FM 88.3 in Quebec City, and since 2007 she has also been its producer.

CHARITY MARSH is the Canada Research Chair in interactive media and performance and an associate professor in the Faculty of Fine Arts at the University of Regina. Her research focuses on Indigenous hip hop cultures in Canada, DJ cultures, the production and performance of popular music in western and northern Canada, interactive social media, and creative media technologies.

SOPHIE MERASTY is from the Dene and Cree nations and comes from Reindeer Lake in northern Manitoba. Since 1983 she has worked extensively in the performing arts across Canada. In theatre, Ms Merasty has acted in plays such as Floyd Favel's *Lady of Silences*, Headline Theatre's *Shattering* (formerly *Meth*), and Marie Clements's *The Unnatural and Accidental Women*. She produces, directs, workshops, and develops new plays. Ms Merasty is also a television, radio drama, and film actor, receiving a Leo Awards nomination for her role in Clements's *Unnatural and Accidental*, directed by Carl Bessai.

GARRY OKER is an innovative designer who integrates cultural mythology with communicative arts for business solutions. He is a leading proponent of "Cultural Design Thinking" – a means of using Indigenous design systems to connect information exchange between people from different cultures. Mr Oker is a member and former chief of Doig River First Nation, located seventy kilometres north-east of Fort St John, British Columbia. He received his master's degree in leadership and training from Royal Roads University in 2005. He is apprenticing under grand master song keepers to learn ancient Dane-ẕaa dreamers' songs. Garry has travelled throughout Canada, the United States, and Europe marketing leading-edge art projects through digital animation, video, art, fashion, and music. He has performed for over twenty years, leading ceremonies and rituals in the community and on the international level.

MARCIA OSTASHEWSKI is an ethnomusicologist whose research and teaching are strongly community-based, collaborative, and service-oriented. She has worked with First Nations and Métis in northern Ontario, British Columbia, and on the Prairies since 2005 and with Ukrainian diaspora communities on several continents since the 1990s. Her research focuses on intersections of music and dance with gender, race and ethnicity, class, region, and language. In 2010–11 she served as Fulbright Research Chair in Canadian Studies at the University of Washington. Her current projects include: the development of music and language corpora for three of the six Salish and Wakashan languages spoken on Vancouver Island; a musical biography arising from investigations of Aboriginal-Ukrainian encounters and relations in Canada; and a collaborative research program with Ukrainian communities on expressive culture in Cape Breton, Nova Scotia. Toward this latter project, she is currently completing through Cape Breton University and the University of Alberta a postdoctoral research fellowship from the Social Science and Humanities Research Council of Canada. She is also an associate member of the Faculty of Graduate Studies at the University of Victoria, where she supervises graduate students in music.

MARY PIERCEY is a doctoral candidate in ethnomusicology at Memorial University of Newfoundland. Her research explores how the Inuit of Arviat, Nunavut, use their musical practices to negotiate social diversity within the community in response to massive sociocultural changes since three distinctive groups were resettled there in the 1950s. Ms Piercey lived, taught music, and conducted ethnomusicological research in Arviat from 2001 to 2007. During this time, she founded and directed the Arviat Imngitingit Community Choir, a mixed-voiced group specializing in traditional and contemporary Inuit music originating from the Kivalliq region of Nunavut. In collaboration with Qitiqliq High School's drama and Inuktitut teachers, Gord Billard and Maggie Manik, respectively, she wrote and directed two musicals, which were performed in Arviat in English and Inuktitut. Ms Piercey holds a master's degree in music education from the University of Toronto, where she studied choral conducting with Dr Doreen Rao and orchestral conducting with Dr Patricia Shand. She is the past director of the Bloor Street United Church Youth Choir, the First Unitarian Congregation Senior Choir, and the Hart House Chorus at the University of Toronto. Mary now lives in Iqaluit, Nunavut, where she directs the Inuksuk Drum Dancers and teaches music at Inuksuk High School.

AMBER RIDINGTON is a doctoral candidate in folklore at Memorial University of Newfoundland. Since 2001 she has collaborated with Aboriginal and community groups in Kentucky, Alaska, and British Columbia to design, produce, and facilitate museum exhibits, new media projects, and documentary videos that showcase cultural landscapes through oral history. Her doctoral work with the Doig River First Nation in north-eastern British Columbia focuses on the situated meanings of Dane-ẕaa dreamers' songs and the role of technology as an agent of both conservatism and dynamism within the tradition. Find more about Ms Ridington and her work at www.amberridington.com.

DYLAN ROBINSON, of mixed Stó:lō-European decent, is a postdoctoral researcher at Royal Holloway, University of London, where he is a member of the Indigeneity in the Contemporary World Project, funded by the European Research Council. He was previously a postdoctoral research fellow in the Faculty of Music at the University of Toronto and in 2010 was a John A. Sproul Fellow in Canadian Studies at the University of California Berkeley. His current research focuses on the aesthetics of reconciliation at performing arts events organized by Canada's Truth and Reconciliation Commission. His previous publications include *Opera Indigene: Re/presenting First Nations and Indigenous Cultures* (2011) and *Collision: Interarts Practice and Research* (2008).

CHRISTOPHER SCALES is an assistant professor of ethnomusicology at Michigan State University. His research focuses on contemporary northern pow-wow culture and musical creation both on the powwow grounds and in Aboriginal recording studios, specifically engaging the effects of technology and mass mediation on powwow performance aesthetics and how the stylistic transformations produced by recording studio practices have become linked to the politics of Native American ethnicity in North America. Aspects of this work have appeared in the journals *Ethnomusicology*, *World of Music*, and *Canadian University Music Review*. He has also been active in collaborating with Native musicians and has produced, recorded, or performed on several powwow and "contemporary Native music" CD projects for Arbor Records and War Pony Records, independent record labels specializing in North American Aboriginal music.

GILLES SIOUI is a singer-songwriter, guitar soloist and accompanist, self-taught musical director and arranger, and special education teacher. He performs contemporary Aboriginal music, as well as Québécois and Canadian blues-folk-rock. He is Huron-Wendat, born in Wendake (Huron Village). A professional musician since 1974, he started his career as a bassist and then drummer, debuting in his brother's band Ook Pik, performing in Quebec bars, and eventually performing as a guitarist with a variety of musicians and bands, including the Stephen Barry Band, Sioui's trio Storm/Soft Rain, the group Kashtin, and Kevin Parent. In the 1990s he also formed the Midnight Riders. He has been involved in the production of over fifty albums and has performed in a multitude of concerts;

he continues to give his fans more than 200 performances every year throughout Quebec. He has recorded three albums, *Gilles C. Sioui and the Midnight Riders* (1997), *Rising Sun* (2000), and *Old Fool* (2004), and he is currently preparing a fourth album. He has also participated in many projects and activities that showcase Aboriginal artists. Since 2008 Gilles Sioui has been the official spokesperson for the Centre de développement de la formation et de la main-d'œuvre Huron-Wendat. In this position, he regularly meets with Aboriginal youth to share his experiences as a singer-songwriter, performer, and musician.

GORDON E. SMITH is a professor of ethnomusicology at Queen's University. Formerly director of the School of Music, he is an associate dean in the Faculty of Arts and Science. A co-editor of *Marius Barbeau: Modelling Twentieth-Century Culture* (2008) and of *Music Traditions, Cultures, and Contexts* (2010), he is the editor of MUSICultures, *the Journal of the Canadian Society for Traditional Music/La Société canadienne pour les traditions musicales*. His current research includes fieldwork in the Mi'kmaw community of Eskasoni, Cape Breton Island, Nova Scotia.

BEVERLY SOULIERE (Manido Taji Memengwe Kijkwe/Spirit of the Butterfly Honoured Woman) is an Algonquin musician and lead singer of the award-winning women's hand-drumming trio Women of Wabano, based in Ottawa, Ontario. She also leads a women's hand-drumming circle at Minwaashin Lodge – Aboriginal Women's Support Centre, and she sings regularly with the church choir at St Michael and All Angel's Church. Beverly has an honours diploma in child and youth work from Northern College of Applied Arts and Technology in Timmins Ontario. After a number of years working in the field with children and their parents, she was appointed by the attorney general of Ontario as a justice of the peace for the Province of Ontario in June 2007.

JANICE ESTHER TULK is the senior research associate for the Purdy Crawford Chair in Aboriginal Business Studies at Cape Breton University. Her recent ethnomusicological research considers the relationship between Mi'kmaw musical expression and the soundscape of Mi'kma'ki (the traditional territory of the Mi'kmaq). Her doctoral dissertation "'Our Strength Is Ourselves': Status, Identity, and Cultural Revitalization among the Mi'kmaq in Newfoundland" (2008) explores the way that contemporary music-making practices such as the powwow are localized to express both Mi'kmaw identity and First Nations identity more broadly.

The recipient of a postdoctoral fellowship and Canada graduate scholarship from the Social Sciences and Humanities Research Council of Canada, Dr Tulk has published in the journals *Newfoundland and Labrador Studies, Canadian Journal for Traditional Music,* and *Culture & Tradition.* She is the producer of the CD *Welta'q – "It Sounds Good": Historic Recordings of the Mi'kmaq* (2009).

FLORENT VOLLANT is Innu, from Mani-utenam, Quebec, and an important figure in the Aboriginal popular music scene in Quebec. He is an artist, a spirit seeker, a proud defender of his culture, and a songwriter, composer, and performer of folk-country-rock/pop music in the Innu-aimun language. His first exposure to music was the traditional songs accompanied by the *teueikan* (Innu drum) that he heard as a child in the heart of Labrador. For nine years he accompanied Philippe McKenzie, most notably on his album *Mistashipu* (1982). In 1984 he formed the group Kashtin (Tornado) with Claude McKenzie, and from 1989 to 1995 they achieved national and international success, issuing three albums that were awarded four Felix awards: *Kashtin* (1989), *Innu* (1991), and *Akua Tuta* (1994). In 1985 he co-founded Innu Nikamu, an Aboriginal music festival in Mani-utenam, and in 1998 he founded Studio Makusham. He has also produced three solo albums, *Nipaiamianan* (1999), which won a Juno award in 2001, *Katak*ᵘ (2003), and *Eku Mamu* (2009). In 1994 he received the title Artist for Peace.

RUSSELL WALLACE, of the Lil'wat nation, is an acclaimed composer and producer of contemporary electronic music and is a traditional Lil'wat singer. In the late 1990s he worked at the Banff Centre with the participants of both the Aboriginal Women's Voices and Aboriginal Dance programs. Wallace's music has been part of a number of film, video, and television soundtracks as well as theatre and dance productions. He has produced CDs that have been nominated for awards at the Junos, the Canadian Aboriginal Music Awards, and the Native American Music Awards in the United States. Currently, Wallace works with his family singing group Tzo'kam, having produced their debut CD, titled *It'em – To Sing,* in 2000 as well as *Journeys* (2004).

Kwagiulth, 223, 238–9, 244, 247
Kwakwa̱ka'wakw, 264
Kyak, Pauline, 222, 234

Labrador, 13, 408, 409, 414, 416, 430
LaFever, K.C., 78, 79
Laforme, Mark, 256
Lake Deer, 79
Lake of the Woods, 89
Lakota, 14, 99–101, 123, 209
Lamon, Jean, 223, 243
Lamont, 327
Langford, Georges, 420
language, 8, 13, 22, 23, 29, 63, 71, 76,
    82, 91–2, 99, 100, 118, 134, 142, 151,
    157, 164, 168, 183, 185, 209, 266,
    219, 273, 278, 283, 306, 317, 329, 355,
    411; musical language, 220, 224,
    29–30, 235–6, 243–6. *See also* Cree;
    Dane-za̱a; Innu-aimun; Inuktitut;
    Métis language; Michif; Mi'kmaq,
    Mi'kmaw language; Ojibwa,
    Ojibway language; Salish; Wendat
Lapointe, Éric, 409
Laramee, Myra, 116
Larivière, Donna, 420
LaRoque, Emma, 367
Latino, 353
Lauzon, Jani, 147, 259
Laveau, Christian Shondak8a, 420
Lawrenchuk, Michael, 250
Leboeuf, Breen, 420
LeBouthillier, Wilfred, 419
LeClercq, Chrestien, 81
Lennox Island First Nation Cultural
    Centre, 81
Lescarbot, Marc, 224–5
libretto, 230
Lillos, Brian, 37, 39
Lil'wat, 6, 215, 218–19. *See also* Salish
localization, 18, 29, 70–88, 182, 256,
    323, 336, 368
Loco Locass, 395
longhouse, 104, 137–8, 222, 236
Longjohn, Marc, 364–5
Loon, Morley, 384, 408, 410

Louisbourg Institute, 80
lullaby, 249, 254, 409
L.W. Conolly Theatre Archives, 250

madrigal, 230
Magowan, Catherine, 223, 229, 230–2
Maillard, Pierre, 81
Maine, 13, 72
Makadahay, Rita, 42, 43
Makénúúnatane, 36, 44, 62, 68
Mak'íhts'ewéswa̱a̱, 62, 68
makushan, 376–8, 384, 388; *makusham*
    dance, 375–99
Maliseet, 20, 72
Mamgark family, 151, 162, 163, 169, 171
"Mamitunenitamun," 386
Mandamin, Isaac, 256
Mandaree, 93
Mani-utenam, 374, 378, 384–7, 390–1,
    397, 410
Manick, Joe, 170
Manido Taji Memengwe Kijkwe, 194
Manitoba, 89, 122, 125, 132, 161, 176,
    177, 179, 185, 190, 213, 256, 300–18,
    336
Manitoban Interlake, 302
Maniwaki, 185
Mannik, Maggie, 160
Marché des Trois Sœurs/Fête des ré-
    coltes, 420
marginalization, 8, 111, 113, 117–22, 132,
    179, 216, 242, 250–1, 254–5, 267, 328,
    367. *See also* racism
Mark Kalluak Community Hall, 166,
    169
Marshall, Albert, 292
Marshall, Murdena, 292
Marshall, Suzie, 292
Martynowych, Orest, 326
"Mary Had a Little Baby," 254–5
Mason, Tina, 253
Maten, 381–2, 397–8
Mathieu, Mireille, 424
Matimekush, 378, 390
Mattawa, 184, 186, 187
Mattes, Catherine, 120

18, 22, 72, 300, 213, 215–17. *See also* Anishnabe
Okatsiak family, 151, 169, 170
Oker, Annie, 50
Oker, Garry, 48–57, 61–9
Oker, Madeline, 38
old-style dance, 98
old-time music, 324, 331, 333–9
Olson, Michelle, 251, 264
Omaha, 78
"On Eagles Wings," 255
Onion Lake, 104
Onondaga, 141
Ontario, 19, 72, 89, 109, 110, 125, 132, 133, 163, 174–80, 185–90, 194, 206, 223, 231, 250, 256, 281, 336, 429
Ontario Ministry of Education, 174, 178, 179, 180
Ook Pik, 419, 425, 427
Ootova, Eliaspie, 223
Oklahoma, 109
Olympics, 134, 227; Olympian, 297
opera, 134, 148, 216, 223, 230, 232, 244, 249, 267, 290
oral history, 17, 21, 55, 73, 151, 363
organ, 159, 169, 331, 365
organum, 222, 232, 234
Original-singing style, 97
Ottawa, 6, 132, 163, 194, 195, 197, 293, 394
Ottawa, Pascal, 420
Ottawa, Sakay, 420
"Our Father." *See Nahhatáá?*
ownership, 13, 28–9, 87, 103, 106. *See also* intellectual property

Pacific Baroque Orchestra, 222, 229, 235, 236, 238, 246
Padlei, 157
Padlirmiut, 151, 153, 157, 165, 169
"La Paix des braves," 394
pan-Indianism, 15, 18, 70, 277. *See also* intertribal
Pappy Johns Band, 256
Parent, Kevin, 419, 425, 430
"Partridge Song," 74

Passamaquoddy, 14, 72
pastiche, 53, 245, 267
Paul, Maggie, 20
Paul, Tom, 82
Paved Arts, 350
peace dance, 239
Peace River, 32, 33
Pelletier, Claire, 409
Pelly Bay, 158
Penobscot, 72
Pessamit, 390
Petersen's Crossing, 42, 48
Petiquay, Arthur, 420
Phillips, Shawn, 420
piano, 52, 66, 159, 170, 280, 423
Piero, Annie Marie, 287
Piétacho, Jean-Charles, 376
Piétacho, Pinip, 376, 383
Pike, Paul, 77, 78, 81
Pine Ridge Indian Reservation, 123
Pinette, Samuel "Pudu," 382
pinguqtitsijiup pilirianga, 164
pipa, 223, 241–2
pisit, 168
Place Where Happiness Dwells. *See* Suunéch'ii Kéch'iige yiné?
Plains, 18, 76–7, 89–106, 109, 209, 327
plunger-fiddle, 324, 330, 333, 334. *See also* fiddle; violin
polka, 334–6, 339
polyvocality, 51
popular music, 84, 158, 217, 226, 251, 255, 282, 347, 368, 372–99
Porter, Murray, 256
postcolonialism, 4, 12, 150, 155, 230, 253, 255, 307, 339
potlatch, 21, 23, 235, 239, 244
Poulette, Thomas George, 20
Powers, William K., 13, 113
powwow, 5–8, 17–18, 20–1, 27–30, 70–84, 89–107, 109–29, 196, 206–13, 257, 264, 279, 347, 366, 429–30; arbour, 71, 94, 101. *See also* honour beats; northern-style singing; southern-style singing; powwow dance

resistance, 13, 31, 35, 36, 57, 121, 180, 232, 328, 338, 347–8, 353, 356, 372, 382; to musical conventions, 256, 263, 308–18
Restigouche, 291
revitalization, 3, 5, 19, 20, 31, 34–5, 37, 43, 50, 56–7, 102, 216, 260, 366, 372–3, 399
ribbon shirt, 78. *See also* regalia
Richard, Zachary, 409, 412, 416
Ridington, Jillian, 32–57
Ridington, Robin, 5, 11, 17, 32–57
Riel, Louis, 176
"The River Runs Red," 311
roach pin, 78. *See also* regalia
Robert Usher Collegiate, 353
Roberts, Helen, 158
Robertson, Robbie, 134, 409
Robi, Roy, 420
Robinson, Angela, 282
Robinson, Lisa, 297
Rock, Kathia, 391
rock 'n' roll, 230, 373, 375, 383, 384
Rocky Mountain Fort, 32
rodeo, 15, 45–6, 49
Ronceria, Alejandro, 140
Roots of Truth, 217
Rosen, Robert, 144
Ross, Ian, 250
Roulston, Kathryn, 181
round dance, 76, 104, 264, 278, 347, 364–5
Royal Canadian Mounted Police, 167, 292
Royal Ontario Museum, 14
Rupert's Land, 328
Rural Forum, 161

Saga of the Greenlanders, 237
Sagard-Théodat, Gabriel, 225, 228
Sagkeeng First Nation, 125
Sainte-Anne de Beaupré, 295–6
Sainte-Marie, Buffy, 21, 408, 411
Sainte-Marie, Chloé, 385, 392, 419

Salish, 218–20, 236, 239, 261, 266, 273, 279–80; language, 279. *See also* Lil'wat
salite, 296
Salteaux, 263
Samian, 394
Sante' Mawio'mi, 71, 286. *See also* Grand Council
sarangi, 223, 241–2
Saskatchewan, 7, 217, 249, 258, 261, 269, 328, 336, 346–68
Saskatchewan Centennial Celebrations, 351
Saskatchewan Jazz Festival, 351
Saskatchewan Native Theatre Company, 261
Saskatoon, 16, 349–53, 357
Schefferville, 384, 390
Schemitzun, 97, 98
school, 8, 32, 41, 45, 89, 92, 132, 138, 150–71, 174, 177–80, 194–5, 207–10, 217, 257, 280, 284–7, 298, 303, 330–1, 349, 352–4, 367, 424. *See also* education; residential school; teaching and learning
Scott Collegiate, 354
Scottish reel, 157
Séguin, Richard, 408, 409, 419
Les Séguin, 423
selfhood, 12, 21, 300, 311, 312, 314, 317
Seneca, 111, 133, 138, 140
Sept-Îles, 383, 384, 387
Se't A'newey School, 75
Sewall, Jason, 420
shamanism, 36, 88, 162, 200, 376
Shappa, June, 223, 240–2
Shared Learnings Program, 179
Sheshatshit, 389
shield, 78–80. *See also* regalia
shuffle dance. *See eskanye*
Sidney, Angela, 17
Sidney, Pete, 17
"Sing Two Songs," 51–3, 57
single-headed snare drum, 39–40, 49–50, 52